Mondrian
De Stijl

Mondrian
De Stijl

Städtische Galerie
im Lenbachhaus und Kunstbau
München

HATJE
CANTZ

Inhalt

Contents

Mondrian und De Stijl – Die Ausstellung für das Lenbachhaus

Die *De Stijl*-Gruppe um Piet Mondrian und Theo van Doesburg hat wie keine andere Kunstbewegung neben dem Bauhaus in der ersten Hälfte des 20. Jahrhunderts unseren Alltag nachhaltig beeinflusst. Mondrian schuf streng geometrische Gemälde, die heute als Ikonen der Moderne gelten. Ihre charakteristische Struktur aus schwarzen orthogonalen Linien und eingepassten rechteckigen Farbflächen in Rot, Gelb und Blau, führt längst ein reges Eigenleben in Kunst und Mode, Werbung und Populärkultur. Auch Möbel wie Gerrit Rietvelds *Rot-Blauer Stuhl* (um 1918) genießen inzwischen den Status von Design-Klassikern. Gegründet 1917 in Leiden, versammelte die Gruppe wechselnde Kunstschaffende und Theoretiker aus den Niederlanden sowie aus Italien, Deutschland, Österreich und der Sowjetunion um die Zeitschrift *De Stijl,* die unter der Herausgeberschaft von Theo van Doesburg bis ins Jahr 1928 erschien.

Wichtigstes Ziel der internationalen Vereinigung war die ›Neue Gestaltung‹ sämtlicher Bereiche der Lebenswirklichkeit. Entsprechend reichte die Palette der Themen, die diskutiert wurden, von bildender Kunst über Architektur und Städtebau bis zu Design. Aber auch Film, Theater, Musik und Literatur fanden Beachtung. Die *De Stijl*-Künstler einte die Auffassung, dass die Grenzen der tradierten Gattungen der Künste immer wieder herausgefordert und überschritten werden müssten.

Die Ausstellung *Mondrian und De Stijl* der Städtischen Galerie im Lenbachhaus ist eine der ersten umfassenden Museumspräsentationen in Deutschland, die sich dieser stilbildenden Avantgarde-Gruppe widmet. Sie ist aus einer Kooperation mit dem Gemeentemuseum in Den Haag entstanden, Heimat der weltweit umfangreichsten Sammlung an Bildern Piet Mondrians. Das Gemeentemuseum hatte im Jahr 2009 die Sammlung *Der Blaue Reiter* des Lenbachhauses zu einer Ausstellung zusammengefasst, welche speziell die frühe Rezeption von Kandinsky in den Niederlanden zum Thema hatte. Nun bildet die Sammlung des Gemeentemuseums die Basis für unsere Ausstellung *Mondrian und De Stijl* im Kunstbau des Lenbachhauses. Dieser Sammlungstausch ist ein kunsthistorisch logischer Schritt. Beide Sammlungen repräsentieren auf sehr umfassende und einzigartige Weise Pioniere der abstrakten Malerei. Den Haag verfügt über die größte Mondrian-Sammlung der Welt und München über die umfassendste Sammlung von Werken des *Blauen Reiters.* Im Lenbachhaus sind es besonders die frühen Werke Wassily Kandinskys, und ebenso liegt der Schwerpunkt der Mondrian-Sammlung in Den Haag auf dem frühen Œuvre des Künstlers. Beide Häuser verfügen über außergewöhnliche Werke, die jeweils Kandinskys und Mondrians eigenen und unterschiedlichen Weg in die Abstraktion dokumentieren. Zudem sind beide Häuser im Besitz einer Sammlung, die das Werk ihrer jeweils zentralen Figuren in den Kontext derjenigen Künstler stellt, die maßgeblich diesen Weg in die Abstraktion begleitet, beeinflusst und ermöglicht haben. In Bezug auf Mondrian waren dies zunächst die Künstler, denen er im niederländischen Domburg begegnete, während seine späteren Kollegen der Gruppe *De Stijl* angehörten; bei Kandinsky waren es die Künstler des *Blauen Reiters* und später die des Bauhauses.

Für das Lenbachhaus ist die Ausstellung *Mondrian und De Stijl* nicht nur eine Herausforderung, sondern eine Verpflichtung, welche sich aus dem Schwerpunkt der eigenen Sammlung ergibt. Im Zentrum des Projekts steht deshalb zum einen der Weg von Piet Mondrian in die Abstraktion: Nach Anfängen im Umfeld der neoimpressionistischen Luministen in Domburg entwickelte Mondrian ab 1912 anhand von Baum- und Architekturstudien zunehmend ungegenständlichere Kompositionen, von denen wichtige Arbeiten gezeigt werden. Aus der späteren, neoplastizistischen Periode sind zahlreiche zentrale Werke vertreten wie das programmatisch als *Tableau I* (1921) betitelte Bild. Zum anderen soll der interdisziplinäre und internationale Ansatz von *De Stijl* anhand von historischen Möbeln, Kleidung, Architekturzeichnungen und -modellen herausgestellt werden. Unseren Besucherinnen und Besuchern wird damit erstmals die Möglichkeit eröffnet, die beiden wirkmächtigsten Künstlerbewegungen des frühen 20. Jahrhunderts miteinander zu vergleichen und ihre Gemeinsamkeiten, Unterschiede und Widersprüche zu entdecken. Dabei ist uns die Darstellung der vielfältigen Querverbindungen der frühen Avantgarden ein besonderes Anliegen. Nicht nur die beiden zentralen Publikationen, der Almanach *Der Blaue Reiter* und die Zeitschrift *De Stijl,* haben diesen Ideentausch durch die gedruckte Form begünstigt. So hatte zum Beispiel auch das Bauhaus eine Plattform geschaffen, auf der die Ideen von *De Stijl* mit denen des *Blauen Reiters* konkurrieren oder zusammengehen konnten.
Nicht zuletzt hat Theo van Doesburgs Lektüre der Schriften Kandinskys seinen Entschluss gefestigt, die Zeitschrift *De Stijl* Wirklichkeit werden zu lassen. Dass beide Bewegungen ihre Ideen und Gedanken immer wieder publiziert haben, führte zu einer bis heute andauernden wechselseitigen Erhellung der Avantgarden über die Grenzen nationalstaatlichen Denkens hinaus. Die theoretischen Darlegungen Kandinskys, Mondrians und van Doesburgs zeigen außerdem deutlich, dass die bahnbrechende Einführung der Abstraktion in die Kunst einer begleitenden Erläuterung bedurfte, die

Mondrian and De Stijl: An Exhibition for the Lenbachhaus

More than any other artistic movement of the first half of the twentieth century and rivaled only by the Bauhaus, the *De Stijl* group around Piet Mondrian and Theo van Doesburg has exercised a lasting influence over our everyday lives. Mondrian created rigorously geometric paintings that are now considered iconic works of modernism. Their characteristic structure of black orthogonal lines forming a grid into which rectangular fields of red, yellow, and blue are set have long come to lead a life of their own in art and fashion, in advertising and popular culture. Works of furniture design such as Gerrit Rietveld's *Red and Blue Chair* (ca. 1918) are likewise praised as design classics. Founded in Leiden in 1917, the group united a varying cast of producers and theorists of art from the Netherlands as well as Italy, Germany, Austria, and the Soviet Union around the magazine *De Stijl,* which appeared until 1928 under the editorial management of Theo van Doesburg.

The most important aim of this international association was the application of *Nieuwe Beelding* or "Neoplasticism" to all domains of everyday reality. Accordingly, the debates covered topics including the visual arts, architecture and urban planning, and design, also addressing issues of film, theater, music, and literature. The artists of *De Stijl* were united in the view that the boundaries of the traditional artistic genres needed to be continuously challenged and transgressed.

The exhibition *Mondrian and De Stijl* at the Städtische Galerie im Lenbachhaus is one of the first comprehensive museum presentations in Germany devoted to this style-setting avant-garde group. It has been produced in collaboration with the Gemeentemuseum, The Hague, home to the world's largest collection of paintings by Piet Mondrian. In 2009, the Gemeentemuseum had presented the Lenbachhaus's collection of works by *Der Blaue Reiter* artists in an exhibition that focused in particular on the early response to Kandinsky's art in the Netherlands. Now the Gemeentemuseum's collection forms the basis for our exhibition *Mondrian and De Stijl* in the Kunstbau section at the Lenbachhaus. This exchange of loans from the collections has much to recommend it. Each collection holds exceptionally comprehensive sets of works from the oeuvres of unique pioneers of abstract painting. The Hague has the world's largest collection of Mondrians; Munich, the most comprehensive collection of works by the artists of *Der Blaue Reiter.* The Lenbachhaus, in particular, possesses many of Wassily Kandinsky's early works; the Mondrian collection in The Hague is similarly focused on the artist's early oeuvre. Both houses have extraordinary works that document Kandinsky's and Mondrian's individual and distinctive paths to abstraction. Both houses, moreover, possess collections that allow them to place the oeuvres of their central protagonists in their respective contexts by showing the works of other artists whose companionship and decisive influence made their paths to abstraction possible. In Mondrian's case, these were the artists he encountered at Domburg (Netherlands), then later his colleagues at the group *De Stijl;* in Kandinsky's case, the members of *Der Blaue Reiter* and, later on, the Bauhaus artists.

To the Lenbachhaus, the exhibition *Mondrian and De Stijl* is not only a challenge; it is also an obligation that derives from the focus of our own collection. One aim of the project is accordingly to retrace Piet Mondrian's path toward abstraction: after beginnings in the orbit of Domburg's neo-Impressionist Luminists, Mondrian's studies of trees and architectures from 1912 on led him to create increasingly non-representational compositions, represented in the exhibition by important works. Numerous central works such as the painting bearing the programmatic title *Tableau I* (1921) exemplify the later Neoplasticist period. A second aim of the show is to highlight the interdisciplinary and international approach of *De Stijl* by displaying historic furniture, apparel, and architectural drawings and models. The exhibition thus provides our visitors with the unprecedented opportunity to compare the two most influential movements in the art of the early twentieth century and discover similarities as well as differences, and contradictions. Of particular interest to us is to illuminate the manifold interconnections within the early avant-gardes. The two central publications, the almanac *Der Blaue Reiter* and the magazine *De Stijl,* fostered this exchange of ideas by committing them to the printed page; but the conversation took place in other media as well. The Bauhaus, for instance, created a platform on which the ideas of *De Stijl* would compete or coalesce with those of *Der Blaue Reiter.* Not the least factor motivating Theo van Doesburg to realize his plans for the magazine *De Stijl* was the experience of reading Kandinsky's writings. By repeatedly publishing their ideas and thoughts, both movements engendered a mutual illumination of the avant-gardes, across the boundaries drawn by those who think in terms of national cultures, that has lasted to this day. Kandinsky's, Mondrian's, and Van Doesburg's theoretical essays also clearly illustrate that the groundbreaking introduction of abstraction into art required a concomitant explanatory discourse that would be able to elucidate the sensual complexity of the work. An artist who sought to meet the growing challenges posed

das Sinnlich-Komplexe des Kunstwerks zu erklären im Stande war. Wer die zunehmende Herausforderung einer immer komplizierter werdenden Welt bewältigen wollte, deren Beziehung zur Kunst nicht mehr in einer einfachen Ähnlichkeitsbeziehung aufgehoben ist, kam ohne die theoretische Spiegelung der eigenen künstlerischen Praxis nicht mehr aus. Die Essays dieses Katalogs widmen sich deshalb der Aufgabe, die Werke der Ausstellung in den Kontext ihrer theoretischen Reflexion zu stellen. Hans Janssen, Franz Kaiser, Michael White, Felicia Rappe und nicht zuletzt Matthias Mühling sei deshalb für ihre erhellenden Beiträge gedankt, Thomas Mayfried und Swantje Grundler für die dem Thema gegenüber formal wie intellektuell sensible Gestaltung des Katalogs und des Ausstellungs-CIs und schließlich Annette Kulenkampff für die begeisterte Aufnahme des Katalogs in das Programm des Hatje Cantz Verlags.

Wir danken allen Mitarbeitern des Gemeentemuseums in Den Haag, die dazu beigetragen haben, dass dieses Projekt Realität geworden ist. Insbesondere Benno Tempel, Hans Janssen und Franz Kaiser, die über die Rolle der großzügigen Leihgeber hinaus bereit waren, ihr enzyklopädisches Wissen über das Thema bereitwillig mit uns zu teilen. Möglich wurde die Ausleihe der empfindlichen Werke aus der Sammlung des Gemeentemuseums in Den Haag erst durch ein aufwendiges Restaurierungsprojekt, welches großzügig durch American Express gefördert wurde – auch dieser Unterstützung gilt unser Dank.

Allen unseren Mitarbeitern, die an der Verwirklichung dieser Ausstellung beteiligt waren, danken wir herzlich, allen voran aber dem Kurator der Ausstellung Matthias Mühling, tatkräftig unterstützt von Felicia Rappe.

Vor allem sind wir jedoch den Leihgebern zu Dank verpflichtet, welche ihre prominenten Werke für die Dauer der Ausstellung zu entbehren bereit waren. Neben dem Gemeentemuseum in Den Haag, welches den Großteil der Leihgaben für die Ausstellung bereitgestellt hat, sind wir den folgenden Museen und Institutionen zu Dank verpflichtet:
Bauhaus-Archiv Berlin
Bayerische Staatsbibliothek München
Centre Pompidou, Musée national d'art moderne – Centre de création industrielle, Paris
Kunstmuseum Basel
Kupferstich-Kabinett, Staatliche Kunstsammlungen Dresden
Niederländisches Architekturinstitut, Rotterdam
Niederländisches Institut für Kulturerbe (RCE), Amsterdam
Staatsgalerie Stuttgart
Stiftung Van Eesteren, Fluck & Lohuizen, Den Haag

Unserem Medienpartner, dem *Münchner Merkur,* danken wir für die Bereitschaft, unser Projekt einer großen Leserschaft zu empfehlen.

Zum wiederholten Male haben wir bei dieser Ausstellung auf die Hilfe eines Sponsors vertrauen können, der uns seit langem hilft, aufwendige Projekte angemessen zu realisieren. Wir sind deshalb sehr dankbar, dass E.ON Energie AG sich erneut als ein verlässlicher Partner des Lenbachhauses erwiesen hat. Für allen Rat und Hilfe möchten wir uns stellvertretend bei Ingo Luge, Hartmut Geldmacher und Bärbel Tannert ganz herzlich bedanken.

Helmut Friedel
Direktor
Städtische Galerie im Lenbachhaus
und Kunstbau München

by an ever more complicated world, a world whose relation to art is no longer safely contained within the confines of simple resemblance, needed the reflection of his own artistic practice in the mirror of theory. The essays in the present catalogue are accordingly dedicated to the task of embedding the works in the exhibition into the context of their theoretical reflections, and I would like to thank Hans Janssen, Franz Kaiser, Michael White, Felicia Rappe, and last but not least Matthias Mühling for their illuminating contributions. I am also grateful to Thomas Mayfried and Swantje Grundler for creating a catalogue design and exhibition corporate identity that evince great formal as well as intellectual sensitivity to the issues under consideration, and to Annette Kulenkampff at Hatje Cantz publishers for the enthusiasm with which she included the catalogue in their program.

We would like to thank the staff at the Gemeentemuseum The Hague who helped make this project a reality; Benno Tempel, Hans Janssen, and Franz Kaiser in particular not only generously organized the loans but also readily shared their encyclopedic knowledge of the art on display with us. The loans of the sensitive works from the Gemeentemuseum's collections would have been impossible without a costly restoration project implemented with generous support from American Express, for which we are deeply grateful.

We would like to express our gratitude to the entire staff at the Lenbachhaus involved in realizing this exhibition, and especially to Matthias Mühling, who curated the show with the untiring assistance of Felicia Rappe.

Most importantly, however, we would like to thank the lenders who were willing to part with prominent works from their collections for the duration of our exhibition. In addition to the Gemeentemuseum The Hague, which provided the majority of the works on display, we are also profoundly grateful to the following museums and institutions:

Bauhaus-Archiv Berlin
Bayerische Staatsbibliothek München
Centre Pompidou, Musée national d'art moderne – Centre de création industrielle, Paris
The Cultural Heritage Agency of the Netherlands (RCE), Amsterdam
Kunstmuseum Basel
Kupferstich-Kabinett, Staatliche Kunstsammlungen Dresden
Netherlands Architecture Institute, Rotterdam
Staatsgalerie Stuttgart
The Van Eesteren, Fluck & Lohuizen Foundation, The Hague

We would like to thank our media partner *Münchner Merkur* for recommending our project to its sizable readership.

As with previous exhibitions, we have been able to rely on the assistance of a sponsor who has long helped us to realize major projects in ways that do justice to great art. We are exceptionally grateful, then, that E.ON Energie AG has again proven a dependable partner to the Lenbachhaus. In lieu of everyone who assisted us, we would like to thank Ingo Luge, Hartmut Geldmacher, and Bärbel Tannert.

Helmut Friedel
Director
Städtische Galerie im Lenbachhaus
und Kunstbau München

Einweihung des Cafés Leo Faust
(Konzeption von Piet Zwart), 36 rue Pigalle, Paris
1926
Vilmos Huszár (vorn links), Piet Mondrian (Mitte) und Piet Zwart (hintere Reihe, zweiter von rechts)
Sammlung RKD Den Haag

Opening of Café Leo Faust
(design by Piet Zwart), 36 rue Pigalle, Paris
1926
Vilmos Huszár (front left), Piet Mondrian (center) and Piet Zwart (back row, second from right)
Collection RKD The Hague

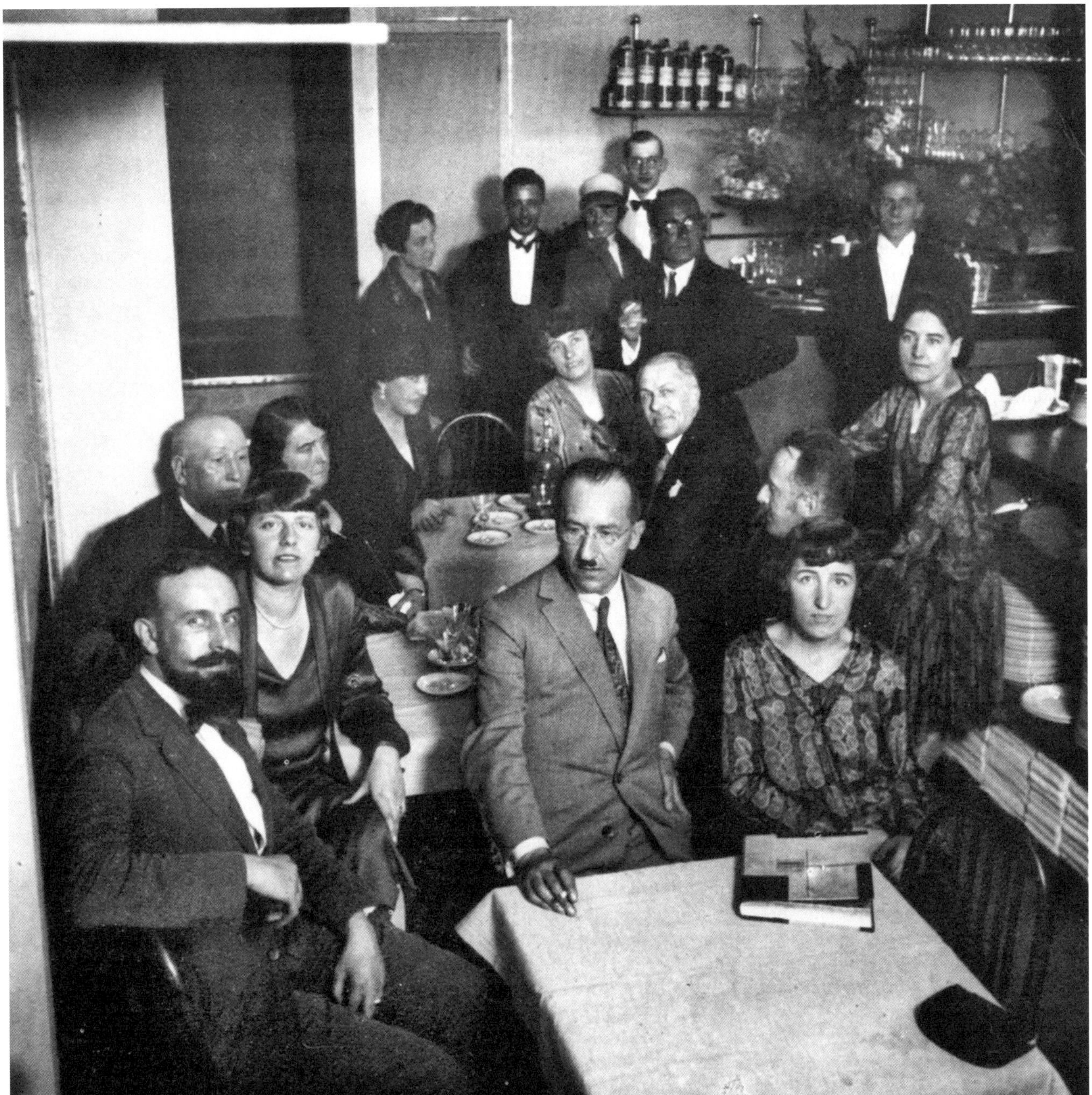

Über ›Bedeutung‹ bei abstrakter Kunst
Franz-W. Kaiser

Die Ausstellung *Mondrian und De Stijl* ergab sich aus einer Zusammenarbeit zwischen dem Gemeentemuseum Den Haag und dem Lenbachhaus in München: Im Frühjahr 2010 war in Den Haag *Kandinsky und Der Blaue Reiter* zu sehen, und im Gegenzug zeigt das Lenbachhaus nun diese Ausstellung.[1] Eine solche Zusammenarbeit lag eigentlich auf der Hand, da die Sammlungen beider Museen über einzigartig umfassende Konvolute jeweils eines der Pioniere der abstrakten Malerei verfügen. Den Haag besitzt die größte Mondrian-Sammlung der Welt und München die umfangreichste Gruppe früher Werke Kandinskys. Das Frühwerk ist ebenfalls der Schwerpunkt des Haager Mondrian-Konvoluts, und so umfassen beide Sammlungen genügend Material, um Kandinskys beziehungsweise Mondrians Weg hin zur Abstraktion darzustellen. Die Sammlungen besitzen darüber hinaus Werke von Künstlern aus dem Umfeld von Mondrian respektive Kandinsky, innerhalb dessen sich deren jeweiliger Werdegang vollzogen hat. Bei Mondrian waren dies zunächst die Künstler, die er im niederländischen Domburg traf, und dann später seine Künstlerkollegen der *De Stijl*-Gruppe; bei Kandinsky waren es die Künstler von *Der Blaue Reiter*.

Man könnte sagen, dass in Den Haag die Wiege der geometrischen beziehungsweise analytischen Abstraktion steht und in München die der lyrischen. Geometrische oder lyrische Abstraktion sind Benennungen für Kunstformen, die erst später im 20. Jahrhundert hervortraten, und wie so oft decken sie sich nicht mit den gemeinten Phänomenen. Jedenfalls steht Mondrian zweifellos am Anfang einer Kunstrichtung, welche danach strebte, die bildnerischen Mittel vernunftmäßig zu analysieren und bis aufs Äußerste zu reduzieren, was letztlich zur Minimal Art führte, während Kandinsky eine andere Entwicklung initiierte, in welcher Ausdruck und Gefühl zentral waren, womit er den Weg bereitete für die lyrische Abstraktion und den Abstrakten Expressionismus der 1950er-Jahre. Doch ist Kunst nie nur das Eine oder das Andere, sondern – ganz im Gegenteil – das Gebiet, in dem hinsichtlich Bedeutung Vernunft und Gefühl nahtlos ineinander übergehen.

Bedeutung

Will man der Frage nachgehen, was ›Bedeutung‹ bei abstrakter Kunst sein kann, dann ist es ratsam, sich zunächst über den Begriff zu verständigen. Denn darüber, was ›Bedeutung‹ eigentlich ist, bestehen verschiedenerlei Auffassungen, die meist stillschweigend vorausgesetzt werden.[2] Eine Definition, welche die Krux des Problems auf elegante Weise deutlich macht, stammt von dem amerikanischen Kognitionswissenschaftler Walter J. Freeman, der in ›Bedeutung‹ das sieht, was »die Beziehung eines jeden Gehirns zur Welt bestimmt.«[3] Zeit unseres Lebens verwenden wir einen Großteil unserer Anstrengungen darauf, die Welt zu verstehen und von anderen verstanden zu werden, und in unserer Auseinandersetzung mit der Welt entstehen in unseren Köpfen Vorstellungen von ihr, die mit Bedeutungen aufgeladen werden. Wir messen sowohl natürlichen als auch kulturellen Gegenständen und Ereignissen Bedeutungen bei, und dies ist ein kontinuierlicher und größtenteils unbewusster Vorgang. Bedeutungen konstituieren sich aus bewussten und unbewussten Erinnerungen, körperlichen Befindlichkeiten, Gefühlen, Wahrnehmungen über alle fünf Sinne gleichzeitig – ein sich ständig änderndes, holistisches Konglomerat, das in jedem Individuum sehr eigene Formen annimmt, viel zu komplex, um als Ganzes mitteilbar sein zu können.[4] Demnach wäre ›Bedeutung‹ Teil eines für

1
Dieser Text ist eine Weiterentwicklung meines Beitrags zum Haager Katalog: Franz-W. Kaiser, »Over de betekenis van abstracte kunst«, in: *Kandinsky en Der Blaue Reiter*, Ausst.-Kat. Gemeentemuseum Den Haag, Den Haag und Zwolle 2010, S. 87 ff.

2
An anderer Stelle habe ich dies ausführlicher dargelegt, als es in diesem Zusammenhang möglich ist, siehe: Franz-W. Kaiser, *Kunst. Wirklichkeit: Untersuchung von Arten der Weltaneignung*, Leiden University Repository, http://hdl.handle.net/1887/5424, 2006), das 4. Kapitel, insbesondere ab S. 229.

3
»[...] meaning, a critical concept that defines the relation of each brain to the world.« Vgl.: Walter J. Freeman, *How Brains Make Up Their Minds*, London 1999, S. 17.

4
Kaiser 2006 (wie Anm. 2), S. 229.

On 'Meaning' in Abstract Art
Franz-W. Kaiser

The exhibition *Mondrian and De Stijl* is the product of a collaboration between the Gemeentemuseum The Hague and the Lenbachhaus Munich. In spring 2010 *Kandinsky and Der Blaue Reiter* was on show in The Hague; in return the Lenbachhaus is now mounting this exhibition.[1] The collaboration was an obvious choice since the two museums possess uniquely comprehensive collections of works by one or other of these two pioneers of abstract painting. The Hague has the biggest Mondrian collection in the world, and Munich the most extensive group of Kandinsky's early works. The Hague's Mondrian collection likewise concentrates on the early work. Thus the two collections contain sufficient material to illustrate Kandinsky's and Mondrian's paths to abstraction. Moreover, the collections also possess works by artists close to Mondrian or Kandinsky, in which circles the development of the artists took place. In the case of Mondrian, these were the artists he met in Domburg in the Netherlands, and later his fellow artists of the *De Stijl* group; in Kandinsky's case it was the artists of *Der Blaue Reiter.*

The Hague, one might say, is the cradle of Geometric and/or Analytical Abstraction, and Munich that of Lyrical Abstraction. Geometric and Lyrical Abstraction denote forms of art that only developed later in the twentieth century and, as so often, the terms coincide but imprecisely with the phenomena they denote. Be that as it may, Mondrian unquestionably stands at the start of an art movement that strove to analyze and to radically reduce the elements of art, which ultimately led to Minimal Art, while Kandinsky initiated a different development in which expression and feeling were central, thus preparing the way for 1950s Lyrical Abstraction and Abstract Expressionism. Art, though, is never just one or the other, but rather the place where, in respect of meaning, reason and feeling merge into each other.

Meaning

Before exploring the subject of 'meaning' in abstract art, it is well to define the concept, for there are different views as to what exactly 'meaning' is, and for the most part they are tacitly taken for granted.[2] A definition that neatly illustrates the crux of the problem is that of the American cognitive scientist Walter J. Freeman, for whom 'meaning' is what "defines the relation of each brain to the world".[3] We spend much of our lives trying to understand the world and to make ourselves understood to others, and, in our dealings with the world, ideas form in our minds and become charged with meaning. In an ongoing, largely unconscious process, we assign meanings to both natural and cultural objects and events. Meanings are assembled from conscious and unconscious memories, bodily states, feelings, perceptions from all five senses, a constantly changing, holistic conglomerate that assumes different forms in each person and is far too complex to be a communicable whole.[4] 'Meaning', in this view, belongs to a discrete consciousness, a view of human consciousness that has dominated modern thinking to date. But more recent findings suggest that underlying this is a common participation in meanings.[5] In order for meanings to be shared, they must be externalized. This occurs by means of symbols, in particular language, man's ubiquitous symbol system, which distinguishes him from his animal relatives more plainly than anything else. But languages are many, and it is not always possible to communicate meanings between them. This blatant contrast between man's universal

1
This text is a development of my article in the Hague catalogue: Franz-W. Kaiser, "Over de betekenis van abstracte kunst," in *Kandinsky en Der Blaue Reiter,* exh. cat. Gemeentemuseum The Hague (Zwolle, 2010), pp. 87ff.

2
I have gone into this at greater length than is possible here in Franz-W. Kaiser, *Kunst. Wirklichkeit / Untersuchung von Arten der Weltaneignung,* Leiden University Repository, http://hdl.handle.net/1887/5424, 2006); see in particular the fourth chapter, from p. 229.

3
Walter J. Freeman, *How Brains Make Up Their Minds* (London, 1999), p. 17.

4
Kaiser 2006 (see note 2), p. 229.

5
Merlin Donald, *A Mind so Rare: The Evolution of Human Consciousness* (New York, London, 2001); Michael Tomasello, *The Cultural Origins of Human Cognition* (Cambridge/MA, London, 1999).

sich selbst stehenden Bewusstseins – eine Auffassung vom menschlichen Bewusstsein, die in der Tat das neuzeitliche Denken bisher weitgehend bestimmt hat. Doch scheint dies neueren Erkenntnissen zufolge überhaupt erst durch die gemeinschaftliche Teilhabe an Bedeutungen entstanden zu sein.[5] Um Bedeutungen miteinander teilen zu können, müssen sie veräußerlicht werden. Das geschieht mittels Symbolen und insbesondere der Sprache, dem allgegenwärtigen Symbolsystem des Menschen, mit dem er sich am deutlichsten von seinen nächsten Verwandten unterscheidet. Der Sprachen aber gibt es viele, und zwischen verschiedenen Sprachen ist die gemeinschaftliche Teilhabe an Bedeutungen oft kaum möglich. Dieser flagrante Widerspruch zwischen der universellen Sprachfähigkeit des Menschen und der Vielfalt existierender Sprachen sowie die Beobachtung, dass jeder Mensch in seinen ersten Lebensjahren gewissermaßen von selbst seine Muttersprache erlernt, hat Noam Chomsky in der Mitte des vergangenen Jahrhunderts auf die Idee gebracht, dass es eine sehr reduzierte, universelle Basisgrammatik geben müsse, auf die alle Sprachen zurückgeführt werden können und die erblich ist. Wie eine solche »generative Grammatik« aussieht und was die der Sprache zugrunde liegenden Regeln sind, ist trotz aller Forschungsanstrengungen von Seiten der durch Chomsky initiierten linguistischen Schule strittig geblieben. Es sieht immer mehr danach aus, als sei die Ursache jener universell menschlichen Fähigkeit zur Sprache woanders zu suchen: im nicht-sprachlichen Austausch von Bedeutungen;[6] und hiermit sind wir im Bereich der Kunst angelangt.

Die triviale Vorstellung von der Bedeutung eines Werks bildender Kunst ist, dass es seinen Bildgegenstand mit visuellen Mitteln – mittels naturalistischer Nachahmung oder symbolischen Verweises – darstellt. Darstellen ist eine Form der Veräußerlichung von ›Bedeutung‹: Einem willkürlichen, äußerlichen Gegenstand – sei er gefunden oder fabriziert, sei es eine Eiche oder die vergängliche Klangwelle eines Sprachgeräuschs, ein geschriebenes Wort, eine mathematische Formel, ein gemaltes Bild etc. – wird eine Bedeutung zuerkannt, was meist unbewusst geschieht; und so wird der Gegenstand zu einem Symbol, das auf etwas anderes – eine ›Bedeutung‹ – verweist. Die Wörter ›Hund‹, ›chien‹ und ›dog‹ haben vom Klang her nichts miteinander gemein, doch verweisen sie auf dieselbe Bedeutung. Um als Wörter funktionieren zu können, sind sie allerdings angewiesen auf eine hinlängliche Kenntnis der jeweiligen Sprache bei den Kommunikationspartnern. Ein naturalistisches Bild oder ein Foto, das einen Hund darstellt, kann dagegen jeder erkennen. Dass naturalistische Darstellungen also universeller sind als Sprache, hat schon Leonardo erkannt,[7] und es wird durch die heutige globale Massenkultur eindrucksvoll bestätigt.

Wie aber passen in diese Skizze verschiedener Symbolsysteme Bilder, die sich dem Verweis auf fest umschriebene Bedeutungen verweigern? Wir brauchen dabei noch nicht einmal unbedingt an abstrakte Bilder zu denken. Poussins arkadische Landschaften etwa verweisen nicht auf konkrete Landschaften, sondern auf Landschafts-Konzepte, und Caspar David Friedrichs *Wanderer über dem Nebelmeer* referiert nicht auf einen bestimmten Mann, sondern auf eine Art Mann-Konzept – etwa ein Betrachter, versunken in ästhetischer Kontemplation. Die Kunstgeschichte ist voll von Bildern mit dergleichen ›unbestimmten Denotationen‹.[8] Unser durch Sprache konditionierter Umgang mit Bedeutungen lässt uns leicht übersehen, wie oft wir auch im Alltag mit unbestimmten Bedeutungsträgern zu tun haben – und natürlich können wir darauf adäquat reagieren: Wenn das ›Was‹ unbestimmt ist, dann verschiebt sich die Aufmerksamkeit auf das ›Wie‹,[9] was gleichkommt einer Verschiebung des Interesses von dem, worauf verwiesen wird, hin zu den intrinsischen Eigenschaften des Bedeutungsträgers. Die Regelmäßigkeit, mit der Cézanne immer wieder dieselben Bildthemen aus seiner nächsten Umgebung behandelte, und die geradezu serielle Systematik, mit der Monet Heuhaufen oder die Fassade der Kathedrale von Rouen malte, macht den Bildgegenstand sekundär, während die Art und Weise, wie er gemalt ist – die Bildeigenschaften – den Ausdruck des Bildes veranschaulichen. So ist »Veranschaulichung« (exemplification) eine andere Form der Bedeutung,[10] der in der bildenden Kunst seit dem 20. Jahrhundert – als Selbstbezug – eine wichtige Rolle zukommt.

Caspar David Friedrich
Wanderer über dem Nebelmeer
um 1818
Hamburger Kunsthalle

Caspar David Friedrich
The Wanderer Above the Sea of Fog
c. 1818
Hamburger Kunsthalle

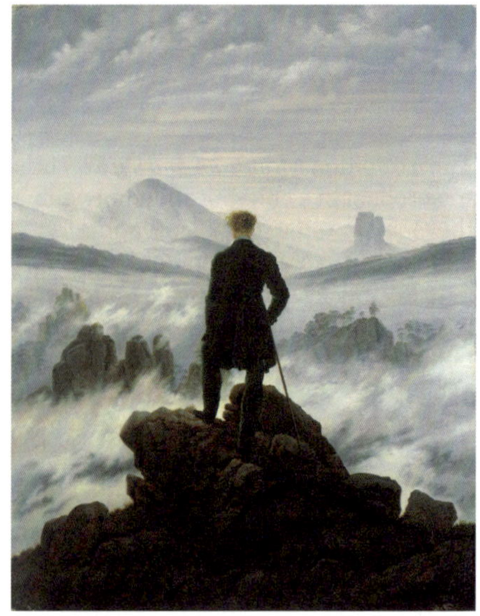

5
Merlin Donald, *A Mind so Rare – The Evolution of Human Consciousness,* New York und London 2001; Michael Tomasello, *The Cultural Origins of Human Cognition,* Cambridge / MA und London 1999.

6
Das Leipziger Max-Planck-Institut für evolutionäre Anthropologie hat in diesem Perspektivenwandel eine Vorreiterrolle. Vgl. hierzu die Schriften eines seiner Direktoren, Michael Tomasello, insbesondere: *Constructing a Language – A Usage-Based Theory of Language Acquisition,* Cambridge / MA und London 2003 sowie *Origins of Human Communication,* Cambridge / MA und London 2008.

7
In seinem Vergleich zwischen Malerei und Wissenschaft schreibt Leonardo ersterer mehr Glaubwürdigkeit zu, da er dem eigenen Sehen mehr vertraute als den Schriften, und eine größere Nützlichkeit, da was man sieht, universell verständlich ist. Martin Kemp (Hrsg.), *Leonardo on Painting,* New Haven und London 1989, S. 14, 18 f.

8
Der amerikanische Philosoph Nelson Goodman hat hierfür den Begriff »Null-Denotation« geprägt; in ders., *Languages of Art* [1968], Indianapolis 1976, S. 21–26.

9
Vgl. hierzu die Symboltheorie von Dan Sperber, *Le Symbolisme en général,* Paris 1974.

10
Goodman 1976 (wie Anm. 8), S. 45–57.

linguistic ability and the multiplicity of existing languages, as well as the fact that we all, in the first years of life, learn our mother tongue more or less alone, prompted Noam Chomsky in the mid-twentieth century to posit the existence of a very reduced, universal basic grammar, from which all languages derive and which is hereditary. What this "generative grammar" looks like and what its underlying rules are remains disputed, despite all the research efforts on the part of the linguistic school initiated by Chomsky. The cause of man's universal linguistic ability must apparently be sought elsewhere, in the nonlinguistic exchange of meanings;[6] and here we have arrived in the realm of art.

The trivial idea of the 'meaning' of a work of art is that it visually represents an object by means of naturalistic imitation or symbolic reference. Depicting is a form of externalizing meaning: an arbitrary object—an oak tree or the transient airwave of a linguistic sound, a written word, a mathematical formula, a painted picture—is assigned a meaning, usually unconsciously, and the object refers symbolically to something else, a 'meaning'. The words 'Hund', 'dog', 'chien' have nothing in common as sounds, yet they have the same meaning. To function as words, though, they depend on the communication partners' having an adequate knowledge of the language in question. A naturalistic picture or photo of a dog, on the other hand, can be recognized by anyone. That naturalistic representations are more universal than language has been known since Leonardo,[7] and contemporary global mass culture impressively confirms it.

But how do pictures that avoid referring to firmly circumscribed meanings fit into this sketch of symbol systems? We need not turn directly to abstract pictures. Poussin's Arcadian landscapes refer to no specific landscapes but to landscape concepts, and Caspar David Friedrich's *Wanderer above the Sea of Fog* does not reference a particular man but a kind of man concept, a beholder sunk in aesthetic contemplation, for instance. Art history is full of such pictures with 'indefinite denotations'.[8] Conditioned as our contact with meanings is by language, we easily overlook how often in everyday life we also deal with indefinite bearers of meaning, and yet we react appropriately: when the 'What' is indefinite, attention shifts to the 'How',[9] in other words, from what is referenced to the intrinsic properties of the bearer of meaning. Cézanne's insistence on handling the same subject-matter in his immediate surroundings, over and over, or Monet's systematic serialism in painting haystacks or the façade of Rouen Cathedral, renders the pictorial object secondary, while the manner of the paintings—their pictorial properties—exemplify what the pictures express. This 'exemplification' is another form of meaning,[10] to which—in the form of self-reference—great importance has been attached in the visual arts since the twentieth century.

Mondrian and Kandinsky

The frequently posed question "Which was the first abstract painting?" is idle, for against the backdrop of the history of mankind naturalism has been the exception rather than the rule.[11] It makes more sense to ask who was the first to develop nonfigurative art, both in terms of practice and theory, and the answer here is Kandinsky. Mondrian also wrote theoretical texts later on. As often with artists, the writings of both are well-nigh incomprehensible. This is hardly surprising given that an artist's primary symbol and thought system is not written language but his own pictorial language, a language, in other words, of a fundamentally different kind.

Kandinsky had developed his abstract pictorial language while still a member of the *Neue Künstlervereinigung München* (NKVM), prior, that is, to *Der Blaue Reiter.* His *Composition V,* which was rejected by the jury of the third NKVM exhibition and led to his break with the NKVM and to the founding of *Der Blaue Reiter,* certainly seems to be abstract. But, as emerges from a lecture he held in Cologne in 1914, the work was evidently meant to depict the theme of 'resurrection'.[12] Kandinsky's work, then, unlike Mondrian's, displays no direct path to abstraction. Even in his later works one can make out occasional landscape fragments, towers, people, and suchlike.

6
The Max Planck Institute for Evolutionary Anthropology in Leipzig has played a pioneering role in this shift of perspective. See the writings of Michael Tomasello, one of the institute's directors, in particular *Constructing a Language: A Usage-Based Theory of Language Acquisition* (Cambridge/MA, London, 2003) and *Origins of Human Communication* (Cambridge/MA, London, 2008).

7
Comparing painting and science, Leonardo allows the former greater credibility, since he trusted his eyes more than he did the written word, and also greater utility, because what is seen is universally understood; see Martin Kemp, ed., *Leonardo on Painting* (New Haven, London, 1989), pp. 14, 18–19.

8
The term "null denotation" was coined by the American philosopher Nelson Goodman; see id., *Languages of Art* [1968], (Indianapolis, 1976), pp. 21–26.

9
See Dan Sperber's symbol theory in id., *Le Symbolisme en général* (Paris, 1974).

10
Goodman 1976 (see note 8), pp. 45–57.

11
A fact that surprises from the point of view of the present. It forms the starting point of Ernst H. Gombrich's *Art & Illusion: A Study in the Psychology of Pictorial Representation* [1956] (London, 1960–1977), and is referred to by him there as the "riddle of style."

12
Magdalena Dabrowski, "Compositions: The Creation of a New Spiritual Realm," in *Kandinsky Compositions* (New York, 1995), p. 34.

Mondrian und Kandinsky

Die oft gestellte Frage nach dem ersten abstrakten Bild ist eigentlich müßig, denn vor dem Hintergrund der Menschheitsgeschichte ist eher der Naturalismus die Ausnahme.[11] Sinnvoller wäre da schon die Frage nach der ersten, sowohl in Praxis als auch in Theorie entwickelten, ungegenständlichen Kunst – und in dieser Hinsicht wäre Kandinsky wohl der Erste. Später hat auch Mondrian theoretische Texte verfasst. Die Schriften beider sind, wie so oft bei Künstlertexten, kaum verständlich. Dies ist auch nicht verwunderlich, denn des Künstlers primäres Symbol- und Denksystem ist nicht Schriftsprache, sondern seine eigene Bildsprache, also eine grundsätzlich andere Art von Sprache.

Kandinsky hat seine abstrakte Bildsprache schon während der Zeit seiner Mitgliedschaft bei der *Neuen Künstlervereinigung München* (NKVM) – also schon vor dem Blauen Reiter – entwickelt. Sein Bild *Komposition V,* das wegen der Abweisung durch die Jury der dritten Ausstellung der NKVM zum Bruch und zur Gründung des *Blauen Reiter* führte, sieht jedenfalls abstrakt aus. Doch wollte er mit dem Werk offenbar, wie wir aus einem im Jahre 1914 in Köln gehaltenen Vortrag folgern können, das Thema ›Auferstehung‹ darstellen.[12] In Kandinskys Werk lässt sich denn auch keine gradlinige Entwicklung hin zur Abstraktion ausmachen, anders als bei Mondrian. Selbst in späteren Werken kann man hier und da Landschaftsfragmente, Türme, Menschen und dergleichen erkennen.

Für einen Russen war der Schritt hin zur Abstraktion wohl weniger problematisch als für einen westeuropäischen Künstler, denn auch Ikonen referieren nicht auf sichtbare Wirklichkeit. So war der dritte Pionier der abstrakten Malerei, Kasimir Malewitsch (1878–1935), wohl nicht zufällig auch ein Russe. Auf dem Land aufgewachsen, war seine erste Begegnung mit einem naturalistischen Bild in einem Kiewer Schaufenster ein Schock. Wie in seiner Biographie zu lesen ist, hatte er bis dahin nur Ikonen gekannt; und nun erkannte er, dass es »zwischen der Kiewer Kunst und der Kunst des Dorfes einen Unterschied gibt.«[13]

Mondrian dagegen musste sich seine Abstraktion mühsam erarbeiten, und dementsprechend war seine Gegenstandslosigkeit radikaler als die Kandinskys. Zur Markierung seines letzten Schritts hin zur völligen Gegenstandslosigkeit wird oft ein Satz aus einem Brief an Theo van Doesburg zu seinem Bild *Rasterkomposition 8: Schachbrettkomposition mit dunklen Farben* (1919) zitiert: »Ich arbeite jetzt an einem Ding, das eine Rekonstruktion eines Sternenhimmels ist, doch mache ich es ohne Anlehnung an die Natur.«[14]

Schon im »Gründungszirkular« der *NKVM* hatte Kandinsky zusammengefasst, was er mit seiner abstrakten Kunst erreichen wollte.[15] Er geht darin von dem Gedanken aus, dass der Künstler neben den Eindrücken, die er von der Außenwelt erfährt, auch innere Erfahrungen sammelt. Auf der Suche nach einer künstlerischen Form muss er danach streben, all diese Erfahrungen miteinander verwoben zum Ausdruck zu bringen; und um einen überzeugenden Ausdruck erreichen zu können, muss er die Form von allen Zufälligkeiten der äußeren Erscheinung befreien. Dies nennt er das Streben nach einer künstlerischen Synthese, womit er eine Verschmelzung von Eindrücken aus der äußeren und der inneren Welt meint.

Kandinsky ging es um einen möglichst unvermittelten Ausdruck von Erfahrungen und inneren Befindlichkeiten. Dieses Anliegen lag seiner Theorie von einer Verwandtschaft zwischen Malerei und musikalischer Komposition zugrunde, die er in seinem Briefwechsel mit Arnold Schönberg gedanklich weiterentwickelte, und worin Dissonanzen eine große Bedeutung zugemessen wird für eine auf die Zukunft gerichtete Kunst. Seine Hervorhebung der Bedeutung von Dissonanzen war unter anderem gegen die zeitgenössische Vorstellung gerichtet, wonach Harmonie in geometrischen Konstruktionen zu suchen sei. Man könnte meinen, dass Kandinsky damit den Weg, den Mondrian kurz danach einschlagen sollte, von vornherein ausschloss. Doch zielte seine Ablehnung wohl eher auf die geometrische Ornamentik primitiver Kulturen oder vielleicht auch auf die akademische Kompositionslehre. In jedem Fall war für ihn nur eine »antigeometrische« und »antilogische« Harmonie akzeptabel.[16]

In seinem Beitrag zum Almanach *Der Blaue Reiter,* »Über die Formfrage«,

11
Diese, aus heutiger Sicht überraschende Tatsache hat Ernst H. Gombrich »Stilrätsel« (Riddle of Style) genannt und zum Ausgangspunkt seines *Art & Illusion – A study in the psychology of pictorial representation* [1956], London 1960–1977 gemacht.

12
Magdalena Dabrowski, »Compositions – The Creation of a New Spiritual Realm«, in: *Kandinsky Compositions,* The Museum of Modern Art, New York 1995, S. 34.

13
Zit. nach Noemi Smolik, »›Die Kunst meines Landes ist ungleich tiefer und vor allem bedeutender als alles, was ich im Westen kenne‹ – Die russische Avantgarde im Spannungsverhältnis zwischen Ost und West«, in: *Chagall, Kandinsky, Malewitsch und die russische Avantgarde,* Ausst.-Kat. Hamburger Kunsthalle; Kunsthaus Zürich, Ostfildern-Ruit, 1998, S. 24.

14
Brief von Piet Mondrian an Theo van Doesburg, 18. April 1919, Van Doesburg Archief, Rijksinstituut voor Kunsthistorische Documentatie, Den Haag.

15
Helmut Friedel, Annegret Hoberg, »Zur Geschichte des ›Blauen Reiter‹«, in: dies., *Der Blaue Reiter im Lenbachhaus München,* München 2007, S. 33 f.

16
Jelena Hahl-Koch (Hrsg.), *Wassily Kandinsky und Arnold Schönberg – Der Briefwechsel* (Korrespondenzen, 3), Stuttgart 1993, S. 15.

The step to abstraction was less problematic for a Russian than for a West European artist, for icons likewise refer to no visible reality. Hence it was not by chance that the third pioneer of abstract art, Kazimir Malevich (1879–1935), was Russian. Malevich grew up in the country, and his first encounter with a naturalistic picture in a Kiev show window came as a shock. Until then, as one reads in his biography, he had known only icons; now he realized that there was "a difference between Kiev art and village art."[13]

Mondrian, in contrast, had to painstakingly elaborate his abstraction and as a result his nonfigurativeness was more radical than Kandinsky's. A sentence in a letter to Theo van Doesburg about his *Composition with Grid 8: Checkerboard Composition with Dark Colors* (1919) is often cited as marking his final step to complete nonfigurativeness: "I'm now working on a thing that is a reconstruction of a starry sky, and yet I'm making it without a given from nature."[14]

Kandinsky had already set out what he wished to achieve with his abstract art in the founding circular of the NKVM.[15] His basic idea was that an artist, alongside the impressions he receives of the external world, also collects memories. In seeking an artistic form, he must try to blend all these experiences and give them expression, and to convincingly achieve such expression he must free the form of everything incidental in external appearances. This he referred to as artistic synthesis, by which he meant a fusion of external impressions and inner experience.

Kandinsky wanted to express experiences and inner states as directly as possible. This concern underlay his theory of the relation of painting and musical composition, elaborated in his correspondence with Arnold Schönberg, in which dissonances were assigned great importance for future-directed art. His stress on dissonances, among other things, was directed against the idea that harmony was to be sought in geometric constructions. This, it might be thought, automatically precluded for Kandinsky the path Mondrian embarked on shortly thereafter. Yet his repudiation was actually aimed more at the geometric ornamentalism of primitive cultures, perhaps also at academic theories of composition. At any rate, only composition that was "antigeometric" and "antilogical" was acceptable for Kandinsky.[16]

In his article in *The Blue Rider Almanac,* "On the Question of Form," Kandinsky invites the reader to consider a letter on the page simply as a 'thing', in other words detached from its normal function as a sign for a tonal element in a word. Once freed of its linguistic function, a letter can also directly express an emotional value. The same holds true for a line, which represents nothing. A line, which refers to no 'thing', itself becomes a 'thing', which directly—one could say bodily—addresses feelings in the same way that music does.[17]

Even the uninitiated can easily grasp Mondrian's direct path to abstraction, simply on the basis of its visual logic. While Mondrian prioritized intuitive working methods and experience in his work, he was fully aware of the rationality inherent in his artistic project.[18] Using the analytic potential of Cubism to dismantle an object's appearance and, as it were, to unfold it onto the planar canvas, he destroyed the traditional illusion of depth and simultaneously restructured the picture surface. These reductionist modes of structuring prefigured in Cubism persisted right into Mondrian's abstract painting. Nine years later, they issued in what he called Neoplasticism. As with Kandinsky, pictorial elements such as line, color, shape, and plane received their own values without having to refer to anything else. Mondrian further subjected them to extreme reduction: only straight vertical or horizontal lines, no diagonals, only primary colors, no non-primary colors as found in nature, and otherwise only the non-colors black, white, and gray. He employed this highly reduced system of pictorial elements as a framework offering little room for variation, rather like a scientific experiment where most of the variables are fixed so that one or two others can be studied. In this sense, one can view Mondrian's Neoplasticism as a sort of laboratory experiment for investigating universal harmony.

As is evident from their writings, both artists felt a need to theoretically underpin their departure from a centuries' old tradition of painting. The ideas they

Wassily Kandinsky
Komposition V
1911
Neue Galerie, New York

Wassily Kandinsky
Composition V
1911
Neue Galerie, New York

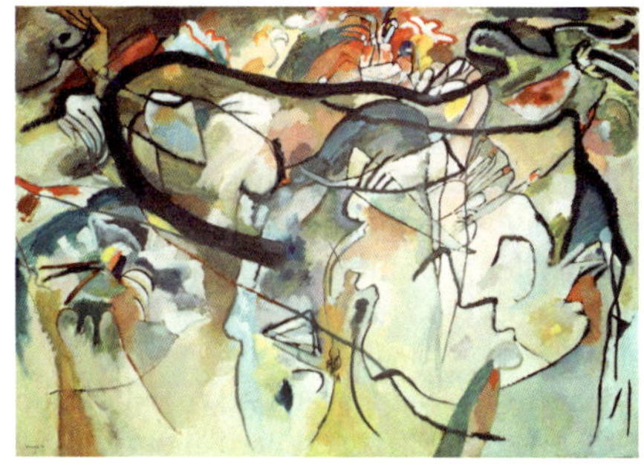

13
Quoted from Noemi Smolik, "'Die Kunst meines Landes ist ungleich tiefer und vor allem bedeutender als alles, was ich im Westen kenne': Die russische Avantgarde im Spannungsverhältnis zwischen Ost und West," in *Chagall, Kandinsky, Malewitsch und die russische Avantgarde,* exh. cat. Hamburger Kunsthalle, Kunsthaus Zurich (Ostfildern-Ruit, 1998), p. 24.
14
Letter from Piet Mondrian to Theo van Doesburg, April 18, 1919, Van Doesburg Archive, Netherlands Institute for Art History, The Hague.
15
Helmut Friedel, Annegret Hoberg, "Zur Geschichte des 'Blauen Reiter'," in id., *Der Blaue Reiter im Lenbachhaus München* (Munich, 2007), pp. 33–34; translated as "The History of the Blue Rider," in *The Blue Rider in the Lenbachhaus* (Munich et al., 2001).
16
Jelena Hahl-Koch, ed., *Wassily Kandinsky und Arnold Schönberg: Der Briefwechsel* (Korrespondenzen, 3) (Stuttgart, 1993), p. 15.
17
Hahl-Koch 1983 (see note 16), pp. 29–30.
18
See, for example, Part Four (on the rationality of Neoplasticism) of his essay "De Nieuwe Beelding in de schilderkunst" published from 1917 to 1918 in twelve numbers of the journal *De Stijl,* reprinted in English in Harry Holtzman and Martin S. James, eds., *The New Art–The New Life: The Collected Writings of Piet Mondrian* (London, 1987), pp. 40ff.

lädt Kandinsky seinen Leser dazu ein, einen Buchstaben auf der Seite einfach als »Ding« zu betrachten – unabhängig also von seiner normalen Funktion als Zeichen für ein Klangelement eines Wortes. Einmal befreit von seiner sprachlichen Funktion kann ein Buchstabe auch unmittelbar einen Gefühlswert ansprechen. Ähnliches gilt für eine Linie, die nichts darstellt: Die Linie, die auf kein ›Ding‹ verweist, wird selbst zu einem ›Ding‹, welches so unmittelbar wie überhaupt möglich – man könnte sagen körperlich – Gefühle anspricht, eben so wie Musik dies tut.[17]

Mondrians gradliniger Weg zur Abstraktion ist selbst für den Laien allein aufgrund seiner visuellen Logik leicht nachvollziehbar. Obwohl Mondrian der intuitiven Erarbeitung und Erfahrung seines Werks immer den Vorrang gab, war er sich der seinem künstlerischen Unterfangen inhärenten Rationalität durchaus bewusst.[18] Er nutzte das analytische Potential des Kubismus, um die Erscheinung eines Gegenstands auseinanderzunehmen, diesen gewissermaßen in die Fläche der Leinwand hinein aufzuklappen, die konventionelle Tiefenillusion zu zerstören und gleichzeitig die Bildfläche ganz neu zu strukturieren. Diese, im Kubismus angelegten reduktionistischen Strukturierungsmöglichkeiten wirkten in Mondrians weiterer Entwicklung fort bis hinein in seine abstrakte Malerei: Neun Jahre später mündeten sie in dem, was er Neoplastizismus nannte. Ganz ähnlich wie bei Kandinsky wurden den bildnerischen Mitteln Linie, Farbe, Form und Fläche eigene Wertigkeiten zuerkannt, ohne dass sie auf etwas anderes zu verweisen brauchten. Bei Mondrian aber wurden sie darüber hinaus aufs Äußerste reduziert: nur noch gerade, vertikale oder horizontale Linien – keine Diagonalen –, nur noch Primärfarben – keine Mischfarben wie in der Natur – und sonst nur noch die Nicht-Farben Schwarz, Weiß und Grau. Dieses extrem reduzierte System bildnerischer Mittel verwendete er als Rahmen, innerhalb dessen nur noch wenig Raum für Variation blieb – beinahe so wie in der wissenschaftlichen Versuchsanordnung eines Labors, wo fast alle Variablen festgelegt sind, sodass die verbliebenen untersucht werden können. In diesem Sinne könnte man Mondrians Neoplastizismus als eine Art Versuchsanordnung zur Erforschung universeller Harmonie betrachten.

Wie ihre Schriften bezeugen, hatten beide Künstler das Bedürfnis, ihr Verlassen einer Jahrhunderte alten Malereitradition theoretisch zu untermauern. Ihre darin formulierten Gedanken zur Kunst sind eingebettet in allgemeine, lebensanschauliche Überlegungen über den Menschen, den Künstler, das anbrechende Zeitalter, und als konzeptueller Referenzrahmen dient ihnen dabei – Mondrian wohl mehr als Kandinsky – die Theosophie, ein um die Jahrhundertwende bei vielen Künstlern beliebtes Lehrgebäude irgendwo zwischen Philosophie, Religion und Wissenschaft. Während Mondrian sich mittels rationeller Methodik von den Zufälligkeiten des Gegenständlichen befreite und zu einer radikalen Abstraktion vorstieß, waren für Kandinsky rein abstrakte Formen nur dekorative Ornamente und als solche überholt. *Zwischen* Naturalismus und Abstraktion dagegen sah er unendlich viele Möglichkeiten.[19] »Die große Abstraktion« muss danach streben, den Naturalismus auszuschalten, indem sie den Inhalt in Formen konkretisiert, die auf nichts außerhalb des Bildes verweisen. »Die große Realistik« muss das »künstlerische Ideal« vermittels einfacher (unkünstlerischer) Referenz auf die Wirklichkeit aus dem Bild verbannen. Beide Imperative gründen auf dem Gedanken, dass sowohl allzu naturgetreue Darstellung, als auch allzu veredelte Ästhetik ablenken vom »inneren Klang« – ein Terminus, der einerseits an die große Bedeutung erinnert, welche die Musik für Kandinkys Auffassung von der Malerei hatte, und andererseits an Kandinskys Begriff von der »inneren Notwendigkeit«.[20] Diese richtet sich aus nach dem »Objektiven in der Kunst« sowie nach der »objektiven Form«.[21] Fast beiläufig wird damit eine subjektive Entscheidung für diese oder jene Farbe beziehungsweise Form objektiviert, und so fand Kandinsky in der »inneren Notwendigkeit« die Universalität, die Mondrian mittels rationaler Analytik anstrebte.

Verdinglichung und Bedeutung

In der erwähnten Passage von »Über die Formfrage« geht Kandinsky selbst so weit, die Linie mit einem Stuhl oder

Wassily Kandinsky

Hartnäckig mit Nachsicht. Die Biegungen sind locker. Der Widerstand von links schwach. Von rechts verdichtete Schichten.

Hartnäckig in steiferer Spannung. Die Biegungen härter. Der Widerstand von rechts stark bremsend. Links lockere »Luft«.

Aus: Wassily Kandinsky, Punkt und Linie zu Fläche – Beitrag zur Analyse der malerischen Elemente [1926] Bern 1973, S. 152

Wassily Kandinsky

Obstinacy mixed with indulgence. Bends are loose. Resistance from the left weak. Denser layer at right.

Obstinacy with stiffer tension. Bends firmer. Sharp braking effect of resistance from right. Free »air« at left.

From: Wassily Kandinsky, Point and Line to Plane, in: Kandinsky. Complete Writings on Art, vol. 2, London 1982, S. 660

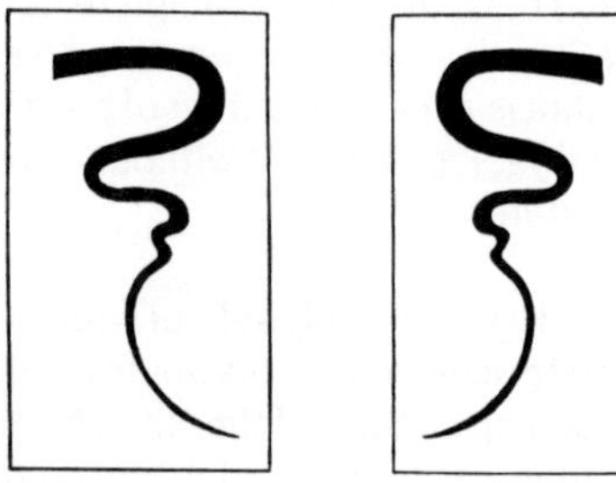

17
Ebd., S. 29 f.
18
Vgl. z.B. den vierten Abschnitt über die Rationalität des Neoplastizismus seines in 12 Folgen der Zeitschrift *De Stijl* zwischen 1917 und 1918 publizierten Aufsatzes »De Nieuwe Beelding in de schilderkunst«, neu herausgegeben in Englisch in: Harry Holtzman und Martin S. James (Hrsg.), *The New Art – The New Life. The Collected Writings of Piet Mondrian,* London 1987, S. 40 ff.
19
Wassily Kandinsky, *Über das Geistige in der Kunst* [1912], Bern, 1952, S. 70 f.
20
Wassily Kandinsky, »Über die Formfrage« [1912], in: Wassily Kandinsky, *Essays über Kunst und Künstler,* Teufen 1955, S. 25.
21
Kandinsky 1952 (wie Anm. 19), S. 128 f.

formulated on art are embedded in general considerations on life, man, the artist, the dawning age, with theosophy—a body of doctrine somewhere between philosophy, religion, and science that was very popular with many artists around the turn of the century—serving, more so for Mondrian than Kandinsky, as conceptual frame of reference. While Mondrian employed reason and method to break free of figurative incidentals, and pushed on to radical abstraction, for Kandinsky abstract shapes were mere decorative ornaments and as such passé. He saw countless possibilities, though, *between* naturalism and abstraction.[19] "The great abstraction" must strive to eliminate naturalism by concretizing content in forms that refer to nothing outside the picture. "The great realism" must ban the "artistic ideal" from the picture by simply (unartistically) referring to reality. Underlying both demands is the idea that excessive truth to nature in representation and excessive aesthetic refinement distract from the "inner sound"—a concept recalling the importance of music in Kandinsky's theory of painting and also his concept of "inner necessity,"[20] a notion pertaining to the "objective in art" and to "objective form."[21] Thus, almost casually, a subjective decision to use a particular color or form was objectivized, "inner necessity" providing Kandinsky with the universality Mondrian sought through analytic rationality.

Objectification and Meaning

To illustrate what he meant by calling a line a thing in the passage of "On the Question of Form" referred to above, Kandinsky compares the line to a chair or a knife. The line acquires its own reality, and an appropriate function. Mondrian summarized this shift of focus from the reality of the external world to that of the artistic means in analogous terms: "However, it can be stated that all art is more or less realism.... Reality here is understood to be the plastic manifestation of forms and not of the events of life."[22] Conversely, in an oft-cited thought experiment, Malevich proposed freeing a chair, a table, and a bed from their normal practical functions and considering them plastically as bearers of expression.[23] Inverting Kandinsky's or Mondrian's reified elements of art opens the way for assigning things the function of such elements, and indeed, Marcel Duchamp (1887–1968) invented the readymade just as the early forms of abstract art were crystallizing out. Utility objects such as a bicycle wheel, a bottle rack, or a urinal were transformed into art simply by his signing or exhibiting them.

The structural analogy and historical simultaneity of these two avant-garde border transgressions—viewing the elements of art as things and using things as art elements—was the occasion for Werner Hofmann's thesis that every radical modernist art movement that breaks free of naturalism must lead to the "objectification" of art, and that this is the defining feature of twentieth-century art.[24]

The thesis is still surprising, shedding, as it does, a different light on the meaning of the readymade for twentieth-century art history, for in using a thing as an art element its properties as a medium ought to be central. However, given the common reception of the readymade, which generally tends to be seen as a found object, this is doubtful. Duchamp's *Fountain* is not held to be the most important twentieth-century work of art[25] for sensitizing us to the beauty of a urinal. Rather, so the often tacit assumption, it is held to be so important because it collapsed the distinction between art and everyday life and, in the process, made fun of the aura of the artwork.[26] Indeed, the surface simplicity of this interpretation of Duchamp's readymade, and its fitting in with the zeitgeist of the latter half of the twentieth century, made it the conceptual foundation for much art and its discourse as of the 1960s—from Andy Warhol to the most successful contemporary artists: Jeff Koons, Damien Hirst, Takashi Murakami.

Did Duchamp's readymades really collapse the distinction between art and everyday life? That cannot be so; for then the distinction would cease to exist and, with it, the readymade. For the distinction lies in the function. In a men's room, a urinal has an unambiguous practical function. In the art context, this practical function persists, at most, as a memory, a connotation that already references the new function: here the urinal has meaning primarily as an exhibit. Viewers meeting with it in this context know

19
Wassily Kandinsky, *Über das Geistige in der Kunst* [1912] (Bern, 1952), pp. 70–71; translated as *Concerning the Spiritual in Art* [1914] (New York, 1977).
20
Wassily Kandinsky, "Über die Formfrage" [1912], in Wassily Kandinsky, *Essays über Kunst und Künstler* (Teufen, 1955), p. 25; translated as "On the Question of Form," in Wassily Kandinsky, *Complete Writings on Art* (New York, 1994).
21
Kandinsky 1952 (see note 19), pp. 128–29.
22
Quoted from Piet Mondrian, "A New Realism" [1942–43], in Holtzman/James 1987 (see note 18), pp. 338–41.
23
"The chair, the bed, the table are not functionalities but the form of plastic sensations"; quoted from Werner Hofmann, *Grundlagen der modernen Kunst* (Stuttgart, 1978), p. 291.
24
Hofmann 1978 (see note 23).
25
According to a survey commissioned by BBC News and conducted in 2004 among 500 art experts, Duchamp's *Fountain* exceeds in importance even Picasso's *Demoiselles d'Avignon:*
http://news.bbc.co.uk/2/hi/entertainment/4059997.stm
26
See e.g. the relevant section of the Encyclopedia Britannica article on Duchamp.

einem Messer zu vergleichen, um nochmals zu betonen, was er mit der Identifizierung einer Linie mit einem Ding meinte: Der Linie erwächst dadurch eine eigene Wirklichkeit mit einer dazugehörigen Funktion. Ganz analog hat Mondrian diese Verlagerung des Interessenschwerpunkts von der Wirklichkeit der Außenwelt hin zu derjenigen der künstlerischen Mittel zusammengefasst: »Nichtsdestoweniger kann gesagt werden, dass jede Kunst mehr oder weniger eine Art von Realismus ist. [...] Realismus ist hierbei zu verstehen als eine plastische Manifestierung von Formen und nicht von Ereignissen des Lebens.«[22] Spiegelbildlich hat Malewitsch in einem oft zitierten Gedankenexperiment vorgeschlagen, einen Stuhl, einen Tisch und ein Bett von ihren normalen, praktischen Funktionen zu befreien und als Ausdrucksträger plastisch zu betrachten.[23] Die Umkehrung von Kandinskys oder Mondrians Verwendung künstlerischer Mittel als Dinge eröffnet so die Möglichkeit, Dingen die Funktion künstlerischer Mittel zuzuerkennen, und tatsächlich hat Marcel Duchamp (1887–1968) in der Zeit, da sich die frühen Positionen der abstrakten Kunst herauskristallisierten, das Readymade erfunden: Er hat Gebrauchsgegenstände wie etwa das Rad eines Fahrrads, einen Flaschentrockner oder ein Urinal zu Kunst gemacht, indem er sie signierte oder schlichtweg ausstellte. Die strukturelle Analogie und historische Gleichzeitigkeit dieser beiden avantgardistischen Grenzüberschreitungen – die Betrachtung bildnerischer Mittel als Dinge sowie die Verwendung von Dingen als bildnerische Mittel – hat Werner Hofmann zum Anlass für seine These genommen, dass jede radikale Kunstbewegung der Moderne, die sich vom Naturalismus befreit, zur »Verdinglichung« der Kunst führen müsse, und dass darin das charakteristische Merkmal der Kunst des 20. Jahrhunderts liege.[24]

Auch heute noch überrascht diese These, da sie ein anderes Licht wirft auf die Bedeutung des *Readymades* für die Kunstgeschichte des 20. Jahrhunderts, denn strikt genommen müssten bei der Verwendung eines Dings als bildnerisches Mittel dessen bildnerische Eigenschaften im Zentrum stehen. Dies ist jedoch eingedenk der gängigen Rezeption des Readymades eher zweifelhaft und gilt allenfalls für das Objet trouvé. Duchamps *Fountain,* sein Urinal-Readymade, wird ja doch wohl nicht als das wichtigste Kunstwerk des vergangenen Jahrhunderts angesehen,[25] weil es uns für die Schönheit eines Urinals sensibilisiert hätte. Vielmehr gilt es als so wichtig, weil es, so wird meist stillschweigend unterstellt, den Unterschied zwischen Kunst und Alltag aufgehoben und dabei auch gleich die Aura des Kunstwerks ins Lächerliche gezogen haben soll.[26] Wohl wegen ihrer vordergründigen Simplizität und weil sie dem Zeitgeist der zweiten Hälfte des 20. Jahrhunderts entgegen kam, ist diese Interpretation von Duchamps Readymade zum konzeptuellen Fundament geworden, auf welchem sich vieles in der Kunst und dem sie begleitenden Diskurs seit den 60er-Jahren gründet – von Andy Warhol bis hin zu den erfolgreichsten Künstlern von heute: Jeff Koons, Damien Hirst und Takashi Murakami.

Hat Duchamp mit seinen Readymades aber wirklich den Unterschied zwischen Kunst und Alltag aufgehoben? Eigentlich kann das nicht so sein, denn gäbe es den Unterschied nicht mehr, dann gäbe es auch kein Readymade. Der Unterschied liegt in der Funktion: Auf der Toilette hat ein Urinal eine eindeutige, praktische Funktion. Im Kontext einer Kunstausstellung besteht diese praktische Funktion allenfalls noch als Erinnerung – als Konnotation, womit schon auf die neue Funktion hingewiesen ist: Als Ausgestelltes hat das Urinal vor allem eine Bedeutung. Das weiß der Betrachter, der ihm innerhalb dieses Kontextes gegenübersteht, was immer die Bedeutung auch sein möge: die Intention des Künstlers oder eine allgemein akzeptierte Interpretation? Was die tatsächlichen Intentionen Duchamps waren, ist hier, so scheint mir, weniger relevant als die Tatsache, dass deren inkonsistente Interpretation so entscheidend den Kunstbegriff von heute geprägt hat.

Bei abstrakter Malerei dagegen ist dieses Missverständnis über die Funktion künstlerischer Mittel ausgeschlossen, denn im Gemälde ist eine Linie zweifellos Teil eines Bedeutungsträgers. Was sollte ein Gemälde sonst sein? Nur geht es hier natürlich nicht um eine einfach zu umschreibende Bedeutung: Für Kandinsky ging es um den inneren Klang – eine Art notwendige Synthese von Erfahrungen aus der Außenwelt

Marcel Duchamp
Fountain
1917
Original verloren; 2. Version: Sidney Janis, New York (1951); 3. Version Galleria Schwarz, Mailand (1964)

Marcel Duchamp
Fountain
1917
Original lost; 2nd version: Sidney Janis, New York (1951); 3rd version Galleria Schwarz, Mailand (1964)

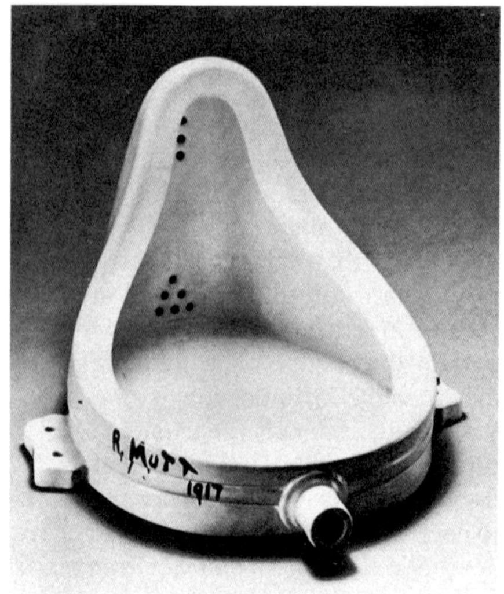

22
»However, it can be stated that all art is more or less realism. [...] Reality here is understood to be the plastic manifestation of forms and not of the events of life.« Zit. nach: Piet Mondrian, »A New Realism« [1942–43], in: Holtzman / James 1987 (wie Anm. 18), S. 338–341.

23
»Der Stuhl, das Bett, der Tisch sind nicht Zweckmäßigkeiten, sondern die Gestalt plastischer Empfindungen.« Zit. nach: Werner Hofmann, *Grundlagen der modernen Kunst,* Stuttgart 1978, S. 291.

24
Ebd., S. 291.

25
Gemäß einer Umfrage des Jahres 2004 im Auftrag der BBC News unter 500 Kunstexperten ist *Fountain,* das *Readymade* von Duchamp, selbst wichtiger als die *Demoiselles d'Avignon* von Picasso: http://news.bbc.co.uk/2/hi/entertainment/4059997.stm

26
Vgl. z. B. das Lemma zu Duchamp in der *Encyclopaedia Britannica.*

this, regardless of any other meanings involved, the artist's intention, for instance, or a conventional interpretation. What Duchamp's actual intentions were is less relevant, in my view, than the fact that their being inconsistently interpreted has so strongly influenced today's concept of art.

In abstract painting, though, one cannot possibly mistake the function of the elements of art, for a line in a painting is manifestly part of a bearer of meaning. What else is a painting meant to be? Only we are not dealing here with an easily conveyable meaning. For Kandinsky, it was a question of the inner sound, a quasi-necessary synthesis of impressions of the external world and inner experience, and he was well aware that this differed for each individual. Mondrian's approach, in contrast, was more universal. He wished to reduce natural forms to constant elements and to discover "*consciously or unconsciously* the fundamental laws hidden in reality."[27] The art of both artists appeals to a proper attitude on the viewer's part, to his openness, as also to his readiness to take some trouble: meaning must be sought somewhere between reason and feeling.

And if we can infer anything from the objectification of art in Hofmann's sense, then it is not so much the collapse of the distinction between art and everyday life as the warning that art, like all symbolic worlds, has its own reality, a fact that is too easily lost sight of in front of the evening television screen.

Translated from the German
by Christopher Jenkin-Jones

27
Quoted from Piet Mondrian, "Toward the True Vision of Reality" [1941], in Holtzman/James 1987 (see note 18), pp. 338–41.

und der Innenwelt –, und er war sich durchaus bewusst, dass dies je nach Individuum verschieden ist. Mondrians Ansatz war dagegen universeller. Er wollte natürliche Formen zurückführen auf konstante Elemente und so »*bewusst oder unbewusst* die in der Wirklichkeit verborgenen, grundlegenden Gesetzmäßigkeiten entdecken«.[27] Beider Kunst appelliert an eine angemessene Haltung seitens des Betrachters, an seine Offenheit sowie auch an seine Bereitschaft, sich ein wenig Mühe zu geben: Irgendwo zwischen Vernunft und Gefühl muss er nach Bedeutung suchen.

Und wenn wir etwas von der Verdinglichung der Kunst im Hofmannschen Sinne folgern können, dann ist dies weniger die Aufhebung der Grenze zwischen Kunst und Alltag als die Mahnung, dass Kunst, wie alle Symbolwelten, eine eigene Wirklichkeit hat – eine Tatsache, die man vor der abendlichen Bildröhre leicht vergisst.

27
»To create pure reality plastically it is necessary to reduce natural forms to the *constant elements.*« Mondrian wollte »... *consciously or unconsciously* the fundamental laws hidden in reality« entdecken. Zit. nach: Piet Mondrian, »Toward the true vision of reality« [1941], in: Holtzman / James 1987 (wie Anm. 18), S. 338–341.

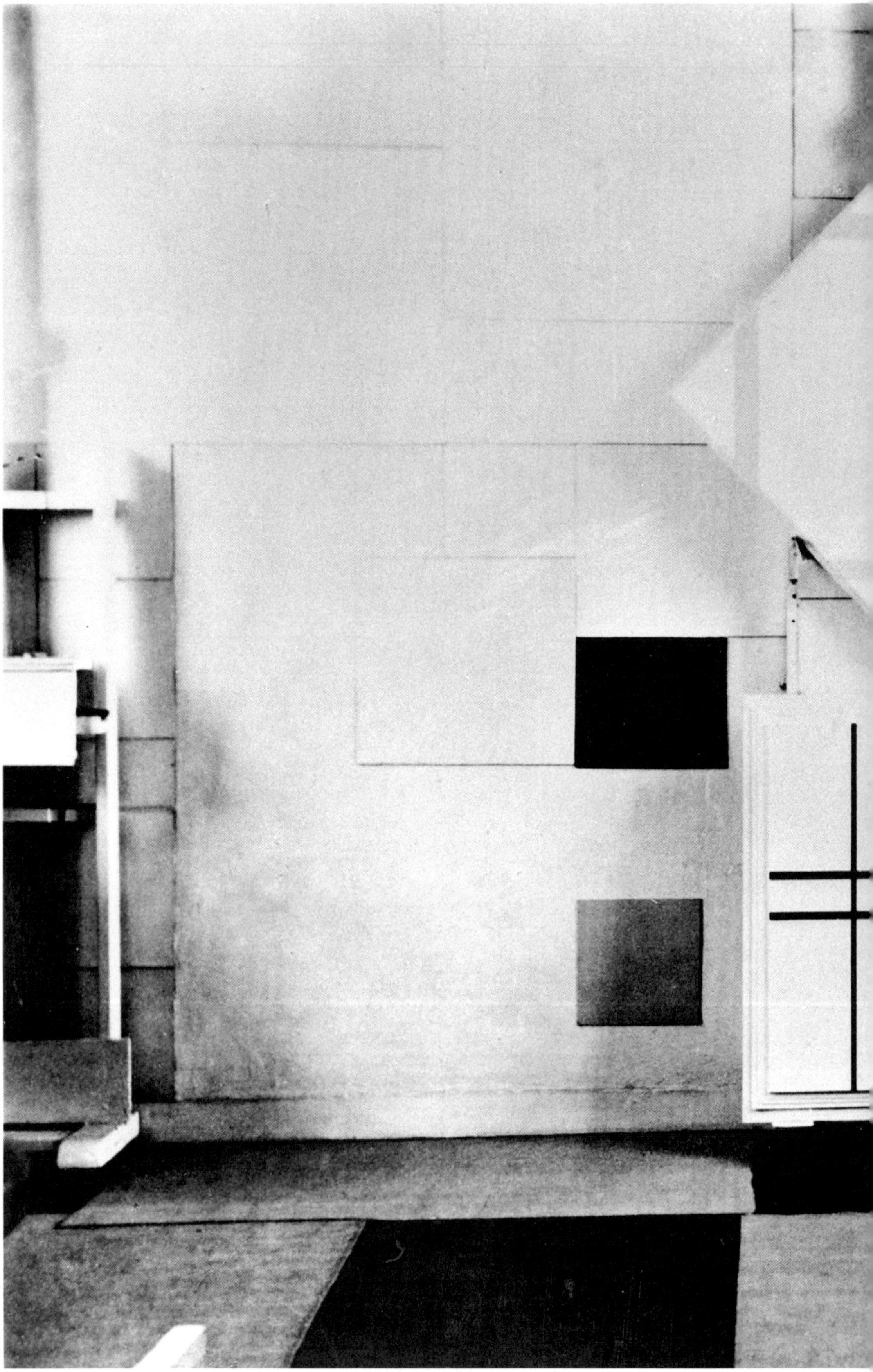

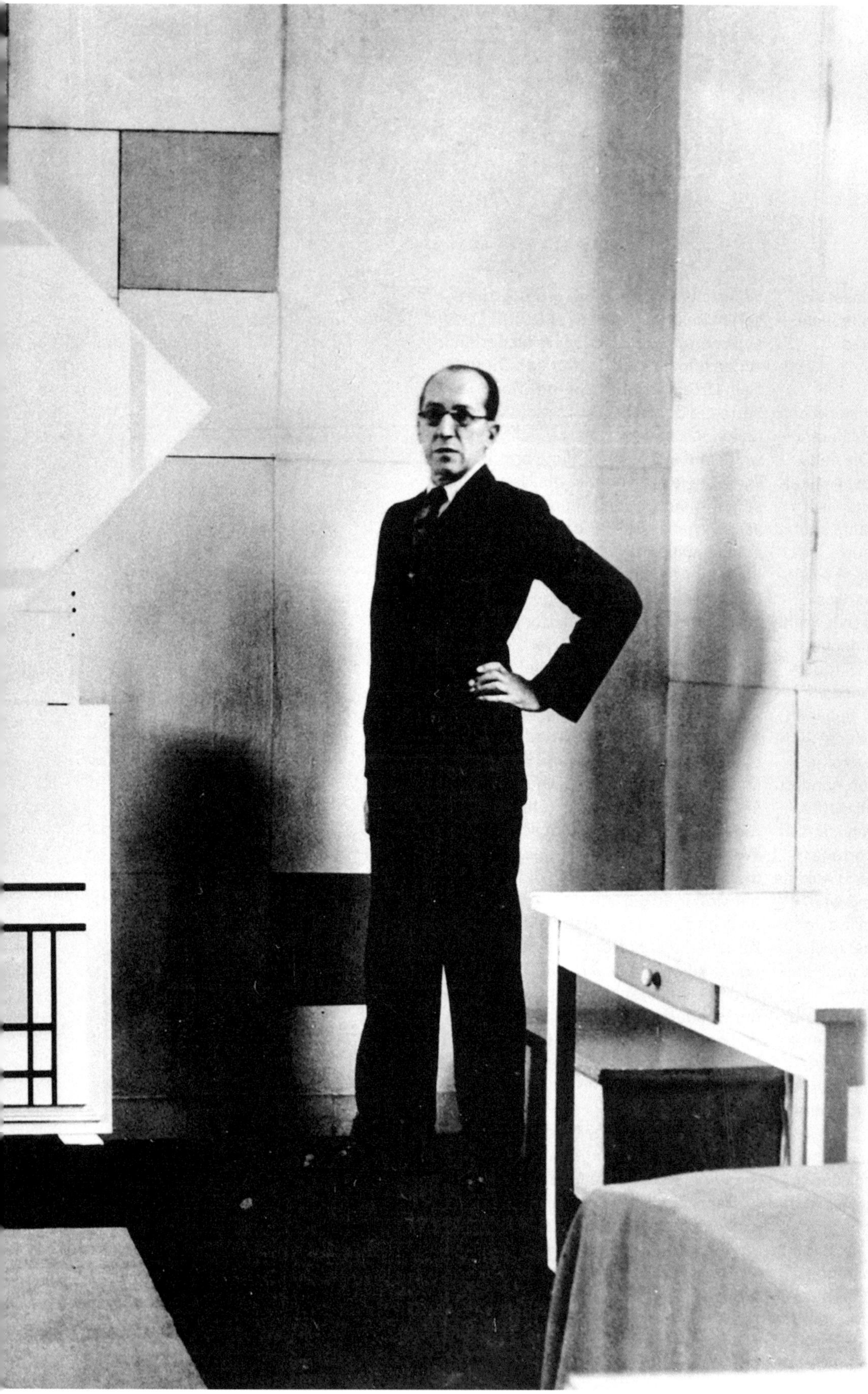

Piet Mondrian in seinem Atelier
26 Rue du Départ, Paris
Oktober 1933
Oben:
Rautenkomposition mit vier gelben Linien (1933)
Unten:
Komposition mit Doppellinien und Gelb (1934)
Foto Charles Karsten
RKD, Archiv Anna Bergman

Piet Mondrian in his studio
26 Rue du Départ, Paris
October 1933
On top:
Lozenge Composition with Four Yellow Lines (1933)
Bottom:
Composition with Double Lines and Yellow (1934)
Photo Charles Karsten
RKD, Archive of Anna Bergman

»Die neue Gestaltung« lesen
Hans Janssen

»Wir wiederholen: Der Inhalt lässt sich nicht beschreiben und ausschließlich durch die Ausführung des Werks verdeutlichen.«[1]

»De nieuwe beelding in de schilderkunst« (»Die neue Gestaltung in der Malerei« – nachstehend abgekürzt als »Die neue Gestaltung«) lautet der Titel der Artikelserie, die Mondrian für die Zeitschrift *De Stijl* verfasste. Etwa drei Jahre später übersetzte er den Begriff »nieuwe beelding« mit der Bezeichnung »Le Néo-Plasticisme« ins Französische, was 1925 im Band 5 der Bauhausbücher-Reihe als »neue Gestaltung« ins Deutsche übertragen wurde. Zwischen Oktober 1917 und Oktober 1918 erschienen elf Fortsetzungsfolgen in *De Stijl,* in denen Mondrian die neue abstrakte Kunst nicht erläuterte, wie er in der vierten Folge noch einmal deutlich hervorhob, sondern ihre Berechtigung nachweisen wollte. Es ist ein außerordentlich komplizierter, hin und wieder überdies verworrener Text, der von unbegreiflicher Terminologie nur so wimmelt und deshalb schwer zugänglich ist. Bis zum heutigen Tag haben sich die meisten Autoren daher noch nicht an das Problem herangewagt, den Inhalt zusammenzufassen.[2] Unter anderem wahrscheinlich auch deshalb, weil Mondrians Gemälde für sich selbst sprechen und es darum gar nicht notwendig ist, sie mit Text zu untermauern. Dieser Meinung bin ich auch. Ich werde daher nicht versuchen, Mondrians Bemühungen zu paraphrasieren, um die ›Essenz des Universellen‹ und der ›veräußerlichten Verinnerlichung‹, der ›exakten Darstellung reiner Beziehungen‹, der ›sauberen, harmonischen Gestaltung‹ und der ›unaufhaltsamen Evolution vom Subjektiven ins Objektive‹ zu formulieren. Allerdings möchte ich versuchen, die Funktion der Artikelserie in Bezug auf Mondrian, aber auch auf seine Leser, etwas weiter zu verdeutlichen.

Während ich über diese erste Artikelserie Mondrians in der Zeitschrift *De Stijl* schrieb, sprach ich mit dem niederländischen bildenden Künstler Jan Dibbets. Sein Urteil war vernichtend: Mondrian hätte die Schreiberei besser lassen sollen. Wenn ein Gemälde nicht gelingen wolle und sich Verzweiflung breitmache, verspüre jeder Künstler die Neigung, seine Absicht dann zumindest zu *formulieren.* Worte bieten einen Ausweg, machen Mut und weisen die Richtung, um Material und Intuition in den Griff zu bekommen. Dibbets zufolge ist dies aber ein Irrtum. Auch als Künstler projiziere man Ideen auf das Kunstwerk, so wie man eine Jacke auf einen Kleiderständer hänge; Ideen, die teils das Produkt von Zeit und Umständen seien, teils Wahnbilder. Das Kunstwerk sei kein Kleiderständer. Das sei der Irrtum. Die Formulierung funktioniere nicht verdeutlichend, sondern geradezu verschleiernd. Sie füge nichts hinzu, sondern schränke das Werk höchstens ein. »Übrigens«, bemerkte Dibbets, »weiß ich die Gemälde, die Mondrian gerade zu jener Zeit schuf, enorm zu schätzen. Das Beste, was der Künstler geschaffen hat, was überhaupt entstanden ist. Die Art von Œuvre, über die sich der Künstler danach selbst nur wundert: ›Hab ich das gemacht?‹ – das passiert einem zwei- bis dreimal im Leben. Solche Schreiberei fügt da nichts hinzu.«[3]

Als Gegenargumente für die Auffassung, »Die neue Gestaltung« sei überflüssig sind zwei Beobachtungen anzuführen. Erstens, dass das Schreiben nicht durch Verzweiflung und Misserfolg eingegeben wurde. Im Gegenteil: Anfang Oktober 1918 war Piet Mondrian an spanischer Grippe erkrankt. Es war »zum Glück nicht schlimm«, schrieb der Künstler an Theo van Doesburg, »aber [...] trotzdem habe ich, außer einem einzigen Tag, ununterbrochen gearbeitet. Heute habe

1
Originalzitat: »We repeat that the content cannot be described, and that it is only through the execution of the work that it can be made apparent.« Piet Mondrian, »Plastic Art and Pure Plastic Art«, in: *Circle: International Survey of Constructive Art,* hrsg. von J. L. Martin, Ben Nicholson, N. Gabo, London 1937, S. 41 ff.
2
Der Kopplung von Schreiben und Schaffen liegt bei Mondrian eine lange und komplizierte Geschichte zugrunde. Darauf näher einzugehen, gehört nicht hierher. Carel Blotkamp befasste sich als einziger Autor detaillierter mit den Schriften von Mondrian in *Mondriaan. Kunst als destructie,* Zwolle 1994, S. 109 ff., und »Mondriaan als literator«, in: *Maatstaf,* 26, 4, April 1978, S. 182 ff.
3
Persönliches Gespräch mit dem Künstler am 2. April 2010.

Reading "The New Plastic"
Hans Janssen

"We repeat that the content cannot be described, and that it is only through the execution of the work that it can be made apparent."[1]

"The New Plastic in Painting" (referred to below as "The New Plastic") is the title of a series of articles that Mondrian wrote for *De Stijl.* Eleven instalments were published between October 1917 and October 1918, in which Mondrian did not attempt to explain the new, abstract art—as he emphasised in the fourth instalment—but did endeavour to show its rationale. These are extremely complex, sometimes even obscure, pieces of writing, larded with incomprehensible terminology which makes them very inaccessible. To date, most authors have avoided any attempt to summarise their contents.[2] For some, the reason for this lies in the fact that Mondrian's paintings speak for themselves, with no need of any support from his writing. I too take this view. I shall not therefore try to paraphrase Mondrian in his attempts to put into words the essence of the universal, or of the 'exteriorised inward', of the exact expression of pure relationship, the pure plastic expression of harmony or the inexorable growth away from the subjective and towards the objective. I should however like to try and shed more light on the role of this series of articles, both for Mondrian and for his readers.

While I was writing about Mondrian's first series of articles in the journal *De Stijl,* I spoke to Dutch artist Jan Dibbets. His assessment was damning: it would have been better if Mondrian had not bothered with all that writing. Every artist, when a painting just will not come together and desperation gets the upper hand, is tempted to at least *put into words* what it is supposed to be. The words provide an escape. They give comfort, direction, a grip on the material and on intuition. But, says Dibbets, this is a mistake. Artists also hang ideas on the work, as if it were a coathanger. To a certain extent, those ideas are the product of the age and of the circumstances. They also describe delusions. A work of art is not a hanger. There lies the mistake. The words do not reveal, they obscure. They add nothing; they merely scratch at the surface. "Make no mistake, though," Dibbets added, "I greatly admire the paintings Mondrian was producing *at that particular time.* They are the best things he ever did, the best one could possibly accomplish. They are the kind of work that makes an artist stand back and ask himself 'Did I do that?'. That happens twice, maybe three times in your life. All that writing adds nothing to that."[3]

Two things belie the idea that "The New Plastic" was superfluous. The first is that the articles were not prompted by desperation and failure. On the contrary. In early October 1918 Mondrian contracted the Spanish flu. It was "not too bad, fortunately", he wrote to Theo van Doesburg "but ... still I continued working, except for one day. Today I looked at my work and was so struck by its clarity that I wrote another article."[4] It was not therefore a *failed* painting, but a *successful* painting that inspired him to write. A painting that brought him closer to his ideal of abstract painting. The jacket was not being hung on the hanger, the hanger had produced the jacket! And it is this amazing experience that Mondrian gives an account of in his writing. This was how he wrote about his work and about abstraction from 1913 onwards at any rate.[5]

There is further evidence of the importance of this series of articles. Almost everyone who has written

1
Piet Mondrian, "Plastic Art and New Plastic Art," in *Circle: International Survey of Constructive Art,* J. L. Martin, Ben Nicholson, N. Gabo, eds. (London, 1937), p. 41.

2
In Mondrian's case, the relationship between writing and creating has a long history. This is not the place to discuss this aspect of Mondrian. The only author who has looked at Mondrian's writing in greater detail is Carel Blotkamp, in *Mondriaan. Kunst als destructie,* (Zwolle, 1994), pp. 109–11, and "Mondriaan als literator", *Maatstaf* 26 (April 1978), pp. 182–86.

3
Personal communication with Jan Dibbets, April 2, 2010.

4
Letter from Piet Mondrian to Theo van Doesburg (written shortly after October 6, 1918). Theo van Doesburg Archive, Netherlands Institute for Art History, The Hague, no. 135.56. Van Doesburg had responded to an anonymous review in *Algemeen Handelsblad* of September 25, 1918 of the *De Branding* exhibition which was held at Haagse Kunstkring in The Hague from September 15 to October 15, 1918. Van Doesburg's response, entitled "The New Plastic Art and Criticism" was published in *Algemeen Handelsblad* on October 6, 1918, with comments from the editor. Van Doesburg's response to these comments was never published.

5
Letter from Piet Mondrian to Theo van Doesburg (written after February 1, 1921), Theo van Doesburg Archive, Netherlands Institute for Art History, The Hague, no. 138.110, in which Mondrian indicated he had found a 1913–14 article about "Representation and subject in art". This is a sign that he had already adopted the habit of writing about his findings in 1913.

ich mein Werk betrachtet und die Klarheit traf mich so sehr, dass ich noch einen Artikel geschrieben habe.«[4] Es war also nicht das ›misslungene‹, sondern gerade das ›gelungene‹ Gemälde, das ihn zum Schreiben inspirierte. Gemälde, die seinem Idealbild zunehmend entsprachen: das abstrakte Gemälde. Die Jacke wird nicht an den Kleiderständer gehängt; der Kleiderständer produziert die Jacke! Und über genau diese grandiose Erfahrung berichtet Mondrian in seinen Schriften – dies ist die Haltung, mit der er ab 1913 über sein Werk und die Abstraktion schreibt.[5]

Es gibt noch weitere Hinweise auf die Bedeutung der Artikelserie. Beinahe alle Autoren, die Mondrians Werk behandeln, beschreiben die Gemälde ab 1917/18 mit Begriffen, die »Der neuen Gestaltung« entlehnt wurden. Yve-Alain Bois zum Beispiel, der sich wie kein anderer in den vergangenen Jahrzehnten darum bemüht hat, Mondrians logischen Werdegang zu präsentieren, setzt bei seinen Erläuterungen fortwährend Wörter und Begriffe mit spezieller Bedeutung in Anführungszeichen: »the universal«, »particularity«, »immutable, which is equilibrated relationships«, »each element is determined by its contrary«, »tensed curve« und »elimination of the particular«. Das sind englische Übersetzungen der niederländischen Begriffe »het universeele« (das Universelle), »bizonderheid« (Besonderheit), »het onveranderlijke, dat evenwichtige verhouding is« (das Unveränderliche, das gleichgewichtige Beziehung ist), »ieder beeldingsmiddel wordt bepaald door zijn tegendeeligheid« (jedes Gestaltungsmittel wird durch seine Gegensätzlichkeit bestimmt), »gespannen lijn« (gespannte Linie) und »vernietiging van het bizondere« (Vernichtung des Besonderen).[6] Mondrians Sprachgebrauch ist noch viel sonderbarer als die englische – oder deutsche – Übersetzung zum Ausdruck bringen kann.

Mondrian verwendet in »Die neue Gestaltung« nicht nur diese, sondern noch weitere Begriffe wie »bepaaldheid« (Bestimmtheit), »veralgemeening« (Verallgemeinerung), »het volstrekte« (das Absolute), »klaarheid« (Klarheit), »verinnerlijking« (Verinnerlichung), »veruiterlijking« (Veräußerlichung) und »uitbreiding« (Ausweitung) auf eine besonders eigensinnige Weise. Sie erhalten eine okkasionelle Bedeutung, und das erfordert selbst im Niederländischen viel Einfühlungsvermögen, um genau nachzuvollziehen, was gemeint war. Darüber hinaus wollte Mondrian mehr Bedeutung zum Ausdruck bringen, als die Wörter selbst vermitteln können. Das geht aus der merkwürdigen Typografie hervor, wobei alles, was im Manuskript unterstrichen war (und das war eine Menge), mit größerem Buchstabenabstand gesetzt wurde (Abb. rechts). Der Text sagt: ›Dies ist gewichtig; dies hat Tiefe‹.

Das wird auch in den ersten Briefen deutlich, die Mondrian mit van Doesburg austauschte. Am 21. Mai 1917 schreibt er: »Ich habe die Kriegszeit bisher damit verbracht, dies zu Papier zu bringen, werde jetzt aber nicht nur noch schreiben. Die ersten Jahre werde ich Dir jedoch durchaus eine – wage ich zu behaupten – gute Stütze sein können. Wir denken so in etwa in die gleiche Richtung und gehen jetzt mit doppelter Kraft immer wieder das gleiche Thema an!! Mein Geschreibsel ist nun so gut wie fertig, muss es ~~also~~ jeden Monat nur noch etwas ausfeilen und kann dir dann regelmäßig sofort eine Kopie schicken. Du wirst mir später dann bestimmt helfen, dies als Buch herauszugeben, denn obwohl ich kein Schriftsteller bin, messe ich meinem Geschreibsel doch Gewicht bei. In einer Aufsatzreihe habe ich die (unsere) Sache aus allen Gesichtspunkten betrachtet, sofern möglich. Was ich sonst noch vergesse, machst Du dann.«[7] Mondrian überarbeitete für jede Ausgabe also erneut den Text, den er schon längst fertig liegen hatte, feilte daran, strich Teile weg, fügte andere hinzu und formulierte immer wieder neu. Das tat er nicht nur aus Unsicherheit (er weist van Doesburg wiederholt darauf hin, dass »sie« [die Leser] an dem Text nichts beanstanden dürfen), sondern auch, weil er sich fortwährend mit Künstlerkollegen, Lesern, Opponenten austauschte. Er reagierte auf andere, suchte aber gelegentlich auch die Konfrontation.

In dieser Hinsicht ist »Die neue Gestaltung« eigentlich kein Text mit einem einzigen Autor. Es laufen implizite Dialoge mit Künstlern aus seinem Umfeld wie Bart van der Leck (über die Farbanwendung und den Status des Gemäldes),

Seite 87 des Artikels der Serie »Natuurlijke en abstracte realiteit« von Piet Mondrian in *De Stijl*, II, 8, 1919, S. 87

Page 87 of an article in Piet Mondrian's series »Natuurlijke en abstracte realiteit« in *De Stijl* II, no. 8 (1919), p. 87

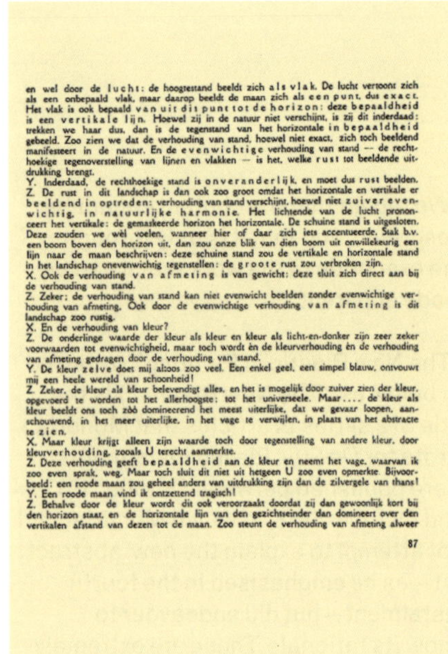

en wel door de lucht: de hoogtestand beeldt zich als vlak. De lucht vertoont zich als een onbepaald vlak, maar daarop beeldt de maan zich als een punt, dus exact. Het vlak is ook bepaald van uit dit punt tot de horizon: deze bepaaldheid is een vertikale lijn. Hoewel zij in de natuur niet verschijnt, is zij dit inderdaad: trekken we haar dus, dan is de tegenstand van het horizontale in bepaaldheid gebeeld. Zoo zien we dat de verhouding van stand, hoewel niet exact, zich toch beeldend manifesteert in de natuur. En de evenwichtige verhouding van stand — de rechthoekige tegenoverstelling van lijnen en vlakken — is het, welke rust tot beeldende uitdrukking brengt.
Y. Inderdaad, de rechthoekige stand is onveranderlijk, en moet dus rust beelden.
Z. De rust in dit landschap is dan ook zoo groot omdat het horizontale en vertikale er beeldend in optreden: verhouding van stand verschijnt, hoewel niet zuiver evenwichtig, in natuurlijke harmonie. Het lichtende van de lucht prononceert het vertikale: de gemaskeerde horizon het horizontale. De schuine stand is uitgesloten. Deze zouden we wèl voelen, wanneer hier of daar zich iets accentueerde. Stak b.v. een boom boven den horizon uit, dan zou onze blik van dien boom uit onwillekeurig een lijn naar de maan beschrijven: deze schuine stand zou de vertikale en horizontale stand in het landschap onevenwichtig tegenstellen: de groote rust zou verbroken zijn.
X. Ook de verhouding van afmeting is van gewicht: deze sluit zich direct aan bij de verhouding van stand.
Z. Zeker; de verhouding van stand kan niet evenwicht beelden zonder evenwichtige verhouding van afmeting. Ook door de evenwichtige verhouding van afmeting is dit landschap zoo rustig.
X. En de verhouding van kleur?
Z. De onderlinge waarde der kleur als kleur en kleur als licht-en-donker zijn zeer zeker voorwaarden tot evenwichtigheid, maar toch wordt èn de kleurverhouding èn de verhouding van afmeting gedragen door de verhouding van stand.
Y. De kleur zelve doet mij altoos zoo veel. Een enkel geel, een simpel blauw, ontvouwt mij een heele wereld van schoonheid!
Z. Zeker, de kleur als kleur belevendigt alles, en het is mogelijk door zuiver zien der kleur, opgevoerd te worden tot het allerhoogste: tot het universeele. Maar .... de kleur als kleur beeldt ons toch zóó domineerend het meest uiterlijke, dat we gevaar loopen, aanschouwend, in het meer uiterlijke, in het vage te verwijlen, in plaats van het abstracte te zien.
X. Maar kleur krijgt alleen zijn waarde toch door tegenstelling van andere kleur, door kleurverhouding, zooals U terecht aanmerkte.
Z. Deze verhouding geeft bepaaldheid aan de kleur en neemt het vage, waarvan ik zoo even sprak, weg. Maar toch sluit dit niet uit hetgeen U zoo even opmerkte. Bijvoorbeeld: een roode maan zou geheel anders van uitdrukking zijn dan de zilvergele van thans!
Y. Een roode maan vind ik ontzettend tragisch!
Z. Behalve door de kleur wordt dit ook veroorzaakt doordat zij dan gewoonlijk kort bij den horizon staat, en de horizontale lijn van den gezichtseinder dan domineert over den vertikalen afstand van dezen tot de maan. Zoo steunt de verhouding van afmeting alweer

87

4
Brief von Piet Mondrian an Theo van Doesburg (kurz nach dem 6. Oktober 1918), Archiv Theo van Doesburg, Rijksbureau voor Kunsthistorische Documentatie, Den Haag, Nr. 135.56. Diese im Grunde unsichere Datierung des Briefs habe ich beibehalten, weil Mondrian darin auf eine Polemik eingeht, die van Doesburg im Hinblick auf eine anonyme Rezension der Ausstellung von De Branding im Kunstkreis Haagse Kunstkring in Den Haag – die vom 15. September bis 15. Oktober 1918 stattfand – in der Zeitung *Algemeen Handelsblad* vom 25. September 1918 geführt hatte. Die Reaktion von van Doesburg erschien am 6. Oktober 1918 unter dem Titel »De nieuwe kunst en de kritiek« in der Zeitung *Algemeen Handelsblad* mit Kommentar von der Redaktion. Van Doesburgs Reaktion auf diesen Kommentar wurde nicht veröffentlicht.
5
Brief von Piet Mondrian an Theo van Doesburg (nach dem 1. Februar 1921), Archiv Theo van Doesburg, Rijksbureau voor Kunsthistorische Documentatie, Den Haag, Nr. 138.110, worin Mondrian angibt, einen Artikel aus dem Jahr 1913/14 über »Die Darstellung und das Thema in der Kunst« gefunden zu haben. Das zeigt, dass er 1913 schon die Gewohnheit hatte, sich über Theorie schriftlich zu äußern.
6
Siehe Hal Foster u. a., *Art since 1900. Modernism, Antimodernism, Postmodernism*, London 2004, S. 148 ff.
7
Brief von Piet Mondrian an Theo van Doesburg vom 21. Mai 1917 aus Laren, Archiv Theo van Doesburg, Rijksbureau voor Kunsthistorische Documentatie, Den Haag, Nr. 134.11.

about Mondrian's work considers and describes the paintings he produced from 1917–18 onwards in terms derived from "The New Plastic". Yves-Alain Bois, for example, who over the past few decades has toiled like no other to describe the development of Mondrian's logic, always places many words and expressions in parentheses: "the universal", "particularity", the "immutable, which is equilibrated relationships", "each element is determined by its contrary", "tensed curve", "elimination of the particular" (translations of "het universeele", "bizonderheid", "het onveranderlijke, dat evenwichtige verhouding is", "ieder beeldingsmiddel wordt bepaald door zijn tegendeeligheid", "gespannen lijn" and "vernietiging van het bizondere").[6] Mondrian's use of the Dutch language is in fact much stranger than the English—or French—translation can ever suggest.

In "The New Plastic" Mondrian uses not only these but also other terms—like "bepaaldheid" ("determinateness"), "veralgemeening" ("generalisation"), "het volstrekte" ("the absolute"), "klaarheid" ("clarity"), "verinnerlijking" ("interiorisation"), "veruiterlijking" ("exteriorisation") and "uitbreiding" ("expansion") in his own obstinately curious way. They acquire an opportunistic meaning, and even in Dutch the reader needs a great deal of empathy to be able to follow his precise meaning. Mondrian also tries to suggest more meaning than is actually intrinsic to the words, as evidenced by his strange typography, whereby everything that was underlined in the manuscript (and that was a great deal) was set in a spaced font (fig. left). The text says: 'This is momentous; this is deep.'

This can also be seen in the first exchange of letters between Mondrian and Van Doesburg. On 21 May 1917 he wrote: "I have now spent the war on all that writing, but I will not keep on writing. These first few years, though—I venture to say—I shall be a great support to you. We think more or less along the same lines and now strike the anvil with double force! My writing is actually done now, ~~so~~ I merely have to review a little every month, and can then send you some copy immediately. You will I hope help me later to publish it as a book, for though I am no man of letters, I do attach great importance to my writing. I have considered the (our) cause from all sides, as far as possible, in a series of essays. The rest, what I forget, you shall have to do".[7] So Mondrian reviews each instalment, written long before, chips away at it, removes and adds things, continually changes the wording. He does this not only out of insecurity (he repeats to Van Doesburg that "they" [the readers], must have nothing to remark on in the writing), but also because he is continually in discussion with fellow artists, readers, opponents. He responds to others, and sometimes also seeks confrontation.

In this respect, "The New Plastic" did not in fact have a single author. It contains hidden dialogues with a number of obvious candidates, like artists Bart van der Leck (about the use of colour and the status of painting), Theo van Doesburg (about the precise nature of abstraction, and how to tackle the common cause), Jacob van Domselaer (about the tragic and the harmonious), Wassily Kandinsky (about revealing the inward, the spiritual and how artists use the intuitive) and J.J.P. Oud (about the relationship between the new art and architecture), and also with artists who had been important to Mondrian in his 'previous life', like Jan Toorop (about the role of the spiritual and the symbolic), Simon Maris (about tradition and the nature of the image), Matthijs Maris (about the expression of an inner truth and of a higher reality that transcends nature) and H.P. Berlage (about the social impact of art). As the series of articles developed the implicit dialogue with this last group, in particular, gradually descended into a more vicious exchange. Within a year, as "The New Plastic" was being written, what began as mere provocation of admired predecessors turned into open conflict. I shall return to this later. At the moment, I merely wish to highlight the unflagging enthusiasm with which Mondrian engaged in his dialogue with the new guard.

These hidden debates had major implications. They prevented the final version from becoming a homogeneous view of the world. The target is often indiscernible. But sometimes the discussion was highly specialised,

6
See Hal Foster et al., *Art since 1900. Modernism, Antimodernism, Postmodernism.* (London, 2004), pp. 148–50.

7
Letter from Piet Mondrian to Theo van Doesburg, sent from Laren on May 21, 1917, Theo van Doesburg Archive, Netherlands Institute for Art History, The Hague, no. 134.11.

mit Theo van Doesburg (über die genaue Art der Abstraktion und die Vorgehensweise bei ihrer gemeinsamen Sache), mit Jacob van Domselaer (über das Tragische und das Harmonische), mit Wassily Kandinsky (über das Sichtbarmachen des Inneren, Geistigen und wie der Künstler die Intuition einsetzt) und mit J.J.P. Oud (über die Beziehung zwischen neuer Kunst und Architektur); so führt Mondrian sie auch mit jenen Künstlern, die ihm aus seinem ›früheren Leben‹ noch etwas bedeuten, nämlich mit Jan Toorop (über die Rolle des Geistigen und Symbolischen), mit Simon Maris (über Tradition und die Beschaffenheit des Bildes), mit Matthijs Maris (über den Ausdruck einer inneren Wahrheit sowie einer höheren Wirklichkeit, die sich über die Natur erhebt) und mit H.P. Berlage (über die Auswirkung von Kunst auf die Gesellschaft). Vor allem wenn nach und nach das ›Gespräch‹ mit letzterer Gruppe die Entwicklung der Artikelserie immer mehr prägt, wird der implizite Dialog grimmiger. Was als Suche nach Zusammenarbeit mit bewunderten Vorgängern begonnen hatte, gerät im Laufe eines Jahres und während des Schreibens von »Die neue Gestaltung« zu einer offenen Auseinandersetzung. Darauf komme ich später noch zurück. Für den Moment ist vor allem auf den nicht nachlassenden Enthusiasmus hinzuweisen, mit dem der implizite Dialog mit der jungen Garde geführt wird.

Diese impliziten Diskussionen ufern aus. Sie verhindern es, dass der letztendliche Text ein homogenes Weltbild vermittelt. Häufig ist der Adressat nicht mehr erkennbar. Hin und wieder geht es aber sehr fachspezifisch um ein einziges Wort. »Ich habe van der Leck meinen Aufsatz vorgelesen. Er ist gegen die rechtwinklige [rechthoekig] Abgrenzung der Farbe und wollte stattdessen eine geradlinige [rechtlijnig] haben«, schreibt Mondrian an van Doesburg. »Dann kann ich aber nicht [...] meiner Überzeugung [folgen] und daher wollte ich es so lassen, wie ich es geschrieben habe. Ich bin sehr froh, Verbesserungen in ›Die neue Gestaltung‹ aufnehmen zu können, sowohl von anderen als auch von mir, jedoch kann ich ein Gefüge <u>geometrischer Figuren</u> nicht anders als <u>näher bei der Natur</u> betrachten. Vielleicht irre ich mich, das Werk wird zeigen, wie es werden muss.«[8] Selbst im heftigsten Streit verliert Mondrian den Leser nicht aus den Augen: »Sollen die Leute, die *De Stijl* lesen, dann doch sagen: Die widersprechen sich. Van der Leck kann nicht anders als seinen eigenen Ideen folgen und ich auch nicht. Übrigens glaube ich nicht, dass er über diese Dinge schreibt. Und ich muss es tun, weil ich dies als prinzipiellen Ausgangspunkt betrachte.«[9]

Meinungsverschiedenheiten zwischen den an der mehrstimmigen Debatte Beteiligten sind zudem produktiv, weil sie Klarheit fördern, so wie für die Anwendung des regelmäßigen Rasters, über dessen Zweckmäßigkeit Mondrian auf der Suche nach einem besseren Begriff mit van Doesburg korrespondiert und mit Huszár debattiert. »Was Huszár erreichte, fand ich durchaus <u>was</u>«, schreibt Mondrian im März 1918 an van Doesburg, »da stimme ich dir zu; ich schrieb nur, dass ich es noch nicht für ›geklärt‹ hielt. Auch ich suche gerade, d.h. ohne suchen zu <u>wollen</u>, bringt mich meine Arbeit weiter. In ein paar Monaten werde ich dich mal um dein Urteil bitten und bin gespannt auf deine Schlussfolgerungen.«[10] Huszár besuchte Mondrian am 7. Juni 1918, und noch keine Woche später berichtet Mondrian, er habe ein ganzes Stück über die Schönheit und die Wahrheit der neuen Gestaltung geschrieben.[11] So funktioniert das.

Es wäre schön zu wissen, welches Gemälde Mondrian sieben Monate später dazu veranlasste, doch noch einen weiteren Artikel zu schreiben, obwohl die Artikelserie gerade abgeschlossen war und er mit spanischer Grippe fieberte. Es muss eine der gleichmäßigen Kompositionen der Gemäldereihe gewesen sein, an der Mondrian seit dem Frühjahr 1918 gearbeitet hatte und in der *Rasterkomposition 3: Rautenkomposition* (Abb. S. 210) einen der Höhepunkte darstellt.[12] Das Besondere ist, dass diese Version der Abstraktion – ein Gemälde nur aus straffen Linien und ohne Farbe – schon nahezu ein halbes Jahr zuvor als Option im dritten Artikel der Serie angesprochen worden war. Dort hatte Mondrian in einer Fußnote die Möglichkeit einer reinen »Gestaltung in Linie« als »die meist erwünschte Erscheinung für abstrakte Gestaltung« formuliert.[13] Dies ist beispielhaft für die Theorie, die der Praxis vorausgeht. Das Gleiche gilt für den letzten Artikel im 2. Jahrgang

8
Brief von Piet Mondrian an Theo van Doesburg an einem Samstagabend (Januar 1918?), Archiv Theo van Doesburg, Rijksbureau voor Kunsthistorische Documentatie, Den Haag, Nr. 135.29. Hier geht es um die 4. Ausgabe von »Die neue Gestaltung«, »Ausdrucksmittel und Komposition« [»De nieuwe beelding«, »Beeldingsmiddel en compositie«], veröffentlicht in: *De Stijl*, I, 4, 1918, S. 41 ff. (siehe insbesondere S. 42 und 43).

9
Ebd.

10
Brief von Piet Mondrian an Theo van Doesburg (März 1918), Archiv Theo van Doesburg, Rijksbureau voor Kunsthistorische Documentatie, Den Haag, Nr. 135.34.

11
Brief von Piet Mondrian an Theo van Doesburg (vom 13. Juni 1918), Archiv Theo van Doesburg, Rijksbureau voor Kunsthistorische Documentatie, Den Haag, Nr. 135.44. Wahrscheinlich handelt es sich hier um den 8. Artikel, »Vom Natürlichen zum Abstrakten, d.h. vom Unbestimmten zum Bestimmten (I)« [»Van het natuurlijke tot het abstracte, d. i. van het onbepaalde tot het bepaald (I)«], in: *De Stijl*, I, 9, Juli 1918, S. 102 ff., die im Juli 1918 erschien.

12
Im Februar/März 1918 ist die Farbflächen-Reihe (B87–B94) mehr oder weniger abgeschlossen. Im Juni 1918 beschäftigte er sich mit Kompositionen mit einem regelmäßigen Raster als Ausgangspunkt. Schon vor dieser Zeit hatte er Kompositionen in Rasterstrukturen erstellt. Im Herbst litt er heftig unter mehreren spanischen Grippeanfällen. Am 6. Januar 1919 schreibt er dem Pfarrer van Assendelft, er sei »[...] mit etwa einem Dutzend [beschäftigt], u.a. in Weiß und Schwarz, natürlich wieder ganz anders, als du sie gesehen hattest. Solche habe ich nicht mehr gemacht, weil ich mich ständig wandle – ohne es zu wollen.« Brief von Piet Mondrian (vom 6. Januar 1919) an Pfarrer Van Assendelft, zit. nach: J.M. Joosten, »Documentatie over Mondriaan (4)«, in: *Museumjournaal*, XVIII, 1973, S. 222.

13
»Die Neue Gestaltung in der Malerei. 3. Die Neue Gestaltung als abstrakt-reale Malerei. Gestaltungsmittel und Komposition« [»De nieuwe beelding in de schilderkunst. 3. De nieuwe beelding als abstract-reële schilderkunst. Beeldingsmiddel en compositie«], in: *De Stijl*, I, 3, 1918, S. 30.

focusing on a single word. "I read my essay to v.d. Leck, who is against rectangular [rechthoekig] delimitation of colour and wants rectilinear [rechtlijnig] instead", Mondrian wrote to Van Doesburg. "But then I could not ... [follow] my convictions and so I wanted to leave it as I had written it. I am very pleased when others beside myself make improvements to the new plastic, but I cannot see a composition of geometrical figures as anything other than closer to nature. Perhaps I am wrong, the work will show it as it should be."[8] In the heat of battle, Mondrian does not lose sight of the reader: "Let the people who read *De Stijl* say: they contradict each other. V.d. Leck cannot help but see it as he does, and nor can I. Incidentally, I do not believe he writes of those things. And I cannot desist, because I believe it is a matter of principle."[9]

Differences of opinion between those involved in a debate with many participants can also be productive, however, because they foster clarity, as for the use of the regular grid, on the merits of which Mondrian corresponded with Van Doesburg, and debated with Huszár, in search of a better understanding. "I did think Huszár achieved something," Mondrian wrote to Van Doesburg in March 1918, "I agree with you on that; I merely wrote that I did not believe it had been 'resolved'. I am also searching, i.e. without meaning to search, I make progress through my work. In a few months I will ask your opinion and be interested in your results."[10] Huszar visited Mondrian on June 7, 1918, and less than a week later Mondrian announced that he had written an entire piece about the 'beauty' and 'truth' of the new plastic.[11] That is how it goes.

It would be nice to know which painting inspired Mondrian to write another article seven months later, even though the series had just been completed, and he was suffering from the Spanish flu. It must have been one of the regular compositions, the series on which he was working from spring 1918, one of the highpoints of which was *Composition with Grid 3: Lozenge Composition* (fig. p. 210).[12] Interestingly, he had mentioned this version of abstraction—a painting with only taut lines and no colour—as a possibility almost six months earlier, in the third article of the series. In a footnote, Mondrian had suggested the possibility of pure "expression through line" as "the most desirable manifestation of abstract plastic".[13] This is an example of theory anticipating practice, just as the final article, "The Determinate and the Indeterminate", the "supplement" to the series, is an example of theory following practice. There was therefore continuous interaction, with jackets hung on hangers and hangers producing jackets. Theory and practice could not be distinguished from each other, particularly at the time "The New Plastic" was written.

This is partly because the paintings from those years in particular served a strategic purpose. Mondrian was deliberately in search of visual forms which allowed him to set himself against what he did 'not' want the image to be—a symbolic construction—and was at the same time seeking rules that could help underpin these dissenting visual forms, experimenting in search of the precise nature of abstraction. He was on a quest for plastic means that no longer had a symbolic meaning independent of the whole, but could only become meaningful, manifest their effect, 'in vivo', in the picture, in combination with other elements. That effect Mondrian referred to in a letter to Van Doesburg written shortly after 6 October 1918 as "clarity" ("klaarheid"). In "The Determinate and the Indeterminate" he called it "determinateness", signifying the use of elements that meet two criteria: they no longer resemble natural forms and colours (they appear "in the manner of art", as Mondrian puts it) and they are defined as purely and radically as possible. Mondrian argues that they express the "universal" in the "absolute", using the Dutch word "volstrekt" ("complete") in a uniquely literal way, as the past participle of the verb "strekken" ("to stretch", "to make flat"), with the prefix "vol-" suggesting completeness, comprehensiveness. This is precisely what happens in *Composition with Grid 3: Lozenge Composition.* The regular division of the plane into colourless grey lines of (almost) equal thickness makes this painting deceptively radical.

Mondrian believed this to be the case, too. He summarised his perception in the

8
Letter from Piet Mondrian to Theo van Doesburg written on a Saturday evening (January 1918?), Theo van Doesburg Archive, Netherlands Institute for Art History, The Hague, no. 135.29. This refers to the fourth instalment of "The New Plastic", "Plastic means and composition", published in *De Stijl* I, no. 4 (1918), pp. 41–45 (see in particular pp. 42–43).
9
ibid.
10
Letter from Piet Mondrian to Theo van Doesburg (March 1918), Theo van Doesburg Archive, Netherlands Institute for Art History, The Hague, no. 135.34.
11
Letter from Piet Mondrian to Theo van Doesburg (June 13, 1918), Theo van Doesburg Archive, Netherlands Institute for Art History, The Hague, no. 135.44. He is probably referring to the eighth article "From the Natural to the Abstract: From the Indeterminate to the Determinate (I)," *De Stijl,* I, no. 9 (1918), pp. 102–07.
12
In February–March 1918 the series of compositions with colour planes (B87–B94) had more or less come to an end. In June 1918 he was working on compositions based on a regular grid. Prior to then he had already laid out some compositions in rhombus form. In the autumn he was suffering badly from repeated bouts of Spanish flu. On January 6, 1919 he wrote to pastor Van Assendelft that he was working "on twelve, including some in black and white, different of course from those which you saw. I have not made any more such, because I am constantly changing—without wishing to". Letter from Piet Mondrian to Pastor van Assendelft (January 6, 1919), J.M. Joosten, "Documentatie over Mondriaan (4)", *Museumjournaal* XVIII (1973), p. 222.
13
"The New Plastic in Painting. 3. The New Plastic as abstract-realist painting. Plastic means and composition," *De Stijl* I, no. 3 (1918), p. 30.

von *De Stijl* »Das Bestimmte und das Unbestimmte«[14], der als »Nachtrag«[15] der Artikelserie beispielhaft für Theorie ist, die auf die Praxis folgt. Es erfolgte also eine fortwährende Wechselwirkung von Jacken, die an Kleiderständer gehängt wurden und von Kleiderständern, die Jacken produzierten. Theorie und Praxis waren – vor allem im Zeitraum von »Die neue Gestaltung« – nicht voneinander zu unterscheiden.

Das liegt zum Teil daran, dass die Gemälde vor allem aus jenen Jahren einem strategischen Interesse dienten. Mondrian suchte geflissentlich nach Bildformen, mit denen er sich von dem distanzieren konnte, was er das Bild nicht sein lassen wollte – eine symbolistische Konstruktion. Auf der Suche nach der richtigen Form von Abstraktion experimentierend, forschte er zugleich nach Regeln, um seine abweichende Bildform damit untermauern zu können. Er suchte Gestaltungsmittel, die nicht länger eine symbolische und vom Gesamtbild unabhängige Bedeutung haben, sondern erst durch die Kombination mit anderen Elementen einen Stellenwert erhalten, welche sich erst im Bild in vivo auswirkt. Diese Wirkung beschreibt er van Doesburg in seinem Brief, den er kurz nach dem 6. Oktober 1918 verfasste, als »klaarheid« (Klarheit). In dem Artikel »Das Bestimmte und das Unbestimmte«[16] bezeichnet er sie darüber hinaus als »Bestimmtheit«, womit er den Standpunkt vertritt, der Einsatz von Bildelementen müsse zwei Voraussetzungen erfüllen: nicht länger natürlichen Formen und Farben ähneln (sie erscheinen »auf die Weise der Kunst«, wie Mondrian es ausdrückt) und so rein und radikal wie möglich definiert sein. Mondrian geht davon aus, dass die Bildelemente mit dem Absoluten – »het volstrekte« – das Universelle zum Ausdruck bringen, wobei er das niederländische Wort »volstrekt« auf eine für ihn typische Weise wortwörtlich nimmt: Mit dem Perfekt des Verbes »strekken« (strecken) wird ›flächig machen‹ suggeriert, mit dem Zusatz »vol-« (voll-) das Totale, das Allumfassende vermittelt. Genau dieses Prinzip scheint die *Rasterkomposition 3: Rautenkomposition* darzustellen. Die regelmäßige Einteilung der Fläche in – beinahe – gleich dicke graue Linien ohne Farbe macht dieses Gemälde erstaunlich radikal.

Das fand Mondrian auch. Schon in dem Titel des Artikels »Das Bestimmte und das Unbestimmte«[17] fasst er seine Erkenntnis zusammen. Es ist eine Umkehrung des Entwicklungsprozesses, den er in der Artikelserie skizziert. Dort beschreibt er, wie sich die Kunst vom »Unbestimmten ins Bestimmte« und vom »Natürlichen ins Abstrakte« aus drei Kräften heraus entwickelt, die Mondrian nicht als solche benennt, die sich jedoch hinter seinen Argumenten verbergen: eine evolutionäre Kraft (das Leben bewegt sich unaufhaltsam in die Richtung der neuen Gestaltung), eine ästhetische Kraft (das universell Schöne wird immer gleichgewichtiger und reiner sichtbar) und eine psychologische Kraft (das Individuelle wird mittels Bewusstwerdung immer weiter in den Hintergrund gedrängt, und die Einheit von Geist und Natur ermöglicht es, mit den alten Formen zu brechen und der Vitalität des modernen Lebensgefühls Ausdruck zu verleihen).

In »Das Bestimmte und das Unbestimmte«[18] dreht er die Sache um. Hier geht er von der Kraft des gelungenen Kunstwerks aus. Er konstatiert (mit der *Rasterkomposition 3: Rautenkomposition* vor Augen?), dass die Wahrnehmung des Schönen ausgeweitet wird, je mehr die Beziehungen im Bild von »Bestimmtheit« gekennzeichnet sind und je gleichgewichtiger die Gestaltung ist. Er zieht Künstlerkollegen zurate, die ihm bei der Bestimmung der Gestaltung schon vorausgegangen waren, reserviert aber die »Ausweitung der Gestaltung« – »uitbreidingsbeelding«, wie Mondrian es nennt – der reinen Beziehung für die neue Gestaltung. Was er mit »uitbreidingsbeelding« genau meint, geht aus dem Kontext dieses Artikels nicht hervor. Dem sachverständigen Leser, wovon es im Dezember 1918 etwa 200 gab, war allerdings deutlich, dass »uitbreiding«, die Ausweitung also, für das ›Sichtbarwerden der aktiven Urkraft‹ steht und grundlegend für räumliche Gestaltung ist.[19] Mondrian zufolge ergeben die rechtwinklig zueinander liegenden Linien wie von selbst eine sich ausweitende, strahlende Wirkung.

Wie in einer Versuchsanordnung ist dies in *Rasterkomposition 3: Rautenkomposition* ganz eindeutig erkennbar. Einige der grauen Linien wurden breiter gemalt,

14
Originaltitel: »Het bepaalde en het onbepaalde«.
15
Originaltitel: »Aanvulling«.
16
Siehe Anm. 14.
17
Siehe Anm. 14.
18
Siehe Anm. 14.
19
De Stijl, I, 4, 1918, S. 42.

very title of the piece: "The Determinate and the Indeterminate." This is a reversal of the development he had outlined in the series of articles, where he described how art develops from the "indeterminate" to the "determinate", from the "natural" to the "abstract", driven by three forces (which Mondrian does not mention as such, though they are implicit in his arguments): an evolutionary force (life moving inexorably towards the new plastic), an aesthetic force (as universal beauty becomes more equilibrated and visible in its pure form) and a psychological force (as awareness causes the individual to recede more and more into the background, and unity of spirit and nature allows old forms to be abandoned and the vitality of the modern spirit of life to be expressed).

In "The Determinate and the Indeterminate" he turns things around, using the power of a successful work of art as the starting point. He observes (perhaps face to face with *Composition with Grid 3: Lozenge Composition*) that one's perception of beauty is stronger, the more "determinate" the relationships in the image, and the more equilibrated the plastic. He refers to fellow artists who preceded him in bringing the plastic to determination, but reserves the plastic expression of expansion, as he calls it, of equilibrated relationship, for the new plastic. What exactly he meant by the "plastic expression of expansion" cannot be discerned from the context. But the initiated reader—of whom there would have been around two hundred in December 1918—knew that "expansion" signified the "exteriorisation of the active primal force", and the cause of spatial appearance.[14] According to Mondrian, the perpendicular relationship of lines appears automatically to produce an expanding, radiating effect.

This can all be seen quite unequivocally in *Composition with Grid 3: Lozenge Composition,* as in a laboratory experiment. A number of grey lines are thicker, causing a rudimentary composition to emerge which has none of the sense of arbitrary wavering that dominated earlier paintings. The grid makes the composition more articulated, what Mondrian calls "determinate". The "plastic expression of expansion" also emerges quite clearly in the way the painting is hung, by one of the corners, leaving the taut, clear network open on all sides. The biggest vertical and the biggest horizontal create an apparently spontaneous ecstatic, expansive radiating effect, which Mondrian had already depicted in so many earlier pieces, and which must always have fascinated him as a basic feature of the picture.

Viewed in this light "The New Plastic" had an articulating effect. So there is an element of Jan Dibbets' "jacket and hanger", with the jacket and hanger regularly trading places. This can also be seen in the way the presentation of the articles develops. The first are tightly structured and solidly argued, extending over four or more pages, with short footnotes added here and there.
From the sixth instalment of May 1918, however, the notes grow into complete lines of reasoning in themselves, covering an entire aspect of the new plastic. They appear after the main body of the text, under the heading "Notes". As a result, their character changes, they become machine-gun fire directed at the reader. While, in the first articles, Mondrian expands on the relationship between the form and content of an artwork—or, if you like, the relationship between the hanger and the jacket—later he writes in short, aphoristic pronouncements, with the idea that the message will get across only if it is repeatedly hammered home. But that is not all, for "The New Plastic" also served another purpose. To understand this more clearly, it is useful to examine the text and Mondrian's use of language from another angle.

Apart from the curious way in which Mondrian uses words and phrases, appearing to impart his own particular meaning to them, he also uses archaic, sometimes weighty language: "tijdloos" ("timeless"), "thans" ("at present"), "aanschouwen" ("contemplate", "behold"), "altoos" ("for aye, always"), words that give the text an air of grandeur and inaccessibility. This was to some extent a defence mechanism. Mondrian realised he was working on something that few people would understand. This is apparent from one of his early letters to Van Doesburg, in

14
De Stijl I, no. 4 (1918), p. 42.

wodurch aus dem Grau die Grundstruktur einer Komposition hervortritt, der nichts mehr von dem willkürlichen, richtungslosen Schweben innewohnt, das bei seinen vorherigen Gemälden den Ton angab. Durch das Raster ist die Komposition ausdrucksvoller, was Mondrian als »bepaald« (»bestimmt«) formuliert. Die »uitbreidingsbeelding« (Ausweitung der Gestaltung) wirkt zudem sehr prägnant, da das Bild an einer seiner Ecken aufgehängt wird und das straffe, klare Netzwerk sich so zu allen Seiten über die Bildgrenzen hinweg fortsetzt. Die größte Vertikale und die größte Horizontale lassen wie von selbst die ekstatische, expansive Strahlenwirkung entstehen, die Mondrian schon in so vielen anderen früheren Werken zum Ausdruck gebracht hatte und was ihn als Basismerkmal des Bildes immer schon unwahrscheinlich fasziniert haben muss.

Aus diesem Blickwinkel hatte »Die neue Gestaltung« eine verdeutlichende, schärfende Funktion – also doch ein wenig Jacke und Kleiderständer, um auf das Sprachbild von Jan Dibbets zurückzukommen, wobei Jacke und Kleiderständer regelmäßig ›Bäumchen, wechsle dich‹ spielen. Das lässt sich auch an der Entwicklung des Aufbaus der Artikel erkennen. Die ersten Artikel sind gut fundierte Erörterungen, die sich über mindestens vier Seiten erstrecken. Hin und wieder werden kurze Fußnoten eingefügt. Ab der 6. Ausgabe im Mai 1918 beginnen die Fußnoten sich bis hin zu selbstständigen Ausführungen auszudehnen, die einen abgeschlossenen (Teil-)Aspekt der neuen Gestaltung behandeln. Die Fußnoten stehen jedoch hinter dem Text unter der Überschrift »Anmerkungen«[20]. Damit verändert sich auch der Charakter. Die Fußnoten verwandeln sich zu Maschinengewehrsalven, mit denen der Leser beschossen wird. Während in den ersten Artikeln die Beziehung zwischen Form und Inhalt des Kunstwerks erläutert wird – oder anders ausgedrückt: die Beziehung zwischen Jacke und Kleiderständer – so finden später auch kurze, aphoristische Mitteilungsformen Anwendung, aufgrund der Überzeugung, der Inhalt könne dem Leser nur durch ständige Wiederholung eingehämmert werden. Damit ist jedoch noch nicht alles gesagt, denn »Die neue Gestaltung« hatte noch eine weitere Funktion. Um dies noch mehr zu verdeutlichen, ist es sinnvoll, sowohl den Text als auch die Ausdrucksweise aus einem weiteren Blickwinkel unter die Lupe zu nehmen.

Abgesehen von der eigensinnigen Art und Weise, wie Mondrian Wörter und Begriffe handhabt und ihnen eine eigene, persönliche Bedeutung andichtet, bedient er sich ebenfalls einer antiquierten sowie hier und da gewichtigen Ausdrucksweise: »tijdeloos« (zeitlos), »thans« (nunmehr), »aanschouwen« (anschauen), »altoos« (immer); Wörter, die dem Text ein ›Air‹ von Würde und Unnahbarkeit verleihen. Das war Teil eines Verteidigungsmechanismus. Mondrian war klar, dass er sich mit etwas beschäftigte, was nicht für viele Menschen nachvollziehbar war. Das ergibt sich aus einem der ersten Briefe an van Doesburg, in dem Mondrian mit gewissem Staunen konstatiert, einen Gleichgesinnten erkannt zu haben: »Ihr Schreiben hat mir besonders gut getan: Selten trifft man auf Menschen, bei denen das Geistige eine positive Form angenommen hat und selten gibt es Künstler, die dies positiv darstellen. [...] Ich bin davon überzeugt, dass es immer mehr solcher Menschen geben und der Materialismus in der Kunst in den Hintergrund treten wird. Wir befinden uns jedoch in einer schwierigen Zeit. Später werden Sie, wenn ich es gut habe, an meiner Schreiberei sicher sehr interessiert sein. Dabei geht es um den Nachweis von Vernunft in unserem Streben.«[21]

Für den Nachweis dieser Vernunft war die Ausdrucksweise nicht hilfreich. Das dafür treffendste Beispiel ist das Wort »beelding« (Gestaltung). Viele haben versucht, diesen unübersetzbaren Begriff näher zu erläutern.[22] Abgeleitet wurde er von dem Verb »beelden«, das es im Niederländischen eigentlich gar nicht gibt. Die niederländischen Wörter »afbeelding« (Abbildung), »uitbeelding« (Darstellung) und »voorstelling« (Darstellung, Idee, Bild, Aufführung) beziehen sich auf den Begriff Repräsentation. Indem er jeweils das »af-« von afbeelding und das »uit-« von »uitbeelding« abtrennt, raubt Mondrian dem Begriff jegliche verweisende Funktion. Ein Wörterbuch von 1881 führt das Wort noch auf und beschreibt es mit »etwas Gegenständliches bilden, um es zu formen«; zugleich enthielt es aber

20
Originaltitel: »Aantekeningen«.
21
Brief von Piet Mondrian an Theo van Doesburg (Oktober 1915) aus Amsterdam, Archiv Theo van Doesburg, Rijksbureau voor Kunsthistorische Documentatie, Den Haag, Nr. 134.2.
22
Am besten gelang dieser Versuch Ina Rike, »Piet Mondrian's Nieuwe Beelding in English«, Amsterdam 1991.

which he noted with some surprise that he had discovered a kindred spirit: "Your writing gave me particular pleasure: it is a rare thing to meet a person in whom the spiritual has taken a positive form and artists who express the positive are rare. ... I am certain that more such people will emerge and that materialism in art will recede into the background. We shall have a difficult time of it, however. Later, I believe, you will surely take great interest in my writing. It is intended to demonstrate the rationality of our intent."[15]

Mondrian's use of language did nothing to help demonstrate the rationality of the cause. This is best exemplified by the word "beelding". Many have attempted to explain this concept, which defies translation.[16] It is derived from the verb "beelden", which does not in fact exist in Dutch. The words "afbeelding" (depiction), "uitbeelding" (portrayal) and "voorstelling" (representation) are all associated with the concept of representation. By removing the "af-" from "afbeelding" and the "uit-" from "uitbeelding", Mondrian robs the concept of any referentiality, however. An 1881 dictionary does still list the word, defining it as "to shape something material, with the intention of giving it form", but already notes that the word is obsolete. "Beelding" in the sense in which Mondrian uses it refers to its usage prior to 1881, and must therefore be regarded as regressive, archaic use of language.[17]

Since the 1950s it has been generally assumed that Mondrian derived the term "nieuwe beelding" ("new plastic"), and therefore the concept of "beelding" ("plastic"), directly from former priest and theosophist Mathieu Schoenmaekers (1875–1944), with whom he associated in Laren.[18] Around 1914 Schoenmaekers had set out a theory decrying the base materialism of his age. He was in search of a modern vision of life which related the spiritual, metaphysical and psychological to the growing individualism of the time. He regarded the inner vision as an intuitive but objective starting point for all reasoning. Mondrian was thinking along similar lines around 1917. He too had taken up arms against materialism, he too was in search of a modern expression of the spiritual.[19] It is therefore only logical that Schoenmaekers should have been identified as the source. But this rather too easily overlooks the fact that Mondrian was using the terms "beelding" and "beelden" much earlier. Mondrian himself indicated that the term had different roots: "I believe I am justified with the perpendicular relationship and radiation. I took it all from the Secret Doctrine (Blavatsky) not Schoenm.[aekers], albeit that he says the same."[21]

There is another source for Mondrian's use of the word "beelding". A brief comparative study of usage in a number of Dutch newspapers and periodicals published between 1909 and 1921 shows that the word was in fact in use.[22] It was found 65 times, mostly in pieces about poetry or theatre, referring invariably to the vivid, direct experience of—while perhaps not directly spiritual—then certainly a spirited reality that one perceives immediately, as an emotional revelation, with a definite psychological element. The slightly archaic connotations of this usage are apparent from the type of authors who used the word. In some cases they were church ministers or religious writers, but the overwhelming majority of them were critics or poets from the ranks of the *Tachtigers,* the *Movement of (Eighteen-) Eighty,* the reform movement in Dutch literature active between 1880 and 1894, which championed Impressionism, inspired chiefly by the French idea of 'l'art pour l'art'. "Beelding" therefore has Symbolist origins.

The most frequent users of the word to emerge from this brief study were Frans Coenen and Frederik van Eeden. Frans Coenen (1866–1936) was an essayist and literary critic who helped the spread of Symbolism in the Netherlands. Frederik van Eeden (1860–1932) was a writer and psychiatrist, an anarchist who wanted to improve the world. In 1890 he wrote a pioneering article on Vincent van Gogh that redefined the way the relationship between the work and the personality of the artist was regarded in the Netherlands.[23] In 1909, however, a different Van Eeden had emerged, more reactionary and Catholic. He viciously described Mondrian's latest work,

15
Letter from Piet Mondrian to Theo van Doesburg (October 1915) written in Amsterdam, Theo van Doesburg Archive, Netherlands Institute for Art History, The Hague, no. 134.2.
16
The best attempt is that by Ina Rika, in *Piet Mondrian's Nieuwe Beelding in English* (Amsterdam, 1991).
17
See Hans Janssen and Joop M. Joosten, "Introduction" in *Mondrian 1892–1914, The Path to Abstraction,* exh. cat. Kimbell Art Museum, Fort Worth and Réunion des Musées Nationaux, Paris (Zwolle, 2002), p. 23.
18
The first one to make this association between Mondrian and Schoenmaekers in relation to the use of the term "beelding" was Michel Seuphor in his "Christen-Calvinist," *Opbouwen,* 10 (1937), n. p., but the relationship was first examined in depth by Hans L. C. Jaffé, *De Stijl 1917–1923. The Dutch Contribution to Modern Art* (London, 1956), pp. 53–62.
19
"I am certain that more such people will emerge and that materialism in art will recede into the background." in: Letter from Piet Mondrian to Theo van Doesburg (October 1915) written in Amsterdam, Theo van Doesburg Archive, Netherlands Institute for Art History, The Hague, no. 134.2, and "We have begun an offensive against the material", Letter from Piet Mondrian to Theo van Doesburg (July 7, 1917), Theo van Doesburg Archive, Netherlands Institute for Art History, The Hague, no. 134.14.
20
Robert P. Welsh and Joop M. Joosten, *Two Mondrian Sketchbooks 1912–1914* (Amsterdam, 1971), p. 23, 32, 38, 39.
21
Letter from Piet Mondrian to Theo van Doesburg (April 1918), Theo van Doesburg Archive, Netherlands Institute for Art History, The Hague, no. 135.38. The remark in the letter refers to the instalment of June 1918, note 5 (De Stijl I, no. 8 (1918), p. 88–90). In his letters, he does not put "new" before "plastic" until May 1917, when plans for the first edition of *De Stijl* were already on the table.
22
The search was conducted in the online archives of *De Amsterdammer, NRC* and *Het Centrum.*
23
De Nieuwe Gids, 6 (January 1891), pp. 263–70. See Jane Beckett, *Colour Theory and Formations of the Dutch Avant-Garde 1900–1926.* Ph.D. diss. (Courtauld Institute, London, 1998), passim.

damals schon den Hinweis, dass der Begriff nicht mehr gebräuchlich sei. »Beelding«, wie Mondrian das Wort verwendet, geht zurück auf den Gebrauch des Wortes vor 1881 und ist daher als regressive, archaische Ausdrucksform anzusehen.[23]

Seit den 1950er-Jahren wird allgemein davon ausgegangen, dass Mondrian den Begriff »nieuwe beelding« (neue Gestaltung) – also auch den Begriff »beelding« – dem Ex-Priester und Theosophen Mathieu Schoenmaekers (1875–1944), mit dem er in Laren in Kontakt stand, direkt entlehnt hatte.[24] Um 1914 hatte Schoenmaekers eine Theorie gegen den platten Materialismus seiner Zeit formuliert und befand sich auf der Suche nach einer modernen Lebenseinstellung, um darin das Spirituelle, das Metaphysische und das Psychologische mit dem wachsenden Individualismus gedanklich zu verknüpfen. Den Blick nach innen betrachtete er dabei als einen intuitiven, wenn auch objektiven Ausgangspunkt jeglicher Argumentation. Mondrian blies mit seinen Auffassungen um 1917 ins gleiche Horn. Auch er zog in den Kampf gegen den Materialismus und auch er suchte eine moderne Bildform für das Spirituelle.[25] Daher ist es durchaus naheliegend, dass Schoenmaekers als Quelle angegeben wird. Allerdings wird dabei zu leicht ignoriert, dass Mondrian den Begriff »beelding« und »beelden« schon viel früher verwendet hatte.[26] Mondrian selbst gibt andere Quellen an: »Ich halte diese rechtwinklige Position und Strahlung wohl für fundiert.
Das alles habe ich aus der Geheimlehre (Blavatzky), nicht von Schoenm.[aekers], obwohl der das Gleiche sagt.«[27]

Für die Anwendung des Wortes »beelding« gibt es noch eine weitere Quelle. Aus einer kurzen Vergleichsstudie über den Wortgebrauch in einer Reihe holländischer Zeitungen und Zeitschriften aus den Jahren 1909 bis 1921 geht hervor, dass dieses Wort offenbar häufiger eingesetzt wurde.[28] Angetroffen wurde es 65 Mal, meist im Kontext von Rezensionen über Poesie oder Theater, wobei es sich dann immer wieder um die lebendige, unmittelbar empfundene Erkenntnis einer nicht unbedingt direkt spirituellen, jedoch mit Sicherheit durchaus schöpferischen Wirklichkeit handelt, die direkt in der Erfahrung, der direkten Erfahrung als offenbarte Betroffenheit, wahrgenommen wird, wobei eine psychologische Komponente bestimmt mit einzubeziehen ist. Dass die Anwendung eine leicht archaische Konnotation enthält, geht auch aus den Autorentypen hervor, die sich des Worts bedienten. In manchen Fällen handelt es sich um Pfarrer oder religiöse Schreiberlinge. Meist sind es aber Kritiker oder Dichter der literarischen Bewegung *Tachtigers,*[29] einer Gruppe niederländischer Künstler, die sich für den Impressionismus und Naturalismus begeisterten und die niederländische Literatur zwischen 1880 und 1894 nach Vorbild der französischen ›L'art pour l'art‹ – sinngemäß: die Kunst um der Kunst willen – von Grund auf erneuerten. »Beelding« hat also einen symbolistischen Ursprung.

Die in der kurzen Studie am häufigsten auftauchenden Verwender des Wortes heißen Frans Coenen und Frederik van Eeden. Frans Coenen (1866–1936) war ein Essayist und Literaturkritiker, der zur Verbreitung des Symbolismus in den Niederlanden beitrug. Frederik van Eeden (1860–1932) war Schriftsteller, Psychiater und anarchistischer Weltverbesserer. 1890 schreibt er einen bahnbrechenden Artikel über Vincent van Gogh, worin er die Beziehung zwischen Kunstwerk und Persönlichkeit des Künstlers in den Niederlanden aufs Neue definiert.[30] 1909 agiert allerdings ein anderer van Eeden aus einem verstärkt reaktionären und katholischen Blickwinkel, indem er Mondrians jüngstes Werk, zum Beispiel *Mühle bei Sonnenlicht,* bösartig als deutliches Symptom geistiger Abweichung beschreibt (Abb. rechts). Was bei van Gogh noch als Ausdruck besonderer Persönlichkeit gebilligt werden konnte, sieht er im Werk von Mondrian nur noch als schwerwiegende Entartung und allgemeinen Kulturverfall.[31] Andere niederländische Kritiker übernahmen dieses Urteil.

Das muss Mondrian mit Sicherheit brüskiert haben, denn Jahre später, in der fünften – irrtümlicherweise als sechste angegebenen – Ausgabe »Das Vernünftige in der Neuen Gestaltung«[32], spricht er dies noch einmal an. Er hebt nachdrücklich hervor, dass ein Künstler ›innerlich‹ anders sieht als visuell: »Sein anderes Sehen ist eine innere Leistung, die trotz der These mancher

23
Siehe Hans Janssen und Joop M. Joosten, »Introduction«, in: *Mondrian 1892–1914, The Path to Abstraction,* Ausst.-Kat. Kimbell Art Museum, Fort Worth und Réunion des Musées Nationaux, Paris, Zwolle 2002, S. 23.
24
Der Erste, der im Hinblick auf den Gebrauch des Begriffs »beelding« die Verbindung zwischen Mondrian und Schoenmaekers herstellte, war Michel Seuphor in seinem »Christen-Calvinist«, Opbouwen, 10, 1937, o. S., aber gründlich untersucht wurde der Bezug zuerst von Hans L. C. Jaffé, *De Stijl 1917–1923. The Dutch Contribution to Modern Art,* London 1956, S. 53 ff.
25
Siehe Anm. 21 für das Zitat im Brief von Piet Mondrian an Theo van Doesburg (Oktober 1915) aus Amsterdam, Archiv Theo van Doesburg, Rijksbureau voor Kunsthistorische Documentatie, Den Haag, Nr. 134.2 und: »Wir haben eine Offensive gegen die Materie eingesetzt«, Brief Piet Mondrian an Theo van Doesburg (vom 7. Juli 1917), Archiv Theo van Doesburg, Rijksbureau voor Kunsthistorische Documentatie, Den Haag, Nr. 134.14.
26
Robert P. Welsh und Joop M. Joosten, *Two Mondrian Sketchbooks 1912–1914,* Amsterdam 1971, S. 23, 32, 38, 39.
27
Brief von Piet Mondrian an Theo van Doesburg (vom April 1918), Archiv Theo van Doesburg, Rijksbureau voor Kunsthistorische Documentatie, Den Haag, Nr. 135.38. Die Bemerkung in dem Brief bezieht sich auf die Ausgabe vom Juni 1918, Anm. 5 (*De Stijl,* I, 8, 1918, S. 88, 90). In seinen Briefen taucht das Adjektiv »nieuwe« (neue) zusammen mit dem Wort »beelding« (Gestaltung) erst ab Mai 1917 auf, in dem Moment, wo die Pläne für die erste Ausgabe von *De Stijl* schon in Vorbereitung sind.
28
Gesucht wurde in den digitalen Archiven der niederländischen Zeitungen *De Amsterdammer, NRC* und *Het Centrum.*
29
»Achtziger«.
30
Zeitschrift *De Nieuwe Gids,* 6, 1, Januar 1891, S. 263 ff. Siehe Jane Beckett, *Colour Theory and Formations of the Dutch Avant-Garde 1900–1926,* unveröffentlichte Dissertation (Courtauld Institute, London, 1998), passim.
31
Frederik van Eeden, »Gezondheid en verval in kunst«, *Op de hoogte,* 6, Februar 1909, S. 79 ff. Auch später noch veröffentlichte van Eeden in einer neuen Zeitschrift *De Samenleving. Nederlandsch Weekblad* einen sehr kritischen Artikel über die Ausstellung St. Lucastentoonstelling, wo Kees van Dongen eine ganz besondere Präsentation erhielt und es die allerneueste Mode zu sein schien, ihn und Vincent van Gogh in starken, kräftigen Farben und grell gemischten Farbstrichen nachzuahmen. Siehe »Bij Sint Lukas«, *De Samenleving,* 1, 49, Juni 1911.
32
Originaltitel: »Redelijkheid der nieuwe beelding«.

for example *Mill in Sunlight,* as a clear symptom of mental aberration (fig. right). What he had approved of in Van Gogh's work as the expression of a unique personality he perceived in Mondrian's work as a severe case of degeneration and general cultural decline.[24] Other Dutch critics concurred.

This must certainly have preyed on Mondrian's mind for, years later, in the fifth instalment, referred to in error as the sixth, which examines the "rationality of the new plastic", he refers to the case again. He emphasises that an artist's inner vision differs from the visual: "this other perception is an inner transformation that one cannot explain by physical abnormality, as some doctors would do (some psychiatrists therefore blame it on mental aberration!)". We cannot say for sure in the case of Frans Coenen but, among those addressed in "The New Plastic in Painting", Van Eeden was certainly an opponent. Use of the word "beelding", "plastic", therefore also refers in an ideological sense to the purer, more original context of the Symbolists and the *Tachtigers*—whose ranks had included the younger Van Eeden.

By adding the adjective "new", Mondrian further emphasised the oppositional element. What he was advertising as "new" was in fact a giant swing away from history, towards purer times that he believed lay ahead. This is in fact consistent with the third 'major user' of the word "beelding", Willem Steenhoff, the art critic, who followed Mondrian's work closely from 1900 onwards and was largely responsible for making the early association between the painter and thinker in Mondrian's work.[25] Steenhoff was slightly older than Mondrian. After 1907 he became one of the leading proponents of Modernism in art. He brought Van Gogh, Cézanne, Picasso and Braque to the Rijksmuseum and in his critiques attempted to identify the connection between perception and the solid structure of the image. He believed the "how" of the image was the place where the immediate, unbreakable connection between the spiritual and the real was forged. He used the term "beelding" in this connection, too. Steenhoff's roots lay in the world of the *Tachtigers.* His relationship with Mondrian was ambiguous: he followed his work closely, encouraging him to fish the "deep idea" out of the art, but at the same time refused to go along with his attempts to hazard the transition to full abstraction. Mondrian's addition of "new" therefore had an element of sly recalcitrance.

These contexts are new. The word "beelding" does not come from Mondrian himself. It belongs to various contexts, some of them mutually enhancing, others mutually exclusive, and in "The New Plastic" it is therefore the result of interaction between multiple voices. Some of those voices belonged to the past, to the 1880s and 1890s. To a younger artist like Theo van Doesburg, the word is new. He used it only after 6 February 1916, the day he met Mondrian at the home of composer Jakob van Domselaer in Laren. Until then, Van Doesburg had been caught up in Expressionism, where the concept of "beelding", with its Symbolist connotations, played no role. To him it was spiritually bound up with the musical, and could be incarnated only in a representational, symbolic way, through line, colour and rhythm. But he would soon put this into perspective, for in the following months he would become familiar with the writings of Schoenmaekers, and come to speak the language that Mondrian, too, spoke.

By then, Mondrian had abandoned Schoenmaekers. The guru in Laren had been significant for Mondrian in the period 1910-14, when he was reading his work. It must have sounded strange to him at first that Schoenmaekers used such expressive terms to put certain concepts into words: "relational thinking" is one, and "unity of opposites", and "beelding", "plastic". Mondrian was inspired, and when they became near neighbours in 1915, he even dragged his paintings through the village to show them to Schoenmaekers, who did not think much of his work. The purely theoretical thinker could not keep up with the artist, who ultimately relied solely on his eyes.

Mondrian did not possess any copies of Schoenmaekers' writings. When, in May 1918, he was juggling all kinds of terms he had taken from Schoenmaekers (whether he should

Piet Mondrian
Mühle bei Sonnenlicht
1908
Öl auf Leinwand
114 x 87 cm
Gemeentemuseum Den Haag

Piet Mondrian
Mill in Sunlight
1908
Oil on canvas
114 x 87 cm
Gemeentemuseum The Hague

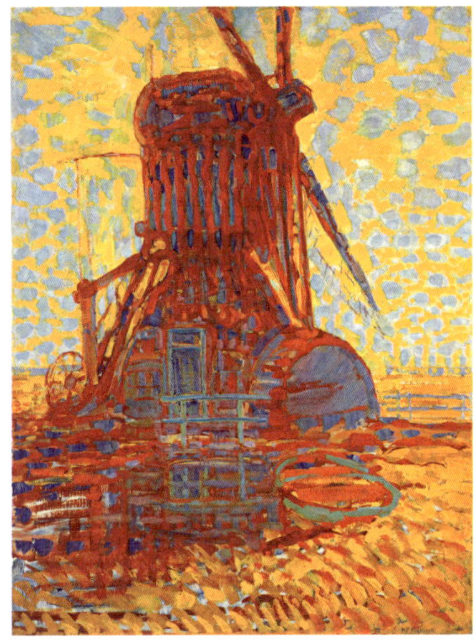

24
Frederik van Eeden, "Gezondheid en verval in kunst", *Op de hoogte,* 6 (February 1909), pp. 79–85. Later, in a new publication entitled *De Samenleving. Nederlandsch Weekblad,* Van Eeden published a highly critical article about the St. Lucas exhibition where Van Dongen had a special presentation and it appeared to be the latest fashion to imitate him and Vincent van Gogh in bright, wild colours and a garish array of paint strokes. See "Bij Sint Lukas", *De Samenleving, 1* (June 1911).
25
Hans Janssen, "'Wanneer men het innerlijke beeldt…', Mondriaan en de invloed van Picasso en Cézanne op zijn werk", in *Cézanne, Picasso, Mondriaan. In nieuw perspectief* (Zwolle, 2009), pp. 57–83.

Ärzte, keiner körperlichen Abweichung untergeschoben werden darf (was so mancher Psychiater daher als geistige Abweichung bezeichnet!).« Von Frans Coenen lässt sich dies nicht mit Sicherheit sagen, aber van Eeden war unter denen, die in »›Die neue Gestaltung‹ in der Malerei« angesprochen waren, auf jeden Fall ein Opponent. Der Gebrauch des Wortes »beelding« verweist daher auch in ideologischem Sinne auf das reinere, ursprünglichere Gedankengut der Symbolisten und der *Tachtigers*[33] – zu denen der frühe van Eeden gehörte, der späte dagegen nicht.

Die Hinzufügung des Adjektivs »nieuwe« (neue) betonte das Oppositionelle noch nachdrücklicher. Denn was als neu bezeichnet wurde, war im Grunde eine auf kommende reinere Zeiten verweisende völlige Kehrtwendung der Geschichte. Das stimmt auch mit dem dritten ›Großverwender‹ des Wortes »beelding« überein: dem Kunsthistoriker Willem Steenhoff, der seit 1900 Mondrians Schaffen intensive Aufmerksamkeit schenkte und großenteils für die frühe Kopplung zwischen Maler und Denker in Mondrians Werk verantwortlich war.[34] Steenhoff war etwas älter als Mondrian. Ab 1907 gehörte er zu den großen Fürsprechern der Moderne in der bildenden Kunst. Er holte van Gogh, Cézanne, Picasso und Braque ins Rijksmuseum Amsterdam und suchte in seinen Kritiken den Zusammenhang zwischen Wahrnehmung und solider Struktur des Bildes. Ihm zufolge war das ›Wie‹ des Bildes für den direkten, unverbrüchlichen Zusammenhang zwischen dem Geistigen und der Wirklichkeit verantwortlich, und in diesem Sinne verwendete er den Begriff »beelding«. Die Wurzeln Steenhoffs lagen ebenfalls in der Welt der *Tachtigers.*[35] Seine Beziehung zu Mondrian war ambivalent: Einerseits folgte er ihm intensiv und bestärkte ihn darin, in die ›Tiefe‹ des Kunstwerks einzudringen, andererseits weigerte er sich aber, sich Mondrians Bestreben anzuschließen, den Schritt in die vollständige Abstraktion zu wagen. Die Hinzufügung des Adjektivs ›neue‹ war daher in gewisser Weise ein trotziger Schachzug.

Diese Zusammenhänge sind neu. Das Wort »beelding« stammt nicht von Mondrian selbst, sondern ist Teil verschiedener, einander manchmal verstärkender, jedoch hier und da auch ausgrenzender Kontexte, und so findet sich in »De nieuwe beelding« – »Die neue Gestaltung« – also das Resultat einer Interaktion vielfältiger Stimmen. Manche dieser Stimmen stammen aus der Vergangenheit, den achtziger und neunziger Jahren des 19. Jahrhunderts. Für einen jungen Künstler wie Theo van Doesburg war das Wort neu. Er verwendete den Begriff erst ab dem 6. Februar 1916, dem Tag, an dem er Mondrian im Hause des Komponisten Jakob van Domselaer in Laren kennenlernte. Van Doesburg war selbst bis zu jenem Moment auf einen Expressionismus fixiert, in dem der Begriff »beelding« mit seinen symbolistischen Konnotationen keine Rolle spielte. Ihm zufolge verband sich das Geistige mit dem Musikalischen und ließ sich nur durch Linie, Farbe und Rhythmus auf eine darstellende, symbolische Weise verkörpern. Dies sollte er jedoch schon schnell relativieren, denn in den darauf folgenden Monaten eignete er sich so manches aus der Lektüre von Schoenmaekers an und begann die Sprache zu sprechen, die auch Mondrian verwendete.

Mondrian hatte Schoenmaekers dann schon hinter sich gelassen. Im Zeitraum 1910–14, als er dessen Schriften las, bedeutete ihm der Guru aus Laren viel. Es muss Mondrian zunächst fremd in den Ohren geklungen haben, dass Schoenmaekers für die Formulierung bestimmter Begriffe solche bildlichen Ausdrücke verwendete: »denken in verhouding« (Denken in Beziehung) ist so einer und »eenheid van tegendeelen« (Einheit von Gegenstücken) und »beelding« (Gestaltung). Mondrian war begeistert, und als sie 1915 in der Nähe voneinander wohnten, schleppte er sogar seine Gemälde quer durch das Dorf, um sie Schoenmaekers zu zeigen. Dieser konnte mit seinen Werken jedoch nichts anfangen. Als rein theoretischer Denker war es ihm letztendlich nicht möglich, diesem einzig und allein von optischen Eindrücken ausgehenden Künstler zu folgen.

Mondrian besaß Schoenmaekers Schriften nicht. Als er im Mai 1918 bei seiner Formung von allerlei Begriffen, die er von Schoenmaekers abgeleitet hatte, den Überblick verlor – ob es nun um »tegendeelen« (Gegenstücke)

33
Siehe Anm. 29.
34
Hans Janssen, Artikel »›Wanneer men het innerlijke beeldt…‹, Mondriaan en de invloed van Picasso en Cézanne op zijn werk«, in: *Cézanne, Picasso, Mondriaan. In nieuw perspectief,* Zwolle 2009, S. 57 ff.
35
Siehe Anm. 29.

use "tegendelen" ("antitheses") or "tegenovergesteldheden" ("opposites") or whether plastic expression of equilibrated relationships should be expressed as outwardness, or in fact as inwardness), he called on a neighbour in Laren to consult Schoenmaekers' book: "I did not have it myself."[26] The dialogue continued less than a month later: "Thus I have to find an answer to the following. I have colour as the opposite of light. According to Schoenmaekers, sound is the opposite of light. If I put inner light, in my view I am justified, but I can also call colour an opposite or antithesis of light, then it will certainly be right."[27] We must exercise caution here, for Mondrian (as a layman) is of course the vulnerable party in this sociolinguistic setting, though that does not detract from his views.

The same goes for the other philosophers—and pseudo-philosophers—who are sometimes linked to "The New Plastic", whether it be Spinoza, Schopenhauer, Hegel or Goethe: Mondrian picked up their names and words from conversations with others, or read about them in the newspaper, and then incorporated them into his own thoughts and writings. "Have I given the title of Kandinsky's book correctly?" he asked Van Doesburg in a letter written in March 1918. "I am no longer sure. Finally, I wanted to ask you if that expression of Spinoza's (at the beginning) was correct. I have none of his works and since you cited it in your last letter to me I came upon the idea of including it because I was talking about truth—further evidence that we think alike. It looks so odd, if I tried to use different words for what Spinoza said."[28]

Mondrian also had such a 'hearsay' relationship, via Schoenmaekers, with G.J.P.J. Bolland (1854–1922), a philosophical exegete who dominated intellectual debate in the Netherlands for a time by popularising the German philosopher Hegel. Mondrian will certainly have derived some of his knowledge of Hegel's ideas about dialectics from Bolland, or from the Hegelian revival that was causing a swing away from neo-Kantism right across the Netherlands at that time, partly thanks to Bolland. But Bolland's actual significance to Mondrian was of another order, particularly if we look at the final sociolinguistic aspect I wish to highlight, the one that is largely responsible for the inaccessibility of the text: the morphological function of words and concepts.[29] In his philosophical writings, Bolland enjoyed exploring the 'real' meaning of words by taking them 'literally'. All kinds of concepts appear to reveal their meaning spontaneously when one examines their morphology. One example is the simple Dutch verb "begrijpen". It means "to understand", though perhaps the most useful English translation in this context is "to grasp", whose literal translation into Dutch is "grijpen", the root of "begrijpen", which therefore appears to be literally associated with "grasping meaning". Or the term "tegendeel", "antithesis", whose literal translation is "counterpart", which appears to embody within itself a different, complementary viewpoint. Bolland actually believed that Dutch was the superior language for higher spiritual matters, concluding matter-of-factly that French, for example, is entirely incapable of reflecting the subtleties of concepts.[29]

Schoenmaekers adopted this way of thinking. He defined the "living meaning" of the word "ontwikkeling" ("development") by dissecting it into "ont" and "wikkel". The prefix "ont-" denotes something passing "from within to without". And "wikkel" means: "wrapping".[30] "Ontwikkeling" thus means a movement from an inner life, that grows from the inside out, outgrowing an earlier form that has become a shroud or wrapping". Perhaps because of its expressive nature, Mondrian became enchanted with this style of reasoning, attempting in "The New Plastic" to use language in the unique manner employed by a certain group of people.

Mondrian also took from Bolland and Schoenmaekers the irritating habit of linking terms and using verbal nouns and whole phrases as nouns thus creating in "The New Plastic" a kind of exponential multiplication of the morphological idea. Terms like "determinate plastic expression of aesthetic relationships", "bringing to determination", "determinate plastic expression of equilibrated relationships", "expression in vagueness", and "the universal as

26
Letter from Piet Mondrian to Theo van Doesburg (early May 1918), Theo van Doesburg Archive, Netherlands Institute for Art History, The Hague, no. 135.37. He is probably referring to part 2 of "The Rationality of the New Plastic", early May 1918 (*De Stijl* I, no. 7 (1918), p. 75).

27
Letter from Piet Mondrian to Theo van Doesburg (June 1918), Theo van Doesburg Archive, Netherlands Institute for Art History, The Hague, no. 134.45.

28
Letter from Piet Mondrian to Theo van Doesburg (March 1918), Theo van Doesburg Archive, Netherlands Institute for Art History, The Hague, no. 135.43. He is referring to the passage in "The Rationality of the New Plastic," *De Stijl* I, no. 5 (1918), p. 50.

29
NRC, 1 May 1912: Avondblad 1.

30
Mathieu Schoenmaekers, *Het Nieuwe Wereldbeeld*, Bussum (Van Dishoeck) 1915, p. 34. Thanks to Marek Wieczorek who, in personal conversations, alerted me to this unusual feature of *"The New Plastic"*.

oder »tegenovergesteldheden« (Gegenüberstellungen) gehen sollte, es sich bei der »verhoudingsbeelding« (Gleichgewichtsgestaltung) um »uiterlijkheid« (Äußerlichkeit) oder nun gerade um »innerlijkheid« (Innerlichkeit) handelte – lief er in Laren kurz bei jemandem vorbei, um in Schoenmaekers Buch nachzuschlagen: »Selbst hatte ich es nicht«.[36] Kaum einen Monat später wird der Dialog fortgesetzt: »Für Folgendes muss ich da was finden. Ich nehme die Farbe als Gegenstück zum Licht. Und Schoenmaekers zufolge ist Klang das Gegenstück zum Licht. Wenn ich inneres Licht nehme, ist das meiner Meinung nach gut vertretbar, aber ich kann ~~die~~ Farbe auch »tegenoverstelling« (Gegenüberstellung) oder »tegenheid« (Gegenwirkung) von Licht nennen [sic], dann ist es sicher gut«.[37] Doch hier sei gewarnt, denn im soziolinguistischen Kontext hat Mondrian natürlich die schwächere Position (im Hinblick auf diesen Sprachgebrauch war er der Laie), was seine eigene Auffassung allerdings nicht im Geringsten abwertet.

Das Gleiche gilt auch für andere (Pseudo-)Philosophen, die im Kontext von »Die neue Gestaltung« erwähnt werden, ob es sich dabei um Spinoza, Schopenhauer, Hegel oder Goethe handelt: Mondrian begegneten ihre Namen und Aussprüche in Gesprächen mit anderen oder in der Zeitung, und er brachte sie dann in seinen eigenen Gedanken und Schriften unter. »Hab ich diesen Titel von Kandinskys Buch gut übernommen?«, fragt er van Doesburg in einem Brief vom März 1918. »Ich weiß es nicht mehr genau. Letztendlich wollte ich dich noch fragen, ob ich diese Äußerung von Spinoza (zu Beginn) gut zitiert habe. Ich besitze keines seiner Werke, aber weil du das in deinem vorigen Schreiben erwähnt hattest, kam ich auf die Idee, es dazu zu setzen, weil es mir gerade um die Wahrheit ging – wohl wiederum ein Beweis für unsere übereinstimmenden Gedankengänge. Es sieht so merkwürdig aus, wenn ich für Spinozas Formulierungen manchmal andere Wörter einsetze.«[38]

Solch einen Berührungspunkt hatte Mondrian – vom Hörensagen via Schoenmaekers – auch mit G.J.P.J. Bolland (1854–1922), einem philosophischen Exegeten, der die intellektuelle Debatte in den Niederlanden einige Zeit fest im Griff hatte, indem er den Philosophen Hegel popularisierte. Mit Sicherheit übernahm Mondrian bestimmte Elemente von Bollands Wissen über Hegels dialektisches Denken und profitierte von der Neubelebung des Interesses an Hegel auf Kosten des Neukantianismus, womit unter anderem Bolland die Niederlande in diesen Jahren überflutete. Bollands tatsächliche Bedeutung für Mondrian liegt allerdings auf einer anderen Ebene, vor allem im Hinblick auf einen letzten soziolinguistischen Aspekt, auf den ich hinweisen möchte. Vor allem aus einem Grund sind die Texte so schwer zugänglich: aufgrund der morphologischen Funktion von Wörtern und Begriffen.

Bolland machte es sich in seiner Philosophie zu einem Sport, die ›wirkliche‹ Bedeutung von Wörtern nachzuempfinden, indem er sie wortwörtlich nahm. Allerlei Begriffe enthüllen ihre Bedeutung wie von selbst, wenn man ihre Morphologie näher unter die Lupe nimmt. Zum Beispiel bezieht sich das einfache Verb »begrijpen« (begreifen) anscheinend buchstäblich auf den Begriff »grijpen« (greifen). Und der Begriff »tegendeel« (Gegenstück) scheint den anderen komplementären Standpunkt buchstäblich in sich selbst einzuverleiben. Bolland meinte in diesem Zusammenhang tatsächlich, dass »Niederländisch als Sprache für höhere geistige Angelegenheiten« die überlegene sei, wobei er lakonisch schlussfolgerte, Französisch sei beispielsweise mitnichten imstande, Gedankengänge in all ihren Finessen wiederzugeben.[39]

Schoenmaekers übernahm diese Art des Denkens. So interpretiert er die »lebende Bedeutung« des Wortes »ontwikkeling« (Entwicklung), indem er erwägt, es ließe sich in »ont« (ent) und »wikkel« (Wicklung) zergliedern. Die Vorsilbe »ont« (ent) stelle etwas dar, was »von innen nach außen« gehe. Und »wikkel« (Wicklung) bedeute »omhulsel« (Umhüllung). Also verkörpere »ontwikkeling« (Entwicklung) die Bewegung eines inneren Lebens, das von innen nach außen wachse, einer früheren Form entwachse, woraus eine tote »wikkel« (Wicklung) beziehungsweise »omhulsel« (Umhüllung) entstanden sei.[40] Mondrian war – womöglich

36
Brief von Piet Mondrian an Theo van Doesburg (Beginn Mai 1918), Archiv Theo van Doesburg, Rijksbureau voor Kunsthistorische Documentatie, Den Haag, Nr. 135.37. Gemeint wird hier wahrscheinlich Teil 2 von »Das Vernünftige in der Neuen Gestaltung« [»De redelijkheid der nieuwe beelding'], Anfang Mai 1918 (*De Stijl*, I, 7, 1918, S. 75).

37
Brief von Piet Mondrian an Theo van Doesburg (Juni 1918), Archiv Theo van Doesburg, Rijksbureau voor Kunsthistorische Documentatie, Den Haag, Nr. 135.45.

38
Brief von Piet Mondrian an Theo van Doesburg (März 1918), Archiv Theo van Doesburg, Rijksbureau voor Kunsthistorische Documentatie, Den Haag, Nr. 135.43. Gemeint ist die Passage in »Das Vernünftige in der Neuen Gestaltung« [»De redelijkheid der nieuwe beelding«], *De Stijl*, I (1918), 5, S. 50.

39
Zeitung *NRC*, 1. Mai 1912: Avondblad 1.

40
Mathieu Schoenmaekers, *Het Nieuwe Wereldbeeld*, Bussum (Van Dishoeck) 1915, S. 34. Hiermit bedanke ich mich bei Marek Wieczorek, der mich in persönlichen Gesprächen auf die Spur dieses typischen Charakterzugs von »Die neue Gestaltung« aufmerksam machte.

mathematical"—rendered as compound nouns in Dutch—are all examples of this complex thinking and articulation.[31] This device occurs frequently in the first instalments of the series. From instalment VII onwards, once Mondrian had abandoned Schoenmaekers, things calm down.

We cannot, however, say that he had also abandoned Symbolism by then. Even in the "Supplement" to "The New Plastic", he refers to the "universal" and the "individual", the "inward" that becomes objectively visible in the work of art, to seeking the truth through "manifold illusions" and to the "essence of beauty", albeit now suddenly isolated from any substance behind the image, from any 'jacket' (and therefore from any hanger, because where there is no jacket, there is no hanger, and vice versa), because it appears as clear as day on the surface—to be "perceived purely", to use Mondrian's words, in the "determination" of the image. In this sense the series can be seen as an account of Mondrian's development, of his ideas about the possible form abstract art might take and the role that meaning would play in it, the place where it should be located. In that sense, he is also settling accounts with the past.

In the "Supplement" Mondrian compares the "clarity" of a work of art to the way in which, in faith, "clarity" lies in the direct contemplation of the religious.[32] This is not so far removed from the discussions he must have had with Jan Toorop in 1908 about the aesthetic and the religious (which to the Symbolist Toorop were almost inextricably bound together) and about the technical aspects of making the spiritual visible. But Mondrian no longer uses the word 'spiritual' in the "Supplement", while the first instalment of "The New Plastic" was teeming with it. From this point of view, it was not appropriate for Jan Toorop—or by the way H.P. Berlage—to have been listed as permanent staff of the journal in the first announcements. They never became permanent, and it was better that way.

In 1920 Van Doesburg wrote to sculptor Georges Vantongerloo describing a curious visit that is relevant in this connection. In response to an exhibition, Toorop had written that "he would so liked to have been at the opening, because he would have liked so much +to speak with me! So I visited him yesterday with the vague illusion that he might be persuaded of the new insights. But he was worse than I anticipated. He is firmly rooted in the ethereal, chimerical ideas of Medieval Mysticism, is too attached to appearance to ever relinquish it.... He is full of enthusiasm for my endeavours and those of *De Stijl* and agreed with my ideas. He is still searching and, as he says himself, is very much "back and forth". It is difficult to find the way in the mist. The thicker the mist, the more difficult. Only those who perpetually destroy what is behind them to rebuild themselves for the future can arrive at the new and the true."[33] This is demonstrated by "The New Plastic".

Translated from the Dutch
by Sue McDonnel

31
These terms can be found in *De Stijl* I, no. 1 (1917), p. 3, I, no. 2 (1917), p. 16 and I, no. 2 (1918), p. 29 respectively.
32
De Stijl II, no. 2 (1918), p. 19.
33
Letter from Theo van Doesburg to Georges Vantongerloo (July 16, 1920), Vantongerloo Archive, Zumikon.

durch den bildhaften Charakter dieser Argumentationsweise – vom Zauber dieser Art zu argumentieren entzückt und suchte in »Die neue Gestaltung« Anschluss an diesen gruppengebundenen Sprachgebrauch.

Übernommen hat Mondrian zudem Bollands und Schoenmaekers irritierende Aneinanderkopplung von Begriffen, die Substantivierung von Verbformen und ganzen Satzteilen, wodurch eine Art exponentielle Vervielfachung des morphologischen Denkens in »Die neue Gestaltung« einzieht. Begriffe wie »aesthetisch in bepaaldheid gebeelde verhouding« (ästhetisch mit Bestimmtheit gestaltete Beziehungen), »tot-bepaaldheid-stelling« (Zur-Bestimmtheits-These), »enkel verhoudingsbeelding in-bepaaldheid« (reine Beziehungsgestaltung in-Bestimmtheit), »beelding-in-vaagheid« (Gestaltung-in-Unbestimmtheit) und das »universeele-als-het-mathematische« (Universelle-als-das-Mathematische) sind Beispiele für diese komplexen Gedankengänge und Formulierungen.[41] In den ersten Folgen der Artikelserie erscheint diese Stilfigur ausgesprochen häufig. Ab Ausgabe VII, dem Moment, wo er Schoenmaekers hinter sich gelassen hatte, gelangt der Text in ruhigeres Fahrwasser.

Es ist keineswegs so, dass der Symbolismus in dem Moment ebenfalls losgelassen wurde. Selbst noch im »Nachtrag«[42] von »Die neue Gestaltung« wird das »Universelle« und das »Individuelle« angesprochen, geht es um das »Verinnerlichte«, das im Kunstwerk objektiv sichtbar wird, um die »erweiterte Erkenntnis« des Wahren und um das »Wesentliche des Schönen«, allerdings mit einem Mal von einer Substanz befreit, die sich hinter dem Bild verbirgt, da es sonnenklar auf der Oberfläche erscheint und in der »Bestimmtheit« des Bildes Mondrian zufolge »rein anzuschauen« ist. In diesem Sinne kann die Artikelserie »Die neue Gestaltung« verstanden werden als Beschreibung von Mondrians Entwicklung, als Abfolge seiner Gedanken über die mögliche Form, die das abstrakte Kunstwerk annehmen könnte, und darüber, welche Rolle Bedeutung dabei übernehmen würde und an welcher Stelle diese zu lokalisieren sei. In diesem Sinne wird hier also auch mit der Vergangenheit abgerechnet.

Im »Nachtrag«[43] vergleicht Mondrian die »Klarheit« des bildenden Kunstwerks mit der Art und Weise wie im Glauben die »Klarheit« in der direkten religiösen Betrachtung wurzelt.[44] Damit bewegt er sich durchaus im Umfeld der Diskussionen, die er 1908 mit Jan Toorop über das Ästhetische und das Religiöse (was für Toorop als Symbolist nahezu unlösbar miteinander verbunden war) sowie über den technischen Aspekt vom Sichtbarmachen des Spirituellen geführt haben muss. Aber dieser letzte Begriff taucht im »Nachtrag«[45] nicht mehr auf, während es in den ersten Ausgaben von »Die neue Gestaltung« davon nur so gewimmelt hatte. Aus dieser Sicht heraus ist es daher auch nicht angemessen, dass Jan Toorop – und übrigens auch H.P. Berlage – in den ersten Ankündigungen der Zeitschrift als feste Mitarbeiter angegeben werden. Soweit kam es nicht, und das war besser so.

1920 schreibt van Doesburg dem Bildhauer Georges Vantongerloo über einen merkwürdigen Besuch, der in diesem Zusammenhang relevant ist. Toorop hatte ihm anlässlich einer Ausstellung geschrieben, »er wäre so gern bei der Ausstellungseröffnung gewesen, weil er mich so gern endlich mal gesprochen hätte! Deshalb habe ich ihn mit der vagen Illusion gestern kurz aufgesucht, er sei noch von der neuen Erkenntnis zu überzeugen. Aber das war eine Enttäuschung. Beharrt geradezu halsstarrig auf schwärmerische, mittelalterlich-mystische Träumereien und verliert sich zu sehr in dieser Vision, als dass er sie jemals loslassen könnte. [...] Von meinen Bemühungen und *De Stijl* ist er vollauf begeistert und stimmte meinen Ideen zu. Er befindet sich noch immer auf der Suche und fühlt sich, wie er selber sagt, sehr ›hin und her‹. Im Nebel lässt sich der Weg ja wohl schwer finden. Je dicker der Nebel – desto schwieriger. Nur wer selbst dauernd hinter sich abbricht, um vor sich erneut aufzubauen, schafft Neues und Wahres.«[46] Genau das vermittelt »Die neue Gestaltung«.

Aus dem Niederländischen übertragen von Sigrid Kullmann

41
Die Originalzitate stehen u. a. in: *De Stijl*, I, 1, 1917, S. 3; I, 2, 1917, S. 16 und I, 3, 1918, S. 29.
42
Originaltitel: »Aanvulling«.
43
Siehe Anm. 42.
44
De Stijl, II, 2, 1918, S.19.
45
Siehe Anm. 42.
46
Brief von Theo van Doesburg an Georges Vantongerloo (vom 16. Juli 1920), Vantongerloo-Archiv, Zumikon.

De Stijl
Umschlag der ersten Nummer
des ersten Jahrgangs
Oktober 1917
gestaltet von Vilmos Huszár

De Stijl
Cover of first number,
first volume
October 1917
designed by Vilmos Huszár

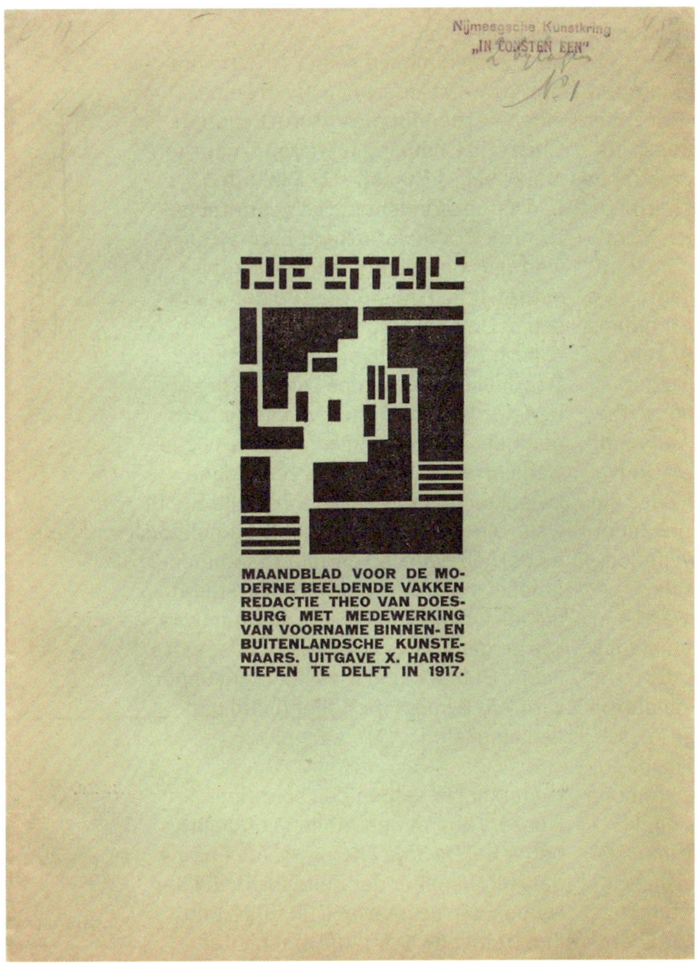

DE STYL

MAANDBLAD VOOR DE MODERNE BEELDENDE VAKKEN REDACTIE THEO VAN DOESBURG MET MEDEWERKING VAN VOORNAME BINNEN- EN BUITENLANDSCHE KUNSTENAARS. UITGAVE X. HARMS TIEPEN TE DELFT IN 1917.

De Stijl: Eine Kunst fürs Volk?
Michael White

Wir schreiben das Frühjahr 1929.
In einigen Monaten werden dramatische Entwicklungen an der New Yorker Aktienbörse dem Boomjahrzehnt ein jähes Ende setzen und eine neue Dekade einläuten, die von Wirtschaftskrisen, politischen Konflikten und Kriegen gezeichnet sein wird. Der in Ungarn geborene Künstler Vilmos Huszár, ein Gründungsmitglied von *De Stijl*, schreibt, die Werbung könne ein ideales Medium zur Verfolgung der künstlerischen Prinzipien bilden, die er und andere in Antwort auf die vorangegangene globale Katastrophe vor gut zehn Jahren entwickelt hatten.[1] Eine Außenwerbetafel biete sich nicht nur als der perfekte Ort an, Malerei und Architektur zusammenzubringen; Werbegestaltung werde darüber hinaus, so glaubt er, umso erfolgreicher sein, je mehr Sorgfalt auf die Beachtung der Prinzipien von Komposition und auf die Beherrschung der Oberfläche verwandt wird, die in der modernen Malerei entwickelt wurden. Der Anspruch, dass ein Werbemittel von universal anziehender Wirkung sein soll, erfordert zweifellos, dass der Künstler sich universaler Merkmale bedient. Huszár verwendet in seiner Diskussion moderner Kunst und Werbung das Wort »beelding«; der Begriff tauchte häufig in den komplexen theoretischen Schriften auf, die in *De Stijl* erschienen, und wurde insbesondere durch Mondrians Beschreibung seiner Praxis als »Nieuwe Beelding« popularisiert – eine Formel, die ins Französische als »Néo-plasticisme« und ins Deutsche als »Neue Gestaltung« übersetzt wurde. »Beelding« ist äußerst schwer zu definieren: Für diese Künstler bedeutet der Begriff so etwas wie die Konzentration auf die Gestaltwerdung (statt der Gestalt) eines Kunstwerks. Geht man aus dieser Perspektive an die Werbung heran, so Huszár, dann kann sie eine schöne Massenkunst sein: »Unmittelbar auf der Straße, unmittelbar vor jener großen Öffentlichkeit, deren überwiegende Mehrheit niemals in eine Kunstsammlung oder ein Museum gehen, unmittelbar vor diesen Leuten sollte man das Höchste, was in der Kunst zu leisten ist, ausstellen. [...] Wer an ›Kunst für das Volk‹ glaubt, kann sein Ziel nicht besser erreichen als mittels der Reklamekunst.«[2]
Im Zusammenhang seiner Argumentation verweist Huszár auch auf seine eigene Arbeit für die Vittoria Egyptian Cigarette Company, für deren Zigarettenmarke »Miss Blanche« er Plakate und Verpackungsmaterial gestaltet hat. Der Ironie, die darin liegt, Zigarettenwerbung als Beispiel für die positive ästhetische Transformation der städtischen Umgebung anzuführen, ist sich Huszár nicht bewusst – er lebt in einer Ära, in der manche noch an eine gesundheitsfördernde Wirkung des Rauchens glauben. Auch nimmt er nicht die mittlerweile offensichtlichen Verbindungen zwischen Kommerz, Begehren und Sucht wahr, die in der Zigarette, der vollendeten modernen Ware, so perfekt zusammengefasst sind. Gerade die Universalität dieses Objekts hat es ihm angetan, das, wie er anmerkt, »von allen gesellschaftlichen Ständen und Klassen« konsumiert wird, ein Symbol für Kollektivität und Geselligkeit.[3]

Ungefähr zur selben Zeit schreibt Huszárs ehemaliger Kollege und Mitarbeiter bei *De Stijl*, Theo van Doesburg – der Herausgeber der Zeitschrift, die den Namen der Gruppe im Titel führt, und ihre treibende Kraft – an einen alten Freund, den holländischen Anarchisten und Antimilitaristen Bart de Ligt darüber, wie es ihm in letzter Zeit ergangen ist und wie sich die Zukunft für *De Stijl* darstellt. Van Doesburg ist wieder in Paris, nachdem er einige Jahre in Straßburg verbracht hat, wo er an der Renovierung eines riesigen historischen

1
Vilmos Huszár, »Reclame als beeldende kunst«, in: *Bouwkundig Weekblad*, 50, 20 (18. Mai 1929), S. 155–160 und 24 (22. Juni 1929), S. 195–198.
2
»Juist op de straat, juist voor het groote publiek, waarvan de meesten nooit naar een kunstverzamelaar of naar de musea gaan, juist voor dezem moet het hoogste wat men in de Kunst bereiken kan, tentoongesteld worden. [...] Wie in ›Kunst voor het Volk‹ gelooft, heeft geen beter middel ter bereiking van zijn doel dan de reclamekunst.« Ebd., S. 155–156.
3
Ebd., S. 196. Eine faszinierende Diskussion des Bildes vom Rauchen im Modernismus und die Unterschiede zwischen Pfeife, Zigarre und Zigarette findet sich in Karel Srp, »An Avant-Gardist's Solitude«, in: *Umění* 48, 1–2, 1995, S. 5–8.

De Stijl: An Art for the People?
Michael White

It is the spring of 1929. In a few months time dramatic events on the New York Stock Exchange will bring an abrupt end to the boom years of this decade and usher in a new one marked by economic crisis, political conflict and war.
The Hungarian-born artist and founder member of *De Stijl,* Vilmos Huszár, is writing about the potential of advertising to be the ideal medium through which to pursue the artistic principles he and others had developed as a response to the last global catastrophe over a decade before.[1] Not only can an outdoor billboard be the perfect site to bring together painting and architecture, in his view, the more an advert is made with due care to the principles of composition and control of the surface that have been developed in modern painting, the more successful it will be. The demand for an advert to appeal universally surely requires an artist to tap into universal qualities. He continues to use the word "beelding" in his account of modern art and advertising, a term that occurs frequently in the complex theoretical writings in *De Stijl* and was made particularly well-known by Mondrian's description of his practice as "Nieuwe Beelding", translated into French as "Néo-plasticisme" and German as "Neue Gestaltung". Very difficult to define, "beelding" for these artists means something like concentrating on the forming (not the form) of an artwork. Approached in this way, Huszár sees that adverts can be a mass fine art: "Right on the street, right in front of the great public, of whom the vast majority never visit an art collection or a museum, right in front of these people should be exhibited the highest that can be achieved in art.... Whoever believes in 'Art for the People', can achieve his aim in no better medium than advertising art."[2]

As part of his discussion Huszár refers to his own work for the Vittoria Egyptian Cigarette Company, for whose brand of Miss Blanche cigarettes he has designed posters and packaging. The irony of utilising cigarette advertising to demonstrate the positive, aesthetic transformation of the urban environment is not evident to Huszár, who lives in an age when some still believe smoking to be beneficial to health. Nor does he perceive the now obvious connections between commerce, desire and addiction so neatly summed up in that perfect modern commodity, the cigarette. It is the universality of the object that appeals to him, "used by every rank and class in society", as he points out, a symbol of collectivity and sociability.[3]

Around the same time, Huszár's former *De Stijl* colleague and collaborator, editor of the journal of the same name and its leading force, Theo van Doesburg, is writing to his old friend, the Dutch anarchist and anti-militarist Bart de Ligt about his recent fortunes and the future for *De Stijl.* Van Doesburg is back in Paris having spent a couple of years in Strasbourg working on the renovation of a massive historic building in the centre of the city known as the Aubette, which he has been involved in transforming into an entertainment complex, featuring a number of cafés, bars, restaurants, dance-halls and a cinema. As he complains to De Ligt, despite the size of the job, the project has left him nearly broke and it has not resulted in the flurry of new commissions he was expecting.[4] He used the opportunity quite literally as a shop window to showcase the wares of *De Stijl,* but publications such as the tenth anniversary issue of the journal and a special issue on the Aubette, which he has financed personally, have put him in debt. Meanwhile the art market, he reports, is sluggish and only those who respond to passing trends are being successful.[5] His experience in Strasbourg

1
Vilmos Huszár, "Reclame als beeldende kunst", *Bouwkundig Weekblad* 50, no. 20 (May 18, 1929), pp. 155–60, no. 24 (June 22, 1929), pp. 195–98.
2
"Juist op de straat, juist voor het groote publiek, waarvan de meesten nooit naar een kunstverzamelaar of naar de musea gaan, juist voor dezem moet het hoogste wat men in de Kunst bereiken kan, tentoongesteld worden.... Wie in 'Kunst voor het Volk' gelooft, heeft geen beter middel ter bereiking van zijn doel dan de reclamekunst." Huszár 1929 (see note 1) pp. 155–56.
3
Huszár 1929 (see note 1), pp. 196. For a fascinating discussion of the image of smoking in modernism and the differences between the pipe, cigar and cigarette see Karel Srp, "An Avant-Gardist's Solitude", *Umění* 48, nos. 1–2 (1995), pp. 5–8.
4
Theo van Doesburg, letter to Bart de Ligt, February 7, 1929, Van Doesburg Archive, Netherlands Institute for Art History, The Hague, no. 110.
5
It is likely that Van Doesburg is referring to the Surrealists with this comment.

Gebäudes in der Innenstadt namens Aubette arbeitete. Das Gebäude wurde unter seiner Mitarbeit in einen Vergnügungskomplex mit mehreren Cafés, Bars, Restaurants, Tanzlokalen und einem Kino umgebaut. De Ligt gegenüber klagt er, dass das Projekt ihn trotz des Umfangs seines Auftrags zuletzt beinahe ruiniert und auch nicht die erhoffte Flut neuer Aufträge ausgelöst habe.[4] Er nutzte die Gelegenheit, in der Aubette ein regelrechtes Schaufenster für die Waren von *De Stijl* einzurichten, aber Veröffentlichungen wie das Heft zum zehnten Jubiläum der Zeitschrift und ein Sonderheft über die Aubette, das er persönlich finanzierte, haben ihn in Schulden gestürzt. Gleichzeitig, so berichtet er, ist der Kunstmarkt träge, und Erfolg haben nur Künstler, die flüchtige Trends bedienen.[5] Aufgrund seiner Straßburger Erfahrungen ist er pessimistischer als Huszár, was die Aussichten auf Förderung aus der Wirtschaft oder von Privatpersonen für Großprojekte angeht, die *De Stijl* an eine größere Öffentlichkeit bringen werden. Interessiert ist er dagegen an den Entwicklungen in Italien. Im selben Jahr wird der Anführer der Futuristen, Filippo Tommaso Marinetti, von Mussolini persönlich zum Mitglied der Accademia d'Italia ernannt.[6] Schon in der Vergangenheit hatte van Doesburg über italienische Architektur und die Förderung des Modernismus durch die faschistische Regierung geschrieben.[7] Nun scherzt er de Ligt gegenüber über den klapprigen Zustand der faschistischen Bewegung in den Niederlanden: »Sie halten nach einem Mussolini Ausschau, aber niemand meldet sich zur Stelle außer ein oder zwei blassen und zerzausten Studenten in Delfter Kragen.«[8] Man fragt sich, was sich van Doesburg wirklich für die Niederlande erhoffte.

Diese Reflexionen zur Politik wie auch die von Huszár zur Massenkultur kommen zu einem Zeitpunkt, da van Doesburg hofft, *De Stijl* durch die Verschmelzung mit einer anderen holländischen Zeitschrift, *i10,* neuen Schwung zu verleihen; unter den Beiträgern zu *i10* waren de Ligt und Huszár sowie viele andere ehemalige Mitglieder von *De Stijl,* namentlich Piet Mondrian, Jacobus Johannes Pieter Oud und Gerrit Rietveld.[9] Seinem Artikel über die Werbung schickte Huszár eine Anmerkung über die Entstehung von *De Stijl* voran sowie über die Notwendigkeit, das Programm der Gruppe zu erneuern.[10] Im Sommer 1929 meldet van Doesburg sogar, dass frühere interne Streitigkeiten beigelegt seien und »Stijlkünstler als geschlossene Gruppe mit einem neuen Organ (Nouveau Plan) an die internationale Kunstwelt appellieren werden.«[11] Kein solches neues Organ ist je erschienen. Van Doesburgs Bestrebungen, die Ziele von *De Stijl* – Kollektivität und Universalität – weiter voranzutreiben, trugen nur sehr begrenzt Früchte im hermetischeren und enger beschränkten Projekt der *Art Concret.* Statt in den öffentlichen Raum auszugreifen, wenden sich seine letzten Überlegungen, wie sie im ihm posthum gewidmeten letzten Heft von *De Stijl* erschienen, der Abgelegenheit und Ungastlichkeit des Ateliers des Künstlers zu, das »die kalte Atmosphäre dreitausend Meter hoher Berge besitzen und von ewigem Schnee bedeckt sein« müsse.[12]

In dem Artikel, der das Wiederauftreten der *De Stijl*-Gruppe ankündigte, erklärte van Doesburg deren Entstehung durch einen Impuls, der einem solchen Rückzug ins Atelier gerade entgegengesetzt ist. Nicht Innenschau, so erinnert sich van Doesburg, sondern der Drang hin zu »kollektiver Konstruktion« veranlasste »radikale Maler« (also Künstler wie Huszár, van der Leck und van Doesburg selbst), die Kooperation mit Architekten zu suchen und ihre Werke im dreidimensionalen Raum und nicht auf der Leinwand zu verwirklichen, um die Öffentlichkeit zu überzeugen, dass ihre Bestrebungen ernst zu nehmen seien. Er fährt fort: »In dem Moment, da die radikalsten Künstler, die damals in Holland arbeiteten, sich vom öffentlichen Kunstleben isolierten, entstand der Gedanke, vermittels eines Organs den Individualismus zu bekämpfen, Klärung über gemeinsame Arbeit zu schaffen und alle schöpferischen Kräfte zu sammeln, welche auf ihrem Gebiet die Konsequenzen des Neuen gezogen hätten.«[13] Dieses »Organ« war *De Stijl.*

Einen deutlich erkennbaren Hinweis darauf, wie van Doesburg den Eingriff von *De Stijl* in den öffentlichen Raum zu erneuern hoffte, finden wir in der Darstellung seiner Arbeit und der von *De Stijl* in seiner Straßburger Schaufenster-

4
Theo van Doesburg, Brief an Bart de Ligt, 7. Februar 1929, Van-Doesburg-Archiv, Rijksbureau voor Kunsthistorische Documentatie, Den Haag, Nr. 110.

5
Mit dieser Bemerkung bezieht sich van Doesburg wahrscheinlich auf die Surrealisten.

6
Caroline Tisdall und Angelo Bozzolla, *Futurism,* London 1977, S. 208.

7
Theo van Doesburg, »Architectuurvernieuwingen in het buitenland«, in: *Het Bouwbedrijf,* 4, 15, 22. Juli 1927, S. 352–355.

8
»Ze zijn op zoek naar een Mussolini doch niemand meldt zich, tenzij dan een of ander goor studentje met delftsch boord en knolharen.« Van Doesbergs Bemerkung bezieht sich auf die traditionelle Kleidung der Mitglieder der Delfter Studententheatergesellschaft.

9
Siehe den Brief von van Doesburg an Oud vom 18. November 1929 (in der Fondation Custodia, Paris), indem er auf die praktischen Aspekte einer Fusion eingeht.

10
Huszár 1929 (wie Anm. 1), S. 155.

11
Theo van Doesburg, »Der Kampf um den neuen Stil«, in: *Neue Schweizer Rundschau,* 22, 7, Juli 1929, S. 541.

12
»uw atelier moet de koude atmospheer hebben van de bergen op 3000 meter hoogte; de eeuwige sneeuw moet er liggen.« Theo van Doesburg, »elementarisme«, *De Stijl,* dernier numéro, 1932, S. 16.

13
Theo van Doesburg, »Der Kampf um den neuen Stil«, in: *Neue Schweizer Rundschau,* 22, 1, Januar 1929, S. 44.

has made him more pessimistic than Huszár about the prospects for commercial or private sponsorship of large scale works that will bring *De Stijl* to a public audience. However he is interested in what is going on in Italy. This is the year that the Futurist leader, Filippo Tommaso Marinetti, is personally appointed by Mussolini to the Accademia d'Italia.[6] Van Doesburg has previously written about Italian architecture and the fascist government's sponsorship of modernism.[7] Van Doesburg jokes to De Ligt about the ramshackle Dutch fascist movement: "They are looking for a Mussolini, but nobody reports for duty other than one or two sallow students with Delft collars and tousled hair."[8] We are left to wonder what Van Doesburg really hopes for The Netherlands.

These reflections on politics, and Huszár's on mass culture, came at a moment when Van Doesburg was hoping to relaunch *De Stijl* by merging it with another Dutch journal, *i10,* to which both De Ligt and Huszár had been contributing, along with many other previous *De Stijl* collaborators, notably Piet Mondrian, Jacobus Johannes Pieter Oud and Gerrit Rietveld.[9] Huszár prefaced his article on advertising with a comment about the formation of *De Stijl* and the need for renewal of its agenda.[10] In the summer of 1929, Van Doesburg even announced that earlier internal conflicts had been resolved and "the artists of De Stijl can face the international world as a united group with a new publication (Nouveau Plan)."[11] Such a thing never appeared. His aspirations for the furtherance of *De Stijl's* ambition for collectivity and universality were only faintly realised in the more hermetic and tightly circumscribed terms of *Art Concret.* Rather than interventions in public space, his last thoughts, as published in the final issue of *De Stijl* dedicated to him posthumously in 1932, concern the remoteness and inhospitability of the artist's studio which "must have the cold atmosphere of mountains three thousand metres high topped with an eternal cap of snow."[12]

In the article which announced the reappearance of the *De Stijl* group, Van Doesburg explained its origins in precisely an opposite impulse to such a retreat into the studio. Rather than introspection, Van Doesburg recollects it was the urge for "collective construction" that prompted "radical painters" (in other words, the likes of Huszár, Van der Leck and himself) to seek collaboration with architects and realise their works in three-dimensional space and not on canvas, "in order to convince the public that their endeavours were serious." As he continues: "At a time when the most radical artists working in Holland were cutting themselves off from public artistic life, the idea was born of making use of an organ to combat individualism, to obtain clarity about common work and to assemble all the creative forces which had taken the consequence of the New in their own fields."[13] This "organ" was *De Stijl.*

As a visual indication of Van Doesburg's desire to renew *De Stijl's* intervention in public space, we can look at how he chose to represent himself and *De Stijl* in his Strasbourg shop window display. There we see prominently positioned a photograph of a model for a monument intended for the northern Dutch town of Leeuwarden, a competition project on which Van Doesburg collaborated with Jan Wils in 1917, just at the moment that the first issues of *De Stijl* were being published. The task involved the redesign of the square outside the town's railway station to include a fountain. The renunciation of individualism and promotion of collective endeavour expressed frequently in theoretical texts in *De Stijl* at the time, and expressed forcefully in the manifesto of the group published in 1918, was given physical shape here in the public placement of an architectonic structure that deliberately renounced the hierarchy of views of a traditional sculptural monument by not privileging any of its faces. Not only that, the single cube at the summit of the tower Van Doesburg designed was not even positioned centrally, reinforcing a dynamic asymmetry evident in its unequal sides.

There was certainly some pressure on Van Doesburg and Wils to succeed in this competition. Prominent on the jury was H.P. Berlage, the leading modern architect in The Netherlands whom Van Doesburg was keen to recruit to *De Stijl* and in whose architectural office

6
Caroline Tisdall and Angelo Bozzolla, *Futurism* (London, 1977), p. 208.

7
Theo van Doesburg, "Architectuurvernieuwingen in het buitenland", *Het Bouwbedrijf* 4, no. 15 (July 22, 1927), pp. 352–55.

8
"Ze zijn op zoek naar een Mussolini doch niemand meldt zich, tenzij dan een of ander goor studentje met delftsch boord en knolharen." Van Doesburg is referring to the traditional outfit of members of the Delft student theatre society.

9
See letter from Van Doesburg to Oud, November 18, 1929, Fondation Custodia, Paris, which discusses the practicalities of a merger.

10
Huszár 1929 (see note 1), p. 155.

11
"In diesem Jahre wurden viele Konflikte, begründet in Auffassungsunterschieden, geschlichtet, sodaß die Stijlkünstler als geschlossene Gruppe mit einem neuen Organ (Nouveau Plan) an die internationale Kulturwelt appellieren werden." Theo van Doesburg, "Der Kampf um den neuen Stil", *Neue Schweizer Rundschau* 22, no. 7 (July 1929), p. 541.

12
"uw atelier moet de koude atmospheer hebben van de bergen op 3000 meter hoogte; de eeuwige sneeuw moet er liggen." Theo van Doesburg, "elementarisme", *De Stijl,* dernier numéro, 1932, p. 16.

13
"In dem Moment, da die radikalsten Künstler, die damals in Holland arbeiteten, sich vom öffentlichen Kunstleben isolierten, entstand der Gedanke, vermittels eines Organs den Individualismus zu bekämpfen, Klärung über gemeinsame Arbeit zu schaffen und alle schöpferischen Kräfte zu sammeln, welche auf ihrem Gebiet die Konsequenzen des Neuen gezogen hätten." Van Doesburg 1929 (see note 11), p. 44.

gestaltung. Dort erscheint an prominenter Stelle die Fotografie eines Modells für ein Denkmal, das für die nordholländische Stadt Leeuwarden bestimmt war. Van Doesburg hatte für dieses Wettbewerbsprojekt im Jahr 1917 mit Jan Wils zusammengearbeitet, just zu der Zeit, da die ersten Ausgaben von *De Stijl* erschienen. Die Aufgabenstellung umfasste die Neugestaltung eines Platzes vor dem Bahnhof der Stadt, wobei ein Brunnen geschaffen werden sollte. Der Ablehnung des Individualismus und der Forcierung kollektiver Bemühungen, wie sie in den theoretischen Schriften der Zeit in *De Stijl* häufig und noch eindringlicher in dem Manifest zum Ausdruck kommen, das die Gruppe im Jahr 1918 veröffentlichte, verleiht der Entwurf physische Gestalt durch die Aufstellung einer architektonischen Struktur im öffentlichen Raum, die bewusst auf die Blickhierarchie eines traditionellen skulpturalen Denkmals verzichtet, indem sie keiner seiner Seiten einen Vorrang zugesteht. Darüber hinaus ist der einzelne Würfel an der Spitze des von van Doesburg entworfenen Turms noch nicht einmal mittig angeordnet, was die in seinen ungleichen Seiten augenfällige dynamische Asymmetrie noch verstärkt.

Van Doesburg und Wils sahen sich zweifellos nicht unerheblichem Druck ausgesetzt, diesen Wettbewerb zu gewinnen. Ein wichtiges Mitglied der Jury war H.P. Berlage, der führende moderne Architekt in den Niederlanden, den van Doesburg nur zu gerne für *De Stijl* gewonnen hätte und in dessen Architekturbüro Wils von 1914 bis 1916 gearbeitet hatte. Die erste Ankündigung des Magazins *De Stijl* im August 1917 versprach Beiträge von Berlage.[14]
Im Herbst 1917 bemerkt ein enttäuschter van Doesburg in einem Brief an einen engen Freund, dass »Berlage und andere, die ihre Unterstützung für *De Stijl* zugesagt hatten, sich zurückgezogen haben. Ich bin ganz auf mich gestellt!«[15] Letztlich gewann van Doesburgs und Wils' Vorschlag den zweiten Preis, allerdings, so wird man sagen müssen, eher für Wils' Planung für den Platz und die Verkehrsregelung als für van Doesburgs Skulptur.[16] Nichts davon jedoch scheint van Doesburgs Ehrgeiz unmittelbar beeinträchtigt zu haben: *De Stijl* sollte ein Reformprojekt vorantreiben, das in den Niederlanden eng mit Berlages Namen verbunden war. Einige Jahre später schrieb van Doesburg an Oud, der auch mit Berlage ein freundschaftliches Verhältnis pflegte, sein Ziel sei es, »zu verwirklichen, was Berlage in der Theorie gepredigt hat: eine *ineinandergreifende Einheit* eines Hauses mit seinem Inhalt, bis hin zum Schreibpapier.«[17]

Wie an anderer Stelle bereits bemerkt wurde, leitete sich wahrscheinlich sogar der Name *De Stijl* selbst aus den umfangreichen und wirkmächtigen Schriften Berlages her.[18] 1917 erschien eine Neuauflage von Berlages einflussreichem erstem Buch, *Over Stijl in bouw- en meubelkunst* (Über Stil in der Bau- und Möbelkunst), eine Studie, die die Ursprünge und Entwicklung von Ornamentik und Möbelgestaltung vom antiken Ägypten bis zur Gegenwart verfolgte. Über diese Überblicksdarstellung hinaus vertritt das Buch ein polemisches Argument: Der industrielle Kapitalismus sei an der Aufgabe gescheitert, eine einheitliche stilistische Identität herauszubilden, wie sie in vergangenen Epochen zu finden sei; erst mit dem Anbruch des Sozialismus werde eine solche Identität wieder möglich werden. In den angewandten Künsten erkennt Berlage die radikalste Form zeitgenössischer kultureller Produktion; er beschreibt sie als eine Bewegung, die sich »mit dem geistigen Wachstum der zukünftigen Kultur befasst, also mit einer Aufgabe, die erst dann vollständig gelöst werden wird, wenn die Trennung des Geistigen vom Materiellen nicht länger bestehen wird und die gesellschaftlichen Beziehungen der Menschen fest auf einen idealen Plan gegründet sein werden.«[19] Die Architektur sollte nach Berlages Auffassung das Zusammentreten aller Künste ermöglichen, um einen sie einigenden Zweck und eine gemeinsame Identität auszudrücken, sodass er in einer einige Jahre später verfassten Schrift mit großer Fantasie das zukünftige Erscheinen eines neuen »religiösen Gemeinschaftsbaus« beschreiben konnte, der dem griechischen Tempel oder der christlichen Kirche ebenbürtig sein würde; in diesem riesigen Baukörper würden Wandgemälde, Skulptur, Musik, Gesang und Tanz sämtlich nicht einen Gott, sondern »die Gleichheit aller Menschen« feiern.[20]

14
In der Zeitschrift *Holland Express,* Ausgabe August 1917. Siehe Evert van Straaten, *Theo van Doesburg 1883–1931,* Den Haag 1983, S. 80f.
15
»Berlage en anderen die hun steun aan den Stijl beloofden hebben zich teruggetrokken. Ik sta helemaal alleen!« Theo van Doesburg, Brief an Antony Kok, 5. Oktober 1917, zit. nach Alied Ottevanger (Hrsg.), *De Stijl overall leiding: De briefwisseling tussen Theo van Doesburg en Antony Kok,* Bussum 2008, S. 213.
16
J.A.N. Patijn et al., »Juryrapport: Prijsvraag tot verfraaing Stationsplein te Leeuwarden«, in: *Bouwkundig Weekblad,* 39, 16, 20. April 1918, S. 97–99.
17
»Mijn doel is inderdaad te bereiken wat Berlage in theorie verkondigde: een in *elkaar grijpende eenheid* van huis en onderdelen tot postpapier toe.« Theo van Doesburg, Brief an J.J.P. Oud, 6. Juli 1919, zit. nach Evert van Straaten, *Theo van Doesburg, constructeur van het nieuwe leven,* Otterlo 1984, S. 11.
18
Paul Overy, *De Stijl,* London 1991, S. 25.
19
»De nu bezige kunstbeweging is dus werkzaam aan de geestelijke groei der komende kultuur, aan een dienovereenkomstige taak, welke eerst dan tot volle uiting zal komen geraken, wanneer de geestelijke en stoffelijke scheiding niet meer zal bestaan; wanneer maatschappelijke verhoudingen der menschen zullen zijn vastgesteld op een ideal plan.« H.P. Berlage, *Over stijl in bouw- en meubelkunst,* 2. Ausg., Rotterdam 1908, S. 131.
20
H.P. Berlage, »Kunst en Maatschappij«, in: *Studies over bouwkunst, stijl en samenleving,* 2. Ausg., Rotterdam 1922, S. 56.

Wils worked from 1914 to 1916. The first announcement of the magazine *De Stijl,* in August 1917, advertised Berlage as a contributor.[14] Writing to a close friend in the autumn of 1917, a disappointed Van Doesburg commented that "Berlage and others who had promised their support to *De Stijl* have withdrawn. I'm standing all on my own!"[15] In the end, Van Doesburg and Wils proposal received second prize, more for Wils's plan for the square and traffic circulation than Van Doesburg's sculpture, it must be said.[16] But none of this appears to have immediately diminished Van Doesburg's ambition that *De Stijl* should continue a reform project with which Berlage's name was very much associated in The Netherlands. Writing a couple of years later to Oud, who was also on friendly terms with Berlage, Van Doesburg commented that his aim was "to realise what Berlage preached theoretically: an *interlocking unity* of a house and its contents down to the very notepaper."[17]

As has been pointed out before, the very choice of name *De Stijl* was probably derived from the extensive and influential writings of Berlage.[18] In 1917, Berlage's influential first book, *Over stijl in bouw- en meubelkunst* (Concerning Style in the Art of Architecture and Furniture Making), was republished, a study which examined the origin and development of ornament and furniture design from ancient Egypt to the near present. Not simply an overview, the book makes a polemical argument that industrial capitalism has failed to produce a coherent stylistic identity, such as could be found in former periods, and that such a thing will only be once more achievable with the dawn of socialism. Berlage identifies the applied arts as the most radical form of contemporary cultural production, describing them as a movement "busy with the spiritual growth of the coming culture, with the task that, accordingly, shall only be entirely achieved when the separation of the spiritual and material no longer exists, when the social relationships of people are firmly placed on an ideal plan."[19] Architecture, in Berlage's view, was to facilitate the coming together of all the arts to express unity of purpose and a common identity, so that, writing a few years later, he could imaginatively describe the future appearance of a new "religious community building," of equivalent status to the Greek temple or the Christian church, whose enormous volume would contain wall painting, sculpture, music, song and dance, all celebrating not a god but "the equality of all people."[20]

Berlage's peculiar combination of religious and socialist imagery, and his appeal to the "community" are both aspects of a contemporary cultural discourse in the Netherlands at the turn of the twentieth century which had crystallised around the term 'gemeenschapskunst' (community art), a term first used by the critic Jan Veth in 1892 to describe wall paintings by Antoon Derkinderen in the town hall of Den Bosch.[21] As Jan Bank and Maarten van Buuren have elegantly summarised, the term 'gemeenschapskunst' was subsequently used to mean rather different things by different people and was mixed with related terms such as 'public art', 'monumental art' and 'art of the people'.[22] Primarily 'gemeenschapskunst' could mean an art of or for the community, in each case implying a direct connection with a public and the use of readily accessible forms and narratives. This version of 'gemeenschapskunst' is associated with a rise in attention to the applied arts during the period and the creation of artworks for public buildings. Opportunities in this area were generated both by the Catholic revival in The Netherlands of the late nineteenth century, which led to the renovation and construction of many churches, and the expansion of urban centres with their concomitant need for new civic buildings. Practices such as stained glass manufacture and wall painting underwent dramatic revivals. The term 'gemeenschapskunst' was also adopted by architects and artists with socialist leanings and positioned against the individualism associated with a late Romantic sensibility. Berlage would be a good example here. Furthermore, the term was used to describe a notion of a community of the arts, the concept that architecture, painting and sculpture should manifest common stylistic traits. And finally, the pursuit of 'gemeenschapskunst' implied that artists, architects and designers should

14
In the magazine *Holland Express* in August 1917. See Evert van Straaten, *Theo van Doesburg 1883–1931* (The Hague, 1983), pp. 80–81.

15
"Berlage en anderen die hun steun aan den Stijl beloofden hebben zich teruggetrokken. Ik sta helemaal alleen!" Theo van Doesburg, letter to Antony Kok, October 5, 1917, quoted in Alied Ottevanger, ed., *De Stijl overall leiding: De briefwisseling tussen Theo van Doesburg en Antony Kok* (Bussum, 2008), p. 213.

16
J.A.N. Patijn et al., "Juryrapport: Prijsvraag tot verfraaing Stationsplein te Leeuwarden", *Bouwkundig Weekblad* 39, no. 16 (April 20, 1918), pp. 97–99.

17
"Mijn doel is inderdaad te bereiken wat Berlage in theorie verkondigde: een in *elkaar grijpende eenheid* van huis en onderdelen tot postpapier toe." Theo van Doesburg, letter to J.J.P. Oud, July 6, 1919, quoted in Evert van Straaten, *Theo van Doesburg, constructeur van het nieuwe leven* (Otterlo, 1984), p. 11.

18
Paul Overy, *De Stijl* (London, 1991), p. 25.

19
"De nu bezige kunstbeweging is dus werkzaam aan de geestelijke groei der komende kultuur, aan een dienovereenkomstige taak, welke eerst dan tot volle uiting zal komen geraken, wanneer de geestelijke en stoffelijke scheiding niet meer zal bestaan; wanneer maatschappelijke verhoudingen der menschen zullen zijn vastgesteld op een ideal plan." H.P. Berlage, *Over stijl in bouw- en meubelkunst* (Rotterdam, 1908) p. 131.

20
H. P. Berlage, "Kunst en Maatschappij", in *Studies over bouwkunst, stijl en samenleving* (Rotterdam, 1922), p. 56.

21
Jan Veth, *Derkinderens wandschildering in het Bossche stadhuis* (Amsterdam, 1892).

22
Jan Bank and Maarten van Buuren, *1900 — The Age of Bourgeois Culture. Dutch Culture in a European Perspective,* vol. 3 (New York, 2004), pp. 139–83.

Berlages eigenartige Verknüpfung von religiöser und sozialistischer Bildlichkeit wie auch die Berufung auf die ›Gemeinschaft‹ sind typisch für einen zeitgenössischen kulturellen Diskurs in den Niederlanden um die Wende zum 20. Jahrhundert, der sich um den Begriff ›gemeenschapskunst‹ (Gemeinschaftskunst) herum herauskristallisiert hatte. Dieser Begriff selbst erscheint zuerst bei dem Kritiker Jan Veth, der ihn 1892 verwendet, um Wandgemälde von Antoon Derkinderen im Rathaus von Den Bosch zu beschreiben.[21] Wie Jan Bank und Maarten van Buuren in einer eleganten Zusammenfassung gezeigt haben, verwendeten in der Folge verschiedene Autoren das Wort ›gemeenschapskunst‹ zur Beschreibung durchaus verschiedener Dinge; Überschneidungen gab es darüber hinaus mit verwandten Begriffen wie ›öffentliche Kunst‹, ›Monumentalkunst‹ und ›Kunst des Volks.‹[22] In erster Linie konnte sich ›gemeenschapskunst‹ auf eine Kunst der Gemeinschaft oder für die Gemeinschaft beziehen – in beiden Fällen implizierte der Begriff eine direkte Verbindung mit einer Öffentlichkeit und die Verwendung allgemein verfügbarer Formen und Erzählmuster. Diese Version von ›gemeenschapskunst‹ steht im Zusammenhang mit der wachsenden Aufmerksamkeit, die die angewandten Künste zur selben Zeit erfuhren, und der Schaffung von Kunstwerken für öffentliche Gebäude. Gelegenheiten dazu entstanden sowohl durch das Wiederaufleben des niederländischen Katholizismus im späten 19. Jahrhundert, das zu zahlreichen Kirchenrenovierungen und -neubauten führte, als auch durch das Wachstum der städtischen Zentren und dem sich daraus ergebenden Bedarf nach neuen öffentlichen Gebäuden. Praktiken wie Glas- und Wandmalerei erlebten einen dramatischen Aufschwung. Auch Architekten und Künstler mit sozialistischen Neigungen nahmen sich des Begriffs ›gemeenschapskunst‹ an und setzten ihn dem Individualismus, den sie mit der Gefühlswelt der Spätromantik verbanden, entgegen; dafür wäre Berlage ein gutes Beispiel. Außerdem wurde der Begriff eingesetzt, um eine Vorstellung von der Gemeinschaft der Künste zu beschreiben, also die Auffassung, dass Architektur, Malerei und Skulptur einheitliche stilistische Züge aufweisen sollten. Schließlich implizierte das Streben nach ›gemeenschapskunst‹, dass Künstler, Architekten und Gestalter in Gemeinschaften arbeiten sollten, die manchmal nach dem Muster mittelalterlicher Gilden beschrieben wurden.

Wie bei vielen Künstlern und Kritikern wurde Berlages idealistische und sozialistische Rhetorik nicht unwesentlich dadurch gedämpft, dass er von Aufträgen von reichen Privatpersonen und großen Unternehmen abhängig war; sein bis heute bekanntester Entwurf ist ironischerweise das Gebäude der Amsterdamer Börse (das allerdings vielleicht das einzige seiner Art ist, in dem der Eingangsbereich mit Bildern geschmückt ist, die der Emanzipation der Frau gewidmet sind). Ein Bereich, in dem Berlage größere Kontrolle ausüben konnte, war die Möbelherstellung, und so war er im Jahr 1900 federführend bei der Einrichtung einer Kooperative in Amsterdam namens 't Binnenhuis (Das Innere des Hauses), deren Zielsetzung war, gelungene Gestaltung in guter Produktqualität einer großen Kundschaft durch einen Laden im Stadtzentrum zugänglich zu machen. Anders als die Konkurrenz im Bereich zeitgenössischer Möbel- und Produktgestaltung verkaufte 't Binnenhuis Artikel, die nicht durchgängig handgefertigt waren, um durch maschinelle Produktion die Kosten zu senken, selbst wenn die Angebote auch dadurch noch nicht für jeden erschwinglich wurden. Interne Streitigkeiten innerhalb der Kooperative führten nach nur zwei Jahren zum Ausscheiden mehrerer Mitglieder, die eine neue Firma namens De Woning (Die Wohnung) gründeten, die verstärkt auf den Massenmarkt abzielte. Diese Spaltung hinderte Vertreter beider Organisationen aber nicht daran, gemeinsam im Jahr 1904 eine neue Gesellschaft zu gründen, die Reformbestrebungen im Gestaltungsbereich fördern und die Interessen der Hersteller wahren sollte, die *Vereniging voor Ambachts- en Nijverheidskunst* (VANK, Vereinigung für Handwerk und Industriekunst). Eines der wichtigsten Projekte dieser Vereinigung war die Ausdehnung des Urheberrechtsschutzes auf die Arbeit von Gestaltern; ein diesbezügliches Gesetz wurde im Jahr 1912 eingeführt. VANK veranstaltete außerdem wichtige Ausstellungen im Amsterdamer Stedelijk Museum, darunter insbesondere eine zu *Kunst en*

21
Jan Veth, *Derkinderens wandschildering in het Bossche stadhuis,* Amsterdam 1892.
22
Jan Bank und Maarten van Buuren, *1900 – The Age of Bourgeois Culture. Dutch Culture in a European Perspective,* Bd. 3, New York 2004, S. 139–183.

work in communities, sometimes described along the lines of medieval guilds.

As was the case with many artists and architects, much of Berlage's idealistic and socialist rhetoric was tempered by his reliance on wealthy individuals and large corporations for commissions and, ironically, his best known building to this day remains the Amsterdam Stock Exchange (even though it may be the only one of its kind to have images dedicated to women's emancipation in its foyer). One area he could have more control over was furniture production and in 1900 he was instrumental in setting up a cooperative in Amsterdam, 't Binnenhuis (The Interior), the aim of which was to bring good quality, well designed products to a large audience sold through a shop in the centre of Amsterdam. Unlike rival outlets for contemporary furniture and design, 't Binnenhuis sold items which were not solely hand crafted allowing machine production to bring down costs, although that still did not bring them within reach of everyone. Disputes in the cooperative led to several members leaving after just two years and setting up another company, De Woning (The Dwelling), aimed more at the mass market. This split did not prevent representatives of both organisations from becoming founder members of a new association established in 1904 to promote design reform and represent the interests of makers, the *Vereniging voor Ambachts- en Nijverheidskunst* (VANK, Association for Craft and Applied Art). The introduction of copyright protection for design was one of the association's most important campaigns, which led to the introduction of new legislation in 1912. VANK also staged important exhibitions at the Stedelijk Museum in Amsterdam, notably one in the year of *De Stijl's* founding, on *Kunst en Reclame* (Art and Advertising).[23]

The precise connections between *De Stijl* and Dutch design reform discourse have yet to be fully unravelled. I have commented previously on the significance of the fact that the very first image to appear in *De Stijl,* as it did on the inside front cover of the first six issues, was an advert.[24] Designed by Vilmos Huszár, with his signature distinctly visible, it promoted the parquet flooring of the Bruynzeel Company and took great delight in using the patterns of the wooden blocks to create abstract compositions. Just as was the case with his later cigarette adverts, Huszár obviously saw the possibility here for the marriage of art and commerce. The precise relationship between Huszár's work for Bruynzeel and VANK needs further investigation. In the spring of 1917 Cornelis van der Sluys, then on the executive board of VANK, redesigned a room in Bruynzeel's family home for his young daughter. Huszár, a close neighbour of the Bruynzeel's in the Voorburg district of The Hague, had already installed a stained glass window in the house the previous year and would go on to design the boys' bedroom in 1919. In his correspondence of the time, Huszár refers to plans among VANK members to form the Dutch equivalent to the *Deutscher Werkbund,* to be called *De Driebond* (The Triple Alliance) as it was to link together industry, business and art. Discussion about the formation of such an organisation was published as a special issue of the magazine *Architectura* in October 1917, edited by Hendricus Theodorus Wijdeveld.[25] As Mienke Simon Thomas has argued, this issue effectively became the prospectus for the journal *Wendingen* which started publication shortly afterwards and became *De Stijl's* major rival and opponent.[26]

Much of the impetus to form *De Driebond* came from the first national trade fair (Jaarbeurs) held in Utrecht in 1917 where many architects designed pavilions and stands for leading manufacturers. Very few were judged to be successful and some were faintly ridiculous. Perhaps for this reason, Bruynzeel commissioned Huszár to design the company stand for the 1918 fair, and Van der Leck would be involved the year after that. For these types of projects *De Stijl* received much public recognition and criticism at the time. In this instance, Van der Leck was singled out for attention in a review of "Art at the Jaarbeurs" written by the designer Piet Zwart for the national circulation magazine *Elseviers Geïllustreerd Maandblad* (Elsevier's Illustrated Monthly), where he was identified as a representative of *De Stijl* and then

23
For some idea of the content of this exhibition see Richard Roland Holst, "Moderne eischen en artistieke bedenkingen", *Wendingen* 2, no. 5 (May 1919), pp. 3–18.
24
Michael White, *De Stijl and Dutch Modernism* (Manchester, 2003), p. 78.
25
Architectura, "Driebond Nummer", vol. 25, nos. 39–40 (October 6, 1917).
26
Mienke Simon Thomas, *Goed in vorm: Honderd jaar ontwerpen in Nederland* (Rotterdam, 2008), p. 76.

Reclame (Kunst und Werbung) im selben Jahr, in dem *De Stijl* gegründet wurde.[23]

Die genauen Zusammenhänge zwischen *De Stijl* und dem niederländischen Reformdiskurs im Gestaltungsbereich harren noch einer ausführlichen Darstellung. Ich selbst habe an anderer Stelle auf die Bedeutung der Tatsache hingewiesen, dass das allererste Bild, das in *De Stijl* abgedruckt wurde – es erschien auf der inneren Umschlagseite der ersten sechs Ausgaben – eine Werbung war, und zwar für die Parkettfußböden der Firma Bruynzeel.[24] Vilmos Huszár, dessen Unterschrift deutlich erkennbar war, hatte sie gestaltet und dabei erkenntlich große Freude daran gehabt, die Muster der Holzblöcke einzusetzen, um abstrakte Kompositionen zu schaffen. Wie bei seinen späteren Zigarettenwerbungen sah Huszár hier offenbar eine Möglichkeit, Kunst und Kommerz zu vermählen. Das genaue Verhältnis zwischen Huszárs Tätigkeit für Bruynzeel und VANK bedarf weiterer Untersuchung. Im Frühjahr 1917 gestaltete Cornelis van der Sluys, damals ein Mitglied des Vorstands von VANK, ein Zimmer im Haus der Familie Bruynzeel für die Tochter des Besitzers. Huszár, der in Voorburg, einem Stadtteil von Den Haag, ganz in der Nähe der Bruynzeels wohnte, hatte in diesem Haus bereits ein buntes Glasfenster angebracht und sollte 1919 das Schlafzimmer der Söhne gestalten. Im Briefverkehr aus dieser Zeit verweist Huszár auf Planungen unter den Mitgliedern von VANK, ein niederländisches Gegenstück zum *Deutschen Werkbund* zu schaffen; die Organisation sollte *De Driebond* (Der Dreibund) heißen und Industrie, Handel und Kunst zusammenführen. Eine Diskussion über den Aufbau einer solchen Vereinigung erschien als von Hendricus Theodorus Wijdeveld herausgegebenes Sonderheft der Zeitschrift *Architectura* im Oktober 1917.[25] Wie Mienke Simon Thomas herausgearbeitet hat, diente diese Ausgabe letztlich als eine Art Programmskizze für die Zeitschrift *Wendingen*, die kurz darauf zu erscheinen begann und zur wichtigsten Rivalin und Gegnerin von *De Stijl* wurde.[26]

Der Impuls zur Gründung des *Driebond* ging vor allem von der 1917 in Utrecht abgehaltenen ersten landesweiten Jaarbeurs (Gewerbeschau) aus, bei der zahlreiche tonangebende Architekten für führende Hersteller Pavillons und Stände gestalteten. Nur wenige dieser Arbeiten galten als erfolgreich; einige waren ein wenig lächerlich. Vielleicht deshalb beauftragte Bruynzeel Huszár mit dem Entwurf des Firmenstandes auf der Messe des Jahres 1918; im darauffolgenden Jahr sollte van der Leck mitarbeiten. Projekte dieser Art trugen *De Stijl* damals viel öffentliche Aufmerksamkeit wie auch Kritik ein. Im konkreten Fall hob der Gestalter Piet Zwart in seiner Rezension der »Kunst auf der Jaarbeurs« in der Publikumszeitschrift *Elseviers Geïllustreerd Maandblad* (Elseviers Illustriertes Monatsblatt) van der Lecks Arbeit hervor, um ihn als Vertreter von *De Stijl* zu bezeichnen und dann den formelhaften Charakter seines Entwurfs zu kritisieren.[27]

Einige Monate zuvor hatte Zwart sich mit Huszár in einer öffentlichen Debatte im *Haagsche Kunstkring* (Haager Kunstkreis), einer großen Kunstvereinigung, der Huszár wie auch Zwart und Bruynzeel angehörten, über zeitgenössische ›Monumentalkunst‹ ausgetauscht.[28]
In einem Bericht über dieses Ereignis nannte Huszár Zwart einen »*Wendingen*-Mann« und offenbarte, dass die Debatte durch einen Vortrag ausgelöst worden war, den er zuvor gehalten hatte und in dem er sich auf einen Vergleich zwischen Arbeiten van der Lecks und Richard Roland Holsts bezogen hatte, der in *De Stijl* erschienen war und in dem er »die Auffassung vertreten hatte, R.H.s sei keine Monumentalkunst.«[29] Das Wandgemälde, das Huszár zum Ziel seiner Polemik nahm, hatte Roland Holst 1907 für das von Berlage entworfene Gebäude der Gewerkschaft der in der Edelsteinindustrie Beschäftigten gestaltet. Das Gebäude gilt als Höhepunkt der ›gemeenschapskunst‹, und so ist kaum eine größere Provokation zu denken als die, seine monumentalen Qualitäten zu bestreiten. Nachdem er die Tradition verteidigt hatte, zu deren gefeiertsten Vertretern Roland Holst gehörte, scheint Zwart eine Art Bekehrung erlebt zu haben; gegen Ende desselben Jahres begann er mit der Herstellung von einfachen Holzmöbeln, in denen der Einfluss Rietvelds erkennbar ist. Einer seiner Stühle wurde im Rahmen einer Ausstellung angewandter Kunst im Museum voor Kunstnijverheid

23
Einen Eindruck vom Inhalt dieser Ausstellung vermittelt Richard Roland Holst, »Moderne eischen en artistieke bedenkingen«, in: *Wendingen,* 2, 5, Mai 1919, S. 3–18.

24
Michael White, *De Stijl and Dutch Modernism,* Manchester 2003, S. 78.

25
Architectura, »Driebond Nummer«, 25, 39–40, 6. Oktober 1917.

26
Mienke Simon Thomas, *Goed in vorm: Honderd jaar ontwerpen in Nederland,* Rotterdam 2008, S. 76.

27
Piet Zwart, »Kunst op de Jaarbeurs«, in: *Elseviers Geïllustreerd Maandblad,* 29, 57, 1919, S. 316–320.

28
Für eine Darstellung dieser Debatte siehe Yvonne Brentjens, *Piet Zwart, 1885–1977: Vormingenieur,* Den Haag 2008, S. 61.

29
Vilmos Huszár, »Aesthetische Beschouwingen IV«, in: *De Stijl* I, 7, Mai 1918, S. 79–84; Vilmos Huszár, Brief an Chris Beekman, 25. Februar 1919, zit. nach Sjarel Ex und Els Hoek, *Vilmos Huszár: Schilder en ontwerper, 1884–1960,* Utrecht 1985, S. 202.

criticised for the formulaic nature of his design.[27]

A couple of months before, Zwart had publically debated contemporary monumental art with Huszár at the *Haagsche Kunstkring* (Hague Art Circle), a large art association of which Huszár, Zwart and Bruynzeel were all members.[28] Relating this event in his correspondence, Huszár called Zwart a "*Wendingen* man" and revealed that the debate was prompted by an earlier talk he had given which utilised a comparison of works by Van der Leck and Richard Roland Holst he had previously published in *De Stijl* where he "argued that R.H. was not monumental art."[29] The wall painting Huszár chose to make his polemical point was one Roland Holst had made in 1907 for Berlage's Diamond Workers Union building in Amsterdam. Considered an apogee of 'gemeenschapskunst', it is difficult to imagine a greater provocation than to deny its monumental qualities. Having defended the tradition of which Roland Holst was one of the most celebrated representatives, Zwart, it seems, experienced something of a conversion and towards the end of the year began making simple wooden furniture inspired by Rietveld. One of his chairs was shown at an applied arts exhibition in October 1919 organised in part by VANK at the Museum voor Kunstnijverheid (Applied Arts Museum) in Haarlem and received lengthy commentary by Van der Sluys in review where he linked Zwart and the chair to the worthy "philosophical considerations" of *De Stijl* but also criticised its workmanship and utility.[30]

Van Doesburg responded to Van der Sluys in characteristic fashion to deny Zwart's connection to *De Stijl* but the point is that his propagandistic efforts had rapidly given the group a level of visibility and association with a certain agenda that belied the number of its realised projects in the field of monumental or applied art at the time.[31] Throughout 1919 and 1920 Van Doesburg continued engaged in a lengthy public debate with Roland Holst on the subject of monumental art. Roland Holst had responded to Huszár's attack on him by referring directly and critically to *De Stijl* in his inaugural lecture as a new Professor of Monumental Art at the Amsterdam Rijksacademie, accusing it of a "mechanisation of the spirit."[32] Van Doesburg reviewed the lecture and played up to Roland Holst's characterisation of *De Stijl* as mechanical and soulless by portraying him and his naturalistic art contrastingly in biological terms of degeneration, retrogression and decay.[33] During 1920 the two men both contributed to the far left journal *De Nieuwe Amsterdammer* where Van Doesburg once more and finally attempted to position the abstraction of *De Stijl* in relation to the concept of monumental art.[34] Somewhat bizarrely, his final article in the series for the journal was on Dada, which he had encountered on his first visit to Paris that year, but it clearly marks the end of his strategy of opposing the vagueness and irrationalism of Roland Holst's version of 'gemeenschapskunst' with *De Stijl's* clarity and geometry.[35]

From this point on Van Doesburg would take *De Stijl* abroad where he discovered international trends unconcerned with the terms of the Dutch context. As Frederic Schwartz has described, the terms 'style' and 'spirit' rapidly disappeared from the debates of *Deutscher Werkbund* after the First World War, just at the point, we have seen, of the attempt to form the Dutch *Driebond*.[36] The gradual disintegration of *De Stijl* as a coherent movement through the 1920s has been well documented.[37] Collaborations between its artists and architects failed and dwindled. So what sense was there in its revival at the end of the decade?

Seen from the perspective of design history, *De Stijl* received its initial impetus and cultural force from campaigning against art and artfulness in production. Contrarily, its second wind came from the desire to preserve aesthetic qualities in the face of functionalism. Van Doesburg had wanted to recruit Berlage to *De Stijl* in 1917 not just because of his profile but because he represented (despite his idealism) a rationalist tendency in Dutch modernism. Intriguingly, another approach was made to the veteran architect in 1928, this time by Rietveld, when the two men met at the first gathering of the Congrès Internationaux d'Architecture Moderne (International Congresses of Modern

27
Piet Zwart, "Kunst op de Jaarbeurs", *Elseviers Geïllustreerd Maandblad 29,* 57 (1919), pp. 316–20.
28
For an account of the debate see Yvonne Brentjens, *Piet Zwart, 1885–1977: Vormingenieur* (The Hague, 2008), p. 61.
29
Vilmos Huszár, "Aesthetische Beschouwingen IV", *De Stijl* I, no. 7 (May 1918), pp. 79–84. Vilmos Huszár, letter to Chris Beekman, February 25, 1919, reprinted in Sjarel Ex and Els Hoek, *Vilmos Huszár: Schilder en ontwerper, 1884–1960* (Utrecht, 1985), p. 202.
30
Cornelis van der Sluys, "Tentoonstelling van aesthetisch uitgevoerde gebruiksvoorwerpen", *De Groene Amsterdammer,* no. 2206 (October 4, 1919), p. 9.
31
See Van der Sluys's retraction a fortnight later in *De Groene Amsterdammer,* no. 2208 (October 18, 1919), p. 3.
32
For a good summary of Van Doesburg and Roland Holst's war of words see Lieske Tibbe, *R.N. Roland Holst, 1868–1938: Arbeid en schoonheid vereend* (Amsterdam, 1994), pp. 236–38.
33
See Theo van Doesburg, "Moderne wendingen in het kunstonderwijs", *De Stijl* II, no. 9 (July 1919), pp. 102–04 and no. 11 (September 1919), pp. 127–32.
34
Theo van Doesburg, "De ontwikkeling van het 'schilderachtige' en 'monumentale' en hun verhouding in de nieuwe beeldende kunst", *De Nieuwe Amsterdammer,* no. 261 (January 3, 1920), p. 4, no. 263 (January 17, 1920), p. 4, no. 274 (April 3, 1920), p. 4.
35
See Van Doesburg's follow-up comments on 'gemeenschapkunst' and the model of Dada as the eradication of an older, sentimental aesthetic in "Is een universeel beeldingsbegrip thans mogelijk", *Bouwkundig Weekblad* 41, no. 39 (September 25, 1920), pp. 230–31. As further articles in the same journal constituted his first public rejection of Berlage: "De taak der nieuwe architectuur", *Bouwkundig Weekblad* 41, no. 50 (December 11, 1920), pp. 278–80, no. 51 (December 18, 1920), pp. 281–85, vol. 42, no. 1 (January 8, 1921), pp. 8–10.
36
Frederic Schwartz, *The Werkbund: Design Theory and Mass Culture before the First World War* (New Haven and London, 1996), pp. 213–22.
37
See Carel Blotkamp, ed., *De vervolgjaren van De Stijl, 1922–1932* (Amsterdam and Antwerp, 1996).

(Museum für Handwerk) in Haarlem, bei deren Organisation VANK mitwirkte, gezeigt und von van der Sluys in einer Rezension ausführlich besprochen, in der er Zwart und den Stuhl mit den wertvollen »philosophischen Überlegungen« von *De Stijl* in Verbindung brachte, zugleich allerdings die Verarbeitung und den Nutzwert des Möbelstücks kritisierte.[30]

Van Doesburgs Antwort auf van der Sluys ist bezeichnend – er bestreitet jede Verbindung zwischen Zwart und *De Stijl* –, aber die Anekdote zeigt, dass seine Propagandabemühungen der Gruppe in kurzer Zeit zu einem Grad an öffentlicher Sichtbarkeit verholfen und sie mit einer bestimmten Programmatik in Verbindung gebracht hatten, die zur Zahl der damals umgesetzten Projekte in den Bereichen ›Monumentalkunst‹ oder angewandte Kunst in keinerlei Verhältnis standen.[31] Im weiteren Verlauf der Jahre 1919 und 1920 setzte sich van Doesburg in einer langen öffentlichen Debatte mit Roland Holst über das Thema ›Monumentalkunst‹ auseinander. Roland Holst hatte auf Huszárs Angriff gegen ihn geantwortet, indem er in seiner Antrittsvorlesung als Professor für ›Monumentalkunst‹ an der Amsterdamer Rijksacademie direkt und kritisch auf *De Stijl* Bezug nahm; er beschuldigte die Gruppe einer »Mechanisierung des Geistes.«[32] Van Doesburg rezensierte die Vorlesung und reagierte auf Roland Holsts Beschreibung von *De Stijl* als mechanisch und seelenlos, indem er den Ball zurückspielte und Holsts naturalistische Kunst im Gegenzug in biologischen Begriffen von Degeneration, Rückentwicklung und Verfall porträtierte.[33] Im Verlauf des Jahres 1920 schrieben beide Männer Beiträge in der politisch linksaußen angesiedelten Zeitschrift *De Nieuwe Amsterdammer,* wobei van Doesburg einen weiteren und letzten Versuch unternahm, die Abstraktion von *De Stijl* im Verhältnis zum Begriff der ›Monumentalkunst‹ zu positionieren.[34] Ein wenig bizarr ist, dass sein letzter Aufsatz in der Serie für diese Zeitschrift sich mit *Dada* beschäftigt, dem van Doesburg im selben Jahr bei seinem ersten Besuch in Paris begegnet war; jedenfalls bezeichnet dies deutlich das Ende seiner Strategie, der Vagheit und dem Irrationalismus von Roland Holsts Version von ›gemeenschapskunst‹ die Klarheit und Geometrie von *De Stijl* entgegenzusetzen.[35]

Von nun an sollte van Doesburg *De Stijl* ins Ausland exportieren, wo er auf internationale Entwicklungen stieß, die mit den Begriffen des niederländischen Zusammenhangs nichts zu tun hatten. Wie Frederic Schwartz beschrieben hat, verschwanden die Begriffe ›Stil‹ und ›Geist‹ nach dem Ersten Weltkrieg schnell aus den Debatten im *Deutschen Werkbund,* just zu der Zeit, wie wir gesehen haben, da es Bemühungen gab, den holländischen *Driebond* zu gründen.[36] Die fortschreitende Auflösung von *De Stijl* als einheitlicher Bewegung im Verlauf der 1920er-Jahre ist ausführlich dokumentiert worden.[37] Kollaborationsprojekte zwischen Künstlern und Architekten innerhalb der Gruppe scheiterten, und die Neigung, sie zu unternehmen, nahm ab. Welchen Sinn konnte also die Wiederbelebung von *De Stijl* am Ende des Jahrzehnts haben?

In Hinblick auf die Geschichte des Designs gab die Kampagne gegen Kunst und Künstlichkeit in der Produktion den ersten Anstoß zu *De Stijl* und der kulturellen Wirkungsmacht der Gruppe. Den Neuaufschwung dagegen verdankte sie dem Bestreben, angesichts des Funktionalismus ästhetische Qualitäten zu bewahren. Van Doesburg hatte Berlage 1917 nicht nur wegen seiner Prominenz für *De Stijl* gewinnen wollen, sondern auch, weil dieser trotz seines Idealismus eine rationalistische Tendenz innerhalb des holländischen Modernismus vertrat. Interessanterweise trat man 1928 erneut an den altehrwürdigen Architekten heran, diesmal durch Rietveld bei einer Begegnung der zwei Männer während der ersten Versammlung der Congrès Internationaux d'Architecture Moderne (Internationale Kongresse Moderner Architektur) im schweizerischen La Sarraz. Wie es scheint, lehnte Berlage das Ansinnen rundweg ab und erwiderte: »Ihr Leute reißt alles nieder, was ich aufgebaut habe.«[38]

Wie auch immer diese Begegnung genau ablief, es ist unwahrscheinlich, dass Berlage Rietvelds kurz zuvor in *i10* erschienenen Aufsatz über »Nutzen, Konstruktion: (Schönheit: Kunst)« gelesen hatte, in dem der Autor ent-

30
Cornelis van der Sluys, »Tentoonstelling van aesthetisch uitgevoerde gebruiksvoorwerpen«, in: *De Groene Amsterdammer,* 2206, 4. Oktober 1919, S. 9.

31
Siehe van der Sluys' Rückzieher zwei Wochen später in: *De Groene Amsterdammer,* 2208, 18. Oktober 1919, S. 3.

32
Eine gute Zusammenfassung des Wortgefechts zwischen van Doesburg und Roland Holst findet sich in Lieske Tibbe, *R.N. Roland Holst, 1868–1938: Arbeid en schoonheid vereend,* Amsterdam 1994, S. 236–238.

33
Siehe Theo van Doesburg, »Moderne wendingen in het kunstonderwijs«, in: *De Stijl,* II, 9, Juli 1919, S. 102–104 und Nr. 11, September 1919, S. 127–132.

34
Theo van Doesburg, »De ontwikkeling van het ›schilderachtige‹ en ›monumentale‹ en hun verhouding in de nieuwe beeldende kunst«, in: *De Nieuwe Amsterdammer,* 261, 3. Januar 1920, S. 4, Nr. 263, 17. Januar 1920, S. 4 und Nr. 274, 3. April 1920, S. 4.

35
Siehe van Doesburgs weiterführende Einlassungen zu ›gemeenschapkunst‹ und das Modell Dada als Auslöschung einer älteren sentimentalen Ästhetik in »Is een universeel beeldingsbegrip thans mogelijk«, in: *Bouwkundig Weekblad,* 41, 39, 25. September 1920, S. 230–231. Ein weiterer Artikel in derselben Zeitschrift enthält seine erste öffentliche Ablehnung Berlages: »De taak der nieuwe architectuur«, in: *Bouwkundig Weekblad,* 41, 50, 11. Dezember 1920, S. 278–280, Nr. 51, 18. Dezember 1920, S. 281–285 und Bd. 42, 1, 8. Januar 1921, S. 8–10.

36
Frederic Schwartz, *The Werkbund: Design Theory and Mass Culture before the First World War,* New Haven und London 1996, S. 213–222.

37
Siehe Carel Blotkamp (Hrsg.), *De vervolgjaren van De Stijl, 1922–1932,* Amsterdam und Antwerpen 1996.

38
Overy 1991 (wie Anm. 18), S. 26–27.

Architecture) in La Sarraz, Switzerland. Apparently Berlage turned him down flat and retorted, "You people are demolishing everything that I have built up."[38]

Whatever the exact nature of this exchange, it seems unlikely that Berlage had read Rietveld's recent article in *i10* on "Utility, Construction: (Beauty: Art)," which argued forcefully for the preservation of art in design.[39] Without great talents as a writer or theorist, Rietveld initially makes his argument by using the words of others and it is striking to read him quote at length texts by Oud, Mondrian and Van Doesburg. It is almost as if he was trying to reconstruct *De Stijl* on paper. Towards the end of the article, he even quotes the philosopher Bolland, who had been an important source for the theory of "Nieuwe Beelding" during the formative years of *De Stijl*. The role of art is not to beautify, Rietveld argues, but to make visible what things really are, using the classic idealist inversion of appearance and reality that informed so much of *De Stijl* theory and supported a view of abstraction not as a flight from reality but as its closest approximation.

In terms of Rietveld's practice, these years are marked by his self-redefinition as an architect and his work on bringing his furniture prototypes into mass production. He was facilitated in doing so by the furniture store Metz & Co., which developed its own manufacturing capability during the 1920s. Its owner Joseph de Leeuw was a personal friend of Bart van der Leck and also worked with Willem Penaat, a former collaborator with Berlage on 't Binnenhuis and founder member and onetime director of VANK, who alongside Van der Sluys established *Kunst aan het Volk* (Art for the People) and *Kunst aan Allen* (Art for Everybody) before the war, organisations which staged didactic design exhibitions. To cap it all, Penaat was currently curator of the Museum for Applied Art in Haarlem.[40] Objects designed by all three were displayed together in the Metz showrooms in Amsterdam and The Hague, creating fascinating echoes of the abstract coloured environments of early *De Stijl* years.

The question remains, though, how does this commercial variant compare to Van Doesburg's design for Bart de Ligt's house in 1919, a photograph of which he also chose for his Strasbourg window display? Is there any significance in Van Doesburg's reutilisation for the Aubette of typography he designed in 1919 and used for, among others, the Lettergieterij Amsterdam (Amsterdam Letter Foundry), a firm that, like Metz & Co., was a member of the *Bond voor Kunst en Industrie* (Association for Art and Industry), another Dutch attempt to form a *Werkbund*-type organisation? Such issues require further thought, along with the overarching problem of *De Stijl's* relationship to 'gemeenschapskunst'. Did *De Stijl,* as Berlage suggested, destroy everything he had built up, or did it actually help to prolong the debate on style and culture, on productive connections between art and society, on dreams of a perfected community, all of which would eventually buckle under the weight of totalitarianism and mass culture?

38
Overy 1991 (see note 18), pp. 26–27.
39
Gerrit Rietveld, "Nut, Constructie: (Schoonheid: Kunst)", *i10* 1, no. 3 (March 1927), pp. 89–92.
40
See Simon Thomas 2008 (see note 26), p. 90.

schieden für die Erhaltung der Kunst in der Gestaltung eintrat.[39] Ohne großes Talent für das Schreiben oder die Theorie zu besitzen, vertritt Rietveld seine Auffassung zunächst, indem er auf die Worte anderer zurückgreift; mit Staunen liest man heute, wie er ausführlich aus Schriften von Oud, Mondrian und van Doesburg zitiert. Es scheint beinahe, als versuche er, *De Stijl* auf dem Papier wiederherzustellen. Gegen Ende seines Artikels zitiert er sogar den Philosophen Bolland, der eine wichtige Quelle für die Theorie des »Nieuwe Beelding« während der prägenden Jahre von *De Stijl* gewesen war. Die Rolle der Kunst ist nicht die Verschönerung, sondern sichtbar zu machen, was die Dinge wirklich sind, schreibt Rietveld unter Rückgriff auf die klassische idealistische Umkehrung von Schein und Wirklichkeit, auf der so große Teile der Theoriebildung von *De Stijl* beruht hatten und nach der Abstraktion als etwas gesehen werden konnte, das, weit entfernt davon, aus der Wirklichkeit zu fliehen, sich dieser gerade so weit wie möglich annäherte.

Was Rietvelds Praxis angeht, sind diese Jahre von der Neuerfindung seiner selbst als Architekt geprägt und von seinem Vorhaben eingenommen, seine Möbelprototypen in die Massenfertigung zu überführen. Dabei half ihm die Möbelhandlung Metz & Co., die in den 1920er-Jahren eigene Produktionskapazitäten aufbaute. Ihr Inhaber, Joseph de Leeuw, war persönlich mit Bart van der Leck befreundet und arbeitete auch mit Willem Penaat zusammen, einem früheren Mitarbeiter Berlages bei 't Binnenhuis und Gründungsmitglied und ehemaligem Direktor von VANK, der vor dem Krieg gemeinsam mit van der Sluys *Kunst aan het Volk* (Kunst für das Volk) und *Kunst aan Allen* (Kunst für alle) gegründet hatte, Organisationen, die didaktische Designausstellungen veranstalteten. Obendrein war Penaat damals auch noch Kurator des Haarlemer Museums für angewandte Kunst.[40] Von den dreien gestaltete Objekte waren gemeinsam in den Verkaufsräumen von Metz in Amsterdam und Den Haag ausgestellt, wodurch sich faszinierende Nachklänge der abstrakten farbigen Environments der frühen Jahre von *De Stijl* ergaben.

Die Frage bleibt jedoch: Wie steht diese kommerzielle Variante im Vergleich zu van Doesburgs Entwurf für Bart de Ligts Haus aus dem Jahr 1919 da, der ebenfalls auf einer Fotografie in seiner Straßburger Schaufenstergestaltung erschien? Welche Bedeutung ist der Tatsache beizumessen, dass er für die Aubette auf typographische Gestaltungen zurückgriff, die er 1919 entworfen und unter anderem für die Lettergieterij Amsterdam (Amsterdamer Letterngießerei) verwendet hatte, eine Firma, die wie Metz & Co. Mitglied des *Bond voor Kunst en Industrie* (Bund für Kunst und Industrie) gewesen war, auch dies ein holländischer Versuch, eine *Werkbund*-ähnliche Organisation zu schaffen? Solche Fragen erfordern weitere Betrachtung, wie auch das übergeordnete Problem des Verhältnisses zwischen *De Stijl* und ›gemeenschapskunst‹. Hat *De Stijl,* wie Berlage nahelegte, alles zerstört, was er aufgebaut hatte, oder half es im Gegenteil die Debatte über Stil und Kultur, über produktive Verbindungen zwischen Kunst und Gesellschaft, über Träume von einer vollkommenen Gesellschaft zu verlängern, bevor all diese Ideen zuletzt unter dem Gewicht von Totalitarismus und Massenkultur zusammenbrechen sollten?

Aus dem Englischen übertragen
von Gerrit Jackson

39
Gerrit Rietveld, »Nut, Constructie: (Schoonheid: Kunst)«, in: *i10,* 1, 3, März 1927, S. 89–92.
40
Thomas 2008 (wie Anm. 26), S. 90.

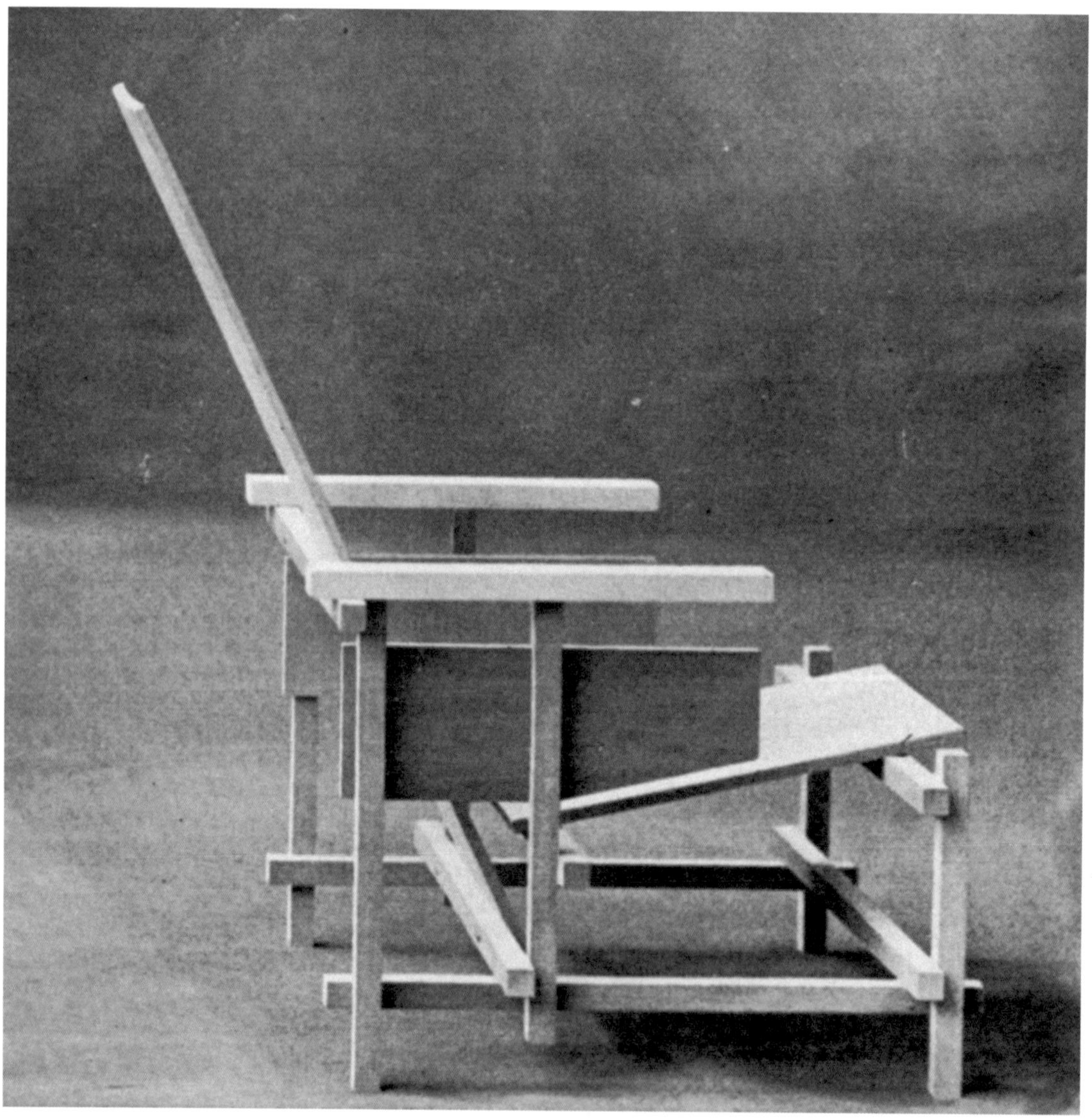

Gerrit Rietveld
Stuhl
Abgebildet in *De Stijl*, II, 11
September 1919

Gerrit Rietveld
Chair
Illustrated in *De Stijl* II, no. 11
(September 1919)

Der Betrachter in Bewegung. Elementarisierung und Standardisierung bei De Stijl

Felicia Rappe

Der sogenannte *Rot-Blaue Stuhl* von Gerrit Rietveld ist eine Ikone der Künstlergruppierung um die Zeitschrift *De Stijl* (Abb. S. 241). Nicht von vornherein trug er die Farben, die ihn heute unverkennbar machen. Er entstand im Jahr 1918 und ist aus wenigen Elementen rechtwinklig zusammengesetzter Holzstreben und schräger Spanholzplatten konstruiert (Abb. S. 60).
Der Designer und Architekt Rietveld stieß erst ein Jahr später zu *De Stijl* und versah nicht vor 1923 unter dem neuen Einfluss die Sitzflächen und Holzstreben mit den Farben Rot, Blau und Gelb.
Theo van Doesburg, der Herausgeber der Zeitschrift *De Stijl*, war es, der die Einheitlichkeit dieser Stilmerkmale vorantrieb. Mit seinen Aufsätzen und Beiträgen bewarb er ein homogenes Erscheinungsbild der Künstler um das Publikationsorgan, mit so viel Erfolg, dass das Bild von *De Stijl* bis heute in erster Linie mit Grundfarben und rechtwinkligen Formen verbunden ist.
Dies sollte der losen Gruppierung von Künstlern mit teils ganz unterschiedlichen ästhetischen Bestrebungen den Anstrich einer zusammenhängenden Gruppe mit charakteristischem Profil verleihen. Eine einheitliche Formensprache wurde noch 1930 von Theo van Doesburg als zentrales Ziel von *De Stijl* formuliert, als die Zeitschrift bereits nicht mehr regelmäßig erschien. Unter der Überschrift »Elementarismus« schrieb er: »Was ist dem Maler das Höchste? Sich selbst als Farbe fühlen, Farbe sein, sonst bleibt das Werk farblos, auch wenn es bunt ist. Farbe sein, Weiß, Rot, Gelb, Blau, Schwarz sein, das heißt Maler sein. [...] als Form genügt ein einziges Element, z.B. das Viereck. Die Linie ist trennend und verbindend zugleich, sie gibt dem Werk Richtung und Kraft. Komposition ist nicht das Höchste. Das Höchste ist der Übergang zu einer universalen Gestaltungsform.«[1]

An eine solche Rhetorik von Artikeln in *De Stijl* lehnte sich die kunstgeschichtliche Forschung lange Zeit an und schrieb auch den Fokus auf Künstler fort, die sich der von van Doesburg als optimal beschriebenen Elemente bedienten.
So denkt man bei van Doesburgs Passus in erster Linie an charakteristische Kunstwerke von Piet Mondrian, wie sie seit Anfang der 1920er-Jahre entstanden sind (Abb. S. 213–215). Dagegen gerieten Künstler und ihre Werke im Umfeld der Zeitschrift aus dem Blick, die statt Rechteck und Primärfarben andere Grundelemente verwendeten oder jenseits völliger Abstraktion figürliche Referenzen beibehielten wie etwa Bart van der Leck. *De Stijl* erweist sich als ein vielfältiges und von Widersprüchen gekennzeichnetes Phänomen.

Schon zur Zeit von *De Stijl* gab es unter den Künstlern Kontroversen darüber, welche Elemente zu verwenden oder aber aus den Kunstwerken fern zu halten seien. Grundsätzlich waren sich Piet Mondrian und Theo van Doesburg zwar über die Verwendung von Primärfarben und rechtwinkligen Rasterstrukturen einig. Theo van Doesburgs Ausführungen über den »Elementarismus« sind jedoch tatsächlich Teil einer Debatte mit Piet Mondrian über sein Verfahren, die Linien des Rasters diagonal anzuordnen, statt horizontal und vertikal, wie Mondrian es tat. Wenn Mondrian auch selbst teilweise mit rautenförmigen Bildformaten experimentierte, verwehrte er sich grundsätzlich gegen diagonale Kompositionen wie sie neben vielen Bildern Doesburgs auch Werke von César Domela oder Friedrich Vordemberge-Gildewart kennzeichnen (Abb. S. 135, S. 64 und S. 273). Bart van der Lecks Kompositionen, in denen er nicht-rechtwinklige Formen verwendete und figürliche Referenzen beibehielt, stießen ebenfalls bald auf Piet Mondrians Kritik, nachdem er sich

1
Theo van Doesburg, »Elementarismus«, geschrieben am 13. Juli 1930, in: *De Stijl*, dernier numéro, 1932, S. 15–16.

The Viewer in Motion:
Elementarization and Standardization in De Stijl

Felicia Rappe

Gerrit Rietveld's *Red and Blue Chair* is an icon of the group of artists associated with the journal *De Stijl* (cf. ill. p. 241). Made in 1918 out of a small number of elements consisting of wooden elements assembled at right angles to one another and obliquely placed pieces of plywood, it did not acquire its unmistakable colors until after 1923 (ill. p. 60). Only under the influence of the *De Stijl* movement, which he joined in 1919, did designer and architect Rietveld decide to make the seat and the rods of the chair red, yellow, and blue. The idea of a uniform style was propagated among the artists connected with the journal by its editor, Theo Van Doesburg—so successfully, in fact, that today the *De Stijl* movement is associated chiefly with primary colors and rectangles. His aim was to bring together loosely connected artists with in some cases quite divergent aesthetic ambitions and to cast them as a homogenous group with a characteristic profile of its own. Even as late as 1930, after the journal had ceased to appear regularly, Van Doesburg was still promulgating a standard formal vocabulary as a central aim of *De Stijl*. Under the heading "Elementarism" he wrote: "What is the highest ideal for a painter? To experience himself as color, to be color, otherwise the work remains colorless even if it is brightly colored. To be color, to be white, red, yellow, blue, or black means to be a painter. ... as a form a single element will suffice, the rectangle, for example. The line both separates and joins at the same time, it gives the work direction and strength. Composition is not the highest ideal. The highest ideal is the transition to a universal form."[1]

Art historians for a long time based their research into abstract art on rhetoric of the kind that appeared in the journal *De Stijl* and continued to focus chiefly on those artists who employed the elements defined as optimal by Van Doesburg. The principles espoused by Van Doesburg primarily call to mind the characteristic works created by Piet Mondrian from the early nineteen-twenties onward (cf. ill. pp. 213–215). Artists such as Bart van der Leck, on the other hand, who, though associated with the journal, founded their work on elements other than the rectangle and primary colors or who retained figural references rather than going all the way down the road to abstraction, tended to be forgotten. *De Stijl* was simply a phenomenon that came in many guises and was beset with contradictions. Even as *De Stijl* was still evolving its artists became involved in controversies about which elements should be used and which excluded from works of art. Mondrian and Van Doesburg were at least in fundamental agreement about the use of primary colors and rectangular grid structures, but indeed Van Doesburg's remarks about "elementarism" were part of the debate he carried on with Mondrian about his practice of arranging the lines of the grid diagonally, rather than horizontally or vertically as Mondrian did. Although Mondrian did sometimes experiment with rhombic formats, he was fundamentally opposed to the diagonal compositions frequently employed by Van Doesburg, César Domela or Friedrich Vordemberge-Gildewart (cf. ill. p. 135 and p. 64 + ill. p. 273). Van der Leck's compositions, which also used non-rectangular forms and retained figural references, soon came in for criticism from Mondrian, even though the latter had for a time allowed himself to be influenced by Van der Leck's painting style. Van der Leck had joined the group of artists around Mondrian and Van Doesburg in 1916 and had written essays for *De Stijl* on the relationship between architecture and painting excerting a

1
Theo van Doesburg, "Elementarism," written on July 13, 1930, and published in *De Stijl*, dernier numéro (1932), pp. 15–16.

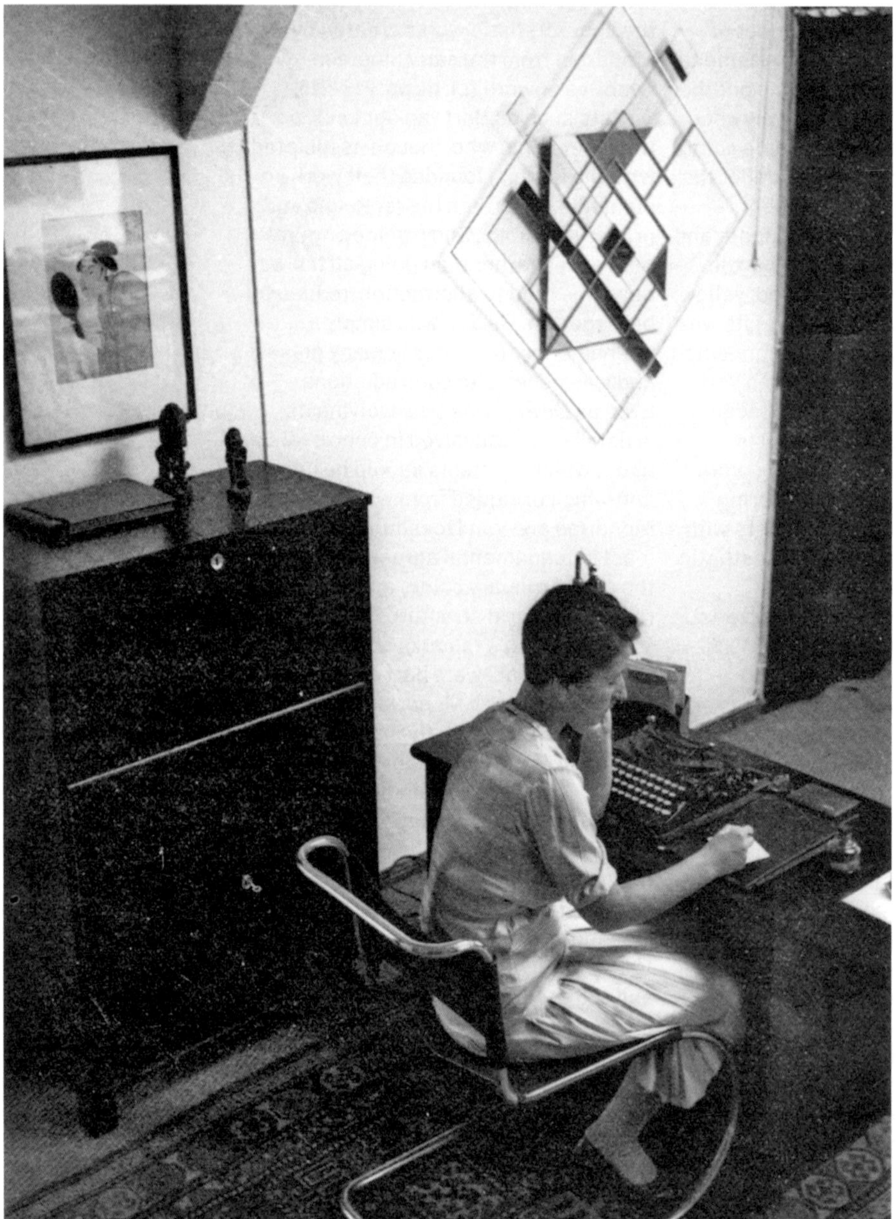

Ruth Domela, Berlin
1933
RKD, Archiv César Domela

Ruth Domela, Berlin
1933
RKD, Archive of César Domela

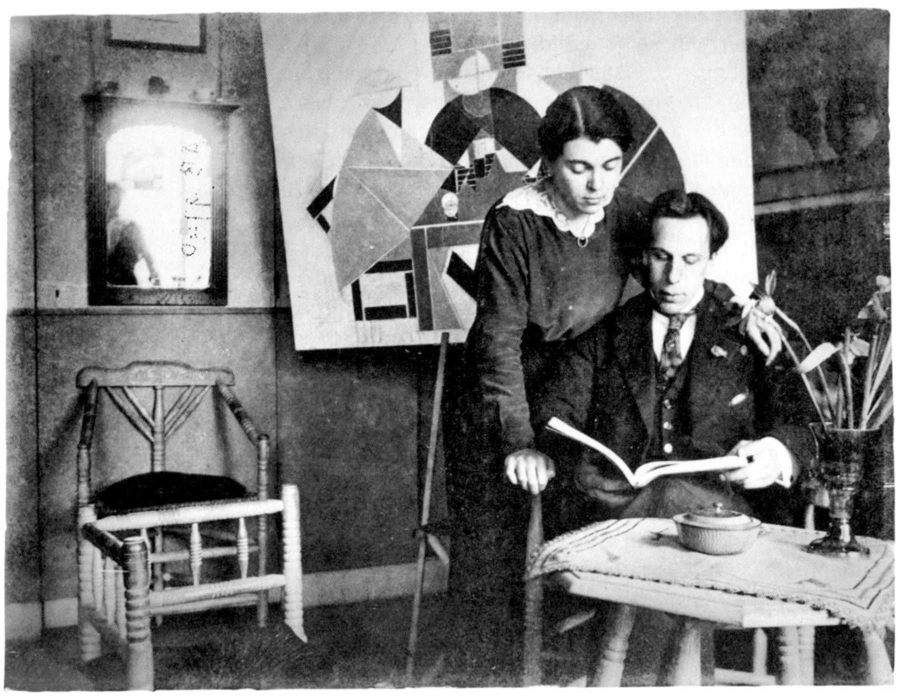

Lena Milius and Theo van Doesburg
in the studio on Kort Galgewater, Leiden
April 1917
Collection RKD The Hague

Lena Milius und Theo van Doesburg
im Atelier, Kort Galgewater, Leiden
April 1917
Sammlung RKD Den Haag

einige Zeit von der Malweise van der Lecks hatte beeinflussen lassen.
Bart van der Leck war 1916 zu den Künstlern um Piet Mondrian und Theo van Doesburg gestoßen. Er verfasste Aufsätze für *De Stijl*, in denen besonders seine Ausführungen über das Verhältnis von Architektur und Malerei Einfluss auf die anderen Künstler um die Zeitschrift hatten. Vor dem Hintergrund der Kontroverse um die unterschiedlichen Bildauffassungen brach Bart van der Leck jedoch mit dem engen Umfeld von *De Stijl* und unterzeichnete das Manifest der Zeitschrift im November 1918 bereits nicht mehr. Er entwickelte daraufhin seine charakteristische Malweise weiter, wie sie etwa in Gemälden *Die Holzfäller* aus dem Jahr 1928 (Abb. S. 181) oder dem 1926 entstandenen *Stillleben* (Abb. S. 180) anzutreffen ist: Er baute seine Bilder aus geometrischen Formen auf, die einander nicht berühren. Rechtecke, Dreiecke und trapezförmige Elemente unterschiedlicher Größe und Maßverhältnisse sind lose auf dem Bildgrund verteilt und scheinen auf diesem zu schweben. Dabei ermöglichen die Titel von Gemälden wie *Die Holzfäller* und *Stillleben* die den Bezeichnungen entsprechenden Motive zu erkennen, in anderen Bildern ist die Formensprache dagegen so abstrakt, dass keine gegenständlichen Referenzen auszumachen sind. Bart van der Leck nutzte zunächst die Primär-farben Blau, Rot und Gelb, die er von Piet Mondrian übernahm. Später ergänzte er sie durch Grau wie in *Die Holzfäller* oder in den Kacheln, die er vermehrt in den 1940er-Jahren entwarf (Abb. S. 183).

Nicht nur die Vorstellung davon, welche Farben und welche Elemente für *De Stijl* stehen, ist durch die Rhetorik von Künstlern wie Theo van Doesburg geprägt, sondern auch das Verständnis, was es für die Geschichte der Malerei bedeutet, dass Künstler zu Beginn des 20. Jahrhunderts von figürlichen Darstellungen Abstand nahmen. Erklärungen des Stellenwerts der Abstraktion bei *De Stijl* in der Kunstgeschichte bezogen sich lange Zeit auf Äußerungen wie diejenigen Theo van Doesburgs, dass dem »Maler das Höchste« sei, »sich selbst als Farbe [zu] fühlen, Farbe [zu] sein«. Diese Rhetorik einer Identifikation des Malers mit der Farbe als das Optimum einer »universalen Gestaltungsform« lebte in Formulierungen fort, wie der, dass die Malerei dann ihrem Wesen am nächsten und insofern an ihrem Ziel- und Höhepunkt angelangt sei, wenn sie die Abbildung von Gegenständen hinter sich lasse, und sich allein auf die dem Maler eigenen Mittel konzentriere: Farbe und Form.[2] Die modernistische Kunstkritik beschrieb diese Malerei als ›Reinigung‹ und Befreiung von der ›Knechtschaft‹, die äußere Wirklichkeit nachzuahmen. Zu solchen teleologischen Beschreibungen verführen Zeugnisse der Künstler auf ihrem Weg zur Abstraktion: So galt es für Theo van Doesburg, mögliche Assoziationen der abstrakten Darstellungen mit Vorbildern in der äußeren Wirklichkeit zu vermeiden und die völlige Abstraktion unter Verwendung weniger Grundelemente in den Mittelpunkt zu stellen. Dies zeigen sein berühmtes Gemälde *Komposition IX, Opus 18. Abstrakte Version der Kartenspieler* aus dem Jahr 1917 (Abb. S. 114) und die Kommentare des Künstlers zu seinem Bild.

Das Bild setzt sich vollständig aus rechteckigen Farbfeldern in schwarz, weiß, blau und grau zusammen. Diese sind miteinander verzahnt und füllen die Leinwand bis zu den Rändern. Der Bildtitel verweist neben der abstrakten Benennung »Komposition IX, Opus 18« auch auf ein konkretes Motiv: die Kartenspieler. Vor diesem Hintergrund wirken die kleineren geometrischen Formen in der Mitte des Bildes wie Spielkarten auf einem Tisch, um den herum Figuren sitzen. Während der Entstehung des Gemäldes schrieb Doesburg in einem Brief: »Ich habe mit einer neuen Lösung für meine Kartenspieler begonnen. Das Ergebnis verspricht sagenhaft kraftvoll und aufregend zu werden«.[3] Er verweist hier auf sein im selben Jahr entstandenes, noch stark figürliches Bild *Die Kartenspieler,* das vier Figuren im Kartenspiel um einen Tisch versammelt zeigt (Abb. rechts). Van Doesburg versuchte, über die Zerlegung dieses figürlichen Motivs eine neue Formensprache zu finden. Der Verweis auf den figürlichen Ursprung des Bildes *Komposition IX, Opus 18. Abstrakte Version der Kartenspieler* fehlt jedoch völlig, wenn sich der Künstler einige Jahre später noch einmal über das abstrakte Bild äußert: Das Gemälde bestehe ausschließlich aus rechteckigen Flächen. Ein Freund habe es daher eine »Kiste

Theo van Doesburg
Die Kartenspieler
1916/17
Öl und Tempera auf Leinwand, 126 x 156 cm
Gemeentemuseum Den Haag
Dauerleihgabe Niederländisches Institut für Denkmalpflege

Theo van Doesburg
The Card Players
1916/17
Oil and tempera on canvas, 126 x 156 cm
Gemeentemuseum The Hague
On permanent loan from the Netherlands Institute for Cultural Heritage

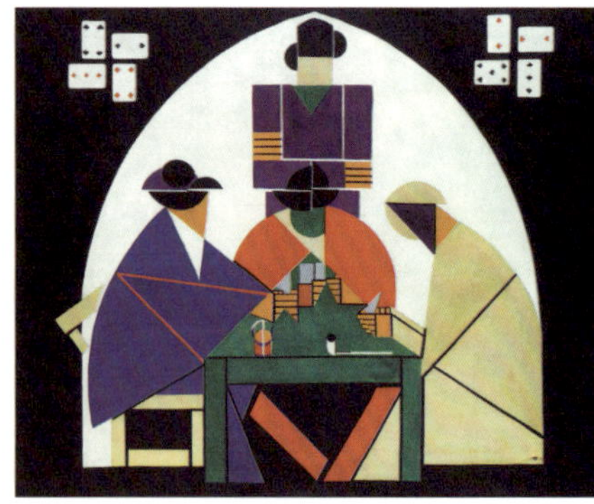

2
Prägend war in Hinblick auf diese Perspektive der US-amerikanische Kunstkritiker Clement Greenberg mit Aufsätzen wie »Modernistische Malerei« (1960) oder »Nach dem abstrakten Expressionismus« (1962), in: *Die Essenz der Moderne. Ausgewählte Essays und Kritiken,* hrsg. von Karlheinz Lüdeking, Amsterdam u.a. 1997.

3
Theo van Doesburg an Antony Kok, 9. September 1917 (Archiv Theo van Doesburg), zit. nach: Els Hoek, *Theo van Doesburg. Oeuvre catalogue,* Utrecht 2000, S. 206.

particularly strong influence on the other artists associated with the journal. Following the controversy over composition, however, van der Leck broke with those most closely associated with *De Stijl* and refused to sign the manifesto published by the journal in November 1918. Instead, he continued to pursue his own characteristic style of painting—as evidenced in such paintings as *Woodcutters* from the year 1928 (cf. ill. p. 181) or *Still Life* painted in 1926 (cf. ill. p. 180)—in which he employed geometric forms that never touched each other. Rectangles, triangles, and trapezoid elements of various sizes and scales scattered loosely over the pictorial ground look as if they were floating on it. The titles of paintings such as *Woodcutters* and *Still Life* serve as an aid to deciphering the motifs to which they refer, while in other pictures the formal language is so abstract that no references to objects can be discerned at all. Initially Van der Leck used the primary colors he had adopted from Mondrian—blue, red, and yellow—later adding gray as in *Woodcutters* or on the tiles that he began producing in increasing quantities during the nineteen-forties (cf. ill. p. 183).

The rhetoric of artists like Van Doesburg not only influenced ideas about which colors and elements should serve as the defining characteristics of *De Stijl* but also served to underline the significance of the fact that artists in the early twentieth century chose to distance themselves from figural representation. Art historians seeking to explain the importance attached to abstraction in the *De Stijl* movement for a long time found their arguments in assertions like Van Doesburg's that "the highest ideal for a painter" was "to experience himself as color, to be color." This identification of the painter with color as the best way to achieve a "universal form" was taken to its logical conclusion in the claim that painting came closest to its true nature—and hence to its ultimate goal and climax—if it abandoned the portrayal of objects and instead concentrated solely on the painterly idioms of color and form.[2] Modernist art critics described this kind of painting as a process of 'purification' and as a liberation from the 'servitude' of having to copy external reality. The temptation to jump to such teleological conclusions was provided by the testimonials of artists on their way to abstraction. Van Doesburg, for instance, strove to avoid any possible associations that abstract paintings might have with models in external reality and tried instead to focus on total abstraction by using just a few basic elements. This is illustrated by his famous painting of 1917 *Composition IX, Opus 18. Abstract Version of the Card Players* (ill. p. 114) and his commentaries on it.

The picture is composed entirely of rectangular color fields in black, white, blue, and gray. Interlocking with one another, they fill the canvas right up to the edges. The title of the painting alludes not only to its abstract quality *(Composition IX, Opus 18)* but also to a concrete motif, the card players. This allusion allows us to interpret the smaller geometric shapes in the middle of the picture as playing cards on a table around which figures are seated. While working on the painting Doesburg wrote in a letter: "I've started on a new solution for my card players. The result should be fantastically powerful and exciting."[3] The reference here is to another, still strongly figural painting he had produced the same year entitled *The Card Players,* which shows four figures around a table playing cards (ill. left). By reducing this figural motif to its component parts Van Doesburg sought to find a new formal language. A few years later the artist once again commented on the abstract painting *Composition IX, Opus 18. Abstract Version of the Card Players,* albeit this time omitting any reference to its figural origins. Instead he said that it consisted exclusively of rectangular fields and that this had even prompted a friend of his jokingly to label the painting a "box of bricks", thus canceling out any idea that it was derived from a figural object.[4] Van Doesburg's retrospective description of the painting in 1925 reveals his ambition to sever any connections it might have with visible reality and to liberate it from any associations with figures or narrative scenes.

Art historians and art critics, who have helped to shape popular conceptions about abstract art, described this 'liberation from the

2
Key criticism representing this perspective were essays by the US art critic Clement Greenberg such as "Modernist Painting" (1960), originally delivered as a radio broadcast on *The Voice of America Forum Lectures: The Visual Arts,* 1960 or "After Abstract Expressionism," *Art International,* 1962.

3
Theo van Doesburg to Antony Kok, September 9, 1917 (Theo van Doesburg Archive), quoted in Els Hoek, *Theo van Doesburg, Oeuvre catalogue* (Utrecht, 2000), p. 206.

4
Theo van Doesburg, quoted in Hoek 2000 (see note 3), p. 206.

voller Bausteine« genannt. Damit seien »alle Gedanken daran beiseite geräumt, dass es auf einen figürlichen Gegenstand zurückgeht.«[4] In dieser nachträglichen Schilderung Theo van Doesburgs aus dem Jahr 1925 zeigt sich sein Bestreben, das Bild jenseits eines Ausgangspunktes in der sichtbaren Wirklichkeit zu positionieren und von Assoziationen mit Figuren oder narrativen Szenen frei zu halten.

Die kunsthistorische Forschung und die Kunstkritik, die auch die populäre Vorstellung von Abstraktion prägt, beschrieb eine solche ›Befreiung vom Gegenstand‹ als den ›Triumphzug der Autonomie der Malerei‹: Farben und Linien seien nicht mehr Mittel zum Zweck, um Gegenstände und Figuren abzubilden, sondern emanzipierten sich von dieser Aufgabe und seien fortan ›autonom‹; statt das Bild als ›offenes Fenster‹ zu konzipieren, verleugne die Leinwand ihre faktische Zweidimensionalität nicht mehr; statt vorzugeben, dass sich im Rahmen der Leinwand ein dreidimensionaler Raum öffne, trete nun die Fläche ins Bewusstsein der Betrachter. So genüge das abstrakte Gemälde letztlich sich selbst, und die Malerei komme zur Deckung mit sich selbst: »Farbe sein [...], das heißt Maler sein«. Mit solchen Formulierungen ist die Idee einer Kunst verbunden, die inwendig wird, sich unabhängig von der Erfahrung des Betrachters auf sich selbst bezieht. Das Ergebnis der Reduktion auf wenige Grundelemente wäre also, dass das ›autonome‹ Bild sich gleichsam fixiert und immobilisiert.

Die Perspektive darauf, was Abstraktion für die Geschichte der Malerei bedeutet, lässt sich durch eine weitere Betrachtungsweise ergänzen, wie Michael White sie in seinem Buch *De Stijl and Dutch Modernism* vorschlägt.[5] Vom Betrachter her gedacht öffnet sich eine andere Möglichkeit, die Bedeutung und Tragweite der Elementarisierung, das heißt der Reduktion auf Grundfarben und -elemente, zu betrachten. Elementarisierung und Standardisierung haben den Effekt, dass der Betrachter vor den Kunstwerken ständig in Bewegung bleibt, anders gesagt: Abstraktion kann verstanden werden nicht als ein ›inwendiges Engführen‹ auf die der Malerei eigenen Mittel, sondern als ein Öffnen zum Umraum hin – eine Öffnung, die durch bestimmte und ganz unterschiedliche ästhetische Verfahren erreicht wird. Sie setzen den Betrachter in eine neuartige Wechselbeziehung zum Kunstobjekt, die im Zusammenhang mit der sich zu Beginn des 20. Jahrhunderts radikal verändernden Lebenswelt gesehen werden kann. Zunächst ein Blick auf Bart van der Lecks Gemälde *Die Holzfäller,* in dem dies besonders augenfällig wird.

Dynamisierungsverfahren bei Bart van der Leck: Das nicht fixierte Motiv

Bart van der Leck studierte in Amsterdam an der Staatlichen Akademie für bildende Künste. Vorausgegangen war dem bereits eine Ausbildung in einer Glaswerkstatt. Seine Erfahrungen in diesem Handwerk haben sich in dem großformatigen Gemälde *Die Holzfäller* aus dem Jahr 1928 niedergeschlagen: Die Bildfläche erinnert an ein Glasfenster, in dem bunte geometrische Glaspartikel zu einer bewegten Oberfläche komponiert sind. Die Formen sind so auf der Bildfläche verteilt, dass man unterstützt durch den Bildtitel zwei symmetrisch gegenübergestellte Figuren imaginieren kann. Sie führen offenbar die gleichen Bewegungen aus: In den zwei längeren grauen Strichen am oberen Bildrand könnte man jeweils ein Axtblatt erkennen, und damit zwei Holzfäller bei der Arbeit. Van der Leck stellt jedoch weder eine bestimmte Landschaft oder eine bestimmte Stimmung dar, in der die Holzfäller arbeiten, noch geht es hier darum, die Faszination von den starken Körpern der arbeitenden Männer zu vermitteln. Stattdessen wirken die sich zu Figuren zusammenschließenden Formen roboterartig. Die Augen des Betrachters wandern über die Bildfläche und fügen das Motiv nach und nach zusammen, springen staccato-artig zwischen den einzelnen Formen, gleichen die beiden annähernd symmetrisch erscheinenden Bildhälften miteinander ab. Der Blick findet keine Ruhe, da die Formen ohne einen Verdichtungspunkt regelmäßig verteilt und alle annähernd gleich groß sind. Dadurch wird das Auge in Bewegung gehalten; im Akt des Sehens kann die ruckartig-gleichförmige Dynamik des Arbeitsprozesses nachvollzogen werden. Der Kritiker und Sammler H.P. Bremmer bemerkte zu van der Lecks *Bergwerktriptychon* von 1916,

4
Theo van Doesburg, zit. nach: Hoek 2000 (wie Anm. 3), S. 206.

5
Die wesentlichen Anregungen für diesen Artikel verdanke ich dieser Publikation. Michael White, *De Stijl and Dutch Modernism,* Manchester 2003. Michael White argumentiert entschieden gegen das Verständnis von Abstraktion als »pursuit of essence« (S. 27).

object' as 'the triumphal march of autonomy in painting' whereby colors and lines are no longer a means to an end—i.e., media for portraying objects and figures—but instead emancipate themselves from this function to become 'autonomous'. Instead of conceiving a picture as an 'open window', the canvas now ceases to deny its *de facto* two-dimensionality, while the viewer, rather than maintaining the illusion that a picture is a three-dimensional space that opens out within the frame of the canvas, now becomes aware of its flatness. The abstract painting thus becomes sufficient onto itself and painting as an art is congruent with what it depicts: Statements like "To be color . . . means to be a painter" are associated with the idea of an art that has turned inwards and that stands in relation to itself regardless of how the viewer sees it. The logical outcome of a reduction to a few basic elements would then be that the 'autonomous' image, would become, as it were, fixed and immobilized.

To this view of what abstraction means for the history of painting we may add another proposed by Michael White in his book *De Stijl and Dutch Modernism.*[5] Seen from the perspective of the viewer, it offers another possibility for considering the significance and far-reaching implications of elementarization—that is, the reduction to primary colors and basic elements. The effect of elementarization and standardization in a work of art is to keep the viewer before it in a state of constant motion. This view posits abstraction not as an 'inward-looking reduction' of painting to its own idiom, but rather as an opening to the surrounding space—an opening that can be achieved via a number of specific and rather different aesthetic processes that cause the viewer to interact with the art object in a new way that might be said to reflect the radically changing world of the early twentieth century. For an exemplary illustration of what we mean, let us begin by taking a look at Bart van der Leck's painting *Woodcutters.*

The Dynamic Process in Bart van der Leck's Painting: the Nonfixed Motif

Bart van der Leck studied at the Academy of Fine Arts in Amsterdam, having previously completed an apprenticeship in a glass workshop. The experience he had gained working with glass found expression in the large-format 1928 painting *Woodcutters:* the pictorial plane reminds one of a glass window in which brightly colored geometric fragments have been composed to create a vibrant surface. The shapes are arranged on the pictorial plane in such a way that together with the clue provided by the picture's title the viewer can imagine two symmetrical figures standing opposite one another. Both are apparently performing the same movements: the two longer gray strokes on the upper edge of the picture might be the blades of two axes, suggesting two woodcutters engaged in their work. Van der Leck portrays neither any particular landscape nor any particular mood in which the woodcutters are working, nor is it his intention to convey the fascination exerted by the strong bodies of two men engaged in physical work. Instead, the figures formed by the colored shapes make a robot-like impression. The eyes of the viewer wander over the pictorial plane, gradually assembling the motif, darting in *staccato movements* from one shape to another, comparing the two apparently symmetrical halves of the picture. The viewer's gaze never comes to rest, for the shapes—which are all about the same size—are evenly distributed with no point of convergence. The eye is thus kept in motion so that in the act of seeing the viewer experiences the jerky but steady dynamic of the work. The critic and collector H.P. Bremmer said of Van der Leck's *Mine Triptych* of 1916, which also takes work as its thematic starting point, that the figures are like "puppets without a will of their own, driven by an invisible force"[6]—a description that the artist explicitly affirmed. In the course of industrialization people had become ever more integrated into standardized and mechanical processes—and this applied to the timber industry too. Modern work was seen as dehumanizing, which is why Van der Leck does not portray his 'woodcutters' as individuals. Instead, he reduces them to geometrical forms that enter into a dynamic relationship with one another on the pictorial plane in a way that conveys their mechanical, synchronized

5
My ideas for this article have been largely inspired by this publication. Michael White, *De Stijl and Dutch Modernism* (Manchester, 2003). Michael White argues decisively against the interpretation of abstraction as the "pursuit of essence" (p. 27).

6
Cees Hilhorst, ed., *Vriendschap op afstand. De correspondentie tussen Bart van der Leck en H. P. Bremmer* (Bussum, 1999), p. 165.

das ebenfalls einen Arbeitsprozess als thematischen Ausgangspunkt nimmt: Die Figuren seien wie »Puppen ohne eigenen Willen, von einer unsichtbaren Kraft getrieben«.[6] Eine Beschreibung, welcher der Künstler explizit zustimmte. Im Zuge der Industrialisierung wurden die Menschen immer mehr in standardisierte und mechanisierte Prozesse eingebunden – das betraf auch die Holzverarbeitung. Moderne Arbeitsprozesse wurden als entmenschlichend verstanden. Entsprechend stellt van der Leck seine »Holzfäller« nicht als Individuen dar. Er reduziert sie stattdessen auf geometrische Formen, die auf der Bildfläche in eine dynamische Beziehung zueinander treten, die mechanische, synchronisierte Bewegungen nachvollziehbar macht. Statt eine plausible Situation in einem fiktiven Raum innerhalb des Bildrechtecks hervorzurufen, wird eine Wirkung beim Betrachter ausgelöst, die das Thema – die Struktur moderner Arbeitsprozesse – über eine rhythmische Seherfahrung vermittelt. Es besteht also ein enger Zusammenhang zwischen der abstrakten Gestalt des Bildes und der Veränderung der sozialen Realität im Zuge der Modernisierung.

Neben der Beschreibung von Abstraktion als selbstreflexive, in sich gekehrte Konfiguration aus Form und Farbe lässt sich die geometrische Reduktion also mit einer von neuartigen Rhythmen geprägten Lebenswelt kontextualisieren, von der das Schauen der Betrachter beeinflusst war. Van der Lecks Verwendung geometrischer Formelemente muss nicht als Mittel zur ›Reinigung‹ der Malerei verstanden werden. Vielmehr ist sie auch so aufzufassen, dass durch sie die entfremdenden Auswirkungen moderner Produktionsverhältnisse auf den menschlichen Körper anschaulich werden.[7]

Bart van der Leck erreicht die Rhythmisierung des Betrachterblicks durch sein ästhetisches Verfahren, die Motive nicht zu fixieren, die kleinen geometrischen Formpartikel sich nicht berühren und den Blick dadurch springen zu lassen. Damit einher geht der Verzicht auf eine Rahmung der Formpartikel, die ohne Konturen meist im Zentrum der weiß grundierten Leinwand vibrieren. Die Randbereiche der Bildfläche lässt er fast durchweg frei. Wenn Gemälde des Künstlers abgedruckt werden sollten, verwehrte er sich stets gegen eine schwarze Umrandung der Illustration. Ein Werbeplakat, das van der Leck für die »Batavier Linie«, eine Fährverbindung des Handelsunternehmens Müller & Co., im Jahr 1916 entwarf, gliedert er noch in sechs gerahmte Boxen (Abb. S. 178), um beispielsweise oben links Arbeiter, die Fracht verladen, rechts oben Passagiere einzufügen. Drei Jahre später hat van der Leck ein Plakat für eine eigene Ausstellung in Utrecht geschaffen (Abb. S. 179), dem jegliche Rahmung fehlt. Das Motiv entlehnte er seinem Gemälde *Der Reiter* (1918), auf dem sich wie zufällig kleine geometrische Formen zu einem anonymen Reiterstandbild zusammen finden. Statt etwa über den kraftvoll gespannten Körper eines Pferdes, das ein repräsentative Stärke und Standhaftigkeit vermittelnder Herrscher im Sattel zu zügeln weiß, Indikatoren von Dynamik abzubilden, findet Bewegung hier maßgeblich auf der Ebene des Betrachterblicks statt. Nur ein blauer Balken oben und ein roter Balken über einem podestartigen Quader scheinen die geometrischen Splitter zusammen zu halten; es wirkt, als könne man die einzelnen Bausteine ohne Weiteres zu einem anderen Motiv verschieben.

Dynamisierungsverfahren bei Piet Mondrian: Der asymmetrische Bildaufbau

Ein berühmtes Gemälde von Piet Mondrian ist von dem Bildaufbau beeinflusst, der für Bart van der Lecks Malweise charakteristisch ist: In *Compositie No. 3, mit Farbfeldern 3* von 1917 (Abb. S. 206) verteilt Mondrian nach dem Vorbild des Künstlerkollegen geometrische Formen über eine grau-weiß grundierte Fläche, elf in hellblau, zwölf in zartrosa, acht in dunkelgelb, ohne sie in einem Raster zu fixieren, wie es bald überwiegend Mondrians Vorgehen sein sollte. Mit dem Bildaufbau dieses Gemäldes zeigte sich Mondrian jedoch bereits während der Entstehung einer ganzen Reihe ähnlicher Kompositionen unzufrieden und resümmierte: »Während ich an der Arbeit saß musste ich feststellen, dass *die Farbfelder* auf einem leeren Hintergrund *in meinen Arbeiten* keine Einheit bilden. Für van der Leck mag das funktionieren, aber er arbeitet anders.«[8] Nicht die Komposition des

6
Cees Hilhorst (Hrsg.), *Vriendschap op afstand. De correspondentie tussen Bart van der Leck en H. P. Bremmer,* Bussum 1999, S. 165.

7
Vgl. White 2003 (wie Anm. 5), S. 20.

8
Piet Mondrian an H.P. Bremmer am 27. Februar 1918, zit. nach Robert P. Welsh, Joop M. Joosten, *Piet Mondrian. Catalogue raisonné,* S. 261.

movements. Rather than showing a plausible situation in a fictive space contained within the rectangle of the picture, the effect is to give the viewer a rhythmic visual experience that reminds him or her of the structure of modern work. In other words, a close relationship exists between the abstract form of the image and the social changes that accompanied modernization.

Abstraction may thus be seen not only as a self-reflexive, inward-looking configuration of form and color, but also, with its characteristic geometrical reduction, as an expression of the new rhythms that were coming to shape the life world of the time and which also influenced the way people perceived art. Seen in this context, Van der Leck's employment of geometrical form elements need not necessarily be interpreted as a way of 'purification' of painting. Rather it can enable the viewer to comprehend the alienating effect of modern production processes on the human body.[7]

Van der Leck uses an aesthetic technique that does not fix the motifs—because the geometric fragments do not touch each other the eye is forced to jump from one to the next—thus achieving rhythm in the way the viewer looks at the painting. This effect is reinforced by his dispensing with any framing of the fragments, so that in the absence of contours they appear to vibrate, mainly in the center of the white grounded canvas, while the areas at the edge of the pictorial plane are left blank almost everywhere. Whenever this painting was printed, the artist always resisted having the image set in a black frame. By contrast, the advertising poster that Van der Leck designed in 1916 for the Batavier Line, a ferry run by the trading company Müller & Co, is divided into six framed boxes (cf. ill. p. 178), with workers loading freight onto the ship portrayed in the top left box and passengers in the top right one. Three years later Van der Leck designed another poster—this time completely without frame—for his own exhibition in Utrecht (cf. ill. p. 179). He borrowed the motif from his painting *The Horseman* (1918), in which, as if by chance, small geometrical forms converge to form an image of an anonymous equestrian statue. Rather than achieving dynamism via the powerful tension of the body of a horse being reined in by the imposing strength and steadfastness of a ruler in the saddle, the movement here takes place chiefly in the eyes of the beholder. The geometrical fragments are apparently held together solely by a blue bar at the top and a red bar above a pedestal-like block at the bottom, creating the illusion that the individual components of the picture could easily be rearranged to form a different motif.

Dynamism in the Work of Piet Mondrian: the Asymmetrical Composition

In *Compositie No. 3, with Color Planes 3* (1917)—one of his more famous paintings—Piet Mondrian was influenced by a style of composition typical of Bart van der Leck's painting (cf. ill. p. 206). Following his fellow artist's lead, Mondrian distributed geometrical forms—eleven in light blue, twelve in pale pink, and eight in dark yellow—over a gray-white ground without fixing them in any kind of grid (he was soon to adopt this latter technique as his standard practice). Yet Mondrian had already expressed dissatisfaction with this composition principle while working on a whole series of other similar compositions: "While at work I found that *the color fields* on an empty background do not form a unity *in my work.* They may do so for Van der Leck, but he works differently."[8] The pictures also earned him criticism from Theo van Doesburg, although it was not the composition to which he took exception but rather the coloration, which he considered "impure". Mondrian defended himself, saying he too preferred pure colors but that he would go on using subdued tones until people had got used to pure colors.[9] Mondrian's use of Van der Leck as a model for the composition shows that his main focus in this painting was in any case on the relationship between color fields and the background and on how to make them into a unified whole. A technical analysis of the material Mondrian used for this picture reveals that he was indeed feeling his way forward very slowly.[10] Initially the forms were grouped around an open center which he subsequently decided to fill in. One particularly conspicuous feature of the composition is that some of the rectangles appear to be cropped at the edge of picture and

7
See White 2003 (see note 5), p. 20.
8
Piet Mondrian to H.P. Bremmer on February 27, 1918, quoted by Robert P. Welsh and Joop M. Joosten in *Piet Mondrian, Catalogue raisonné*, p. 261.
9
Piet Mondrian to Theo van Doesburg on February 13, 1919, Netherlands Institute for Art History, The Hague, quoted by Hans Janssen in *Piet Mondrian. Vom Abbild zum Bild* (The Hague, 2008), p. 208.
10
See Janssen 2008 (see note 9). Janssen refers to the examination of the painting's technique documented in: P. Van der Werf, "The working methods of Piet Mondrian," *kM Kunstenaarsmaterialen* 12 (Winter 1994), pp. 31-35.

Bildes erfuhr indes Kritik, sondern die Farbigkeit, an deren ›Unreinheit‹ Theo van Doesburg Anstoß nahm. Mondrian verteidigte sich: Auch er bevorzuge die reinen Farben, verwende aber dezente Töne, solange die meisten Menschen noch nicht an die reinen Farben gewöhnt seien.[9] Mondrians Orientierung an Bart van der Lecks Bildaufbau zeugt davon, dass der Fokus des Künstlers bei diesem Gemälde ohnehin auf dem Verhältnis zwischen Farbfeldern und Hintergrund lag sowie auf dem Ziel, beide zu einer Einheit zu verbinden. Aus einer materialtechnischen Untersuchung des Bildes geht hervor, dass sich Mondrian in der Tat Schritt für Schritt vorantastete.[10] Er legte die Formen zunächst um ein offenes Zentrum herum an, bevor er dieses schließlich ebenfalls mit Farbfeldern ausfüllte. Auffällig an der Komposition ist aber vor allem eines: Die Rechtecke scheinen vom Bildrand abgeschnitten zu sein und über den Rahmen hinaus wegzudriften. Dies geschieht nur auf der linken und der unteren Seite – eine dezidiert asymmetrische Komposition. Anders als van der Leck, der seine Motive stets im Zentrum der Bildfläche situiert, provoziert Mondrians Gemälde durch die Dezentralisierung der Bildelemente eine Desorientierung des Betrachterblicks weg vom geometrischen und traditionell zugleich inhaltlichen Bildzentrum. Diese Asymmetrie regt dazu an, das Motiv über die Ränder der Leinwand hinaus weiterzudenken und suggeriert einen unbegrenzten Raum des Kunstwerks. Diese Desorientierung und Dezentralisierung ist ein Merkmal, das auch bei anderen Gemälden Mondrians augenfällig wird, die nicht durch schwarze Raster strukturiert sind, wie die 1933 entstandene *Rautenkomposition mit vier gelben Linien* (Abb. S. 219 und S. 24/25). Die gelben Linien, die über jede der vier Ecken des auf die Spitze gestellten Quadrats verlaufen, lassen sich über die Leinwand hinaus ergänzen – gedanklich entsteht ein fiktives, gelbes Quadrat. Eine besondere Wirkung wird dadurch erzielt, dass die gelben Linien unterschiedlich breit sind: Die breiteren Linien treten hervor, die schmaleren weichen weiter zurück. Was zunächst flach und statisch wirkt, gerät so in Bewegung; was auf den ersten Blick symmetrisch wirkt, erweist sich als aus dem erwarteten Gravitationszentrum verschoben. Mondrian hat an der Rückseite des Gemäldes eine Ecke mit »TOP« bezeichnet, gibt dadurch vor, an welcher Ecke das Bild aufzuhängen sei, und ergänzt außerdem, dass die untere Ecke der Raute auf Augenhöhe hängen solle. Das räumliche Zusammentreffen von Kunstwerk und Betrachter wird von Mondrian also von vornherein in die Konzeption des Bildes miteinbezogen und eine Öffnung zum Umraum mitgedacht. Dies steht der modernistischen Rhetorik eines abgeschlossenen Kunstwerks entgegen, das von der Perspektive des Betrachters unabhängig sei.
Ähnliche Merkmale, die zu einem veränderten Verhältnis von Betrachter und Kunstwerk führen, können auch in der Architektur von Jacobus Johannes Pieter Oud als Effekte der Elementarisierung und Standardisierung beschrieben werden.

Dynamisierungsverfahren bei J.J.P. Oud: Die repetierte Fläche

Der Architekt Jacobus Johannes Pieter Oud begann im Jahr 1921 damit, die Wohnsiedlung Tusschendijken in Rotterdam zu entwerfen.[11] Oud konzipierte komplett standardisierte Wohnblöcke, die einen teils privat, teils öffentlich nutzbaren Innenhof einschlossen (Abb. S. 76/77).[11] Dadurch, dass die einzelnen Häuser allesamt mit Flachdächern versehen waren, konnten sie problemlos zu Blöcken aneinandergefügt werden.
Die Gründe für die Standardisierung und daraus folgende Wiederholung der immer selben Elemente waren in der Architektur auch ökonomische. Entsprechend sollten die Fassaden nicht dekoriert, sondern höchstens durch vertikale Akzente betont werden, um ein Gegengewicht zur horizontalen Lagerung der Häuserblocks zu schaffen.
Die Fassaden, die so entstanden, waren flache Ebenen – im Gegensatz zur Tradition der vielfältigen, die Flächen gliedernden und belebenden Dekoration wie sie zum Beispiel die Bauten der Amsterdam School auszeichnete.
Die Seitenfassaden unterschieden sich dadurch kaum von den Hauptfassaden – von der Perspektive einer Straßenkreuzung aus ein starker Effekt der Desorientierung. Auch die traditionell stark hervorgehobenen Haupteingänge als zentrale Elemente symmetrisch aufgebauter Fassaden verschwanden in Ouds Entwürfen von der angestammten

9
Piet Mondrian an Theo van Doesburg am 13. Februar 1919, Rijksbureau voor Kunsthistorische Documentatie, Den Haag, zit. nach: Hans Janssen, *Piet Mondrian. Vom Abbild zum Bild,* Den Haag 2008, S. 208.

10
Vgl. dazu Janssen 2008 (wie Anm. 9), S. 208. Janssen beruft sich auf die Dokumentation einer materialtechnischen Untersuchung in: P. Van der Werf, »The working methods of Piet Mondrian«, in: *kM Kunstenaarsmaterialen,* 12, 1994, S. 31-35.

11
Vgl. Michael Whites Ausführungen in: White 2003 (wie Anm. 5), S. 57 ff.

to be drifting out beyond the frame. Mondrian does this only on the left and the bottom edges of the picture, however, producing a decidedly asymmetrical effect. Unlike Van der Leck, who always centers his motifs in the pictorial plane, Mondrian decentralizes his pictorial elements. This asymmetry is disorientating for the viewer's gaze, which is drawn away from the geometrical center where traditionally the main content of the picture would be and encouraged instead to imagine the motif going beyond the confines of the canvas as if the work of art occupied infinite space. We find this disorientation and decentralization in other paintings by Mondrian that are not structured with black lines, such as the *Lozenge Composition with Four Yellow Lines* (cf. ill. p. 219 + ill. pp. 24–25) produced in 1933. The yellow lines running across each of the four corners of the diagonally placed square appear to go beyond the edges of the canvas, creating an imaginary yellow square. The artist achieves a further effect by making the yellow lines of different thicknesses, so that the thicker lines appear more prominent, while the thinner ones recede into the background. Thus an image that at first glance appears to be flat and static starts to move, and what initially looked symmetrical turns out to be shifted from the expected center of gravity. To indicate at which corner the painting should be hung, Mondrian wrote "TOP" on the back of one corner of the painting and also gave instructions that the bottom corner of the lozenge be hung at eye level. Thus, in defiance of the modernist rhetoric of a self-contained work of art that is independent of the viewer's perspective, Mondrian's concept from the outset takes into account the space in which the work of art and the viewer meet and how the painting should open into the surrounding space. Similar features leading to an altered relationship between viewer and work of art, that might be described as effects of elementarization and standardization, can also be identified in the architecture of Jacobus Johannes Pieter Oud.

Dynamism in the Work of J.J.P. Oud: Repetition of Surfaces

The architect Jacobus Johannes Pieter Oud's design for the residential district of Tusschendijken in Rotterdam, which he began working on in 1921, consisted of completely standardized apartment blocks built around an internal courtyard that was partly private and partly used as public space (ill. pp. 76–77).[11] Since all the houses had flat roofs it was not difficult to combine them into blocks. The reason for this standardization in architecture and the consequent repetition of the same elements over and over again was mainly economic, and was also the reason why Oud's design envisaged facades that would not be decorated but at most furnished with vertical accents in order to provide a counterweight to the horizontal arrangement of the apartment blocks. Oud's flat facades contrasted with the tradition of decoration espoused, for instance, by the Amsterdam School, which used a variety of elements to break up the planes and make them more lively. The side facades thus scarcely differed from the main facades, which when seen from the perspective of a crossroads produced a highly disorientating effect. Main entrances had traditionally occupied a prominent place as central elements in symmetrically constructed facades, but these disappeared from their original place in Oud's designs. The effect on people walking along the street must have been disconcerting, for instead of being able to direct their gaze and movements toward hierarchically structured architectural elements they were forced into a rhythm of permanent flux. It was a time when the infrastructure of cities in the Netherlands and elsewhere had changed radically in response to their inhabitants' ever-increasing needs for greater mobility: commuter trains now connected areas of apartment buildings with industry on the periphery of cities, transporting masses of people from one point to another within an extensive geographical network on a daily basis. In the context of such changes abstraction can be understood as a commentary on "the effects of industrialization on the body."[12] The ways of seeing promoted by the new aesthetic processes redefined the relationship between works of art and viewers and must therefore be discussed in these terms. The elementarization and reduction of motifs in painting and the

11
Michael White writes extensively on this topic. White 2003 (see note. 5), p. 57 ff.
12
Ibid., p. 13.

Stelle. Die Wirkung auf die Menschen, die sich der Straße entlang bewegten, muss irritierend gewesen sein, wenn Blick und Bewegung sich nicht auf hierarchisch strukturierende Architekturelemente richten konnten und stattdessen der Rhythmus eines stetigen Flusses provoziert wurde. Die Infrastruktur nicht nur der niederländischen Städte hatte sich radikal verändert und reagierte auf die steigenden Anforderungen an die Mobilität der Bewohner: Pendlerzüge verbanden Wohnblockareale mit der Industrie in der Peripherie der wachsenden Städte und bewegten tagtäglich Menschenmengen entlang der weitläufig gespannten geografischen Koordinaten. Im Kontext solcher Veränderungen kann Abstraktion verstanden werden als ein Kommentar der »Auswirkungen der Industrialisierung auf den Körper«[12] – Die Sehweisen, die durch die neuen ästhetischen Verfahren gefordert wurden und das Verhältnis zwischen Kunstwerk und Betrachter neu bestimmten, müssen also auch in diesem Zusammenhang diskutiert werden. Elementarisierung und Motivreduzierung in der Malerei sowie die Standardisierung in der Architektur sind aus dieser Perspektive nicht nur als Konzentration und als Auf-sich-selbst-Richten der künstlerischen Mittel zu verstehen. Vielmehr findet aus der Perspektive des Betrachters eine Erschließung des Umraums statt. Im Raum vor dem Kunstwerk halten die durch Form und Farbe rhythmisch strukturierten, asymmetrischen oder repetitiven Oberflächen den Betrachter ständig in Bewegung.

12
Vgl. White 2003 (wie Anm. 5), S. 13.

standardization adopted by architecture should hence be understood not merely as a concentration on the artistic means used or a focus of painting on its own idiom. Rather, from the perspective of the viewer, the understanding of abstraction is now extended to include the surrounding space as well.
In the space in front of a work of art, the asymmetrical or repetitive surfaces rhythmically structured via form and color keep the viewer in a state of constant motion.

Translated from the German by Tradukas GbR (Melanie Newton and Nicola Morris)

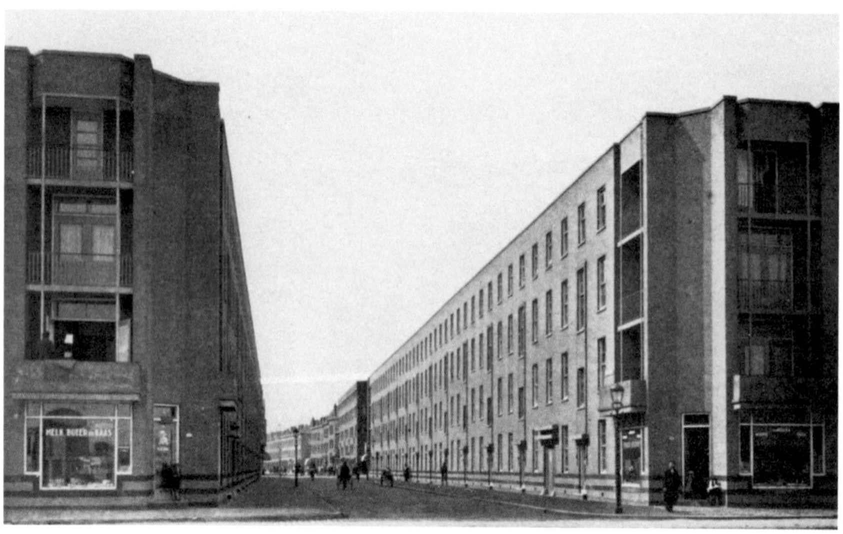

J.J.P. Oud
Wohnsiedlung Tusschendijken in Rotterdam
1920
Abgebildet in
J.J.P. Oud, *Holländische Architektur,*
(*Bauhausbücher*, 10), München 1926, S. 54

J.J.P. Oud
Tusschendijken housing blocks in Rotterdam
1920
Illustrated in
J.J.P. Oud, *Holländische Architektur,*
vol. 10: *Bauhausbücher* (Munich, 1926), p. 54

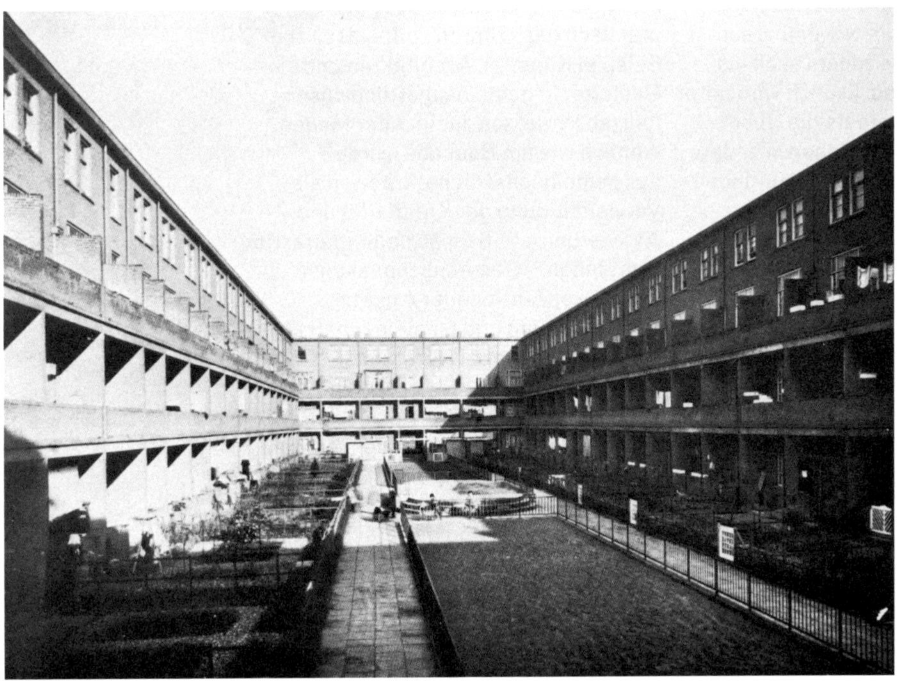

J.J.P. Oud
Courtyard
at Tusschendijken in Rotterdam
1920
Illustrated in
J.J.P. Oud, *Holländische Architektur*,
vol. 10: *Bauhausbücher* (Munich, 1926), p. 55

J.J.P. Oud
Innenhof der
Wohnsiedlung Tusschendijken in Rotterdam
1920
Abgebildet in
J.J.P. Oud, *Holländische Architektur*,
(*Bauhausbücher*, 10), München 1926, S. 55

De Stijl und die Entgrenzung der Künste

Matthias Mühling

Die Rede von der Entgrenzung der Künste prägt die Zeitschrift *De Stijl* und die so unterschiedlichen Protagonisten in ihrem Umkreis. Damit ist zuerst einmal der rein utopische Gedanke angesprochen. Jedoch ganz praktisch hatte Theo van Doesburg schon von der ersten Ausgabe an der Publikation eine dezidiert interdisziplinäre und internationale Ausrichtung gegeben.
Die regelmäßig verwendeten Sprachen waren Niederländisch, Deutsch, Französisch und Italienisch. Das erste Manifest, erschienen in der Novemberausgabe von 1918, wurde zudem auch ins Englische übertragen. Explizit wird unter Punkt III dieses Manifests die Übersetzung internationaler Ideen in andere Sprachen als eine der ersten Aufgaben von *De Stijl* formuliert. Die Themen umfassten alle denkbaren Gattungen der Künste: Malerei, Skulptur, Architektur, Dichtkunst, Musik, Theater, Tanz, Film und angewandte Gestaltung.
Die Beiträge selber, auch wenn sie noch disziplinär gebunden angelegt waren, hatten fast immer eine gedankliche Ausrichtung, die eine Entgrenzung zwischen den Künsten befördern wollte. Die einzelnen Gattungen, die bis dato noch streng hierarchisch geordnet waren und deren Demarkationslinien zum Teil noch argwöhnisch verteidigt wurden, sollten sich eben nicht nur gegenseitig befruchten, sondern mehr noch synästhetisch ineinander aufgehen. Die Ambitionen von *De Stijl* richteten sich jedoch auch auf einen Entgrenzungsprozess gegenüber außerkünstlerischen Feldern wie etwa der Politik oder des Wissens und nicht zuletzt des vielbeschworenen ›Lebens‹.

Auch der Schlüsselbegriff der Publikation, »De nieuwe beelding«, kann als Motor dieser Entgrenzungsprozesse gedeutet werden. In diesem Begriff ist ein gemeinschaftliches und transdisziplinäres Engagement aller Künste enthalten.[1] Im Einzugsbereich der Logik dieser Vorstellungen befindet sich der von *De Stijl* propagierte Begriff der ›gemeenschapskunst‹. Sein Einsatz bestand selbstverständlich darin, die Vorstellung einer synästhetischen Gemeinschaft der Künste zu behaupten und zu propagieren. Im Kontext dieses Begriffs war es jedoch genauso bedeutend, dass die einerseits utopisch formulierte Forderung einer ›gemeenschapskunst‹ andererseits ganz praktisch dazu führen sollte, dass zum Beispiel Künstler, Architekten und Gestalter in gemeinschaftlich ausgeführten Projekten zueinander fanden. Ähnlich wie am Bauhaus wurde das gemeinschaftliche Arbeiten als Vervielfältigung der Kreativität und Aktivierung positiver sozialer Interaktion verstanden.[2] ›Gemeenschapskunst‹ war ein konzeptioneller Ansatz, der Gestaltung und Gemeinschaft als politische Aufgaben verstand.

Theo van Doesburg fand in *De Stijl* ein universelles Prinzip, indem er, wie Mondrian, die sichtbare Welt auf ein autonomes System aus horizontalen und vertikalen Linien und Flächen zurückführte. Er brach mit allen mimetischen Konventionen der Kunst und suchte seine Entdeckung alsbald auf die Architektur und angewandten Künste zu übertragen. Van Doesburgs unermüdlicher Einsatz für eine Kunst, die der sichtbaren Welt mit rein abstrakten Mitteln gegenübertritt, führte bald zu ausgedehnten Propagandareisen im Dienste von *De Stijl*. Er und seine dritte Ehefrau Nelly suchten zunächst in Berlin, dann in Weimar, später in Paris sowie auf Abstechern in andere europäische Metropolen die damals wirkmächtigen Kulturproduzenten, Künstler und Intellektuellen für ihre Sache zu gewinnen. Erwähnenswert sind van

1
Zur genaueren Erläuterung des Begriffs vgl. den Essay »›Die neue Gestaltung‹ lesen« von Hans Janssen in der vorliegenden Publikation.

2
Zur ›gemeenschapskunst‹ vgl. den Essay »De Stijl: Eine Kunst fürs Volk?« von Michael White in der vorliegenden Publikation.

De Stijl and the Integration of the Arts

Matthias Mühling

The aim of dissolving the boundaries separating the arts is a defining trope in the magazine *De Stijl* and the writings of the protagonists in its environment, however divergent their views may otherwise be. The idea it raises is *prima facie* purely utopian. In quite practical terms, however, Theo van Doesburg's publication pursued a decidedly interdisciplinary and international program from its very first issue.
The magazine routinely included writing in Dutch, German, French, and Italian. The first manifesto, published in the November 1918 issue, was also translated into English. In its third article, the same manifesto describes the translation of international ideas into different languages as one of the most pressing tasks of *De Stijl*. The magazine's thematic foci include all conceivable genres of the arts: painting, sculpture, architecture, poetry, music, theater, dance, film, and applied design.
The contributions themselves, even when they were recognizably rooted in traditional disciplines, almost always evinced an intellectual orientation toward fostering integration of the arts. The individual genres, which many practitioners and critics had continued to distinguish within a rigorously hierarchical system, warily defending their respective lines of demarcation, were not just supposed to cross-fertilize; *De Stijl*'s vision ultimately called for their synaesthetic fusion. The group's ambitions also envisaged a process in which other boundaries would dissolve as well—those separating art from extra-artistic fields such as politics or knowledge and, perhaps most importantly, a much-invoked concept: 'life' itself.

The magazine's key term, "De nieuwe beelding," can also be read as propelling these processes of integration. The concept implies a concerted and trans-disciplinary commitment of all the arts.[1] This logic brings another concept *De Stijl* championed into play, that of 'gemeenschapskunst', or 'community art'. Its purpose was, of course, to assert and advertise the idea of a synaesthetic communion of the arts. A no less important aspect of the concept's context, however, was the desire that the call for a 'gemeenschapskunst', however utopian the terms in which it might be couched, would quite practically generate projects implemented in collaboration between, say, artists, architects, and designers. Not unlike the Bauhaus, *De Stijl* understood working in a community of artists as a way to potentiate creativity and activate positive social interaction.[2] 'Gemeenschapskunst' was a conceptual approach that conceived design and community as a political mission.

In *De Stijl*, Theo van Doesburg found a universal principle: like Mondrian, he reduced the visible world to an autonomous system of horizontal and vertical lines and surfaces. He broke with all mimetic conventions in art and soon sought to apply his discovery also to architecture and the applied arts. Van Doesburg's indefatigable dedication to the cause of an art that would confront the visible world with purely abstract means soon led him to undertake extensive propaganda trips in the service of *De Stijl*. With his third wife, Nelly, he moved first to Berlin, then to Weimar and later to Paris, with excursions to other major European cities, seeking at each stop to enlist the support of the era's most influential cultural producers, artists, and intellectuals. Notable instances of these efforts to promote *De Stijl* include a highly promising class he taught at the Bauhaus, numerous lectures, and the

1
For a more detailed discussion of this concept see Hans Janssen's Essay "Reading 'The New Plastic'" in the present volume.
2
On 'gemeenschapskunst' see Michael White's essay "De Stijl: An Art for the People?" in the present volume.

Theo van Doesburg
»Das Bauhaus von De Stijl erobert«
Van Doesburg schickte die Ansichtskarte des Weimarer Bauhaus am 12. September 1921 an Antony Kok
Sammlung RKD Den Haag

Theo van Doesburg
"The Bauhaus conquered by De Stijl"
Van Doesburg sent this postcard of the Bauhaus in Weimar to Antony Kok on September 12, 1921
Collection RKD The Hague

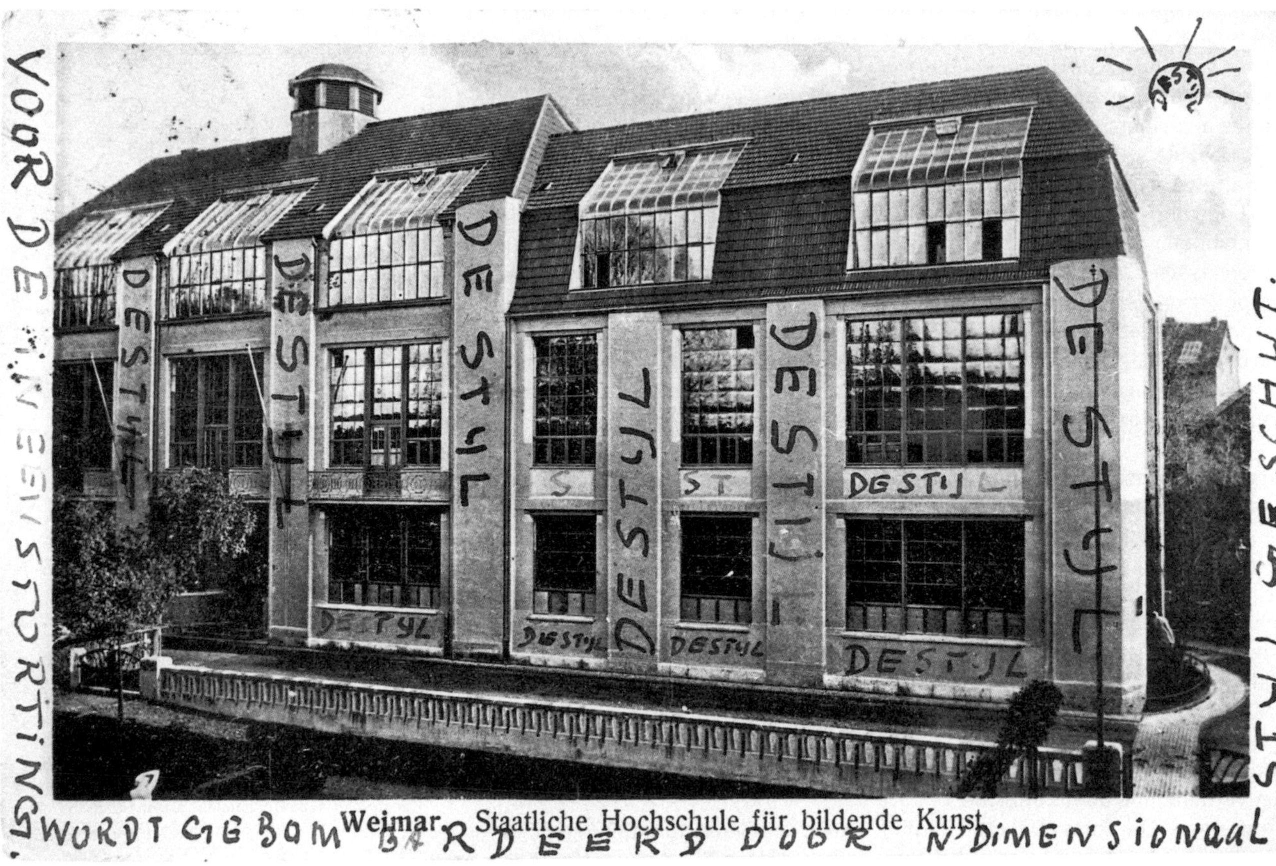
Weimar. Staatliche Hochschule für bildende Kunst
WORDT GEBOMBARDEERD DOOR N'DIMENSIONAAL
STIJL GESCHUT.
DE STIJL

Doesburgs vielversprechender Studienkurs am Bauhaus, seine zahlreichen Vorträge und die Organisation eines internationalen Konstruktivisten-Kongresses. Die Grundmotivation seiner Bestrebungen und seiner publizistischen Tätigkeit, also van Doesburgs ästhetische Prinzipien, lassen sich beschreiben als unbedingten Willen, einen internationalen Stil zu etablieren. Gleichermaßen streng wie einfach sind die Gestaltungsmittel dieser Internationalisierungsbestrebung, die auf die horizontale und vertikale Linie, die Grundformen des Quadrats und des Rechtecks, reduziert werden. Das Universale scheint dabei in der radikalen Einfachheit der Reduktion aufgehoben, die gerade die Anschlussfähigkeit an viele Disziplinen gewährleisten konnte: Architektur, Malerei, Skulptur, die Gestaltung von Gebrauchsgegenständen, Werbung, Tanz, Theater oder Film. Alle Gattungen lassen sich innerhalb dieser definierten Basisoperationen gestalten. So verwundert es auch nicht, dass sich bis heute in der Populärkultur von der Produktgestaltung über die Mode bis zur Werbung und Popmusik immer wieder Grundmuster der ›destijlschen‹ Ästhetik finden lassen. *De Stijl* ist zum ›Marketingtool‹ avanciert, welches sich immer wieder zur rechten oder falschen Zeit aus dem so imaginären wie copyrightfreien Werkzeugkasten der Gestaltungsbranchen hervorzaubern lässt.

Zu den Autoren, die im Laufe der Jahre Beiträge für das von van Doesburg herausgegebende Organ verfasst haben, gehören der italienische Maler Gino Severini genauso wie der US-amerikanische Komponist George Antheil und Friedrich Kiesler, Architekt und Bühnenbildner aus Österreich. Werner Graeff beschäftigte sich mit der Gestaltung von Automobilen oder dem Film, und Antony Kok bemühte sich um die Neuverhandlung poetologischer Programme. Der Russe Valentin Parnac (Parnakh) steuerte mit seinen *Histoires Extraordinaires. Danses* eine tanztheoretische Schrift bei, und aus italienisch-futuristischer Perspektive wurde das Theater in einem gemeinschaftlich von F.T. Marinetti, Emilio Settimelli und Bruno Corra verfassten Textbeitrag mit dem Titel »Le Théâtre Futuriste Synthétique« zum Thema. Aus Moskau sandte El Lissitzky 1920 einen Text, in dem er sein Konzept einer dreidimensionalen Raumstruktur, den Proun, beschrieb. Dass der Tanz zu den Interessengebieten von *De Stijl* zählte, beweist zudem Vilmos Huszárs Objekt *Mechanisch tanzende Figur* von 1920 (Abb. S.166 und S. 85). Die aus geometrisch reduzierten Flächen zusammengesetzte Figur besteht aus schwarzem Aluminium. Einzelne ausgeschnittene Rechtecke in diesen Flächen sind mit transparentem Material in Rot oder Grün hinterlegt. Wie bei einem Schattenspiel wurde diese Puppe angestrahlt, so dass sich ihre Umrisse auf einer weißen Leinwand abzeichneten. Eine komplizierte Bewegungsmechanik, die Huszár in drei Jahren Arbeit entwickelt hatte, ermöglichten dem Spieler der Figur unterschiedliche Posen zur Darstellung zu bringen. Mittels Tasten ließen sich Arme, Beine und Kopf bewegen. Die *Mechanisch tanzende Figur* – unsere Ausstellung zeigt eine Rekonstruktion – wurde innerhalb der *De Stijl*-Bewegung jedoch nicht nur als eine Beschäftigung mit dem Tanz verstanden. Als Huszár 1917 an der Figur zu arbeiten begann, verstand van Doesburg diese Bemühungen als eine Verzeitlichung der Malerei: »Er hat etwas völlig neues erfunden, sich bewegende Malerei«.[3] Die *Mechanisch tanzende Figur* ist Huszárs Bemühungen geschuldet, Zeit, Bewegung und Malerei als Einheit zu denken. Aufführungen der *Mechanisch tanzenden Figur* erfolgten in einer theaterartigen Situation als Schattenbild vor einem Wandschirm (Abb. S. 84). Huszár selbst hatte eine kurze Beschreibung in Kurt Schwitters' Zeitschrift *Merz* formuliert: »Jede Bewegung wird in einem rechten Winkel ausgeführt und nichts ist zufällig. [...] Das Ziel ist es, mit jeder Pose eine plastische Komposition zu erzeugen und den Zwischenraum des Hintergrundes in die Komposition aufzunehmen.«[4]

Auch der Dada-Künstler und Filmemacher Hans Richter veröffentlichte in *De Stijl* und setzte sich mit seinen Arbeiten und in seinen Texten mit den Möglichkeiten einer Verzeitlichung der Malerei auseinander.[5] Die Ansätze seiner neuen Bewegungskunst verwirklichte er in den Filmen *Rhythmus 21* von 1921–1924 (Abb. S. 236) und *Rhythmus 23* von 1922–1924, mit denen er zu einem Pionier des abstrakten Films werden

3
Brief von Theo van Doesburg an Antony Kok (14. Juli 1917), Archiv Theo van Doesburg, Rijksbureau voor Kunsthistorische Documentatie, Den Haag, zit. nach Michael White, *De Stijl and Dutch Modernism*, Manchester 2003, S. 39. Übertragung aus dem Niederländischen von Agnes Thum.
4
Vilmos Huszár, »Mechanische Dansfiguur«, in: *Merz*, 1, Januar 1923, S. 13. Übertragung aus dem Niederländischen von Agnes Thum.
5
Gladys Fabre, »A Universal Language for the Arts: Interdisciplinary as a Practice, Film as a Model«, in: *Van Doesburg and the International Avantgarde. Constructing a New World*, hrsg. von Gladys Fabre und Doris Wintgens Hötte, Ausst.-Kat. Stedelijk Museum De Lakenhal, Leiden und Tate Modern, London 2009, S. 46–57.

organization of an international Constructivist Congress. The fundamental motivation of his undertakings and activities as a publicist, that is to say, Van Doesburg's aesthetic principles, can be summed up as the unbending will to establish an international style. The formal vocabulary deployed by this aspiration to internationalism is as rigorous as it is simple, stripped down to horizontal and vertical lines, the basic forms of square and rectangle. Its universalism appears to be contained in the radical simplicity of reduction, which served to safeguard the possibility of adapting it to many disciplines: architecture, painting, sculpture, product design, advertising, dance, theater, or film. All genres of art allow for creative expression within the limits set by these clearly defined fundamental operations. Little wonder, then, that basic patterns of the '*De Stijl* aesthetic' can be found to this day in products of popular culture, ranging from product design to fashion and from advertising to pop music. *De Stijl* has become a 'marketing tool' unprotected by any copyright that the design industry pulls from its imaginary toolbox at moments opportune as well as inopportune.

Over the years, authors who wrote contributions for the organ published by Van Doesburg included the Italian painter Gino Severini and the American composer George Antheil as well as Friedrich (Frederick) Kiesler, an Austrian architect and stage designer. Werner Graeff wrote about automobile design or film, and Antony Kok sought to reopen the debate over poetological programs. The Russian writer Valentin Parnac (Parnakh) contributed his *Histoires Extraordinaires. Danses,* a dance-theoretical essay, and the theater was examined from an Italian Futurist perspective in a contribution entitled "Le Théâtre Futuriste Synthétique" co-written by F. T. Marinetti, Emilio Settimelli, and Bruno Corra. In 1920, El Lissitzky sent an essay from Moscow in which he described his conception of a three-dimensional spatial structure, the Proun. That dance was among *De Stijl*'s fields of interest is also demonstrated by Vilmos Huszár's object *Mechanical Figure Dancing* (1920; p. 166, p. 85). The figure is composed of geometrically reduced plane elements made of black aluminum. Red or green transparent material is set into several rectangular cutouts in these elements. The puppet was then illuminated with spotlights as though in shadow puppetry so that its outlines would appear on a white canvas. A complicated kinetic mechanism Huszár had developed in three years of work enabled the operator of the figure to make it present various poses, moving the arms, legs, and head by pressing keys. Within the *De Stijl* movement, however, the *Mechanical Figure Dancing*—our exhibition features a reconstruction—was read not only as a study of dance. When Huszár began working on it in 1917, Van Doesburg took his aim to be to lend painting a temporal dimension: "He has invented something totally new, moving painting."[3] *The Mechanical Figure Dancing* is the product of Huszár's efforts to think time, motion, and painting in union. For performances, the work was staged in a theatrical setting, casting a silhouette on a screen (p. 84). Huszár himself wrote a short description of the figure for Kurt Schwitters's magazine *Merz:* "All motions are performed at right angles, and nothing is left to chance .... The aim is to present a pictorial composition in any position and to include the interstices in the backdrop in this composition."[4]

The Dadaist artist and filmmaker Hans Richter, too, published in *De Stijl*; his works and writings study possible ways of adding a temporal dimension to painting.[5] His efforts to create a new art of motion bore fruit in the films *Rhythmus 21* (1921–1924; p. 236) and *Rhythmus 23* (1922–1924), with which he became a pioneer of abstract film. Richter, in whose oeuvre the ideas of motion and rhythm form leitmotifs, was born in Berlin in 1888 and began to study art in Weimar in 1909. Early on, he came into contact with *Der Blaue Reiter* and the editors of *Der Sturm.* After returning from service in World War I, he had his first solo exhibition at Galerie Hans Goltz, Munich, in 1916. He soon began an intense exchange of ideas with the Dada movement in Zurich, where he then moved. In 1918, he met the Swedish painter Viking Eggeling, and in late 1919, Richter and Eggeling with his wife moved to Klein Kölzig in Lusatia, where his parents had a country estate. Inspired by their study of the principles

3
Letter from Theo van Doesburg to Antony Kok (July 14, 1917), Theo van Doesburg archive, Rijksbureau voor Kunsthistorische Documentatie, Den Haag, quoted in Michael White, *De Stijl and Dutch Modernism* (Manchester, 2003), p. 39.

4
Vilmos Huszár, "Mechanische Dansfiguur", *Merz* 1 (January 1923), p. 13.

5
Gladys Fabre, "A Universal Language for the Arts: Interdisciplinary as a Practice, Film as a Model," in *Van Doesburg and the International Avantgarde. Constructing a New World,* eds. Gladys Fabre and Doris Wintgens Hötte, exh. cat. Stedelijk Museum De Lakenhal, Leiden and Tate Modern (London, 2009), pp. 46–57.

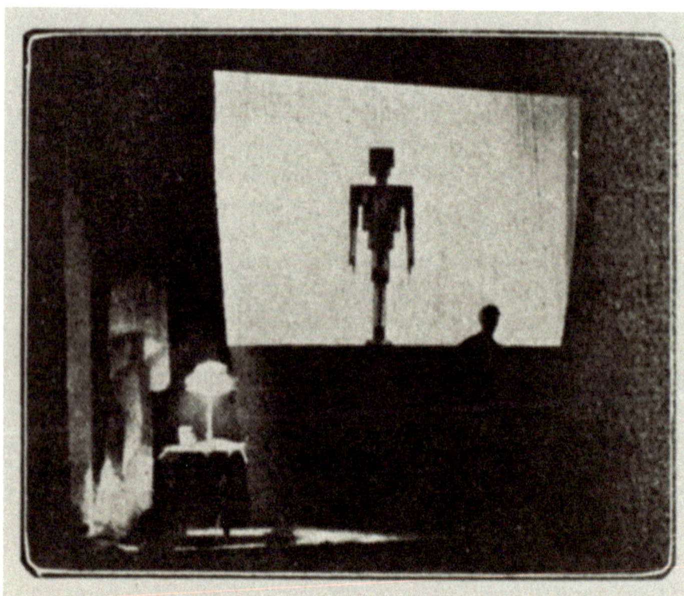

Vilmos Huszár
Mechanisch Tanzende Figur
auf eine Leinwand projiziert während der Dada-Soirée in Bellevue
19. Januar 1923
Abgebildet in *Het Leven* vom 27. Januar 1923

Vilmos Huszár
Mechanical Figure Dancing
projected onto a screen during the Dada-Soirée at Bellevue
January 19, 1923
Illustrated in *Het Leven* from January 27, 1923

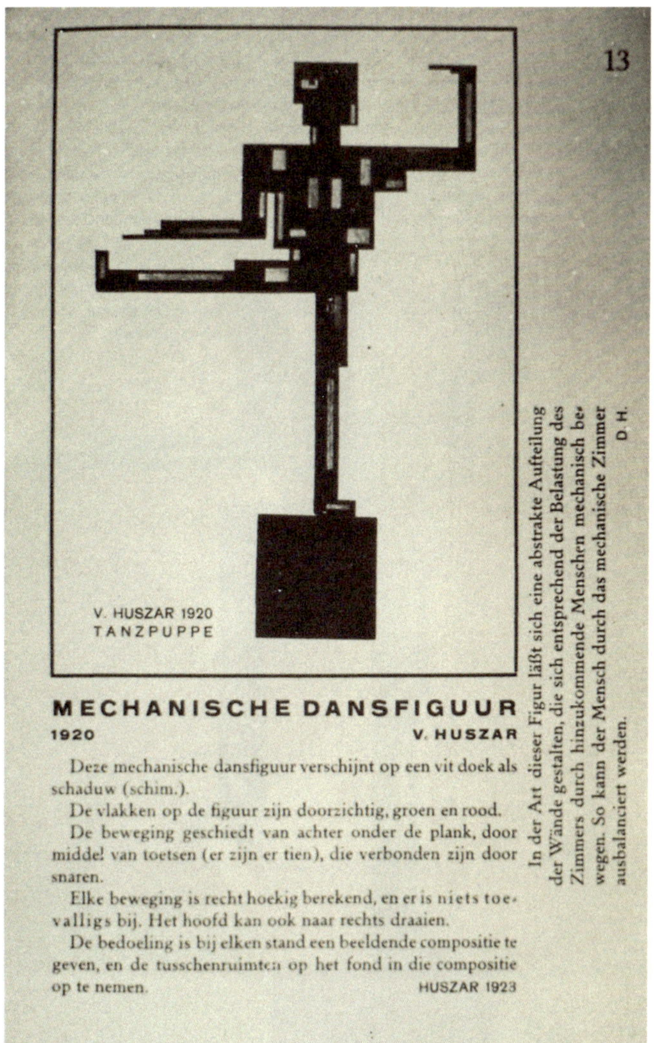

13

MECHANISCHE DANSFIGUUR

1920 **V. HUSZAR**

Deze mechanische dansfiguur verschijnt op een vit doek als schaduw (schim.).

De vlakken op de figuur zijn doorzichtig, groen en rood.

De beweging geschiedt van achter onder de plank, door middel van toetsen (er zijn er tien), die verbonden zijn door snaren.

Elke beweging is recht hoekig berekend, en er is niets toevallig bij. Het hoofd kan ook naar rechts draaien.

De bedoeling is bij elken stand een beeldende compositie te geven, en de tusschenruimten op het fond in die compositie op te nemen.

HUSZAR 1923

In der Art dieser Figur läßt sich eine abstrakte Aufteilung der Wände gestalten, die sich entsprechend der Belastung des Zimmers durch hinzukommende Menschen mechanisch bewegen. So kann der Mensch durch das mechanische Zimmer ausbalanciert werden.

D. H.

Vilmos Huszár
Mechanical Figure Dancing
Illustrated in
Merz, no. 1 (January 1923)

Vilmos Huszár
Mechanisch Tanzende Figur
Abgebildet in
Merz, 1, Januar 1923

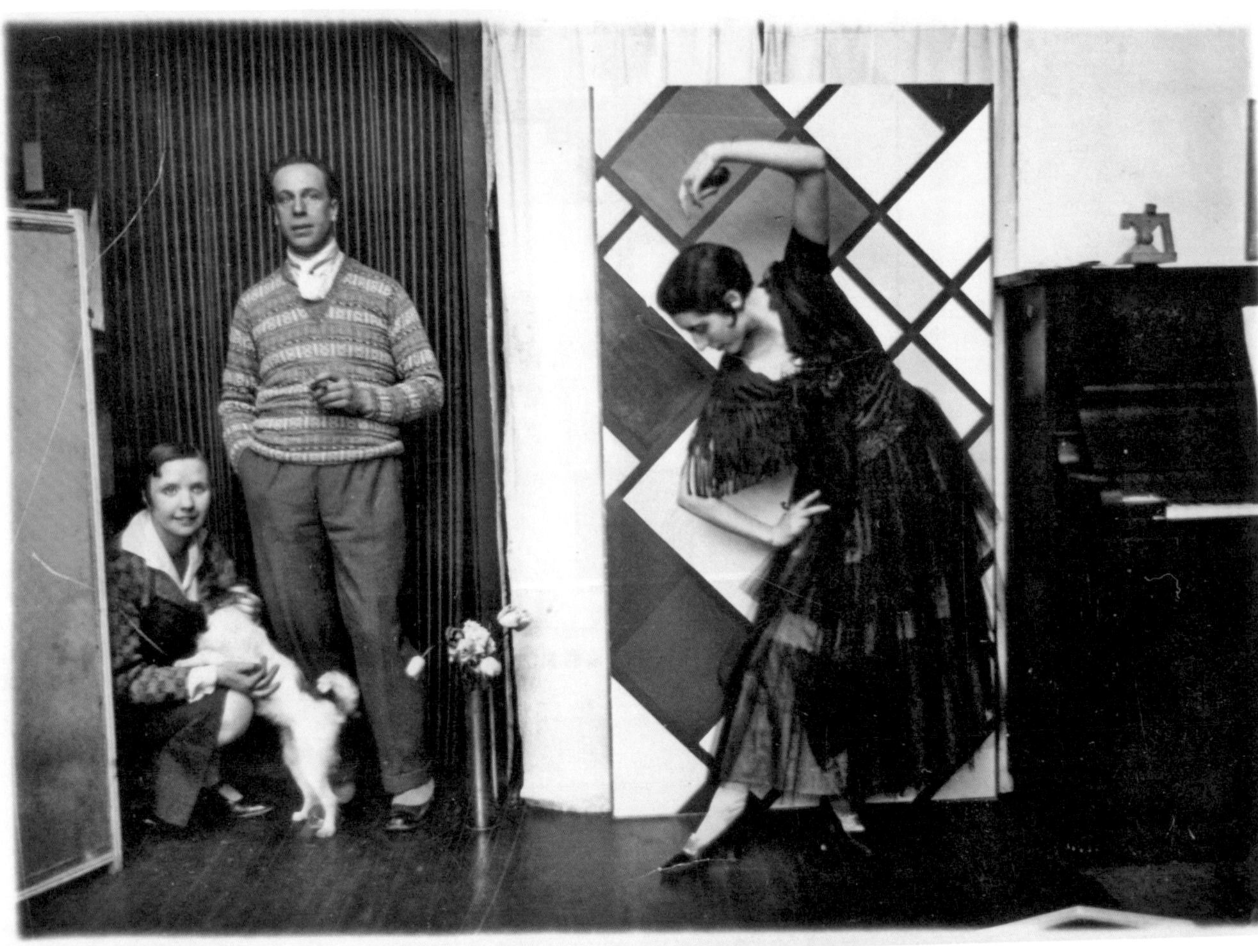

Nelly und Theo van Doesburg,
der Hund Dada und die Tänzerin Kamares
vor *Kontrakomposition XVI*, Paris
1925
RKD, Archiv Theo und Nelly van Doesburg
(Schenkung van Moorsel)

Nelly and Theo van Doesburg,
the dog Dada and dancer Kamares
in front of *Counter-Composition XVI*, Paris
1925
RKD, Archive of Theo and Nelly van Doesburg
(Donation Van Moorsel)

sollte. Richter, dessen Werk sich leitmotivisch auf die Begriffe Bewegung und Rhythmus bezieht, wurde 1888 in Berlin geboren und begann 1909 sein Kunststudium in Weimar. Er hatte früh Kontakte zum *Blauen Reiter* und zum *Sturm*. Nach seiner Rückkehr aus dem ersten Weltkrieg richtete 1916 die Galerie Hans Goltz in München seine erste Einzelausstellung aus. Wenig später hatte er intensiven Kontakt zur Dada-Bewegung in Zürich, wohin er auch übersiedelte. 1918 lernte er den schwedischen Maler Viking Eggeling kennen. Ende 1919 zog Richter mit dem Ehepaar Eggeling nach Klein Kölzig in der Lausitz auf den Landsitz seiner Eltern. Die Auseinandersetzung mit den Prinzipien des Kontrapunkts bei Ferruccio Busoni inspirierte Richter und Eggeling dazu, ihre Leinwände rhythmisch in Schwarzweiß zu organisieren. Dabei hatte sich die in der fernöstlichen Kunst gebräuchliche Form der Gemälderolle als formaler Gestaltgeber angeboten. Entlang einer Leserichtung von links nach rechts entwickelten sie eine erste Chronologie ihrer abstrakten Figuren. Die ersten Experimentalfilme lösen die Versprechen einer zeitlichen und räumlichen wie auch in Bewegung befindlichen Abstraktion endgültig ein. Insofern ist der von Richter angewandte Begriff und Werktitel *Rhythmus* in Analogie zur musikalischen Bedeutung des Begriffs zu verstehen.

Die Zusammenarbeit der Freunde Richter und Eggeling gilt als die Urszene des abstrakten Films. Theo van Doesburg hatte die beiden in Klein Kölzig für drei Wochen im Dezember 1920 und Januar 1921 besucht. Seitdem gehörten Richter und Eggeling zu den Autoren von *De Stijl*. Van Doesburg hatte das erste anderthalbminütige Filmexperiment gesehen, welches auf Dezember 1920 datiert und welches er später auf einer Vortragsreise in Paris zeigte. Die Eindrücke des Besuchs in Klein Kölzig hatten van Doesburgs Interesse am Medium Film intensiviert und führten auch zu seinem theoretischen Text »Abstracte Filmbeelding«, den er im Mai 1921 in *De Stijl* veröffentlichte.

Richter drehte nach der Trennung von Eggeling einen zweiten Film, *Rhythmus 23* (1922–24), der teilweise auf den horizontalen und farbig angelegten Rollenbildern *Fuge 23* und *Rhythmus 23* basiert. Nach der Premiere in Paris im Jahr 1923 schnitt er den Film noch mehrmals um. In der musikalischen Bewegung entfaltet dieser Film eine räumliche Suggestivkraft, die gegenüber *Rhythmus 21* jedoch deutlich reduziert erscheint. Hier kommt erstmals der Diagonalen eine zentralere Rolle zu. Die Linie wird als Motiv den bewegten Flächen gegenübergestellt. Anders als Richter konzipierte Eggeling seinen Film *Symphonie Diagonale* von 1924 vollständig auf der Basis seiner Rollenbilder (Abb. S. 143). Das Tempo erscheint schneller, die filmische Progression stärker gezeichnet und ihre Morphologie deutlich komplexer als bei Richter. Der Kunsthistoriker Paul Ferdinand Schmidt war bei der ersten öffentlichen Aufführung von *Symphonie Diagonale* anwesend. Er urteilte: »Wir wissen nun, daß es möglich ist, den Film als Kunstwerk zu gestalten. Eggeling hat das Prinzip des Films: Bewegung und Licht, von aller Naturnachahmung abstrahiert und auf sich gestellt, er hat den Rhythmus der Bewegungsfolge auf klare Formen gebracht, die etwa so zum Spielfilm stehen, wie ein kubistisches Gemälde zur Naturphotographie [...]. Für heutige Augen noch ungewohnt ist der ruckartige Wechsel im Rhythmus, die Überfülle der sich ablösenden Formfolgen, deren Sinn man nur musikalisch erfassen kann, aber nicht durch das Ohr, sondern durch das Auge [...].«[6]

Richter wie Eggeling hatten mit ihren Filmen einen Endpunkt der Abstraktion berührt. Von hier aus hätten sich nur immer andere Morphologien und Formenkombinationen, jedoch keine grundsätzlich anderen Gedanken mehr entwickeln lassen. Selbstverständlich hatten sie keinerlei Möglichkeit, das etablierte und vom Theater inspirierte Präsentationsmodell des Kinos in Frage zu stellen. Erst die Museen unserer Gegenwart zeigen die Filme von Richter und Eggeling in kinematographischen Installationen.

Grundsätzlich ließe sich natürlich darüber spekulieren, ob und wie der Entgrenzungsbegriff von *De Stijl* bereits ein frühes Verständnis von ›Installationskunst‹ entwickelt hat. Sicherlich sind die Architekturen von Friedrich Kiesler der beste Beweis dafür, wie stark unser zeitgenössisches Verständnis von

6
P. F. Schmidt, »Eggelings Kunstfilm«, in: *Das Kunstblatt*, 8, 1924, S. 381, zit. nach Louise O'Konor, *Viking Eggeling. 1880–1925. Artist and film-maker, life and work*, Stockholm 1971, S. 52.

of counterpoint in Ferruccio Busoni, Richter and Eggeling organized their canvases in a rhythmical arrangement of black and white. The painted scroll, a medium that is customary in the art of the Far East, presented an obvious fundamental formal choice; by imposing a reading direction from left to right, it enabled them to develop an initial chronology of their abstract figures. The first experimental films then fully make good on the promise of an abstraction in time and space that is also in motion. Richter's use of the concept "rhythm" in the titles of his works must thus be read as analogous with the musical meaning of the same term.

The friendship and collaboration between Richter and Eggeling is considered the primal scene of abstract film. Theo van Doesburg had visited the two in Klein Kölzig for three weeks in December 1920 and January 1921. Since then, Richter and Eggeling were among the authors of *De Stijl*. Van Doesburg had seen an initial ninety-second filmic experiment created in December 1920 that he would later screen during a lecture tour to Paris. The impressions he had received while visiting in Klein Kölzig had heightened his interest in the medium of film and led him to write the theoretical essay "Abstracte Filmbeelding," which appeared in the May 1921 issue of *De Stijl*.

After parting ways with Eggeling, Richter made a second film, *Rhythmus 23* (1922–1924), based in part on the horizontal colorful scroll paintings *Fuge 23* and *Rhythmus 23*. Richter re-edited the film several times after its 1923 premiere in Paris. In its musical motion, this work develops a power of spatial suggestion, though significantly less so than *Rhythmus 21* had. For the first time, diagonals play a more central role. The line as a motif is contrasted with the moving surfaces. Unlike Richter, Eggeling conceived his film *Symphonie Diagonale* (1924) entirely on the basis of his scroll paintings (p. 143). The pace seems quicker than in Richter's work, the filmic progression is more distinct and its morphological vocabulary much more complex. The art historian Paul Ferdinand Schmidt, who attended the first public screening of *Symphonie Diagonale,* came to the following assessment: "We now know that it is possible to create a film that is a work of art. Eggeling has abstracted the principle of film—movement and light—from all imitation of nature and made it autonomous, reducing the rhythm of the sequence of movements to clear forms that relate to the feature film roughly as the Cubist painting relates to nature photography .... Still unfamiliar to today's eyes are the sudden shifts between rhythms and the overabundance of sequences of forms superseding one another; their meaning must be apprehended in musical terms, but through the eye, not the ear .... "[6]

Like Richter's, Eggeling's films touched upon an endpoint of abstraction from which artists could have developed forever different morphologies and formal combinations, but no fundamentally new ideas. Of course, it was beyond their means to call the established theater-based model of cinematic presentation in question. Only now do museums show Richter's and Eggeling's films set in cinematographic installations.

In principle, we might certainly speculate about whether and to what extent the concept of the integration of the arts championed by *De Stijl* already gave rise to an early conception of 'installation art'. The architectures created by Friedrich Kiesler are surely the best evidence of the degree to which *De Stijl* has influenced our contemporary understanding of the 'environment' or of 'installation art'. Besides Kurt Schwitters and other prominent representatives of the modernist avant-garde theater, Kiesler created the most intelligent and formally persuasive prefigurations of 'installation art'.

In Kiesler's architectonic thinking, previously solid and immutable architectures are to be transformed into dynamically flexible spaces. The first trial run of this conception was the interactive and technologically complex equipment he created for the stage of Karel Čapek's drama *R. U. R. (Rossum's Universal Robots).* The international avant-garde seems to have met in the audience when the play was produced at Berlin's Theater am Kurfürstendamm in 1923; shortly after the opening performance, Kiesler came into contact with Hans Richter, Theo van Doesburg, László Moholy-Nagy,

6
Paul Ferdinand Schmidt, "Eggelings Kunstfilm," *Das Kunstblatt* 8 (1924), p. 381, quoted in Louise O'Konor, *Viking Eggeling. 1880–1925. Artist and film-maker, life and work* (Stockholm, 1971), p. 52.

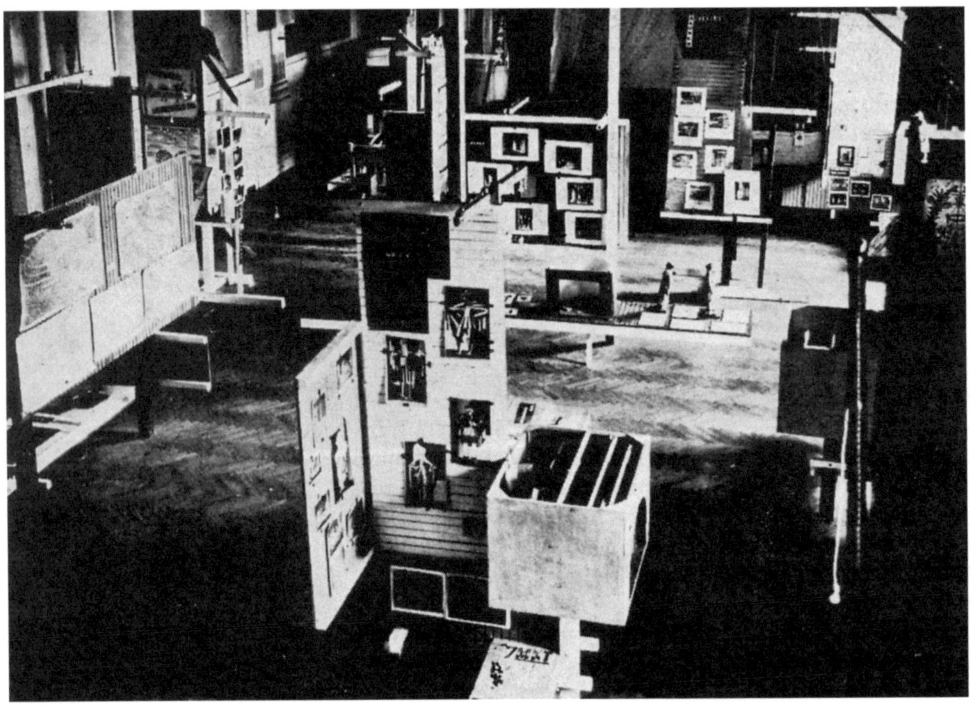

Friedrich Kiesler
Internationale Ausstellung neuer Theatertechnik in Wien
1924
Abgebildet in
De Stijl, VI, 10/11, 1925, S. 140

Friedrich Kiesler
International Exhibition of new Theater Technics in Vienna
1924
Illustrated in
De Stijl VI, no. 10/11 (1925), p. 140

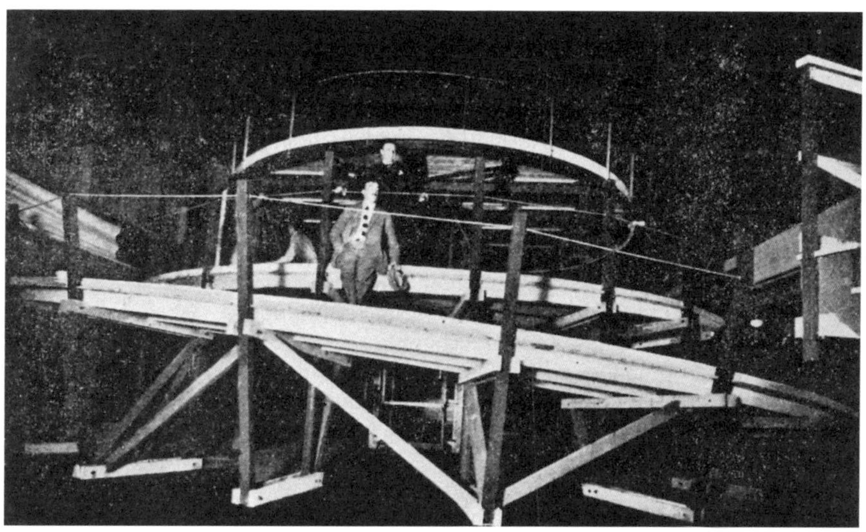

Friedrich Kiesler
Raumbühne
1924
Illustrated in
De Stijl VII, no. 75/76 (1926/27), p. 53

Friedrich Kiesler
Raumbühne
1924
Abgebildet in
De Stijl, VII, 75/76, 1926/27, S. 53

›Environment‹ oder ›Installationskunst‹ von *De Stijl* beeinflusst ist. Neben Kurt Schwitters und weiteren prominenten Figuren der Theateravantgarde der Moderne hat Kiesler die intelligentesten und formal überzeugendsten Präfigurationen der ›Installationskunst‹ geliefert.

In Kieslers architektonischem Denken sollten bisher solide und unveränderliche Architekturen in dynamisch bewegliche Räume überführt werden. Erstes Trainingsfeld war seine interaktiv angelegte und technisch komplex ausgestattete Bühnengestaltung für Karel Čapeks Drama *R.U.R. (Rossum's Universal Robots).* Während der Aufführung im Berliner Theater am Kurfürstendamm im Jahr 1923 muss die internationale Avantgarde im Publikum gesessen haben. Denn bereits nach der ersten Aufführung kam Kiesler mit Hans Richter, Theo van Doesburg, László Moholy-Nagy und El Lissitzky in Kontakt. Insbesondere zwischen van Doesburg und Kiesler entstand eine intensive Künstlerfreundschaft, die bis zu van Doesburgs plötzlichem Tod im Frühjahr 1931 andauerte.[7] Van Doesburg hat entscheidend dazu beigetragen, dass Kieslers Ideen mit Hilfe seiner Zeitschrift verbreitet werden konnten.

Ganz analog zu einer Reform der Architektur oder des Staffeleibildes beschäftigte sich Kiesler mit der Neudefinition der Guckkastenbühne. Sein formales Ziel war die Überwindung eines Theaters, in dem die perspektivische Trennung zwischen Bühne und Zuschauerraum als konstitutiv gilt. Kiesler wollte beide Bereiche miteinander verschränken wie die Kunst mit dem Leben: »Erster Versuch einer elektromechanischen Kulisse. Die Bildstarre ist zum Leben erweckt. Die Kulisse ist aktiv, spielt mit. De la nature morte vivante. Mittel der Verlebendigung sind: Bewegung der Linien, grelle Kontrastierung der Farben. Überleitung von Flächen in Relief-Formen bis zur Rundplastik Mensch (Schauspieler). Bewegungsspiel farbiger Lichter und Scheinwerfer auf der Kulisse. Rhythmisch akzentuiert, dem Sprechen und Bewegen der Schauspieler koordiniert …«[8]

In den folgenden Jahren gelang es Kiesler, sich durch zwei Ausstellungsprojekte ganz vorne in der europäischen Avantgarde zu etablieren. 1924 organisierte er in Wien die *Internationale Ausstellung neuer Theatertechnik* (Abb. S. 90). Er entwarf hierfür eine den theoretischen Gedanken der *De Stijl*-Gruppe verpflichtete Ausstellungsarchitektur und entwickelte außerdem einen konsequent neuartigen Typus der Theaterbühne, den er als »Raumbühne« bezeichnete. Diese Raumbühne war inspiriert von alltäglichen Orten der Unterhaltung wie zum Beispiel der Achterbahn oder dem Boxring. Die Raumbühne war eine Reaktion auf das in der Krise befindliche Modell der traditionellen Guckkastenperspektive und die Konventionen des Frontaltheaters. Die nun im Zentrum befindliche Spielfläche, vollständig umgeben vom Zuschauerraum, sollte aktuellere und körperbezogene Darstellungsformen wie Akrobatik, Tanz oder Pantomime im Theater etablieren helfen. Konkret bestand die Raumbühne aus einer spiralförmigen Rampe, die sich unter und um ein zentrales, höhergelegenes Kreiselement nach oben windet (Abb. S. 91).

Allerdings konnte die Raumbühne nicht unmittelbar zu einer tatsächlichen Veränderung der Theaterpraxis führen, nicht zuletzt deshalb, weil die Bühnen- und Raumkonzeption auch den von Kiesler geforderten »Dichter-Ingenieur« implizierte, der mittels eines »Bewegungsdramas« die Raumbühne erst ihrer Bestimmung zuführen konnte. Ein solcher ließ jedoch bis dato auf sich warten. Kaum ein Theaterexperiment hat jedoch am Ende so nachhaltig die performativ experimentelle Theaterpraxis nach 1945 beeinflusst wie Kieslers Raumbühne.

Ebenfalls im Rahmen einer Ausstellung präsentierte Kiesler 1925 in Paris sein erstes utopisches und bis heute wirkmächtiges Architekturprojekt, die *City in Space,* eine zwischen fast schwebenden Trägern frei im Raum hängende Stadt-Installation. Die utopischen Ansprüche seiner Projekte erläuterte Kiesler 1925 in *De Stijl*: »Die neue Stadt wird die Lösung des Verkehrs- und Hygieneproblems bringen, die Mannigfaltigkeit des Privatlebens ermöglichen und die Freiheit der Masse. Sie ist nicht gebaut, um zu genügen, sondern aus straffster Oekonomie der Mittel grösstmöglichsten Überfluss zu schaffen.«[9] Kieslers

7
Zur Künstlerfreundschaft mit Theo van Doesburg und den vielfältigen Verbindungen Kieslers zur internationalen Avantgarde vgl: Barbara Lesák, *Die Kulisse explodiert: Friedrich Kieslers Theaterexperimente und Architekturprojekte 1923–1925,* Wien 1988.

8
Friedrich Kiesler, „Als ich die Raumbühne erfand" [ca. 1924], Österreichische Friedrich und Lilian Kiesler Privatstiftung [www.kiesler.org, 07.02.2011].

9
Friederich Kiesler, »Manifest. Vitalbau – Raumstadt – Funktionelle Architektur«, in: *De Stijl,* VI, 10/11, 1925, S. 141–147, hier S. 146.

and El Lissitzky. Van Doesburg and Kiesler, in particular, formed an intense friendship that lasted until Van Doesburg's sudden death in the spring of 1931.[7] By featuring Kiesler's work in the pages of *De Stijl*, Van Doesburg decisively helped popularize his ideas.

In precise analogy to the efforts to reform architecture or the easel painting, Kiesler worked on redefining the picture-frame stage. His formal goal was to overcome a theatrical tradition in which the perspectival separation between the stage and the audience room is considered a constitutive element. Kiesler sought to integrate the two spheres, just as art was to be integrated with life: "First attempt to design an electro-mechanical scenery. The frozen scenery has come to life, has become active, takes part in the play. De la nature morte vivante. The means to bring the stage to life are: movement of lines, garish contrasts of colors. The transformation of surfaces into relief and hence into rounded human forms (actors). Play of moving lights and spotlights of various colors on the scenery, rhythmically accentuated and coordinated with the speech and movements of the actors ...."[8]

Over the years that followed, Kiesler implemented two successful exhibition projects that established him at the very forefront of the European avant-garde. In 1924, he organized the *International Exhibition of New Theater Technology* (p. 90), for which he designed an exhibition architecture that owed much to the theoretical ideas of the *De Stijl* group as well as a rigorously novel type of theatrical stage he called "Space Stage." This stage was inspired by lowbrow entertainment venues such as roller coasters or boxing rings. The Space Stage responded to the crisis of the traditional picture-frame stage and the conventions of frontal-view theater. The stage, now located at the center of the house and surrounded on all sides by audience seating, aimed to help establish more contemporary and physically intense forms of performance such as acrobatics, dance, or pantomime in the theater. The Space Stage itself more specifically consisted of a spiral-shaped ramp that twisted upward beneath and around a central elevated circular element (p. 91).

However, the Space Stage did not lead to an immediate revolution in the theatrical practice; the most important obstacle was that Kiesler's conception of the stage and the theatrical space also required what he described as a "poet-engineer," whose "motion-drama" would employ the novel stage in accordance with its true purpose. No such "poet-engineer" emerged in Kiesler's own time. Yet few theatrical experiments ultimately exercised greater influence over experimental theatrical and performance practices after 1945 than Kiesler's Space Stage.

Another project of Kiesler's whose influence can be felt even today was again presented as part of an exhibition, this time in Paris; in 1925, Kiesler showed his first utopian architecture design, the *City in Space,* an urban installation loftily suspended between pillars that almost seem to float. That same year, Kiesler explained the utopian aspirations of his designs in *De Stijl*: "The new city will bring the solution of the problems of traffic and hygiene, allow for a wide diversity of forms of private life, and set the masses free. It is constructed not to be sufficient, but to create the greatest possible superabundance out of the most rigorous economy of means."[9] Kiesler's *City in Space* clearly shows how the central elements of his creative work have taken definite form as early as the mid-1920s. Exhibition design, stage design, and more or less utopian architectures would consistently be at the focus of his numerous projects. Transcending the traditional genres, his structures are exemplary illustrations of the ambitions of *De Stijl*, propelled by the idea of dissolving the boundaries between the arts. His ideas about the theater made history and continue to inspire new forms of physically intense theater even in our own time. His ideas about the city, his architectures, and his proposals for forms of presentation have remained crucial sources of inspiration for a critical reflection on the conventions that govern the various disciplines at any particular moment.

Translated from the German
by Gerrit Jackson

7
On the artists' friendship between Theo van Doesburg and Friedrich Kiesler and Kiesler's wide network of acquaintances among the international avant-garde cf. Barbara Lesák, *Die Kulisse explodiert: Friedrich Kieslers Theaterexperimente und Architekturprojekte 1923–1925* (Vienna, 1988).

8
Friedrich Kiesler, "Als ich die Raumbühne erfand" [ca. 1924], Austrian Frederick and Lilian Kiesler Private Foundation (www.kiesler.org, February 7, 2011).

9
Friederich Kiesler, "Manifest. Vitalbau—Raumstadt—Funktionelle Architektur," *De Stijl* VI, no. 10/11 (1925), pp. 141–47, quote p. 146.

City in Space demonstriert deutlich, wie sich bereits Mitte der zwanziger Jahre die wichtigsten Bereiche seines Schaffens herauskristallisiert hatten. Ausstellungsdesign, Bühnenbildnerei und mehr oder minder utopische Architekturen standen immer wieder im Mittelpunkt seiner zahlreichen Projekte. Ganz besonders deutlich treten in Kieslers gattungsübergreifenden Anordnungen die von der Entgrenzungsidee getriebenen Ambitionen von *De Stijl* hervor. Seine Vorstellung vom Theater hat Geschichte geschrieben und beeinflusst bis in unsere Gegenwart neue Formen körperintensiven Theaters. Seine Vorstellung von Stadt, seine Architekturen und seine Präsentationsvorschläge sind wichtige Impulsgeber für eine kritische Reflektion der jeweils geltenden Konventionen der Disziplinen geblieben.

Abbildungen / Biografien

Plates / Biographies

PETER ALMA

Peter Alma wird 1886 in Medan auf Sumatra geboren. Von 1904 bis 1906 studiert er an der Kunstakademie in Den Haag, geht dann nach Paris und schreibt sich in der Académie Humbert ein. Er lernt Fernand Léger, Diego Rivera, Henri Le Fauconnier und Piet Mondrian kennen, die alle auf ihre Art nach neuen Ausdrucksformen suchen. Diese sollen dem zeitgemäßen Kunstbewusstsein verpflichtet sein, das sich durch das ›Gemeinschaftliche‹, das ›Universelle‹ auszeichnet. Nach 1910 treibt Alma die Verbreitung des Kubismus voran. Er malt mit Lodewijk Schelfhout in Belgien, schließt sich der Vereinigung *Moderne Kunstkring* an – eine Vereinigung avantgardistischer Künstler der Niederlande – und schickt seine Arbeiten zur *Sonderbund*-Ausstellung nach Köln sowie zum Salon des Indépendants in Paris. Während des Ersten Weltkriegs entwickelt Alma in der Künstlerkolonie Laren eine auf elementare Formen reduzierte Bildsprache im Stile Bart van der Lecks, immer auf der Suche nach einer allgemeingültigen Gemeinschaftskunst, die sich von jeglichem Individualismus lossagt. 1916 begegnet er Theo van Doesburg, der Laren mit dem Ziel besucht, Piet Mondrian kennenzulernen. Alma schwärmt damals schon für marxistische Ideen, etwa davon, dass die Kunst sich in den Dienst der industrialisierten Massenproduktion stellen solle. 1919 wird er Mitglied der Kommunistischen Partei der Niederlande. Er verfasst Artikel für das Parteiorgan *De Tribune* und liefert sich eine Auseinandersetzung mit van Doesburg, der ihn in *De Stijl* nicht nur wegen seiner Ansichten scharf kritisiert, sondern auch wegen seiner Formensprache, die zugunsten einer stilisierten, aber stets figürlichen Darstellungsweise nie ganz zur Abstraktion übergegangen war: »Wenn der Herr Alma diesem Verlangen der Massen nachgeben möchte, sollte er sein Künstlerdasein aufgeben, denn jede Kunst entspringt dem Verlangen nach Abstraktion und der Befreiung aus dem Natürlichen.« Alma konzentriert sich in späteren Jahren auf Radierungen und Wandmalereien, in denen er seine dienende Haltung der Partei gegenüber noch besser zum Ausdruck bringen kann. Er unternimmt eine Reise in die Sowjetunion und trifft dort Kandinsky, Lissitzky, Tatlin und Malewitsch. Noch 1927 polemisiert Alma in der Zeitschrift *i10* gegen die Kunst von *De Stijl*, die er »isoliert vom wirklichen Leben« empfindet und der er vorwirft, sich nicht an ein breites Publikum zu richten. 1969 stirbt Peter Alma in Amsterdam.

Peter Alma – born 1886 in Medan, Sumatra.
After attending the Koninklijke Academie in The Hague from 1904 to 1906 he moved to Paris, where he studied at the Académie Humbert. He became acquainted with Fernand Léger, Diego Rivera, Henri Le Fauconnier and Piet Mondrian, all of whom were, in their own way, searching for an art form determined by a new consciousness and committed to common and universal needs. From 1910 Alma helped spread the influence of Cubism, and he painted with Lodewijk Schelfhout in Belgium. He became a member of the *Moderne Kunstkring*—an association of avant-garde artists in the Netherlands—and submitted work to the *Sonderbund* exhibition in Cologne and the Salon des Indépendants in Paris. During World War I, in the small artist colony of Laren, he developed elementary forms in the style of Bart van der Leck and embarked on his own quest for a universal art, devoid of any trace of individualism. In 1916 he met Theo van Doesburg, who had come to Laren in order to visit Piet Mondrian. Even then, Alma enthused over Marxist ideas of art's subservience to industrial mass production. In 1919, Alma became a member of the Dutch Communist Party. He began to write for the party newspaper *De Tribune,* and became involved in a polemic with Van Doesburg, who lectured him in *De Stijl* not only because of his views, but also because of the visual language he chose, in which imagination and illusion continued to play a key role: "If Mr. Alma intends to succumb to this desire of the masses, he will have to cease being an artist, for all art springs from the need for the abstract and the liberation from the natural". In the years that followed Alma produced etchings and murals, which he felt were better suited to express his subservient attitude to the communist party.
He traveled to the Soviet Union where he met Kandinsky, Lissitzky, Tatlin and Malevich. He was still criticizing the *De Stijl* movement in 1927, describing it in the journal *i10* as "isolated from real life" and accusing it of not wishing to speak to the public. Peter Alma died 1969 in Amsterdam.

Peter Alma
Transport
1924
Öl auf Leinwand
46 x 130,5 cm
Gemeentemuseum Den Haag

Peter Alma
Transport
1924
Oil on canvas
46 x 130,5 cm
Gemeentemuseum The Hague

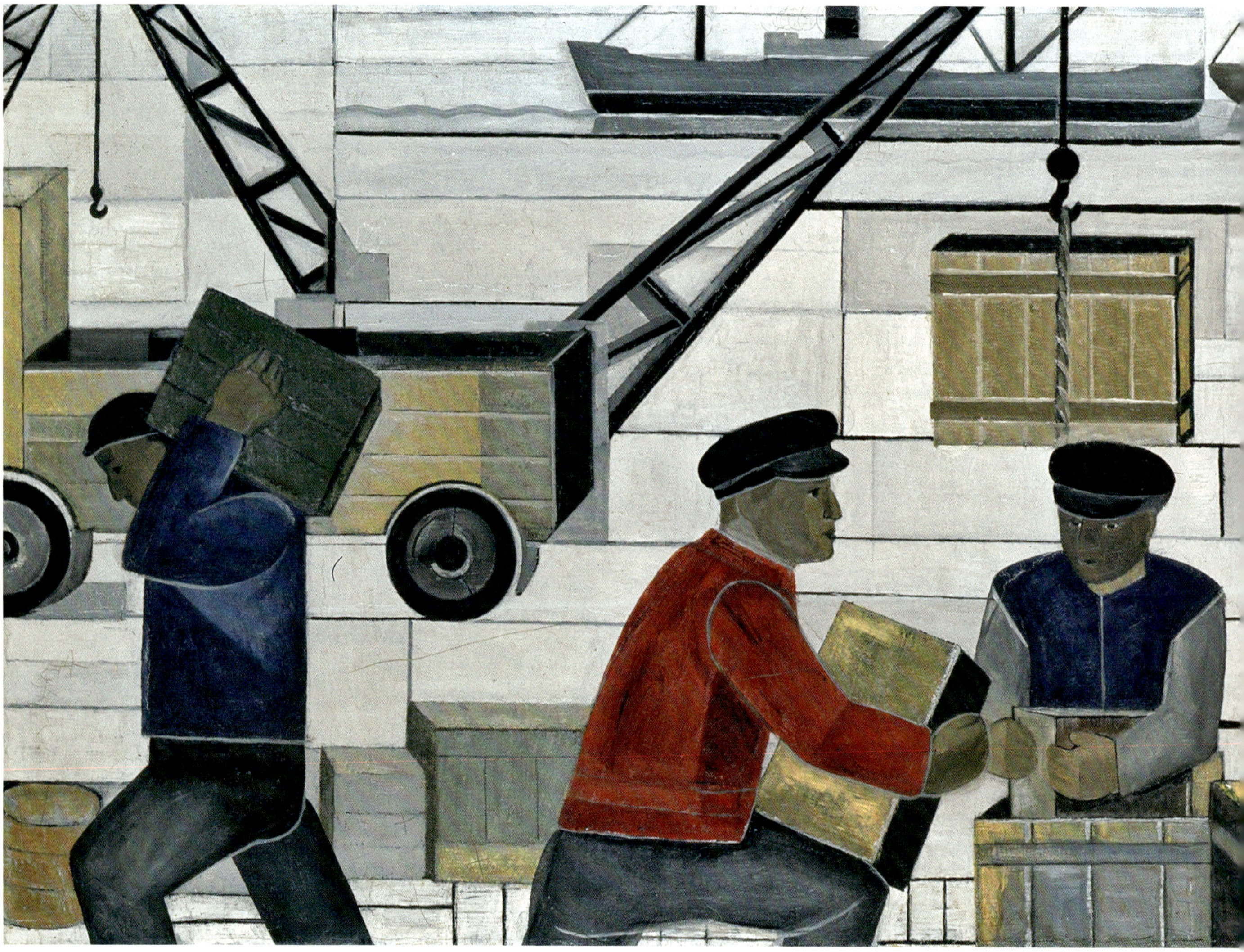

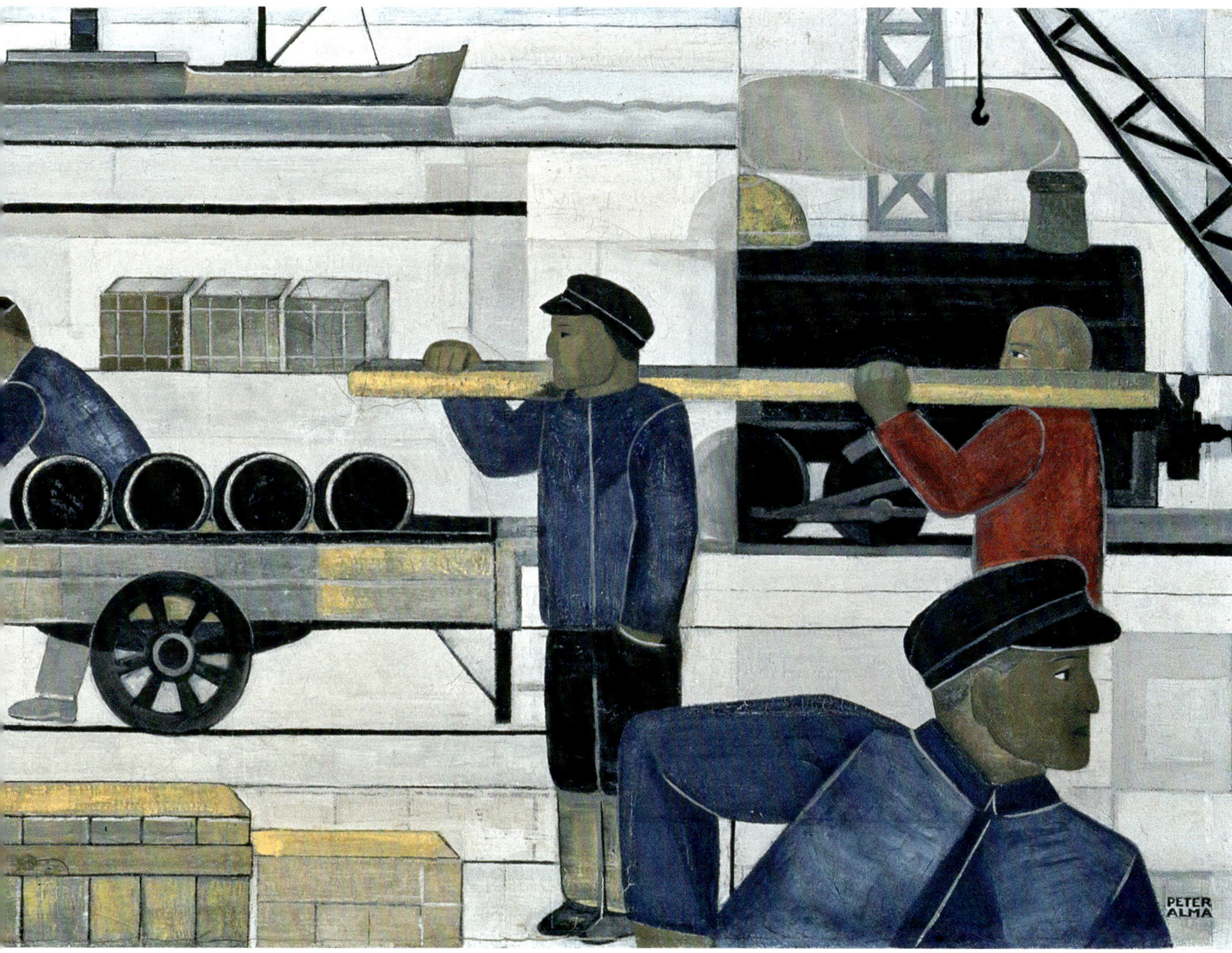
PETER
ALMA

HANS ARP

Hans Arp wird 1886 in Straßburg geboren. Er besucht zunächst die Kunstgewerbeschulen in seiner Geburtsstadt und in Weimar, bevor er ab 1907 sein Studium in Paris an der Académie Julian fortsetzt. Arp befreit sich mit den Jahren zusehends von den tradierten Kunstauffassungen und den damit einhergehenden Formensprachen. Im Jahr 1909 trifft er Paul Klee, und drei Jahre später beteiligt er sich mit eigenen Arbeiten an einer Ausstellung der Künstlergruppe *Der Blaue Reiter*. So kommt er auch mit Künstlern aus den Kreisen um *Der Sturm* in Berlin in Berührung. 1915 zieht Arp nach Zürich, wo er seine spätere Frau, die Künstlerin Sophie Taeuber, kennen lernt. Ihre Art der Abstraktion übt großen Einfluss auf ihn und seine Kunst aus; gemeinsam arbeiten sie an ersten Collagen. 1916 ist Arp einer der Mitbegründer der Dada-Bewegung im Cabaret Voltaire. In den folgenden Jahren verbreiten er und gleichgesinnte Künstler den Dadaismus in ganz Europa; auf Einladung Theo van Doesburgs nehmen Tristan Tzara und Arp im September 1922 am ersten Internationalen Kongress der Konstruktivisten und Dadaisten in Weimar teil und fordern die Konstruktivisten durch ihre Dada-Manifestationen heraus. In den darauf folgenden Monaten reist er mit Theo van Doesburg durch Deutschland und schreibt Beiträge für verschiedene avantgardistische Zeitschriften, etwa für *G, Mécano, Merz* und *Der Sturm.* Ab 1925 erweitert Arp sein Arbeitsfeld: Er nimmt in der Galerie Pierre in Paris an einer der ersten surrealistischen Ausstellungen teil und in Berlin an der Ausstellung der *Novembergruppe.* 1926 übernimmt Arp gemeinsam mit van Doesburg den Auftrag für die Innengestaltung des Kultur- und Vergnügungszentrums Aubette in Straßburg. Hierfür entwickeln sie Entwürfe für Wände, Decken und Möbel, für die Beschriftung und Beleuchtung. Im selben Jahr zieht Arp nach Paris und arbeitet an Collagen, bei denen die Wirkung des Unterbewussten zu einem immer wichtiger werdenden Bestandteil seiner abstrakten Formensprache wird. Im Februar 1931 finden van Doesburg und Arp noch einmal zueinander: Arp tritt der Gruppe *Abstraction-Création* bei, die unter anderem von van Doesburg in diesem Jahr in Paris gegründet wird und zu deren Mitgliedern Künstler wie Piet Mondrian, Sonia und Robert Delaunay sowie Kurt Schwitters zählen. Hans Arp stirbt 1966 in Basel.

Hans Arp – born 1886 in Strasbourg, where he attended the École des Arts et Métiers before moving to the Kunstgewerbeschule in Weimar and, in 1907, to the Académie Julian in Paris. In the years that followed Arp made his first attempts to liberate himself from traditional representation and the visual language associated with it. He became acquainted with Paul Klee in 1909, and in 1912 he participated in the *Der Blaue Reiter* exhibition, which brought him into contact with the *Der Sturm* circle in Berlin. He moved to Zurich in 1915, where he met Sophie Taeuber, whom he would later marry. Her use of abstraction had a lasting impact on him, and they began to produce collages together. He was there when the Dada movement emerged at the Cabaret Voltaire in 1916. In the years that followed Arp joined like-minded artists in spreading Dada throughout Europe. On the invitation of Theo van Doesburg Arp, Tristan Tzara and Hans Richter participated in the 1922 International Congress of Constructivists and Dadaists in Weimar challenging Constructivists El Lissitzky, László-Maholoy-Nagy, Alfreéd Kemény and others. During the following months he traveled around Germany with Van Doesburg, contributing to a range of avant-garde magazines, including *G, Mécano, Merz* and *Der Sturm.* In 1925 Arp broadened his field of activity, participating in the first Surrealist exhibition at Galerie Pierre in Paris and in the *Novembergruppe* exhibition in Berlin. In 1926 he and Van Doesburg undertook a joint commission to design the interior of the Aubette entertainment center in Strasbourg, developing integrated plans for the walls, ceilings, furnishing, lettering and lighting. Arp settled in Paris that same year, and began producing collages, in which the workings of the subconscious increasingly influenced his abstract form language. In February 1931 Van Doesburg and Arp worked together again, and Arp joined a new association, *Abstraction-Création,* established by Van Doesburg, which included Piet Mondrian, Sonia and Robert Delaunay and Kurt Schwitters among its members. Hans Arp died 1966 in Basel.

Hans Arp
Wolkenblumen
1932
Holz
78,8 x 58,5 cm
Gemeentemuseum Den Haag

Hans Arp
Cloud Flowers
1932
Wood
78,8 x 58,5 cm
Gemeentemuseum The Hague

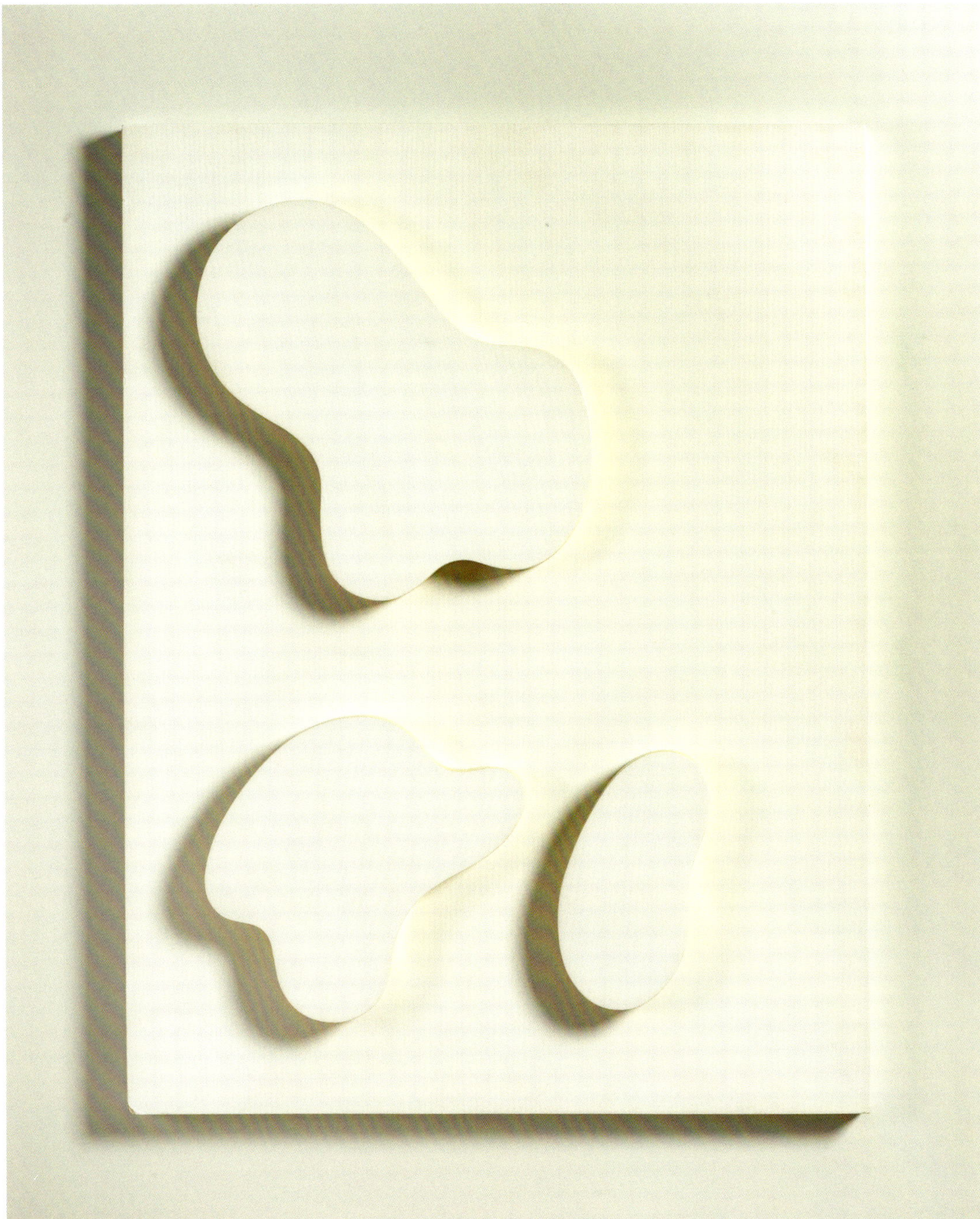

CHRIS BEEKMAN

Chris Beekman, 1887 in Den Haag geboren, beginnt seine Laufbahn mit dreizehn Jahren bei der Porzellanmanufaktur Rozenburg. Die florale Jugendstilornamentik der Keramik, die er dort als Porzellanmaler anfertigt, beruht größtenteils auf Entwürfen von T.A.C. Colenbrander. Sowohl seine Kollegen aus der Fabrik als auch sein älterer Cousin, der Bildhauer und Anarchist Jan Altorf, fördern seine künstlerischen Ambitionen und beeinflussen seine Denkweise. Beekman sympathisiert mit den sozialistischen Ideen von Ferdinand Domela Nieuwenhuis. Ab 1909 studiert er an der Kunstakademie seiner Heimatstadt. 1913 geht er nach Paris, wo er die derzeitigen Kunstströmungen kennen lernt. Seine Bildsprache und seine politischen Überzeugungen verschmelzen bald miteinander. Über den Kunstkritiker Henk Bremmer lernt er Bart van der Leck kennen. Die beiden jungen Künstler ziehen in die nordholländische Provinz nach Eemnes bei Laren. Beekman malt zunächst noch figurative Werke mit vereinfachten Formen und Motiven, bevor er sich um 1916 der abstrakten Bildsprache von *De Stijl* bedient. Er freundet sich mit Alma, Huszár und van 't Hoff an und übt im Jahr 1919 großen Einfluss auf Theo van Doesburg aus, der seine Sympathie für den Kommunismus anfangs noch teilt. Gemeinsam planen sie eine ›Internationale‹ von politisch engagierten Künstlern, die van Doesburg schon vorab »Beeldend Europa« tauft. Van Doesburg bittet Beekman, seine Ansichten und Ideen in *De Stijl* zu veröffentlichen und bietet ihm an, Reproduktionen seiner Gemälde mit in die Zeitschrift aufzunehmen. Doch ein solcher Beitrag kommt nie zustande. Beekman, der den Kontakt mit russischen Künstlern sucht, ist es wichtiger, sich politisch zu engagieren. Van Doesburg ist hingegen der Ansicht, dass Kunst nicht der Revolution zu dienen habe und hält Beekman und dessen aktivistische Freunde zunehmend für ungeeignet, um, wie er es ausdrückt: »das Neue in der Gestaltung in sich aufzunehmen [und] an ihrer Verinnerlichung zu arbeiten«. Beekman hingegen kritisiert die bürgerliche Ausrichtung von *De Stijl,* die nicht im Geringsten revolutionär sei, und arbeitet fortan wieder figurativ. Er malt proletarisch-revolutionäre Darstellungen und widmet sich der Gründung einer Künstlergewerkschaft. 1964 stirbt Chris Beekman.

Chris Beekman – born 1887 in The Hague, as a thirteen-year-old Beekman went to work at the Rozenburg Royal Delftware Factory in The Hague, where he painted Art Nouveau-influenced floral décor largely designed by T.A.C. Colenbrander. Both his fellow workers at the factory and his older cousin Jan Altorf, a sculptor and anarchist, influenced his thinking and encouraged his emerging aspiration to become an artist. He was sympathetic to Ferdinand Domela Nieuwenhuis's socialist ideas. In 1909 Beekman went to study at the Koninklijke Academie, and in 1913 he traveled to Paris, where he was exposed to modern art trends. His visual language and political convictions began to converge. Critic H.P. Bremmer introduced Beekman to Bart van der Leck. The two young artists moved to Eemnes near Laren, in the Het Gooi region of the Netherlands. Beekman focused on figurative painting with simplified forms and motifs before converting to the abstract form language of *De Stijl* around 1916. He befriended Alma, Huszár and Van 't Hoff, and in 1919 had a major influence on Theo van Doesburg, who initially shared his sympathy for communism. They intended to establish an 'Internationale' of artistically and politically engaged artists, which Van Doesburg dubbed "Beeldend Europa" ("Plastic Europe"). Van Doesburg invited Beekman to publish his ideas in *De Stijl,* alongside reproductions of his paintings. But nothing came of it, partly because Beekman prefered to take political action and make contact with Russian artists, and also because Van Doesburg did not believe that art should serve the revolution. He came to regard Beekman and his activist friends as increasingly less suited, as he put it "to assimilate the new in plastic art [and] to strife for its internalization." Beekman returned to figurative art, convinced that *De Stijl* was not revolutionary, but bourgeois. He painted proletarian, revolutionary images and dedicated himself to establishing a trade union for artists. He died in 1964.

Chris Beekman
Komposition
1920
Öl auf Leinwand
48 x 28 cm
Gemeentemuseum Den Haag

Chris Beekman
Composition
1920
Oil on canvas
48 x 28 cm
Gemeentemuseum The Hague

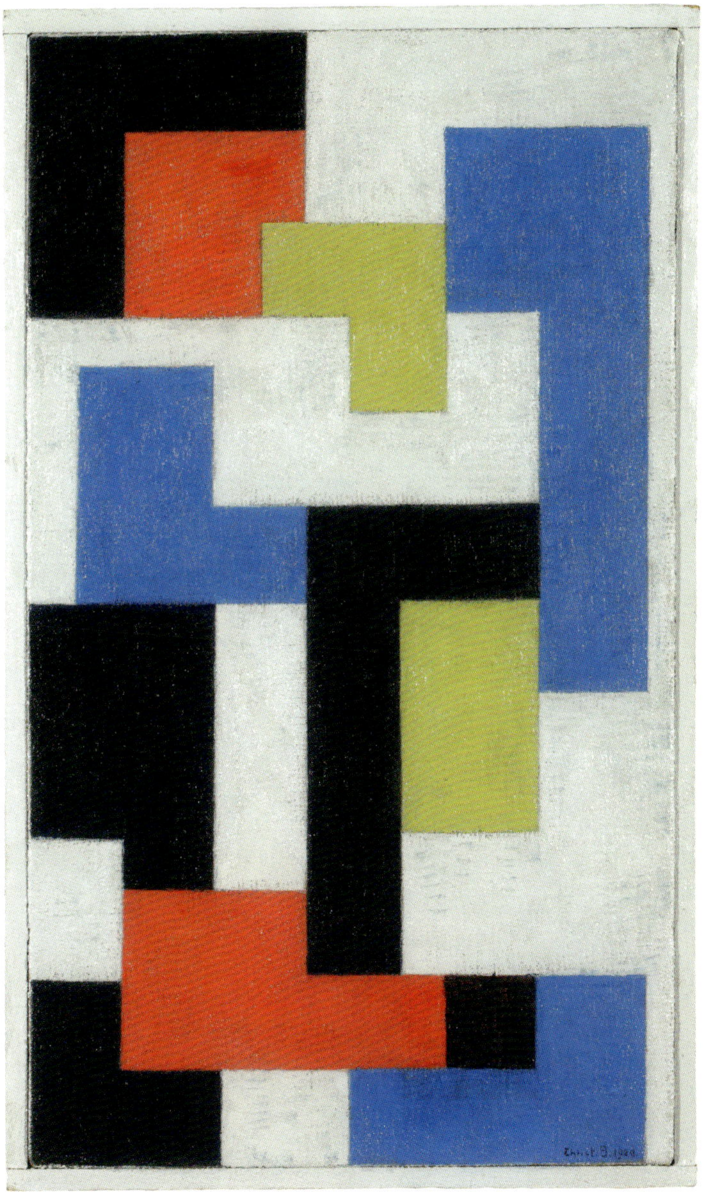

THEO VAN DOESBURG

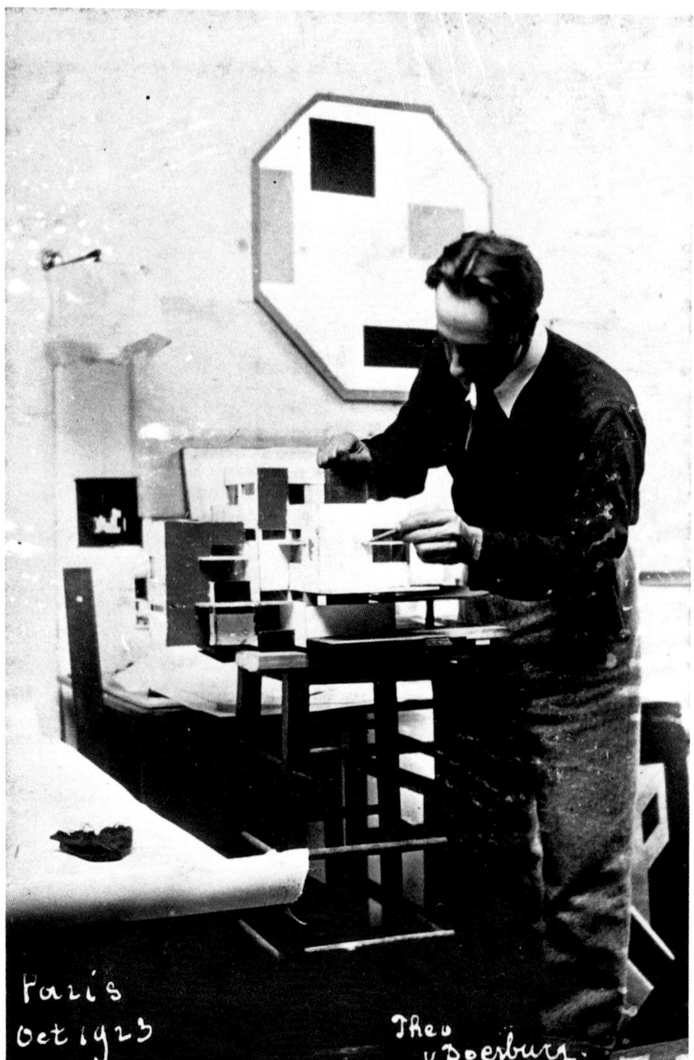

Theo van Doesburg arbeitet an einem Modell des Maison Particulière in seinem Atelier in der Rue du Moulin Vert in Paris
1923
RKD, Archiv Theo und Nelly van Doesburg (Schenkung van Moorsel)

Theo van Doesburg working on a model of Maison Particulière at his studio, Rue du Moulin Vert, Paris
1923
RKD, Archive of Theo and Nelly van Doesburg (Donation Van Moorsel)

Theo van Doesburg wird 1883 als Christian Emil Maria Küpper in Utrecht geboren. Er studiert kurz an der Schauspielschule in Amsterdam, ehe er 1902 den Wunsch hegt, bildender Künstler zu werden. Er nimmt den Namen Theo van Doesburg an und gibt sich damit eine neue Identität. 1903 geht er zum Militär und sucht auch hier nach Wegen, wie er sagt, den »Schleier«, der sein »geistiges Dasein verborgen hält, zur Seite zu schieben und der Welt zu zeigen, was in mir verborgen ist«. Im Jahr 1916 macht er Bekanntschaft mit J.J.P. Oud, Jan Wils, Vilmos Huszár und Piet Mondrian, mit denen er ein Jahr später und gemeinsam mit seiner zweiten Frau Lena Milius die Zeitschrift *De Stijl* gründet. Van Doesburg legt sich allerlei Pseudonyme zu – wie I.K. Bonset und Aldo Camini – die er seinen verschiedenen, oft parallel verfolgten künstlerischen Strategien zuordnet. In vielerlei Hinsicht handelt es sich dabei um Reaktionen auf die Arbeiten anderer Künstler, die er, ähnlich der endlosen Polemiken, die er mit seinen Künstlerkollegen führt, dazu benutzt, seine eigenen Denkweisen zu schärfen. 1920–1922 bemüht sich van Doesburg um eine Anstellung am Bauhaus in Weimar. Als ihm dies nicht gelingt, reist er gemeinsam mit seiner dritten Frau Nelly quer durch Europa, wo er viele Kontakte knüpft und dafür sorgt, dass sich die Niederlanden in kultureller Hinsicht für die internationalen Bewegungen öffnen. 1923 initiiert er gemeinsam mit Kurt Schwitters und Nelly van Doesburg eine Dada-Tour in den Niederlanden. Er zieht mit Nelly nach Paris und organisiert zusammen mit Cornelis van Eesteren eine Aufsehen erregende Architekturausstellung in der Galerie Rosenberg. 1925 bricht er mit Piet Mondrian und entwickelt den sogenannten »Elementarismus«: Die Formensprache ist stark reduziert wie bei Mondrian, beinhaltet aber statt nur horizontal und vertikal angeordneter Linien diagonale Rasterstrukturen und stellt sich auch dadurch entschieden gegen Mondrians »Neoplastizismus«. Gemeinsam mit Hans Arp fertigt van Doesburg Entwürfe für das Kultur- und Vergnügungszentrum Aubette in Straßburg an. Bis 1931 gründet er immer wieder neue Bewegungen und Zeitschriften wie *L'Art Concret*, oder schließt sich anderen Künstlergruppen an, wie etwa *Abstraction-Création*, in der Absicht, der abstrakten Kunst neues Leben einzuhauchen. 1931 stirbt Theo van Doesburg als eine ›Ein-Mann-Künstlergruppe‹ in Davos.

Theo van Doesburg – born Christian Emil Maria Küpper in Utrecht in 1883. Having studied drama for a short time at the School voor Vocale en Dramatische Kunsten in Amsterdam, in 1902 he developed a desire to become a visual artist, and reinvented himself, adopting the name Theo van Doesburg. In 1903 he entered military service, but continued to search for ways to "push aside [the veil] that had hidden my spiritual existence and to show the world what was hidden within me."
In 1916 he met J.J.P. Oud, Jan Wils, Vilmos Huszár and Piet Mondrian and, a year later, established the journal *De Stijl*, together with his second wife Lena Milius. He began to use all kinds of pseudonyms, including I.K. Bonset and Aldo Camini, to create a distinct profile for each of his different artistic strategies. It was not until 1919 that he dared to show the world his own paintings. In many respects they were responses to the work of others, just as he used the polemics in which he repeatedly became involved with other artists to sharpen his own ideas. In 1920–1922 he applied for a position at the Bauhaus. When he was rejected, he traveled through Europe with Nelly, his third wife, making many new contacts and single-handedly opening up the Netherlands to the cultural influences of international movements. In 1923 he organized a Dada-tour of the Netherlands, together with Kurt Schwitters and Nelly van Doesburg. He and Nelly moved to Paris, where he and Cornelis van Eesteren organized a first-of-its-kind exhibition on architecture at Galerie Rosenberg. In 1925 he split with Piet Mondrian and launched "Elementarism", introducing the diagonal as the main compositional element, which signified a radical departure from Mondrian's "Neoplasticism", in which the horizontal and vertical ruled supreme. In 1926 Van Doesburg designed the Aubette in Strasbourg, collaborating with Hans Arp. He would continue his efforts to breathe new life into abstract art until his death in 1931, establishing movements and magazines such as *L'Art Concret*, and associating with *Abstraction-Création*. However, he remained a 'one-man movement' for the rest of his life. Theo van Doesburg died 1931 in Davos.

Theo van Doesburg
Komposition
April 1917
Bleistift, Tinte und Gouache auf Transparentpapier,
bemaltes Passepartout
21,1 x 19 cm
Gemeentemuseum Den Haag

Theo van Doesburg
Composition
April 1917
Pencil, ink, and gouache on transparent paper,
painted passepartout
21,1 x 19 cm
Gemeentemuseum The Hague

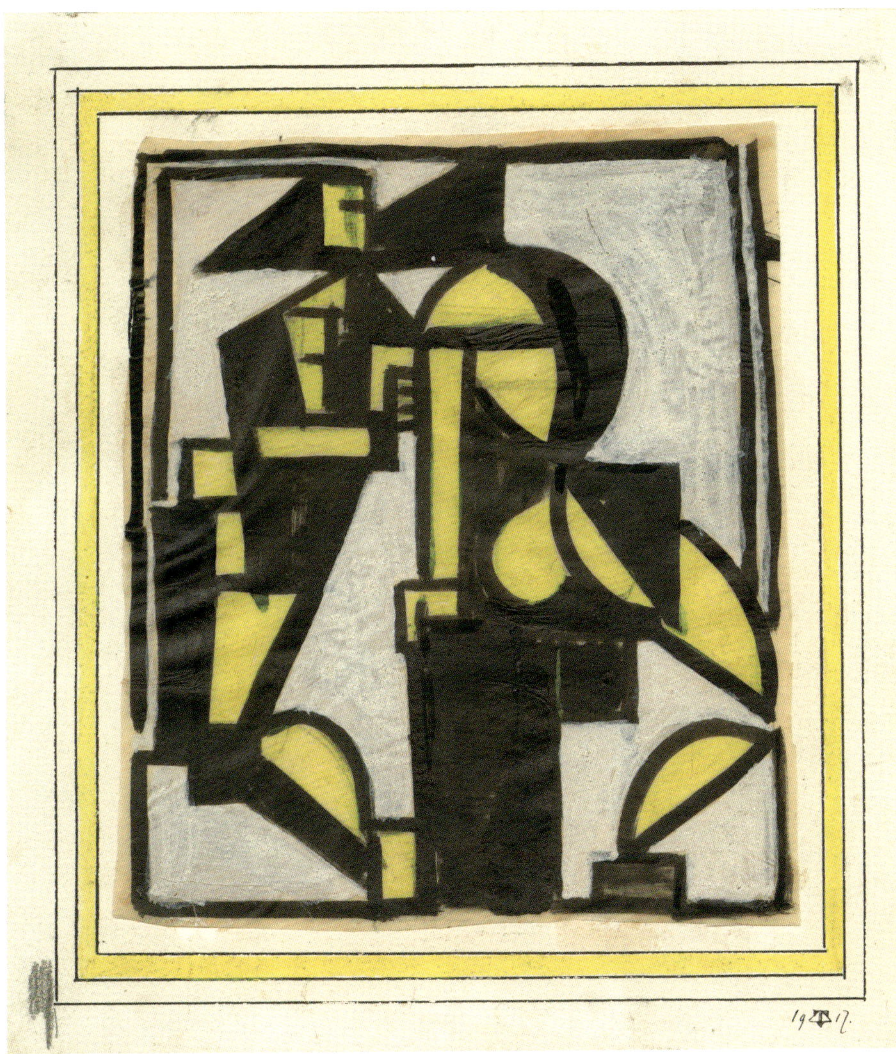

Theo van Doesburg
Komposition IX, Opus 18:
Abstrakte Version der »Kartenspieler«
1917
Öl auf Leinwand
116 x 106,5 cm
Gemeentemuseum Den Haag

Theo van Doesburg
Composition IX, Opus 18:
Abstract Version of "Card Players"
1917
Oil on canvas
116 x 106,5 cm
Gemeentemuseum The Hague

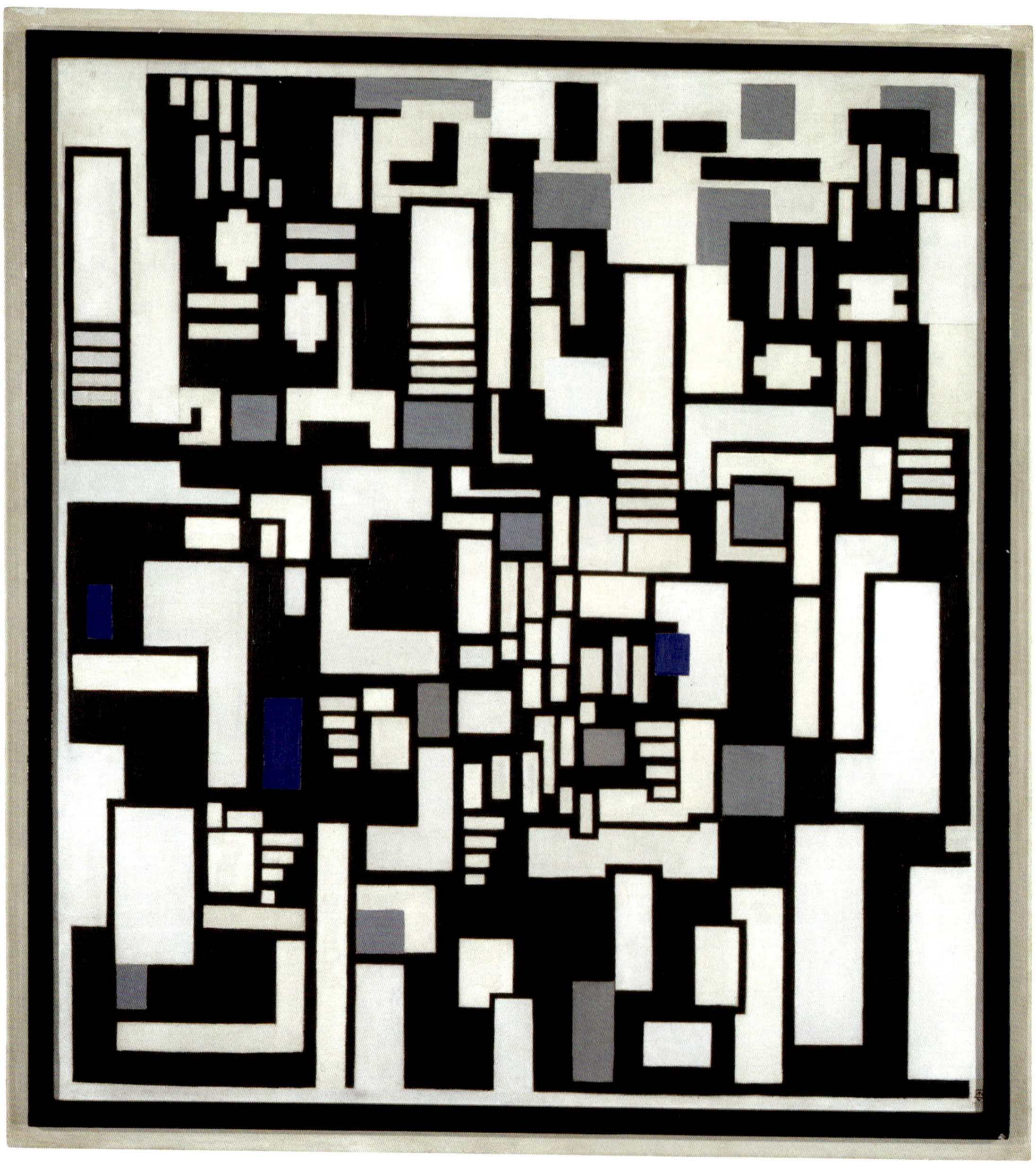

Theo van Doesburg
Komposition XVII
1919
Öl auf Leinwand
50 x 50 cm
Gemeentemuseum Den Haag

Theo van Doesburg
Composition XVII
1919
Oil on canvas
50 x 50 cm
Gemeentemuseum The Hague

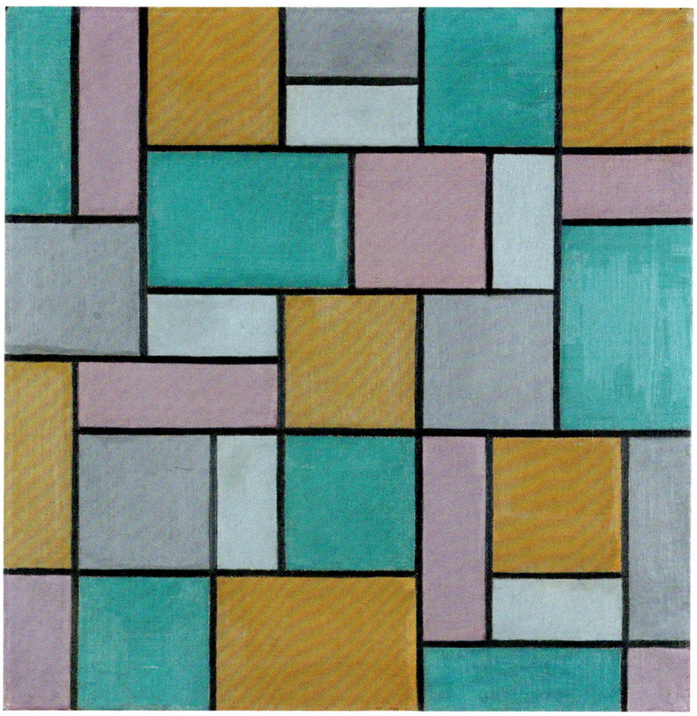

Theo van Doesburg
Kontrakonstruktion
1923
Bleistift, Gouache und Kreide
aufTransparentpapier
36 x 38 cm
Niederländisches Architekturinstitut, Rotterdam
Dauerleihgabe des Niederländischen Instituts
für Kulturerbe (RCE)

Theo van Doesburg
Contra-Construction
1923
Pencil, gouache and crayon
on transparent paper
36 x 38 cm
Netherlands Architecture Institute, Rotterdam
On permanent loan from the Cultural Heritage Agency
of the Netherlands (RCE)

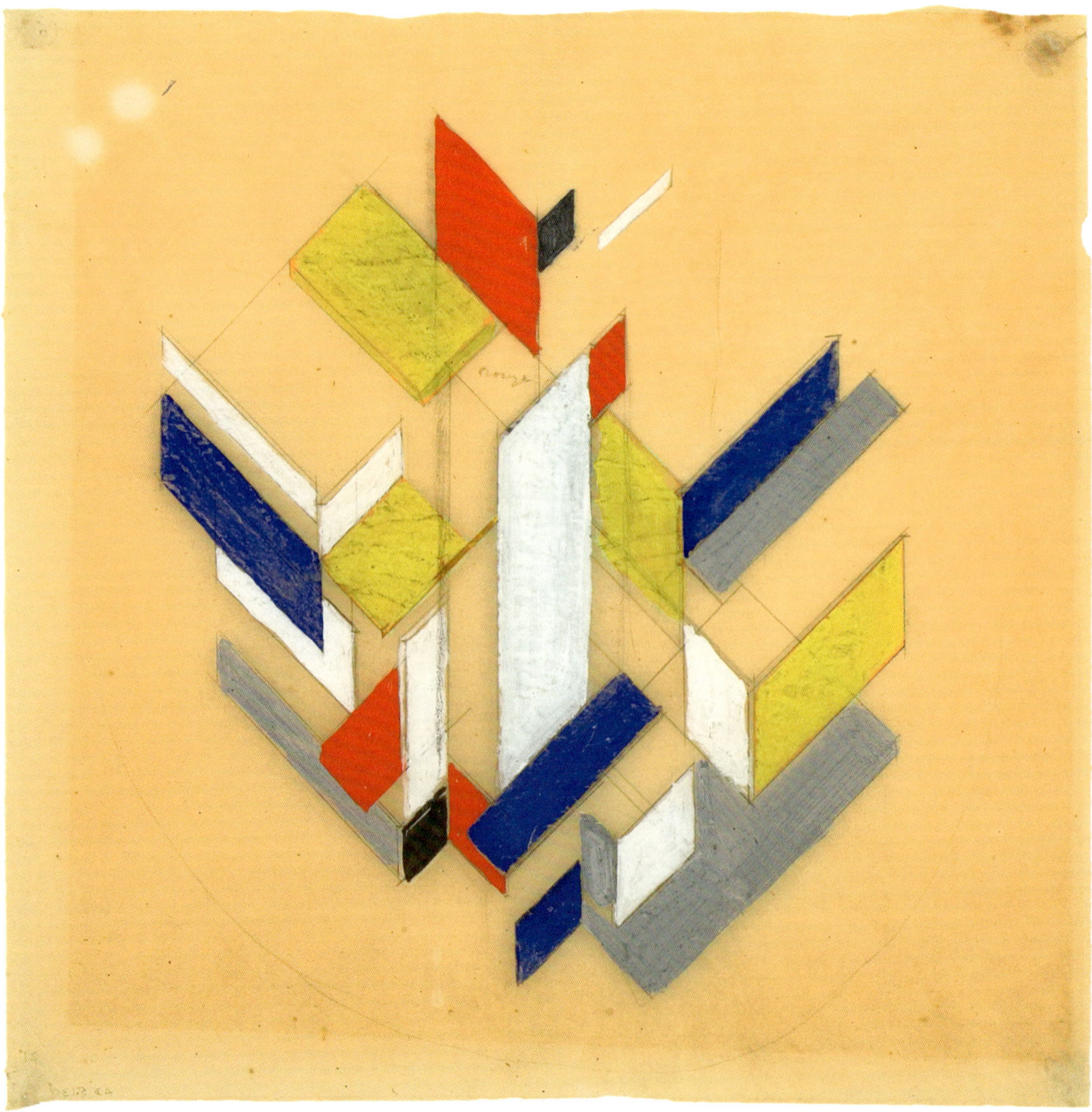

Theo van Doesburg
Kontrakonstruktion
1923/24
Bleistift, Gouache, Tusche und Collage
auf Transparentpapier
54,5 x 40,5 cm
Niederländisches Architekturinstitut, Rotterdam
Dauerleihgabe des Niederländischen Instituts
für Kulturerbe (RCE)

Theo van Doesburg
Contra-Construction
1923/24
Pencil, ink, gouache and collage
on transparent paper
54,5 x 40,5 cm
Netherlands Architecture Institute, Rotterdam
On permanent loan from the Cultural Heritage Agency
of the Netherlands (RCE)

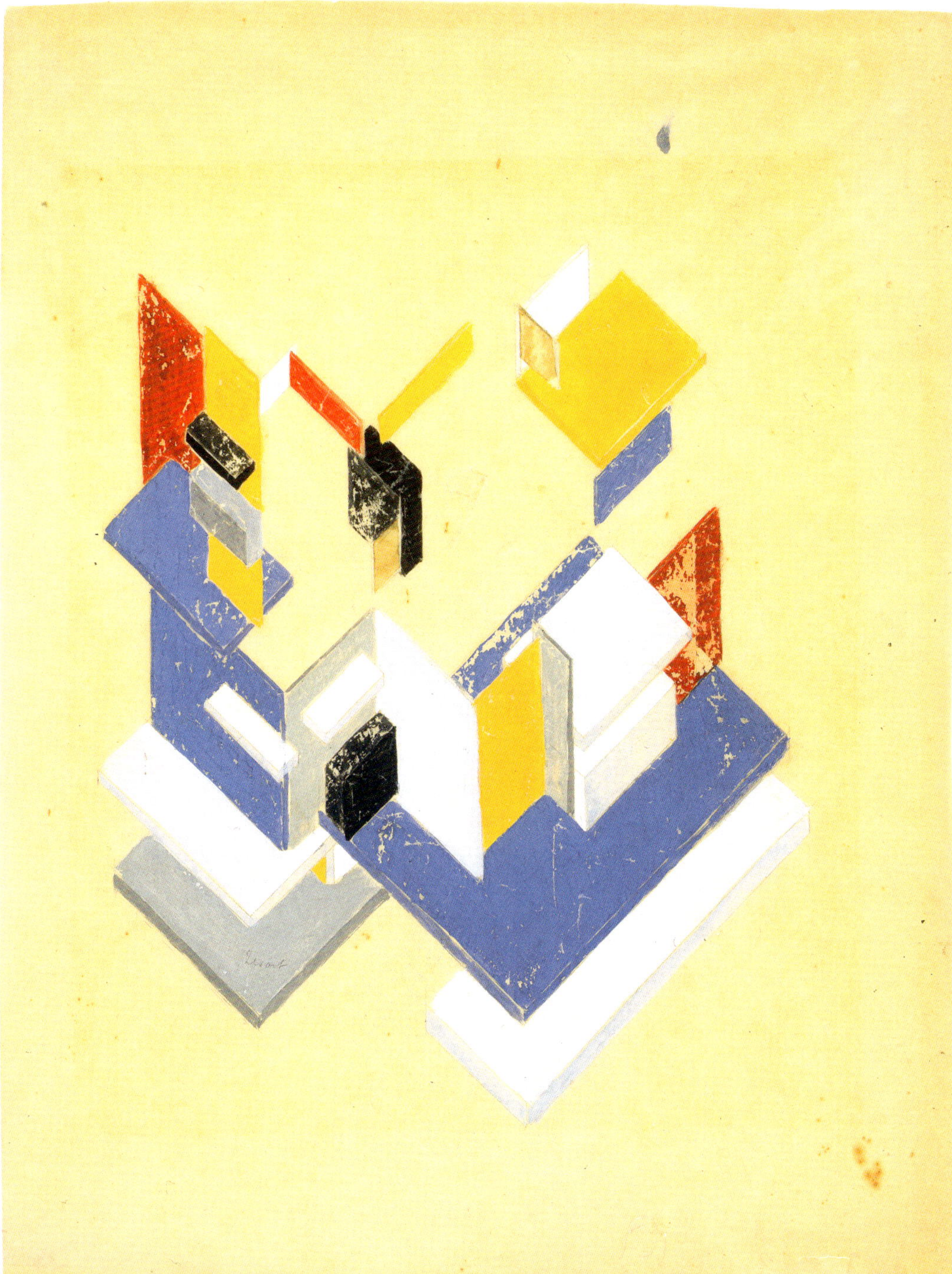

Zwischen 1925 und 1930 erschienen vierzehn Bände der von Walter Gropius und László Moholy-Nagy herausgegebenen *Bauhausbücher*. Moholy-Nagy gestaltete die Umschläge.
Für das Titelblatt von *Grundbegriffe der neuen gestaltenden Kunst* verwendete Moholy-Nagy einen Plakatentwurf von Theo van Doesburg.

J.J.P. Oud
Holländische Architektur
(Bauhausbücher, 10), München 1926

Piet Mondrian
Neue Gestaltung
(Bauhausbücher, 5), München 1925

Theo van Doesburg
Grundbegriffe der neuen gestaltenden Kunst
(Bauhausbücher, 6), München 1925

Bauhaus-Archiv Berlin und
Bayerische Staatsbibliothek München

Between 1925 and 1930 fourteen volumes of the *Bauhausbücher* were published, edited by Walter Gropius and László Moholy-Nagy. Their covers were designed by Moholy-Nagy.
He based the cover of *Grundbegriffe der neuen gestaltenden Kunst* by Theo van Doesburg on a design by the latter for an exhibition poster.

J.J.P. Oud
Holländische Architektur,
vol. 10: Bauhausbücher (Munich, 1926)

Piet Mondrian
Neue Gestaltung
vol. 5: Bauhausbücher (Munich, 1925)

Theo van Doesburg
Grundbegriffe der neuen gestaltenden Kunst
vol. 6: Bauhausbücher (Munich, 1925)

Bauhaus-Archiv Berlin and
Bayerische Staatsbibliothek München

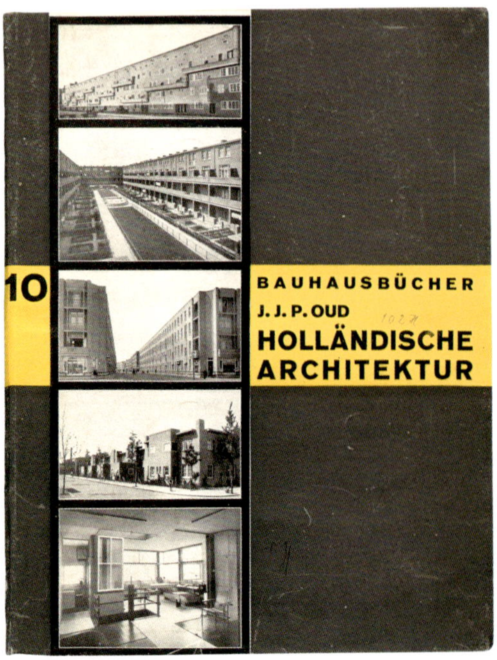

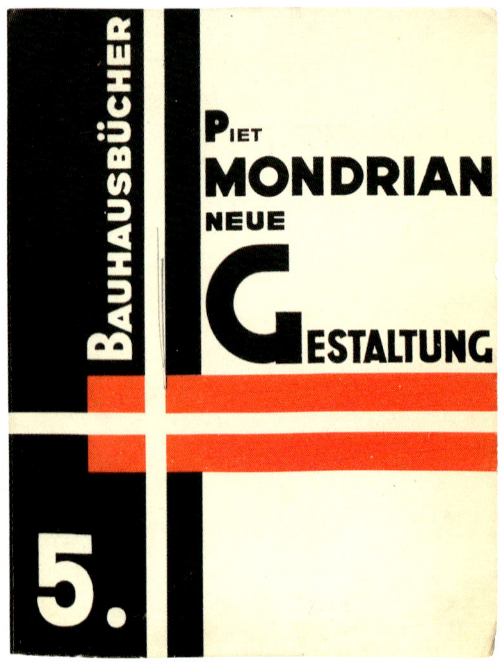

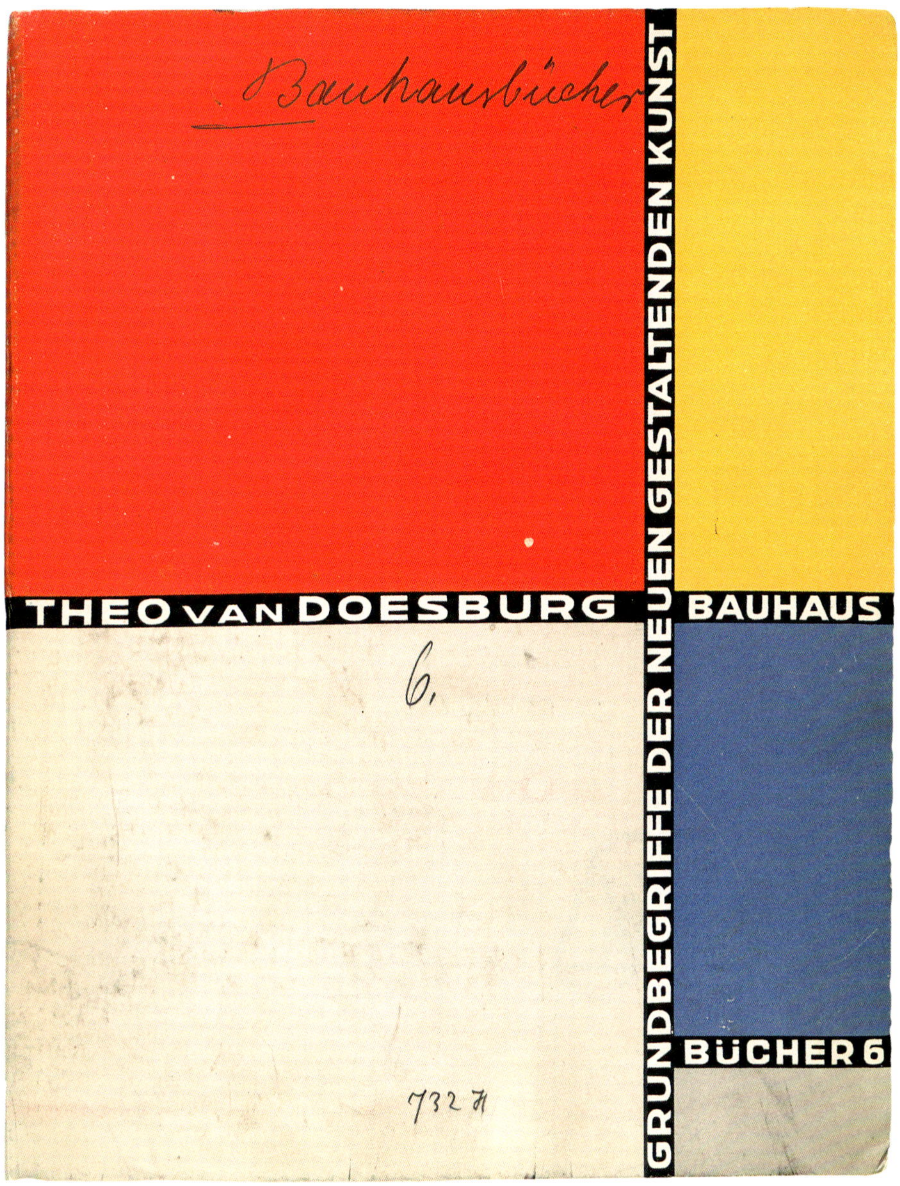
Bauhausbücher
GRUNDBEGRIFFE DER NEUEN GESTALTENDEN KUNST
THEO VAN DOESBURG
BAUHAUS
BÜCHER 6
6.

THEO VAN DOESBURG

CORNELIS VAN EESTEREN

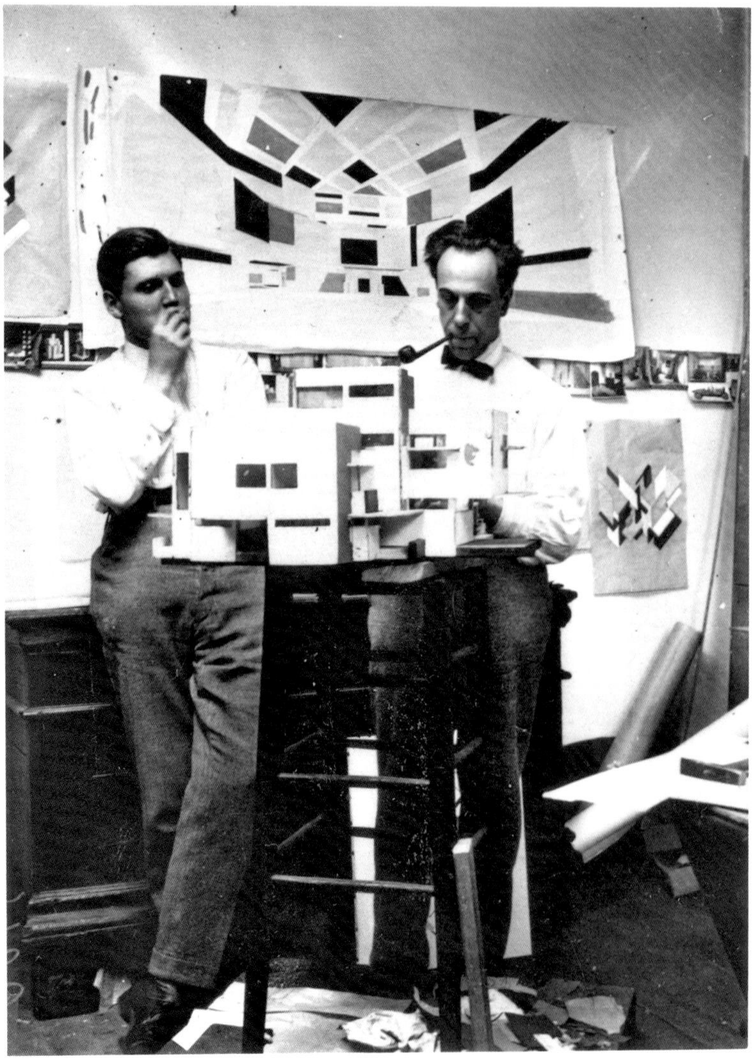

Cornelis van Eesteren und Theo van Doesburg arbeiten an einem Modell des Maison Particulière im Atelier in der Rue du Moulin Vert in Paris
1923
RKD, Archiv Theo und Nelly van Doesburg (Schenkung van Moorsel)

Cornelis van Eesteren and Theo van Doesburg work on the model of Maison Particulière at the Studio at Rue du Moulin Vert in Paris
1923
Archive of Theo and Nelly van Doesburg (Donation Van Moorsel)

Cornelis van Eesteren, 1897 in Kinderdijk bei Rotterdam als ältester Sohn eines Bauunternehmers geboren, beginnt seine Laufbahn als Zimmermann, Bauaufseher und Bauzeichner. 1914 besucht er in Rotterdam die Academie van Beeldende Kunsten en Technische Wetenschappen, nicht aber um Architekt zu werden, sondern um dort als künftiger Bauunternehmer die Entwurfsplanung zu erlernen. Eine Zeit lang zeichnet van Eesteren für verschiedene Architekten. Er gewinnt den Prix de Rome mit dem Entwurf eines Universitätsgebäudes für den Amsterdamer *Plan Süd*. Das Preisgeld ermöglicht ihm eine ausgedehnte Reise nach Deutschland. In Weimar lernt er Theo van Doesburg kennen, der ihn in die konstruktivistischen Künstlerkreise einführt. 1923 erarbeiten sie für die Galerie de l'Effort Moderne in Paris die Konzeption einer Ausstellung über *De Stijl* und Architektur, bei der eine Fülle von Reformen in der Entwurfspraxis vorgestellt werden. Zurück in Amsterdam zeichnet er für Jan Wils einige Entwürfe für das neue Olympiastadion. Mit van Doesburg gerät er in Streit, als dieser ein Manifest über die neue neoplastische Architektur veröffentlicht und van Eesterens Namen darin nicht nennt. Van Doesburg findet diese Reaktion übertrieben. Doch arbeiten die beiden eine Weile miteinander an verschiedenen Projekten, unter anderem an einer Ladenpassage in Den Haag. In den Entwürfen, die van Eesteren für die Neugestaltung des Rokin, einer wichtigen Verkehrsader in der Amsterdamer Innenstadt, zeichnet, zeigt sich, dass er von van Doesburgs »Elementarismus« beeinflusst ist. Zwischen 1927 und 1929 schreibt van Eesteren einige Beiträge für die Zeitschrift *i10*, was ihm wiederum van Doesburg übel nimmt. 1929 legt van Eesteren Pläne für die Stadterweiterung von Amsterdam vor, die international Beachtung finden und die die Grundlage für neue Architekturauffassungen beim Städtebau bilden. Im darauf folgenden Jahr wird er Vorsitzender der CIAM (Internationale Kongresse für moderne Architektur). Cornelis van Eesteren stirbt 1988 in Amsterdam.

Cornelis van Eesteren – born in 1897 in Kinderdijk, near Rotterdam, the eldest son of a builder, Van Eesteren began his career as a joiner, building supervisor and draftsman. He attended the Rotterdam Academie van Beeldende Kunsten en Technische Wetenschappen in 1914, not to become an architect, but to get acquainted with the design process for his future career as a builder. For a time he worked as a draftsman for various architects, winning the Prix de Rome with a design for a university building in Berlage's *Plan Zuid* expansion plan for Amsterdam. He used the prize money to travel to Germany where, in Weimar, he met Theo van Doesburg, who introduced him to Constructivist circles. Together, Van Eesteren and Van Doesburg organized an exhibition for Galerie L'Effort Moderne in Paris on the *De Stijl* and architecture, an exhibition that presented many reforms and dynamic innovations in design practice. After returning to Amsterdam, Van Eesteren produced some of the designs for the new Olympic Stadium by Jan Wils. He came into conflict with Van Doesburg when the latter published a manifesto on new plastic architecture without mentioning Van Eesteren's name. Van Doesburg regarded his response as exaggerated. However, they continued to work together on several projects, including a shopping arcade in The Hague. Van Eesteren also appears to have been influenced by Van Doesburg's "Elementarism" in plans he developed for the restructuring of Het Rokin, a major thoroughfare in the heart of Amsterdam. Between 1927 and 1929 Van Eesteren contributed to the journal *i10*, which Van Doesburg held against him. In 1929 Van Eesteren presented his urban development plans for Amsterdam, which met with international approval and laid the foundations for a new perspective on urban planning. The following year he became president of CIAM (International Congresses of Modern Architecture). Cornelis van Eesteren died 1988 in Amsterdam.

Theo van Doesburg
Cornelis van Eesteren
Modell für das Maison d'artiste
1923
Rekonstruktion 1983
Plexiglas, Polystyrol, Klebefolie, Holz
62 x 60 x 60 cm
Gemeentemuseum Den Haag

Theo van Doesburg
Cornelis van Eesteren
Model for Maison d'artiste
1923
Reconstruction 1983
Plexiglass, polystyrene, adhesive foil, wood
62 x 60 x 60 cm
Gemeentemuseum The Hague

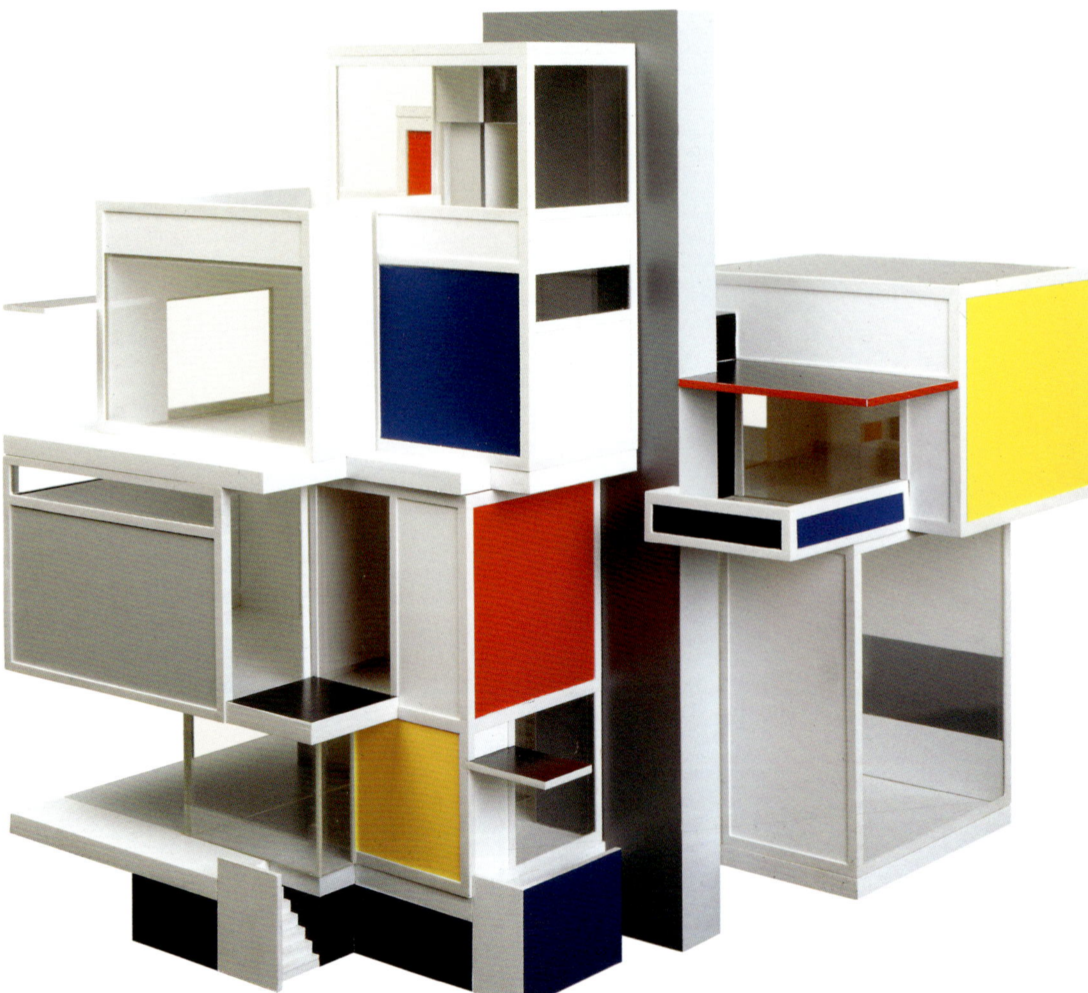

Theo van Doesburg
Cornelis van Eesteren
Modell für das Maison particulière
1923
Rekonstruktion 1982
Holz, Plexiglas
60,5 x 90 x 90 cm
Gemeentemuseum Den Haag

Theo van Doesburg
Cornelis van Eesteren
Model for Maison particulière
1923
Reconstruction 1982
Wood, plexiglass
60,5 x 90 x 90 cm
Gemeentemuseum The Hague

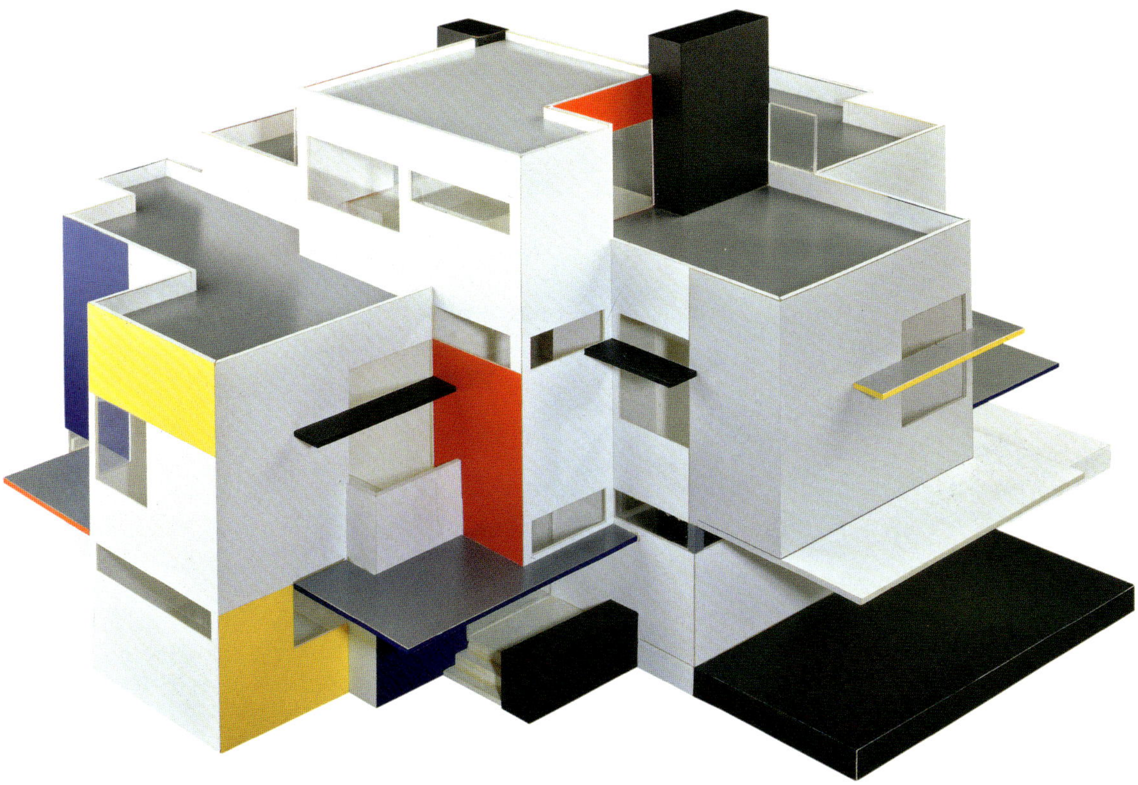

Theo van Doesburg
(Farbkonzept)
Cornelis van Eesteren
(Architektur)
Universitätshalle
Farbentwurf für die Decke
1923
Gouache auf Papier, montiert auf Karton
56 x 32,5 cm
Niederländisches Architekturinstitut, Rotterdam
Dauerleihgabe der Stiftung Van Eesteren,
Fluck & Lohuizen, Den Haag

Theo van Doesburg
(Color design)
Cornelis van Eesteren
(Architecture)
University hall
Color design for the ceiling
1923
Gouache on paper mounted on cardboard
56 x 32,5 cm
Netherlands Architecture Institute, Rotterdam
On permanent loan from the Van Eesteren,
Fluck & Lohuizen Foundation, The Hague

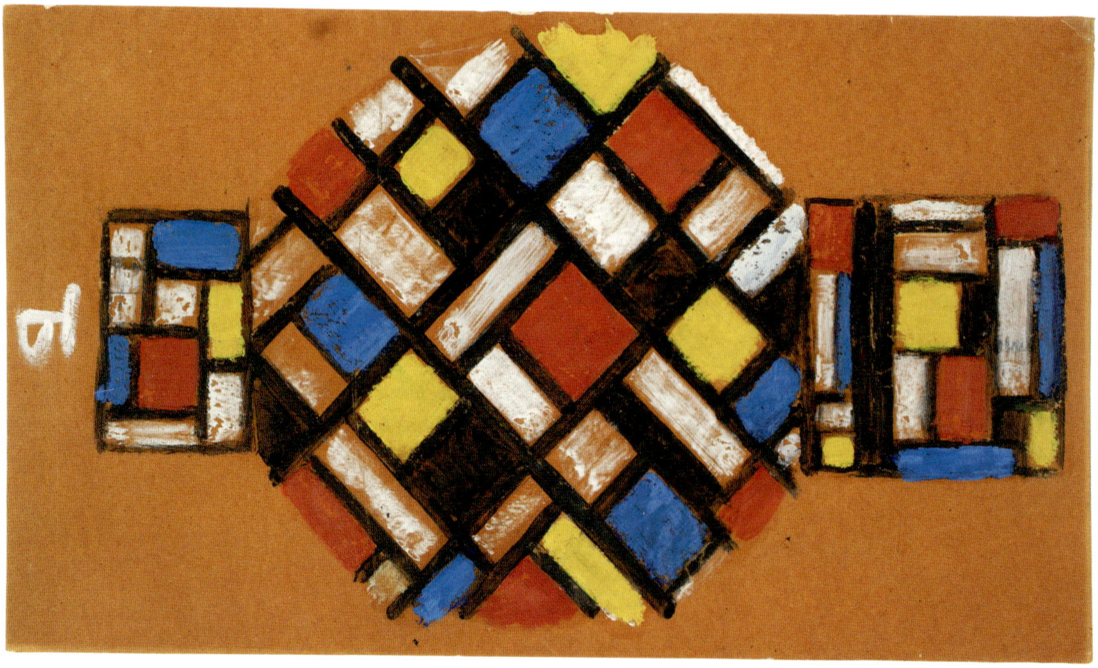

Theo van Doesburg
(Farbkonzept)
Cornelis van Eesteren
(Architektur)
Oben:
Universitätshalle,
perspektivische Darstellung in Richtung Treppe
1923
Ostindische Tusche und Gouache
auf Transparentpapier
61,5 x 144 cm
Unten:
Universitätshalle,
perspektivischer Farbentwurf in Richtung Treppe
1923
Bleistift, Gouache und Collage auf Papier
62 x 144 cm
Niederländisches Architekturinstitut, Rotterdam
Dauerleihgabe der Stiftung Van Eesteren,
Fluck & Lohuizen, Den Haag

Theo van Doesburg
(Color design)
Cornelis van Eesteren
(Architecture)
Top:
Perspective of university hall
towards staircase
1923
East Indian ink and gouache
on transparent paper
61,5 x 144 cm
Bottom:
Perspective in color of university hall
towards staircase
1923
Pencil, gouache and collage on paper
62 x 144 cm
Netherlands Architecture Institute, Rotterdam
On permanent loan from the Van Eesteren,
Fluck & Lohuizen Foundation, The Hague

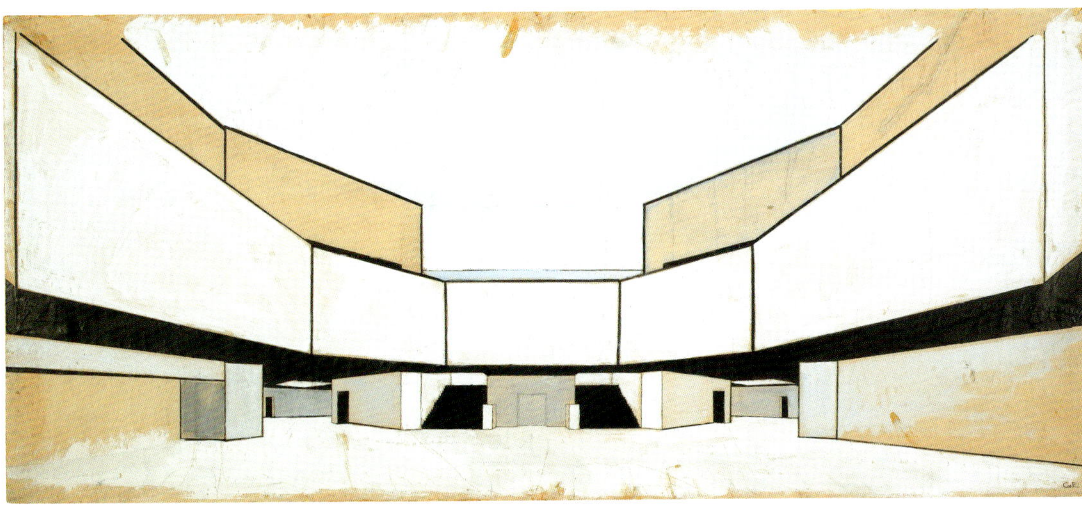

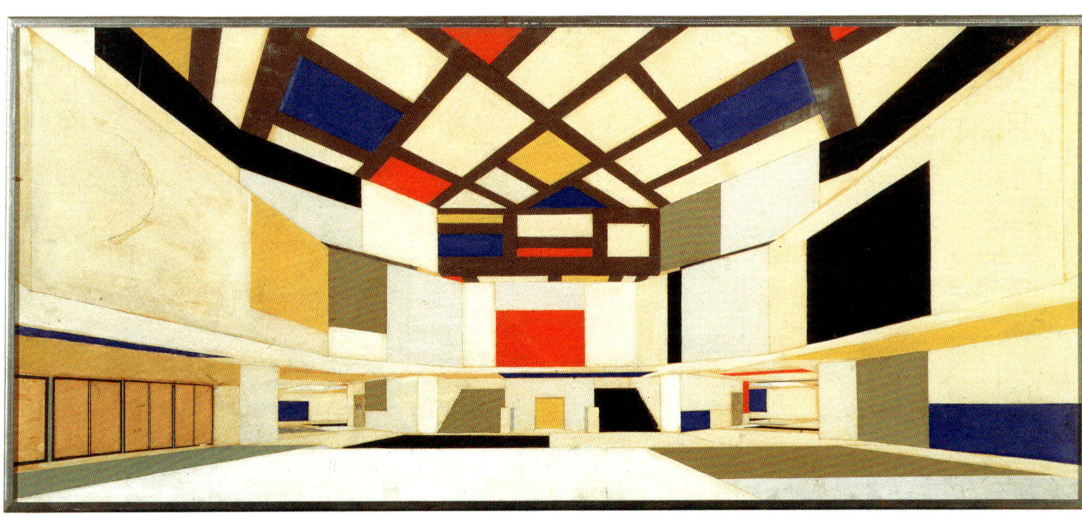

Theo van Doesburg
(Farbkonzept)
Cornelis van Eesteren
(Architektur)
Einkaufszentrum mit Bar-Restaurant
Axonometrische Darstellung und Fassade
mit endgültigem Farbkonzept
1924
Ostindische Tusche, Gouache und Collage
auf Lichtpause
35,5 x 72 cm
Niederländisches Architekturinstitut, Rotterdam
Dauerleihgabe der Stiftung Van Eesteren,
Fluck & Lohuizen, Den Haag

Theo van Doesburg
(Color design)
Cornelis van Eesteren
(Architecture)
Shopping arcade with bar-restaurant
Axonometric projection and facade
with final color design
1924
East Indian ink, gouache and collage
on blueprint
35,5 x 72 cm
Netherlands Architecture Institute, Rotterdam
On permanent loan from the Van Eesteren,
Fluck & Lohuizen Foundation, The Hague

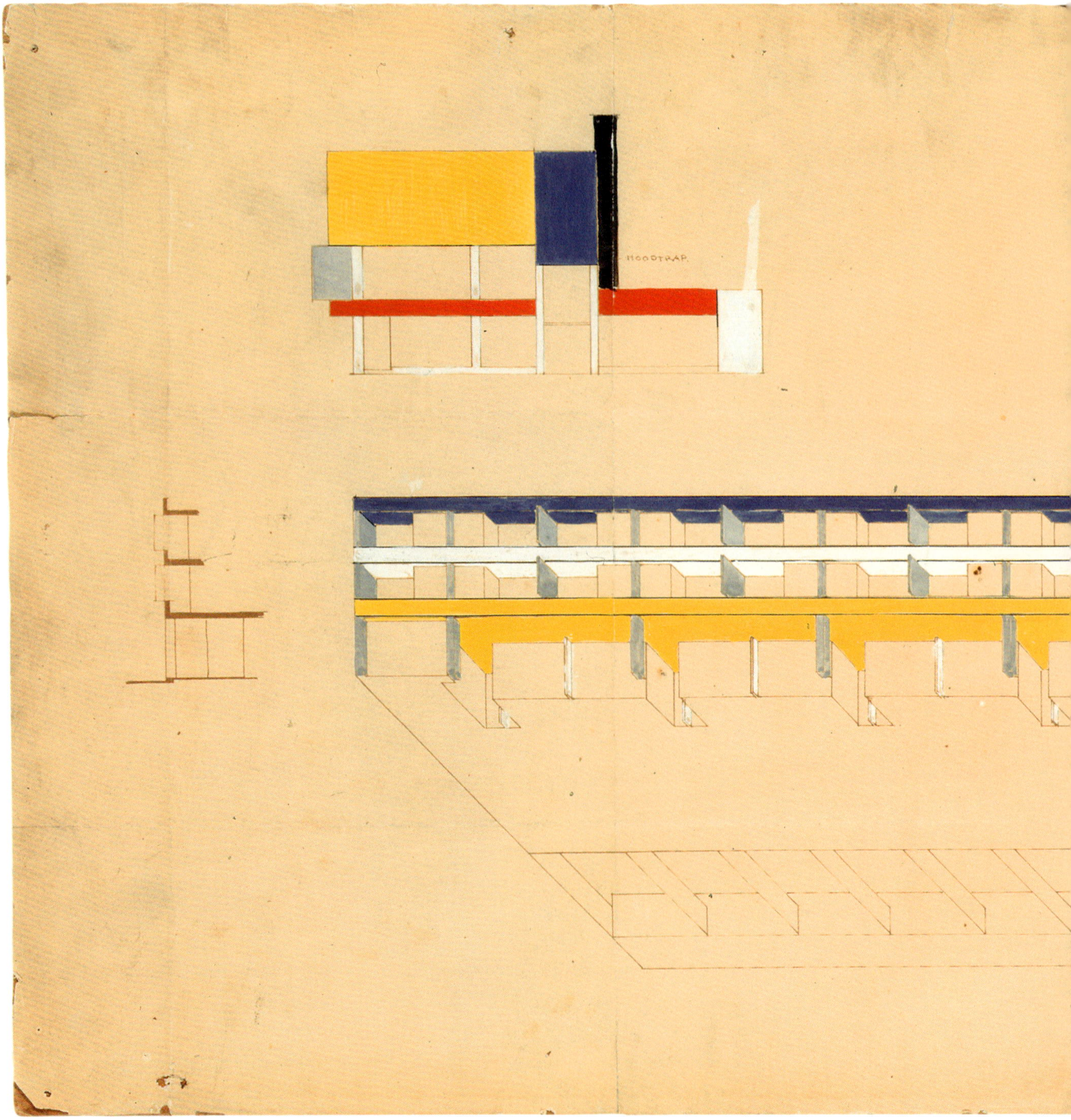

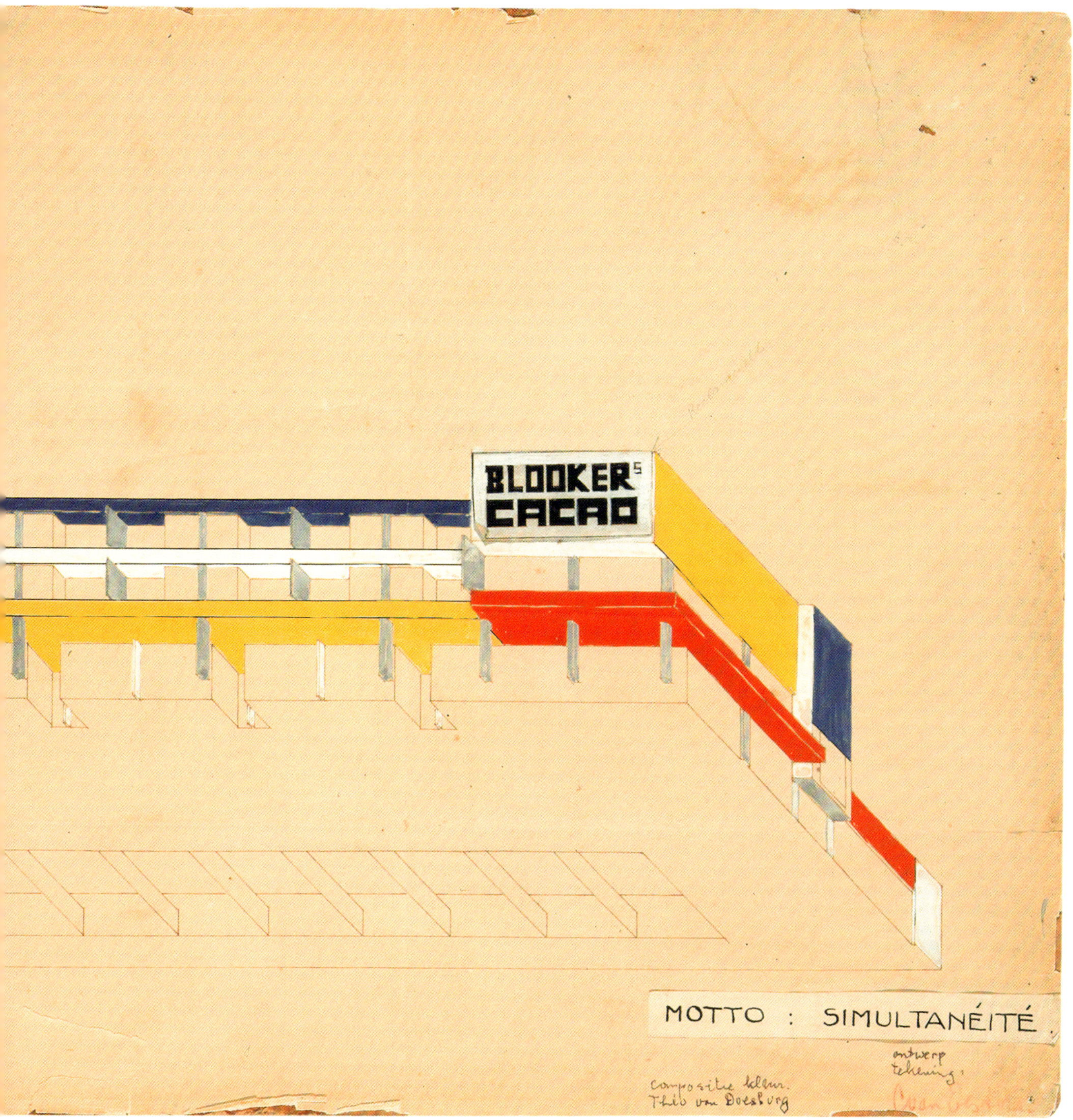
BLOOKER'S
CACAO
MOTTO : SIMULTANÉITÉ
ontwerp
tekening
compositie kleur.
Theo van Doesburg

THEO VAN DOESBURG

KURT SCHWITTERS

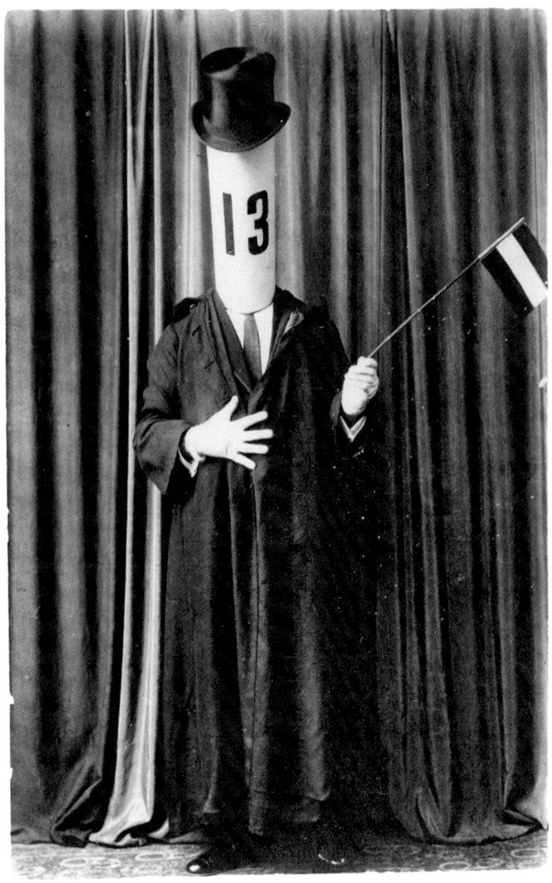

Photograph sent by Theo van Doesburg
to Antony Kok as a postcard with a picture of himself:
"Does à la micarême", Weimar
1922
RKD, Archive of Theo and Nelly van Doesburg
(Donation Van Moorsel)

Fotografie von Theo van Doesburg,
gesendet als Postkarte von van Doesburg an
Antony Kok: »Does à la micarême«, Weimar
1922
RKD, Archiv Theo und Nelly van Doesburg
(Schenkung van Moorsel)

Kurt Schwitters, 1887 in Hannover geboren, studiert dort erst an der Kunstgewerbeschule, bevor er sich an der Akademie der Künste in Dresden einschreibt. Nach dem Vorbild seiner Professoren malt Schwitters naturalistische und spätimpressionistische Bilder. Erst von 1918 an präsentiert er in der *Sturm*-Galerie in Berlin regelmäßig abstrakte Arbeiten. Die Zeitschrift *Der Sturm* veröffentlicht 1919 sein Gedicht »An Anna Blume«. In dieser Zeit arbeitet Schwitters in einer Metallfabrik als technischer Zeichner. Unter der Bezeichnung »Merzbilder« entstehen Schwitters Collagen und Assemblagen. Hans Richter stellt ihn 1920 Theo van Doesburg vor, der begeistert ist von der lebendigen Art und Weise, mit der Schwitters bei seinen Auftritten das Publikum in seinen Bann zieht. Ab 1921 veranstaltet Schwitters »Merzabende«, bei denen Texte vorgetragen werden und befreundete Künstlerkollegen auftreten. Ab den 1920er-Jahren sucht Schwitters in seinem Atelier nach Möglichkeiten, »alle Dinge der Welt miteinander zu verbinden«: Er errichtet eine Säule, aus der mit der Zeit kontinuierlich der *Merzbau* erwächst – eine raumfüllende Installation, die dem Betrachter den Orientierungssinn nimmt, ihn aber in eine aus Fragmenten zusammengesetzte Wunderwelt eintauchen lässt. Schwitters veröffentlicht in der vierten und der siebten *De Stijl*-Ausgabe. Mit Theo van Doesburg, Vilmos Huszár und Nelly van Doesburg organisiert er eine Dada-Tour durch die Niederlande. Für van Doesburgs Zeitschrift *Mécano* schreibt er Beiträge und gibt 1923 mit Merz selbst eine Zeitschrift heraus. Gleich in der ersten Ausgabe berichtet er von den Abenteuern, die er in den Niederlanden erlebt hat. Er verfasst Aufsätze und Gedichte für *G, i10, Pasmo, Fronta* und *Blok*, und in Zusammenarbeit mit van Doesburg entsteht das Kinderbuch *Die Scheuche*. 1928 rufen César Domela, Max Burchartz, El Lissitzky, László Moholy-Nagy und Schwitters den *Ring Neuer Werbegestalter* ins Leben. Er stellt bei der Vereinigung *Cercle et Carré* aus und schließt sich der Künstlergruppe *Abstraction-Création* an. 1936 besucht Schwitters in Paris Hans Arp und Piet Mondrian, ein Jahr später flüchtet er ins Exil nach Norwegen. 1940 folgt die Flucht nach England, wo er einen letzten Versuch unternimmt, sein Lebenswerk *Merzbau* aufzubauen. Kurt Schwitters stirbt 1948 in Kendal.

Kurt Schwitters – born 1887 in Hanover, Schwitters first studied at the Kunstgewerbeschule in Hanover and later enrolled at the Akademie der Künste in Dresden. After the example of his professors he painted in a Naturalist and Post- impressionist manner. Only in 1918 did he first show abstract works at the *Der Sturm* gallery in Berlin. His famous poem "An Anna Blume" was first published in 1919 in the magazine associated with the gallery. At that time Schwitters worked as a technical draftsman in a metal factory. He was making collages and assemblages, which he called "Merzbilder". In 1920 Hans Richter introduced him to Theo van Doesburg, who was fascinated by Schwitter's stage presence and the lively way Schwitters captivated his audience. As of 1921 he had organized "Merz evenings", at which texts were recited and artist friends gave performances. In his search for a way to "connect all things in the world" he set up a pillar in his studio from which over time the *Merzbau* grew–an installation filling an entire space in which the viewer looses his sense of orientation in exchange for immersion in a 'wonderworld' of fragments. Schwitters published articles in the fourth and seventh editions of *De Stijl*. Together with Theo van Doesburg, Vilmos Huszár and Nelly van Doesburg, Schwitters organized a Dada-tour of Germany and the Netherlands, and he also contributed articles to Van Doesburg's publication *Mécano*. In 1923 he launched the magazine Merz, with an account of his Dutch adventures in the first edition. He supplied articles and poems for *G, i10, Pasmo, Fronta* and *Blok* and produced a children's book, with Van Doesburg, entitled *Die Scheuche*. In 1928 Schwitters founded the *Ring Neuer Werbegestalter*, together with César Domela, Max Burchartz, El Lissitzky and László Moholy-Nagy. He took part in the *Cercle et Carré* group's exhibitions and joined the artists' association *Abstraction-Création*. In 1936 he traveled to Paris to visit Hans Arp and Piet Mondrian, the following year he went into exile in Norway before fleeing to England in 1940, where he renewed his efforts to breathe new life into his *Merzbau* project. Kurt Schwitters died 1948 in Kendal.

Theo van Doesburg
Kurt Schwitters
Poster für eine kleine Dada-Soirée
1922
Lithographie auf Papier
30,4 x 30,4 cm
Gemeentemuseum Den Haag

Theo van Doesburg
Kurt Schwitters
Poster for Small Dada Soirée
1922
Lithograph on paper
30,4 x 30,4 cm
Gemeentemuseum The Hague

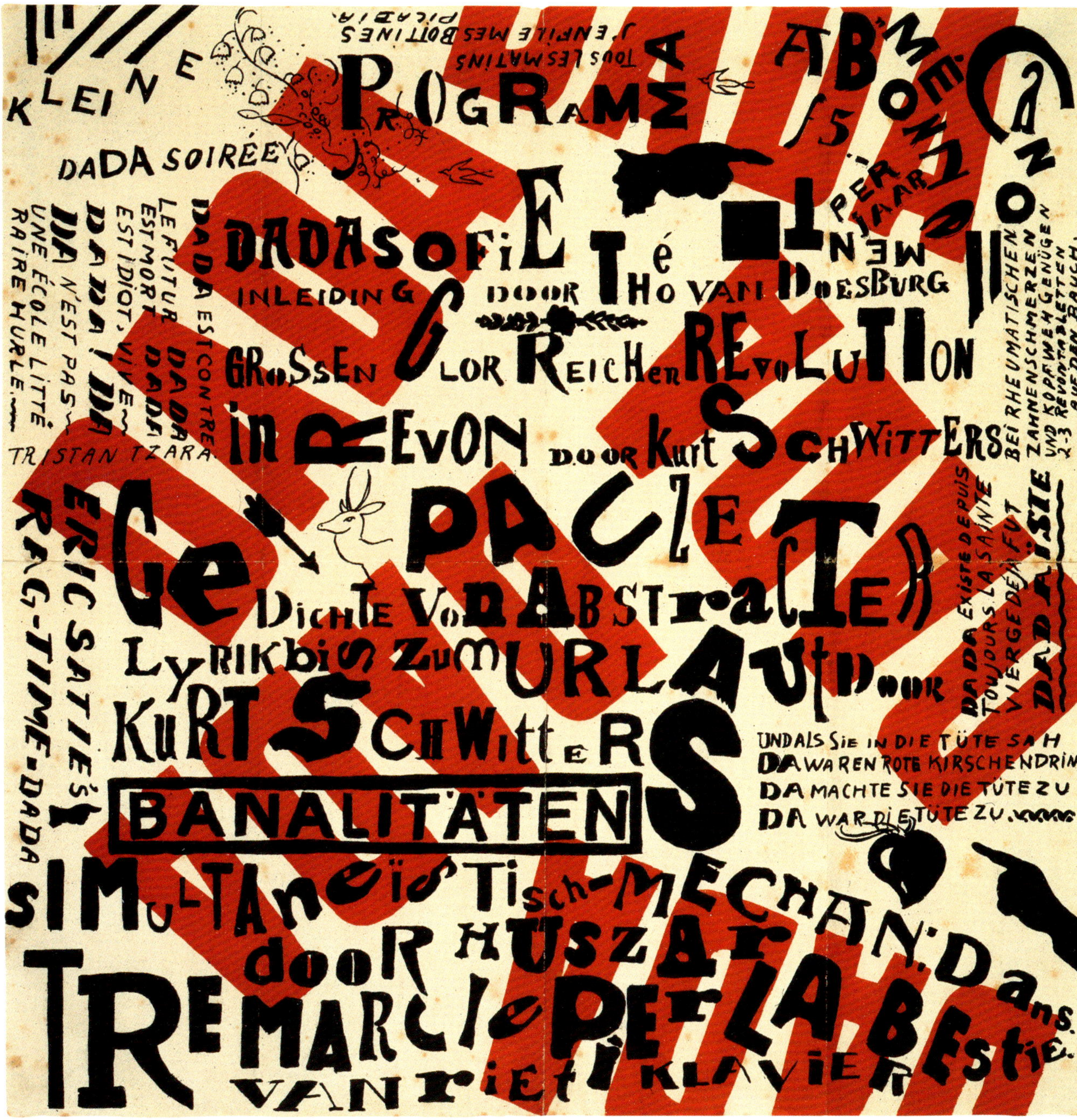

CESAR DOMELA

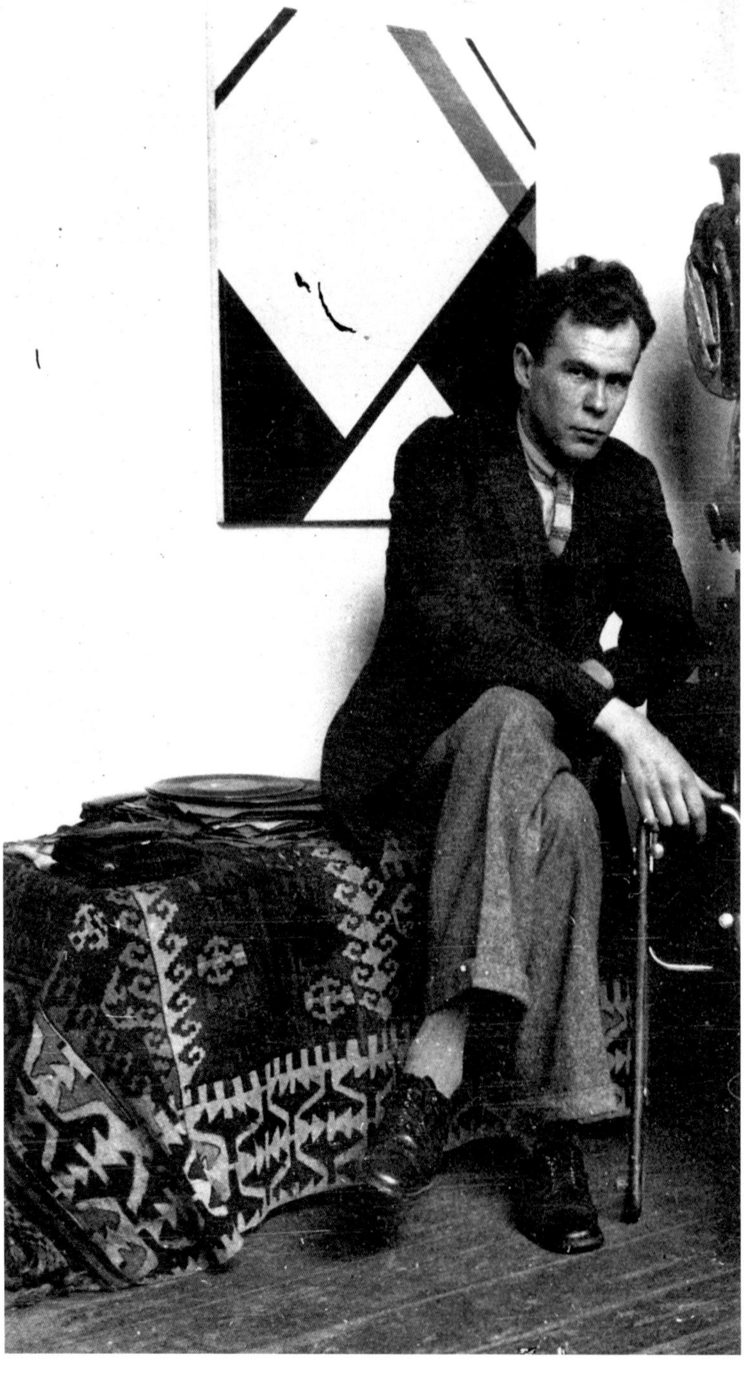

Porträt César Domela
Sammlung RKD Den Haag

Portrait César Domela
Collection RKD The Hague

César Domela, wird 1900 in Amsterdam als Sohn des sozialistischen Politikers Ferdinand Domela Nieuwenhuis geboren. Er sieht seinen Vater nur selten, braucht aber sehr lange, um sich von dem übermächtigen Selbstbewusstsein des Vaters zu befreien.
1914, bei einem Aufenthalt in Paris, kommt er mit Kunst und Künstlern in Berührung. Domela kann aber erst nach dem Tod des Vaters seinen Plan ausführen, selbst Künstler zu werden: 1919 geht er nach Ascona, wo er mit der Künstlerkolonie am Monte Verità den Widerwillen gegen materialistische Tendenzen in der industrialisierten Gesellschaft teilt. Er begegnet dort Hans Richter, Hans Arp und Hugo Ball. Domela beginnt sich nun ernsthaft mit Malerei zu beschäftigen.
In Berlin erlernt er 1923 in linksradikalen Kreisen die Techniken der Fotomontage und der Typografie. 1924, wieder in Paris, trifft er Mondrian und van Doesburg das erste Mal. Domela arbeitet fortan neoplastisch und nimmt an verschiedenen Ausstellungen teil. In seinen Bildern werden nun die Horizontalen und Vertikalen von Diagonalen abgelöst. Dabei hält er sich jedoch nicht an die elementaristischen Werke von van Doesburg, bei denen die Diagonale ebenfalls ein wesentliches Formelement darstellt. 1927 arbeitet er an einigen Ausgaben der Zeitschrift *i10* mit. Durch seine Beherrschung der Typografie und der Fotomontage und wegen seines ausgeprägten Materialgefühls schafft er Gemälde, die immer räumlicher werden: Ab 1930 bringt er Materialien wie Plexiglas, Metall und Holz in einer gemalten Umgebung zusammen und bricht damit die vorgegebenen Grenzen eines Bildträgers auf. Domela schließt sich der Künstlergruppe *Cercle et Carré* an und macht wie Vantongerloo nun die gebogene Linie zum Hauptmotiv seiner Skulpturen. Damit wendet er sich endgültig von den rechtwinkligen Strukturen der Kunst Mondrians ab. César Domela stirbt 1992 in Paris.

César Domela – born 1900 in Amsterdam, the son of socialist leader Ferdinand Domela Nieuwenhuis. Though he rarely saw his father, it took him many years to wrestle free of his overbearing ego. In 1914 he spent time in Paris, where he first came into contact with artists, but it was only after his father's death that he was able to pursue his ambition of becoming an artist himself. Domela traveled to Ascona, where he associated with the Monte Verità circle, with whom he shared an aversion to the materialist tendencies of industrialized society. It was there he met Hans Richter, Hans Arp and Hugo Ball. Domela began to devote himself seriously to painting. In leftist circles in Berlin he learned the techniques of photomontage and typography. In 1924 he was in Paris, where he met Mondrian and Van Doesburg. He began to work in a neoplastic style, and participated in several exhibitions, displaying works in which the horizontal and vertical were replaced by diagonals. He did not, however, identify with Van Doesburg's Elementarism, where the diagonal also played an essential role. In 1927 he collaborated on several editions of *i10*. Influenced by his typographical work and photomontage, as well as his keen feeling for materials, his paintings became increasingly spatial, and from 1930 onward they incorporated materials such as plexiglass, metal and wood in a painted setting—also going beyond the confines of the painting. Domela became a member of the *Cercle et Carré* artists' association and, together with Vantongerloo, introduced the curve as the main motif of his sculptures thus distancing himself from Mondrian's neoplastic rectangular structures. César Domela died 1992 in Paris.

César Domela
Relief néoplastique no. 10
1930
Öl auf Holz, Plexiglas, Messing
110 x 110 cm
Gemeentemuseum Den Haag

César Domela
Neoplastic relief no. 10
1930
Oil on wood, plexiglass, brass
110 x 110 cm
Gemeentemuseum The Hague

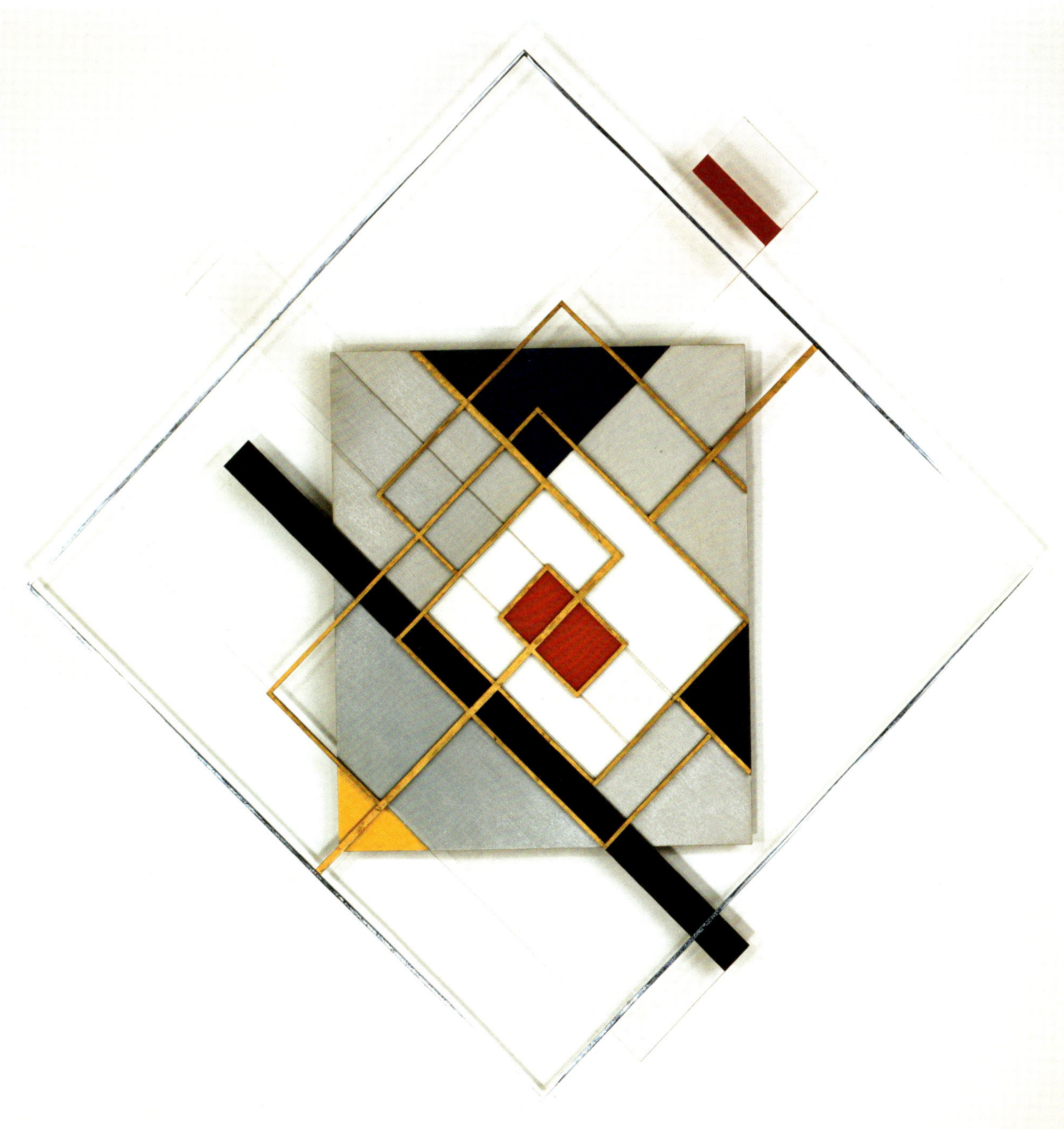

César Domela
Stills aus einem Reklamefilm für ein Elektrizitätsunternehmen
1927
Fotopapier
17 x 24 cm
Gemeentemuseum Den Haag

César Domela
Stills from an advertising film for an electricity company
1927
Photographic paper
17 x 24 cm
Gemeentemuseum The Hague

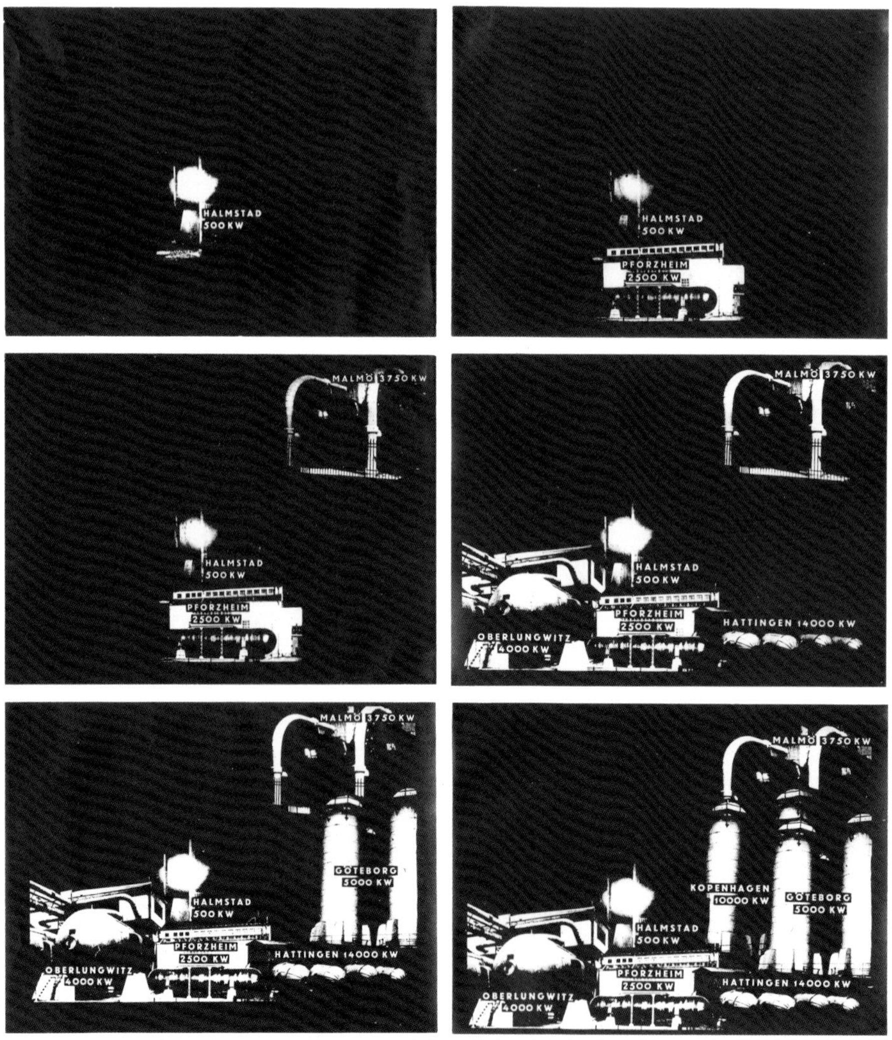

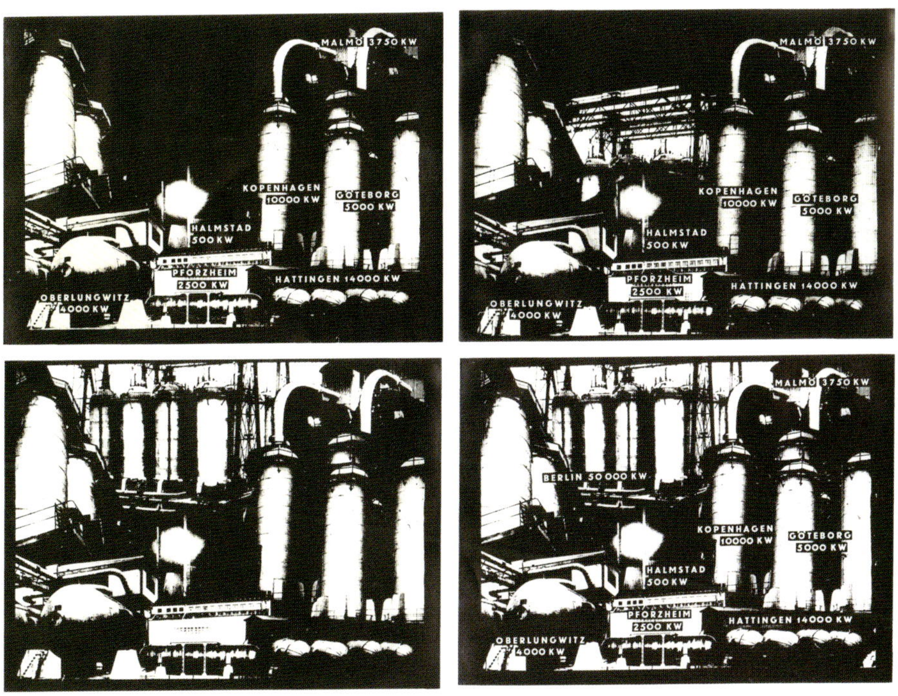
MALMÖ 3750 KW
KOPENHAGEN 10000 KW
GÖTEBORG 5000 KW
HALMSTAD 500 KW
PFORZHEIM 2500 KW
HATTINGEN 14000 KW
OBERLUNGWITZ 4000 KW
MALMÖ 3750 KW
KOPENHAGEN 10000 KW
GÖTEBORG 5000 KW
HALMSTAD 500 KW
PFORZHEIM 2500 KW
HATTINGEN 14000 KW
OBERLUNGWITZ 4000 KW
MALMÖ 3750 KW
BERLIN 50 000 KW
KOPENHAGEN 10000 KW
GÖTEBORG 5000 KW
HALMSTAD 500 KW
PFORZHEIM 2500 KW
HATTINGEN 14000 KW
OBERLUNGWITZ 4000 KW

César Domela
Fotomontage für die Firma Ruths-Speicher
1928
Vintageaufnahme einer Fotomontage,
auf Karton geklebt
44,5 x 38 cm
Gemeentemuseum Den Haag

César Domela
Photomontage for the Ruths-Speicher Company
1928
Vintage photo of a photomontage,
mounted on cardboard
44,5 x 38 cm
Gemeentemuseum The Hague

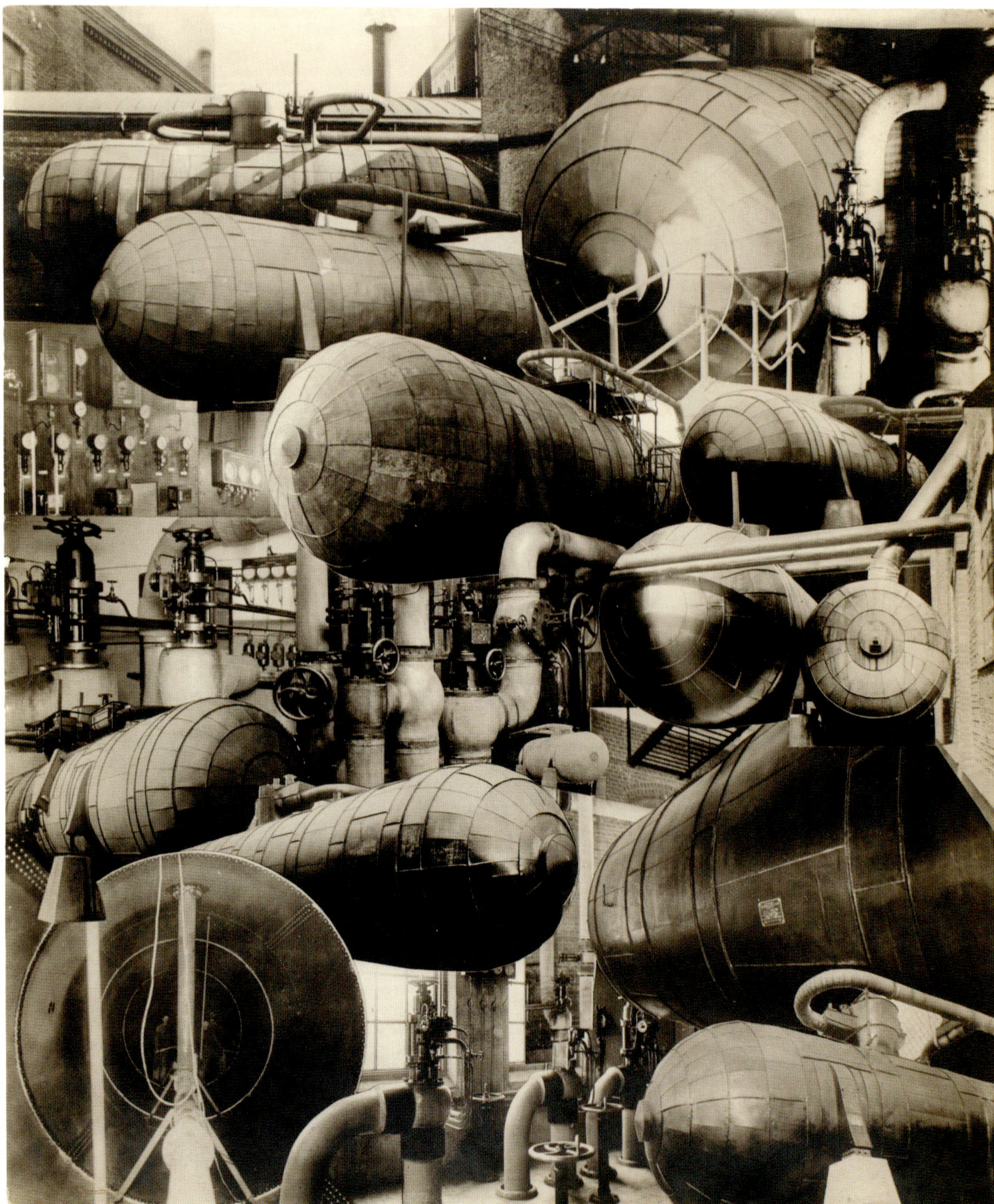

César Domela
Fotomontage für die Firma Ruths-Speicher
1928
Vintageaufnahme einer Fotomontage,
auf Karton geklebt
47,3 x 34,4 cm
Gemeentemuseum Den Haag

César Domela
Photomontage for the Ruths-Speicher Company
1928
Vintage photo of a photomontage,
mounted on cardboard
47,3 x 34,4 cm
Gemeentemuseum The Hague

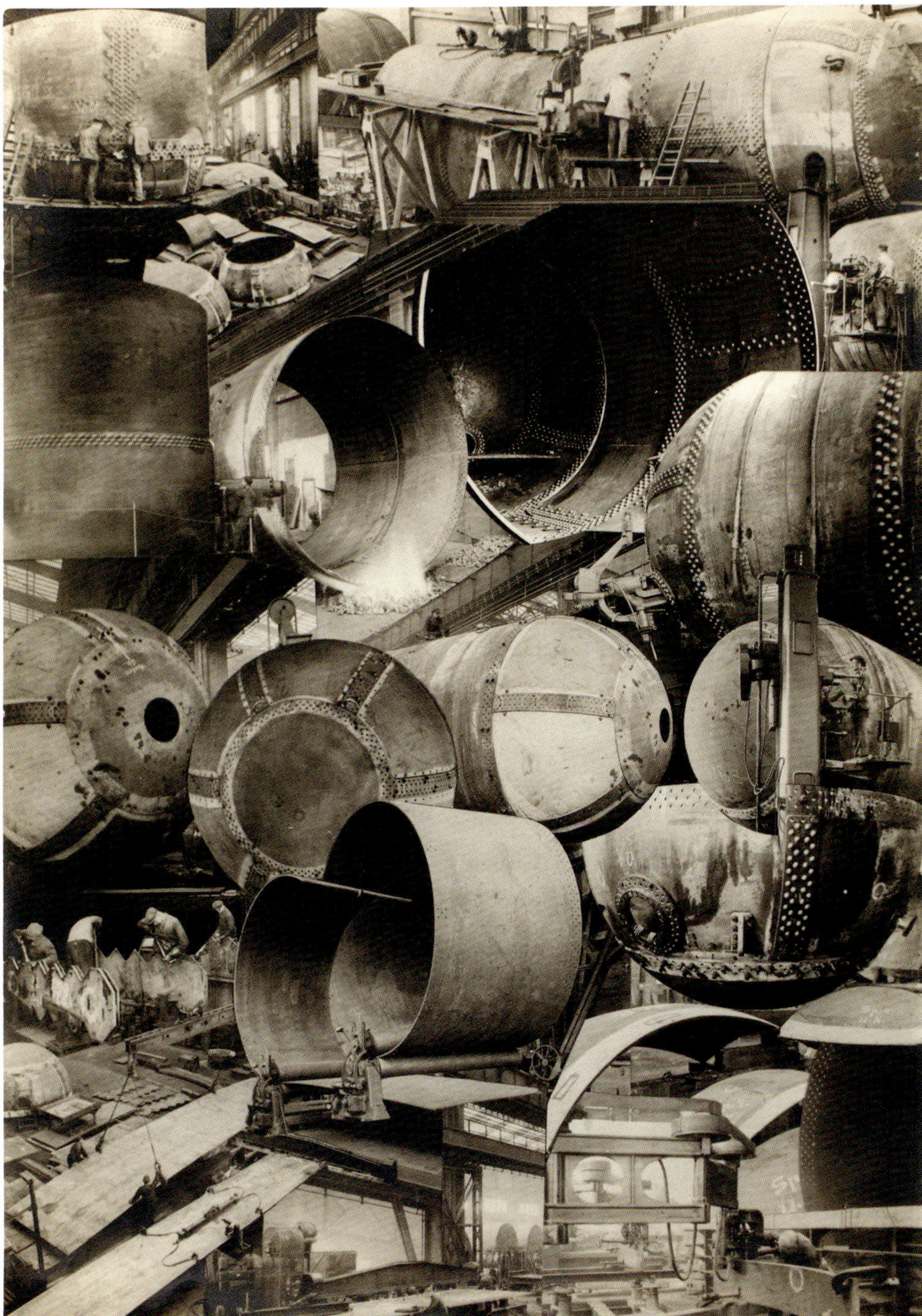

VIKING EGGELING

Viking Eggeling wird 1880 in Lund, Schweden, als Sohn deutscher Eltern geboren. 1897 siedelt er nach Deutschland über, studiert Kunstgeschichte und arbeitet als Buchhändler. Ab 1911 verbringt er viel Zeit in Paris, wo er auf Hans Arp und Friedrich Kiesler trifft. Auch Ascona besucht er oft, da er der Künstlerkolonie am nahegelegenen Monte Verità angehört: Man isst vegetarisch, lebt die Spiritualität und widmet sich der Bewegung und dem Ausdruckstanz. In dieser Zeit malt Eggeling kubistische Bilder. Ab 1915 wohnt er in Zürich, wo er an detaillierten Studien über geometrische Elemente arbeitet. Eggeling schließt sich der Züricher Dada-Bewegung an und tritt im Cabaret Voltaire auf. Tristan Tzara stellt ihm Hans Richter vor, mit dem er über mehrere Jahre zusammenarbeiten wird. 1919 hält Eggeling in Zürich einen bahnbrechenden Vortrag über elementare Gestaltung und abstrakte Kunst. In Deutschland arbeitet er später an einer Vielzahl von Zeichnungen mit geometrischen Formelementen, Verschiebungen und Richtungsänderungen. Er nennt dies den »Generalbass der Malerei«. Mit dieser Bezeichnung verweist er darauf, dass geometrische Formen so angeordnet werden können, dass sie als Bewegung in der Zeit wahrnehmbar werden und daher mit der rhythmischen Wahrnehmung von Musik vergleichbar sind. Das bringt ihn zu ersten Filmexperimenten, in denen Rhythmus und Bewegung auf der Leinwand erzeugt werden. 1920 sieht Theo van Doesburg diese Filmexperimente und schreibt in *De Stijl* begeistert über »Abstrakte Filmbilder«. Viking Eggeling stirbt 1925 in Berlin.

Viking Eggeling – born 1880 of German parents in Lund, Sweden. In 1897 the family returned to Germany where Viking Eggeling took a job as a bookseller and studied art history. From 1911 he made several trips to Paris, where he came into contact with Hans Arp and Friedrich Kiesler. He also paid regular visits to Ascona, where he joined an artist colony at Monte Verità that practiced vegetarianism, and explored spirituality and the meaning of dance and movement. He was then painting in a Cubist style. In 1915 he moved to Zurich, where he began an in-depth study of geometric elements.
He was part of the Zurich Dada movement and performed at the Cabaret Voltaire. Tristan Tzara introduced him to Hans Richter, and they began a collaboration that would last for several years. In 1919 Eggeling gave a groundbreaking lecture in Zurich on elementary design and abstract art. In Germany over the next few years he worked on a variety of drawings with geometric elements, shifts, and changes of direction based on his "Generalbass der Malerei". His way of arranging geometric shapes so they become perceptible as if in movement was similar to the rhythmic experience of music. This led Eggeling to experiment with film, creating rhythm and movement on the screen. Theo van Doesburg saw these experiments in 1920 and published an enthusiatic article about "abstract film images" in *De Stijl.* Viking Eggeling died 1925 in Berlin.

Viking Eggeling
Symphonie Diagonale
1921–1924
Filmstreifen, 35 mm, schwarz-weiß (Stummfilm)
Privatsammlung

Viking Eggeling
Symphonie Diagonale
1921–1924
Filmstrip, 35 mm, black and white (silent film)
Private Collection

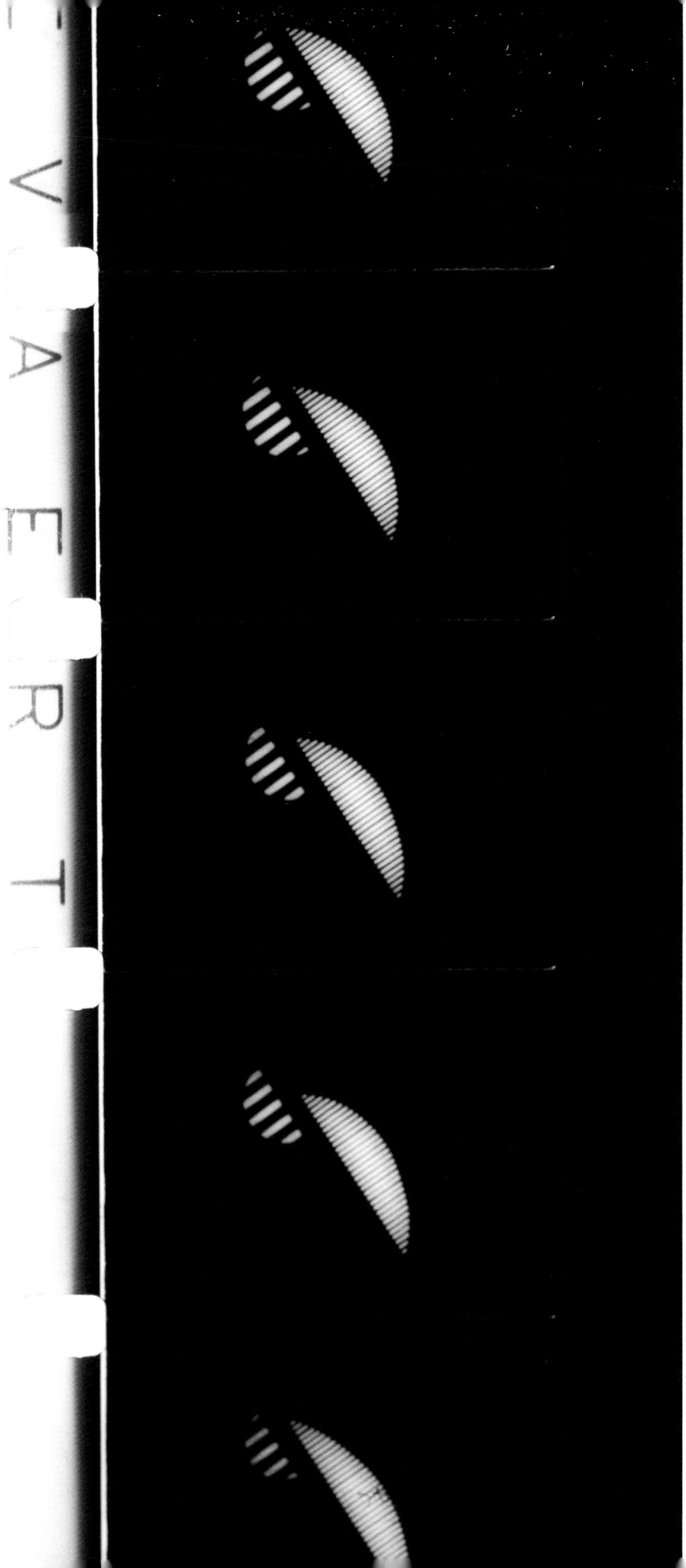

HENRI LE FAUCONNIER

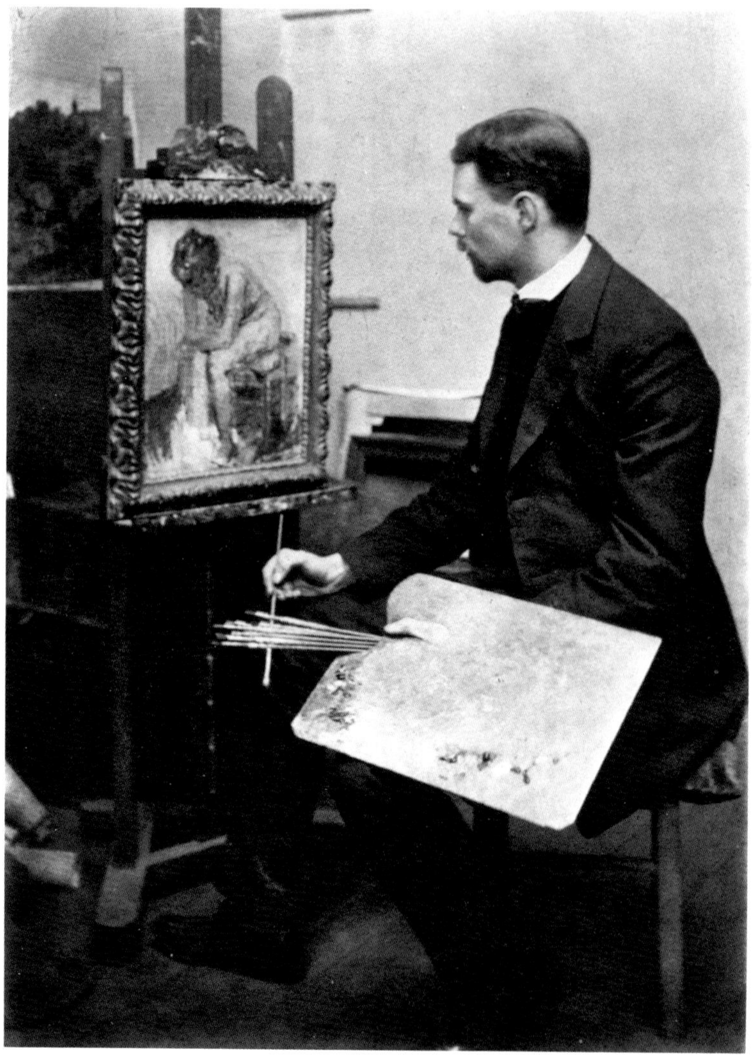

Henri Le Fauconnier
Collection RKD The Hague

Henri Le Fauconnier
Sammlung RKD Den Haag

Henri Le Fauconnier, 1881 im nordfranzösischen Hesdin als Henri Fauconnier geboren, zieht 1901 nach Paris, um Jura zu studieren. Dort angekommen, beschließt er, Maler zu werden; 1905 nennt er sich »Le Fauconnier«. Er schreibt sich an der Académie Julian ein und beteiligt sich am Salon des Indépendants mit einem Gemälde, das ganz dem Stil von Henri Matisse verpflichtet ist. 1907/08 wohnt Le Fauconnier in der Bretagne. Er lernt 1910 Conrad Kickert kennen, der in den Niederlanden gerade eine neue Künstlervereinigung aufbaut. Im selben Jahr trifft er auch Wassily Kandinsky. Le Fauconnier verfasst daraufhin einen theoretischen Beitrag über neue Kunst für den Katalog der zweiten Ausstellung der Münchener *Neuen Künstlervereinigung* und stellt dort selbst einige kubistische Gemälde aus, die zuvor schon im Saal 41 im Pariser Salon des Indépendants für Furore gesorgt hatten. 1911 wurden Bilder von Le Fauconnier in Amsterdam ausgestellt, unter anderem das großformatige Bild *Der Überfluss.* So kam unter anderem Piet Mondrian in Kontakt mit der Malerei Le Fauconniers. Der Kubismus Le Fauconniers zeichnet sich dadurch aus, dass Gegenstand oder Figur gerade noch zu erkennen sind; Apollinaire nennt es einen »physischen Kubismus«. Nach 1912 wendet sich Le Fauconnier vom Kubismus ab und widmet sich stattdessen einem figurativen Expressionismus. Damit entfernt er sich sehr weit von *De Stijl.* 1946 stirbt Henri Le Fauconnier in Paris.

Henri Le Fauconnier – born Henri Fauconnier in Hesdin near Calais in northern France, 1881. In 1901 he went to Paris intending to study law, but soon decided to become a painter. He enrolled at Académie Julian, changed his name to "Le Fauconnier", and showed work in the style of Matisse at the Salon des Indépendants. In 1907 and 1908 he worked in Brittany, and in 1910 he became acquainted with Conrad Kickert, who was at that time establishing a new artists' association in the Netherlands. That same year he met Kandinsky, who asked him to write an essay on the theory of modern art for the catalogue of the second exhibition staged by the *Neue Künstlervereinigung* in Munich. To this exhibition, Le Fauconnier also contributed several Cubist paintings which had previously caused a stir in Paris at the gallery 41 of the Salon des Indépendants. In an exhibition of Le Fauconnier's in Amsterdam in 1911, where he showed, among others, the large-format painting *Abundance,* Piet Mondrian also saw Le Fauconnier's work. In Le Fauconnier's Cubist paintings, the subject or figure remained only just recognizable; Apollinaire called it "physical Cubism". After 1912 he rejected Cubism, turning toward a figurative Expressionism that took him far away from *De Stijl.* In 1946 Henri Le Fauconnier died in Paris.

Henri Le Fauconnier
Der Überfluss
1910
Öl auf Leinwand
191,5 x 123 cm
Gemeentemuseum Den Haag

Henri Le Fauconnier
Abundance
1910
Oil on canvas
191,5 x 123 cm
Gemeentemuseum The Hague

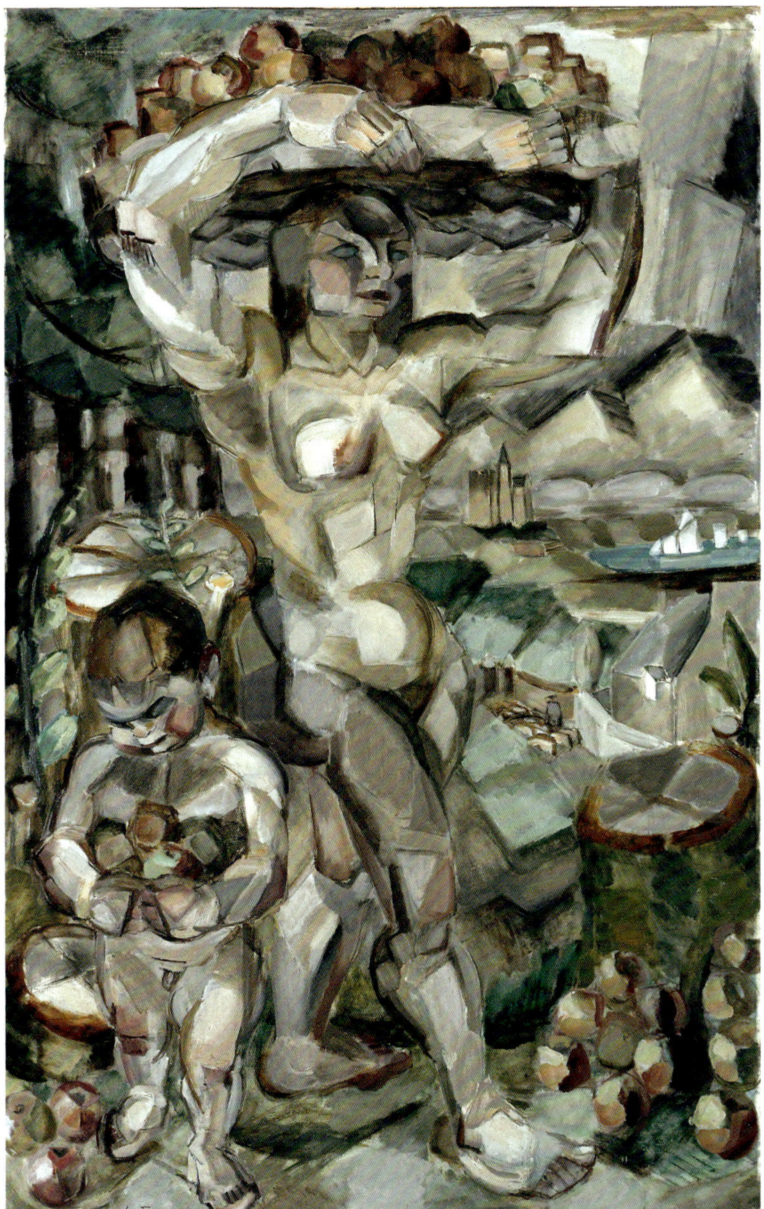

JEAN ALBERT GORIN

Jean Albert Gorin, geboren 1899 in Saint-Emilien-de-Blain bei Nantes, besucht als 14-Jähriger Paris und stößt dort bereits erstmals auf kubistische Kunst. 1916 wird er zum Militärdienst eingezogen und an die Front geschickt. Nach dem Krieg lebt er wieder in der Nähe von Nantes. Er fängt zu malen an und orientiert sich dabei an Matisse, van Gogh und Cézanne. 1922 wendet er sich dem Kubismus zu und arbeitet fortan abstrakt. In der Zeitschrift *Vouloir* sieht er Werke von Piet Mondrian, Theo van Doesburg und Vilmos Huszár. Gorin korrespondiert mit Georges Vantongerloo und besucht Mondrian 1927 in dessen Atelier, was ihn entscheidend beeinflusst; er ist von der Ästhetik von *De Stijl* begeistert. Vor diesem Hintergrund versucht er, das Gemälde in ein dreidimensionales Kunstwerk, ein Relief, zu transformieren. 1926 oder 1927 beginnt er, nach einer Begegnung mit Michel Seuphor, neoplastische Möbel und Interieurs zu gestalten, die er 1928 in Lille ausstellt. Sein Interesse für Architektur wächst. Gorin steht in intensivem Austausch mit Hans Arp und Georges Vantongerloo. Theo van Doesburg trifft er nie persönlich und doch ist Gorin von dessen Ideen und Werken äußerst beeindruckt. Erst nach dessen Tod reist Gorin nach Meudon und besucht das Haus seines Idols. 1981 stirbt Jean Albert Gorin in Niort.

Jean Albert Gorin – born 1899 in Saint-Emilien-de-Blain near Nantes. At the age of 14 Gorin traveled to Paris where he saw Cubist art in the galleries on Rue de la Boétie. In 1916 he was drafted into the army and sent to the front. After the war he settled near Nantes and began to paint in the manner of Matisse, Van Gogh and Cézanne. In 1922 Gorin turned to Cubism and from then on worked in an abstract manner. He also saw work by Piet Mondrian, Theo van Doesburg and Vilmos Huszár in the magazine *Vouloir*. He started corresponding with Georges Vantongerloo and in 1927 met Mondrian in his studio, an event which had a great impact on his work. Under the influence of *De Stijl* aesthetics he tried to transform painting into a three-dimensional art form, a relief. In 1926-27 he met Michel Seuphor and started designing neoplastic furniture and interiors. He exhibited the latter in Lille and developed an interest in architecture. Gorin maintained an intensive exchange of ideas with Hans Arp and Georges Vantongerloo. Although he never met Theo van Doesburg, Gorin was impressed by his ideas and style. It was not until after Van Doesburg's death that he traveled to Meudon, to visit the house where his idol had lived. In 1981 Jean Albert Gorin died in Niort.

Jean Albert Gorin
Composition néoplastique à lignes en creux N 29
1931
Holz, Farbe
66,7 x 66,7 x 2,5 cm
Gemeentemuseum Den Haag

Jean Albert Gorin
Composition néoplastique à lignes en creux N 29
1931
Wood, paint
66,7 x 66,7 x 2,5 cm
Gemeentemuseum The Hague

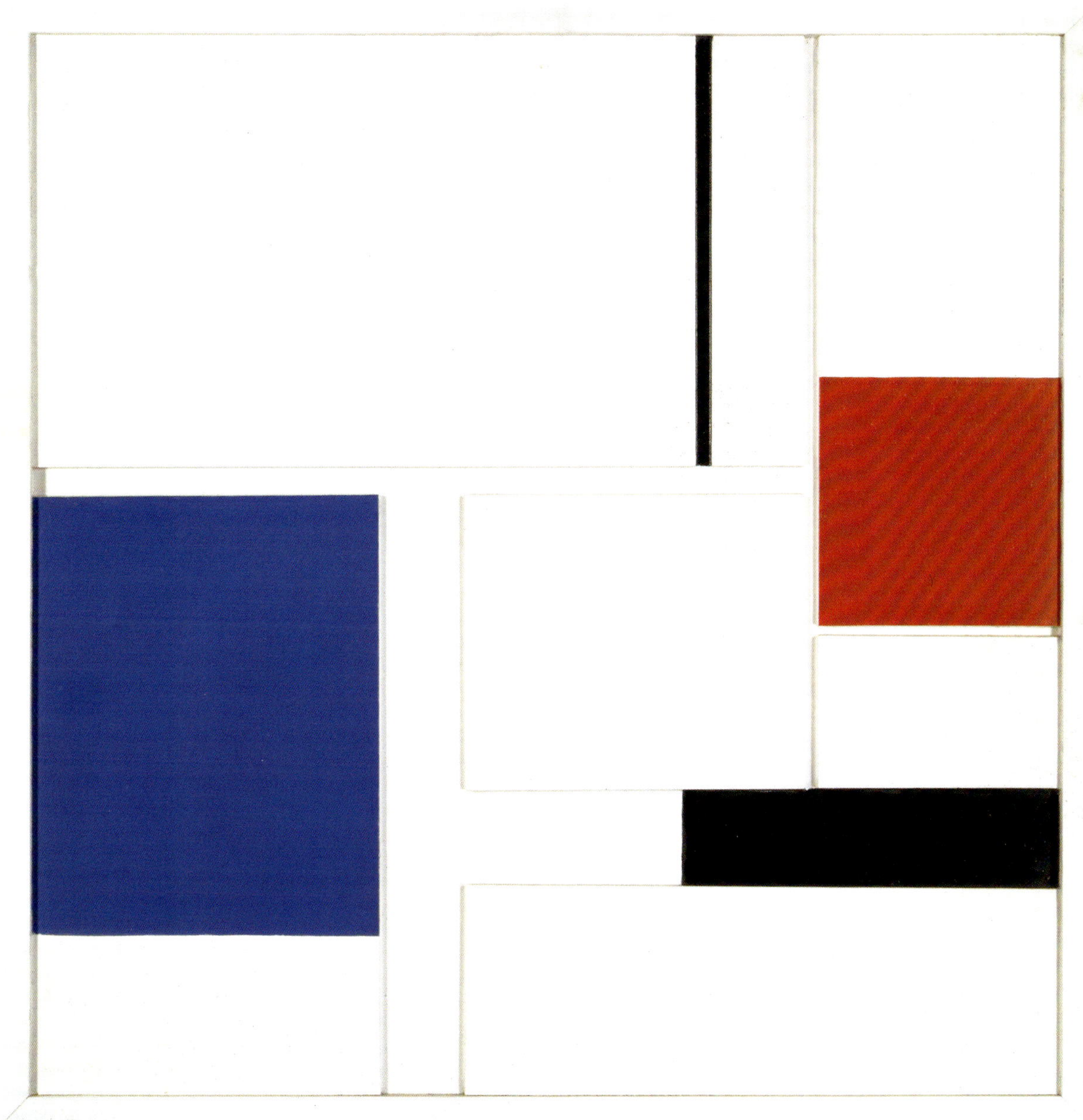

JACOBA VAN HEEMSKERCK

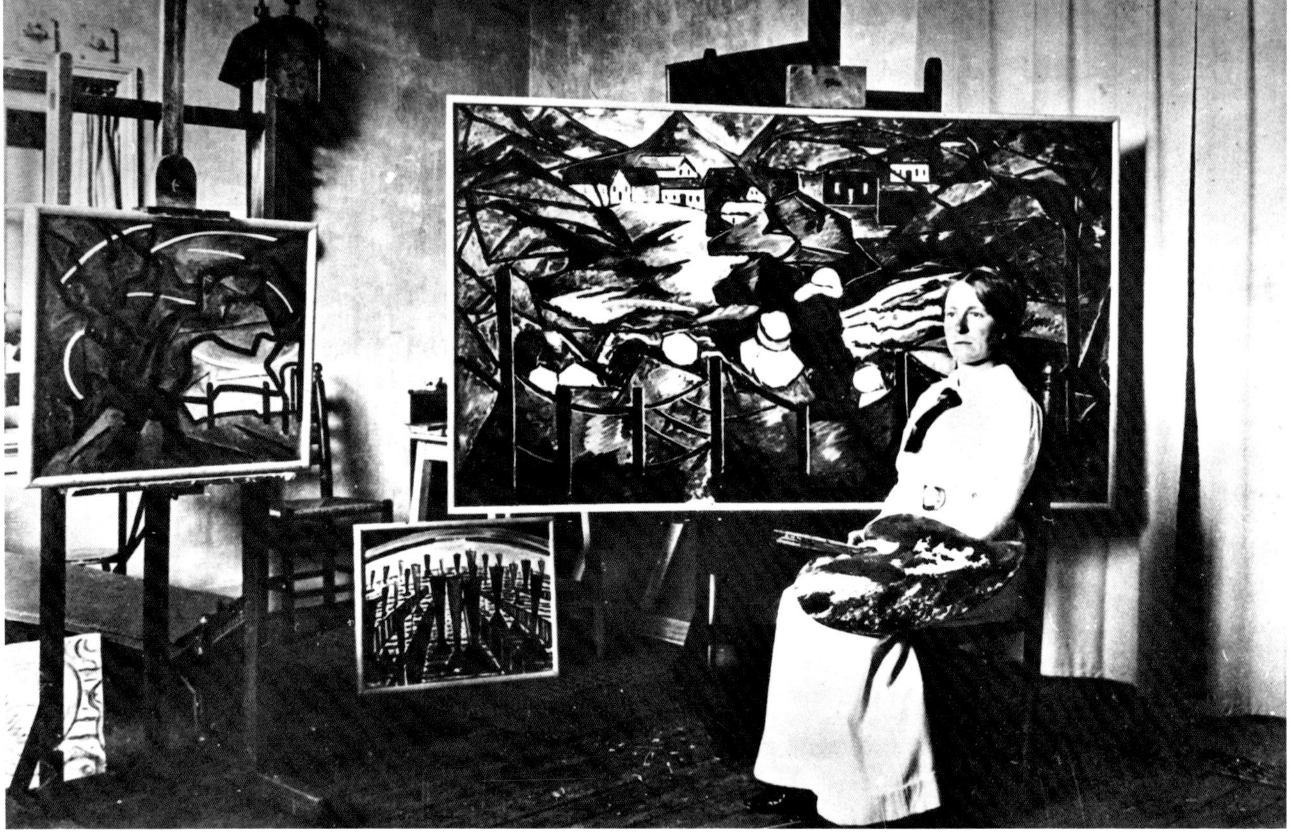

Jacoba van Heemskerck, geboren 1876 in Den Haag, fasst schon in jungen Jahren den Entschluss, Malerin zu werden. Anfangs malt sie symbolistische Darstellungen von Bauern und Fischern. Das ändert sich ab 1904, als sie Marie Tak van Poortvliet trifft, eine wohlhabende Tochter aus vornehmer Familie, die große Ländereien auf der Halbinsel Walcheren in Zeeland besitzt. Tak van Poortvliet verehrt Richard Wagner abgöttisch und ist auch sonst an Kunst und Theosophie interessiert. Die beiden jungen Frauen schließen Freundschaft fürs Leben. Sie lassen sich im mondänen Badeort Domburg ein Wohn- und Atelierhaus errichten, wo Tak van Poortvliet damit beginnt, Kunst zu sammeln und Jacoba van Heemskerck darin unterstützt, sich als Künstlerin einen Namen zu machen. Van Heemskerck zeigt ihre Arbeiten bei den Ausstellungen der Künstlervereinigung *St. Lucas* in Amsterdam und begegnet dort Piet Mondrian, der bald zum Malen nach Domburg reist. Es entsteht – vor dem Hintergrund der Theosophie – ein reger Ideenaustausch über die moderne Kunst. Diese Gespräche helfen Mondrian, seine Ideen über abstrakte Kunst schärfer zu umreißen. Jacoba van Heemskerck beteiligt sich an Ausstellungen in Amsterdam, wo gleich neben Mondrians Arbeiten ihre Bilder zu sehen sind, in denen sie mit einer neuen Formensprache experimentiert. 1910 ist sie dabei, als die Vereinigung avantgardistischer niederländischer Künstler, der *Moderne Kunstkring,* ins Leben gerufen wird, und ein Jahr später zeigen Mondrian und van Heemskerck ihre kubistischen Gemälde im Salon des Indépendants in Paris. 1912 und 1913 halten die beiden Künstler engen Kontakt, wenn Mondrian auf Walcheren zu Gast ist. Und doch tritt eine Entfremdung zwischen ihnen ein. Mondrians Kunst konzentriert sich zusehends auf strengere Linien, während sich van Heemskerck immer mehr an der Bildsprache der deutschen Expressionisten orientiert. Sie zeigt ihre Werke in Ausstellungen bei *Der Sturm,* der Berliner Künstlergruppe um Herwarth Walden. Durch den Einsatz von ungewohnt grellen Farben und ihrer ganz eigenen Art figurativer Abstraktion wird ihre Kunst zu einer der radikalsten von *Der Sturm.* In ganz Deutschland stellt sie ihre Bilder aus und verkauft sie. 1917 experimentiert van Heemskerck mit den Techniken der Bleiglasmalerei. Dies beeinflusst ihre anderen Arbeiten hinsichtlich einer gewissen neuen Strenge; die offensichtlich anthroposophische Thematik entfernt sie von der Kunst von *De Stijl.* Mondrian äußert später sein Bedauern darüber, dass van Heemskerck sich nicht mit ihm in seine Richtung weiterentwickelt hat. 1923 stirbt Jacoba van Heemskerck in Domburg.

Jacoba van Heemskerck – born 1876 in The Hague, Jacoba van Heemskerck's ambition to become a painter developed at an early age. She started out painting symbolist portraits of farmers and fishermen. In 1904 she met Marie Tak van Poortvliet, the daughter of a wealthy patrician family that owned large tracts of land on the island of Walcheren in Zeeland. Tak van Poortvliet idolized Wagner, and was interested in art and theosophy. The two women formed a life-long friendship, and built a house with a studio in the fashionable coastal resort of Domburg. Tak van Poortvliet started an art collection, and supported Jacoba van Heemskerck's career as an artist. Van Heemskerck participated in exhibitions organized by the *St. Lucas* artists' association in Amsterdam, where she met Piet Mondrian. He visited her in Zeeland, and painted there. Based on their commen belief in theosophy they began an exchange of ideas on modern art that would last their entire lives. Their discussions helped Mondrian to hone his ideas about abstract art. Jacoba van Heemskerck took part in exhibitions in Amsterdam, showing Modernist experimental works alongside Mondrian. She was one of the founders of the *Moderne Kunstkring,* established in 1910, and in 1911 Mondrian and Van Heemskerck showed their Cubist paintings at the Salon des Indépendants in Paris. In 1912 and 1913 the two artists were in close contact when Mondrian stayed in Walcheren. And yet they became enstranged as Mondrian began to think increasingly in terms of more rigid lines, while Van Heemskerck shifted toward German Expressionism. She exhibited at Herwarth Walden's gallery *Der Sturm.* With her excessive use of bright, uncompromising color and her ideosyncratic form of figurative abstraction, she became one of the most radical artists of *Der Sturm,* exhibiting and selling her work all over Germany. In 1917 she embarked on experiments with stained glass which introduced a new severity into her work, but the openly anthroposophical nature of her work set her apart from *De Stijl.* Mondrian later regretted the fact that she had not evolved along with De Stijl. In 1923 Jacoba van Heemskerck died in Domburg.

Jacoba van Heemskerck
Collection RKD The Hague

Jacoba van Heemskerck
Sammlung RKD Den Haag

Jacoba van Heemskerck
Zwei Bäume
1908–1910
Öl auf Leinwand
70,5 x 88,2 cm
Gemeentemuseum Den Haag

Jacoba van Heemskerck
Two trees
1908–1910
Öl auf Leinwand
70,5 x 88,2 cm
Gemeentemuseum The Hague

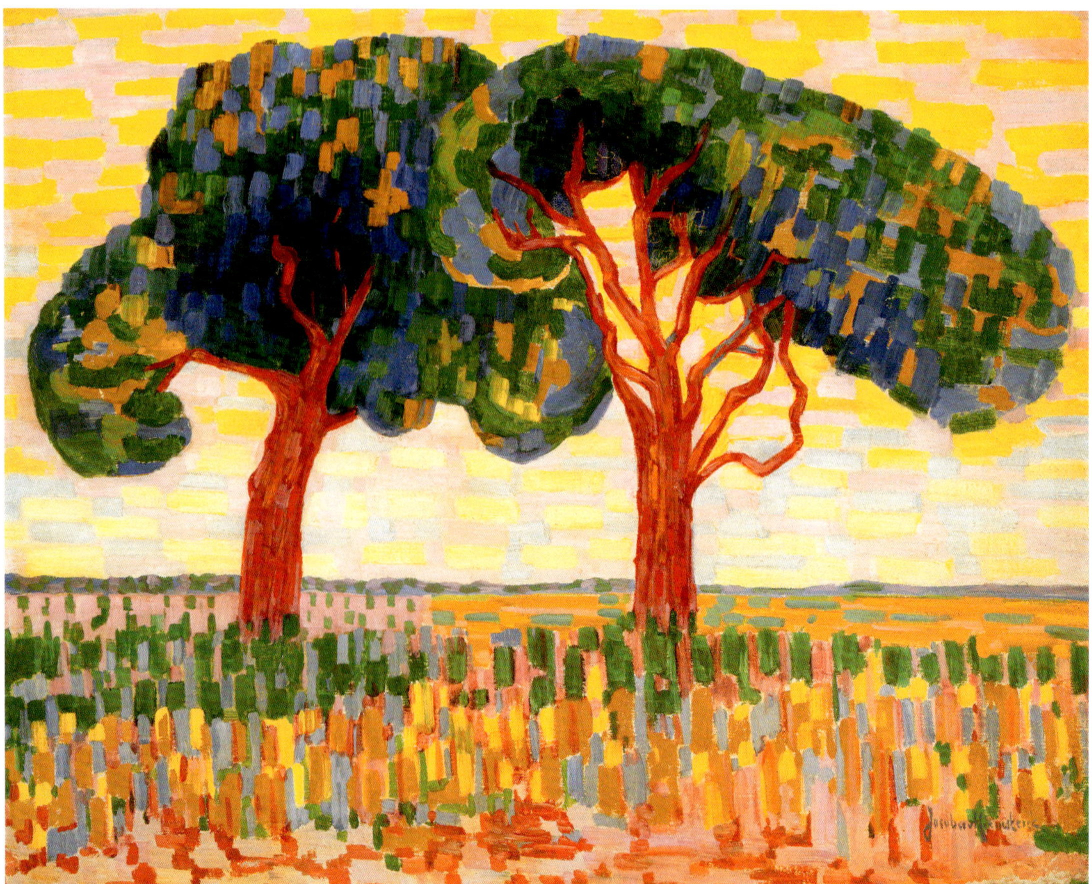

Jacoba van Heemskerck
Baum
1914–1915
Öl auf Leinwand
105 x 78 cm
Gemeentemuseum Den Haag

Jacoba van Heemskerck
Tree
1914–1915
Oil on canvas
105 x 78 cm
Gemeentemuseum The Hague

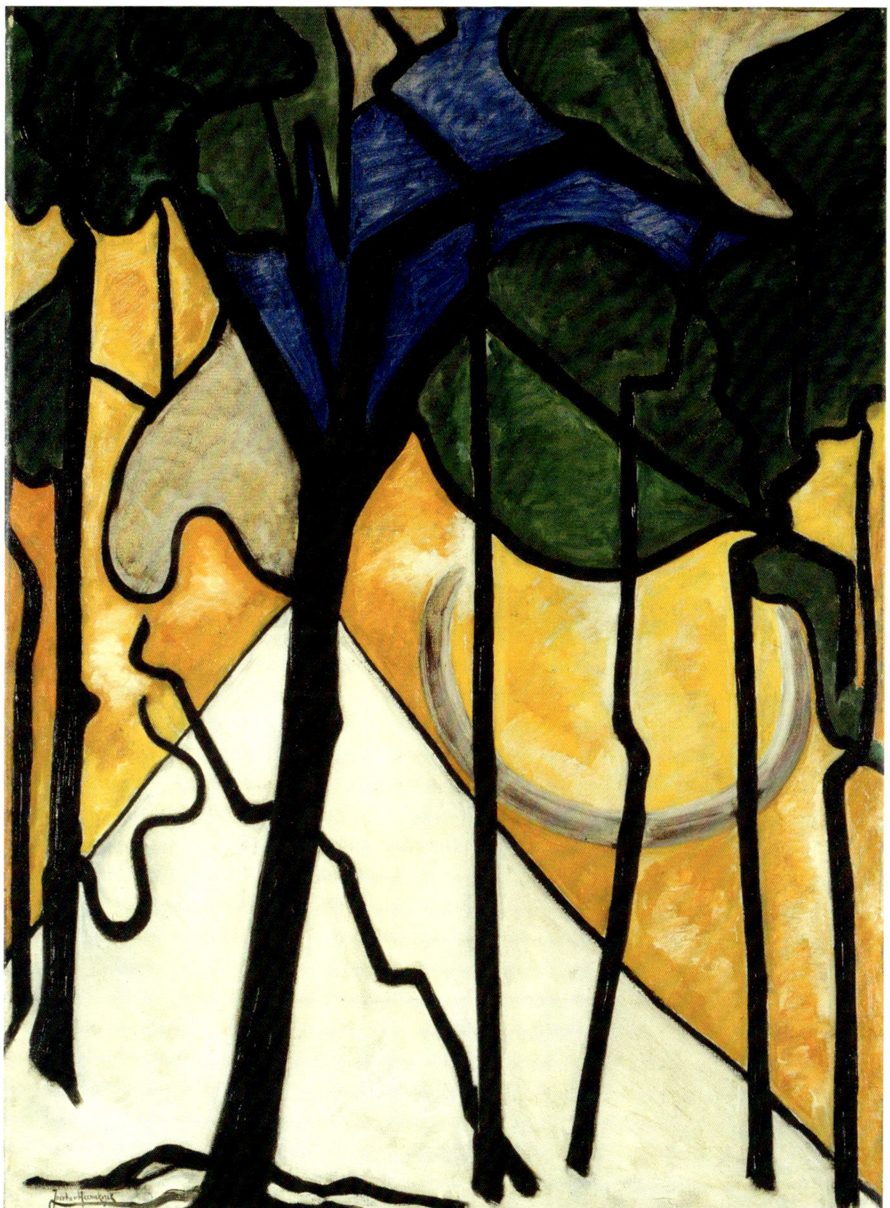

Jacoba van Heemskerck
Komposition Nr. 1
1911–1913
Öl auf Leinwand
100,1 x 80,4 cm
Gemeentemuseum Den Haag

Jacoba van Heemskerck
Composition No. 1
1911–1913
Oil on canvas
100,1 x 80,4 cm
Gemeentemuseum The Hague

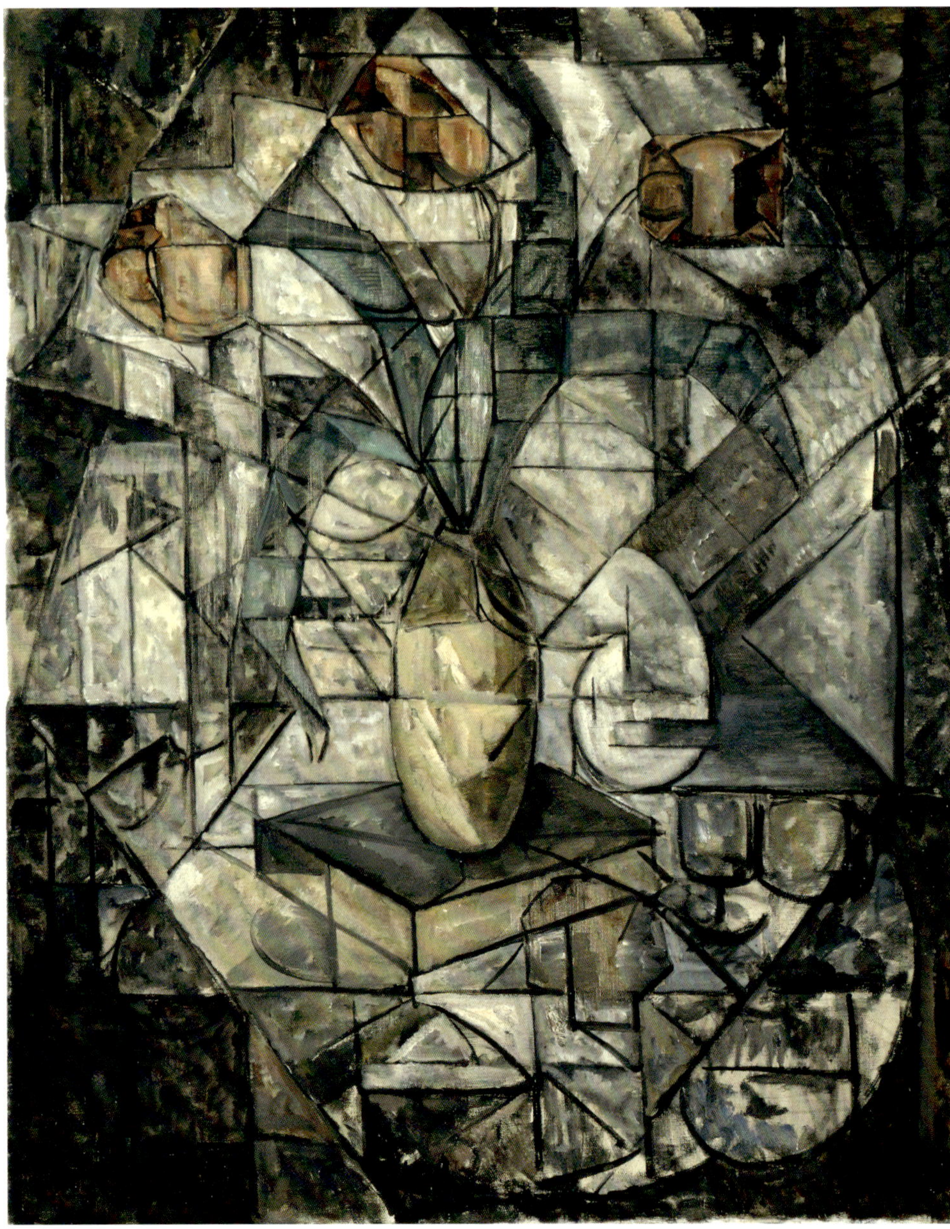

Jacoba van Heemskerck
Komposition Nr. 2
1912–1913
Öl auf Leinwand
80 x 60,5 cm
Gemeentemuseum Den Haag

Jacoba van Heemskerck
Composition No. 2
1912–1913
Oil on canvas
80 x 60,5 cm
Gemeentemuseum The Hague

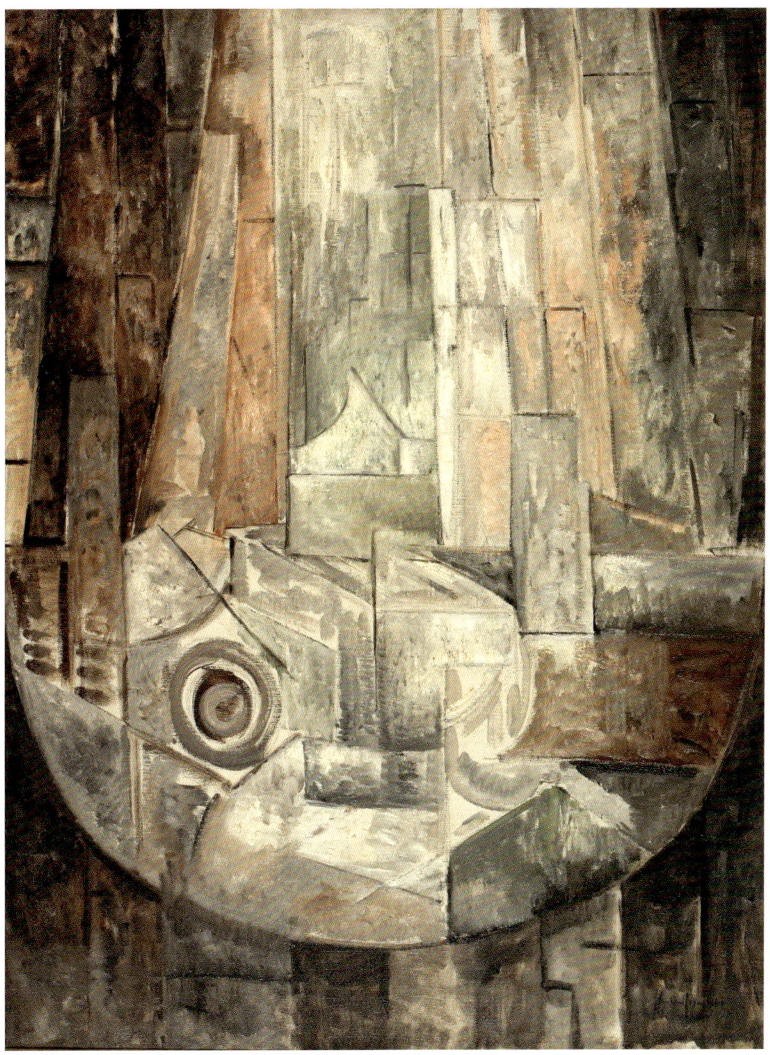

VILMOS HUSZAR

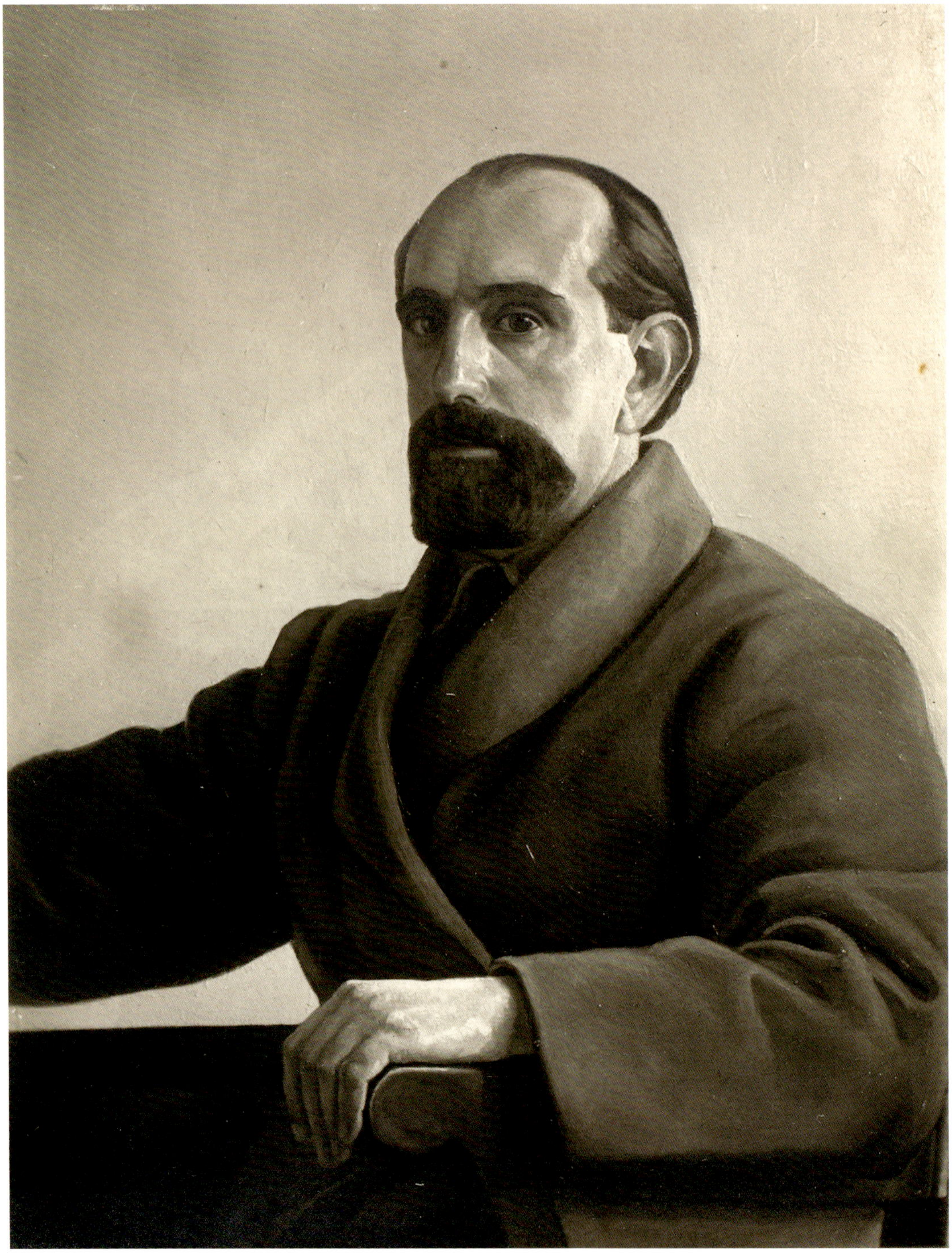

Vilmos Huszár
Collection RKD The Hague

Vilmos Huszár
Sammlung RKD Den Haag

Vilmos Huszár, 1884 in Budapest geboren und dort an der Kunstschule zum Wanddekorateur ausgebildet, studiert 1904 an der Kunstakademie in München, wo er mit niederländischen Künstlern zusammentrifft.
Er unternimmt eine Reise nach Den Haag und besucht dort unter anderem Jozef Israëls in seinem Atelier. Dieser gibt ihm den Rat, die künstlerische Laufbahn einzuschlagen. 1906 zieht er nach Den Haag, lernt den Kunstkritiker und -pädagogen H.P. Bremmer kennen, der ihn in die ›besseren Kreise‹ einführt – Bremmer lehrt ihn, dass bildende Kunst ein Mittel für Künstler ist, um »immer höher zu streben«. Huszár schätzt van Gogh und beschäftigt sich eingehend mit dessen künstlerischen Bestrebungen. Die Idee des »objektiven Sehens«, für das Bremmer eintritt, beeinflusst Huszárs Weg hin zu einer flächigen Stilisierung seiner Kunstwerke, die zeitweise von einer Beschäftigung mit dem um 1914 weit verbreiteten Kubismus geprägt sind.
Erst im Mai 1916 beteiligt er sich nach längerer Pause wieder an Ausstellungen, nachdem Theo van Doesburg seine neuen Bilder gesehen und befürwortend besprochen hatte. Huszár ist von den Arbeiten Mondrians sehr angetan, und wird 1917 einer der Mitbegründer der Zeitschrift *De Stijl*. Huszár beschäftigt sich zu diesem Zeitpunkt schon eine Weile mit neuen Ausdrucksformen in Hinblick auf die Bleiglasmalerei, Entwürfe von Logogrammen, Typografien und Reklame sowie Innenausstattung. Zwischen 1917 und 1920 arbeitet er an einer ›Malerei in Bewegung‹, bei der Theaterelemente einbezogen werden: Es entstehen Kunstwerke wie die *Mechanisch Tanzende Figur*. Huszár eröffnet mit Piet Mondrian eine Diskussion über das Vorder- und Hintergrundproblem in malerischen Kompositionen, die Verwendung von Rastern und die Systematisierung von Farben, wobei ihm sein Wissen über die ungarische Volkskunst zugute kommt. In den folgenden Jahren arbeitet er fast ausschließlich an Interieurentwürfen für den Möbeltischler Cornelis Bruynzeel und andere Auftraggeber; und er nimmt die Art der flachen Stilisierung wieder auf, die an die Malerei von Bart van der Leck erinnert. Huszár nimmt van Doesburgs Einladung an, eine Dada-Tour durch die Niederlande zu unternehmen. Obwohl er nach 1924 den Kontakt zu van Doesburg abbricht, hegt er doch zeitlebens Sympathien für *De Stijl*. Dies zeigt sich darin, dass er insbesondere nach 1950 mittlerweile historische Werke noch einmal ausführt. Vilmos Huszár stirbt 1960 in Harderwijk.

Vilmos Huszár – born in Budapest in 1884, where he trained as a muralist and interior decorator. In 1904 Huszár enrolled at the art academy in Munich, where he met several Dutch artists. During a visit to The Hague he called on the painter Joseph Israëls, who encouraged him to continue his career as a painter. Huszár settled in The Hague in 1906, becoming acquainted with the art critic and educator H.P. Bremmer, who introduced him to refined society and taught him that art was a way for artists to "strive for ever greater things". Huszár was a great admirer of Van Gogh, and engaged himself with the painter's artistic objectives. Bremmer's exhortations to "see objectively" brought Huszár to a flat stylization, which was also influenced by French Cubism. He stopped exhibiting until May 1916, when Theo van Doesburg had seen and discussed his new paintings. Huszár appreciated Mondrian's work and in 1917 Huszár became one of the founder members of *De Stijl*. At that time, Huszár had experimented with new forms of expression in stained glass, in designs for logograms and typography, and in advertisements and interior designs. Between 1917 and 1920 he even worked on "paintings in motion", incorporating theatrical elements, experiments which culminated in the *Mechanical Figure Dancing*. He opened up a discussion with Mondrian about the issues of foreground and background in compositions, the use of the grid and the systematization of colors, drawing on his background in Hungarian folk art. In the years that followed he worked mainly in interior design for the furniture manufacturer Cornelis Bruynzeel and other clients. He began painting again, in a style marked by flat stylization reminiscent of Van der Leck's, and he accepted Van Doesburg's invitation to participate in a Dada-tour of the Netherlands. Although he had no more contact with Van Doesburg after 1924, he remained sympathetic to *De Stijl*, as became particularly apparent after 1950, when he did not hesitate to recreate some historically important works. Vilmos Huszár died 1960 in Harderwijk.

Vilmos Huszár
Komposition mit weißem Kopf
1917
Öl und Tempera auf Sperrholz
50,5 x 44,5 cm
Gemeentemuseum Den Haag

Vilmos Huszár
Composition with White Head
1917
Oil and distemper on plywood
50,5 x 44,5 cm
Gemeentemuseum The Hague

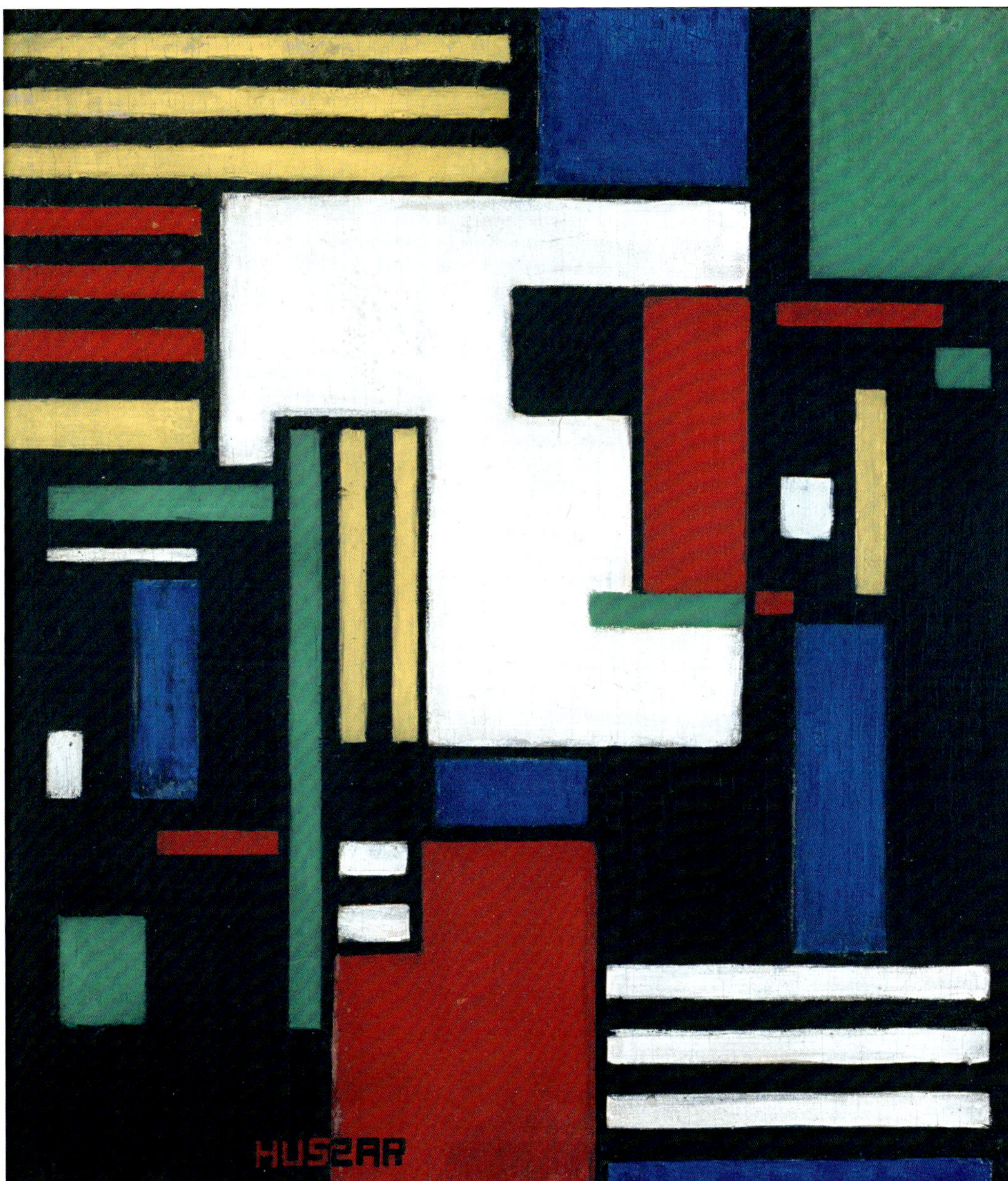

Vilmos Huszár
Komposition (Hammer und Säge)
ca. 1917
Öl auf Holz
42 x 53 cm
Gemeentemuseum Den Haag

Vilmos Huszár
Composition (Hammer and Saw)
ca. 1917
Oil on wood
42 x 53 cm
Gemeentemuseum The Hague

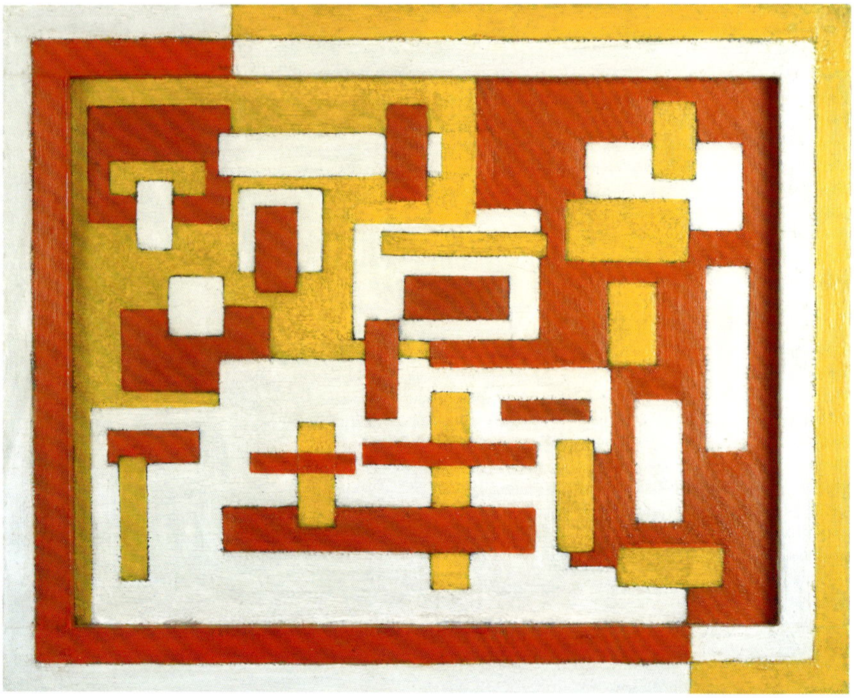

Vilmos Huszár
Komposition in Grau
1918
Öl auf Leinwand
68 x 52,5 cm
Gemeentemuseum Den Haag

Vilmos Huszár
Composition in Gray
1918
Oil on canvas
68 x 52,5 cm
Gemeentemuseum The Hague

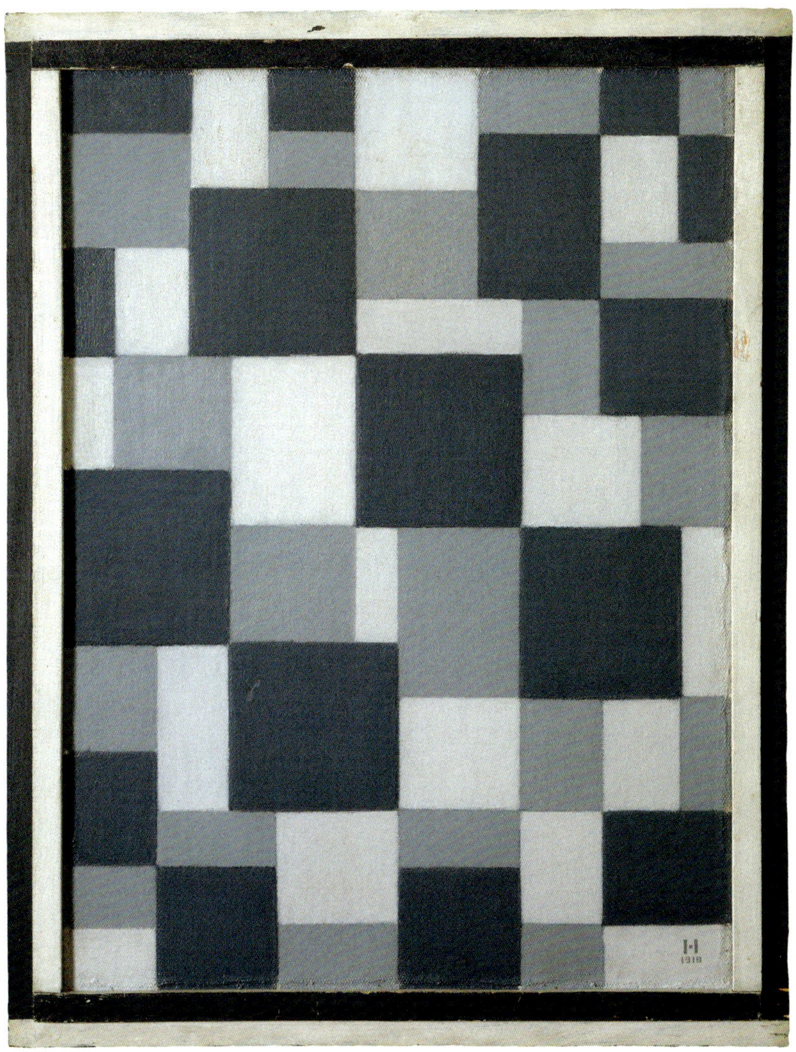

Vilmos Huszár
Umschlag für eine Mappe mit Entwürfen von Sozialwohnungsbauprojekten, herausgegeben vom »Haagsche Kunstkring«
1919
Buchdruck auf Papier
42,7 x 32,2 cm
Gemeentemuseum Den Haag

Vilmos Huszár
Cover for portfolio containing designs for social housing projects, edited by the "Haagsche Kunstkring"
1919
Letterpress on paper
42,7 x 32,2 cm
Gemeentemuseum The Hague

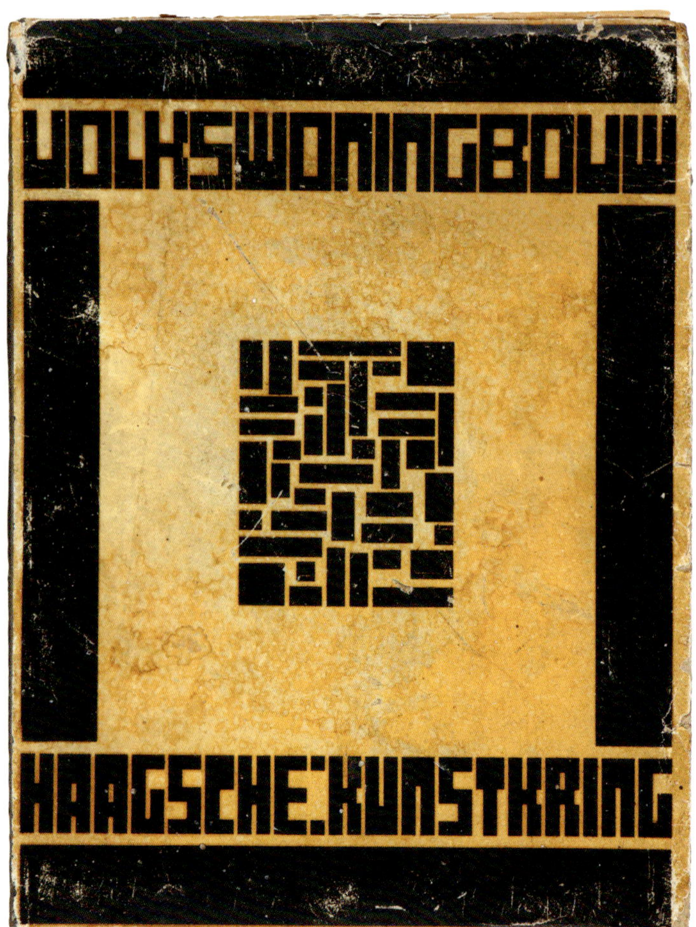

Vilmos Huszár
Komposition ›De Stijl‹
1950–1955
Öl auf Leinwand
66,7 x 57 cm
Gemeentemuseum Den Haag

Vilmos Huszár
Composition 'De Stijl'
1950–1955
Oil on canvas
66,7 x 57 cm
Gemeentemuseum The Hague

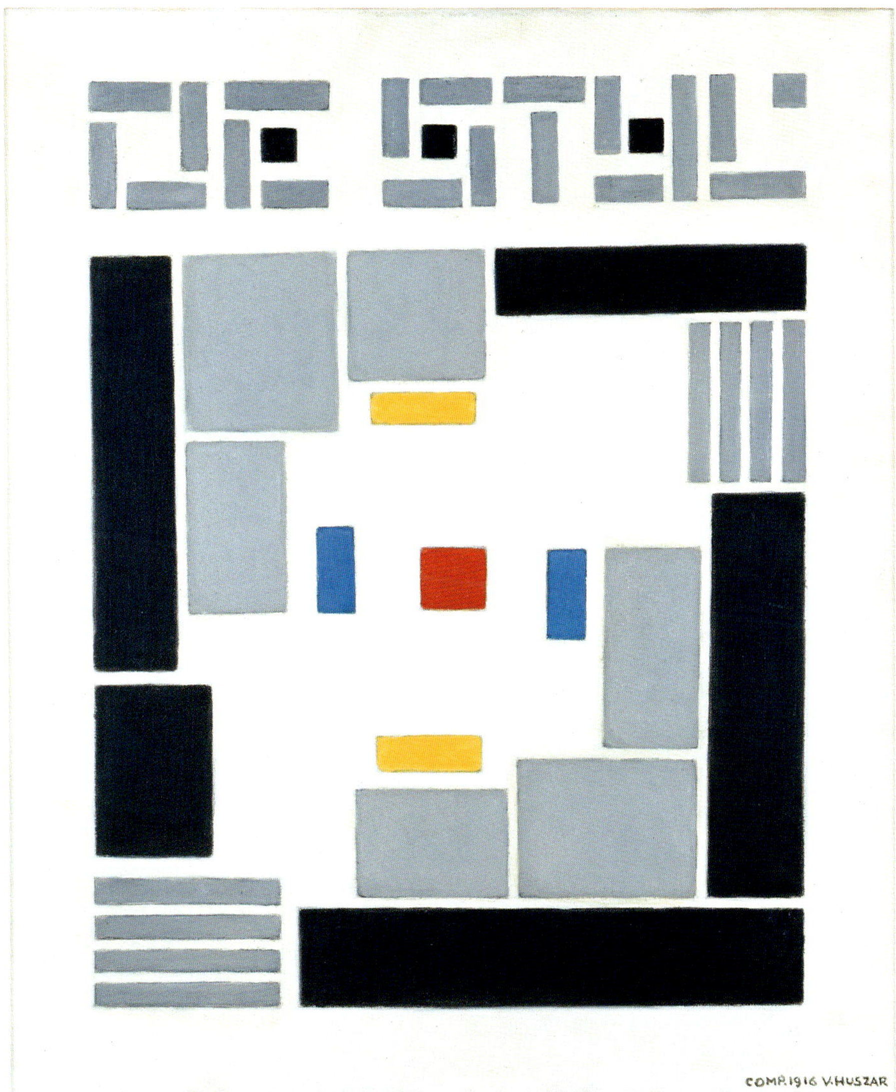

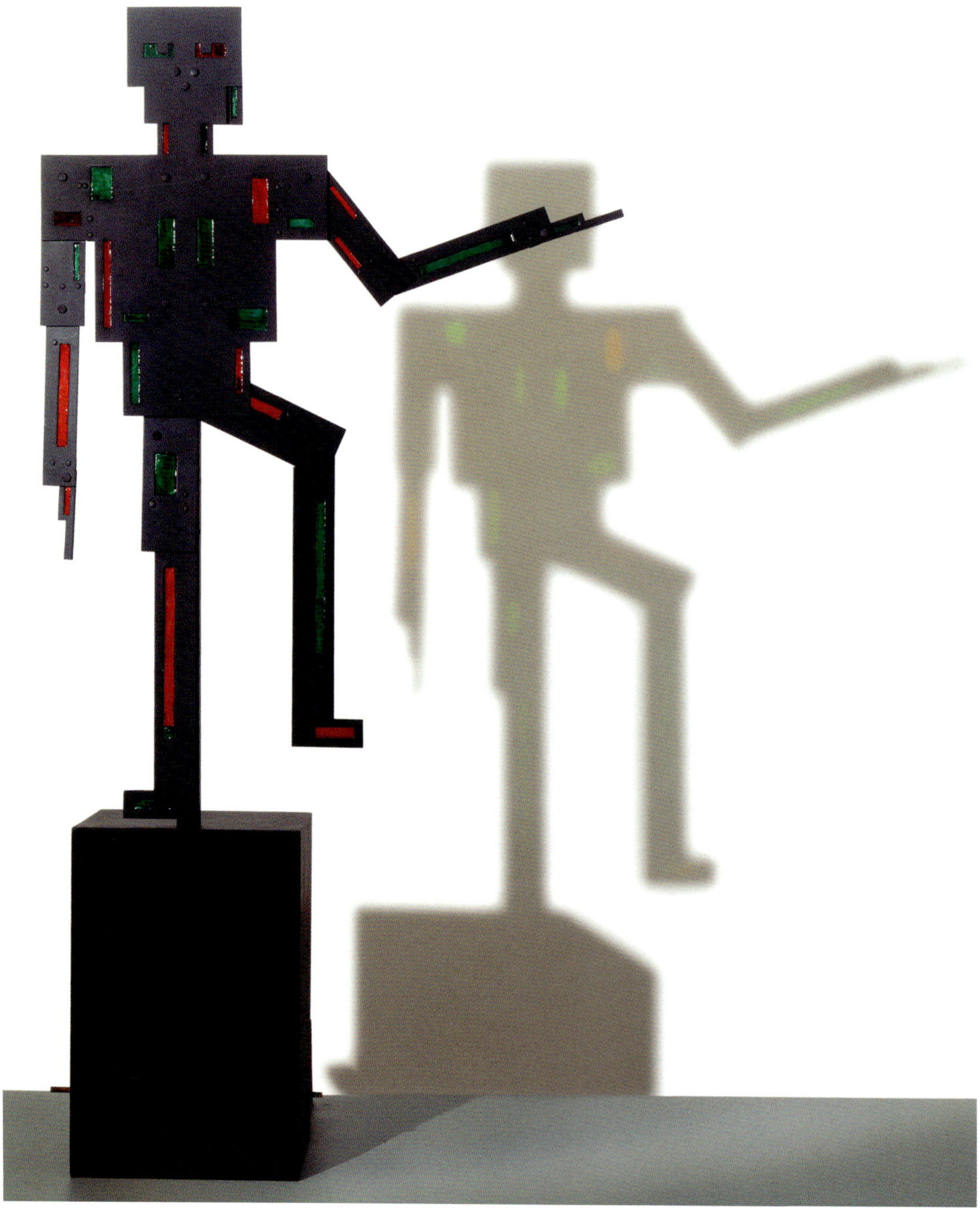

Vilmos Huszár
»Mechanisch tanzende Figur«
1920
Rekonstruktion
von Andy Kowalski und Robert Pachowski, 1984/85
Glimmer, Aluminium, Holz
72 x 26,5 x 4 cm
Gemeentemuseum Den Haag

Vilmos Huszár
"Mechanical Figure Dancing"
1920
Reconstruction
by Andy Kowalski and Robert Pachowski, 1984/85
Mica, aluminum, wood
72 x 26,5 x 4 cm
Gemeentemuseum The Hague

Vilmos Huszár
Tanzpaar
ca. 1928
Öl auf Holz
46,5 x 30,5 cm
Gemeentemuseum Den Haag

Vilmos Huszár
Dancing Couple
ca. 1928
Oil on wood
46,5 x 30,5 cm
Gemeentemuseum The Hague

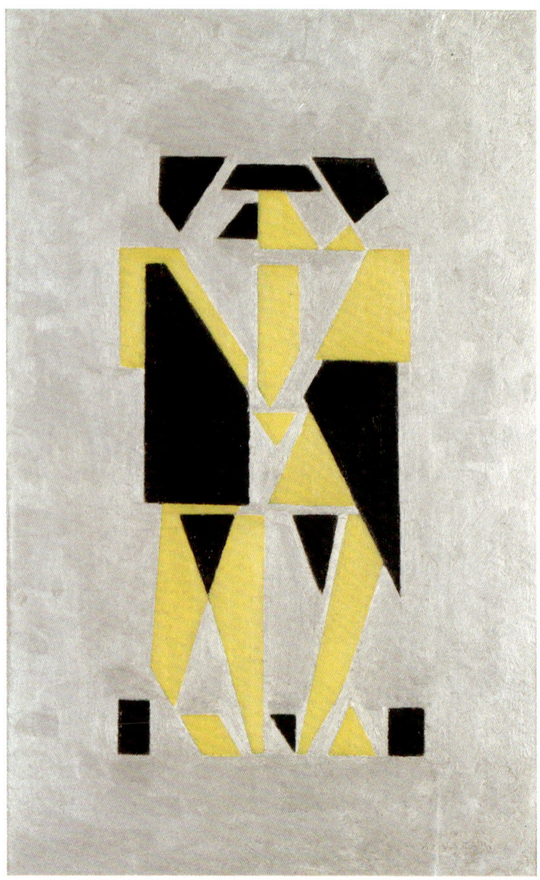

Vilmos Huszár
Tanzpaar
1938/39
Öl auf Leinwand
100 x 60 cm
Gemeentemuseum Den Haag

Vilmos Huszár
Dancing Couple
1938/39
Oil on canvas
100 x 60 cm
Gemeentemuseum The Hague

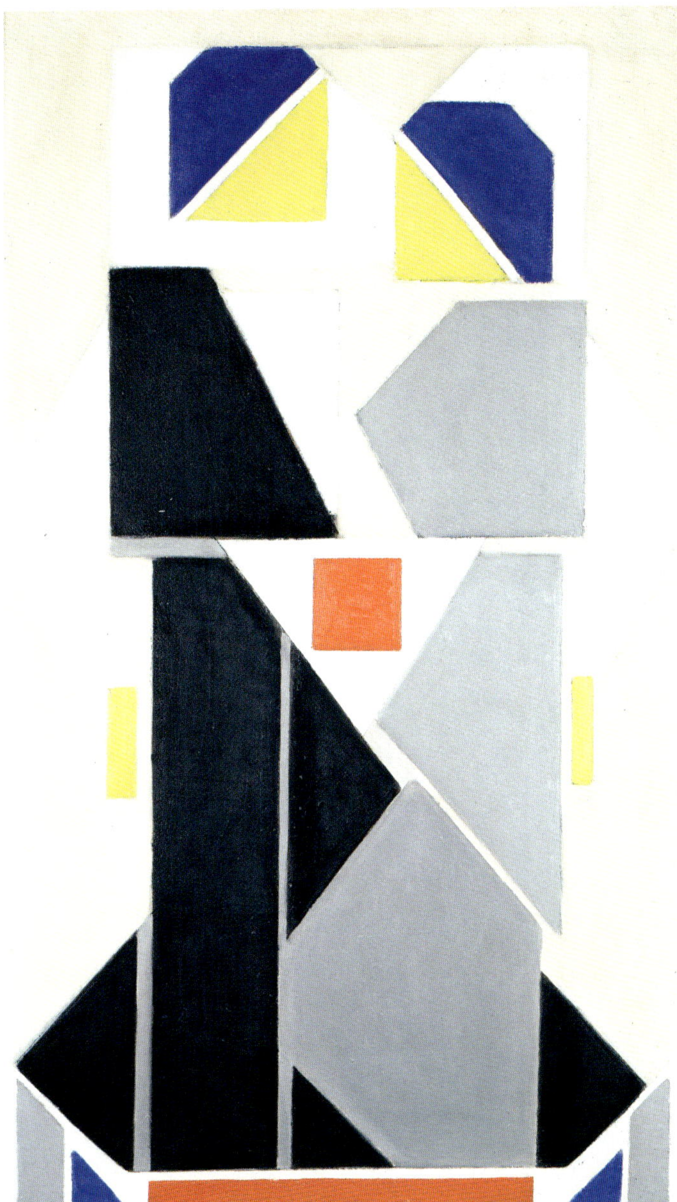

Vilmos Huszár
Glasfenster für das Jungenschlafzimmer
für die Familie Bruynzeel
1919
Glas in Bleirahmen
jeweils 114,5 x 32 cm
Gemeentemuseum Den Haag

Vilmos Huszár
Stained-glass window for the boys' bedroom
for the Bruynzeel family
1919
Leaded window
each 114,5 x 32 cm
Gemeentemuseum The Hague

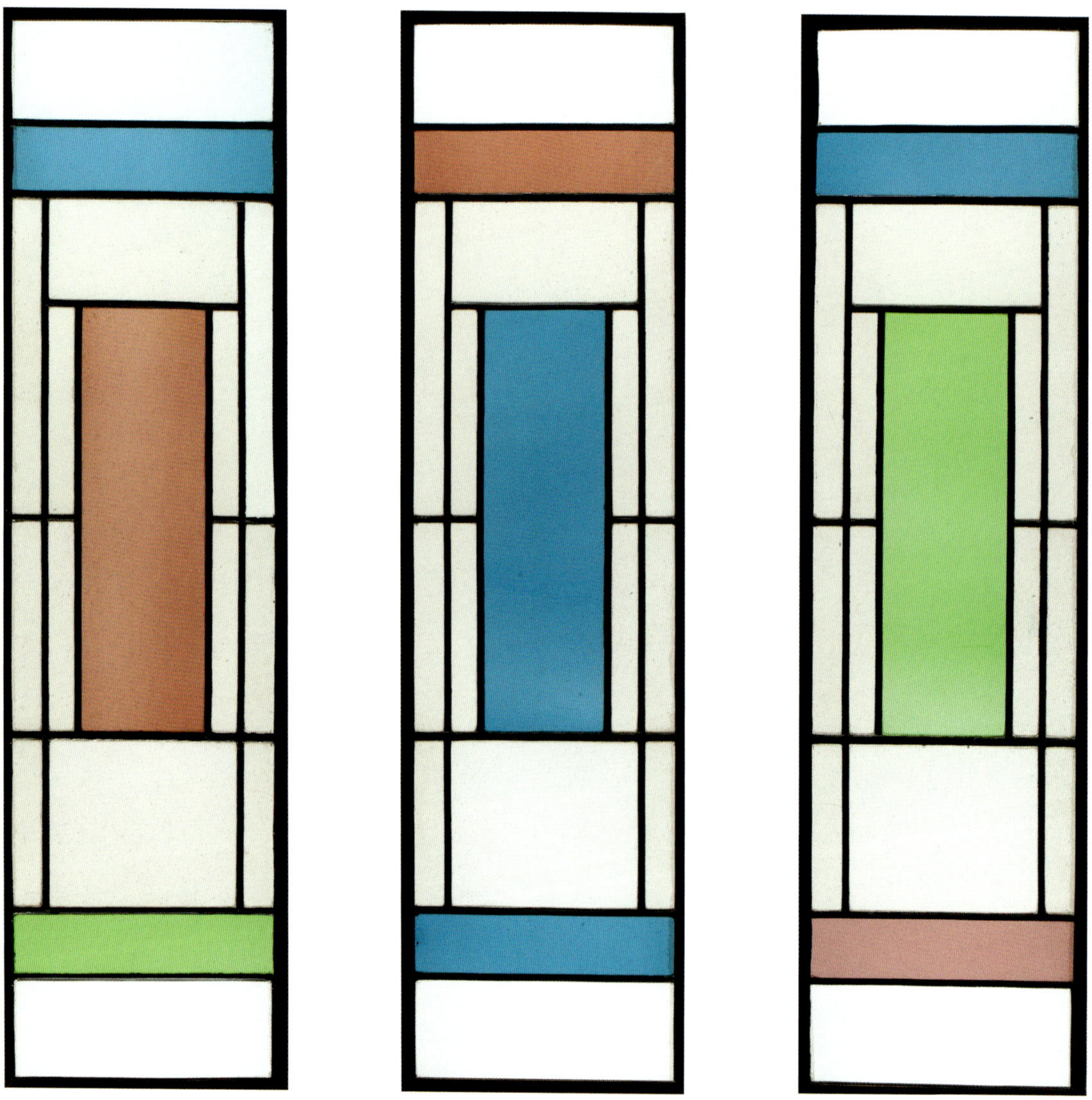

Vilmos Huszár
Liegende Figur
ca. 1937
Glas in Bleirahmen (Industrieglas)
61 x 84,5 cm
Gemeentemuseum Den Haag

Vilmos Huszár
Reclining Figure
ca. 1937
Leaded window (industrial glass)
61 x 84,5 cm
Gemeentemuseum The Hague

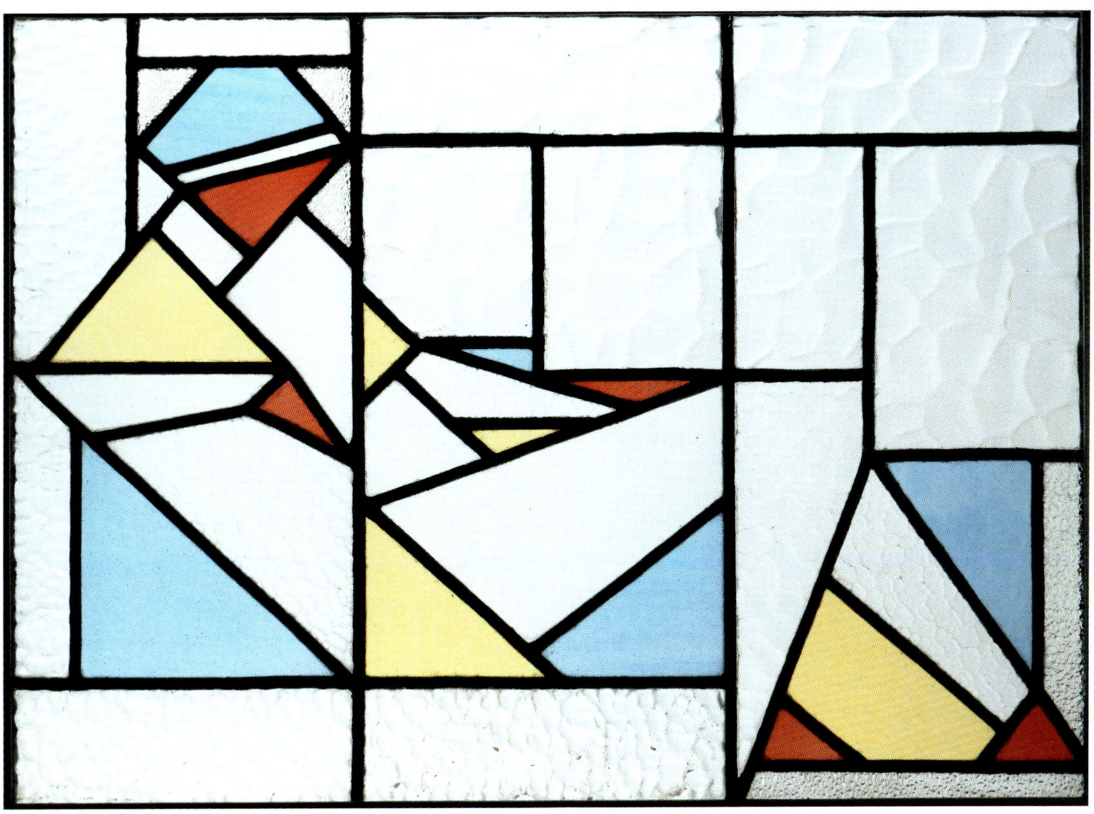

VILMOS HUSZAR

PIET KLAARHAMER

Der Architekt und Möbeldesigner Pieter Jan Christophel (Piet) Klaarhamer wird 1874 in Zwiep geboren. Er besucht die Ambachtsschool (Kunstgewerbeschule) in Utrecht. Anschließend lernt er die Architekten Petrus Josephus Hubertus Cuypers und Hendrik Petrus Berlage in Amsterdam kennen, für deren Werkstätten er tätig ist. Ab 1902 etabliert sich Klaarhamer als Architekt und lehrt bis 1903 Materialwissenschaft an der Utrechter Kunstgewerbeschule. Seine Möbel zeichnen sich bereits sehr früh durch die Forderung nach schlichten Typenentwürfen aus, die für eine industrielle Massenproduktion geeignet sind. Seit 1893 verbindet Klaarhamer und Bart van der Leck eine enge Freundschaft. Beide teilen sich ein Atelier und arbeiten zusammen an zahlreichen Möbelprojekten. Dadurch kommt Klaarhamer mit *De Stijl* in Kontakt, ohne sich allerdings die Ideen der Gruppe komplett anzueignen. Seine Möbelkunst übt außerdem einen gewissen Einfluss auf Gerrit Rietveld aus, der in seinen Lehrjahren Unterricht bei Klaarhamer genommen hat. Als Freund van der Lecks und als Lehrer Rietvelds stellt Klaarhamer ein Bindeglied zwischen Berlage und *De Stijl* dar. Eines seiner populärsten Projekte ist das 1919 gemeinsam mit Vilmos Huszár entworfene Jungenschlafzimmer für die Familie Bruynzeel. Klaarhamers schlichtes Mobiliar aus elementaren Formen und Huszárs auf Harmonie zielendes Farbkonzept ergänzen sich in diesem Projekt: Abstraktion und Massenkultur treffen hier aufeinander. Bekannt ist Klaarhamer auch für seine Jugendstil-Vasen, die er unter anderem für die berühmte Keramikfabrik Mobach anfertigt. Der Künstler stirbt 1954 in Ede.

The architect and furniture designer Pieter Jan Christophel (Piet) Klaarhamer was born 1874 in Zwiep. After attending the Ambachtsschool (School of Arts and Crafts) in Utrecht, he worked for the architects Petrus Josephus Hubertus Cuypers and Hendrik Petrus Berlage in Amsterdam. Klaarhamer established himself as an architect in his own right in 1902, but he continued to teach materials sciences at the Ambachtsschool until 1903. From a very early stage his furniture designs were notable for their simple style that made them suitable for industrial mass production. Klaarhamer first met Bart van der Leck in 1893, the beginning of a friendship that was to last many years. They shared a studio and designed many items of furniture together. Klaarhamer first encountered *De Stijl* through his friend, but he did not entirely adopt the group's ideas. His furniture also exercised a certain influence on Gerrit Rietveld, who had taken lessons with Klaarhamer during his apprenticeship. As van der Leck's friend and Rietveld's teacher, Klaarhamer provided a link between Berlage and *De Stijl*. One of his most popular projects was a boys' bedroom designed jointly with Vilmos Huszár for the Bruynzeel family in 1919. Klaarhamer's simple furniture with its elementary forms and Huszár's color concept complemented one another—it was abstraction and mass culture coming together. Klaarhamer was also well known for his Art Nouveau vases, which he designed for companies such as the celebrated ceramics factory Mobach. He died 1954 in Ede.

Vilmos Huszár
(Entwurf des Farbschemas)
Pieter Jan Christophel Klaarhamer
(Möbelentwurf)
Historische Fotografien des Jungenschlafzimmers
für die Familie Bruynzeel
1919
Gemeentemuseum Den Haag

Vilmos Huszár
(Design for the color scheme)
Pieter Jan Christophel Klaarhamer
(Furniture design)
Historical photographs of the boys' bedroom
for the Bruynzeel family
1919
Gemeentemuseum The Hague

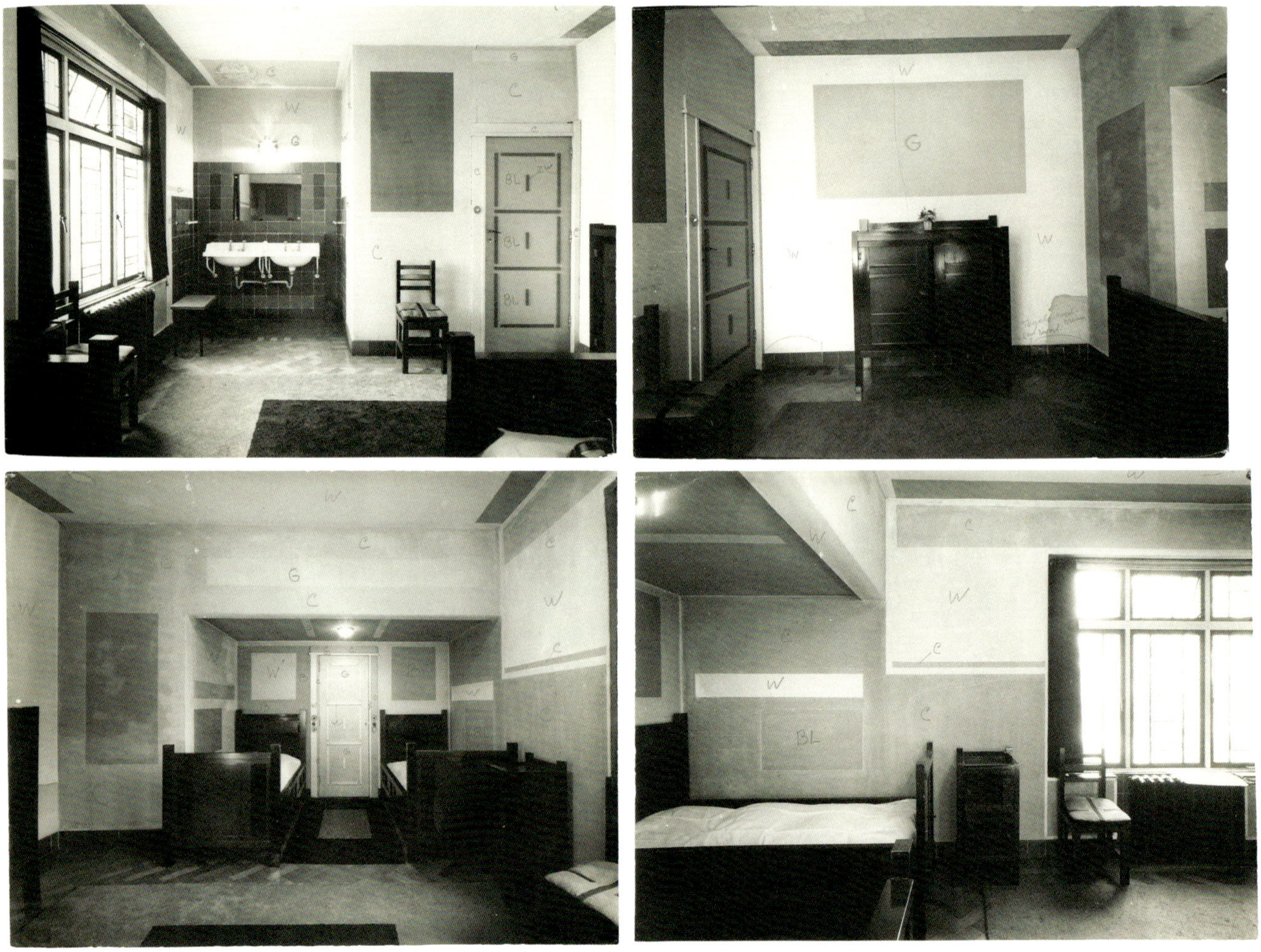

Vilmos Huszár
(Entwurf des Farbschemas und Teppich)
Pieter Jan Christophel Klaarhamer
(Möbelentwurf)
Jungenschlafzimmer für die Familie Bruynzeel
Oben: Historische Fotografie
1919
Gemeentemuseum Den Haag

Vilmos Huszár
(Design for the color scheme and carpet)
Pieter Jan Christophel Klaarhamer
(Furniture design)
Boys' bedroom for the Bruynzeel family
Top: Historical photograph
1919
Gemeentemuseum The Hague

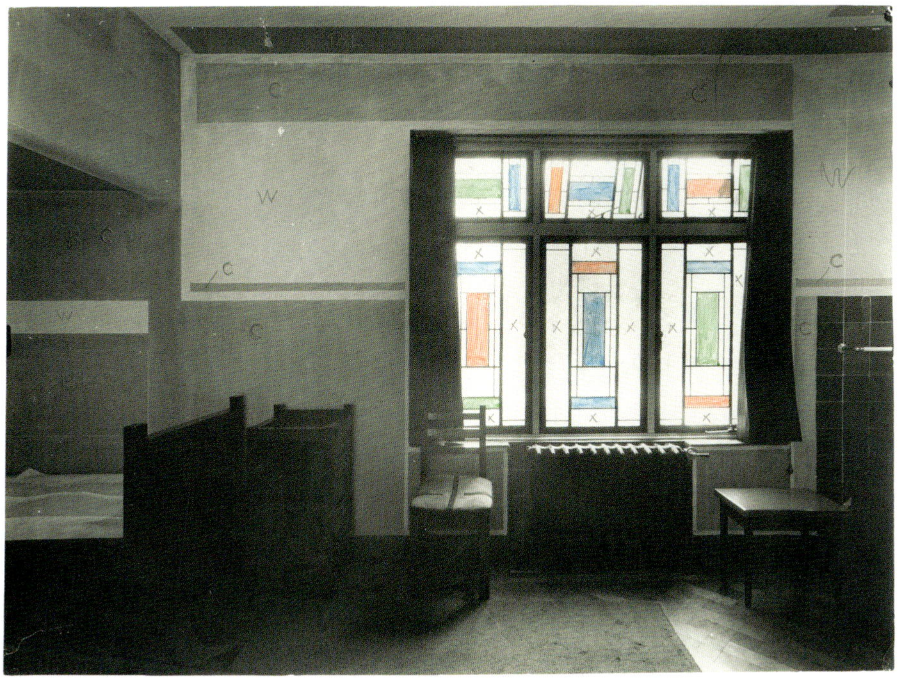

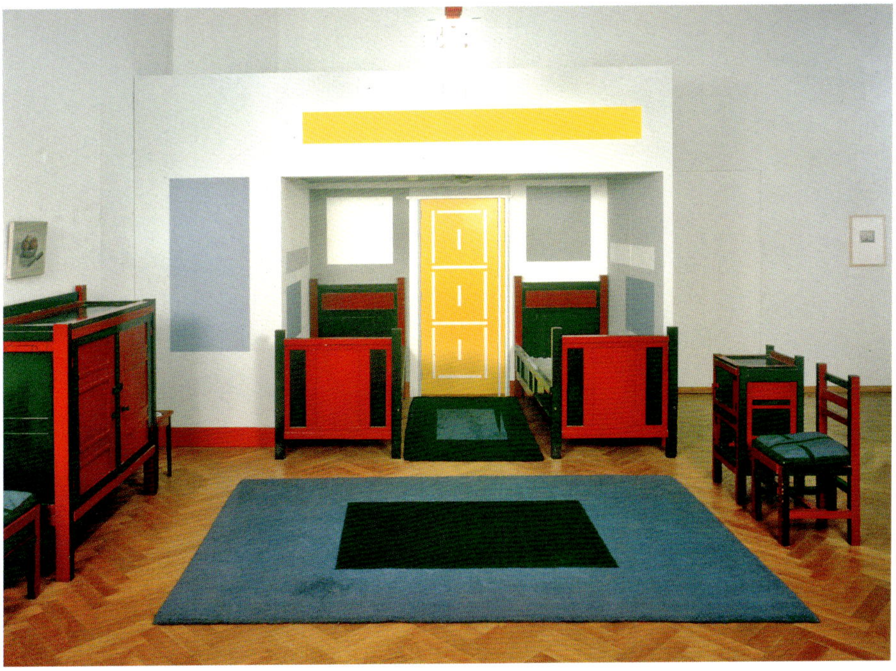

BART VAN DER LECK

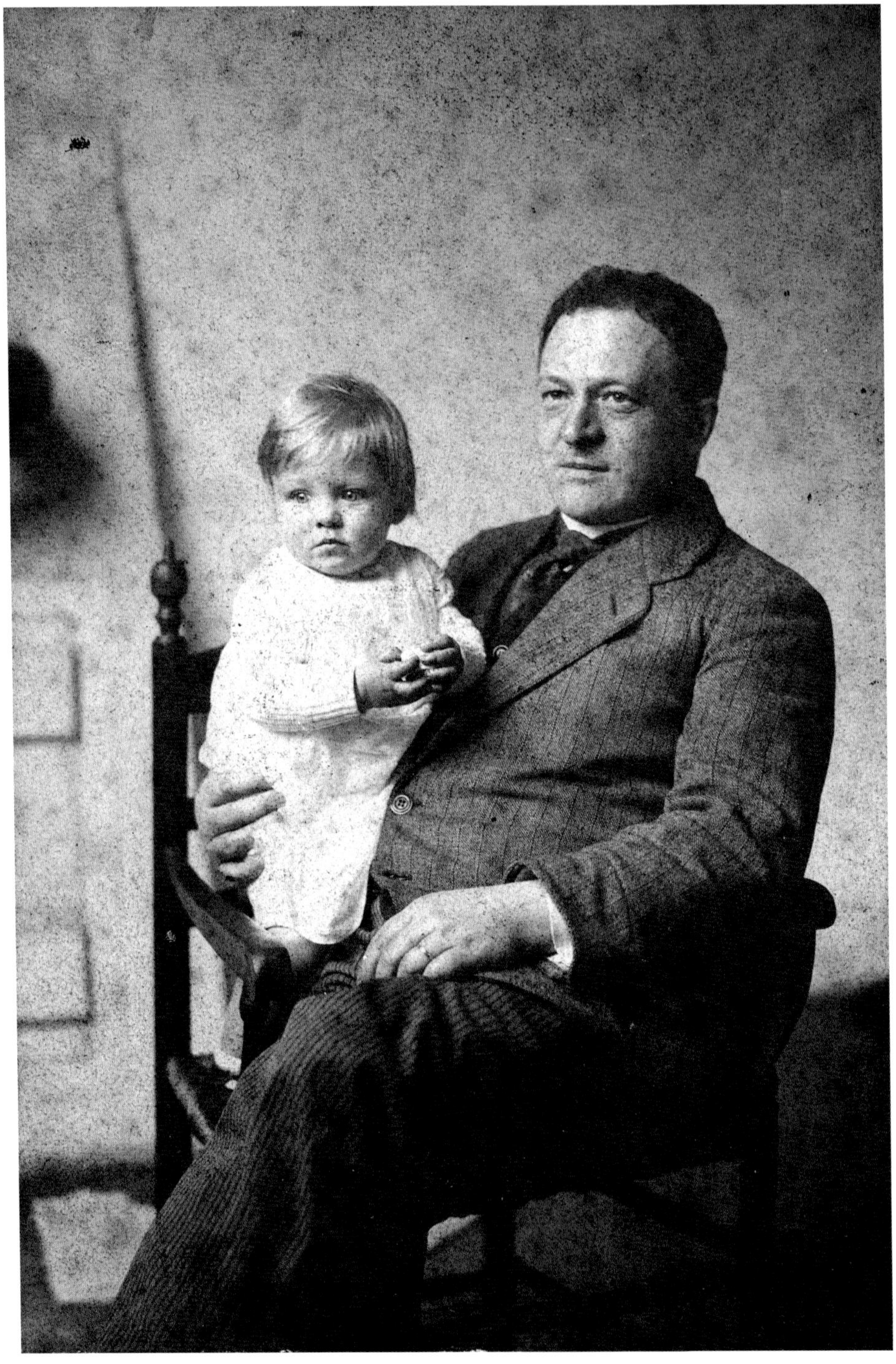

Bart van der Leck
Collection RKD The Hague

Bart van der Leck
Sammlung RKD Den Haag

Bart van der Leck wird 1876 in Utrecht als Sohn eines Anstreichers geboren. Mit 15 Jahren arbeitet er als Glasmaler in einer Werkstatt, die hauptsächlich für Kirchen tätig ist. Van der Leck aber will Künstler werden. Er lernt den Architekten Piet Klaarhamer kennen, der seine künstlerischen Ambitionen fördert. Ein paar Jahre später wird Klaarhamer Gerrit Rietveld unterrichten. In Amsterdam besucht van der Leck zunächst die Quellinusschool voor decoratieve kunsten, danach die Rijksacademie. Er entwickelt anfänglich eine Vorliebe für eine bewusst flach gehaltene, dekorative Kunst, die im öffentlichen Raum erbauliche Botschaften klar und direkt verkünden soll. Van der Leck ist auf der Suche nach einer Art monumentaler Gemeinschaftskunst, in der alle Kunstformen miteinander verschmelzen, und die der Gesellschaft dient. Der Kunstkritiker H.P. Bremmer tritt mit ihm in Kontakt, kauft einige seiner Werke und verhilft ihm zu Aufträgen.
In der Zwischenzeit stilisiert van der Leck seine Arbeiten weiter, bis alles Gegenständliche aus ihnen verschwunden ist und schließlich ein abstraktes Spiel aus Primärfarben und geometrischen Formen vor weißem Hintergrund entsteht. Seine Auffassung, dass ein Bild offen und räumlich sein muss, macht ihn 1916 erst für Mondrian und später auch für van Doesburg zu einem gefragten Künstlerkollegen. Bei van Doesburg avanciert er schnell zu einem wichtigen Mitarbeiter. Mondrian wird von van der Lecks Kunstauffassungen nachhaltig und maßgeblich beeinflusst. Van der Leck verfasst ein paar Beiträge für die erste Ausgabe von *De Stijl,* wendet sich aber bald wieder von der Bewegung ab. Für ihn ist ein Kunstwerk noch immer stark mit der Wirklichkeit verbunden. Er steht, wie er es nennt, mit beiden Beinen fest auf dem Boden: »Keine Illusion, keine Stimmung, keine Faszination schweben mir vor, sondern monumentale Klarheit«. Nach seinem Bruch mit van Doesburg und Mondrian, besonders wegen der Art und Weise, wie van Doesburg seinen Freund Peter Alma wegen dessen figurativem Stil attackiert, sucht van der Leck, wenn auch etwas widerwillig, wieder seinen eigenen Weg. Das bringt ihn einmal mehr zur Gegenständlichkeit – als Ausgangs- und Endpunkt seines Werks. Van der Leck wird einen Unterschied dieser Werke mit den Arbeiten seiner gänzlich abstrakten Periode 1917–1918 stets leugnen, erst recht als 1951 *De Stijl* als eine Bewegung wiederentdeckt wird, in der er eine bedeutende Rolle gespielt hat. Bart van der Leck stirbt 1958 in Blaricum.

Bart van der Leck – born 1876 in Utrecht, the son of a house painter. At the age of fifteen Van der Leck apprenticed to a glass painter who worked mainly for churches. But Van der Leck decided to become an artist. He met architect Piet Klaarhamer, who encouraged his ambition—a few years later Klaarhamer would also teach Gerrit Rietveld. In Amsterdam, he attended the Quellinusschool voor Decoratieve Kunst and later the Rijksakademie. He developed an initial preference for flat, decorative art for public spaces that was to clearly and directly convey edifying messages. Van der Leck was on a quest for a monumental, communal art, in which all forms of art should participate and unite in the service of society. The art critic H.P. Bremmer made contact with Van der Leck, bought some of his work and helped him obtain commissions. Meanwhile, his work was becoming steadily more stylized, until all figurative elements completely diappeared, giving way to an abstract interplay of lines and planes in primary colors and geometric shapes against a white background. His conviction that the image must be open and spatial made him an attractive partner for Mondrian in 1916, and afterwards for Van Doesburg, who soon 'recruited' him as an important collaborator. Mondrian was permanently and decisively influenced by Van der Leck's ideas. Van der Leck wrote several contributions to the first edition of *De Stijl* but soon turned away from the movement. For him, the image was still strongly related to reality. Life always had him "in its grip", as he put it. "No illusion, no mood, no fascination, just a monumental lucidity is in my mind." After his controversy with Van Doesburg and Mondrian, mainly over the way in which Van Doesburg had attacked his friend Peter Alma for his figurative style, Van der Leck somewhat reluctantly went his own way. This took him back to figuration— the starting and end points of his work, though he would always deny the difference between this late work and his truly abstract period of 1917 to 1918, particularly after 1951 when *De Stijl* came to be regarded as a movement in which he had played a key role. Bart van der Leck died 1958 in Blaricum.

Bart van der Leck
Plakat für die »Batavier Linie«
1916
Lithographie
Blatt: 75 x 110,4 cm
Bild: 71,5 x 108,5 cm
Gemeentemuseum Den Haag

Bart van der Leck
Poster for the "Batavier Line"
1916
Lithograph
Sheet: 75 x 110,4 cm
Image: 71,5 x 108,5 cm
Gemeentemuseum The Hague

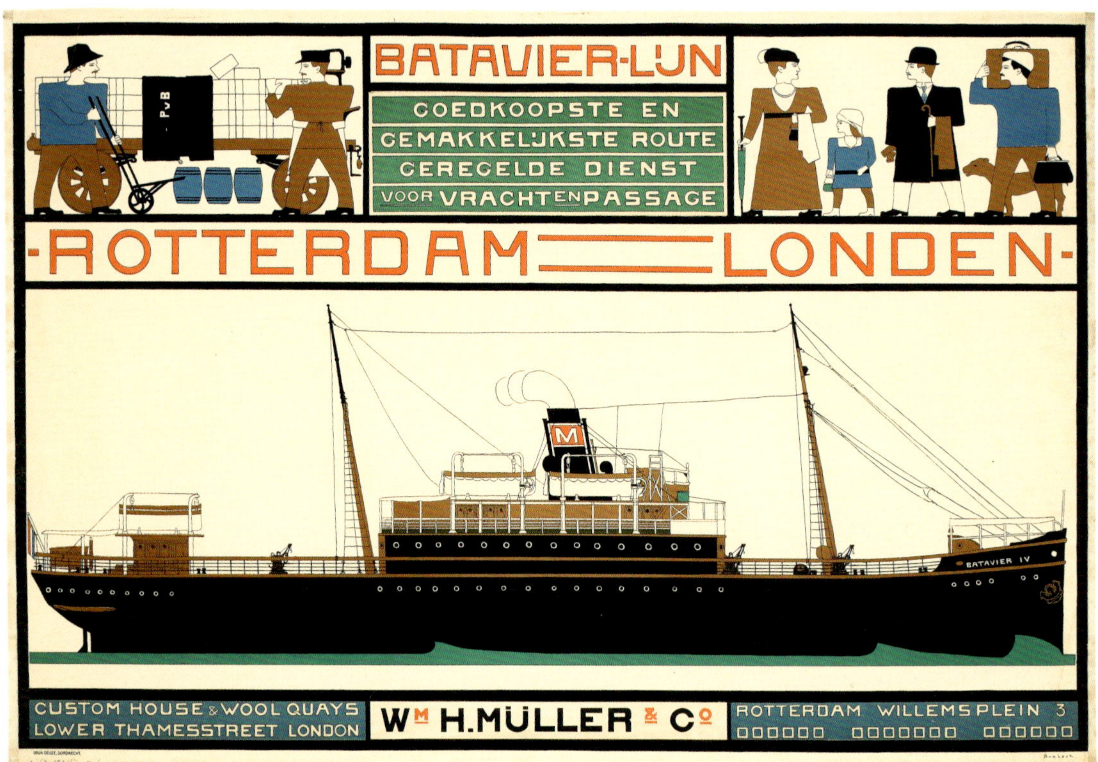

Bart van der Leck
Plakat für die van der Leck-Ausstellung
»Voor de Kunst« in Utrecht
1919
Lithographie auf Papier
116 x 55 cm
Gemeentemuseum Den Haag

Bart van der Leck
Poster for the Van der Leck Exhibition
"Voor de Kunst" in Utrecht
1919
Lithograph on paper
116 x 55 cm
Gemeentemuseum The Hague

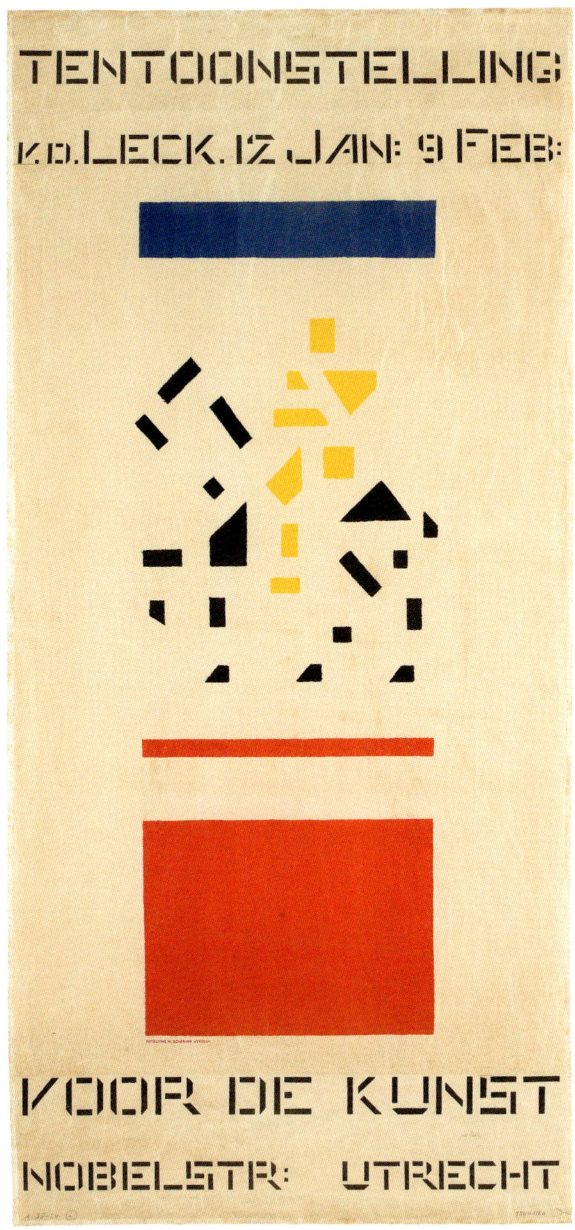

Bart van der Leck
Stillleben
1926
Öl auf Leinwand
29 x 36,5 cm
Gemeentemuseum Den Haag

Bart van der Leck
Still Life
1926
Oil on canvas
29 x 36,5 cm
Gemeentemuseum The Hague

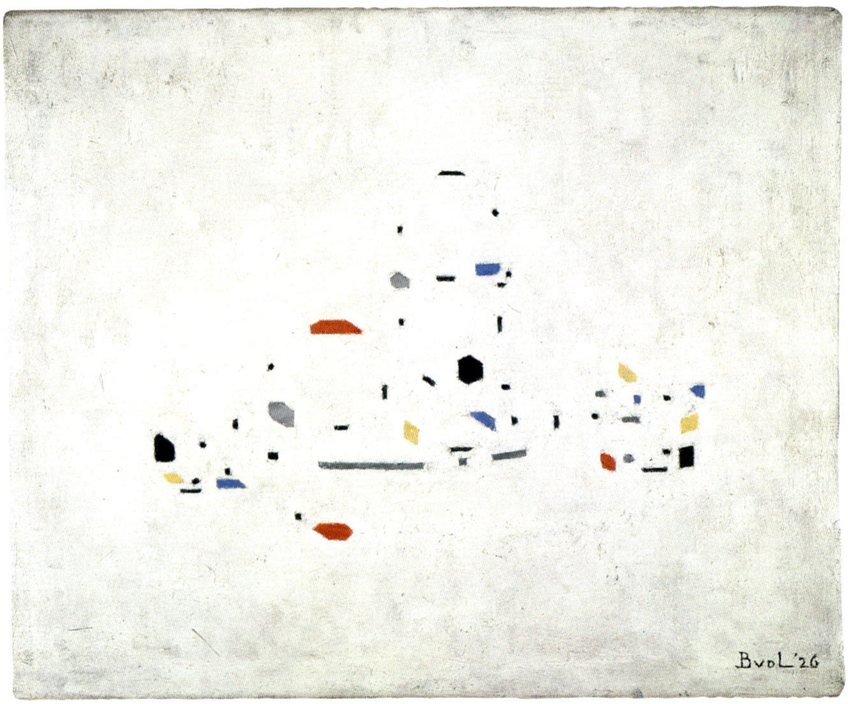

Bart van der Leck
Die Holzfäller
1928
Öl auf Leinwand
140 x 166,5 cm
Gemeentemuseum Den Haag

Bart van der Leck
Woodcutters
1928
Oil on canvas
140 x 166,5 cm
Gemeentemuseum The Hague

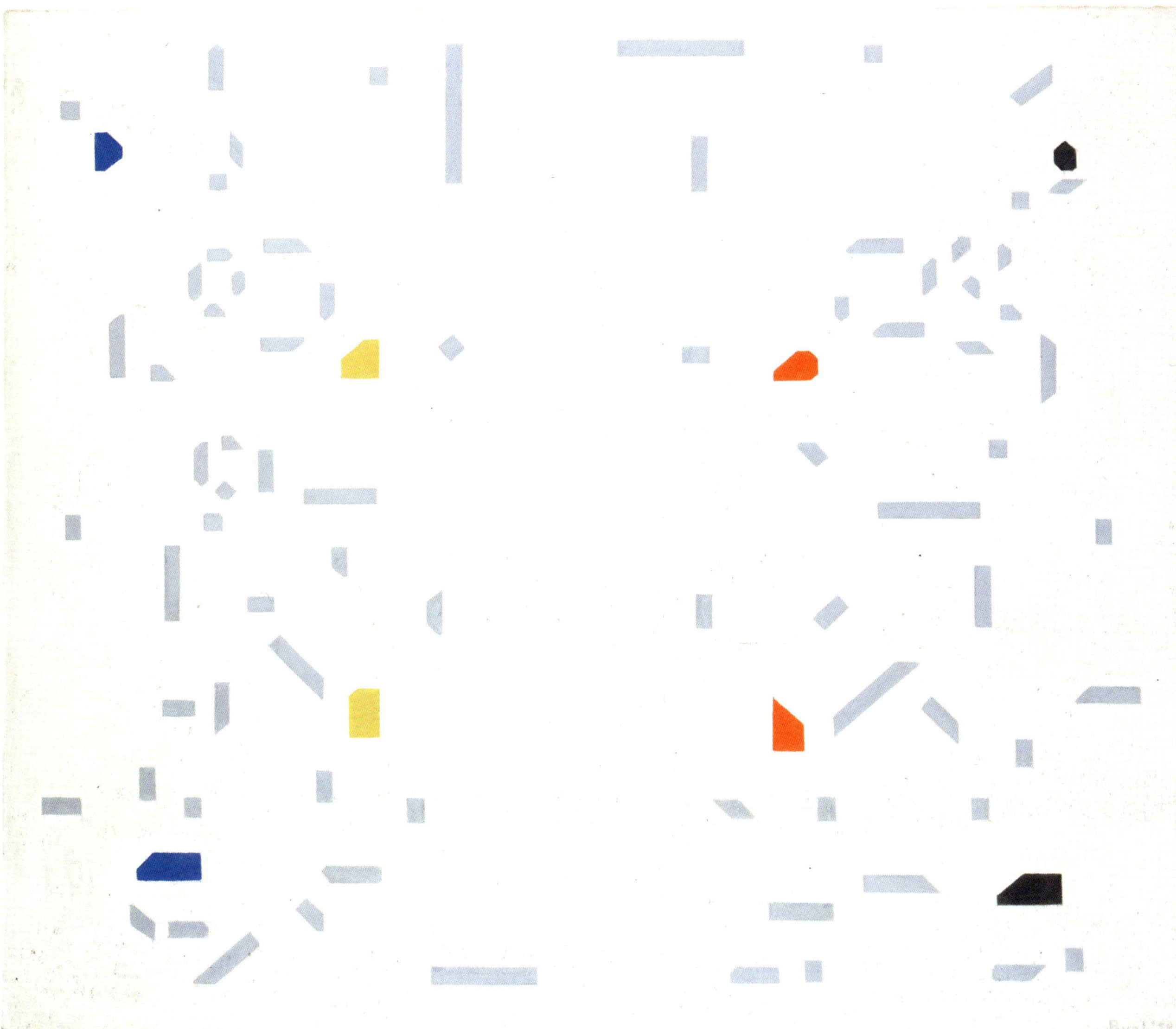

Bart van der Leck
Schale
1939
Glasiertes Steingut
Durchmesser 30 cm
Gemeentemuseum Den Haag

Bart van der Leck
Dish
1939
Glazed earthenware
Diameter 30 cm
Gemeentemuseum The Hague

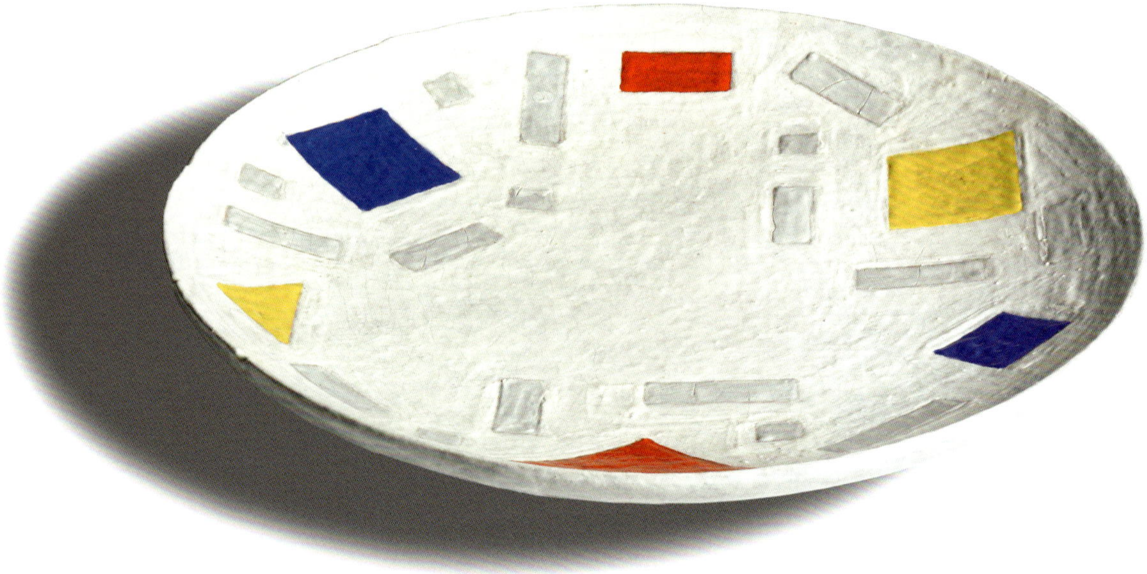

Bart van der Leck
Oben:
Kachel mit Bienenkorb-Motiv
1942
Glasiertes Steingut
12,5 x 12,5 cm
Gemeentemuseum Den Haag
Unten:
Kachel mit Kalbskopf-Motiv
1946
Glasiertes Steingut
12 x 12 cm
Gemeentemuseum Den Haag

Bart van der Leck
Top:
Tile with Beehive décor
1942
Glazed earthenware
12,5 x 12,5 cm
Gemeentemuseum The Hague
Bottom:
Tile with calf's head décor
1946
Glazed earthenware
12 x 12 cm
Gemeentemuseum The Hague

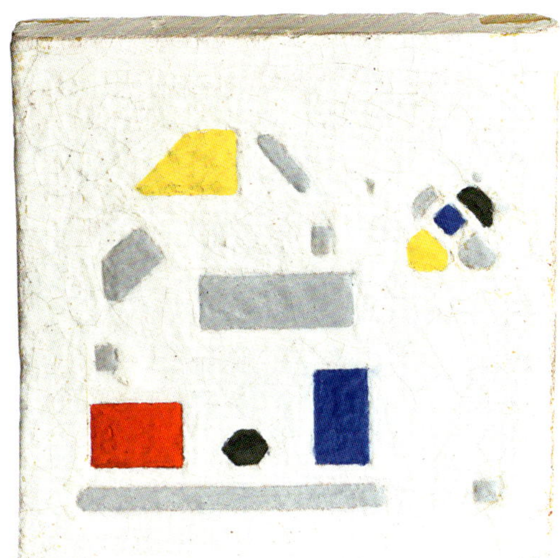

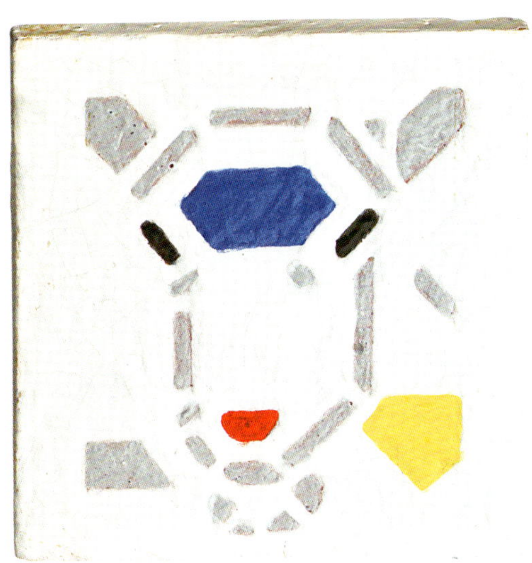

PIET MONDRIAN

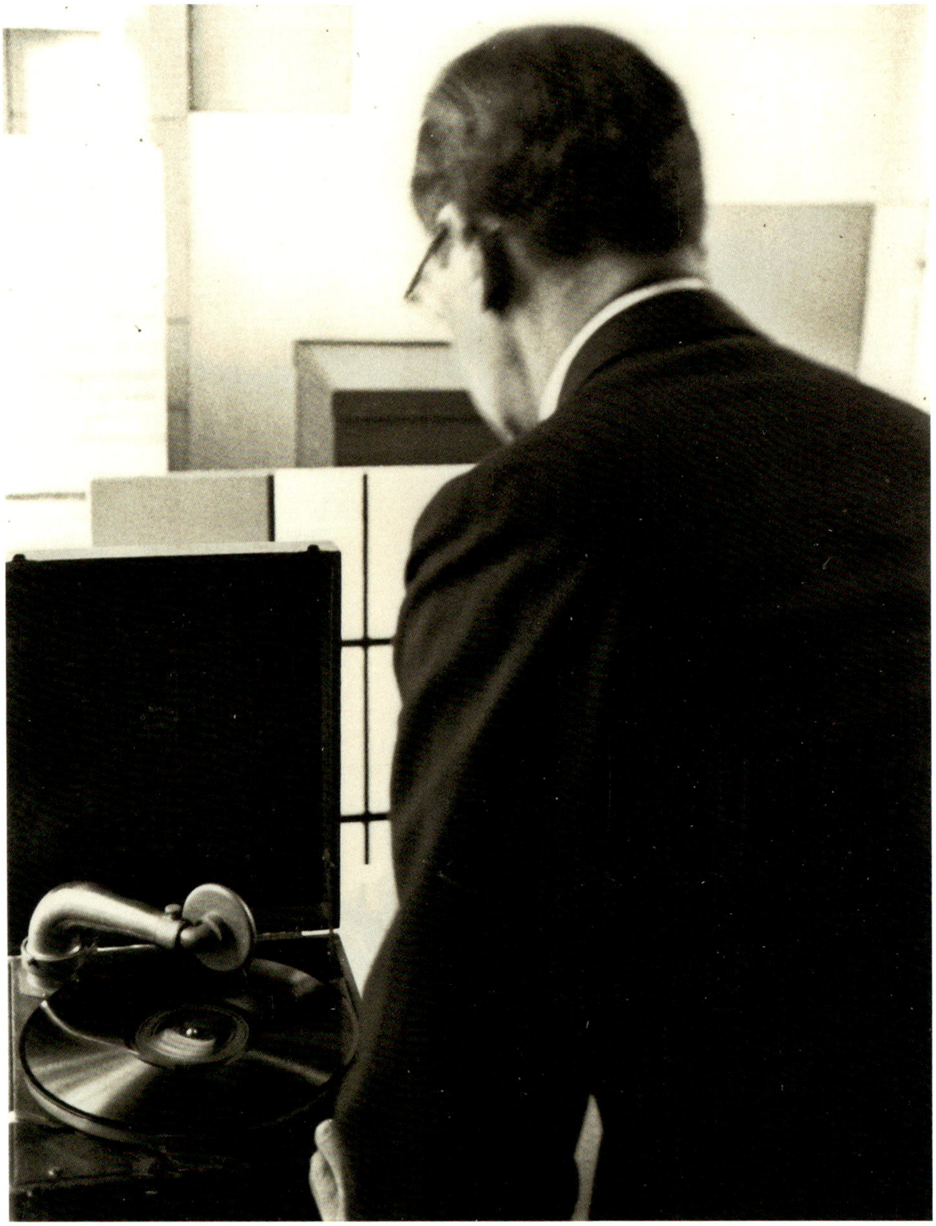

Mondrian in seinem Pariser Studio
1934
Foto Eugene Lux
©Trust of Dennis and Judith DeStefano

Mondrian in his Paris studio
1934
Photo Eugene Lux
©Trust of Dennis and Judith DeStefano

Piet Mondrian wird 1872 in Amersfoort als ältester Sohn eines Lehrers geboren, der sich politisch in der konservativen, calvinistischen Bewegung von Abraham Kuyper engagiert, aber zugleich auch eine große Liebe für das Zeichnen und Malen hegt. Um 1886 fasst Mondrian den Entschluss, Künstler zu werden und schreibt sich in der Rijksakademie in Amsterdam ein. 1894 tritt er der Künstlervereinigung *Arti et Amicitiae* bei und wird 1897 Mitglied der Amsterdamer Künstlervereinigung *St. Lucas,* so dass er an ihren Ausstellungen teilnehmen kann. Mondrian malt Landschaften in der Art von Willem Maris. 1908 lernt er im mondänen Badeort Domburg Jan Toorop und die Gruppe avantgardistischer Künstler um die Sammlerin Marie Tak van Poortvliet kennen. Sein Interesse für zeitgenössische Kunstströmungen, die Gefühle zum Ausdruck bringen sollen, ist geweckt. 1910 sitzt Mondrian im Vorstand des gerade von Conrad Kickert gegründeten *Moderne Kunstkring,* in dem sich alle avantgardistischen Künstler der Niederlande zusammenschließen. Er macht die Bekanntschaft mit den Werken von Pablo Picasso und Henri Le Fauconnier, geht nach Paris und führt mit Jakob van Domselaer intensive Gespräche über die Berührungspunkte von Musik und Malerei. Mondrian geht dazu über, für seine Bilder vollkommen neutrale Titel zu wählen, um die Vorstellungskraft zu unterdrücken und die ästhetische Empfindung anzuregen. 1914 besucht er in den Niederlanden seinen kranken Vater und ist gezwungen, dort zu bleiben: Der Erste Weltkrieg ist ausgebrochen. Zu dieser Zeit notiert Mondrian verstärkt seine Ideen, die er veröffentlichen möchte, und arbeitet in Domburg an einigen Zeichnungen. 1915 findet er eine günstige Unterkunft in der Künstlerkolonie Laren. In diesem Jahr lernt er Theo van Doesburg kennen, der lobend über eine seiner völlig abstrakten Kompositionen schreibt; 1916 macht er Bekanntschaft mit Bart van der Leck. Mondrian arbeitet intensiv an einem Aufsatz über Entwicklung und Funktion in der Kunst, der 1917 als Vorlage für Publikationen im ersten Jahrgang der neuen Zeitschrift *De Stijl* dient. Zwei Jahre später ist Mondrian wieder in Paris. Aus seinen Gemälden sind alle Hinweise auf die äußere Wirklichkeit verschwunden, und aus seinen Texten geht hervor, dass er nicht länger »Intentionen ausdrücken«, sondern nur noch »Relationen sichtbar machen« möchte. Er experimentiert in seinem Atelier mit farbigen Papieren, die er an der Wand zusammensetzt, und ist mit dem Effekt seiner Arbeit zufrieden. Außerdem schreibt Mondrian an einem Buch über seine Kunst, die er als »Neoplastizismus« bezeichnet. 1921 ist sein nach *De Stijl*-Prinzipien eingerichtetes Atelier durch zahlreiche Artikel einem breiteren Publikum bekannt und in aller Munde. Er stellt in Deutschland aus und verkauft, unterstützt von seinen deutschen Kollegen, einige Arbeiten, unter anderem an das Provinzialmuseum Hannover. 1925 löst er die Freundschaft zu van Doesburg. Immer mehr Kunstinteressierte suchen ihn in seinem Atelier auf, um seine Bilder zu betrachten und zu erwerben. Ab 1926 verkauft er seine Kunstwerke an Sammler in Deutschland, in der Schweiz und in den Vereinigten Staaten. Mondrian kündigt an, nie wieder einen Fuß in die Niederlande setzen zu wollen, falls man dort den Charleston verbieten sollte; für ihn stellt der offene Rhythmus des Jazz, genau wie seine Kunst, ein Vorbild für alles Neue dar. 1931 schreibt er an dem Buch *Kunst, Leben und Gesellschaft.* Im folgenden Jahr experimentiert er mit einer Auflösung der geschlossenen Struktur der schwarzen Linie, indem er sie in zwei Teile aufspaltet und sie verdoppelt. Langsam verschwindet auch die Farbe aus Mondrians Bildern, und bald dominieren in seinen Gemälden weiße Flächen und schwarze Linien, die immer rhythmischer werden. Mondrian hat Gelegenheit, in England auszustellen – zwischen 1938 und 1940 lebt er in London – und knüpft Kontakte in den Vereinigten Staaten, in die er 1940 emigriert. 1944 stirbt Piet Mondrian in New York.

Piet Mondrian – born 1872 in Amersfoort, the eldest son of a teacher who was politically active in Abraham Kuyper's conservative Calvinist movement, but also had a great love of drawing and painting. Around 1886 Piet Mondrian decided to study art and enrolled at the Rijksakademie in Amsterdam. In 1892 he became a member of *Arti et Amicitiae* and in 1897 of *St. Lucas,* two art associations, which enabled him to exhibit his work. He painted landscapes in the style of Willem Maris. When in 1908 he met Jan Toorop and the group of avant-garde artists associated with collector Marie Tak van Poortvliet in the fashionable coastal resort of Domburg his interest was raised in all contemporary movements that sought to visualize expressions of feeling. In 1910 he was a board member of Conrad Kickert's recently established *Moderne Kunstkring,* which many progressive Dutch artists joined.
He became acquainted with the work of Picasso and Le Fauconnier, moved to Paris and met Jakob van Domselaer, with whom he had intensive discussions about the affinities of music and painting. He began to assign neutral titles to his works in order to subdue figurative imagination and heighten aesthetic sensibility. In 1914 he returned to the Netherlands to visit his sick father, and was forced to remain there when World War I broke out. At this time he began to put his ideas down in writing for later publication, and he worked on a series of drawings in Domburg. In 1915 he found cheap lodgings in the artist colony of Laren. He met Bart van der Leck and Theo van Doesburg, who wrote enthusiastically about his completely abstract compositions. Mondrian was working hard on an essay about the development and function of art, which in 1917 provided the basis for the first volume of the new magazine *De Stijl.* He returned to Paris in 1919, by which time his paintings bore no more reference to reality, and his writings also made clear that he no longer wished to "express intentions", but merely to "make relations visible". He experimented in his studio with pieces of colored paper which he assembled on the wall, and was pleased with the effect on his work. He wrote a book about his art, which he dubbed "Neoplasticism". In 1921 a number of articles featured the *De Stijl* design of his studio and made it widely known. Thanks to exhibitions in Germany and the interest of his German fellow artists he was able to sell some pieces, among others, to the Provinzialmuseum in Hanover. In 1925 Mondrian broke off contact with Van Doesburg. More and more visitors came to his studio looking to buy his work. From 1926 he sold to collectors in Germany, Switzerland and the United States. Mondrian declared he would never return to the Netherlands if the Charleston were banned there, because he regarded the free rhythm of Jazz as a model for everything new, just like his own art. In 1931 he wrote his book *Art, Life and Society.* From 1932 Mondrian experimented with breaking up the closed structure of black lines, splitting them in two and doubling them. Gradually all color disappeared from his paintings, they became dominated by white fields and black lines increasingly infused with rhythm. Mondrian took advantage of opportunities to exhibit his work in the United Kingdom–from 1938 to 1940 he lived in London— and established contacts in the United States, where he emigrated in 1940. He died 1944 in New York.

Bemerkung

zu den Titeln der Werke von Piet Mondrian: Die von Piet Mondrian selbst gegebenen Titel sind in Großbuchstaben gekennzeichnet, die in Anführungzeichen gesetzten Titel sind ebenfalls auf Piet Mondrian zurückzuführen (dokumentarische Quellen). Im Laufe der Zeit zugewiesene Titel sind in Kleinbuchstaben aufgeführt.

Note

on the work titles of Piet Mondrian: Piet Mondrian's own titles are capitalized, other historically documented titles are put in quotation marks, and titles established later are uncapitalized.

Piet Mondrian
BOSCH (Wald)
1908
Öl auf Leinwand
128 x 158 cm
Gemeentemuseum Den Haag

Piet Mondrian
BOSCH (Woods)
1908
Oil on canvas
128 x 158 cm
Gemeentemuseum The Hague

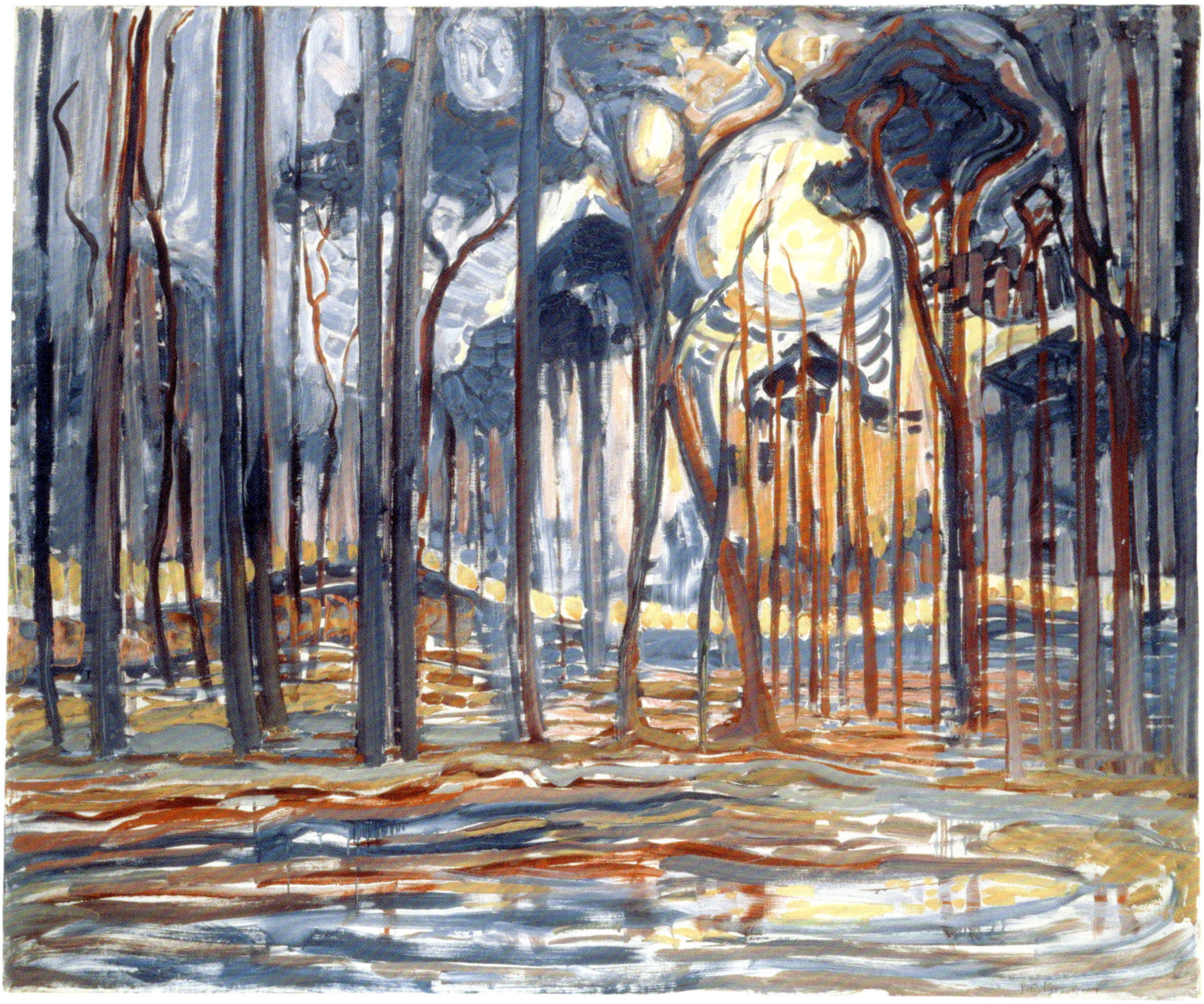

Piet Mondrian
ZOMERNACHT (Sommernacht)
1907
Öl auf Leinwand
71 x 110,5 cm
Gemeentemuseum Den Haag

Piet Mondrian
ZOMERNACHT (Summer Night)
1907
Oil on canvas
71 x 110,5 cm
Gemeentemuseum The Hague

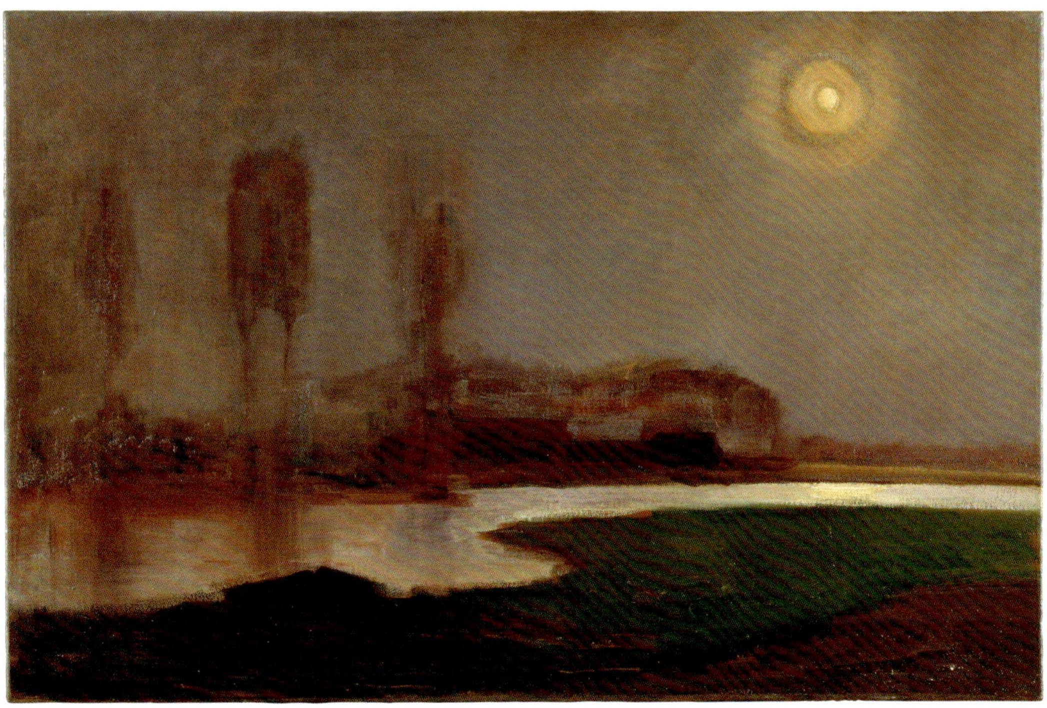

Piet Mondrian
Große Landschaft
1907–08
Öl auf Leinwand
75 x 120 cm
Gemeentemuseum Den Haag

Piet Mondrian
Large Landscape
1907–08
Oil on canvas
75 x 120 cm
Gemeentemuseum The Hague

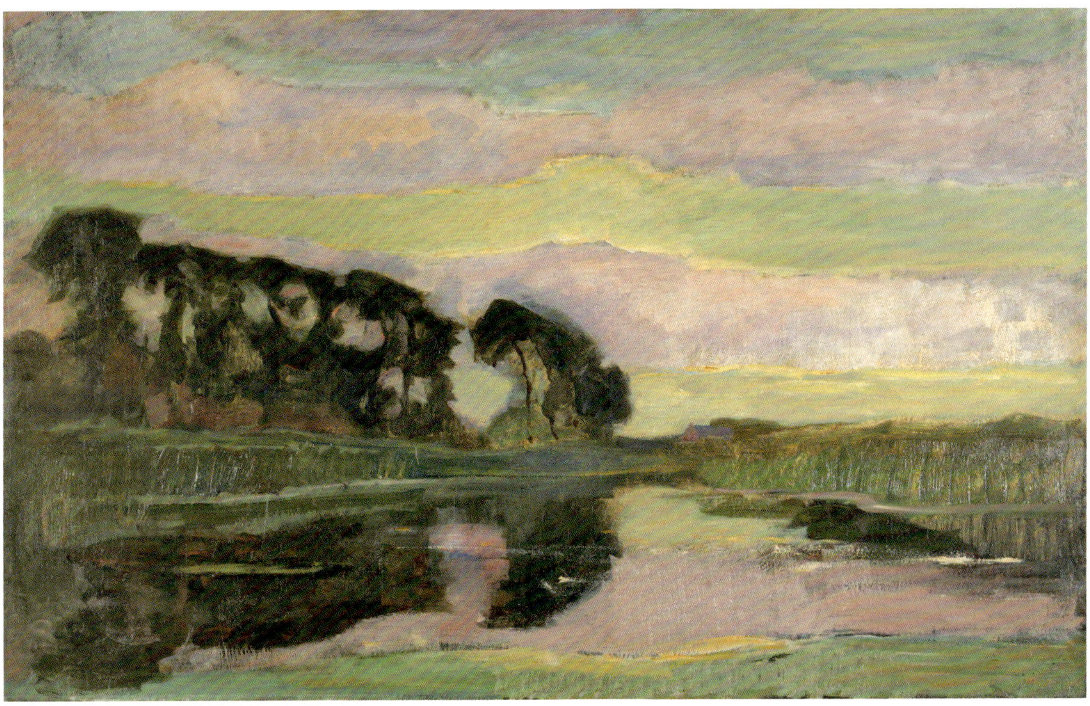

Piet Mondrian
Meer vor dem Sonnenuntergang
1909
Öl auf Pappe
41 x 76 cm
Gemeentemuseum Den Haag

Piet Mondrian
Sea toward Sunset
1909
Oil on cardboard
41 x 76 cm
Gemeentemuseum The Hague

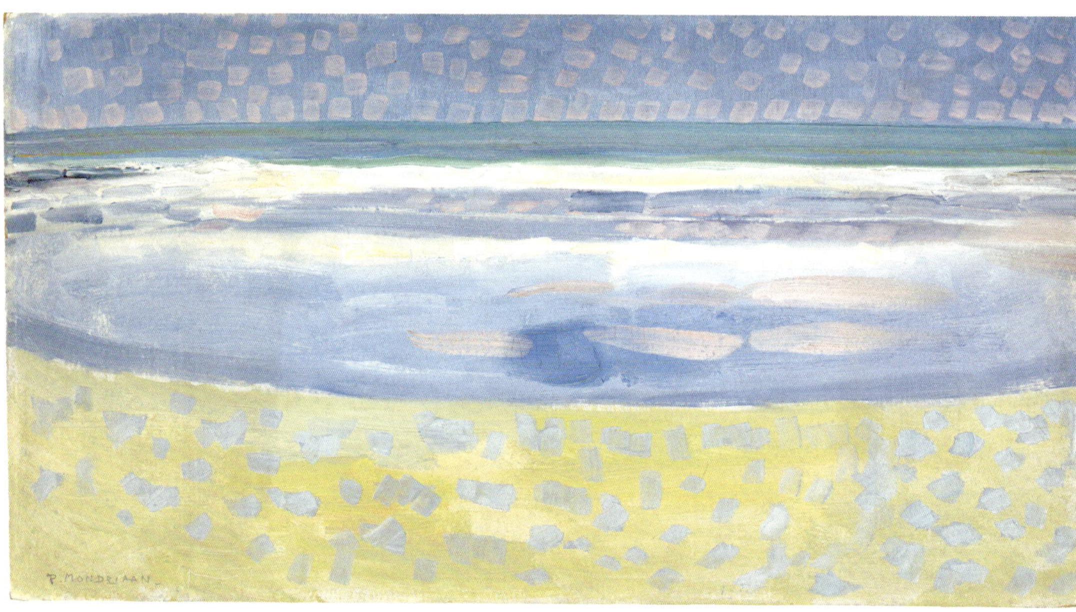

Piet Mondrian
METAMORPHOSE (Metamorphose)
1908
Öl auf Leinwand
84,5 x 54 cm
Gemeentemuseum Den Haag

Piet Mondrian
METAMORPHOSE (Metamorphosis)
1908
Oil on canvas
84,5 x 54 cm
Gemeentemuseum The Hague

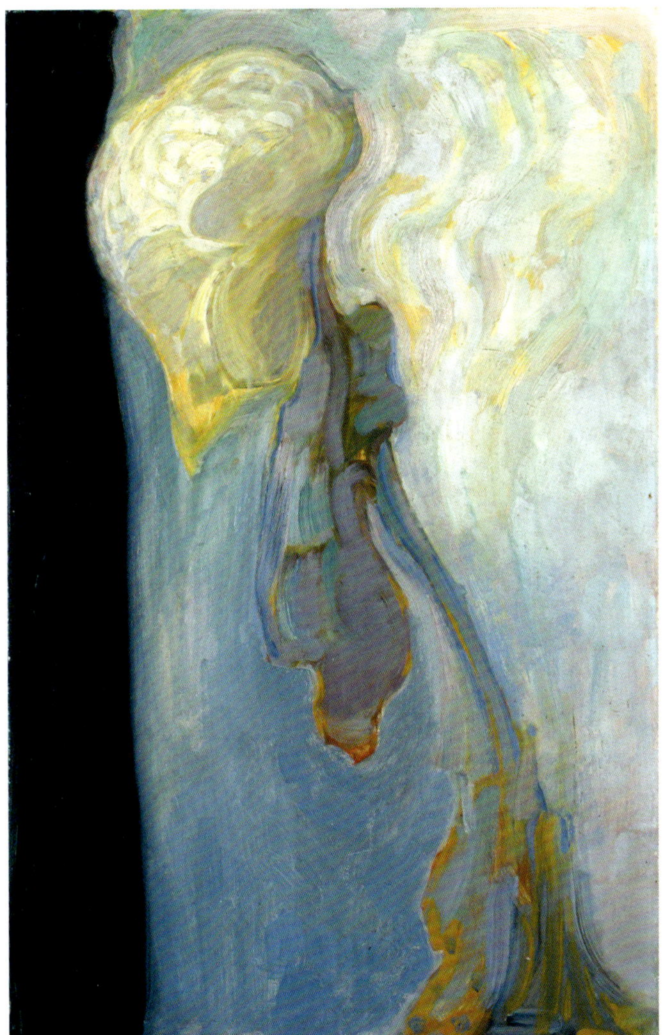

Piet Mondrian
ZEEUWS(CH)E BOER (Bauer aus Zeeland)
1909
Öl auf Leinwand
69 cm x 53 cm
Gemeentemuseum Den Haag

Piet Mondrian
ZEEUWS(CH)E BOER (Zeeland farmer)
1909
Oil on canvas
69 cm x 53 cm
Gemeentemuseum The Hague

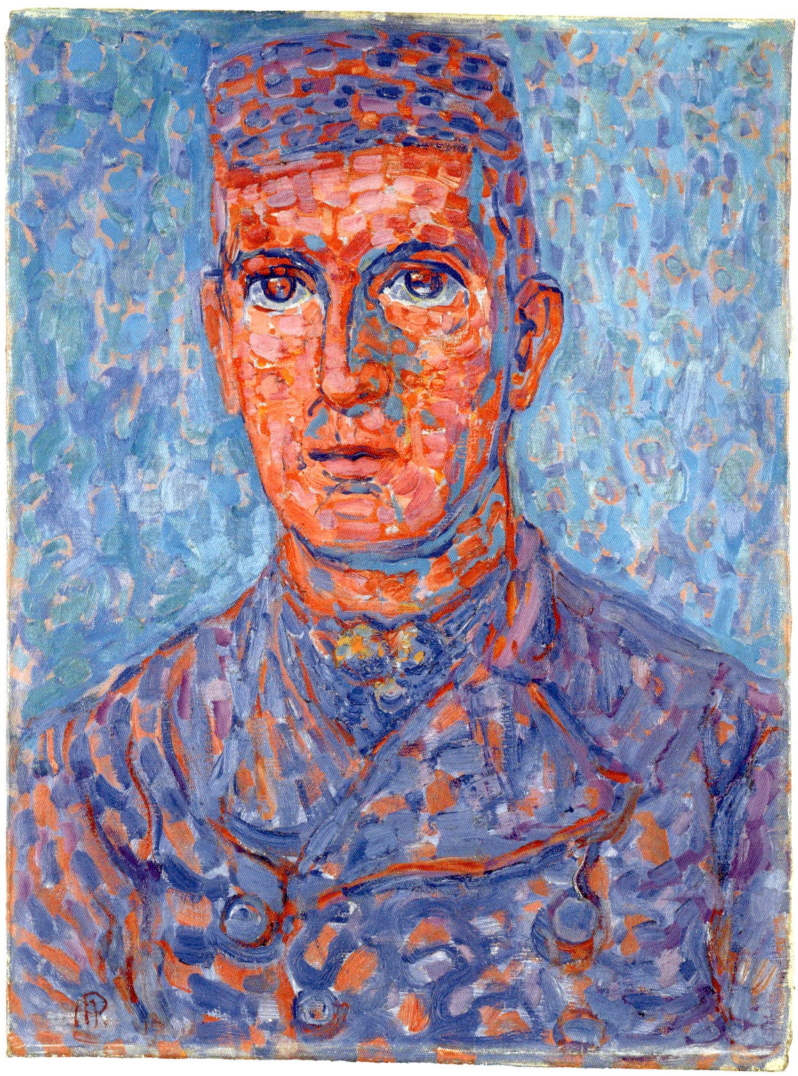

Piet Mondrian
HUISJE BIJ ZON (Kleines Haus im Sonnenlicht)
1909
Öl auf Leinwand
52,5 x 68 cm
Gemeentemuseum Den Haag

Piet Mondrian
HUISJE BIJ ZON (Little House in Sunlight)
1909
Oil on canvas
52,5 x 68 cm
Gemeentemuseum The Hague

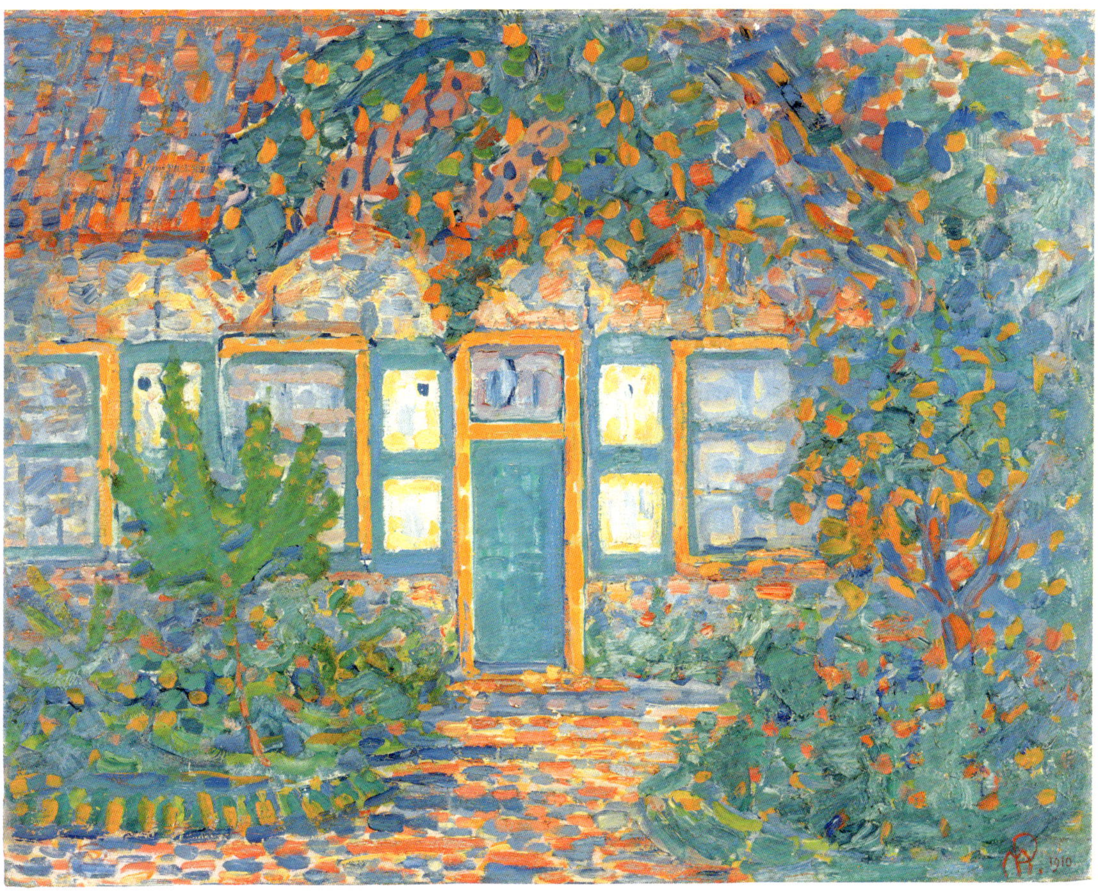

Piet Mondrian
ZEEUWS(CH)E KERKTOREN
(Kirchturm in Zeeland)
1911
Öl auf Leinwand
114 x 75 cm
Gemeentemuseum Den Haag

Piet Mondrian
ZEEUWS(CH)E KERKTOREN
(Zeeland Church Tower)
1911
Oil on canvas
114 x 75 cm
Gemeentemuseum The Hague

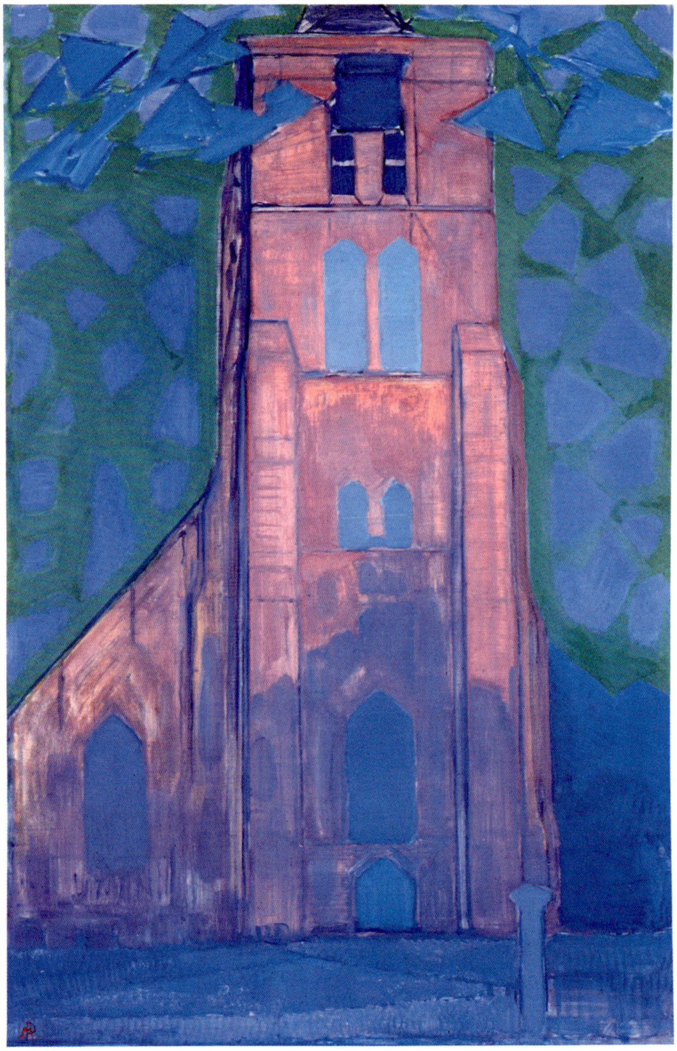

Piet Mondrian
DUINLANDSCHAP (Dünenlandschaft)
1911
Öl auf Leinwand
141 x 239 cm
Gemeentemuseum Den Haag

Piet Mondrian
DUINLANDSCHAP (Dune Landscape)
1911
Oil on canvas
141 x 239 cm
Gemeentemuseum The Hague

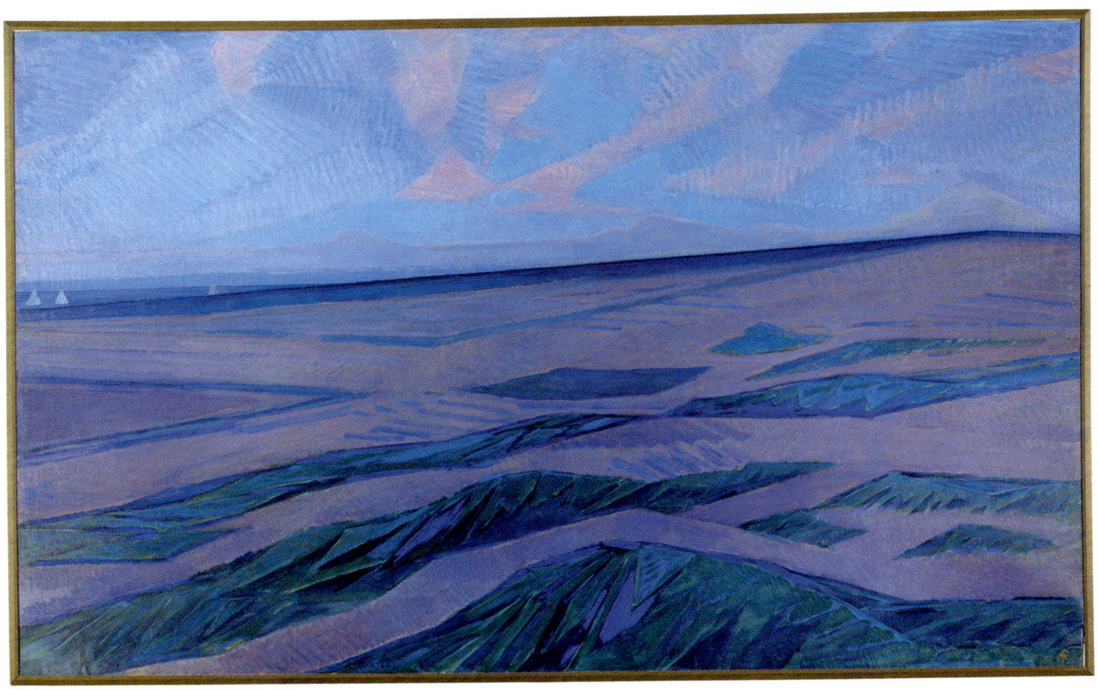

Piet Mondrian
»Paysage« (Landschaft)
1912
Öl auf Leinwand
63 x 78 cm
Gemeentemuseum Den Haag

Piet Mondrian
»Paysage« (Landscape)
1912
Oil on canvas
63 x 78 cm
Gemeentemuseum The Hague

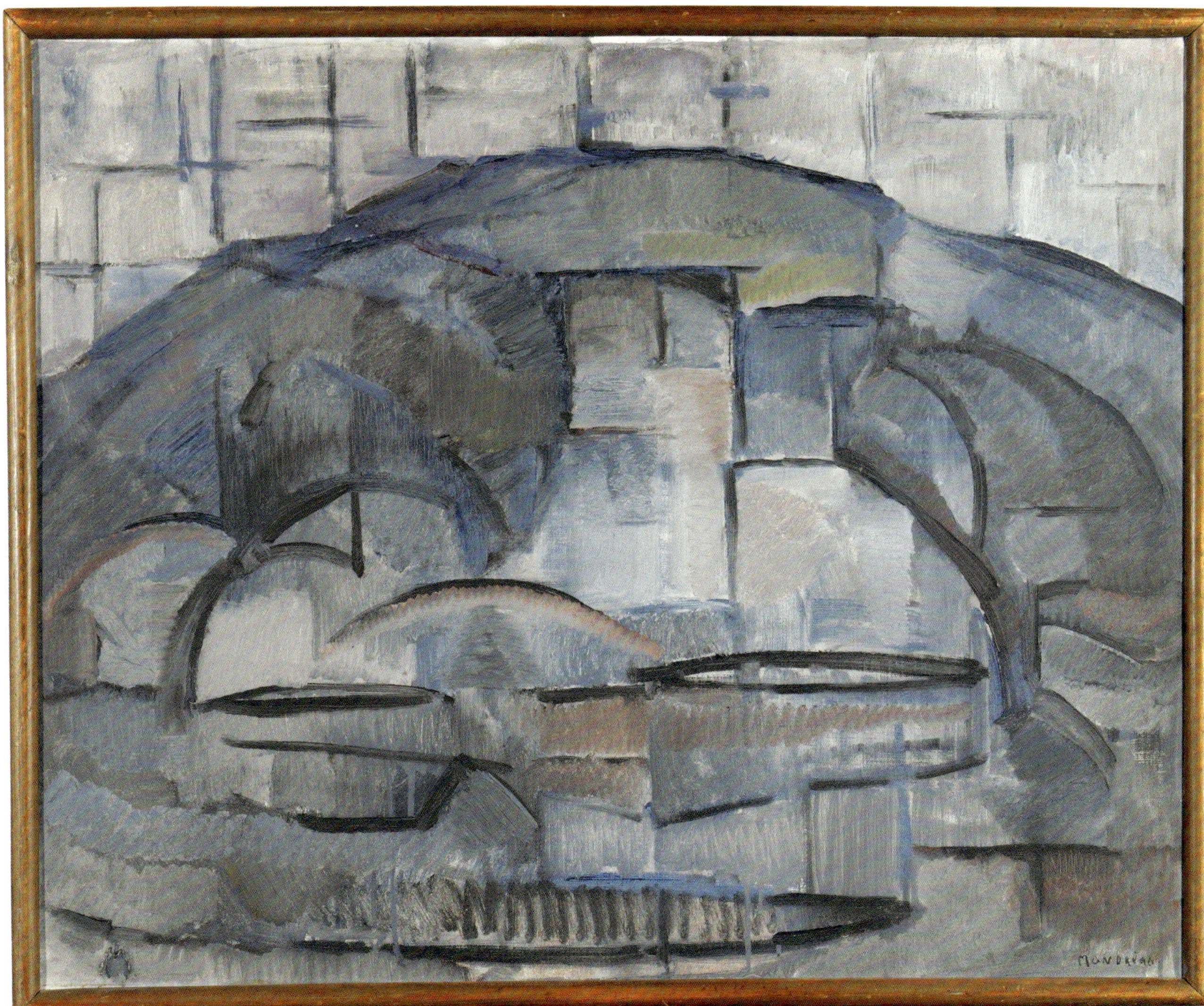

Piet Mondrian
»The Large Nude« (Der große Akt)
1912
Oil on canvas
140 x 98 cm
Gemeentemuseum Den Haag

Piet Mondrian
»The Large Nude«
1912
Oil on canvas
140 x 98 cm
Gemeentemuseum The Hague

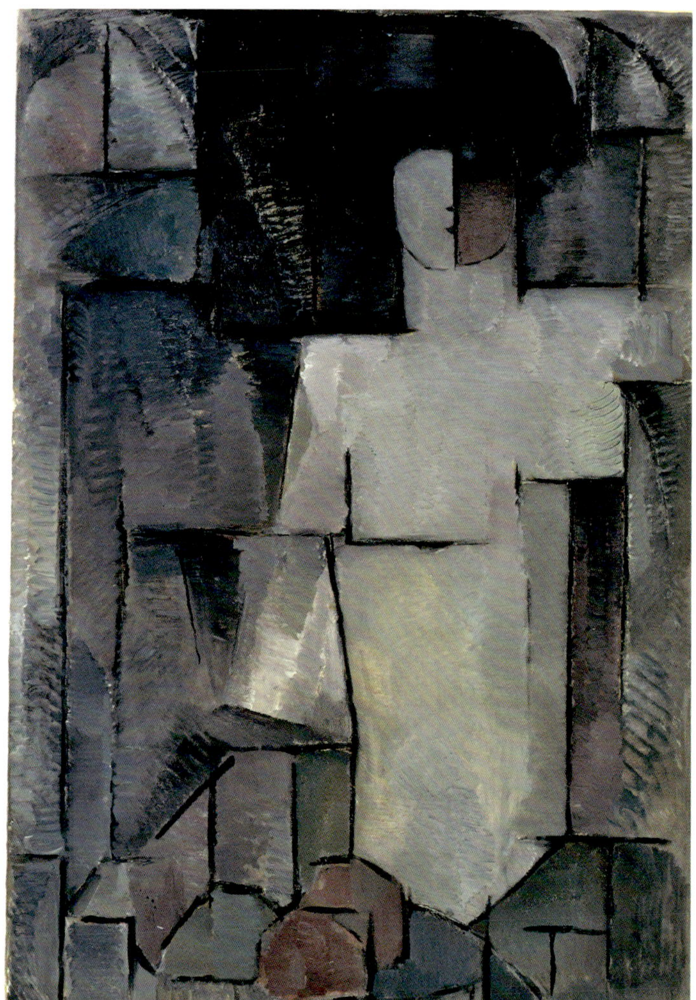

Piet Mondrian
Selbstporträt
1918
Öl auf Leinwand
88 x 71 cm
Gemeentemuseum Den Haag

Piet Mondrian
Self-Portrait
1918
Oil on canvas
88 x 71 cm
Gemeentemuseum The Hague

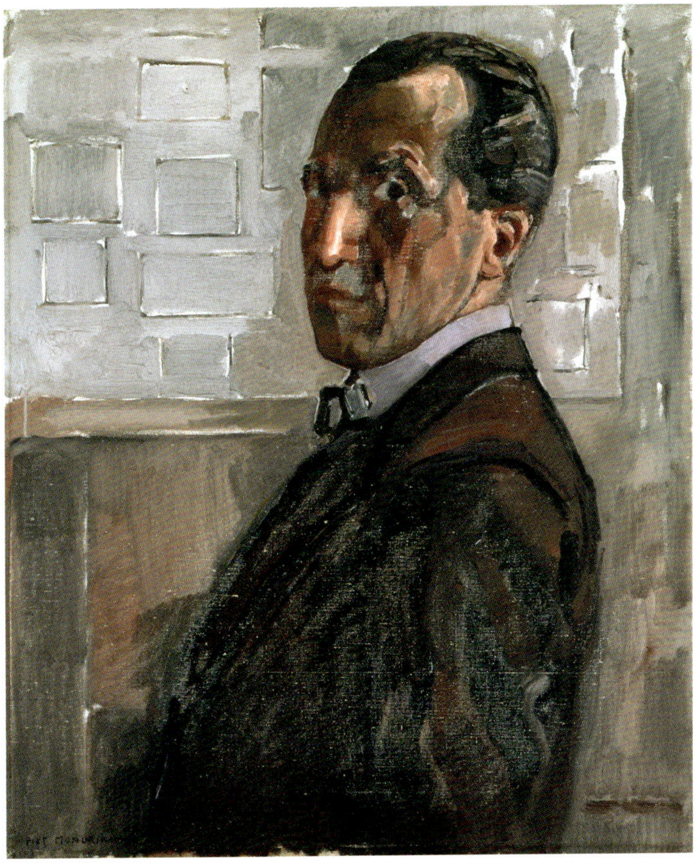

Piet Mondrian
Der graue Baum
1911
Öl auf Leinwand
79,7 x 109,1 cm
Gemeentemuseum Den Haag

Piet Mondrian
The Gray Tree
1911
Oil on canvas
79,7 x 109,1 cm
Gemeentemuseum The Hague

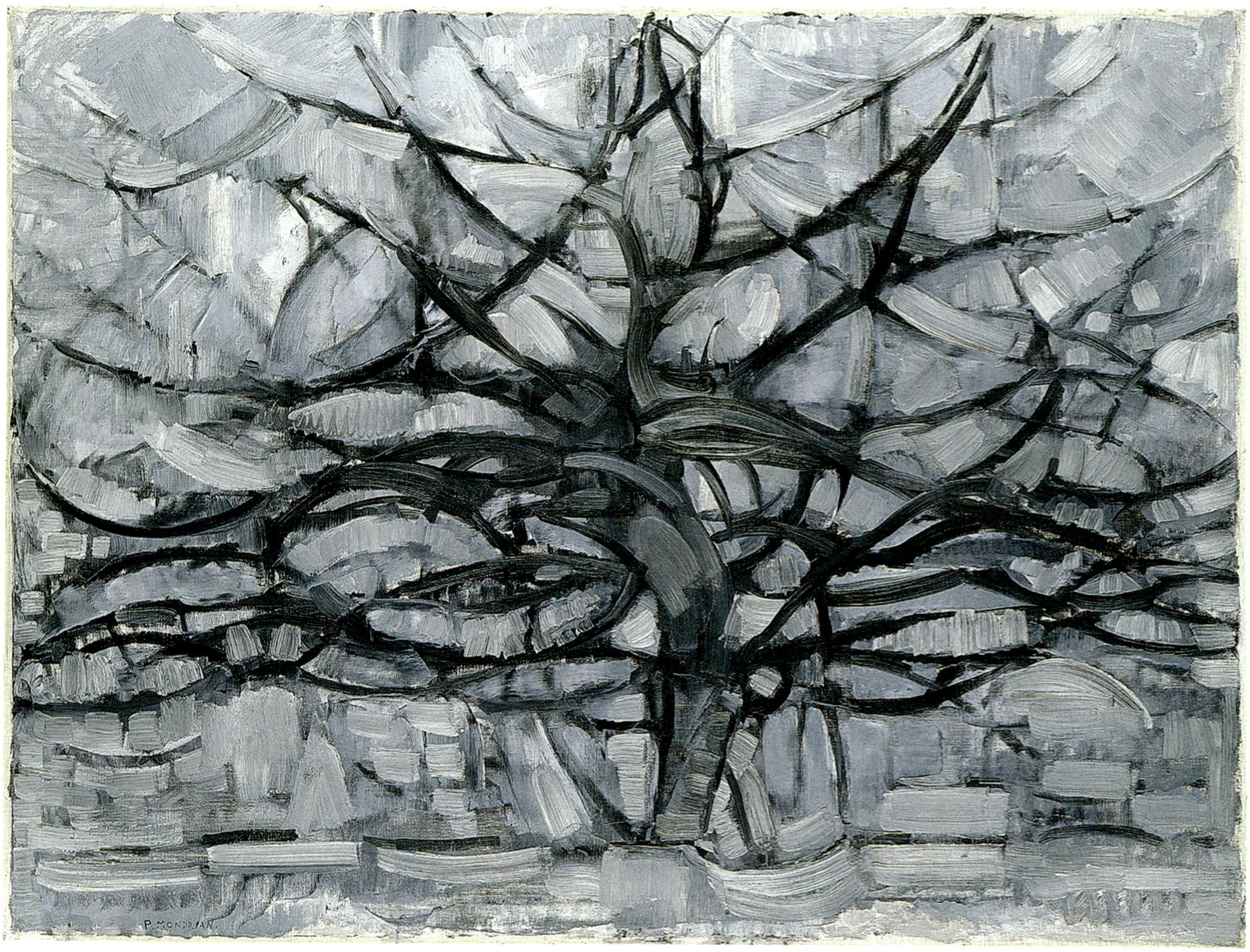

Piet Mondrian
BLOEIENDE APPELBOOM
(Blühender Apfelbaum)
1912
Öl auf Leinwand
78,5 x 107,5 cm
Gemeentemuseum Den Haag

Piet Mondrian
BLOEIENDE APPELBOOM
(Flowering Appletree)
1912
Oil on canvas
78,5 x 107,5 cm
Gemeentemuseum The Hague

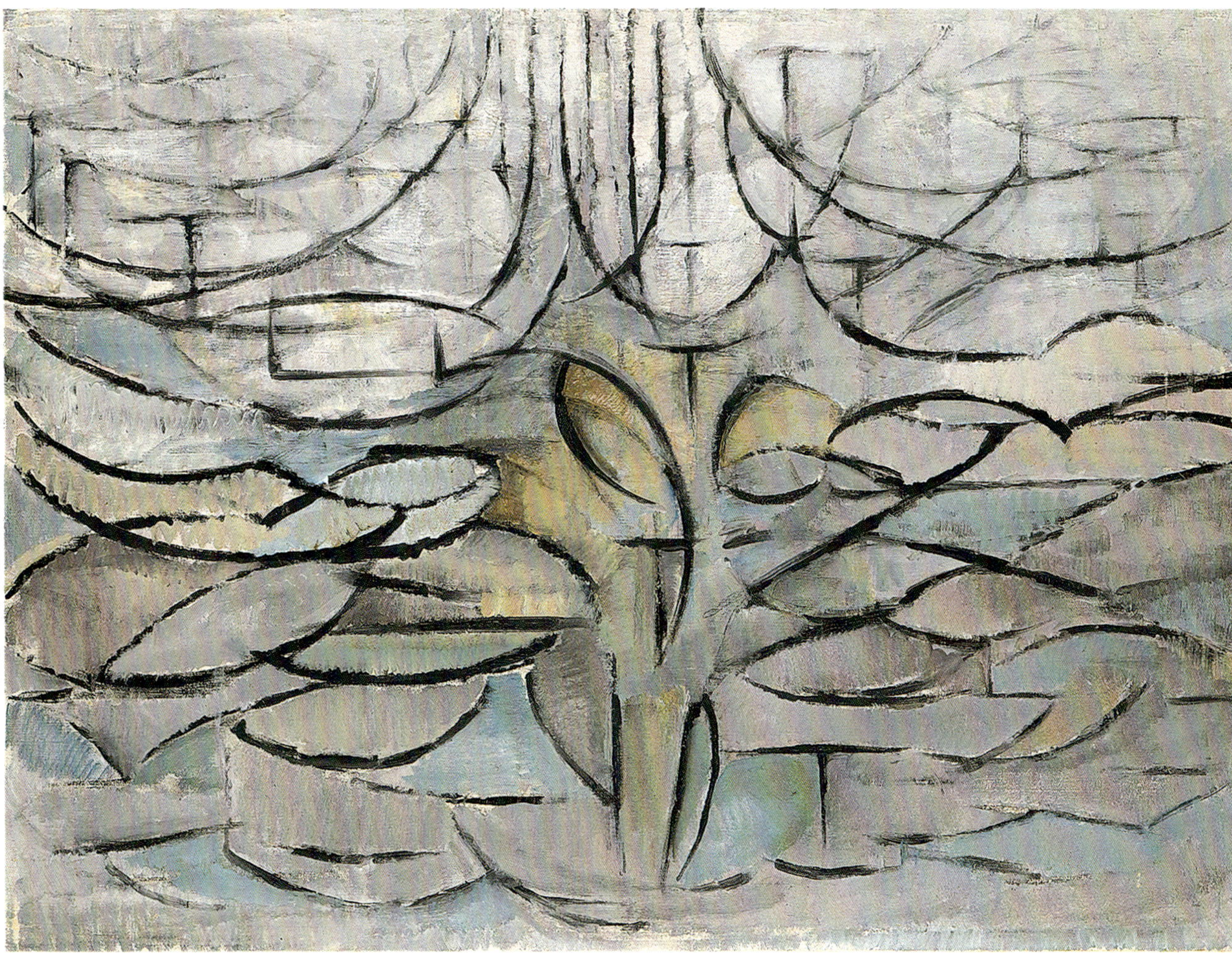

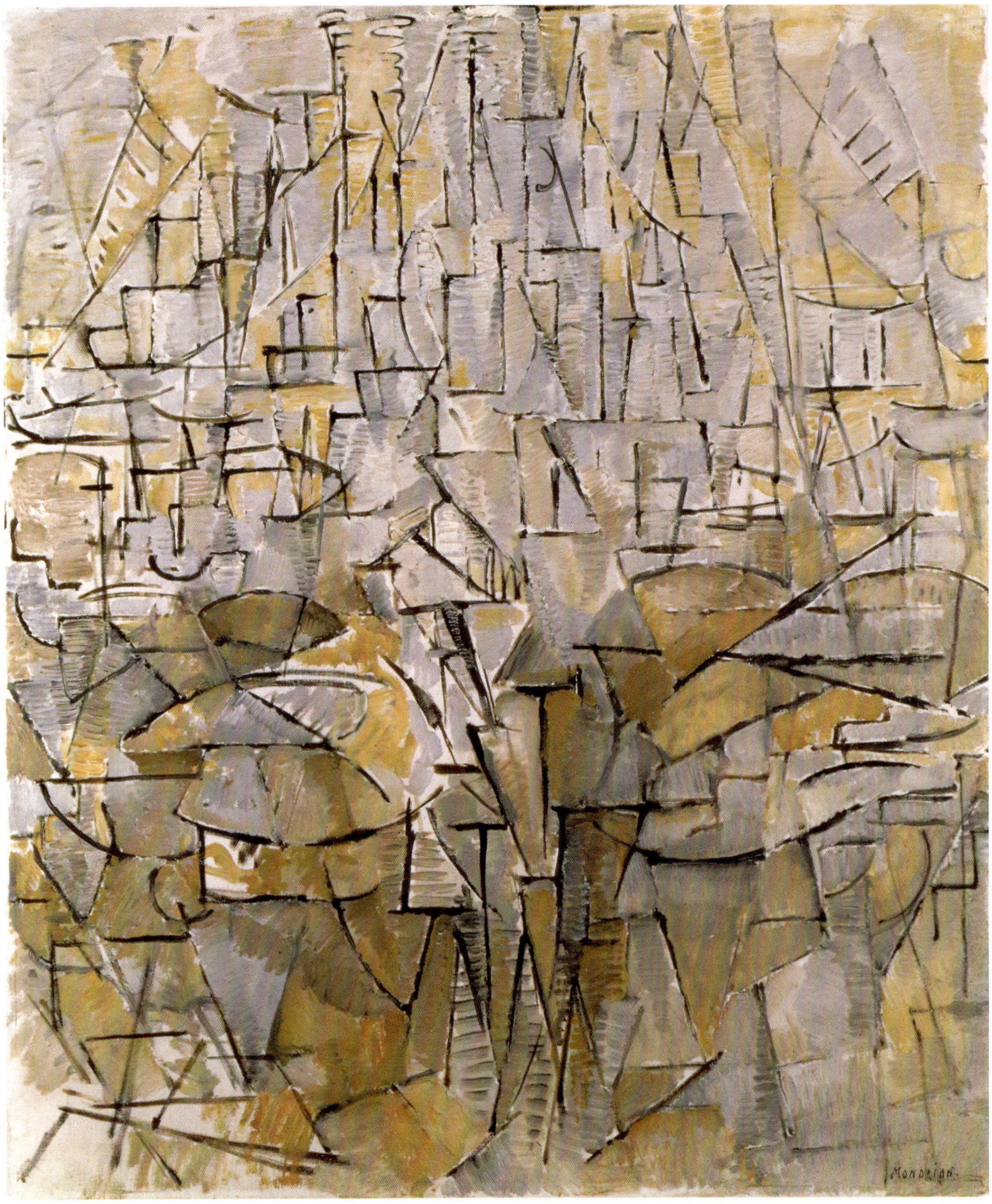
MONDRIAN

Piet Mondrian
TABLEAU NO. 4 / COMPOSITION NO. VIII / COMPOSITIE 3
1913
Öl auf Leinwand
95 x 80 cm
Gemeentemuseum Den Haag

Piet Mondrian
TABLEAU NO. 4 / COMPOSITION NO. VIII / COMPOSITIE 3
1913
Oil on canvas
95 x 80 cm
Gemeentemuseum The Hague

Piet Mondrian
COMPOSITION NO. IV / COMPOSITIE 6
1914
Öl auf Leinwand
88 x 61 cm
Gemeentemuseum Den Haag

Piet Mondrian
COMPOSITION NO. IV / COMPOSITIE 6
1914
Oil on canvas
88 x 61 cm
Gemeentemuseum The Hague

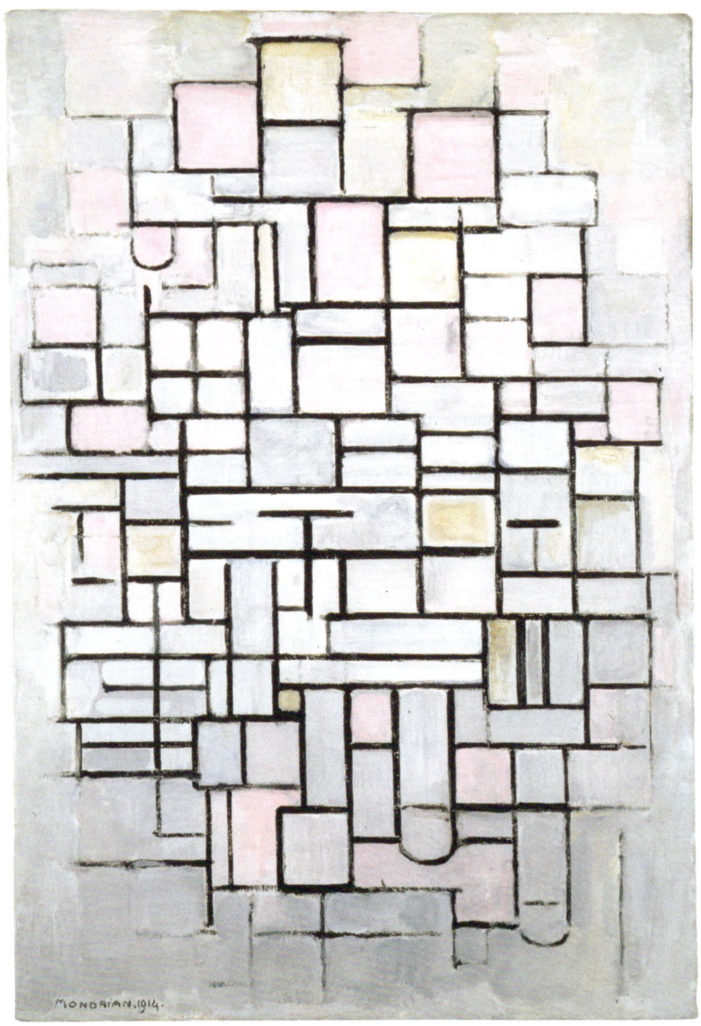

Piet Mondrian
Komposition im Oval mit Farbfeldern 2
1914
Öl auf Leinwand
113 x 84,5 cm
Gemeentemuseum Den Haag

Piet Mondrian
Composition in Oval with Color Planes 2
1914
Oil on canvas
113 x 84,5 cm
Gemeentemuseum The Hague

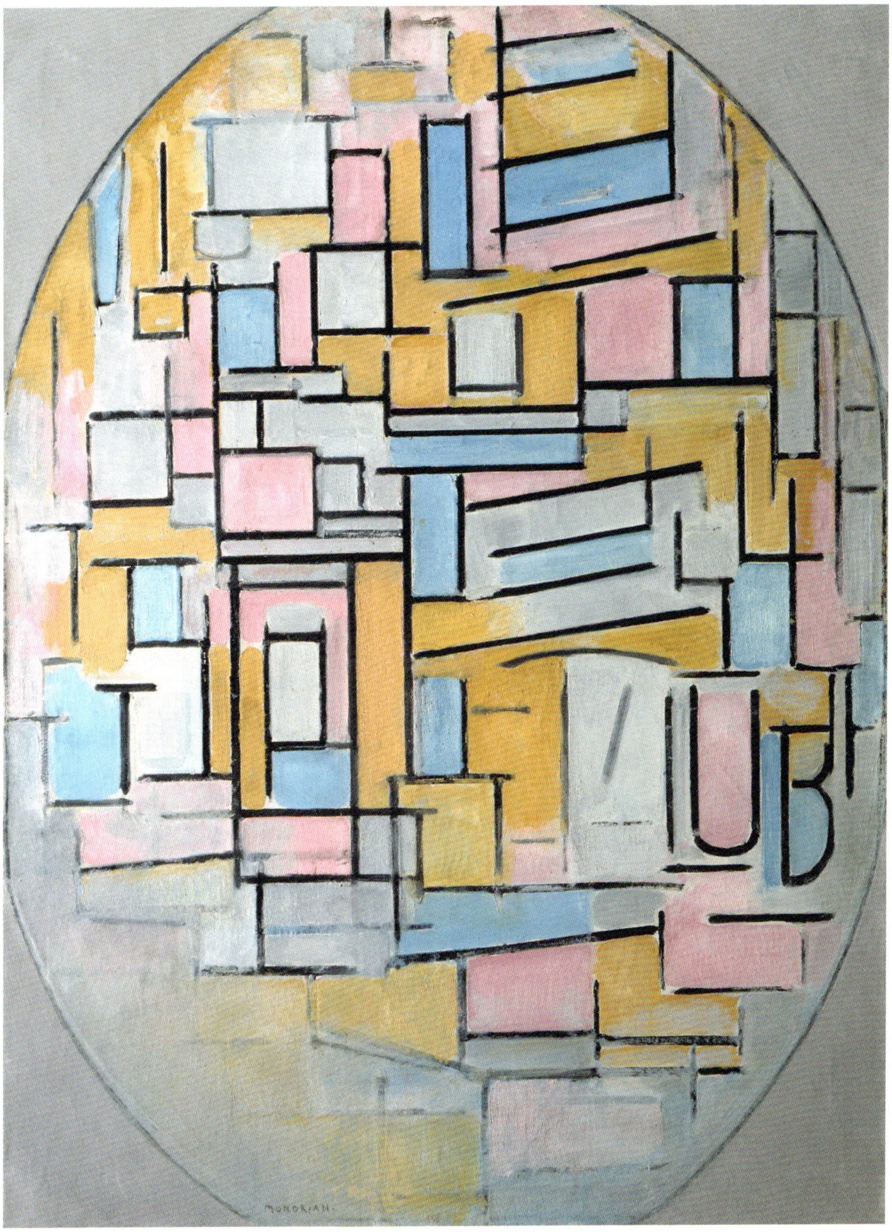

Piet Mondrian
COMPOSITIE NO. 3, mit Farbfeldern 3
1917
Öl auf Leinwand
48 x 61 cm
Gemeentemuseum Den Haag

Piet Mondrian
COMPOSITIE NO. 3, with Color Planes 3
1917
Oil on canvas
48 x 61 cm
Gemeentemuseum The Hague

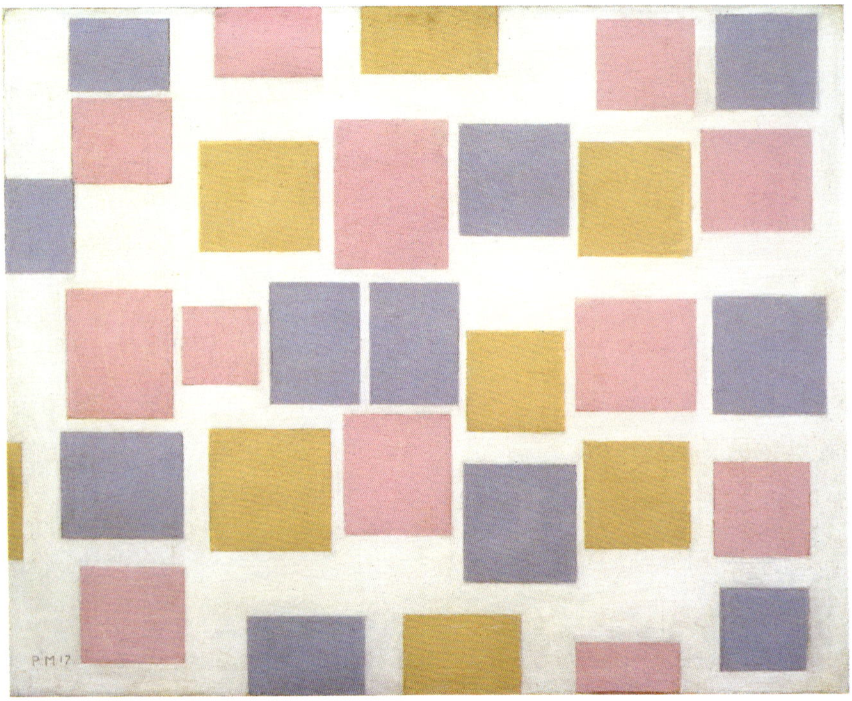

Piet Mondrian
Rasterkomposition 7
1919
Öl auf Leinwand
49 x 49 cm
Kunstmuseum Basel,
Schenkung Marguerite Arp-Hagenbach 1968

Piet Mondrian
Composition with Grid 7
1919
Oil on canvas
49 x 49 cm
Kunstmuseum Basel,
Gift of Marguerite Arp-Hagenbach, 1968

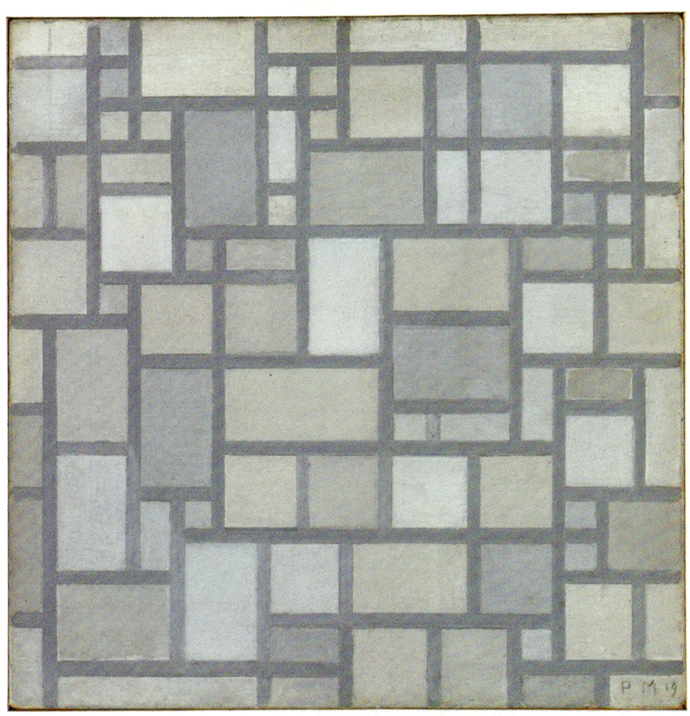

Piet Mondrian
Rasterkomposition 8: Schachbrettkomposition mit dunklen Farben
1919
Öl auf Leinwand
84 x 102 cm
Gemeentemuseum Den Haag

Piet Mondrian
Composition with Grid 8: Checkerboard Composition with Dark Colors
1919
Oil on canvas
84 x 102 cm
Gemeentemuseum The Hague

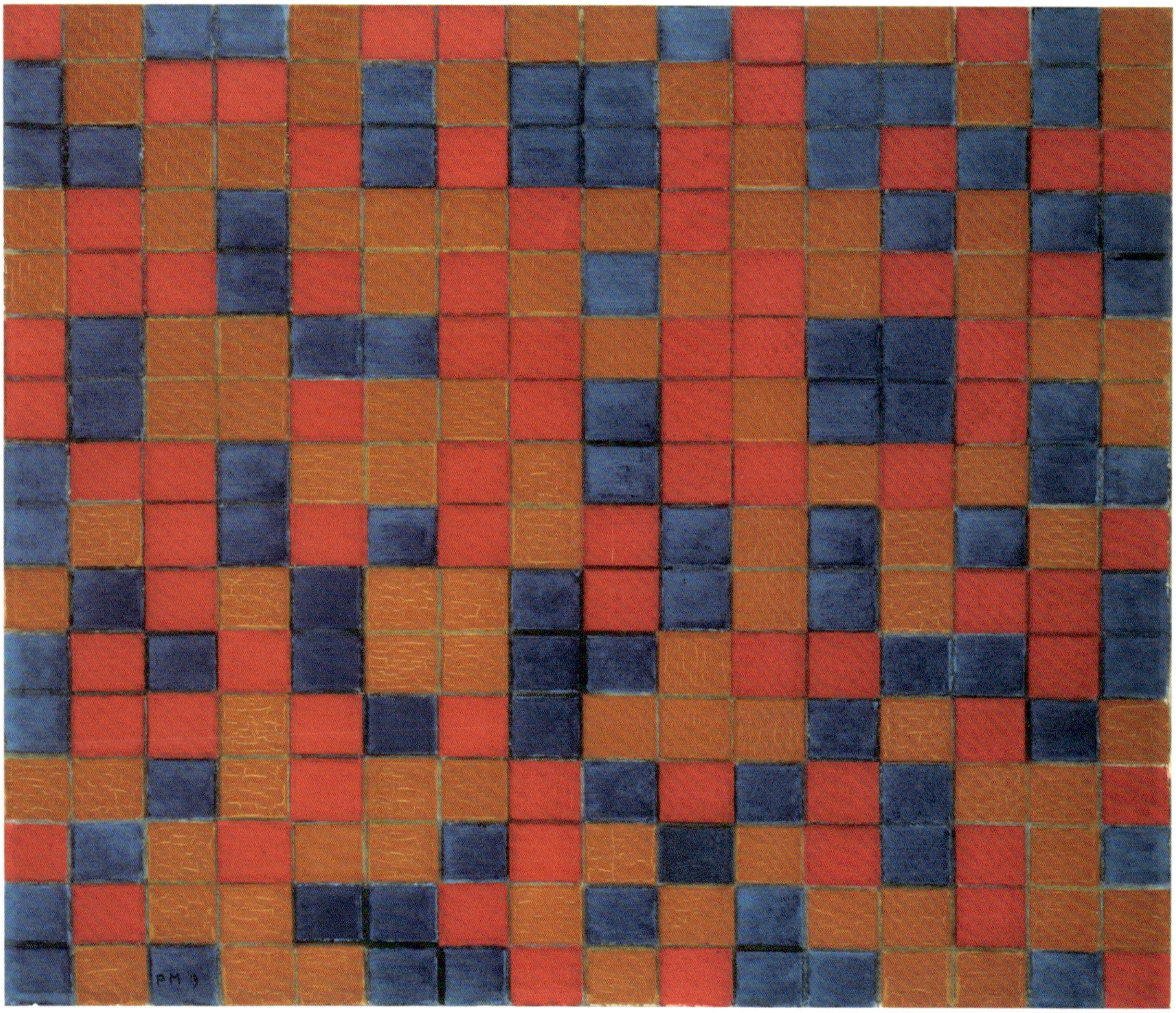

Piet Mondrian
Rasterkomposition 9: Schachbrettkomposition mit hellen Farben
1919
Öl auf Leinwand
86 x 106 cm
Gemeentemuseum Den Haag

Piet Mondrian
Composition with Grid 9: Checkerboard Composition with Light Colors
1919
Oil on canvas
86 x 106 cm
Gemeentemuseum The Hague

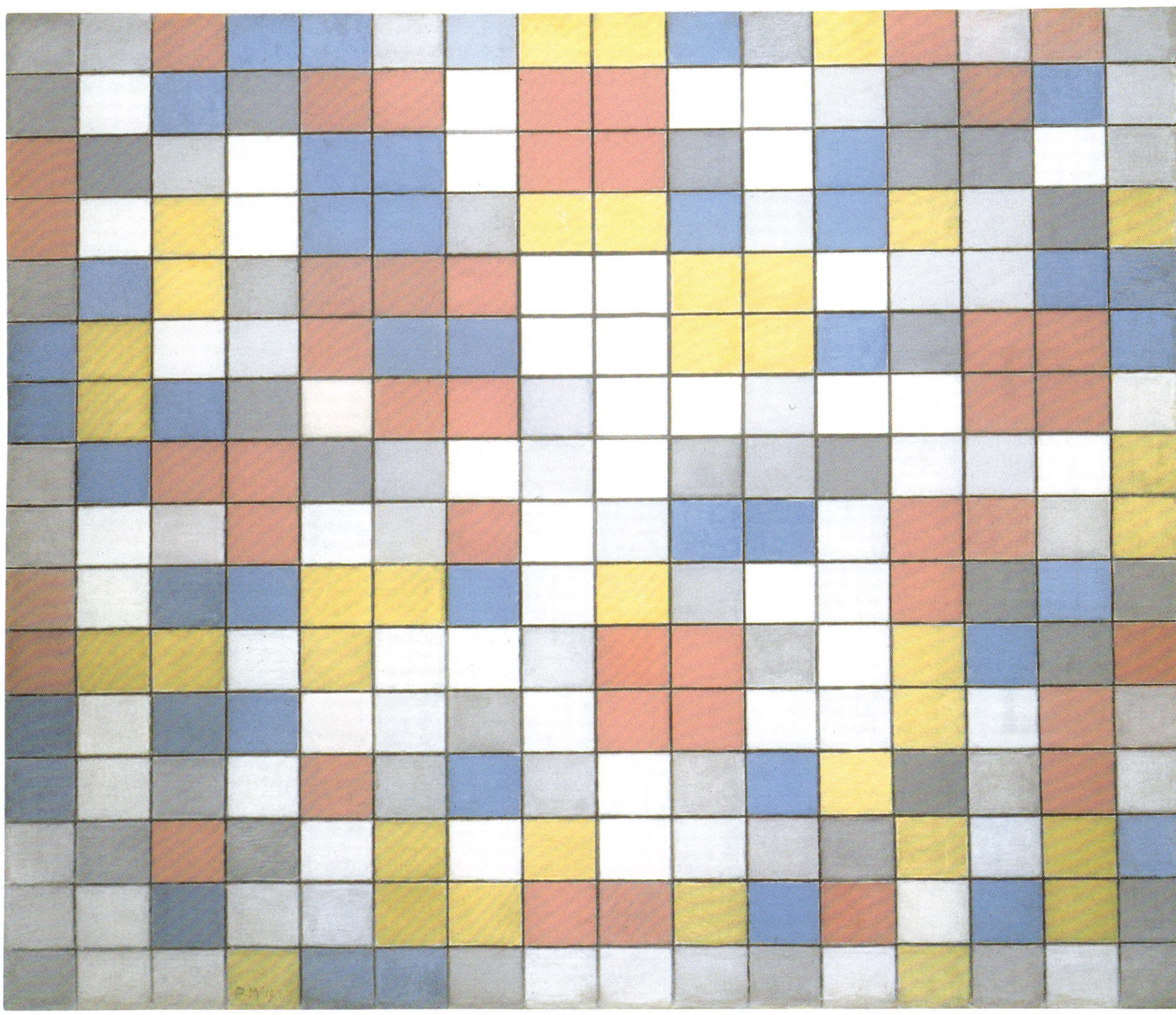

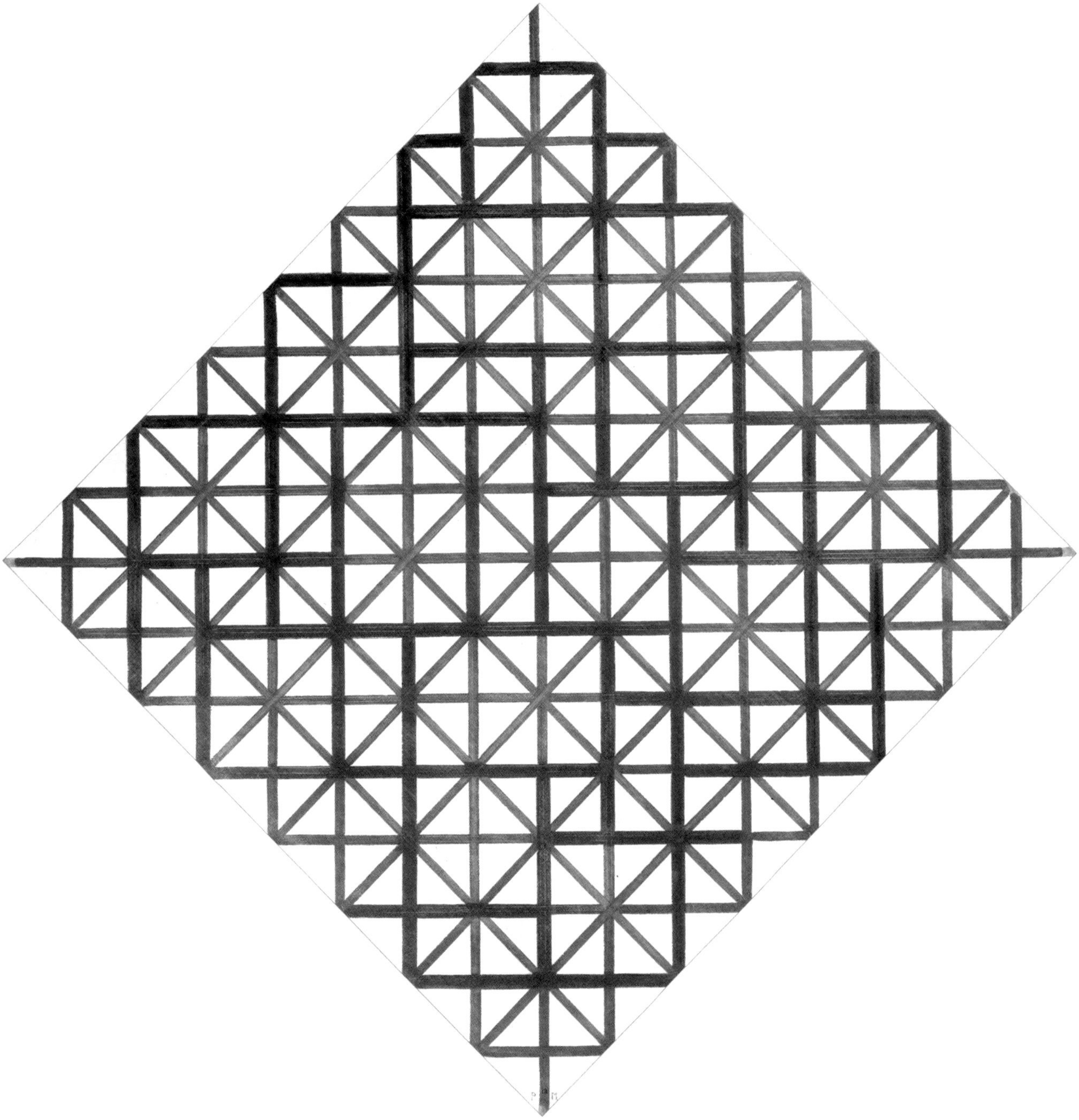

Piet Mondrian
Rasterkomposition 3: Rautenkomposition
1918
Öl auf Leinwand
Diagonale: 121 cm, Seiten: 84,5 cm
Gemeentemuseum Den Haag

Piet Mondrian
Composition with Grid 3: Lozenge Composition
1918
Oil on canvas
Diagonal: 121 cm, Sides: 84,5 cm
Gemeentemuseum The Hague

Piet Mondrian
Komposition mit Rot, Schwarz, Gelb, Blau und Grau
1921
Öl auf Leinwand
80 x 50 cm
Gemeentemuseum Den Haag

Piet Mondrian
Composition with Red, Black, Yellow, Blue, and Gray
1921
Oil on canvas
80 x 50 cm
Gemeentemuseum The Hague

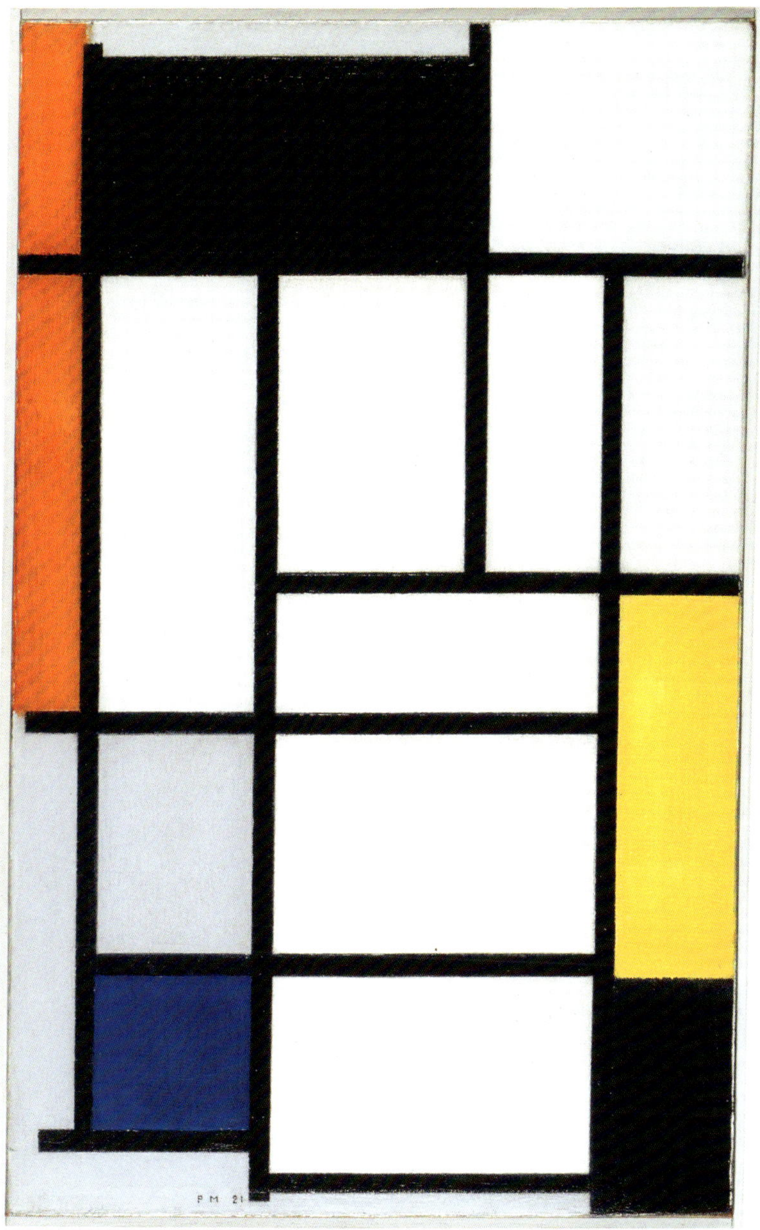

Piet Mondrian
TABLEAU I, mit Rot, Schwarz, Blau und Gelb
1921
Öl auf Leinwand
103 x 100 cm
Gemeentemuseum Den Haag

Piet Mondrian
TABLEAU I, with Red, Black, Blue and Yellow
1921
Oil on canvas
103 x 100 cm
Gemeentemuseum The Hague

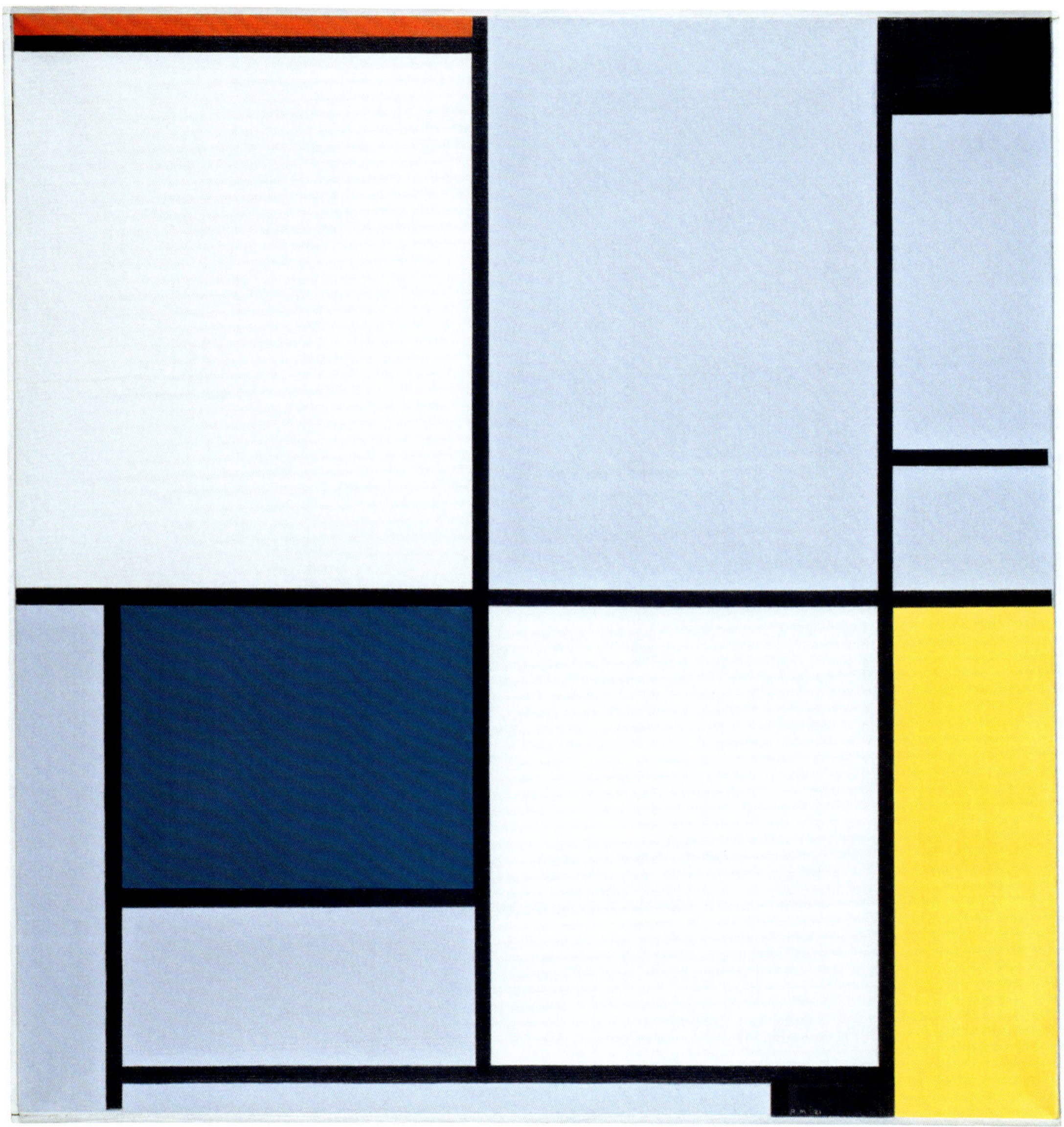

Piet Mondrian
Komposition mit Blau, Gelb, Schwarz und Rot
1922
Öl auf Leinwand
53 x 54 cm
Staatsgalerie Stuttgart

Piet Mondrian
Composition with Blue, Yellow, Black, and Red
1922
Oil on canvas
53 x 54 cm
Staatsgalerie Stuttgart

Piet Mondrian
Entwurf für einen Salon von Ida Bienert
(sogenannter »SALON DE MADAME B...,
À DRESDEN«)
Auseinandergezogene Darstellung
1926
Bleistift und Gouache auf Papier
75 x 75 cm
Kupferstich-Kabinett,
Staatliche Kunstsammlungen Dresden

Piet Mondrian
Design for the Library-Study of Ida Bienert,
the so-called »SALON DE MADAME B...,
À DRESDEN«
Exploded box plan
1926
Pencil and gouache on paper
75 x 75 cm
Kupferstich-Kabinett,
Staatliche Kunstsammlungen Dresden

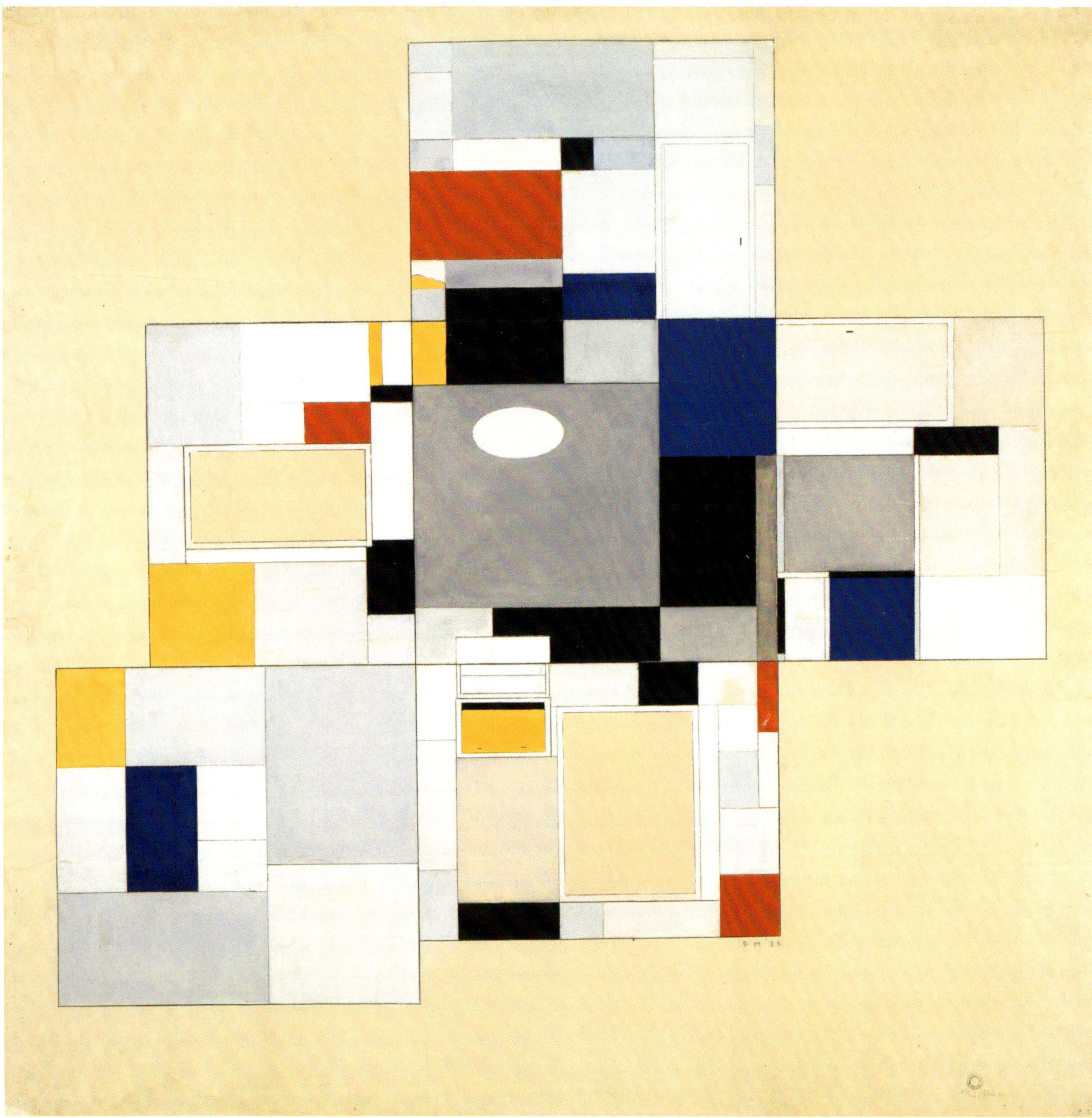

Piet Mondrian
Entwurf für einen Salon von Ida Bienert
(sogenannter »SALON DE MADAME B...,
À DRESDEN«)
Links:
Axonometrische Darstellung
von Boden, Bett und Tisch
1926
Bleistift und Gouache auf Papier
37,3 x 56,5 cm
Kupferstich-Kabinett,
Staatliche Kunstsammlungen Dresden

Rechts:
Axonometrische Darstellung
von Decke, Bücherschrank und Kabinett
1926
Bleistift und Gouache auf Papier
37,6 x 56 cm
Kupferstich-Kabinett,
Staatliche Kunstsammlungen Dresden

Piet Mondrian
Design for the Library-Study of Ida Bienert,
the so-called »SALON DE MADAME B...,
À DRESDEN«
Left:
Axonometric View
with Floor, Bed, and Table
1926
Pencil and gouache on paper
37,3 x 56,5 cm
Kupferstich-Kabinett,
Staatliche Kunstsammlungen Dresden

Right:
Axonometric View
with Ceiling, Bookcase, and Cabinet
1926
Pencil and gouache on paper
37,6 x 56 cm
Kupferstich-Kabinett,
Staatliche Kunstsammlungen Dresden

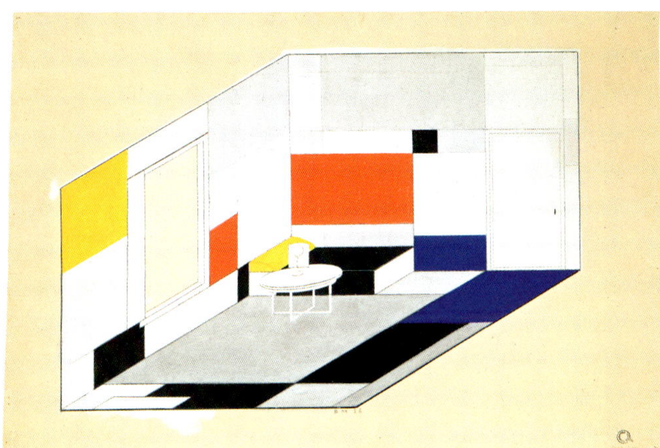

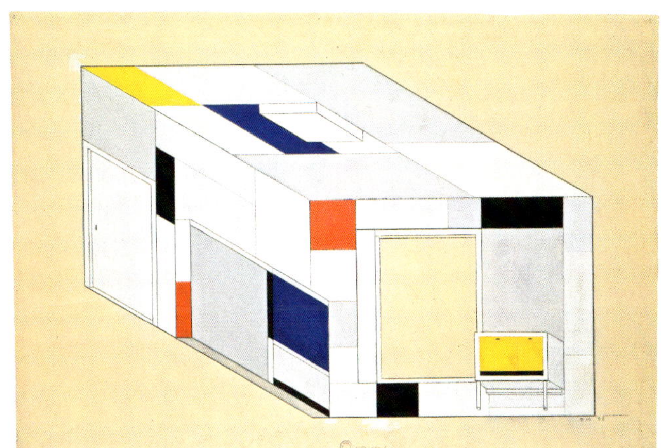

Piet Mondrian
Rautenkomposition mit vier gelben Linien
1933
Öl auf Leinwand
Diagonale: 112,9 cm, Seiten: 80,2 x 79,9 cm
Gemeentemuseum Den Haag

Piet Mondrian
Lozenge Composition with Four Yellow Lines
1933
Oil on canvas
Diagonal: 112,9 cm, Sides: 80,2 x 79,9 cm
Gemeentemuseum The Hague

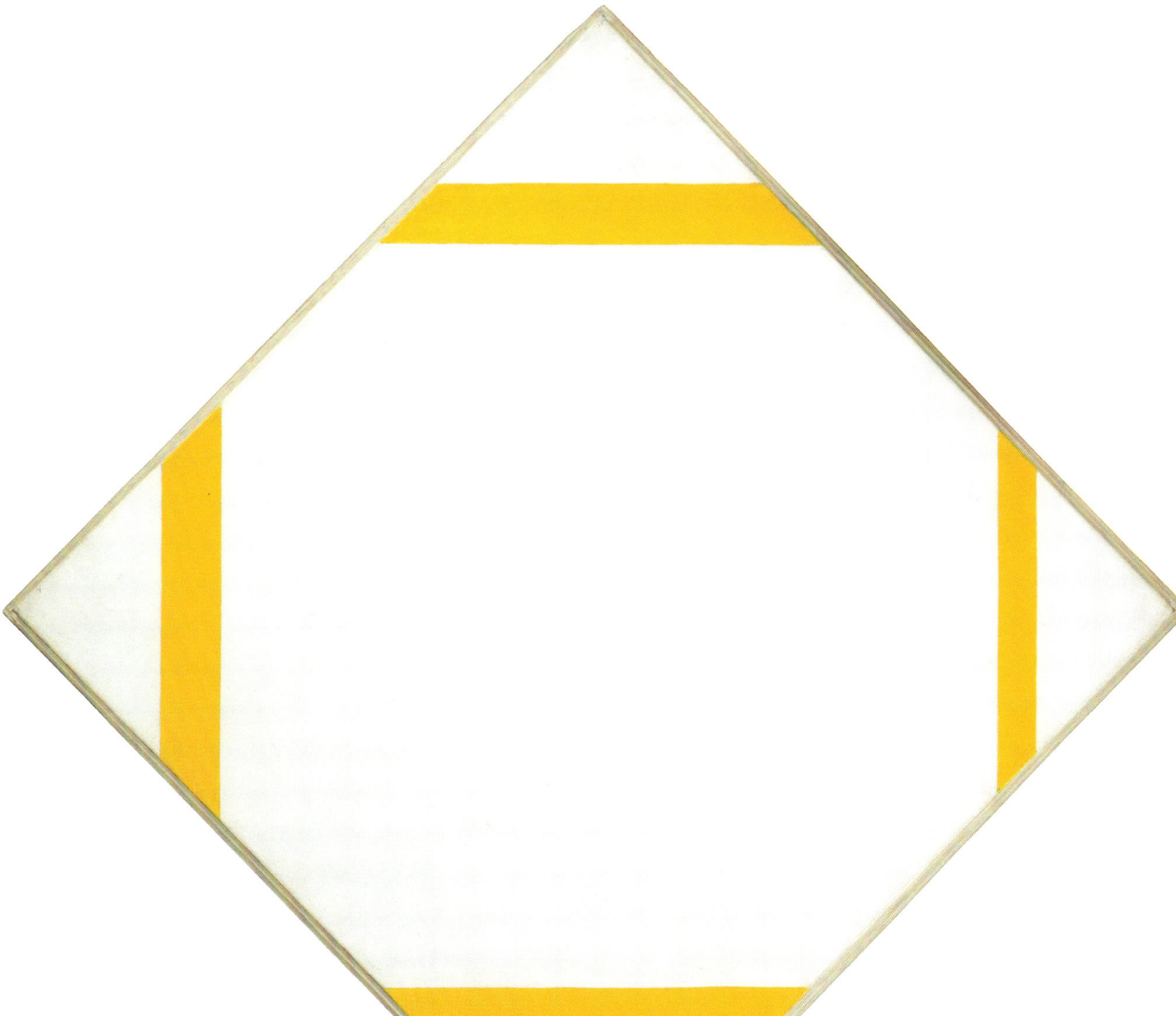

Piet Mondrian
COMPOSITION DE LIGNES ET COULEUR: III
(Komposition aus Linien und Farbe: III)
1937
Öl auf Leinwand
80 x 77 cm
Gemeentemuseum Den Haag

Piet Mondrian
COMPOSITION DE LIGNES ET COULEUR: III
(Composition of Lines and Color: III)
1937
Oil on canvas
80 x 77 cm
Gemeentemuseum The Hague

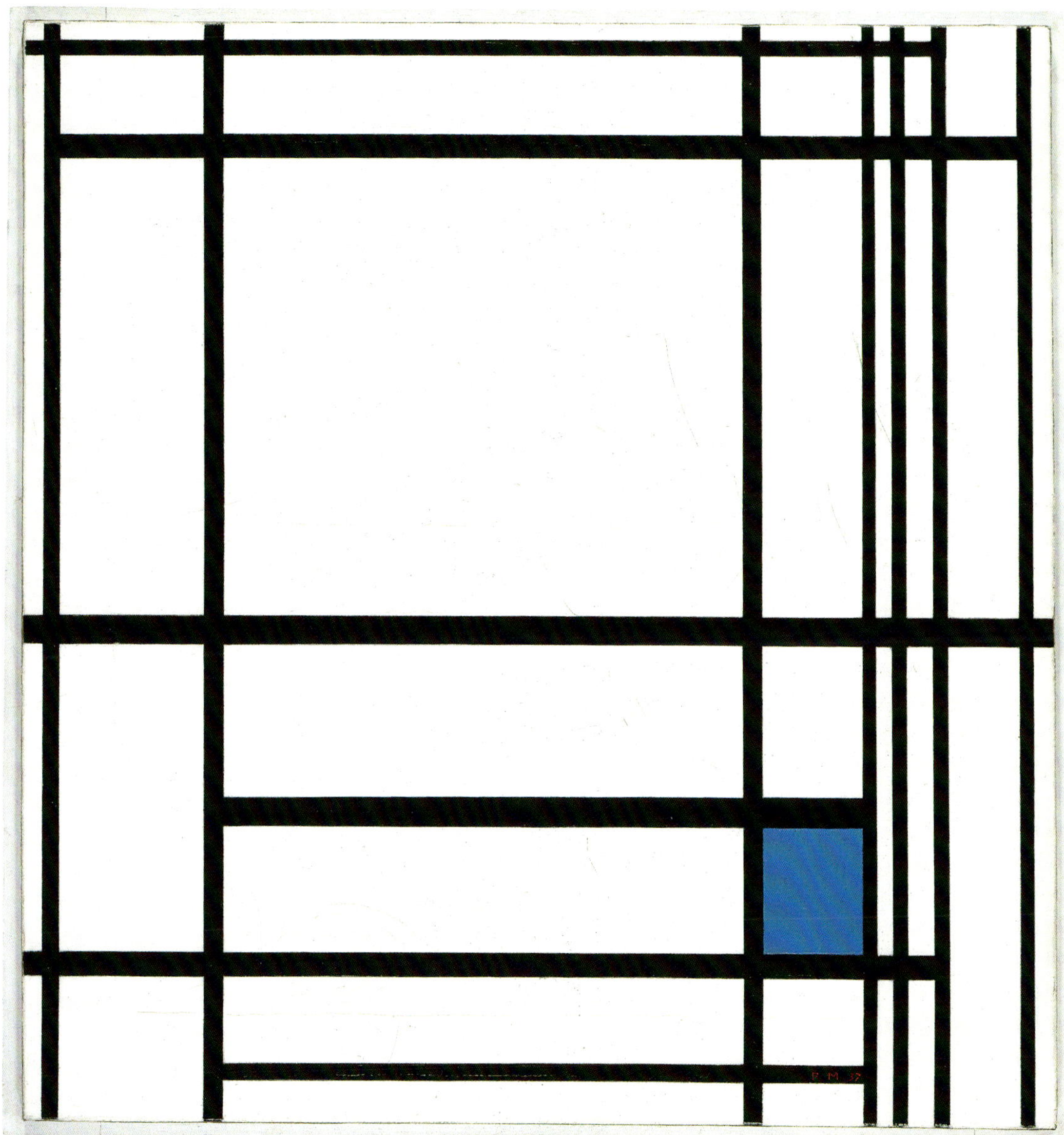

MARLOW MOSS

Marlow Moss, 1889 im englischen Kilburn als Marjorie Jewel Moss geboren, geht gegen den Willen ihrer Eltern 1916 nach London, um dort erst an der St. John's Wood School of Art und dann an der Slade School of Fine Art Malerei zu studieren. 1919 lässt sie sich in Cornwall nieder. Vier Jahre später verlegt sie sich auf die Kunst der Bildhauerei, um ab 1926 wieder mit dem Malen zu beginnen. Zu dieser Zeit ändert sie ihre äußere Erscheinung. Sie trägt das Haar kurz, kleidet sich wie ein Mann mit Einstecktuch und Reithosen und nennt sich ab jetzt Marlow. Ein Jahr später geht sie nach Paris, wo ihr Nettie Nijhoff begegnet, mit der sie ihr ganzes Leben eine Liebesbeziehung unterhält. Moss besucht Kurse an der Académie Moderne als Schülerin von Fernand Léger und Amedée Ozenfant, aber erst die Begegnung mit Mondrian und dessen Werk lässt sie ihren eigenen künstlerischen Stil finden. Ihre Arbeiten orientieren sich später auch an den Reliefs und Skulpturen Georges Vantongerloos und Jean Gorins und treten mit ihnen in Dialog. Doch vor dem Zweiten Weltkrieg widmet sie sich vor allem der Malerei. Moss malt, ganz im neoplastischen Sinne Mondrians, abstrakte Gemälde mit einfachen horizontalen und vertikalen Linien und Flächen in Primärfarben. 1932 entstehen Bilder, bei denen sie die horizontalen Linien dünner, dafür aber doppelt zeichnet.
So kann der entstehende Zwischenraum als schmale weiße Fläche wahrgenommen werden, erscheint aber zugleich selbst als Linie. Mondrian fühlt sich herausgefordert und erkennt dabei die Möglichkeit, die statische klassische Ruhe, die sein Werk auszeichnet, durch ein viel dynamischeres Gleichgewicht zu ersetzen und außerdem den strengen Gegensatz zwischen Fläche und Linie aufzugeben. Es entwickelt sich ein reger Briefwechsel zwischen Mondrian und Jean Gorin, einem der wenigen Künstlerkollegen, der diese Veränderung in Mondrians Arbeiten überhaupt wahrnimmt. Marlow Moss treibt unterdessen die Abstraktion ihrer Gemälde so weit, dass sie beinahe nur noch weiße Flächen sind, an deren Ränder sich Linien und Flächen ins Bild schieben. Erst Jahre später wird sich Moss bewusst, welch enormen Einfluss ihre Kunst auf das Werk eines der Begründer von *De Stijl* ausgeübt hat. Marlow Moss stirbt 1958 in Penzance.

Marlow Moss – born Marjorie Jewel Moss in Kilburn, an area of London, in 1889. In defiance of her parents' wishes, in 1916 she attended St. John's Wood School of Art and later the Slade School of Fine Art. In 1919 she moved to Cornwall. Four years later she took up sculpture but returned to painting in 1926. Moss started to dress as a man (short hair, pocket handkerchief and riding breeches) and called herself Marlow. A year later she went to Paris, where she became friends with Netty Nijhoff, with whom she was to have a lifelong relationship. Moss took courses at the Académie Moderne, as a student of Fernand Léger and Amedée Ozenfant, but it was not until she encountered Piet Mondrian and his work that she found her own path as an artist. She produced reliefs and sculptures, partly under the influence of, and in dialogue with, Georges Vantongerloo and Jean Gorin. But prior to World War II her primary interest was in painting. She produced largely abstract paintings with simple horizontal and vertical lines and planes of primary color, in line with Mondrian's neoplastic works. In 1932 Moss produced a number of paintings, in which she made the horizontal lines thinner and doubled them, thus suggesting that a line could also be a narrow white plane. Mondrian saw this as a challenge: he recognized the potential for replacing the static, classic calm in his work with a much more dynamic balance, and he felt impelled to renounce the sharp contrast between plane and line in his work. An exchange of letters ensued between Mondrian and Jean Gorin, one of the few artists who noticed the radical change in Mondrian's paintings. Marlow Moss continued to empty her paintings until they were virtually just white planes with lines and planes sliding into the image along the edges. It was not until later that she would become aware of the huge influence she had had on the work of one of the founders of *De Stijl*. Marlow Moss died 1958 in Penzance.

Marlow Moss
Weiß, Schwarz, Rot und Grau
1932
Öl auf Leinwand
54 x 45 cm
Gemeentemuseum Den Haag

Marlow Moss
White, Black, Red, and Gray
1932
Oil on canvas
54 x 45 cm
Gemeentemuseum The Hague

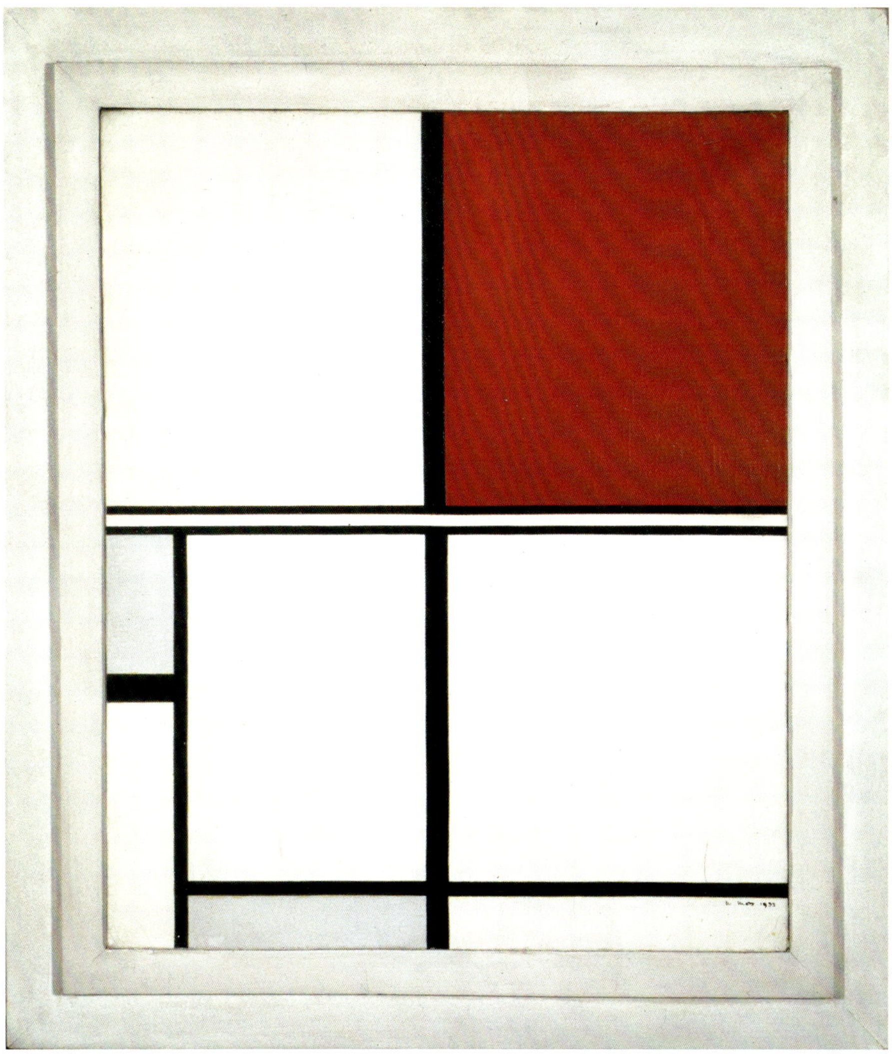

J.J.P. OUD

Jacobus Johannes Pieter Oud, geboren 1890 in Purmerend, wird an der Quellinusschool voor decoratieve kunst in Amsterdam ausgebildet und findet im Anschluss Arbeit bei Pierre Cuypers, dem Architekten, der gemeinsam mit Berlage seit Ende des 19. Jahrhunderts die ästhetischen Kriterien innerhalb der niederländischen Baukunst maßgeblich prägt. Oud arbeitet bereits als selbstständiger Architekt, als Berlage ihn 1912 auf Frank Lloyd Wrights Arbeiten aufmerksam macht. Der junge Architekt ist begeistert. 1913 zieht er nach Leiden, drei Jahre später lernt er Theo van Doesburg kennen, der gerade dabei ist, den Leidener Kunstclub *De Sphinx* zu gründen. Oud unterstützt van Doesburg darin und macht dadurch Bekanntschaft mit Vilmos Huszár, Bart van der Leck und dem Architekten Robert van 't Hoff. Diese Künstler werden kaum ein Jahr später die Zeitschrift *De Stijl* ins Leben rufen. 1918 wird Oud zum Stadtarchitekten von Rotterdam berufen, unter anderem mit der Aufgabe, Pläne für ganze Wohnviertel zu entwickeln. Für die Belebung der soliden, aber eintönigen Wohnblöcke im Stadtteil Spangen bezieht er van Doesburg mit ein – eine letztlich scheiternde Zusammenarbeit, die eine heftig geführte Debatte in *De Stijl* über das Verhältnis von Architektur und bildender Kunst entfacht.
1920 verlässt Oud *De Stijl* und gründet die Künstlervereinigung *Opbouw.* Schon ein Jahr später vertritt er die Meinung, dass das Theoretisieren über Architektur nur wenig Sinn hat, geht aber keiner Diskussion mit van Doesburg aus dem Weg. Oud beteiligt sich an der Architekturausstellung von *De Stijl* in der Galerie de l'Effort Moderne in Paris und entwirft einige Bauwerke, die zu den Hauptwerken von *De Stijl* zu zählen sind, wie etwa das Direktionsgebäude im Viertel Oud-Mathenesse oder die Fassade des Cafés De Unie in Rotterdam. Er hält den Kontakt zu Piet Mondrian und Georges Vantongerloo, obwohl die beiden noch utopistischer über das Verhältnis der Architektur zur bildenden Kunst denken als van Doesburg. Zu seinem Bekanntenkreis zählen auch Walter Gropius, László Moholy-Nagy und Kurt Schwitters. Durch die vielfältigen Kontakte zu anderen Künstlern gelingt es Oud, seine künstlerische Praxis immerfort neu zu beleben. Er beteiligt sich an der Internationalen Bauausstellung in Stuttgart und arbeitet als Redakteur der Zeitschrift *i10.* 1963 stirbt J.J.P. Oud in Wassenaar.

Jacobus Johannes Pieter Oud – born 1890 in Purmerend, north of Amsterdam, Oud attended the Quellinusschool voor Decoratieve Kunst in Amsterdam and went to work for Pierre Cuypers, the architect who, along with Berlage, had defined the aesthetics of Dutch architecture since the late nineteenth century. In 1912, by which time Oud was already working as an independent architect, Berlage made him aware of the work of Frank Lloyd Wright which enthralled the young architect. Having moved to Leiden in 1913, he got to know Theo van Doesburg in 1916, while the latter was organizing the art club *De Sphinx* in order to increase his artistic influence there. Oud helped him in this venture, which brought him into contact with Vilmos Huszár, Bart van der Leck and architect Robert van 't Hoff. Less than a year later, these artists would establish the magazine *De Stijl.* In 1918, Oud was appointed municipal housing architect in Rotterdam, where his new responsibilities included designs for entire residential areas. He involved Van Doesburg in his efforts to liven up the solid, monotonous blocks of apartments in the Spangen district, a collaboration that failed for diverging aesthetic preferences, and only served to sharpen the debate within the *De Stijl* movement on the relationship between art and architecture. Oud left *De Stijl* in 1920 and set up his own group, *Opbouw.* A year later he maintained that there was no point in theorizing about architecture, though he did not shrink from the debate with Van Doesburg.
He contributed to the *De Stijl* exhibition on architecture at Galerie de L'Effort Moderne in Paris, as well as designing a number of buildings, which today are regarded as key examples of *De Stijl.* They include the superintendent's office for the area Oud-Mathenesse and the façade of café De Unie in Rotterdam. Despite their notions of the relationship between art and architecture being even more fundamental and utopian than Van Doesburg's, he continued his exchange with Piet Mondrian and Georges Vantongerloo. Oud was also acquainted with Walter Gropius, László Moholy-Nagy and Kurt Schwitters. He participated in the Internationale Bauausstellung in Stuttgart and edited the magazine *i10.* His various contacts with artists enabled Oud to continually reinvigorate his own design practice. He died 1963 in Wassenaar.

Jacobus Johannes Pieter Oud
Esstisch mit vier Stühlen
1927
Replik von Ecart International nach 1979
Metall, Holz
75 x 90 x 140 cm (Tisch)
90,7 x 42,3 x 45 cm (Stühle)
Gemeentemuseum Den Haag

Jacobus Johannes Pieter Oud
Dining table with four chairs
1927
Replica by Ecart International after 1979
Metal, wood
75 x 90 x 140 cm (Table)
90,7 x 42,3 x 45 cm (Chairs)
Gemeentemuseum The Hague

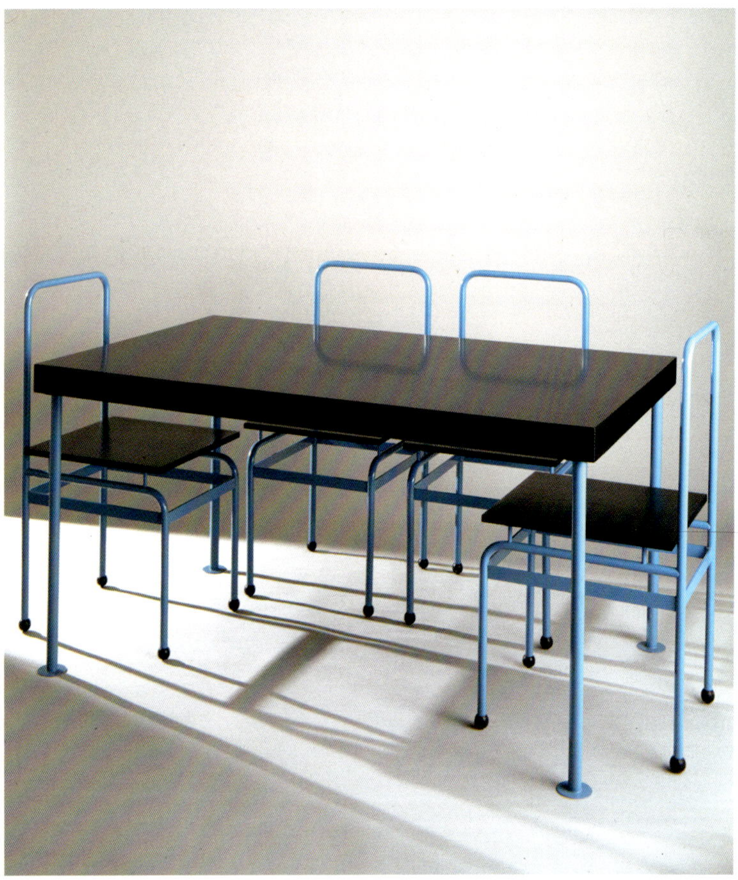

Jacobus Johannes Pieter Oud
Modell für das Café-Restaurant De Unie
1924
Rekonstruktion 1984
Holz
63 x 53 x 20 cm
Gemeentemuseum Den Haag

Jacobus Johannes Pieter Oud
Model for Café-restaurant De Unie
1924
Reconstruction 1984
Wood
63 x 53 x 20 cm
Gemeentemuseum The Hague

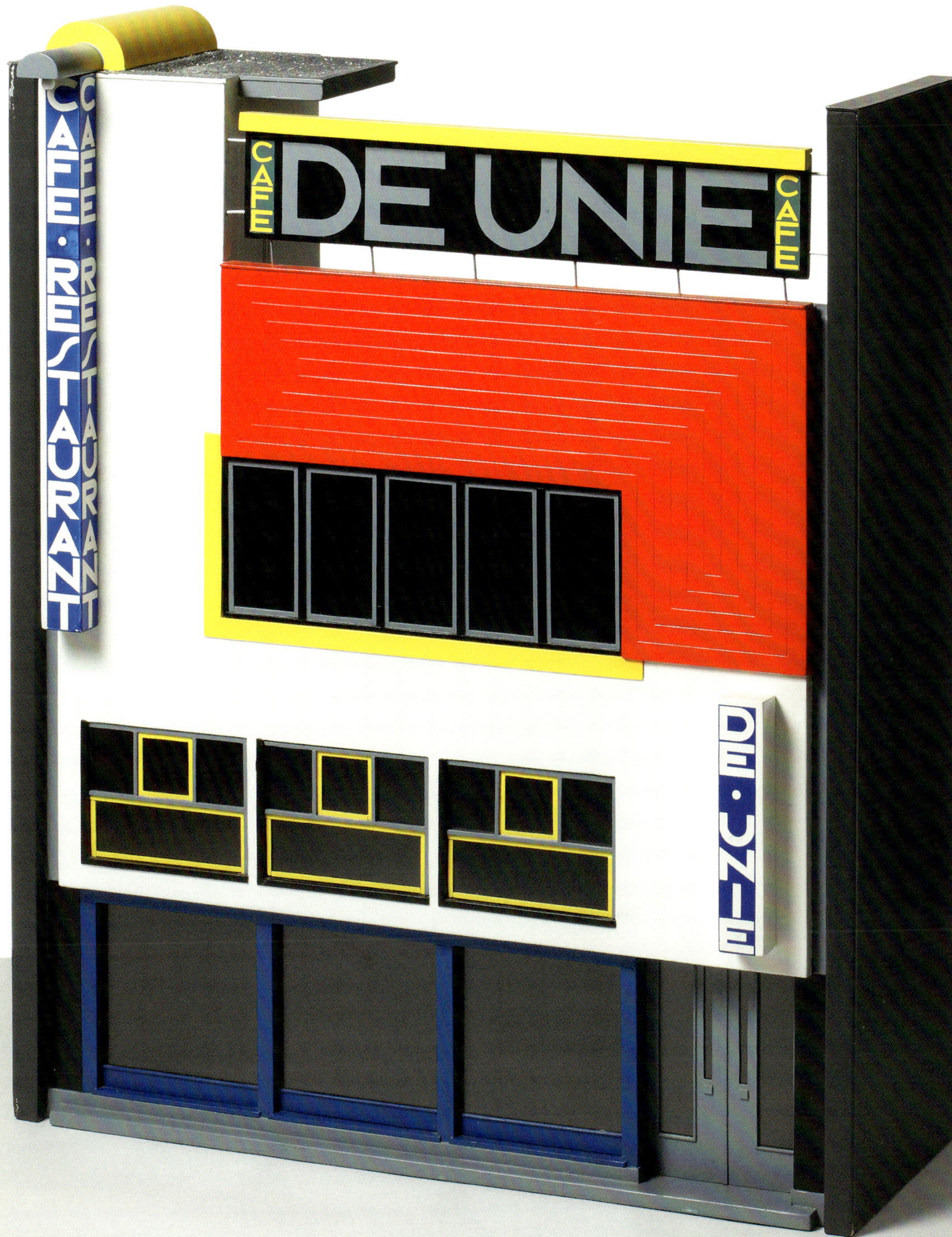

OTTO VAN REES

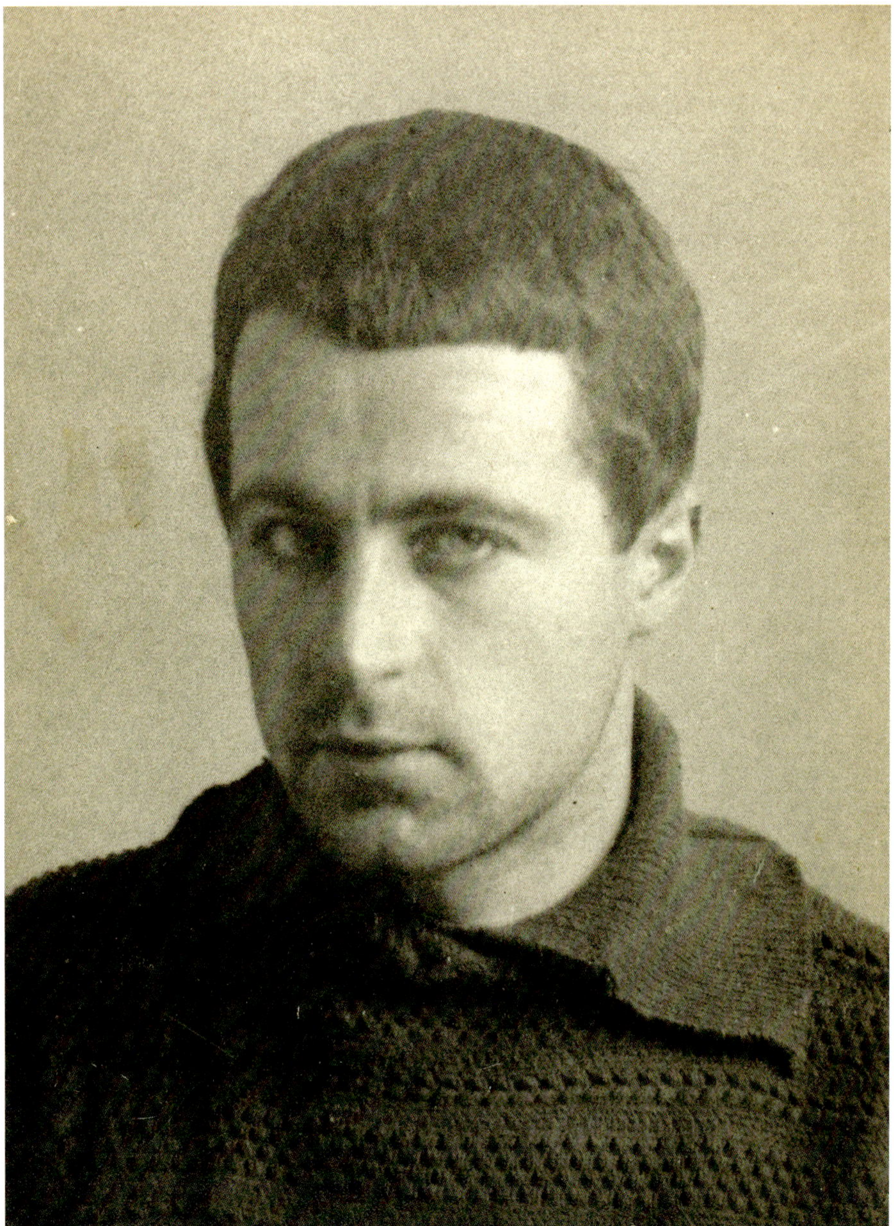

Otto van Rees
Collection RKD The Hague

Otto van Rees
Sammlung RKD Den Haag

Otto van Rees, geboren 1884 in Freiburg im Breisgau, wächst in einem intellektuellen Elternhaus in Amsterdam auf, in dem die Kontakte zu Künstlern, Sozialisten und Anarchisten im In- und Ausland vielfältig sind. 1899 gründet van Rees' Vater eine kooperative Lebensgemeinschaft zwischen den Gemeinden Laren und Blaricum, in der Ideale der Reformbewegung in die Praxis umgesetzt werden sollen. Van Rees beginnt zu malen und reist auf Anraten Jan Toorops, der großen Einfluss auf den jungen Künstler hat, nach Paris. Er schreibt sich in der Academie Carrière ein, begegnet dort Otto Freundlich und Georges Braque, der ihn in den Kreis junger Maler von Montmartre einführt. Van Rees nimmt sich ein Atelier im Bateau-Lavoir, gleich neben Picasso. Um 1910 sieht man ihn in Gesellschaft von Peter Alma, Henri Le Fauconnier und Lodewijk Schelfhout auf den Jours bei Conrad Kickert, der mit Piet Mondrian gerade dabei ist, den *Moderne Kunstkring* ins Leben zu rufen – eine Vereinigung, die die moderne Kunst in den Niederlanden fördern soll.
Über Jahre hinweg besuchen Mondrian und Otto van Rees einander. 1915 reist van Rees nach Ascona, wo er in den Freundeskreis von Arthur Segal, Otto Freundlich, Hans Arp, Tristan Tzara und Hugo Ball aufgenommen wird. Im Herbst fährt die Gruppe gemeinsam nach Zürich, wo van Rees Hans Richter und das Cabaret Voltaire kennen lernt. Van Rees ist beseelt von der Suche nach einer vergeistigten, religiös bestimmten Harmonie der Farben. Intensiv arbeitet er mit Hans Arp zusammen, immer auf der Suche nach einer besseren und gerechteren Welt. 1919 setzt er sich mit dem modern, doch figurativ arbeitenden niederländischen Maler Mathieu Wiegman in Verbindung. Van Rees ist wieder bei der figurativen Malerei angekommen.
Erst Ende der 1920er-Jahre bekennt er sich erneut zur abstrakten Kunst. 1928 besucht er Piet Mondrian, im Jahr darauf stellt er gemeinsam mit ihm und van Doesburg bei der Galería Dalmau in Barcelona aus, und 1931 zeigt er abstrakte Arbeiten bei einer Schau der Künstlervereinigung *Cercle et Carré.* 1957 stirbt Otto van Rees in Utrecht.

Otto van Rees – born 1884 in Freiburg im Breisgau, Germany, Van Rees grew up in Amsterdam, his father was a professor and the family set great store by literacy and creativity. They associated with many artists, socialists and anarchists both in the Netherlands and abroad. In 1899 his father helped establish a cooperative commune on a piece of land between Laren and Blaricum, where ideals of a reformed life were put into practice. Van Rees began to paint and traveled to Paris on the advice of Jan Toorop, who was a major influence on the young artist. He took lessons at Académie Carrière, where he met Otto Freundlich and Georges Braque. The latter introduced him to the circle of young painters at Montmartre. He rented a studio next to Picasso's in the Bateau-Lavoir. Around 1910 he frequented Conrad Kickert's jours in the company of Peter Alma, Henri Le Fauconnier and Lodewijk Schelfhout. Kickert was at that time collaborating with Piet Mondrian on the establishment of the *Moderne Kunstkring,* an association for the promotion of modern art in the Netherlands. Mondrian and Otto van Rees continued to visit each other for many years. In 1915 Van Rees traveled to Ascona, where he was taken into a circle of friends that included Arthur Segal, Otto Freundlich, Hans Arp, Tristan Tzara and Hugo Ball. In the autumn they traveled to Zurich where Van Rees came into contact with Hans Richter and the Cabaret Voltaire. He was in search of spiritual, religiously informed harmonies of color, and worked closely with Hans Arp, on a continuous quest for a better and fairer world. In 1919 he established contact with the Dutch figurative yet modern painter Mathieu Wiegman. He himself reverted to figurative representation, and it was not until the late 1920s that he would resume abstract art. In 1928 he visited Piet Mondrian, and a year later they exhibited together with Van Doesburg at Galería Dalmau in Barcelona. In 1931 Van Rees showed his abstract works at an exhibition staged by the artists' association *Cercle et Carré.* Otto van Rees died 1957 in Utrecht.

Otto van Rees
Frauenkopf
1911
Gips, Holz
36 cm, Durchmesser 25 cm
Gemeentemuseum Den Haag

Otto van Rees
Woman's Head
1911
Plaster, wood
36 cm, Diameter 25 cm
Gemeentemuseum The Hague

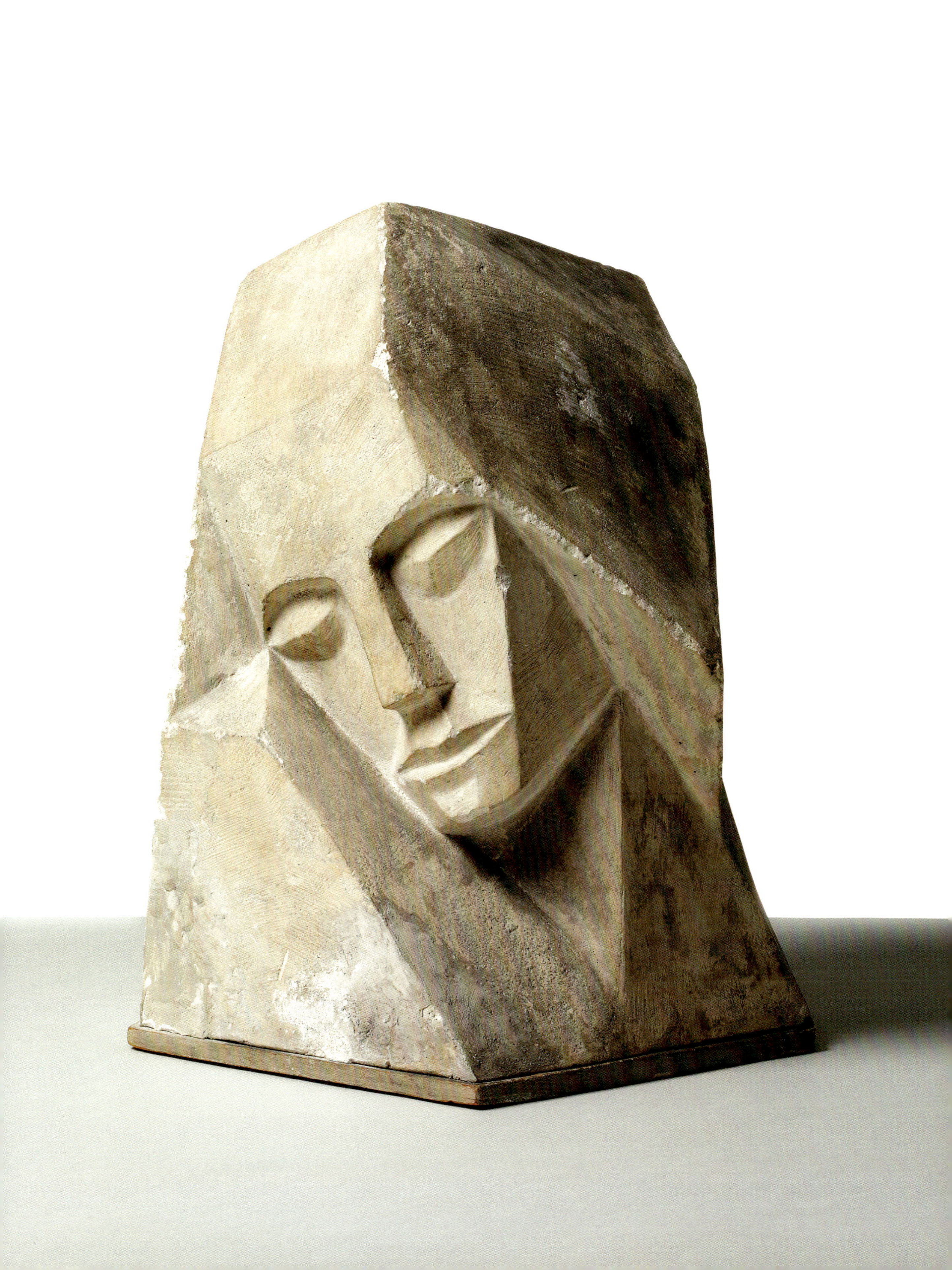

HANS RICHTER

Hans Richter wird 1888 in Berlin geboren. Er absolviert zunächst eine Zimmermannslehre und schreibt sich für ein Architekturstudium ein. Nachdem er mit der avantgardistischen Zeitschrift *Der Sturm* in Berührung gekommen ist, studiert Richter an den Kunsthochschulen zunächst in Berlin, dann in Weimar. Er malt kubistisch und verfasst Beiträge für die Zeitschrift *Die Aktion.* Nach zwei Jahren kehrt er 1916 kriegsversehrt aus dem Ersten Weltkrieg zurück. Er zieht nach Zürich und schließt sich der Dada-Bewegung an. Richter glaubt fest daran, dass ein Künstler politisch und pazifistisch sein solle und alle revolutionären Bewegungen unterstützen müsse. 1917 verschreibt er sich der abstrakten Kunst. Er trifft zum ersten Mal Viking Eggeling, mit dem er, nachdem beide wieder in Deutschland wohnen, experimentelle Filme realisiert. In Deutschland begegnet ihnen Theo van Doesburg. Richter verfasst nun regelmäßig Artikel für *De Stijl* und stellt van Doesburg Kurt Schwitters vor. Ab 1921 produziert er mit *Rhythmus 21* seinen ersten abstrakten Film. Im Jahr darauf beteiligt sich Richter in Düsseldorf gemeinsam mit van Doesburg und Lissitzky am Ersten Internationalen Kongress fortschrittlicher Künstler; sie verlassen jedoch aus Protest den Kongress und fordern eine entschiedene Absage an die in ihren Augen zu »individualistische« Haltung der Organisatoren. Richter gibt gemeinsam mit Lissitzky, Mies van der Rohe und Werner Graeff die Publikation *G: Zeitschrift für elementare Gestaltung* heraus, in der Künstler von Dada, *De Stijl* und vom Internationalen Konstruktivismus eingeladen sind mitzuwirken. Die erste Ausgabe enthält den Artikel »Zur elementaren Gestaltung« von Theo van Doesburg. Nach 1925 gibt Richter die Malerei ganz auf und verlegt sich auf seine Filmexperimente. Um seinen Lebensunterhalt zu verdienen, entwirft er Reklame. Nach van Doesburgs Tod im Jahr 1932 ist er für einige Monate zu Gast bei Nelly van Doesburg, Hans Arp und Sophie Taeuber-Arp in Meudon. 1976 stirbt Hans Richter in Minusio, Schweiz.

Hans Richter – born 1888 in Berlin, Richter initially trained as a carpenter and studied architecture, but after he had come under the influence of avant-garde artists associated with *Der Sturm,* he enrolled at the art academies of Berlin and Weimar. He started out painting in a Cubist style and wrote articles for the magazine *Die Aktion.* During World War I Richter was wounded and sent home, and from there went to Zurich, where he got involved in the Dada movement. He firmly believed that artists should be politically active and pacifist, and support all revolutionary movements. In 1917 he began to devote himself to abstract art, and met Viking Eggeling, with whom he produced experimental films, after they had both returned to Germany. There they became acquainted with Theo van Doesburg. Richter began to write regularly for *De Stijl* and introduced Kurt Schwitters to Van Doesburg. In 1921 he produced *Rhythmus 21,* his first abstract film. In 1922 Richter, Van Doesburg and Lissitzky took part in the First International Congress of Progressive Artists in Düsseldorf but left under protest—rejecting what they considered the far too individualistic attitudes of the organizers. Together with Lissitzky, Mies van der Rohe and Werner Graeff, Richter established the magazine *G: Zeitschrift für Elementare Gestaltung* which invited the participation of artists involved with Dada, *De Stijl* and International Constructivism. The first edition included the article "Zur elementaren Gestaltung" by Theo van Doesburg. Richter stopped painting altogether after 1925, in order to concentrate on his film experiments, while designing advertisements for a living. In 1932, after Van Doesburg's death, he spent several months in Meudon, living with Nelly van Doesburg, Hans Arp and Sophie Taeuber-Arp. Hans Richter died 1976 in Minusio, Switzerland.

Hans Richter
Rhythmus 21
1921–1924
Filmstreifen, 35 mm, schwarz-weiß (mit Tonspur)
Städtische Galerie im Lenbachhaus
und Kunstbau München

Hans Richter
Rhythm 21
1921–1924
Filmstrip, 35 mm, black and white (with sound)
Städtische Galerie im Lenbachhaus
und Kunstbau München

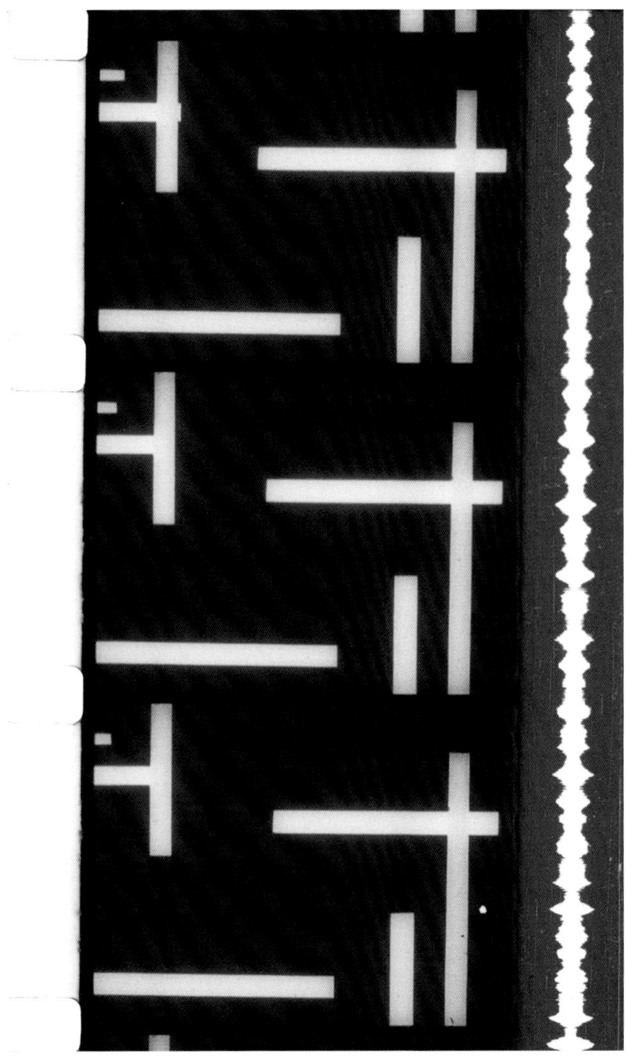

Hans Richter
Rhythmus 23
1922–1924
Filmstreifen, 35 mm, schwarz-weiß (mit Tonspur)
Hans Richter Estate

Hans Richter
Rhythm 23
1922–1924
Filmstrip, 35 mm, black and white (with sound)
Hans Richter Estate

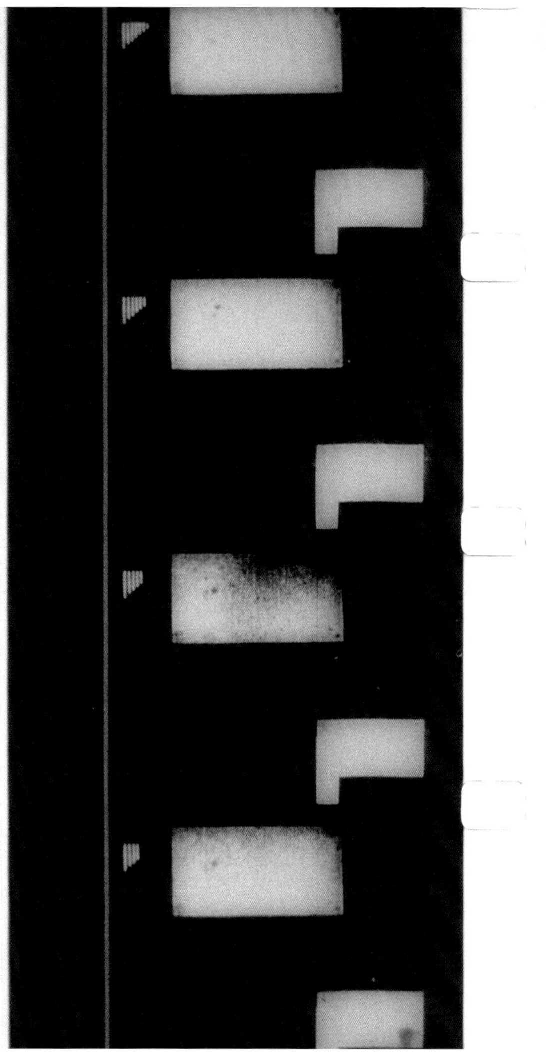

GERRIT RIETVELD

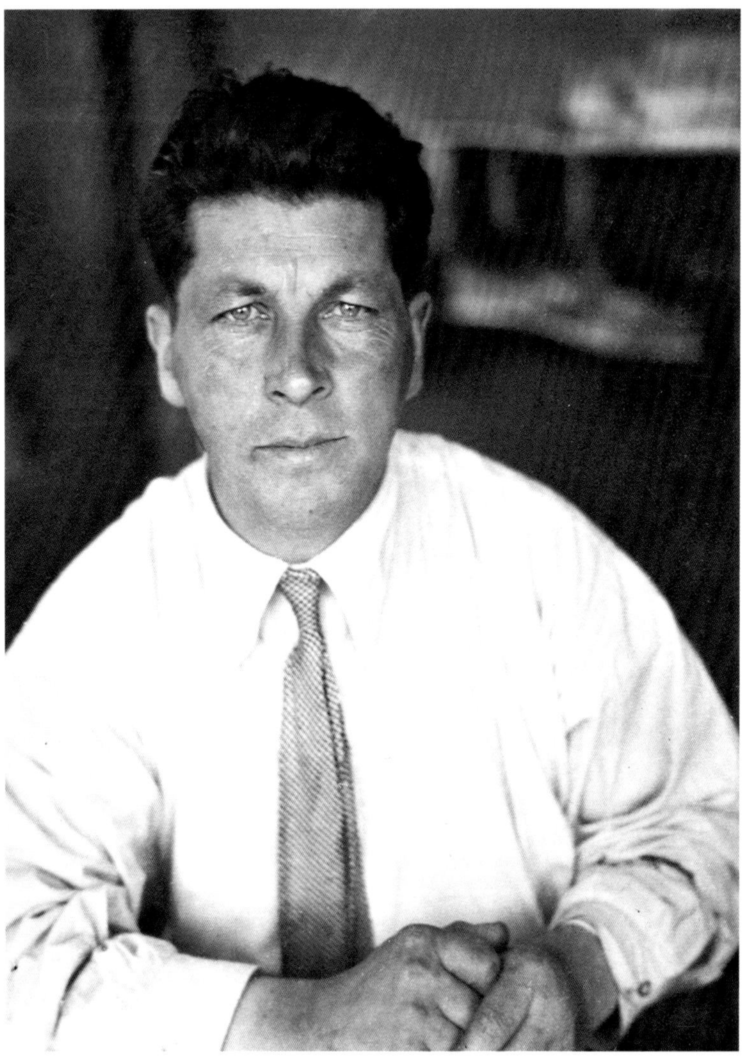

Gerrit Rietveld
Collection RKD The Hague

Gerrit Rietveld
Sammlung RKD Den Haag

Gerrit Rietveld wird 1888 in Utrecht geboren, wo er auch den größten Teil seines Lebens verbringt. Er absolviert im väterlichen Betrieb eine Tischlerlehre, träumt aber davon Künstler zu werden. Um dieses Ziel zu erreichen, besucht er Abendkurse für Bauzeichnen und wird Mitglied der *Vereiniging Kunstliefde.* Schon 1913 entstehen erste recht ausgefallene Möbelstücke, bei denen er ungewöhnliche Materialien verwendet und mit neuen Techniken zur Verbindung der einzelnen Bestandteile experimentiert. 1914 entwirft Rietveld die Möbel für ein Sommerhaus, das der Architekt Robert van 't Hoff im Auftrag der Familie Verloop baut. Van 't Hoff ist gerade aus den Vereinigten Staaten zurückgekehrt, wo ihn die Bauten von Frank Lloyd Wright sehr beeindruckt haben. Auch Rietveld bezieht sich bei seinen Möbelentwürfen auf den Amerikaner.
1917 eröffnet er eine eigene Möbeltischlerwerkstatt. Mit der Zeit entwickelt er eine neue Art der Verbindungstechnik: Die einzelnen Holzteile werden nicht mehr miteinander verzapft, sondern mit Dübeln zusammengehalten. Das ermöglicht ihm, die geschlossene Möbelstruktur hinter sich zu lassen und stattdessen einzelne, frei im Raum stehende Elemente in visuell dynamische Beziehungen zueinander zu setzen.
Zu seinem eigenen Vergnügen baut Rietveld einen Armlehnstuhl sowie einen Kinderstuhl aus Holzlatten, die fotografiert und in *De Stijl* veröffentlicht werden. Van Doesburg ist derart begeistert, dass er darüber eine poetische Kritik verfasst. Rietveld verlegt seine Haupttätigkeit in den folgenden Jahren auf die Konzeption und Neugestaltung von Innenausstattungen und ganzen Wohnungen. Als eingetragener Architekt beteiligt er sich 1923 an der *De Stijl*-Ausstellung, die van Doesburg in der von Léonce Rosenberg geführten Galerie de l'Effort Moderne in Paris organisiert.
1924 entwirft Rietveld gemeinsam mit Truus Schröder ein Wohnhaus, das ein Jahr später am Stadtrand von Utrecht gebaut wird. Die offene, fragmentarische Konstruktion des Hauses sowie die vielfältigen Lösungen, die sich durch verschiebbare Raummodule eröffnen, machen es zu einem verblüffenden Gebäude. Das Rietveld-Schröder-Haus wird zu einer Ikone der *De Stijl*-Architektur, in dem viele Künstler zu Gast sind, um Inspiration zu finden – Lissitzky etwa, Oud und Mart Stam. 1928 bricht Rietveld mit van Doesburg und *De Stijl.* Anfang der 1930er-Jahre entwickelt er für die Stadt Utrecht standardisierte Bauelemente, die als Fertigteile auf unterschiedliche Weise angeordnet und zu Wohneinheiten verbunden werden können.
1930–1932 entwirft er für die Wiener *Werkbund*-Ausstellung eine Wohnzeile mit Musterwohnungen, die sich zur Massenproduktion anbieten. Rietveld ist Gründungsmitglied der CIAM (Internationale Kongresse für moderne Architektur). Gerrit Rietveld stirbt 1964 in Utrecht.

Gerrit Rietveld – born 1888 in Utrecht, where he would live his entire life. Trained as a furniture maker by his father, Rietveld long dreamed of becoming an artist. He took evening classes in architectural drawing and joined the artists' association *Vereniging Kunstliefde.*
In 1913 he began to make furniture in his own unique style, experimenting with unusual materials and new ways of joining the parts. The following year he designed the furniture for a summerhouse that architect Robert van 't Hoff was building for the Verloop family.
Van 't Hoff had just returned from the United States where he had remained impressed with the work of Frank Lloyd Wright. Rietveld's furniture also drew on the example of the American architect. In 1917 he opened his own workshop and began to manufacture furniture in which the normal mortise and tenon joints were substituted by dowels. Solid blocks of furniture were replaced by composite elements distributed throughout the room while visually relating to each other. For his own amusement, he made from slats an easy chair and a child's chair which were featured in *De Stijl.* Van Doesburg was extremely enthusiastic and waxed lyrical in his commentary accompanying the photographs. In the years that followed Rietveld specialized in designing interiors and entire new homes. As a registered architect he participated in the *De Stijl* exhibition that Van Doesburg organized in 1923 at Léonce Rosenberg's Galerie de L'Effort Moderne in Paris. In 1924 he designed a house with Truus Schröder which was built the following year on the outskirts of Utrecht. The house was startling in its openness, fragmentation and spatial solutions, enabled by flexible modules, and it became an icon of *De Stijl* visited by many artists in search of inspiration, including Lissitzky, Oud and Mart Stam. In 1928 Rietveld broke with Van Doesburg and *De Stijl.* The City of Utrecht commissioned him in the early 1930s to develop standardized construction units that could be arranged in different ways and combined into living units.
1930–1932 he presented rows of show apartments at the Wiener *Werkbund*-Exhibition, designed to be mass-produced. Rietveld was a founder member of the CIAM, the International Congresses of Modern Architecture. He died 1964 in Utrecht.

Gerrit Rietveld
Rot-blauer Stuhl
ca. 1918
Ausführung von Gerard van de Groenekan
nach 1918
Bemaltes Buchenholz, Sperrholz
87,5 x 60 x 76 cm
Gemeentemuseum Den Haag

Gerrit Rietveld
Red and Blue Chair
ca. 1918
Realization by Gerard van de Groenekan
after 1918
Painted beechwood, plywood
87,5 x 60 x 76 cm
Gemeentemuseum The Hague

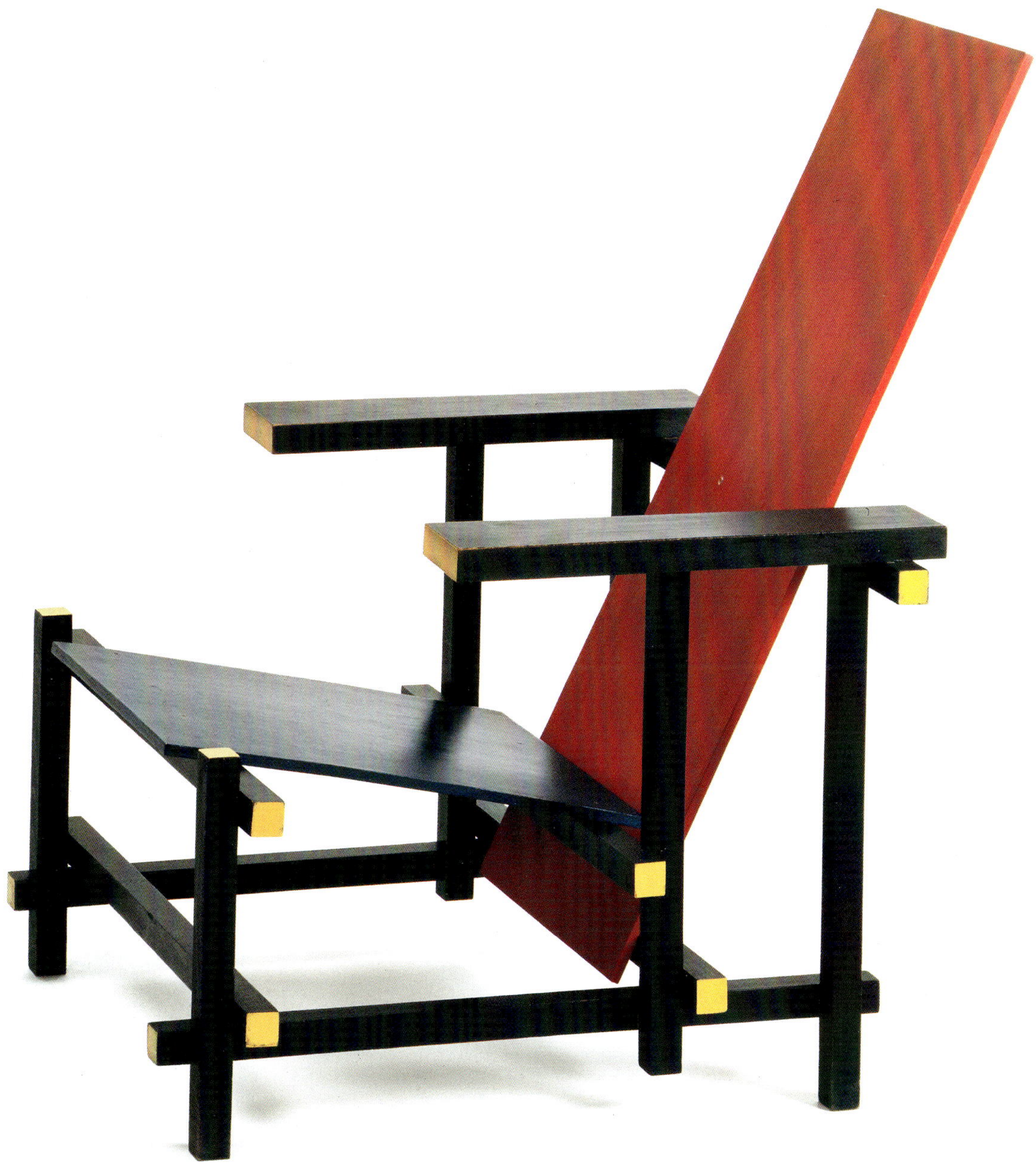

Gerrit Rietveld
Anrichte
1919
Ausführung von Gerard van de Groenekan 1972
Holz, Buchenholz, Farbe
100 x 120 x 45 cm
Gemeentemuseum Den Haag

Gerrit Rietveld
Sideboard
1919
Realization by Gerard van de Groenekan 1972
Wood, beechwood, paint
100 x 120 x 45 cm
Gemeentemuseum The Hague

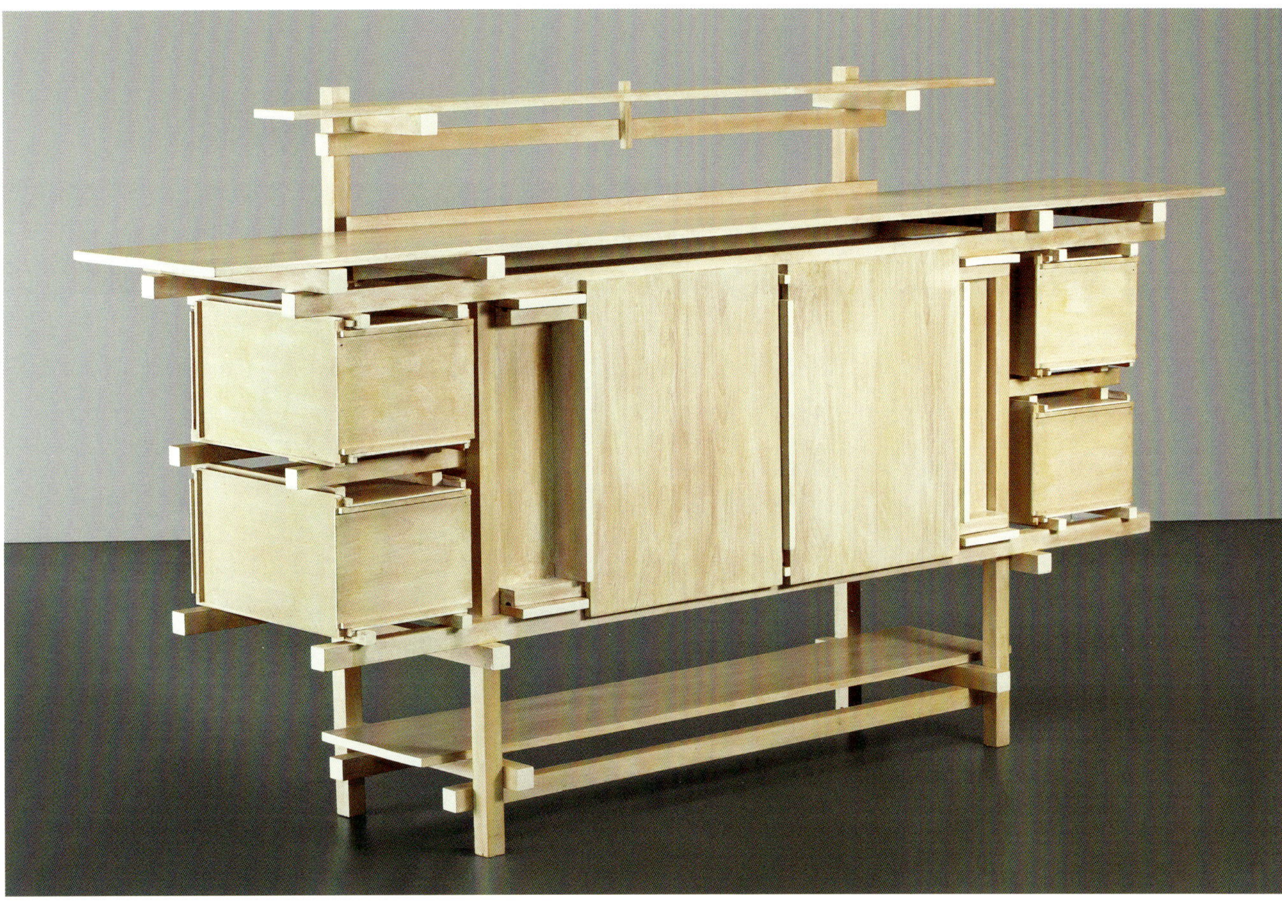

Gerrit Rietveld
Lampe
1920
Replik 2011
Glas, Holz
110 x 40 cm
Gemeentemuseum Den Haag

Gerrit Rietveld
Lamp
1920
Replica 2011
Glass, wood
110 x 40 cm
Gemeentemuseum The Hague

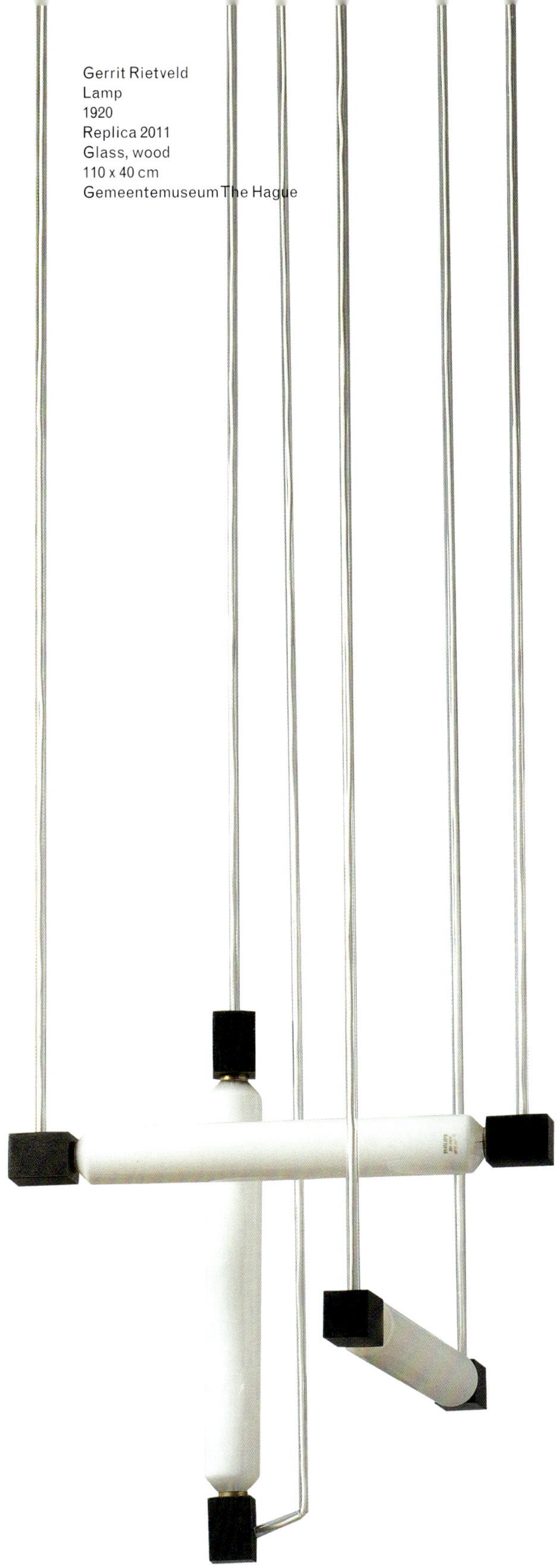

Gerrit Rietveld
Kinderstuhl
ca. 1921
Ausführung von Gerard van de Groenekan 1965
Fichtenholz, Leder
90 x 35 x 40 cm
Gemeentemuseum Den Haag

Gerrit Rietveld
Child's chair
ca. 1921
Realization by Gerard van de Groenekan 1965
Fir wood, leather
90 x 35 x 40 cm
Gemeentemuseum The Hague

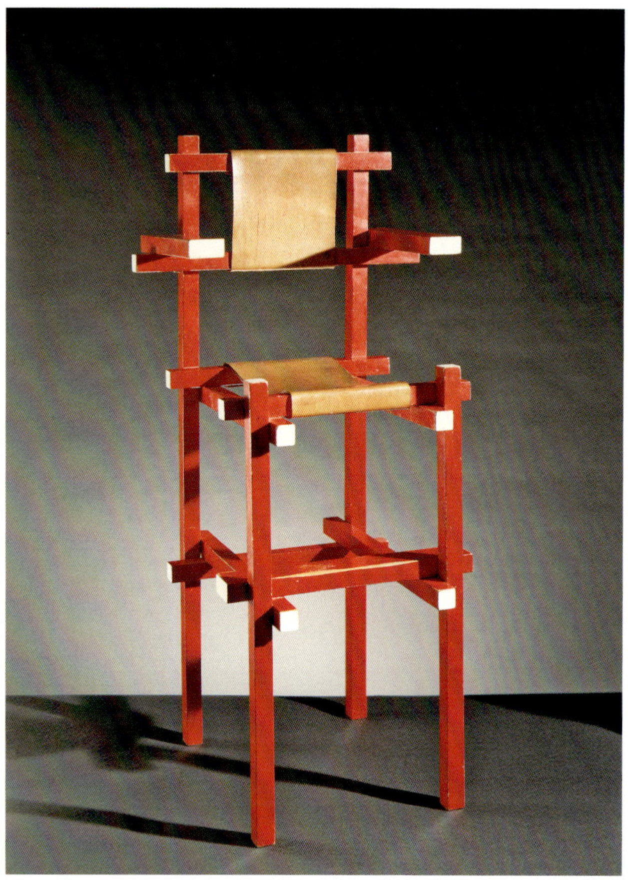

Gerrit Rietveld
Berlin Stuhl
1923
Nachbau von Egbert Rietveld und Ries Seijler nach leicht vom Original abweichenden Zeichnungen Rietvelds von 1960, 2011
Bemaltes Holz
106 x 69,9 x 54,9 cm
RIETVELD by rietveld collection

Gerrit Rietveld
Berlin Chair
1923
Reconstruction by Egbert Rietveld and Ries Seijler after Rietveld's drawings of 1960 slightly differing from the original, 2011
Painted wood
106 x 69,9 x 54,9 cm
RIETVELD by rietveld collection

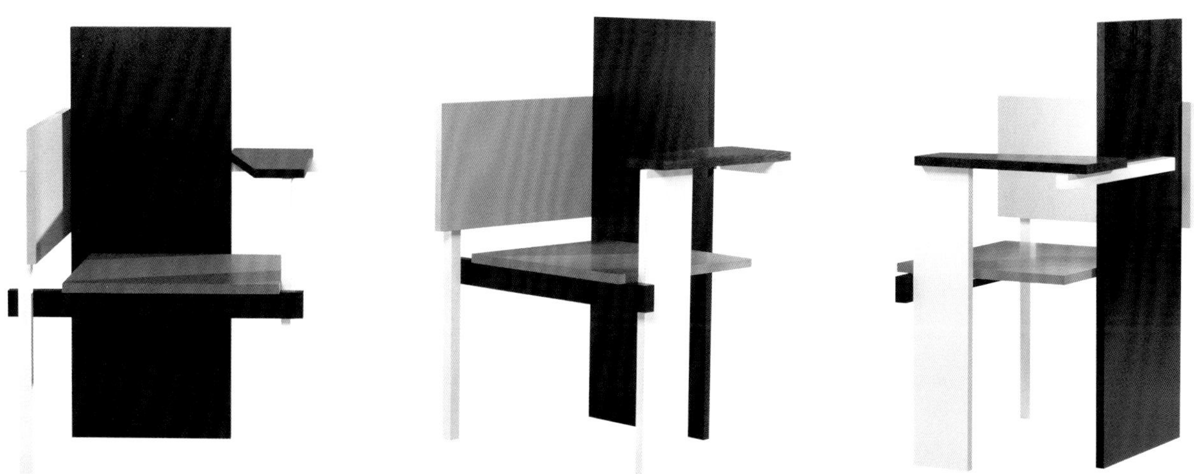

Gerrit Rietveld
Möbel »Militär«
1923
Nachbauten von Egbert Rietveld und Ries Seijler nach leicht vom Original abweichenden Zeichnungen Rietvelds von 1960, 2011
Bemaltes Holz
Maße variabel
RIETVELD by rietveld collection

Gerrit Rietveld
Furniture "Military"
1923
Reconstructions by Egbert Rietveld and Ries Seijler after Rietveld's drawings of 1960 slightly differing from the original, 2011
Painted wood
Variable dimensions
RIETVELD by rietveld collection

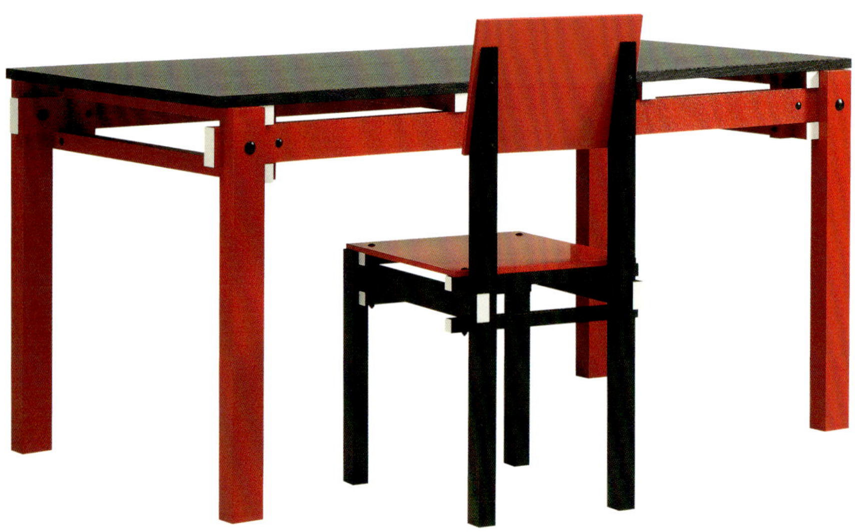

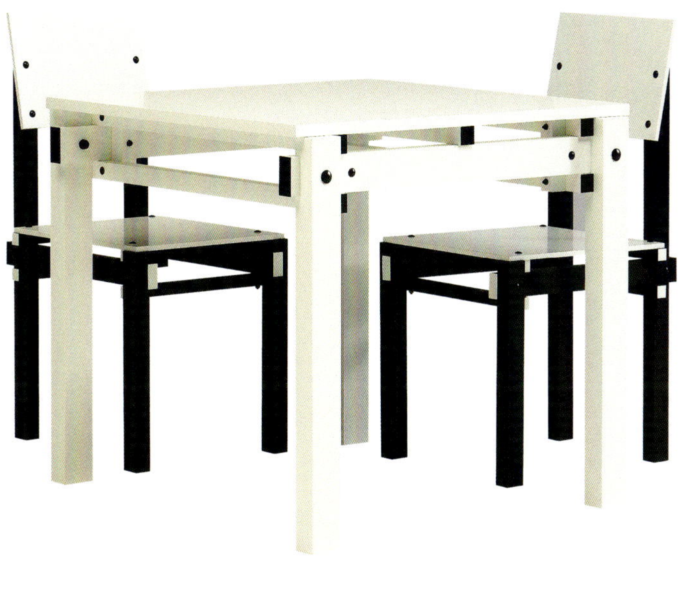

Gerrit Rietveld
Beugelstoel (Stuhl mit Stahlrohrrahmen)
1927
Ausführung 1932
Stahlröhren, Vulkanfiber, Buchenholz
72,5 x 40 x 56 cm
Gemeentemuseum Den Haag

Gerrit Rietveld
Beugelstoel (Tubular steel frame chair)
1927
Realization 1932
Steel tubes, fibreboard, beechwood
72,5 x 40 x 56 cm
Gemeentemuseum The Hague

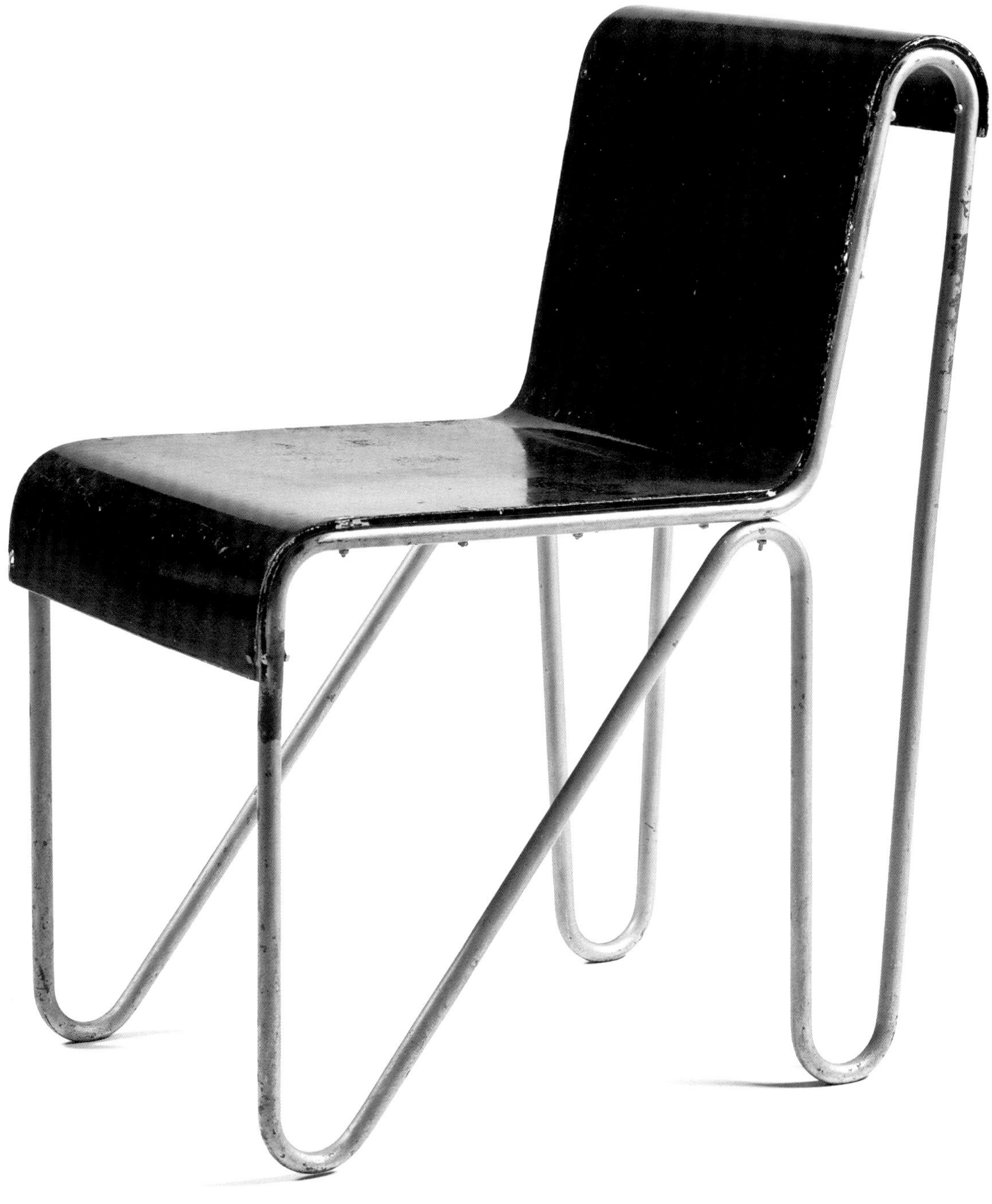

Gerrit Rietveld
Modell des Rietveld-Schröder-Hauses
1924
Rekonstruktion von Otto Lange 1981
Plexiglas, Polystyrol, Siebdruck
33,2 x 40,9 x 31 cm
Gemeentemuseum Den Haag

Gerrit Rietveld
Model of the Rietveld Schröder House
1924
Reconstruction by Otto Lange 1981
Plexiglas, polystyrene, screen printing
33,2 x 40,9 x 31 cm
Gemeentemuseum The Hague

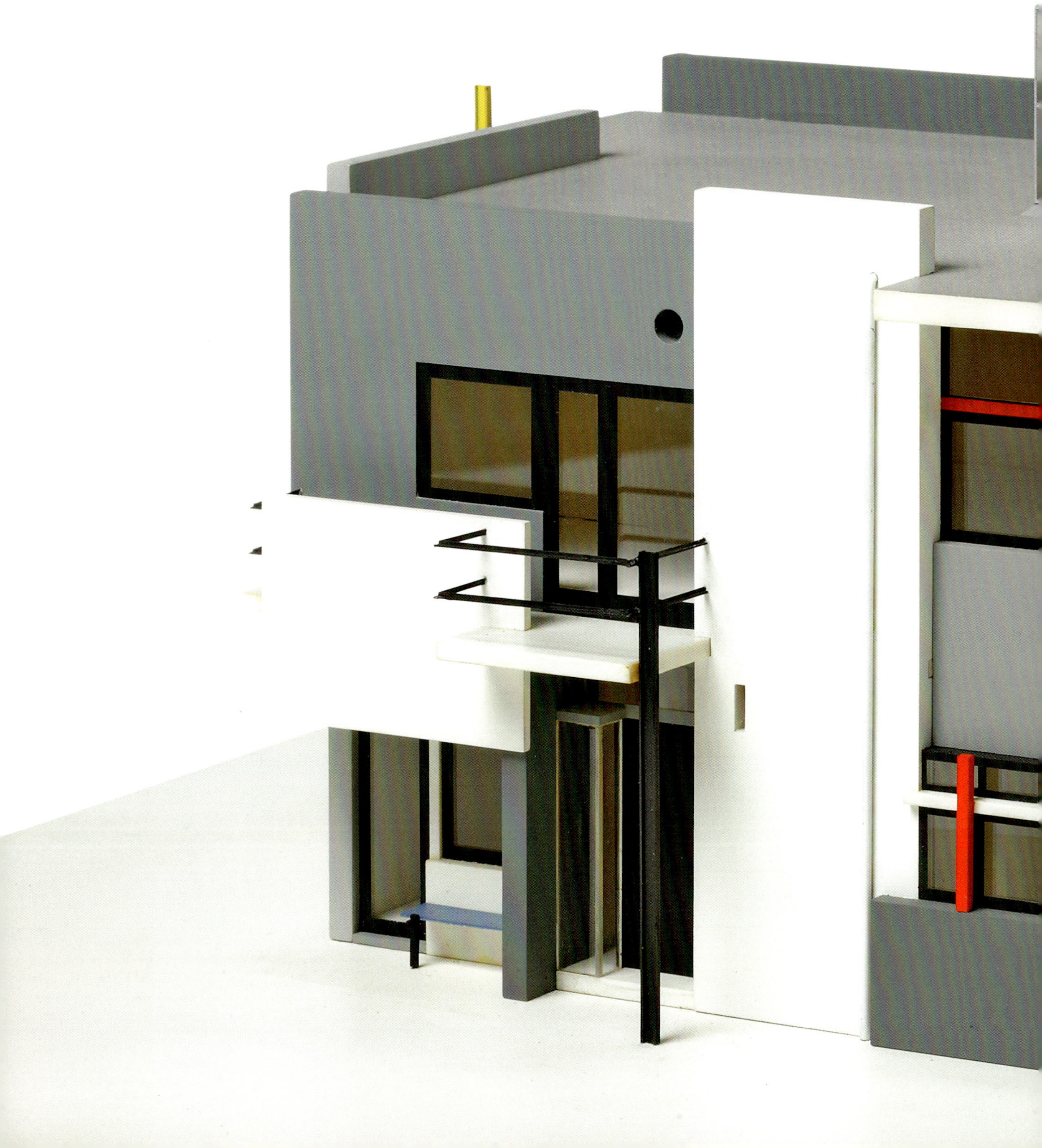

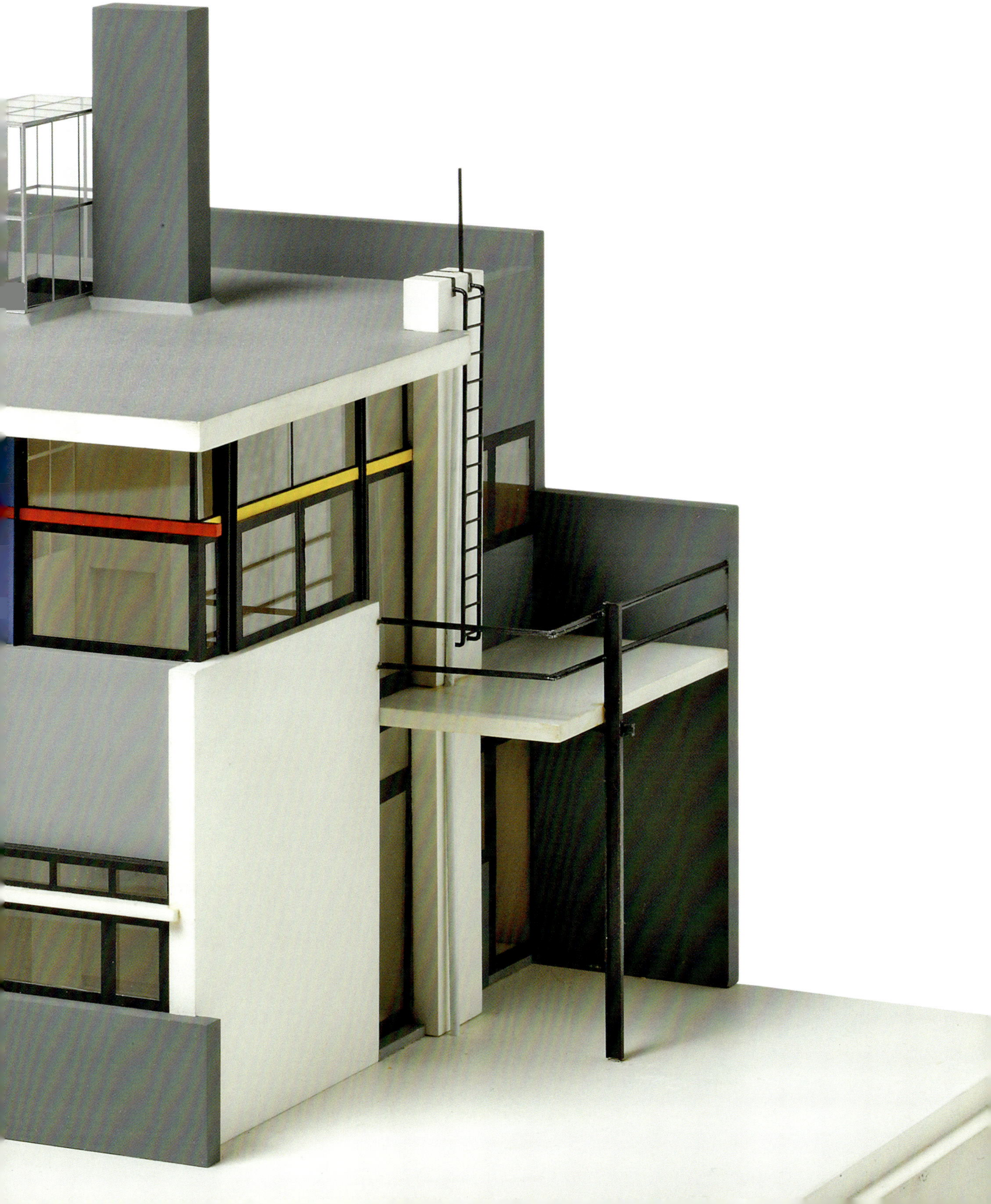

GINO SEVERINI

Gino Severini wird 1883 im italienischen Cortona geboren. In seinem Heimatort wird er als 15-Jähriger der Schule verwiesen, weil er Prüfungsunterlagen gestohlen hat. So geht er bereits 1899 nach Rom und entdeckt dort das Malen und Zeichnen für sich. Er nimmt Unterricht und lernt bald Umberto Boccioni kennen, der ihn in das Atelier von Giacomo Balla einführt. Beide Künstler werden später, wie Severini selbst, zu den berühmtesten Futuristen zählen. Dadurch kommt Severini mit den neuen Strömungen in der Malerei in Berührung; er wird mit der Technik nebeneinander gesetzter, kontrastierender und ungemischter Farben vertraut, die die Oberfläche eines Gemäldes akzentuieren und einer Illusionswirkung des Bildes entgegenarbeiten. 1906 zieht es ihn nach Paris, wo er, wie er sagt »neu geboren wird«. Hier begegnet er der gesamten Avantgarde seiner Zeit. Filippo Marinetti bittet ihn darum, das *Futuristische Manifest* zu unterschreiben, das 1910 in Paris veröffentlicht wird. Severini macht durch seine Ausstellungen in verschiedenen Ländern die Futuristen in ganz Europa bekannt. Er beschäftigt sich mit Mathematik und stellt Überlegungen zu kompositorischen Regeln an. Der niederländische Dichter Dop Bles vermittelt 1917 den Kontakt zu Piet Mondrian. Zudem korrespondiert Severini mit Theo van Doesburg, der sehr davon angetan ist, mit welcher Professionalität Severini in der Öffentlichkeit auftritt. Severini erhält die Möglichkeit, einige seiner Artikel in *De Stijl* zu publizieren; er ist sogar der erste ausländische Künstler, der an der Zeitschrift mitarbeitet.
Die geometrische Stilisierung seiner Gemälde nimmt zu dieser Zeit immer mehr zu, ohne dass Severini dabei die kubistische Formensprache und die Andeutung von Illusion aufgibt. Als van Doesburg nach Paris kommt, besucht er Severini. Allerdings wendet sich Severini da bereits wieder radikal seinen künstlerischen Ursprüngen zu: Nach 1921 gibt es für ihn nur noch die figurative Malerei. *De Stijl* macht nur eine kurze Periode in seinem Künstlerleben aus. Severini beschäftigt sich mit religiöser Kunst und malt für Kirchen in der Schweiz, in Frankreich und Italien große Wandgemälde im Stile Giottos. 1966 stirbt Gino Severini in Paris.

Gino Severini – born 1883 in Cortona, Italy, where he attended technical college until, at the age of fifteen, he was expelled for having stolen some exam papers. In 1899, in Rome, he became interested in painting. He started to frequent art lessons, and soon after met artist Umberto Boccioni, who took him to Giacomo Balla's studio. This brought Severini into contact with new trends in painting, and he became familiar with the use of juxtaposed, contrasting, unmixed colors employed to emphasize the surface of the painting and undermine illusionistic effects. In 1906 he moved to Paris where, as he put it, he was "born again" and came into contact with the avant-garde of the time. Filippo Marinetti invited him to sign the *Futurist Manifesto* which was published in Paris in 1910. Wherever he exhibited he tried to promote the cause of Futurism. He studied mathematics and the rules of composition. In 1917 Dutch poet Dop Bles put Severini in contact with Piet Mondrian, and Severini started corresponding with Theo van Doesburg, who was impressed with the professional way Severini performed in public. Severini was given the opportunity to publish a number of articles in *De Stijl,* and was the first non-Dutch artist to collaborate on the magazine. Geometric stylization came to dominate his paintings, though he did not relinquish the visual language of Cubism and traces of illusionistic representation. During his first visit to Paris Van Doesburg sought out Severini, by which time however, the Italian was reconsidering his artistic originis, which after 1921 would lead to a radical return to figurative painting. *De Stijl* proved to be only a phase in Severini's artistic life. He became interested in religion and began producing large murals in the style of Giotto for churches in Switzerland, France and Italy.

Gino Severini
Obstschale
ca. 1916
Öl auf Holz
61 x 50 cm
Gemeentemuseum Den Haag

Gino Severini
Fruit bowl
ca. 1916
Oil on wood
61 x 50 cm
Gemeentemuseum The Hague

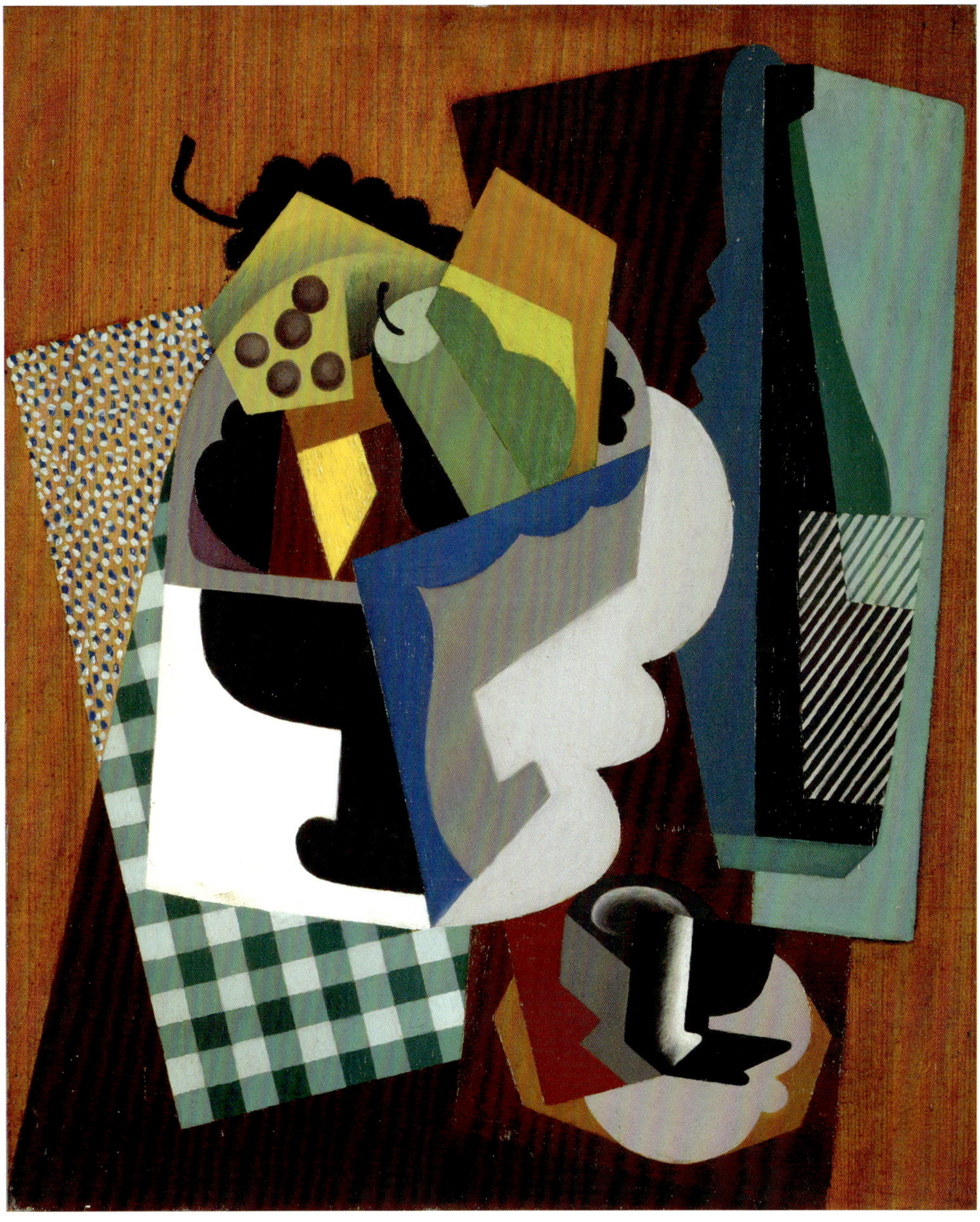

JAN TOOROP

Jan Toorop wird 1858 in Poerworedjo auf Java geboren. 1869 geht er in die Niederlande, erst für kurze Zeit nach Den Haag, dann nach Leiden, um dort die Schule zu besuchen. Ab 1875 nimmt er Zeichen- und Malunterricht bei H. J. van der Weele, der ihm einige Künstler der *Haager Schule* vorstellt. Toorop setzt seine Ausbildung in Amsterdam an der Rijksacademie und an der École des Arts Décoratifs in Brüssel fort. Hierbei lernt Toorop die wichtigsten Maler und Dichter seiner Zeit kennen. Er stellt bei der belgischen Künstlervereinigung *Les Vingt* aus und bewundert James Ensors eigenwillige Maltechnik. Unermüdlich öffnet er sich neuen Einflüssen und lernt, in unterschiedlichen Stilrichtungen zu arbeiten. Zunächst malt er neoimpressionistisch, in den 1890er-Jahren bricht eine Periode an, in der er ausschließlich linear arbeitet, in einer Art, die teilweise an javanische Darstellungen erinnert, zum Teil aber auch an den Jugendstil. Die Wirkung ist so neuartig, dass der Einfluss in ganz Europa, sogar in den Werken von Gustav Klimt in Wien, zu finden ist. Von 1897 an verbringt Toorop die Sommermonate in Domburg und ist vom einfachen Leben der Fischer so fasziniert, dass er beschließt, in Katwijk zu wohnen, wo er mit seiner Kunst wieder eine neue stilistische Richtung einschlägt. Sein Ziel ist, die Verbreitung der Idee einer ›wahrhaft modernen Kunst‹ in so vielen Bereichen wie möglich durchzusetzen. Für die Amsterdamer Börse etwa entwirft er Fliesenbilder, in denen er die Ideen der ›Gemeinschaftskunst‹ meisterhaft umsetzt. Van Doesburg hofft lange, Jan Toorop zur Mitarbeit an *De Stijl* bewegen zu können, muss schließlich aber einsehen, dass Toorop zu sehr der Vergangenheit angehört, als dass er noch einen Beitrag für die Moderne leisten könne. Jan Toorop stirbt 1928 in Den Haag.

Jan Toorop – born 1856 in Purworejo, Java, in the Dutch East Indies. In 1869 he came to the Netherlands, initially to The Hague, and then attended school in Leiden. From 1875 onward he took lessons in drawing and painting with H. J. van der Weele, who introduced him to some artists of the *Hague School*. Three years later Toorop enrolled at the Rijksakademie and after that at the École des Arts Décoratifs in Brussels. He became acquainted with many important painters and poets of his era. He exhibited at the artists' association *Les Vingt* and admired the idiosyncratic painting technique of James Ensor. Toorop continually sought out new stimuli and influences and learned to work in different styles. First he painted in a Neo-impressionist style and then– in the 1890s–he worked exclusively in a linear manner, partly reminiscent of Javan images, partly of Art Nouveau. The effect was lively and so innovative that its influence can be traced throughout Europe, as far as Vienna and the work of Gustav Klimt. From 1897 he spent summers in Domburg, and was so fascinated by the simple lives of the fishermen that he decided to live in Katwijk, where his art entered another stylistic phase. His next objective was to spread the idea of a 'truly modern art' to as many areas of life as possible. He designed pictures executed in tiles for Berlage's Commodities Exchange in Amsterdam which made him a champion of community art. Van Doesburg long cherished hopes of persuading Toorop to work for *De Stijl,* but he ultimately had to admit that Toorop belonged too much to the past to be able to contribute to modernity. Jan Toorop died 1928 in The Hague.

Jan Toorop
Der Aufstieg mit Widerstand; die Moderne Kunst
1893
Farbstift und Kreide auf Papier
in ornamentiertem Rahmen
41,7 x 47 cm, mit Rahmen 70,5 x 76, 4 cm
Gemeentemuseum Den Haag

Jan Toorop
Rise with Counteraction; Modern Art
1893
Colored pencil and chalk on paper
in an ornamented frame
41,7 x 47 cm, with frame 70,5 x 76, 4 cm
Gemeentemuseum The Hague

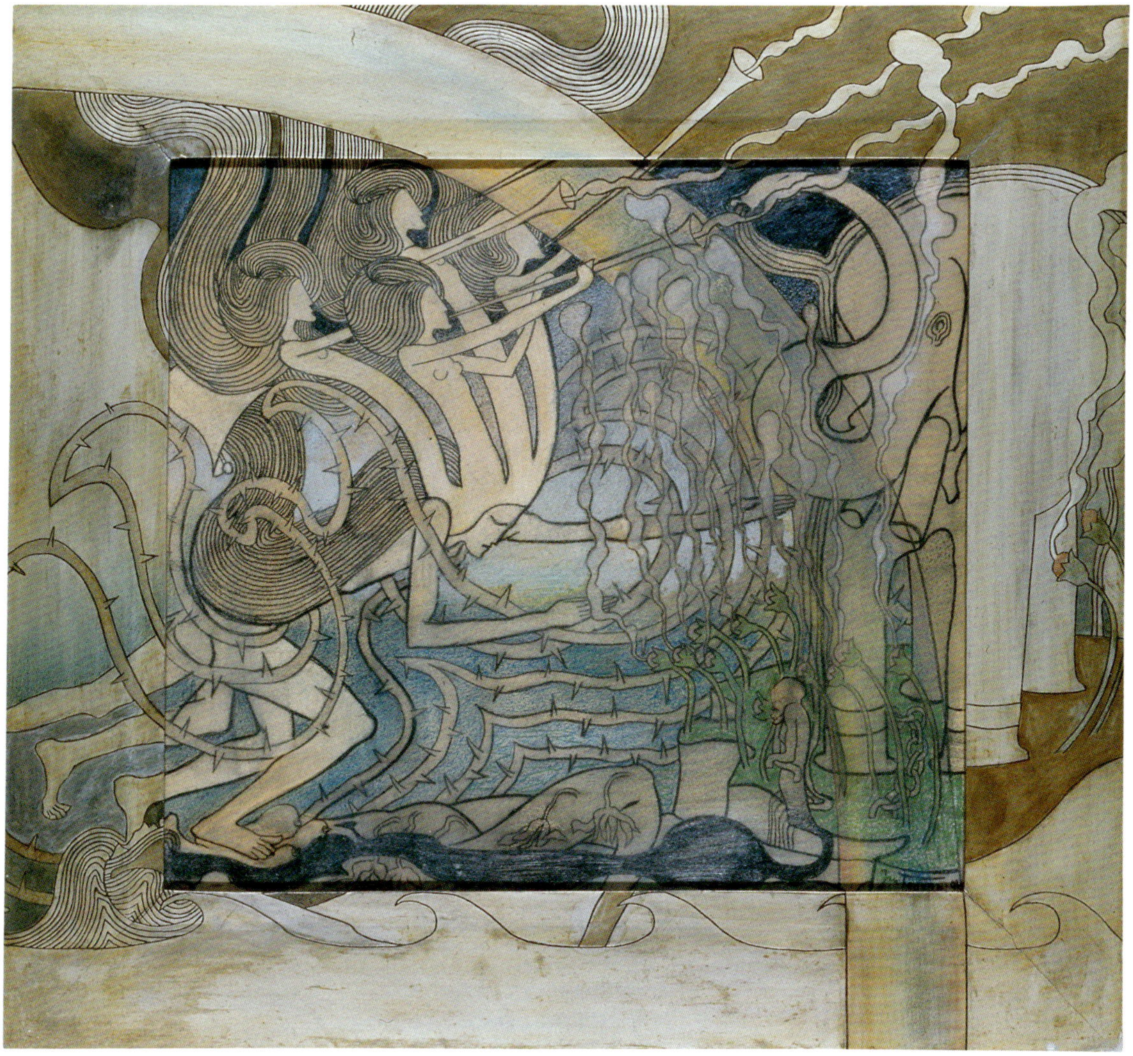

Jan Toorop
Plakat »Delftsche Slaolie«
für die »Niederländischen Ölfabriken« in Delft
1894
Lithographie auf Papier
87 x 66,5 cm
Gemeentemuseum Den Haag

Jan Toorop
Poster "Delftsche Slaolie"
for "Dutch Oil factories" in Delft
1894
Lithograph on paper
87 x 66,5 cm
Gemeentemuseum The Hague

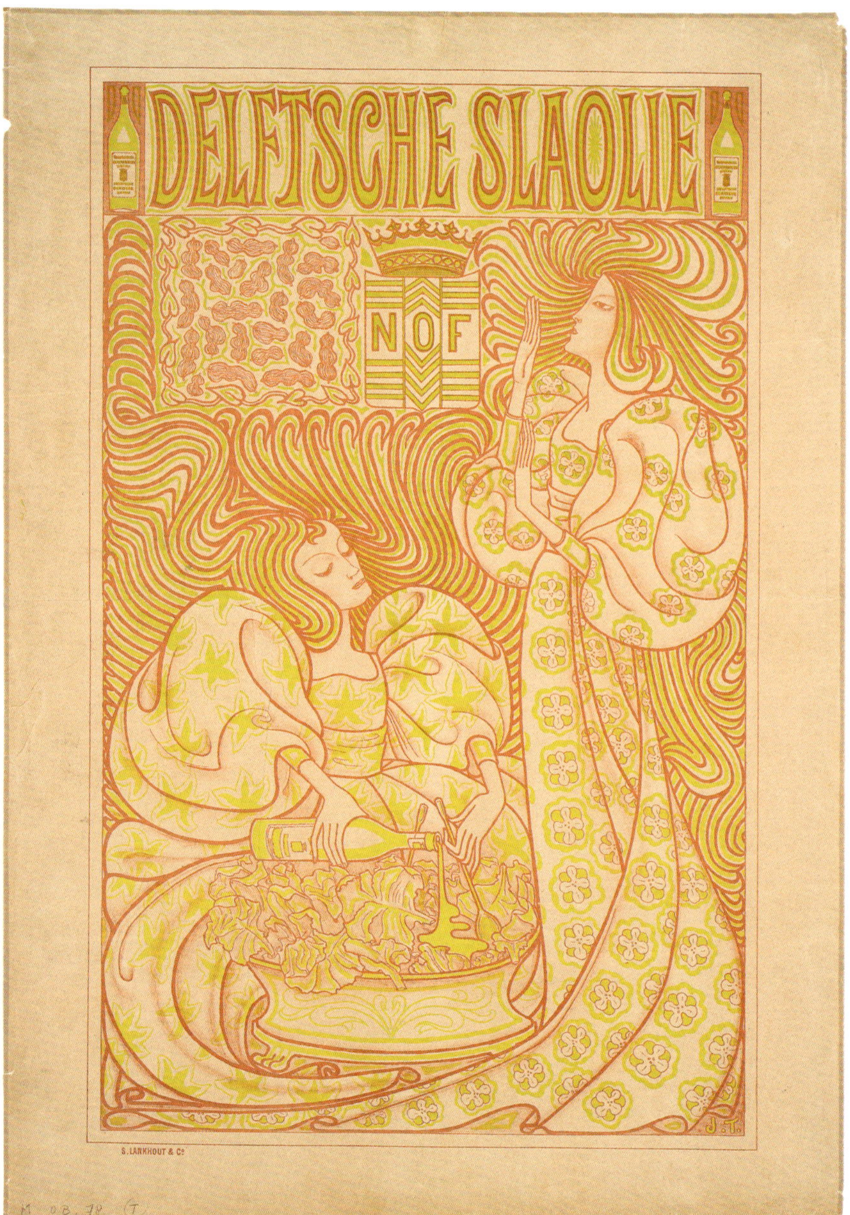

Jan Toorop
Plakat »Arbeit für die Frau«
1898
Lithographie auf Papier
89 x 64,7 cm
Gemeentemuseum Den Haag

Jan Toorop
Poster "Labour for Women"
1898
Lithograph on paper
89 x 64,7 cm
Gemeentemuseum The Hague

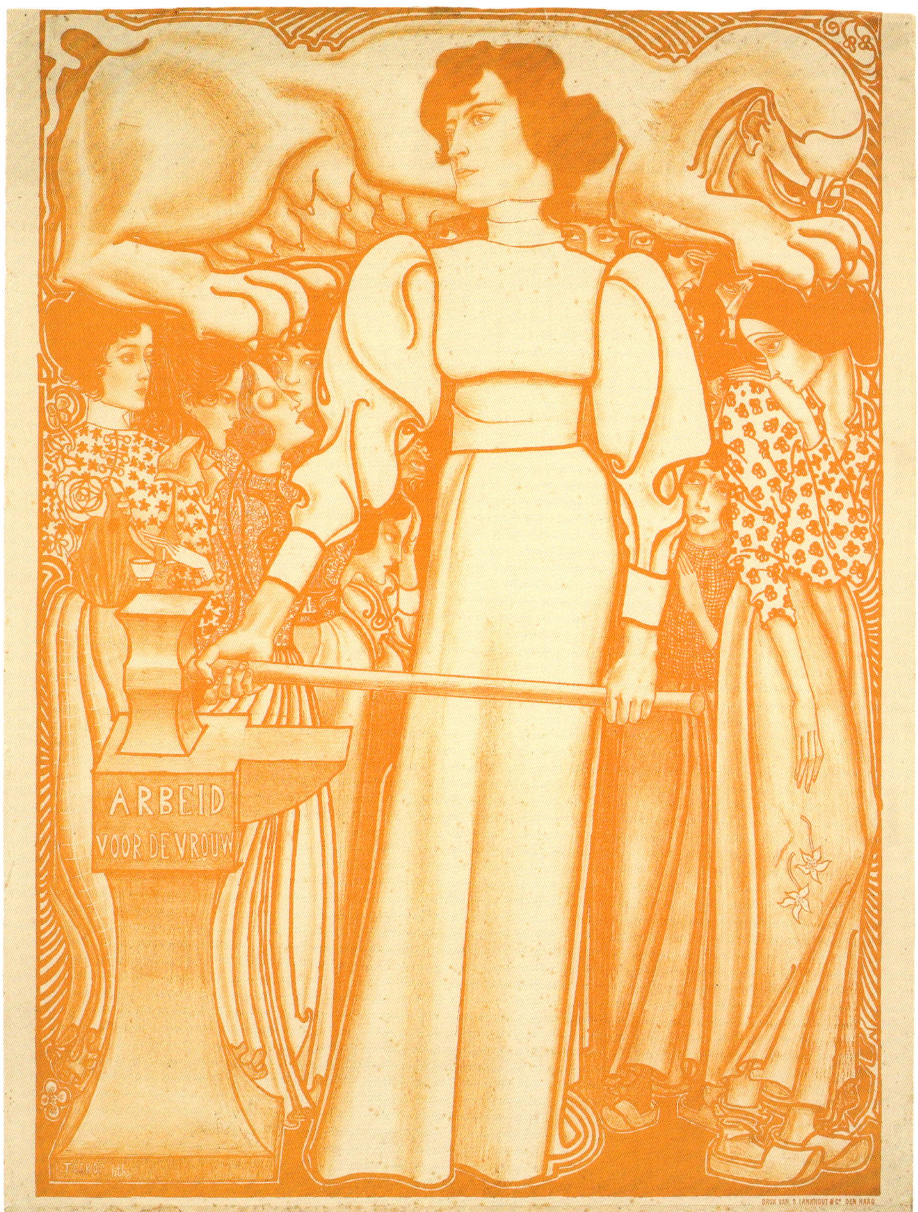

Jan Toorop
Kachelbild »Jong Holland« (Junges Holland)
1903
Handgefertigte Keramik, glasiertes Steingut
105 x 160 cm
Gemeentemuseum Den Haag

Jan Toorop
Tableau with tiles "Jong Holland" (Young Holland)
1903
Handcrafted pottery, glazed earthenware
105 x 160 cm
Gemeentemuseum The Hague

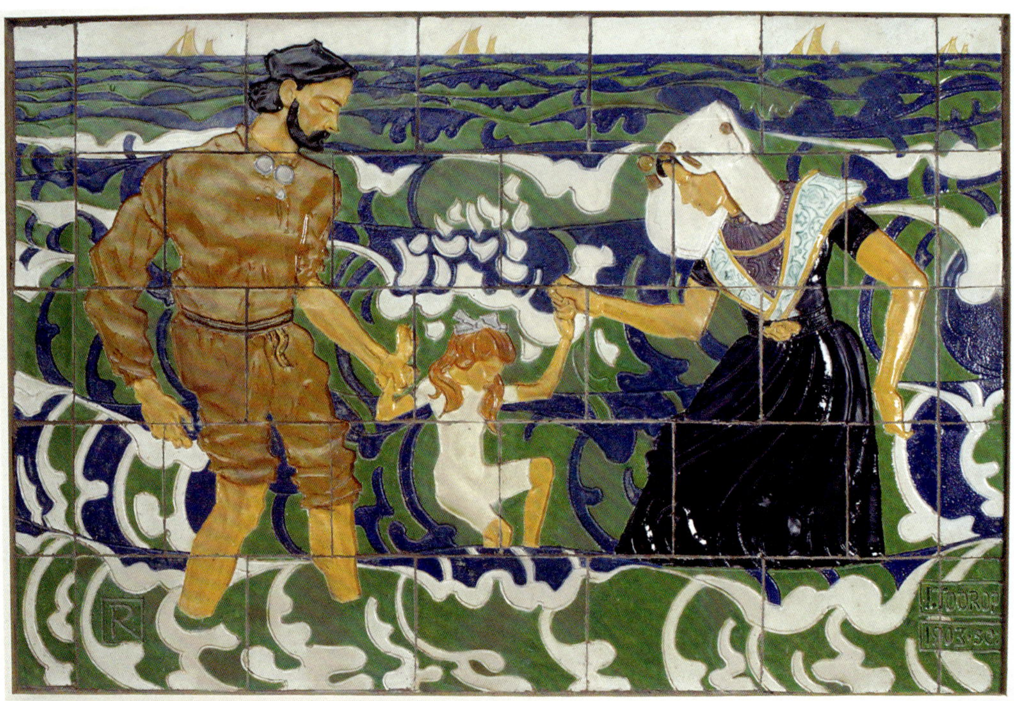

Jan Toorop
Dünen und Meer bei Zoutelande
1907
Öl auf Pappe
62,6 x 76,4 cm
Gemeentemuseum Den Haag

Jan Toorop
Dunes and Sea at Zoutelande
1907
Oil on cardboard
62,6 x 76,4 cm
Gemeentemuseum The Hague

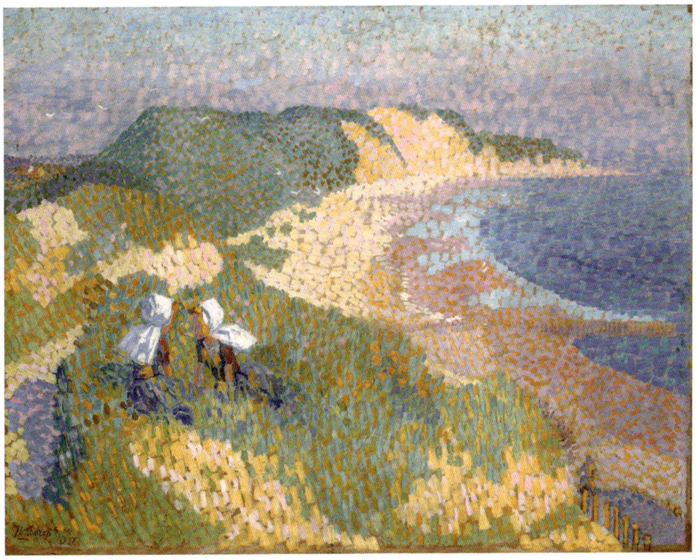

GEORGES VANTONGERLOO

Georges Vantongerloo wird 1886 in Antwerpen geboren. An den Kunstschulen in Antwerpen und Brüssel studiert er Bildhauerei. 1914 wird er zum Militär eingezogen. Als Kriegsversehrter vorzeitig entlassen, geht er nach Den Haag. Dort hofft er, auf eine Bildhauerkunst zu treffen, die seinem Verlangen nach Aufbruchstimmung entspricht und nicht mehr an das vergangene Jahrhundert erinnert. Er lernt Jan Wils und Vilmos Huszár kennen, später auch Theo van Doesburg, mit dem ihn bald eine enge Freundschaft verbindet. Für van Doesburg war es wichtig, Vantongerloo für die Mitwirkung an der Zeitschrift *De Stijl* zu gewinnen, um die Vielfalt der in *De Stijl* vereinten Künste um die Bildhauerei ergänzen zu können. Vantongerloo widmet sich darüber hinaus ernsthaft der Malerei und der Zeichenkunst und befasst sich auch theoretisch mit moderner Kunst, was 1924 zu der Abhandlung »L'art et son avenir« führt, in der er seine Ideen über die Mathematik als Grundlage der abstrakten Kunst darlegt. Ohne einander begegnet zu sein, führen Vantongerloo und Mondrian einen regen Briefwechsel über die Verwendung von Farben in der Malerei. Es entsteht eine Freundschaft, die noch vertieft wird, als sich Vantongerloo 1926 in Paris niederlässt. Zunächst legt Vantongerloo die Bildhauerei auf Eis, konzentriert sich bis 1926 auf das Kunsthandwerk und fertigt zahlreiche Möbel an. Von 1926 an entwickelt er Architekturpläne für Flughäfen und Brücken. Erst 1929 wendet er sich wieder der Bildhauerkunst zu. Zwischenzeitlich haben sich van Doesburg und Vantongerloo überworfen, vor allem wegen der Artikel, die der Belgier für *i10* verfasst. Vantongerloo wird schließlich Mitbegründer von *Abstraction-Création* und weigert sich konsequent, an der letzten Ausgabe von *De Stijl* mitzuwirken, die nach van Doesburgs Tod zu dessen Ehren herausgegeben wird. Georges Vantongerloo stirbt 1965 in Paris.

Georges Vantongerloo – born in Antwerp, Belgium in 1886, Vantongerloo trained as a sculptor at the art academies of Antwerp and Brussels. In 1914 he was drafted but soon discharged after being wounded. He settled in The Hague and began searching for a new form of sculpture in keeping with modern times rather than with the tradition of the past century. He met Jan Wils, Vilmos Huszár and, eventually, Theo van Doesburg, who became a close friend. Van Doesburg thought it important to attract Vantagerloo as a collaborator on *De Stijl* in order that sculpture should be represented in the range of subjects covered by the magazine. But Vantongerloo also took up painting and drawing, and developed his own philosophy of art. His study "L'Art et son avenir" published in 1924 set out his ideas about the mathematical foundations of art. In this sense, his thinking was in line with that of Huszár, Van Doesburg and Mondrian. Without ever having met, in 1921 Mondrian and Vantongerloo embarked on a lively exchange of ideas about the use of color in painting. Their friendship deepened when Vantongerloo moved to Paris in 1926. Vantongerloo abandoned sculpture, and until 1926 focused on applied arts and furniture. From 1926 onward he produced architectural designs for airports and bridges. Vantongerloo took up sculpting again in 1929. In the meantime he had fallen out with Van Doesburg, mainly because of his contributions to *i10.* He founded *Abstraction-Création* and refused to contribute to the final edition of *De Stijl,* which was published in honor of Van Doesburg. Georges Vantangerloo died 1965 in Paris.

Georges Vantongerloo
Schreibtisch
1920
Bemaltes Holz
70 x 140 x 70 cm
Gemeentemuseum Den Haag

Georges Vantongerloo
Desk
1920
Painted wood
70 x 140 x 70 cm
Gemeentemuseum The Hague

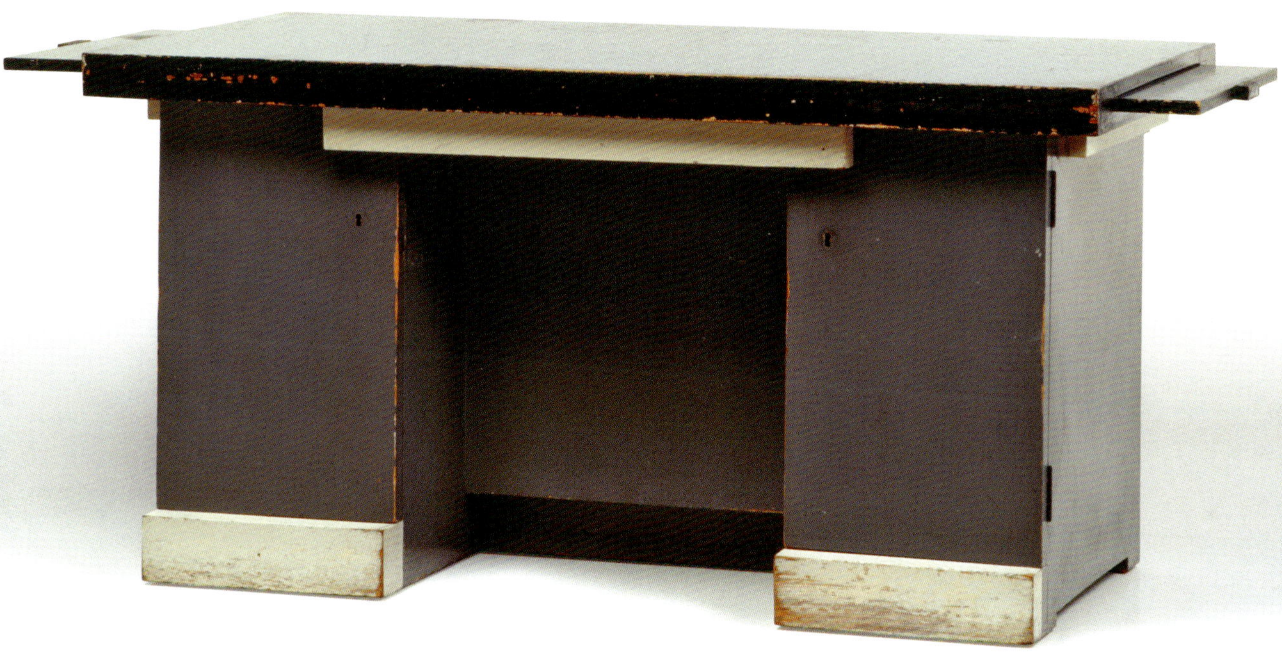

Georges Vantongerloo
S x R/3
1933/34
Eisen
100 x 100 x 100 cm
Centre Pompidou, Musée national d'art moderne –
Centre de création industrielle,
Schenkung Max Bill 1980

Georges Vantongerloo
S x R/3
1933/34
Iron
100 x 100 x 100 cm
Centre Pompidou, Musée national d'art moderne –
Centre de création industrielle,
Donation Max Bill 1980

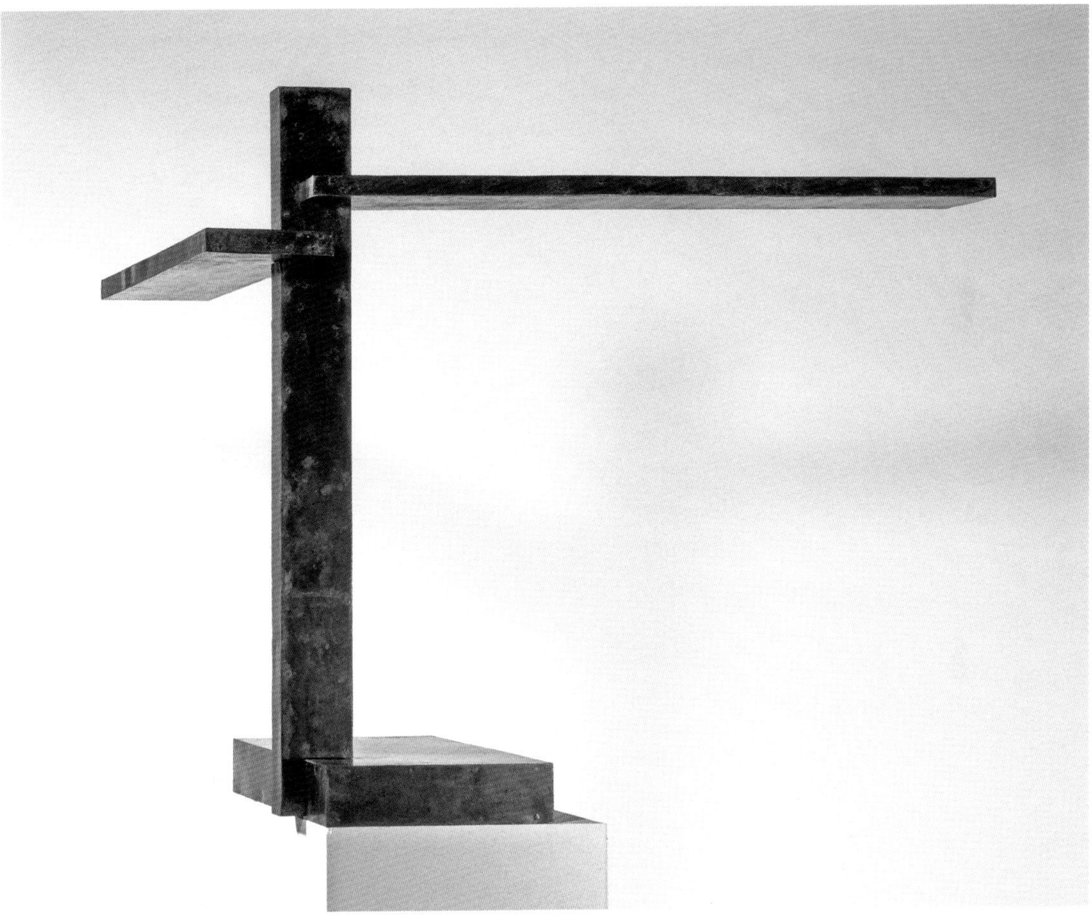

FRIEDRICH VORDEMBERGE-GILDEWART

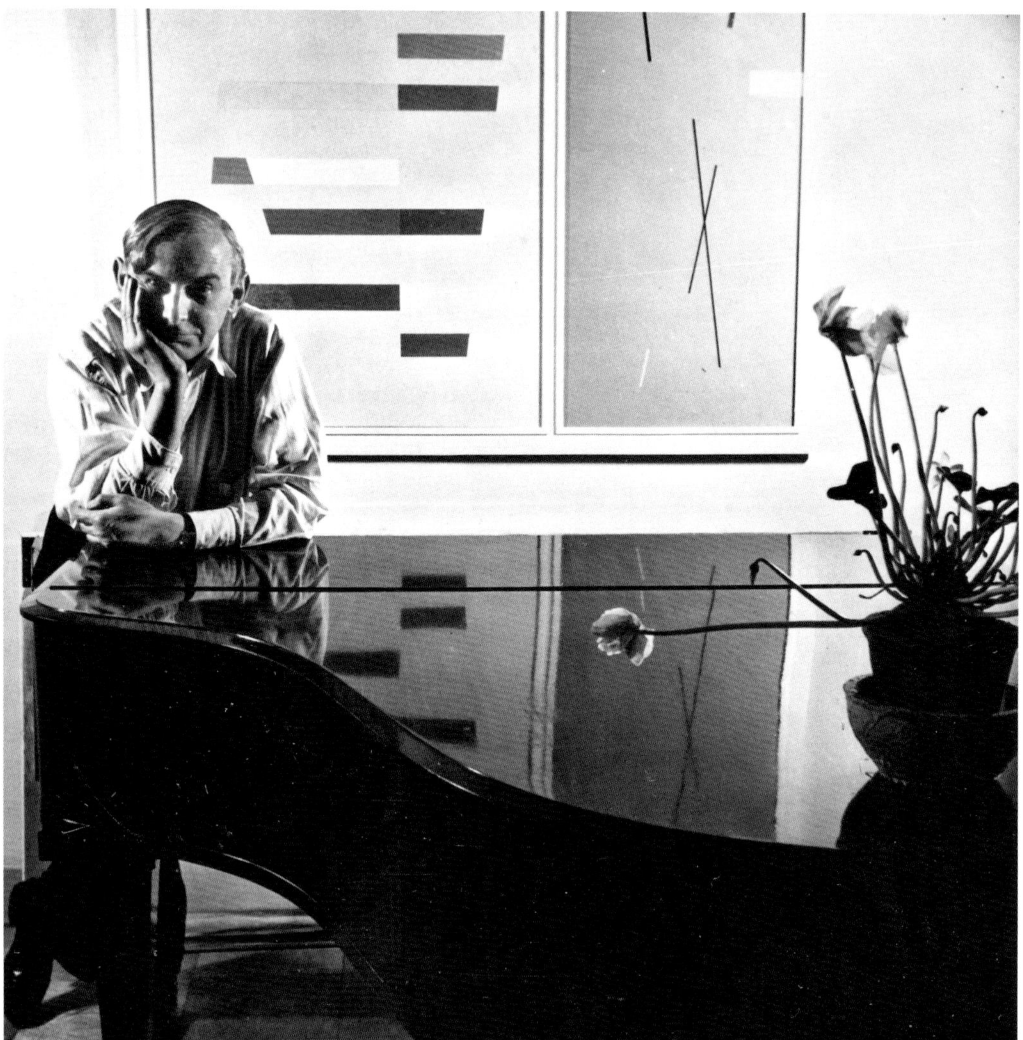

Friedrich Vordemberge-Gildewart wird 1899 in Osnabrück als Sohn eines Möbeltischlers geboren. Er geht an die Kunstgewerbeschule in Hannover, um Innenarchitekt zu werden. Bei seinen figurativen Reliefs orientiert er sich sowohl am Expressionismus als auch am Kubismus, und um 1922 hat er seine Werke so weit stilisiert, dass nur noch gerade und gebogene Linien sowie Farbflächen übrig sind. Im selben Jahr lernt er Kurt Schwitters kennen. Durch ihn und seine Dada-Soirées kommt er in Kontakt mit Hans Arp, Theo und Nelly van Doesburg sowie László Moholy-Nagy. Noch eine Begegnung prägt ihn entscheidend: 1923 trifft er El Lissitzky und sieht zum ersten Mal dessen Arbeiten. Vordemberge-Gildewart verlegt sich auf die Formensprache des russischen Konstruktivisten und ist funktionalistischer Architektur gegenüber äußerst aufgeschlossen. Mit Hans Nitzschke gründet er 1924 die Künstlervereinigung *Gruppe K*. Er ist nun der Ansicht, dass ein Maler nur noch mit elementaren Mitteln »konstruieren« darf. Im selben Jahr wird er gebeten, an *De Stijl* mitzuarbeiten. Wie Lissitzky und van Doesburg setzt er die Diagonale in seinen Arbeiten sehr vielfältig ein. Er verwendet der Malerei nicht verpflichtete Mittel wie hölzerne Quadrate und Kugeln, die das dynamische Element seiner Werke noch verstärken sollen. Ab 1927 ist er einer der angesehensten Künstler von *De Stijl*. Seine Werke werden nahezu überall in Europa und den Vereinigten Staaten gezeigt.
Er ist Gründungsmitglied zahlreicher Vereinigungen, zum Beispiel von *Ring Neue Werbegestalter* und von *Abstraction-Création*. Mit der Zeit wird seine Kunst zurückhaltender und entwickelt eine ganz eigene, einfache Ausdruckskraft. 1962 stirbt Friedrich Vordemberge-Gildewart in Ulm.

Friedrich Vordemberge-Gildewart – born in Osnabrück in 1899, the eldest son of a furniture maker, Vordemberge-Gildewart decided to become an interior designer and enrolled at the Kunstgewerbeschule in Hanover. He created figurative reliefs influenced by both Expressionism and Cubism. By 1922 his works had become so stylized that only straight and curved lines and planes of colors remained. That same year he met Kurt Schwitters at one of his Dadaist soirées, and came into contact with Hans Arp, Theo and Nelly van Doesburg and László Moholy-Nagy. He was also greatly influenced by the work of El Lissitzky, whom he met personally in 1923. He began to adopt the form language of the Russian Constructivists and developed an interest in functionalist architecture. He established *Gruppe K* with Hans Nitzschke, believing that painters should "construct" using only elementary means.
In 1924 he accepted an invitation to contribute to *De Stijl*. Like Lissitzky and Van Doesburg, Vordemberge-Gildewart used diagonals in in his compositions, as well as three-dimensional elements such as wooden blocks and balls that served to reinforce the dynamic element in his work. From 1927 onward he began to be regarded as one of the most important artists of the *De Stijl* movement, and his work was exhibited all over Europe and the United States. He helped to found various associations, including the *Ring Neue Werbegestalter* and *Abstraction-Création*. His compositions eventually became more restrained as he developed a simple idiom of his own. Vordemberge-Gildewart died 1962 in Ulm.

Friedrich Vordemberge-Gildewart
Collection RKD The Hague

Friedrich Vordemberge-Gildewart
Sammlung RKD Den Haag

Friedrich Vordemberge-Gildewart
Komposition Nr. 31
1927
Öl auf Leinwand
100 x 132 cm
Gemeentemuseum Den Haag

Friedrich Vordemberge-Gildewart
Composition No. 31
1927
Oil on canvas
100 x 132 cm
Gemeentemuseum The Hague

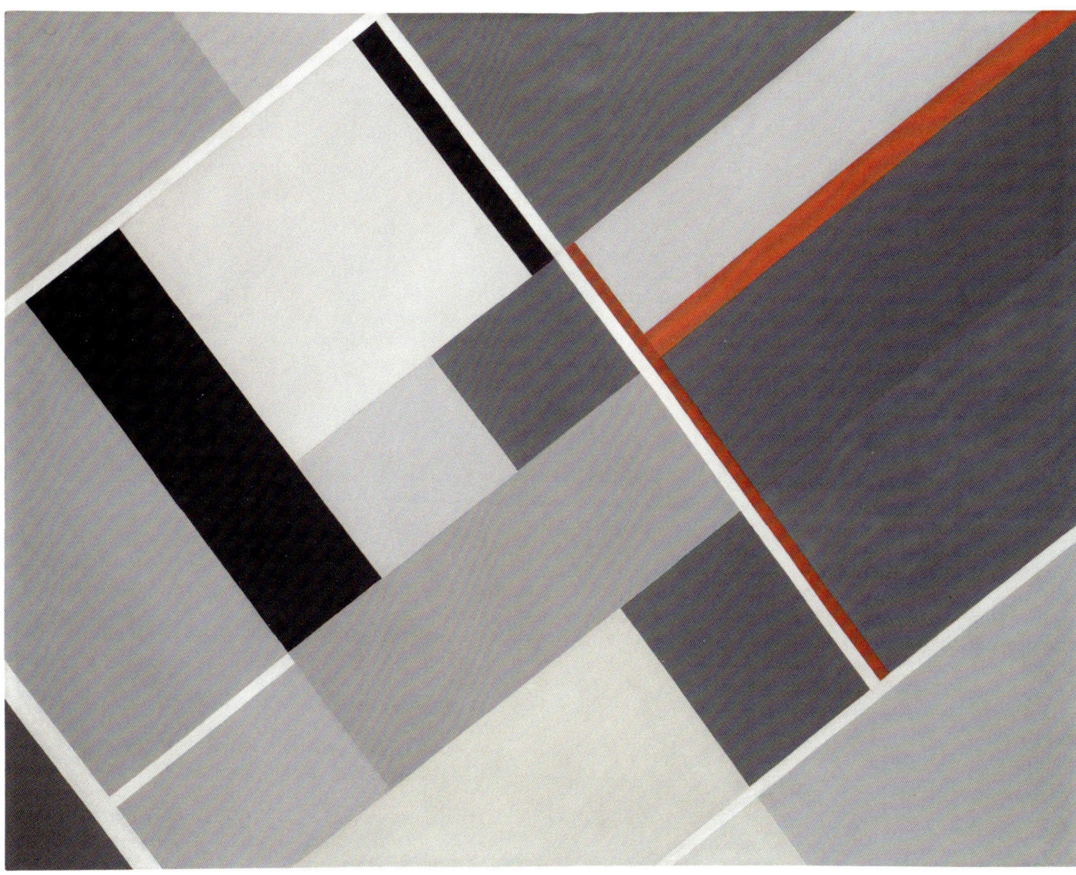

JANUS DE WINTER

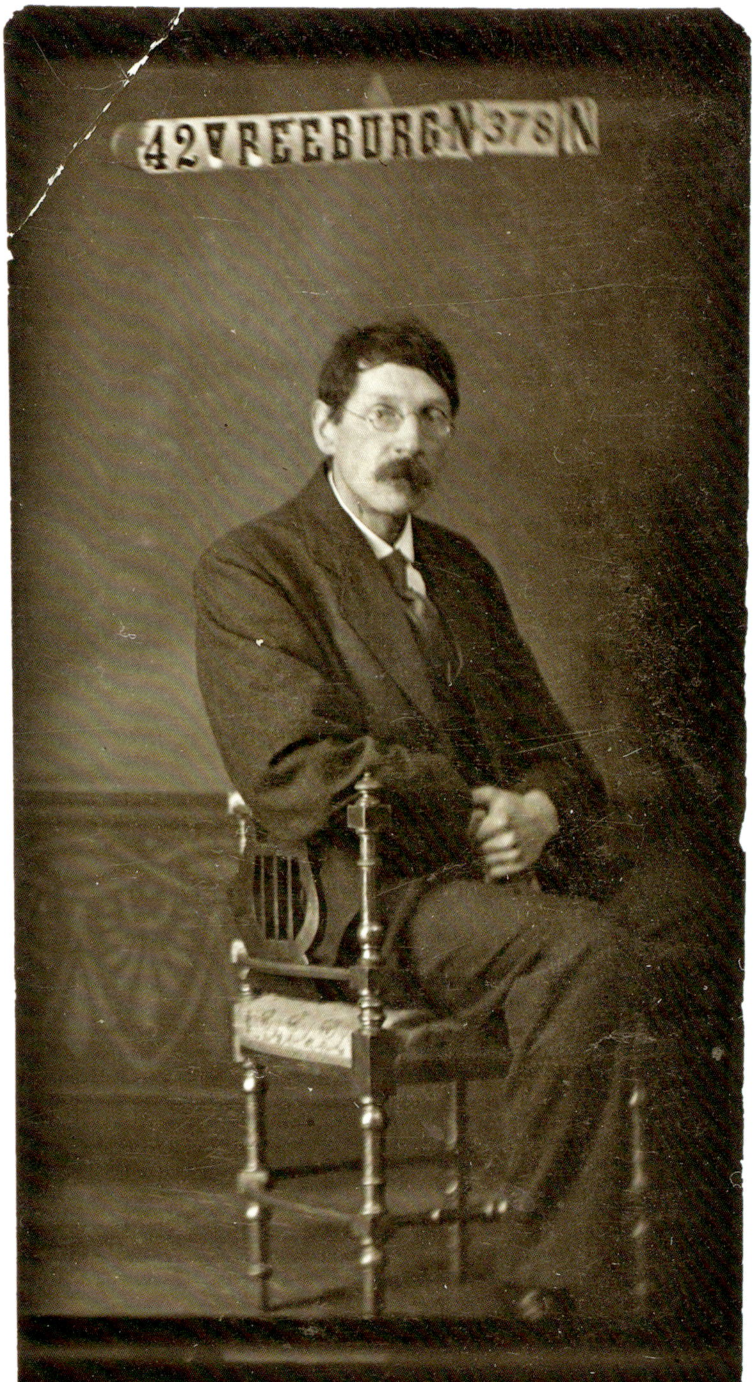

Janus de Winter
Collection RKD The Hague

Janus de Winter
Sammlung RKD Den Haag

Janus de Winter, geboren 1882 in Utrecht, betreibt Zeichnen und Malen zunächst als Hobby. Zwar nimmt er Zeichenunterricht, entwickelt sich jedoch vor allem als Autodidakt. 1907 malt er seine ›Traumphantasien‹ und orientiert sich dabei an der ›wilden‹ Malweise Vincent van Goghs. Er freundet sich mit dem Dadaisten Erich Wichman an, der schon früh mit Herwarth Walden, dem Herausgeber der Zeitschrift *Der Sturm,* in Kontakt steht, am *Ersten Deutschen Herbstsalon* teilnimmt und für eine antibürgerliche Kunst eintritt. Über Wichman lernt Janus de Winter 1915 Theo van Doesburg kennen, der ihm sofort zugetan ist: In seinen Augen scheint es de Winter zu gelingen, Form und Farbe psychologische Inhalte zu verleihen. Van Doesburgs Interesse an seinen Kunstwerken bewahrt de Winter davor, die Malerei ganz aufzugeben, wie er es aufgrund des geringen allgemeinen Interesses an seiner Kunst erwog. De Winter wird Mitglied in van Doesburgs Künstlervereinigung *De Anderen.* Van Doesburg protegiert ihn und rühmt de Winters »innere Wahrnehmung«, die ganz aus der Theosophie erwachse. De Winters Bekanntschaft mit dem Schriftsteller und Psychiater Frederik van Eeden bewirkt allerdings eine Distanzierung von van Doesburg. Er ist noch der Welt des Symbolismus verhaftet und sagt seit 1909 allen modernistischen Strömungen in der Kunst den Kampf an. Van Doesburgs Interesse für die Malerei de Winters nimmt auch deshalb ab, weil er in der Zwischenzeit Mondrian kennengelernt hat und sein Interesse sich nun auf dessen Kunst richtet: auf eine Malerei, die konsequent mit Horizontalen, Vertikalen und monochromen Farbflächen arbeitet. Janus de Winter stirbt 1951 in Den Helder.

Janus de Winter – born 1882 in Utrecht, De Winter first pursued drawing and painting as a pastime. He had some drawing instruction, but was largely self-taught. From 1907 he began painting 'dream fantasies' in a passionate, 'wild' style reminiscent of Van Gogh. De Winter became friends with Erich Wichman, a Dadaist who had early contacts with Herwarth Walden the editor of *Der Sturm,* contributed to the *Erster Deutscher Herbstsalon,* and advocated an anti-bourgeois role for art. In 1915 Wichman introduced De Winter to Theo van Doesburg, who was immediately taken with his work for its capacity to give a psychological dimension to form and color. De Winters had been depressed by the lack of interest in his work, and Van Doesburg's interest dissuaded him from giving up painting altogether. Van Doesburg made him an important figure of his artists' association *De Anderen,* supported him, and praised his "inner perceptions" growing out of theosophical sources. However, Van Doesburg and De Winter became estranged when the latter made contact with Frederik van Eeden, a writer and psychiatrist informed by nineteenth-century Symbolism, who radically and publicly opposed modernist tendencies dissociated from that movement. Van Doesburg had by then met Mondrian and refocused his interest on an art form, which consistently used the horizontal, the vertical and monochrome planes. Janus de Winter died 1951 in Den Helder.

Janus de Winter
Sensitive Verbildlichung eines dröhnenden Motors
1916
Öl und Papier auf Pappe (geklebt)
67 x 91 cm
Gemeentemuseum Den Haag

Janus de Winter
Sensitive Image of a Throbbing Engine
1916
Oil and paper on cardboard
67 x 91 cm
Gemeentemuseum The Hague

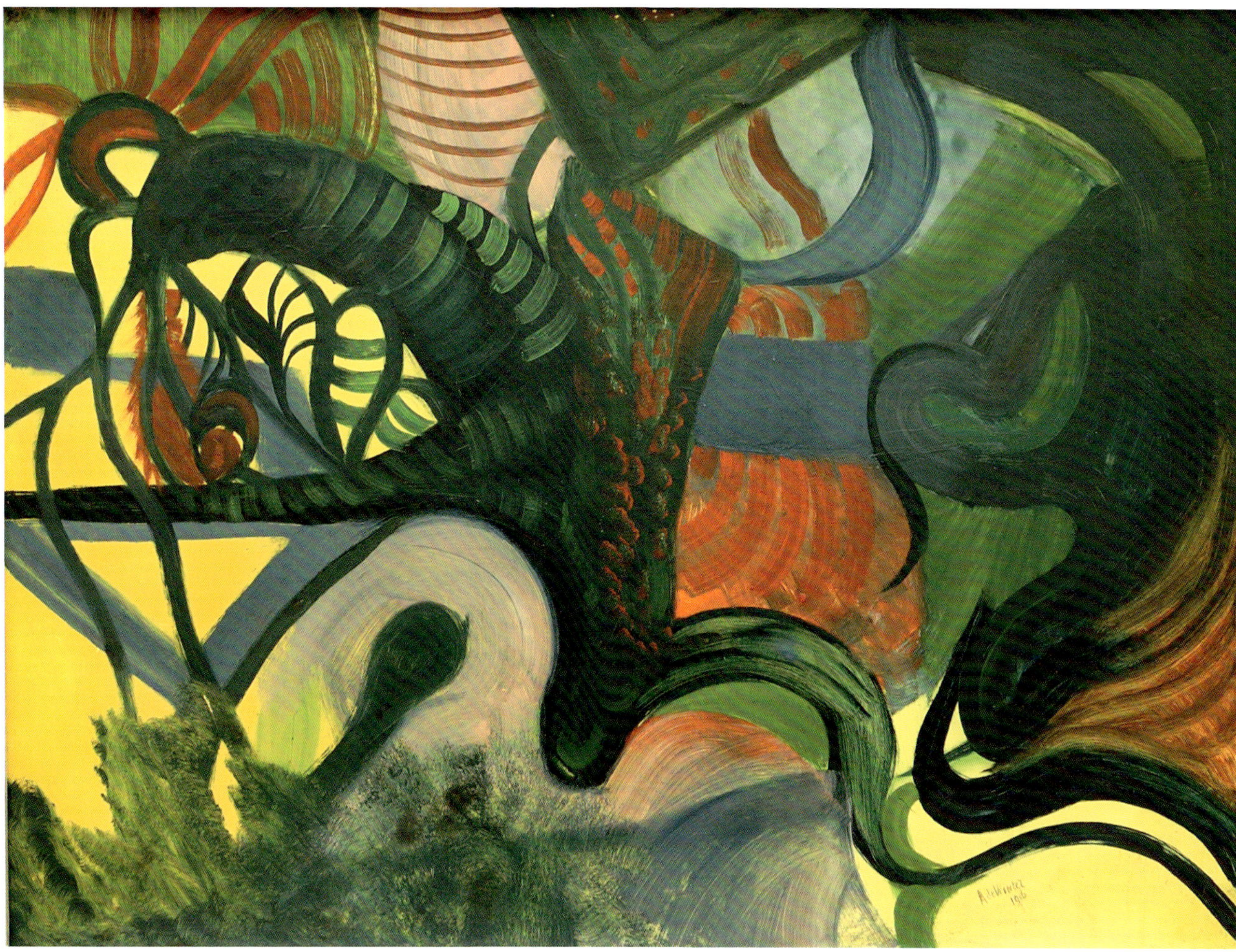

PIET ZWART

Piet Zwart wird 1885 im nordholländischen Zaandijk geboren. Er studiert an der Kunstgewerbeschule in Amsterdam, wo er sich unter anderem mit den Schriften John Ruskins und mit William Morris' *Arts & Crafts*-Bewegung befasst; eine kunsthandwerkliche Reform, die sich gegen industrielle Herstellung wendet. Später wird er sich davon distanzieren, weil die beiden Engländer seiner Meinung nach den Konservatismus kultiviert und ›Wahnideen‹ gefördert haben. Zwart selbst glaubt felsenfest an die moderne Mechanisierung. 1909 entstehen seine ersten Entwürfe für Möbel und Interieurs. Er lässt sich in Voorburg nieder, einem Vorort von Den Haag, wo er auf Theo van Doesburg und Jan Wils trifft, die gerade dabei sind, die Zeitschrift *De Stijl* ins Leben zu rufen. Als die Künstlervereinigung *Haagse Kunstkring* 1918 ein figuratives Wandgemälde ausschreibt, ist dies Anlass für Zwart, sich auf eine engagiert geführte Diskussion mit Vilmos Huszár über monumentale Kunst einzulassen. Zwart strebt nach einer Kunst, die sich als lebendiger, reger Bestandteil der Moderne entwickeln soll, und beschuldigt Huszár und *De Stijl*, ein trocken abgefasstes ästhetisches Konzept zu idealisieren. Dies erbost van Doesburg derartig, dass er Zwart verbal heftig angreift. Und doch kommt Zwart mit seinen Entwürfen der Kunst von *De Stijl* recht nahe, als er ab 1920 verstärkt für die Firma Bruynzeel arbeitet, ein marktführendes Unternehmen auf dem Gebiet moderner Holzverarbeitungstechnik. Er entwirft ›unbequeme‹ Stühle und Möbel, die dem *De Stijl*-Stil entsprechen. Zwart ist aber zu individualistisch, um wirklich Teil der Bewegung zu sein. 1923 konzipiert er einen Messestand, bei dem Bretter und Flächen in einer offenen Konstruktion zu schweben scheinen. Das erinnert an Arbeiten von El Lissitzky, die van Doesburg kurz zuvor in den Niederlanden bekannt gemacht hat; die Fotogramme und -montagen des russischen Künstlers haben Zwart tief beeindruckt. Im Laufe der 1920er-Jahre verlegt er sich auf die Typografie und kommt darüber mit vielen Künstlern in Kontakt, etwa mit Kurt Schwitters, Hans Richter und Jan Tschichold, immer auf der Suche nach der »strikten Lesbarkeit«, nach der die Reklame der modernen Zeit seiner Ansicht nach verlangt. Fotografie und Film sind dabei willkommene Hilfsmittel. Aus seinen Entwürfen für Innenausstattungen spricht ein sehr weit getriebener Rationalismus; Zwarts Streben nach Standardisierung führt schließlich zu seinen ergonomischen Entwürfen für modulare Küchen. Piet Zwart stirbt 1977 in Wassenaar.

Piet Zwart – born 1885 in Zaandijk, north of Amsterdam, Zwart studied at the Rijksschool voor Kunstnijverheid in Amsterdam, where he was first exposed to John Ruskin's and William Morris's ideas about traditional craftsmanship. Later he would speak of these ideas only in fiercely negative terms, because he thought they cultivated conservatism and reinforced delusions. Zwart was to become a functionalist and materialist thinker with an unshakable faith in modern mechanization. He produced his first designs for furniture and interiors in 1909. He moved to Voorburg a suburb of The Hague and met Theo van Doesburg and Jan Wils, who were just establishing the magazine *De Stijl*. When the *Haagse Kunstkring* invited designs for a figurative mural in 1918, a heated debate ensued between Zwart and Vilmos Huszár over monumental art. Zwart felt that art should develop as a vivid, active component of the modern, and he accused Huszár and *De Stijl* of idealizing a dry aesthetic formula. This enraged Van Doesburg, who launched a fierce verbal attack on Zwart. However, Zwart came close to the *De Stijl* artists when, from 1920, he also began to design for Bruynzeel, a company employing the most modern wood-manufacturing methods in the Netherlands. He designed 'uneasy' chairs and furniture that were entirely consistent with the *De Stijl* idiom. Nevertheless, Zwart was too individualistic to participate in the movement. In 1923 he designed a stand for a trade fair with slats and planks floating in an open structure. It was inspired by the work of El Lissitzky, which Van Doesburg had just introduced in the Netherlands. Zwart was deeply affected by the Russian artist's photograms and photomontages. During the 1920s Zwart also turned his attention to typography, an interest that brought him into contact with Kurt Schwitters, Hans Richter, Jan Tschichold and many others. To fulfill the demands of modern advertising Zwart developed types for a "bold readability" and employed photography and film as expedient means. Zwart also championed radical standardization in interior design, resulting, among other things, in his ergonomic designs for modular kitchens. Piet Zwart died 1977 in Wassenaar.

Piet Zwart
Entwurf für das Esszimmer von Nanne Ottema
1912
Aquarell auf Papier
31,1 x 30,8 cm
Gemeentemuseum Den Haag

Piet Zwart
Design for the dining room of Nanne Ottema
1912
Watercolor on paper
31,1 x 30,8 cm
Gemeentemuseum The Hague

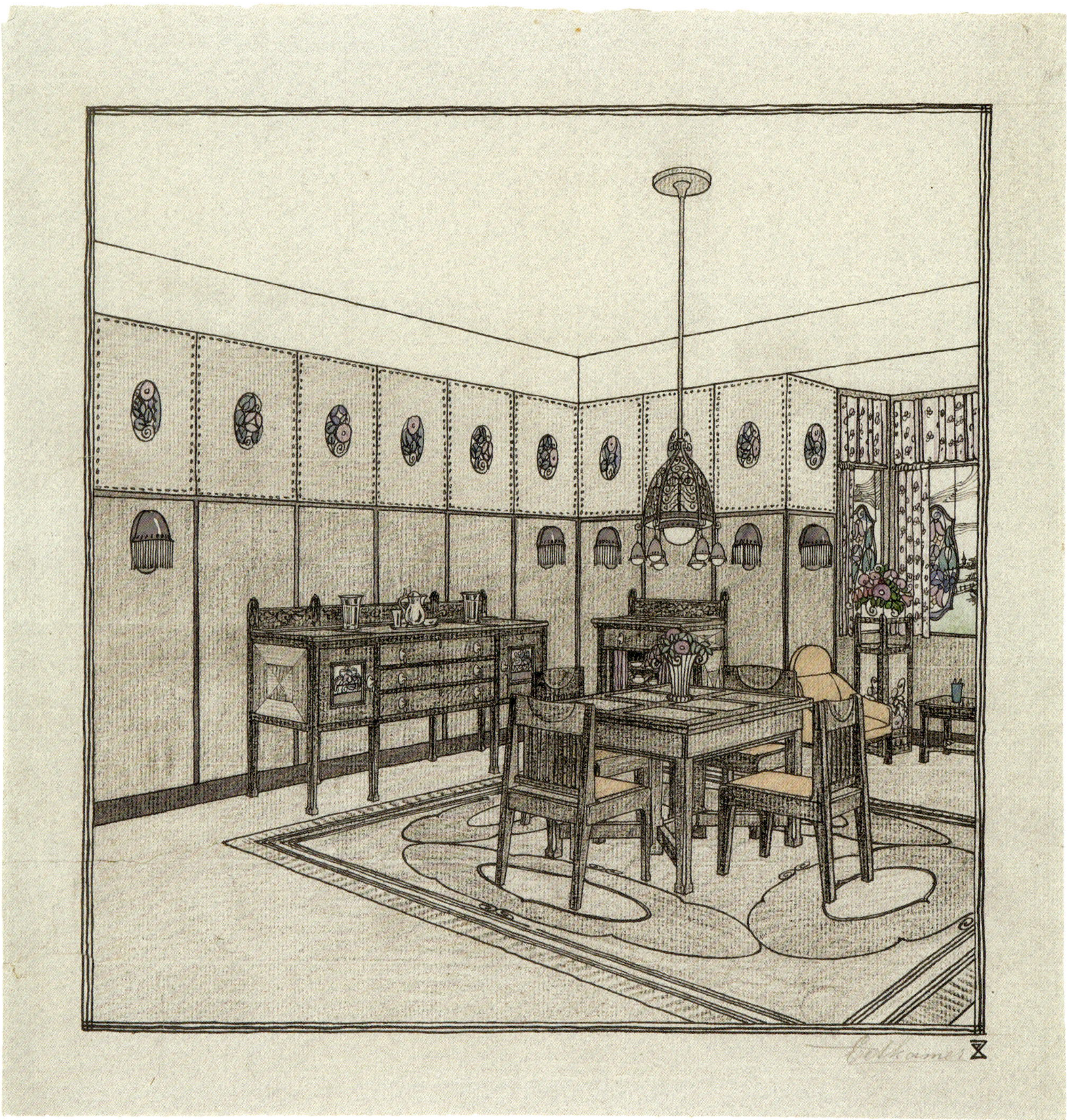

Piet Zwart
Entwurf für das Wohnzimmer für das Haus Cramer
1921
Bleistift und Farbstift auf Papier
23,2 x 30,1 cm
Gemeentemuseum Den Haag

Piet Zwart
Design for a living room for Cramer House
1921
Pencil and colored pencil on paper
23,2 x 30,1 cm
Gemeentemuseum The Hague

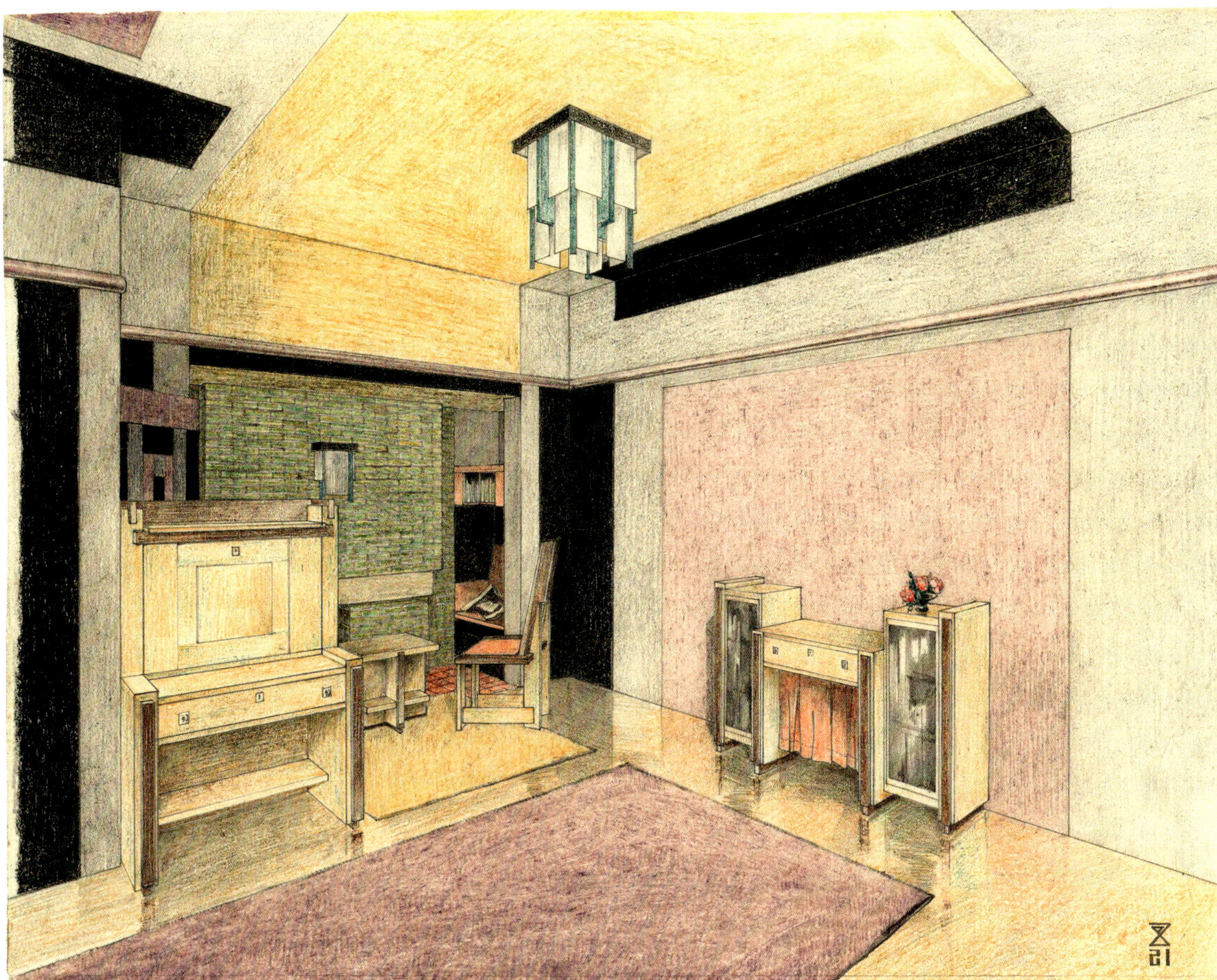

Piet Zwart
Entwurf für einen Messestand
1921
Bleistift und Aquarell auf Papier
23 x 28,5 cm
Gemeentemuseum Den Haag

Piet Zwart
Design for fair stand
1921
Pencil and water color on paper
23 x 28,5 cm
Gemeentemuseum The Hague

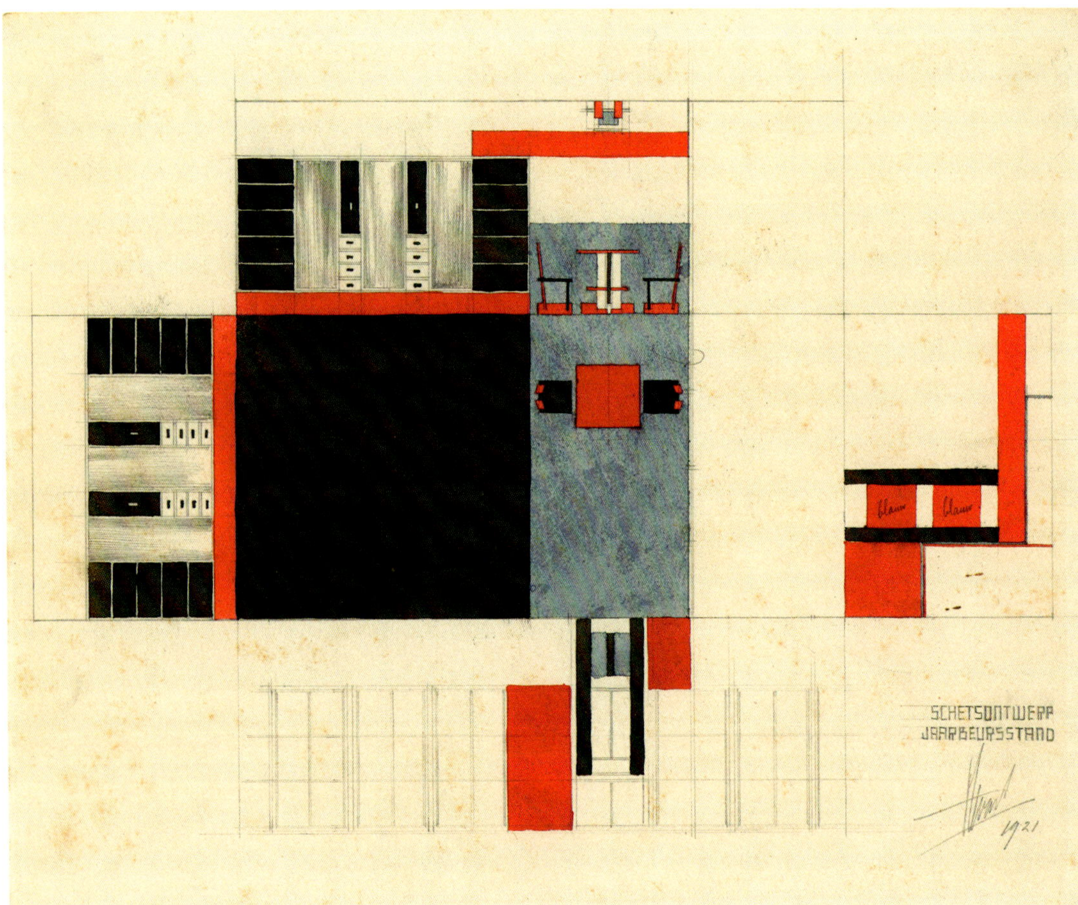

Piet Zwart
Entwurf für einen Messestand
für den Zelluloidhersteller
»Eerste Nederlandsche Celluloidwarenfabriek«
in Hilversum
1921
Bleistift und Farbstift auf Papier
21,5 x 33,4 cm
Gemeentemuseum Den Haag

Piet Zwart
Design for fair stand
for celluloid manufacturer
the "Eerste Nederlandsche Celluloidwarenfabriek"
in Hilversum
1921
Pencil and colored pencil on paper
21,5 x 33,4 cm
Gemeentemuseum The Hague

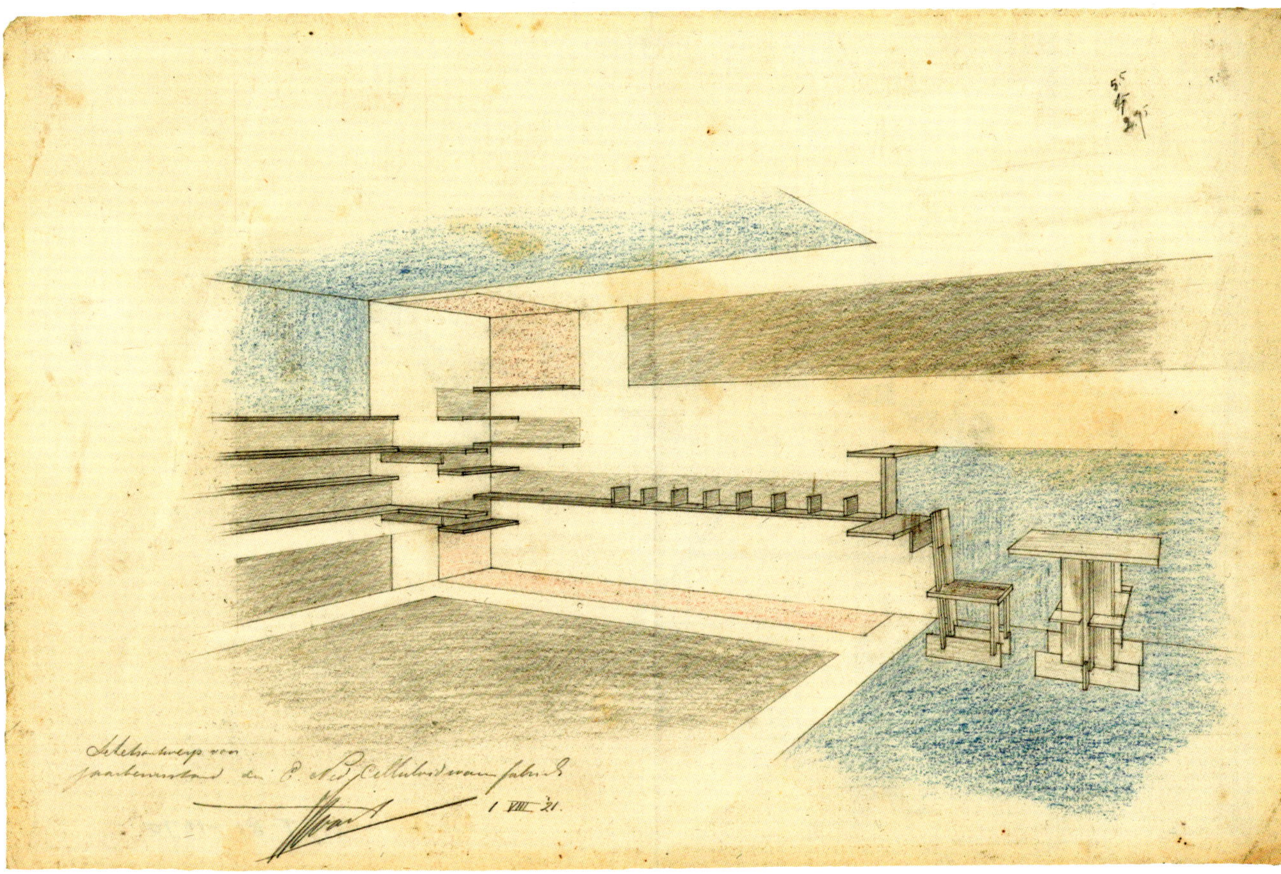

Piet Zwart
Entwurf für einen Messestand
ca. 1923
Modellausfertigung von Helmut Salden
für eine Piet Zwart-Ausstellung
vor 1940
Bemaltes Holz
25 x 39 x 55 cm
Gemeentemuseum Den Haag

Piet Zwart
Design for fair stand
ca. 1923
Model built by Helmut Salden
for a Piet Zwart exhibition
before 1940
Painted wood
25 x 39 x 55 cm
Gemeentemuseum The Hague

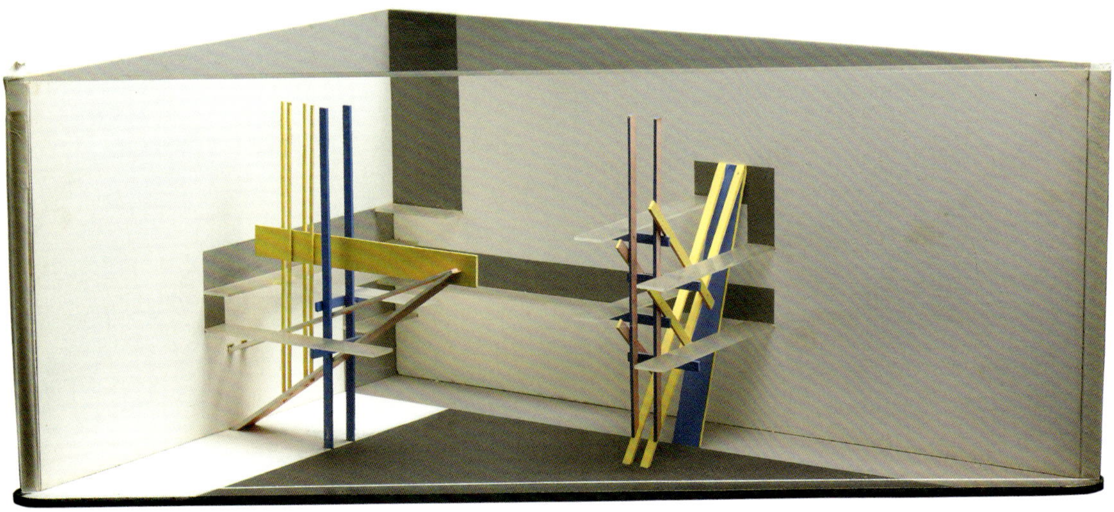

Piet Zwart
Entwurf für einen Messestand
ca. 1923
Aquarell, Tusche und Farbstift auf Papier
auf Pappe
45,5 x 64,7 cm
Gemeentemuseum Den Haag

Piet Zwart
Design for fair stand
ca. 1923
Watercolor, India ink and colored pencil on paper
on cardboard
45,5 x 64,7 cm
Gemeentemuseum The Hague

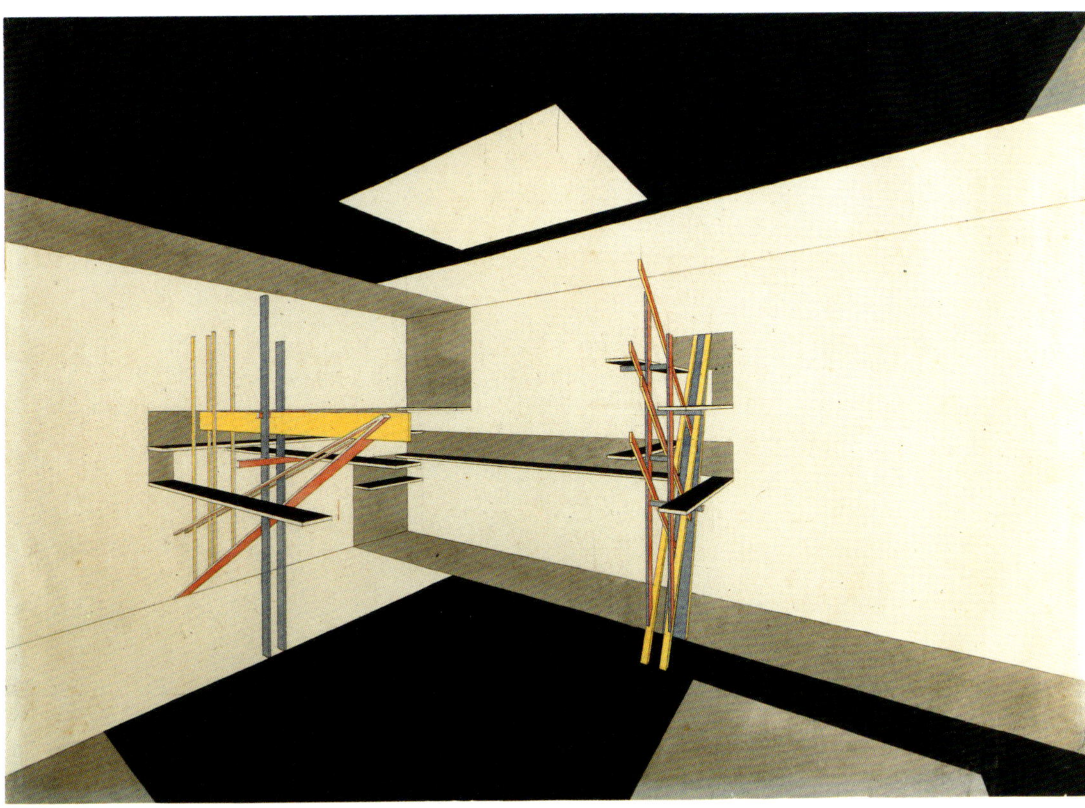

Piet Zwart
Entwurf für einen Teppich
1923
Gouache auf Papier
23,8 x 24 cm
Gemeentemuscum Den Haag

Piet Zwart
Design for a carpet
1923
Gouache on paper
23,8 x 24 cm
Gemeentemuseum The Hague

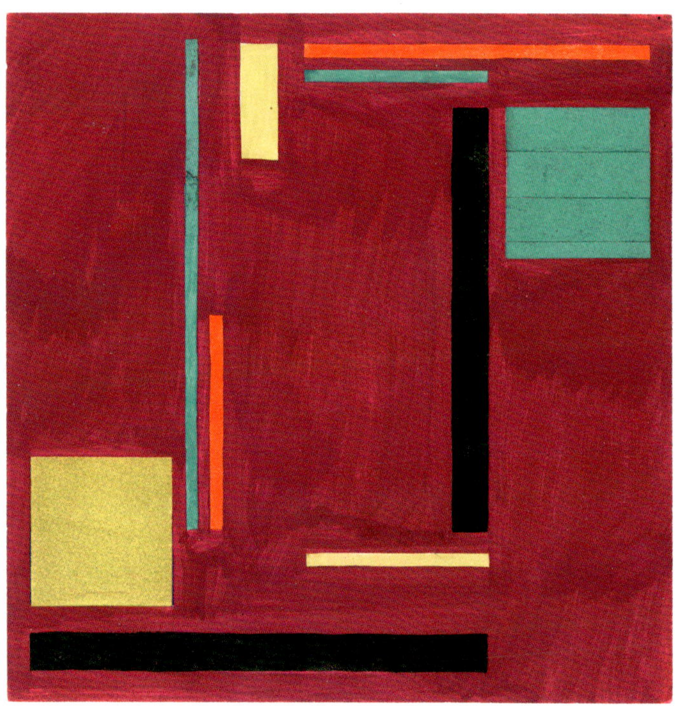

Piet Zwart
Entwurf für einen Teppich
1923
Gouache auf Papier
24,7 x 25 cm
Gemeentemuseum Den Haag

Piet Zwart
Design for a carpet
1923
Gouache on paper
24,7 x 25 cm
Gemeentemuseum The Hague

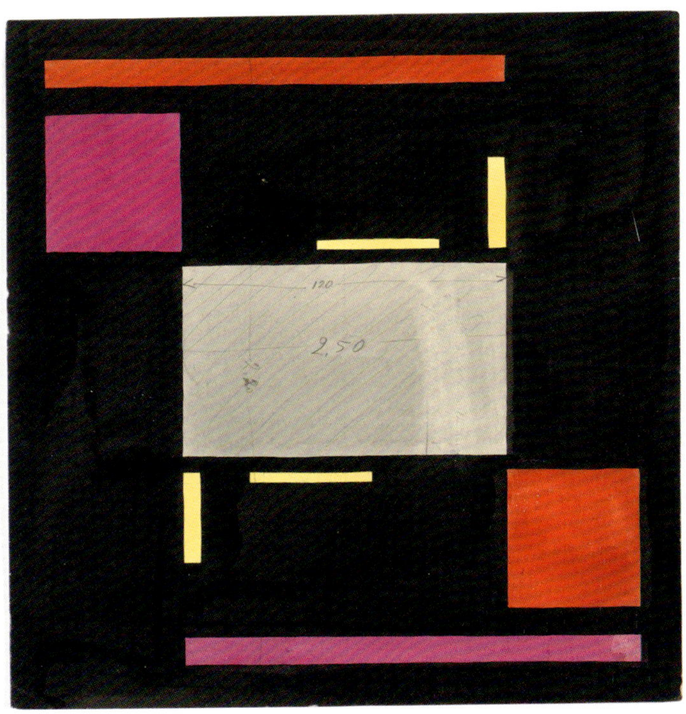

Piet Zwart
Entwurf für einen Teppich
für das Haus De Stormhoek
ca. 1924
Gouache auf Papier
49,1 x 50,9 cm
Gemeentemuseum Den Haag

Piet Zwart
Design for a carpet
for De Stormhoek House
ca. 1924
Gouache on paper
49,1 x 50,9 cm
Gemeentemuseum The Hague

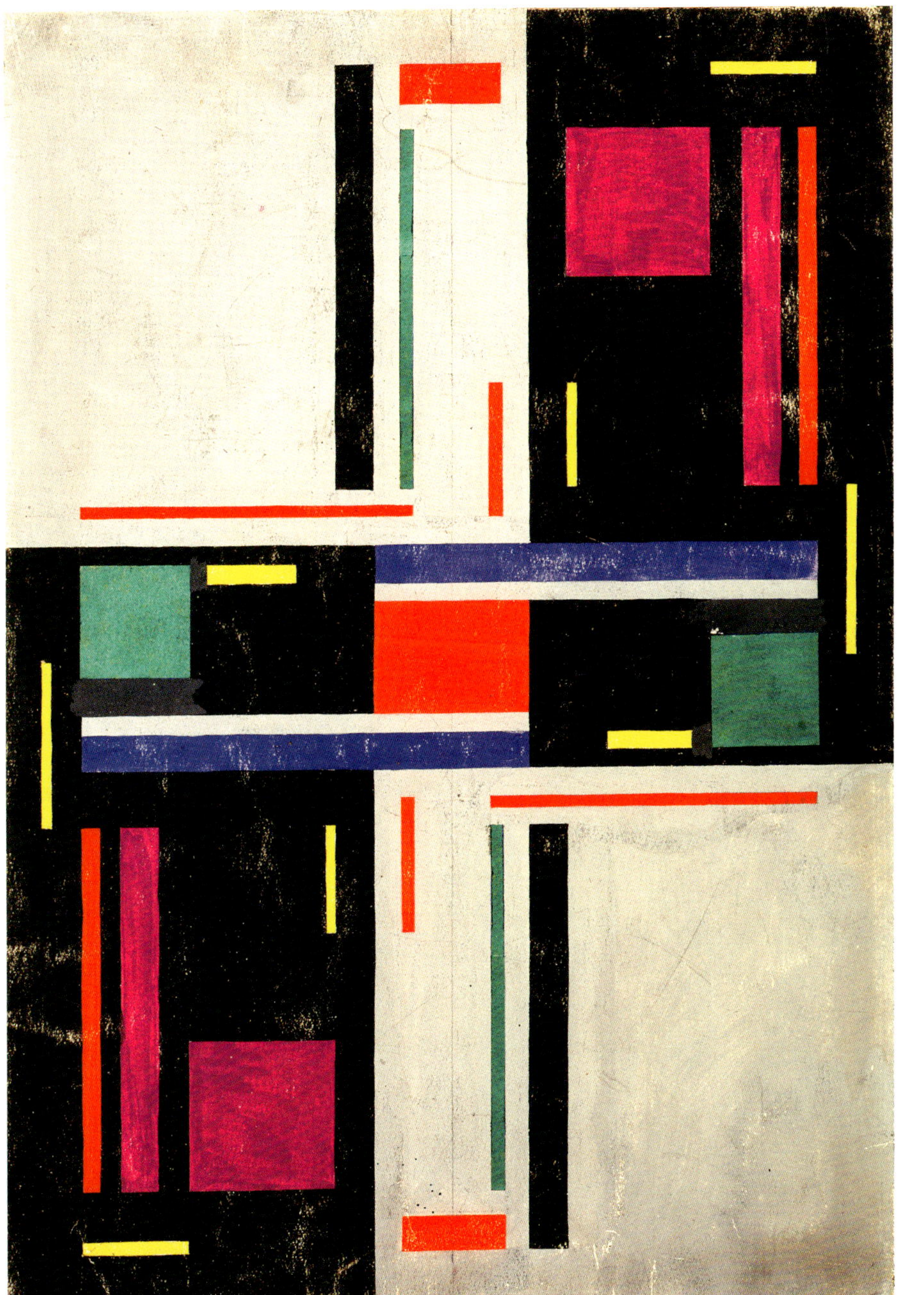

Piet Zwart
Bordürenentwurf für ein Oberteil
1916
Gouache auf Papier
48,7 x 71,6 cm
Gemeentemuseum Den Haag

Piet Zwart
Design for a decorative element for a dress
1916
Gouache on paper
48,7 x 71,6 cm
Gemeentemuseum The Hague

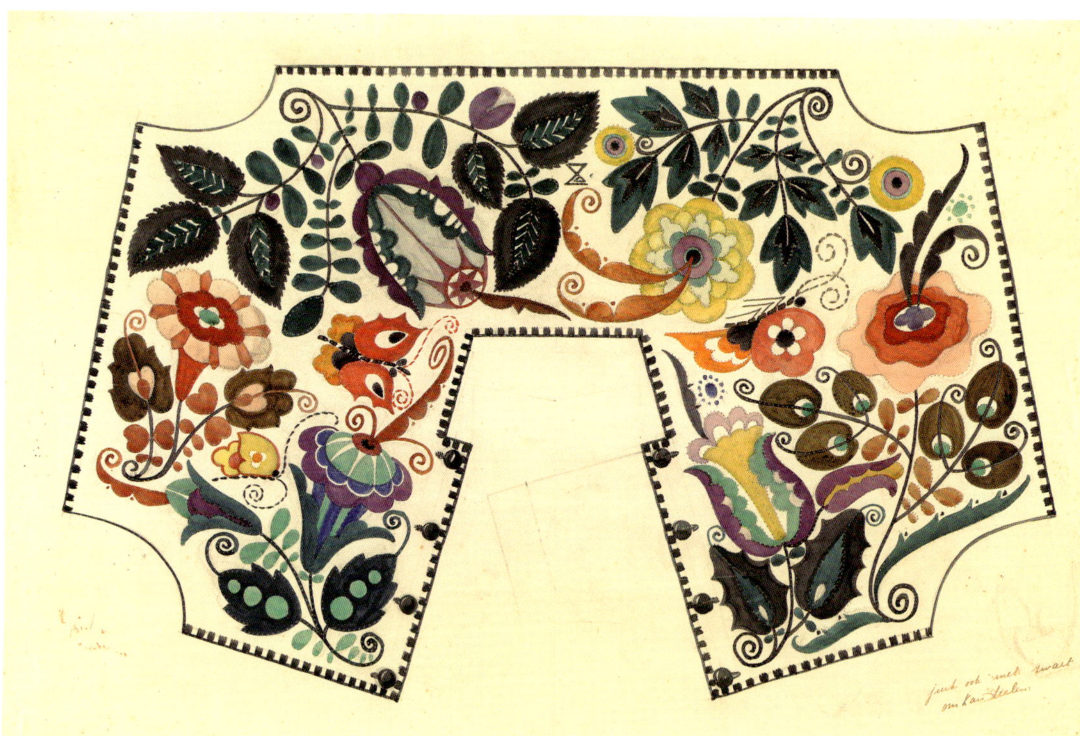

Piet Zwart
Ausführung von Rie Zwart-Ketjen
Links:
Kinderkleid
ca. 1934
Wolle, Kunststoff, 60 x 70 cm
Rechts:
Kinderkleid
ca. 1915–1917
Leinen, Wolle, 50 x 55 cm
Mütze
1915–1918
Wolle, Seide, 25 x 18 cm
Gemeentemuseum Den Haag

Piet Zwart
Realization by Rie Zwart-Ketjen
Left:
Child's dress
ca. 1934
Wool, synthetic fabric, 60 x 70 cm
Right:
Child's dress
ca. 1915–1917
Linen, wool, 50 x 55 cm
Cap
1915–1918
Wool, silk, 25 x 18 cm
Gemeentemuseum The Hague

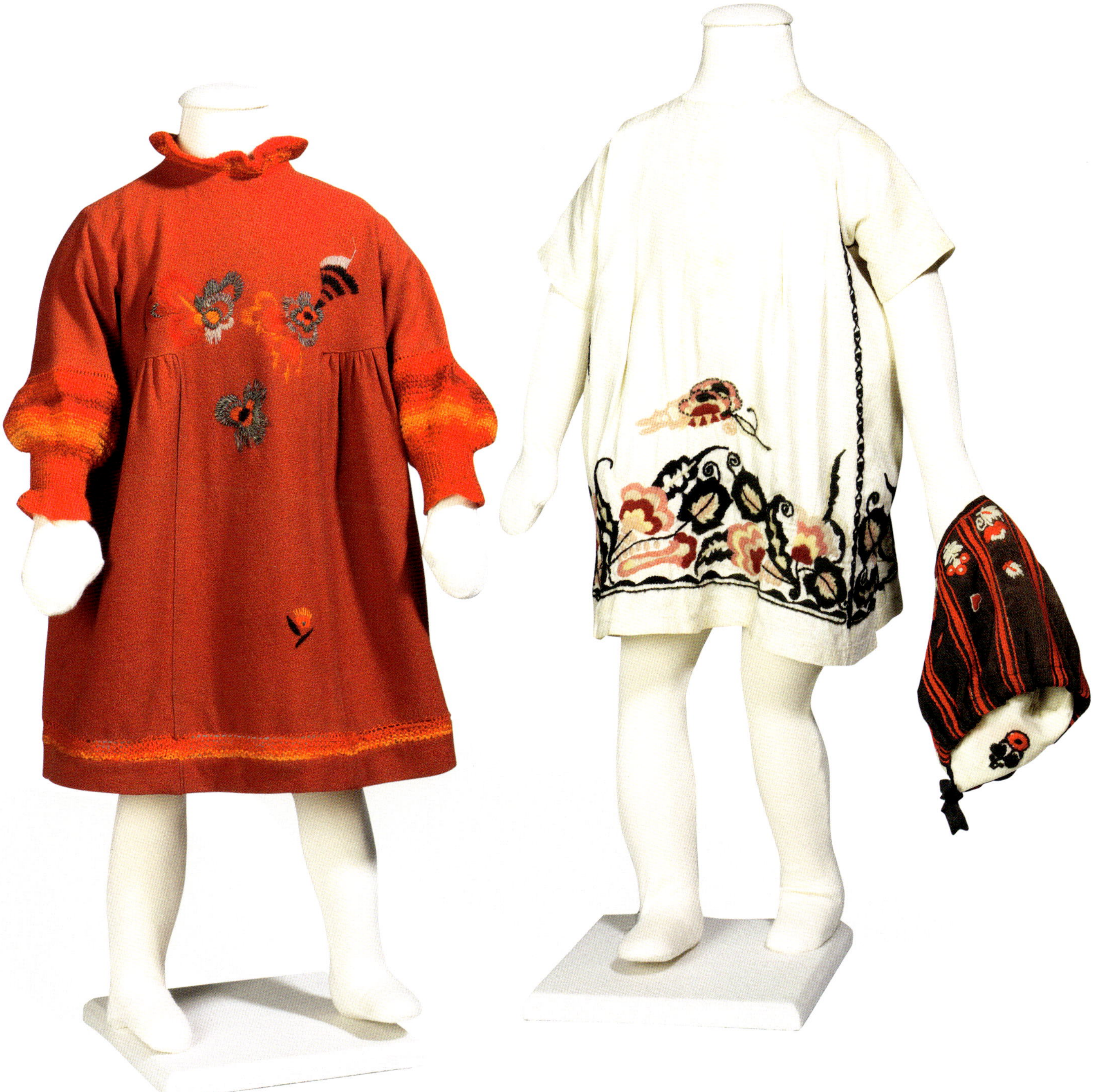

Piet Zwart
Links:
Tänzer
1920
Gouache auf Papier
32,6 x 22,3 cm
Rechts:
Tänzer
1920
Gouache auf Papier
31,3 x 22,2 cm
Gemeentemuseum Den Haag

Piet Zwart
Left:
Dancer
1920
Gouache on paper
32,6 x 22,3 cm
Right:
Dancer
1920
Gouache on paper
31,3 x 22,2 cm
Gemeentemuseum The Hague

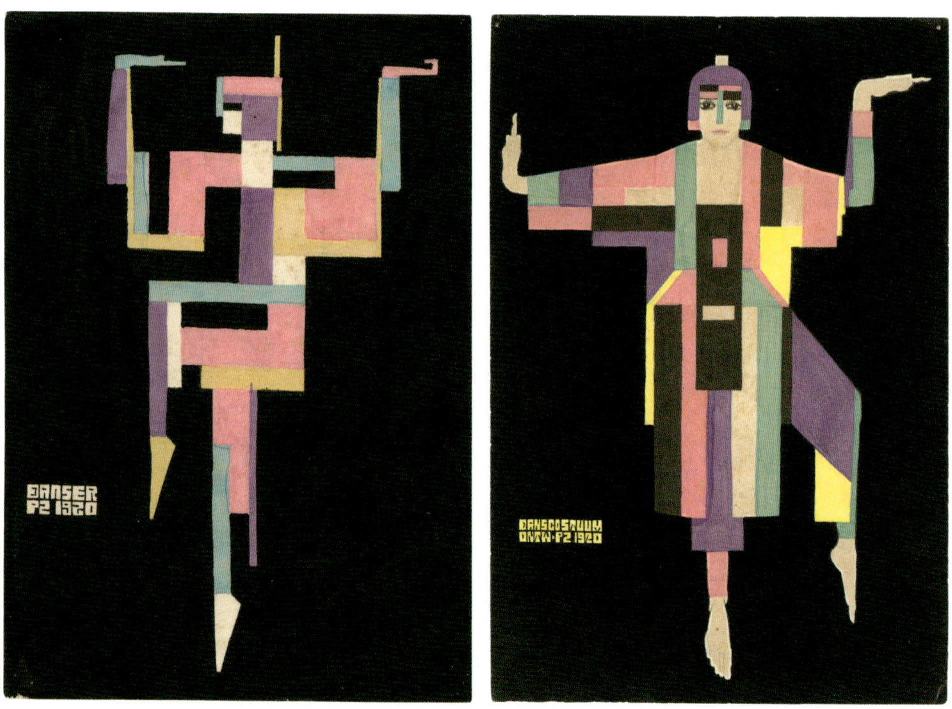

Piet Zwart
Links:
Tänzer
1920
Gouache auf Papier
18,4 x 26,5 cm
Rechts:
Tänzer
1920
Gouache auf Papier
18,5 x 25,5 cm
Gemeentemuseum Den Haag

Piet Zwart
Left:
Dancer
1920
Gouache on paper
18,4 x 26,5 cm
Right:
Dancer
1920
Gouache on paper
18,5 x 25,5 cm
Gemeentemuseum The Hague

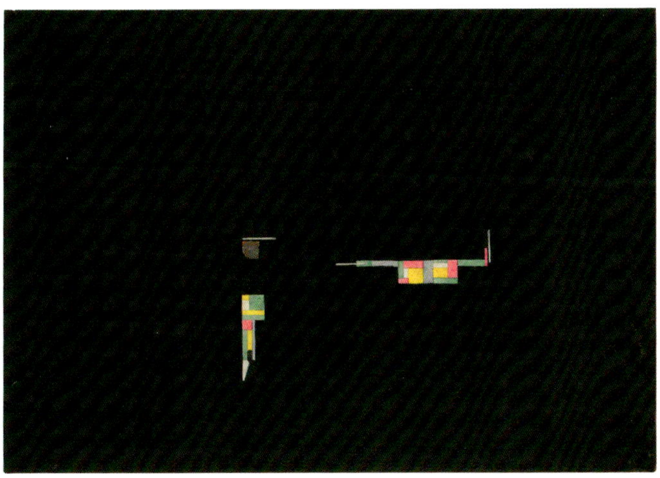

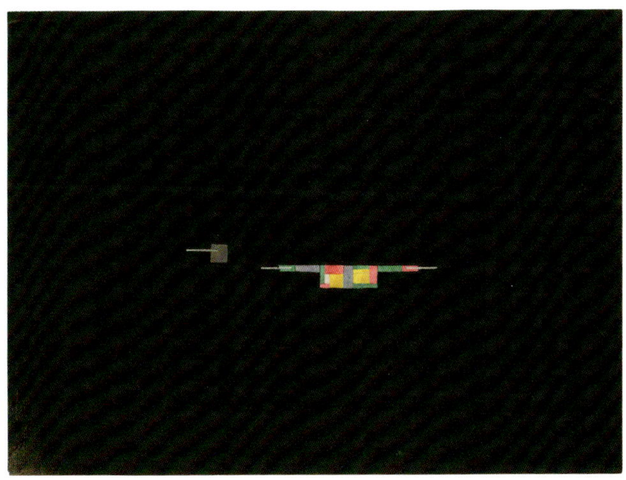

PIET ZWART

HENDRIK PETRUS BERLAGE

Hendrik Petrus Berlage wird 1856 in Amsterdam geboren. In Zürich studiert er Architektur an der Eidgenössischen Polytechnischen Hochschule, wo er sich auch mit den von Gottfried Semper und Eugène Viollet-le-Duc aufgestellten Theorien über Architektur und Ornamentik auseinandersetzt. Sempers Anliegen war, dass ein Architekt, ähnlich wie ein Handwerker, der die Eigenschaften von Holz, Metall und Stein genau kennt und sie sich zunutze macht, seine Baumaterialien exakt ihrer Funktionalität nach einsetzt. Von Viollet-le-Duc übernimmt Berlage den Lehrsatz von der vorrangigen Bedeutung einer klaren Konstruktion und kombiniert diese Einsicht mit eigenen radikal-liberalen Ideen, die sozialdemokratisches Gedankengut vorwegnehmen. In seinen Entwürfen für Möbel und Gebrauchskunst, für Bauwerke, Stadtviertel und für die Stadtplanung, die ganz der Gemeinschaft und dem Rationalismus verpflichtet sind, entwickelt Berlage eine strenge, funktionale Struktur. Um 1890 ist er ein angesehener Architekt in den Niederlanden. Architektonische Neuerungen um die Jahrhundertwende (kühle Sachlichkeit ohne jegliches Ornament, Industrialisierung und Standardisierung, Komfort und Hygiene) werden in den Niederlanden dann akzeptiert, wenn Berlage sie gutheißt. Berlages bekanntestes Bauwerk ist die 1903 in Amsterdam eröffnete Börse, bei der er das enge Zusammenwirken von bildender Kunst und Architektur so eindrucksvoll umsetzt, dass es der folgenden Künstler- und Architektengeneration zum Vorbild wird. Während eines Besuchs in den Vereinigten Staaten im Jahr 1911 faszinieren Berlage die Arbeiten von Frank Lloyd Wright. 1917 fertigt er Entwürfe für einen Museumsbau für die Kunstsammlung des Ehepaars Kröller-Müller, nachdem die Pläne sowohl von Peter Behrens als auch von Ludwig Mies van der Rohe von den Sammlern abgelehnt wurden. Dieses Projekt wird allerdings so nie realisiert. Später wird Berlage jedoch von der Gemeinde Den Haag den Auftrag erhalten, ein Museum für moderne Kunst zu entwerfen: das Gemeentemuseum, das 1935 – nach Berlages Tod im Jahr 1934 – eröffnet wird.

Hendrik Petrus Berlage – born 1856 in Amsterdam, Berlage studied at the Eidgenössische Technische Hochschule in Zurich where he was exposed to Gottfried Semper's and Eugène Viollet-le-Duc's views on architecture and ornamentation. Semper encouraged architects to use materials in keeping with their functionality, in the manner of a craftsman who knows the intrinsic properties of wood, metal and stone. Berlage adopted from Viollet-le-Duc's architectural writings the principle of the primacy of clear structures, and combined this with his own radical-liberal ideas, which can be regarded as anticipatory of social democratic concepts. He developed an austere functional structure in his designs for furniture, applied arts, buildings, entire district- and urban development plans, which were committed both to the community and to Rationalism. Around 1890, his star began to rise in the Dutch architectural world. All turn-of-the-century architectural innovations (unadorned functionalism, industrialization and standardization, comfort and hygiene) were accepted in the Netherlands as long as Berlage approved them. His most famous building was the Amsterdam Beurs (Amsterdam stock exchange), completed in 1903, on which he collaborated effectively with artists, making it an example to an entire generation of artists and architects. During a visit to the United States in 1911 Berlage was fascinated by the work of Frank Lloyd Wright. After Peter Behrens's and Ludwig Mies van der Rohe's designs for a museum to house the collection of Anton Kröller and Helene Kröller-Müller had been rejected, Berlage was invited to submit his design in 1912. Though his project was not realized, Berlage later had the opportunity to put forward his ideas for a museum of modern art when The Hague city council commissioned him to design the Gemeentemuseum, which opened the year after Berlage's death, in 1935.

Piet Zwart
Hendrik Petrus Berlage
Frühstücksservice
1924–1927
Pressglas
Gemeentemuseum Den Haag

Piet Zwart
Hendrik Petrus Berlage
Breakfast service
1924–1927
Pressed glass
Gemeentemuseum The Hague

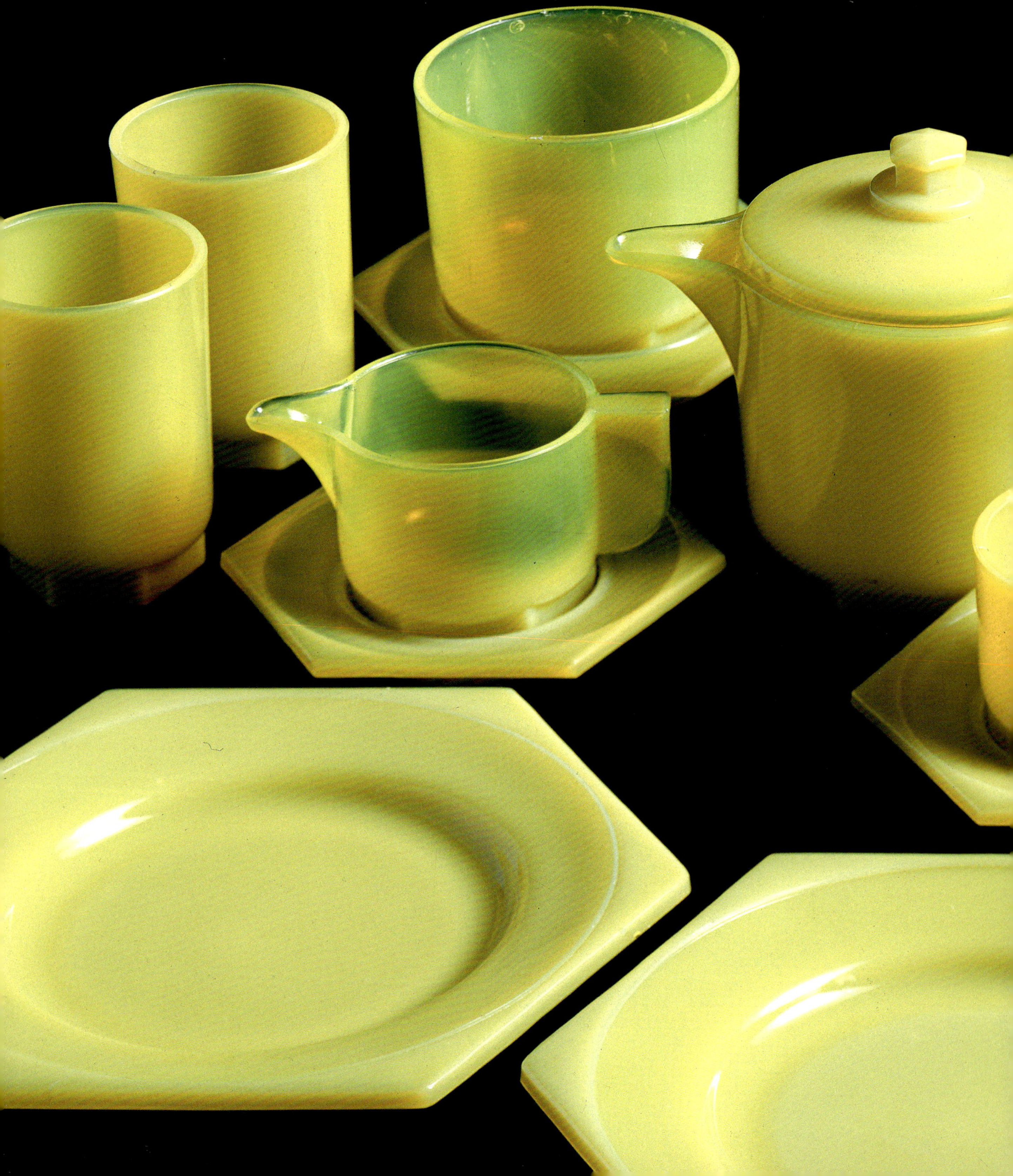

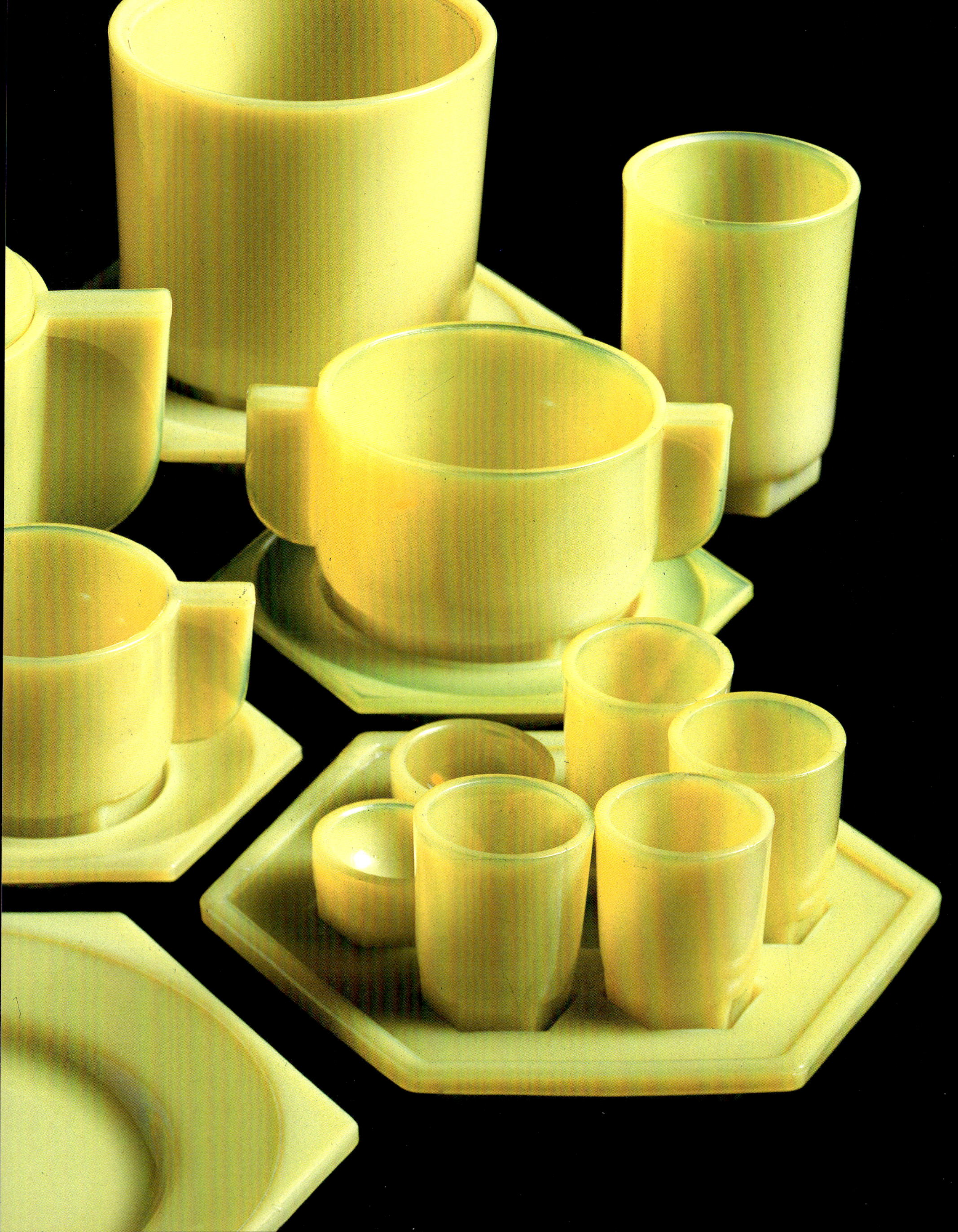

PIET ZWART

VILMOS HUZAR

Piet Zwart
Vilmos Huszár
Entwurf für einen Stuhl
für das Ledigenheim für Frauen in Den Haag
1920
Aquarell und Tusche auf Papier
51,3 x 34 cm
Gemeentemuseum Den Haag

Piet Zwart
Vilmos Huszár
Design for a chair
for the home for single women in The Hague
1920
Water color and India ink on paper
51,3 x 34 cm
Gemeentemuseum The Hague

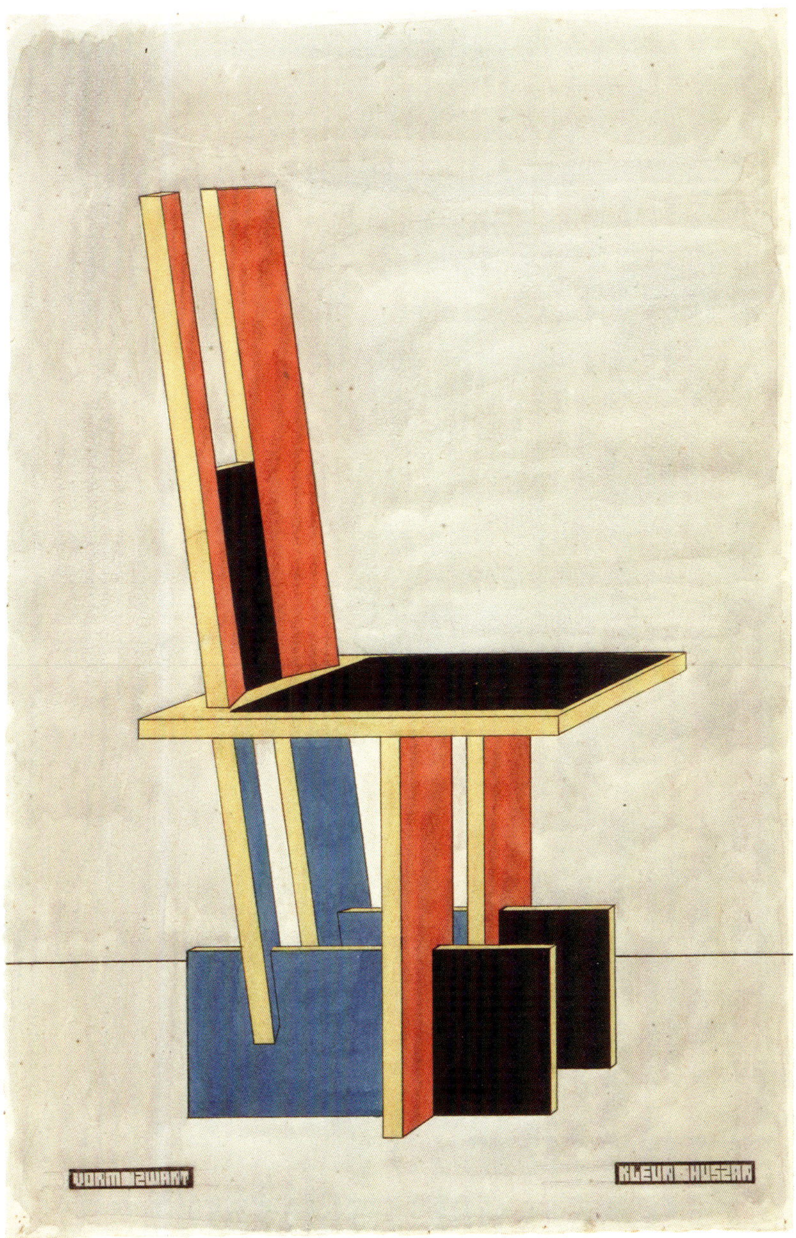

Danksagung / Acknowledgments

Wies van Moorsel, Amsterdam; Bernhard Mendes Bürgi, Nina Zimmer, Charlotte Gutzwiller, Kunstmuseum Basel; Annemarie Jaeggi, Klaus Weber, Monika Tritschler, Bauhaus-Archiv Berlin; Sven Beckstette, TEXTE ZUR KUNST, Berlin; Rudi E.O. Ekkart, Wietse Coppes, RKD – Rijksbureau voor Kunsthistorische Documentatie Den Haag / Netherlands Institute for Art History The Hague; Benno Tempel, Franz Kaiser, Hans Janssen, Doede Hardeman, Madelief Hohé, Ruth Hoppe, Lidwien Speleers, Frans Peterse, Erna Onstenk, Peter Couvee, Ap Gewald, Elmar Groen, Peter Houtman, Gemeentemuseum Den Haag / The Hague; Bernhard Maaz, Petra Kuhlmann-Hodick, Claudia Schnitzer, Yvonne Brandt, Kupferstich-Kabinett, Staatliche Kunstsammlungen Dresden; Erven Vilmos Huszár; Marion von Hofacker, Icking-Irschenhausen, Hans Richter Estate; Egon Bruhin-Seiler, Stiftung Vordemberge-Gildewart, Lachen/Schweiz; Agnes Thum, München; Rolf Griebel, Hanne Schweiger-Schimang, Bayerische Staatsbibliothek München; Alfred Pacquement, Brigitte Léal, Aurélien Lemonier, Frédéric Migayrou, Hervé Derouault, Corinne Picarello, Centre Pompidou, Musée national d'art moderne – Centre de création industrielle, Paris; Ole Bouman, Pascale Pere, Niederländisches Architekturinstitut / Netherlands Architecture Institute, Rotterdam; Sean Rainbird, Ina Conzen, Peter Frei, Staatsgalerie Stuttgart; Hilary Richardson, Mondrian/Holtzman Trust, c/o HCR International Virginia USA; Egbert Rietveld, RIETVELD by rietveld, Voorburg.

Impressum / Imprint

Diese Publikation erscheint anlässlich
der Ausstellung
This catalogue is published in conjunction
with the exhibition

Mondrian und De Stijl / Mondrian and De Stijl

16. April bis 15. August 2011
April 16 until August 15, 2011

Städtische Galerie im Lenbachhaus
und Kunstbau, München
Luisenstrasse 33
80333 München
Tel. +49 89 233 320-00 / Fax +49 89 233 320-03
www.lenbachhaus.de

Partner des Lenbachhauses
e·on | Energie

Ausstellung / Exhibition

Kuratoren / Curators:
Helmut Friedel, Matthias Mühling
Assistenzkuratorin / Assistant Curator:
Felicia Rappe
Organisation / Coordination:
Karin Dotzer
Restaurierung / Conservators:
Iris Winkelmeyer, Daniel Oggenfuss, Isa Päffgen
Kommunikation / Communication:
Anuschka Koos, Clara Eggebrecht
Technische Leitung / Technical administration:
Andreas Hofstett

Direktor / Director:
Helmut Friedel
Geschäftsführer / Managing director:
Kurt Laube
Sekretariat / Secretary:
Lore Thürheimer
Kommunikation / Communication:
Anuschka Koos, Clara Eggebrecht, Nicola Harenberg
Kuratoren / Curators:
Karin Althaus, Annegret Hoberg, Matthias Mühling
Volontariat / Assistant Curators:
Helena Pereña, Felicia Rappe
Restaurierung / Conservation:
Iris Winkelmeyer, Daniel Oggenfuss, Isa Päffgen,
Judith Ortner
Registrare / Registrars:
Susanne Böller, Karin Dotzer, Karola Rattner
Fotoatelier / Photo studio:
Simone Gänsheimer, Ernst Jank
Bibliothek / Library:
Ursula Keltz, Christa Stegemann
Archiv / Archive:
Irene Netta, Lisa Kern
Verwaltung / Administration:
Sonja Schamberger, Elisabeth Faber,
Siegfried Häusler, Beate Lanzinger, Helga Lieberam,
Yvonne Martin, Anahita Martirosjan, Monika Neumann,
Barbara Schleicher
Technik / Technicians:
Andreas Hofstett, Klaus-Peter Henke,
Patrick Naumann, Hermann Vorderegger

Katalog / Catalogue

Herausgeber / Editors:
Helmut Friedel und Matthias Mühling
Städtische Galerie im Lenbachhaus und Kunstbau
München

Biografien / Biographies:
Hans Janssen

Lektorat / Copyediting:
Felicia Rappe, Karin Althaus, Susanne Böller,
Ursula Keltz, Matthias Mühling, Helena Pereña

Übersetzungen / Translations:
Birgit Erdmann, Sue McDonnell (Biografien /
Biographies), Gerrit Jackson (Helmut Friedel)

Grafische Gestaltung / Graphic design:
Thomas Mayfried Visual Communication
München / Munich

Schrift / Typeface:
Architype Van Doesburg, nach einem Entwurf von /
after a design by Theo van Doesburg (1919),
herausgegeben von / edited by The Foundry, London

Reproduktionen / Reproductions:
LVD Gesellschaft für Datenverarbeitung mbH, Berlin

Verlagsherstellung / Production:
Christine Stäcker

Druck / Printing:
Dr. Cantz'sche Druckerei, Ostfildern

Buchbinderei / Binding:
Conzella Verlagsbuchbinderei, Urban Meister GmbH,
Aschheim-Dornach bei München

Erschienen im / Published by
Hatje Cantz Verlag
Zeppelinstrasse 32
73760 Ostfildern
Deutschland / Germany
Tel. +49 711 4405-200 / Fax +49 711 4405-220
www.hatjecantz.de

Hatje Cantz books are available internationally at
selected bookstores. For more information about our
distribution partners please visit our homepage at
www.hatjecantz.com

Buchhandelsausgabe / Trade edition:
Leinen mit Schutzumschlag / Cloth with jacket,
ISBN 978-3-7757-3023-5
Museumsausgabe / Museum edition:
Leinen / Cloth

Printed in Germany

Fotonachweis / Photocredits

Gemeentemuseum Den Haag / The Hague:
S. 37, 66, 100–109, 113–115, 122–123, 131, 135–139, 147–151,
154–157, 161–175, 178–183, 187–206, 208–214, 219–229, 233,
241–244, 249–267, 273, 277–301
Sammlung / Collection RKD Den Haag / The Hague:
S. 11, 81, 132, 144, 152, 158, 176, 230, 238, 270, 274
RKD Den Haag / The Hague, Archiv Theo und Nelly van
Doesburg (Schenkung van Moorsel) / Archive of
Theo and Nelly van Doesburg (Donation Van Moorsel):
S. 65, 86, 110, 120, 128
RKD Den Haag / The Hague, Archiv / Archive of
César Domela:
S. 64
RKD Den Haag / The Hague, Archiv / Archive of
Anna Bergman:
S. 24–25
Neue Galerie, New York:
S. 17
bpk / Hamburger Kunsthalle / Elke Walford:
S. 14
bpk | CNAC-MNAM | Christian Bahier |
Philippe Migeat:
S. 20
bpk | CNAC-MNAM:
S. 143, 236–237, 269
Kunstmuseum Basel, Martin P. Bühler:
S. 207
Staatsgalerie Stuttgart:
S. 215
Städtische Galerie im Lenbachhaus und Kunstbau:
S. 18, 60, 76–77, 84–85, 90–91
Netherlands Architecture Institute, Rotterdam/
collection Van Eesteren-Fluck & Van Lohuizen
Foundation, The Hague:
S. 124–127
Netherlands Architecture Institute, Rotterdam:
S. 116–117
Kupferstich-Kabinett, Staatliche Kunstsammlungen
Dresden, Herbert Boswank:
S. 216–217
Bayerische Staatsbibliothek München:
S. 118–119
RIETVELD by rietveld collection:
S. 245–247
Eugene Lux, Trust of Dennis and Judith DeStefano:
S. 184